READING MAIMONIDES' *MISHNEH TORAH*

THE LITTMAN LIBRARY OF
JEWISH CIVILIZATION

'*Get wisdom, get understanding:*
Forsake her not and she shall preserve thee'

PROV. 4: 5

The Littman Library of Jewish Civilization is a registered UK charity
Registered charity no. 1000784

READING MAIMONIDES'
MISHNEH TORAH

◆

DAVID GILLIS

Oxford · Portland, Oregon
The Littman Library of Jewish Civilization
2015

The Littman Library of Jewish Civilization
Chief Executive Officer: Ludo Craddock
Managing Editor: Connie Webber

PO Box 645, Oxford OX2 OUJ, UK
www.littman.co.uk
———

Published in the United States and Canada by
The Littman Library of Jewish Civilization
c/o ISBS, 920 NE 58th Avenue, Suite 300
Portland, Oregon 97213-3786

A catalogue record for this book is available from the British Library

Library of Congress Cataloging-in-Publication Data
Gillis, David, 1954–
Reading Maimonides' Mishneh Torah / David Gillis.
pages cm. – (The Littman library of Jewish civilization)
Includes bibliographical references and index.
1. Maimonides, Moses, 1135–1204. Mishneh Torah.   2. Jewish law.   I. Title.
BM520.84.G55 2014
296.1'812–dc23   2014015171

ISBN 978-1-906764-06-7

Publishing co-ordinator: Janet Moth
Copy-editing: Agnes Erdos
Indexing: David Gillis
Production, design, and typesetting by Pete Russell, Faringdon, Oxon.
Printed in Great Britain on acid-free paper by
CPI Antony Rowe, Chippenham, Wiltshire

For Sally

Acknowledgements

THIS STUDY was a long time in the making. Twenty-odd years ago Rabbi Shlomo Levin of South Hampstead Synagogue in London suggested to the dozen or so of us who would turn up to services on Shabbat afternoons that we should study *Sefer hamada* (*The Book of Knowledge*), the first book of Maimonides' code of Jewish law, *Mishneh torah*. Since he lived far from the synagogue and did not usually attend at those times, we had to arrange this by ourselves. It fell to me to start leading the study sessions, and as we went through the text line by line, I began to sense something happening between the lines. I am ever grateful to Rabbi Levin, and to all those who kindly listened and commented as my thoughts about *Mishneh torah* first started to take shape. Later, I was given a platform to air those thoughts at Yakar in London.

The way this study evolved has some bearing on its claims. It asserts that the form of *Mishneh torah* is an artistic representation of philosophical ideas. I developed this view through reading *Mishneh torah*, independently of Maimonides' other writings. When I eventually came to study his later, overtly philosophical work, *The Guide of the Perplexed*, I found substantiation for it. Naturally, from then on, my understanding of each work was enriched by the other, as well as by exploration of the rest of Maimonides' oeuvre, not to mention the secondary literature. Nevertheless, although it refers to *The Guide of the Perplexed* a great deal, the argument put forward in this book about the significance of *Mishneh torah*'s form is much as originally conceived; it is not a reading of the later work into the earlier one.

Several people were kind enough to read initial attempts to put my thoughts into writing or, later on, to help on specific points. I thank, in chronological order, Rabbi Feitel Levin, Professor Moshe Halbertal, Rabbi Shimon Felix, Professor Menachem Lorberbaum, Dr Hillel Newman, Dr Moshe Lavee, and Professor Moshe Idel. Professor Lorberbaum particularly gave generously of his time on several occasions. I have also had the benefit of the reports by the examiners of the doctoral dissertation on which this book is based, Professor James Diamond and Professor Lenn Goodman. My brother Dr Michael Gillis has given much-appreciated advice on matters both of substance and of presentation. Of course none of these people is in any way responsible for the result, except insofar as it is the better for their comments and suggestions.

The dissertation was written at the University of Haifa under the supervision of Professor Menachem Kellner. I am thankful for my good fortune in encountering so wise and generous-spirited a scholar and teacher when I did, and for his immediate willingness to take on the project. I could not have wished for a truer guide or a more warmly encouraging mentor. The most rewarding outcome of my doctoral studies is that our association in Maimonides research continues.

Maimonides is so central a figure in the Jewish heritage, and so much fought over, that it would be hard to approach him dispassionately. Much of what I bring to the study of him I owe to my late parents, Pauline and Charles Gillis, and to their conviction, manifest in word and deed, that Judaism, culture, and a spirit of enquiry belong together. Moreover, a remark by my father on reading an initial essay ostensibly on Maimonides' use of biblical citation, that I might as well be frank about its grander designs, was a spur to this endeavour.

I am grateful to Eitan Madmon, CEO of my employer, *Globes* newspaper, for showing the understanding and flexibility that enabled me to pursue my studies. I also thank my friend Tali Schwarzstein for helping me to understand material in German.

It was Professor Kellner who introduced me to the Littman Library—one more reason that I am in his debt. It has been a pleasure to work with all concerned there. Heartfelt thanks to Connie Webber for her initial backing and for her advice throughout, to Ludo Craddock for his friendly efficiency, to Janet Moth for her wonderful attention to detail, and to Agnes Erdos for her skilful and considerate editing. Thanks also to Pete Russell for the typesetting and the stunning jacket design.

My wife Sally has provided immeasurable support in every way—not least in her willingness to read and criticize one draft after another. That the book is dedicated to her is, besides much else, a token of deep gratitude. Our children too deserve thanks; they have helped more than they know.

Tel Aviv   D.G.
May 2014

Contents

Tables

Note on Transliteration

THE TRANSLITERATION of Hebrew in this book reflects consideration of the type of book it is, its content, purpose, and readership. The system adopted therefore reflects a broad approach to transcription, rather than the narrower approaches found in the *Encyclopaedia Judaica* or other systems developed for text-based or linguistic studies. The aim has been to reflect the pronunciation prescribed for modern Hebrew, rather than the spelling or Hebrew word structure, and to do so using conventions that are generally familiar to the English-speaking reader.

In accordance with this approach, no attempt is made to indicate the distinctions between *alef* and *ayin, tet* and *taf, kaf* and *kuf, sin* and *samekh*, since these are not relevant to pronunciation; likewise, the *dagesh* is not indicated except where it affects pronunciation. Following the principle of using conventions familiar to the majority of readers, however, transcriptions that are well established have been retained even when they are not fully consistent with the transliteration system adopted. On similar grounds, the *tsadi* is rendered by 'tz' in such familiar words as barmitzvah. Likewise, the distinction between *ḥet* and *khaf* has been retained, using *ḥ* for the former and *kh* for the latter; the associated forms are generally familiar to readers, even if the distinction is not actually borne out in pronunciation, and for the same reason the final *heh* is indicated too. As in Hebrew, no capital letters are used, except that an initial capital has been retained in transliterating titles of published works (for example, *Shulḥan arukh*).

Since no distinction is made between *alef* and *ayin*, they are indicated by an apostrophe only in intervocalic positions where a failure to do so could lead an English-speaking reader to pronounce the vowel-cluster as a diphthong—as, for example, in *ha'ir*—or otherwise mispronounce the word.

The *sheva na* is indicated by an *e*—*perikat ol, reshut*—except, again, when established convention dictates otherwise.

The *yod* is represented by *i* when it occurs as a vowel (*bereshit*), by *y* when it occurs as a consonant (*yesodot*), and by *yi* when it occurs as both (*yisra'el*).

Names have generally been left in their familiar forms, even when this is inconsistent with the overall system.

Note on Sources and Conventions

Translation

The following English editions of non-English works have been cited throughout unless stated otherwise in the notes. Translations not listed here are cited where appropriate; other translations are my own.

In the case of *Mishneh torah*, translations have occasionally been emended. This has been done without comment where a more literal rendering was required in order to make a point, and in cases of slight disagreement with the translator. More substantial emendations are discussed in the notes.

Works by Maimonides

Mishneh Torah

Introduction and *Book of Knowledge*, trans. Moses Hyamson (Jerusalem, 1965). *The Code of Maimonides*, 13 vols. (New Haven, 1949–2004): *The Book of Agriculture*, trans. Isaac Klein (1979); *The Book of Cleanness*, trans. Herbert Danby (1954); *The Book of Judges*, trans. A. M. Hershman (1949); *The Book of Love*, trans. Menachem Kellner (2004); *The Book of Offerings*, trans. Herbert Danby (1950); *The Book of Seasons*, trans. Solomon Gandz and Hyman Klein (1961); *The Book of Temple Service*, trans. Mendel Lewittes (1957); *The Book of Torts*, trans. Hyman Klein (1954); *The Book of Women*, trans. Isaac Klein (1972).

Other Works

Book of the Commandments [Sefer hamitsvot], trans. Charles B. Chavel, 2 vols. (London, 1940).

'Eight Chapters' [Shemonah perakim] (introd. to commentary on Mishnah *Avot*), trans. in Raymond L. Weiss and Charles E. Butterworth (eds.), *Ethical Writings of Maimonides* (New York, 1975).

'Epistle to Yemen', trans. in Abraham Halkin and David Hartman, *Epistles of Maimonides: Crisis and Leadership* (Philadelphia, 1985), 91–131.

'Essay on Resurrection', trans. in Abraham Halkin and David Hartman, *Epistles of Maimonides: Crisis and Leadership* (Philadelphia, 1985), 209–33.

Guide of the Perplexed [Arab.: Dalalat al-ḥa'irin; Heb.: Moreh nevukhim],
    trans. Shlomo Pines, 2 vols. (Chicago, 1963).
Treatise on Logic, trans. Israel Efros (New York, 1938).

Other Classical Works

Aristotle, *The Complete Works of Aristotle: The Revised Oxford Translation*, ed.
    Jonathan Barnes, 2 vols. (Princeton, 1984).
Plato, *Complete Works*, ed. John M. Cooper (Indianapolis, 1997).
Soncino Babylonian Talmud, ed. Rabbi Dr Isidore Epstein, 36 vols. (London,
    1935–52).

Citations

Mishneh torah is divided into books, sections (treatises), chapters, and *halakhot*
(paragraphs). Citation is in the traditional way, by section, chapter, and
halakhah. A table of books and sections is given in Appendix I. Maimonides
himself numbered chapters, but not *halakhot*; such numbering came into use
in the early printed editions. See the preface to the Or Vishua edition, p. 10
(*Mishneh torah*, ed. Yohai Makbili (Haifa, 2006)).

The Pines translation of the *Guide of the Perplexed* is cited as *Guide*, followed
by part, chapter, and, in parentheses, page number.

References to Maimonides' *Commentary on the Mishnah* are by order and page
number in the Hebrew translation by R. Kafih (*Commentary on the Mishnah*
[Mishnah im perush rabenu moshe ben maimon], ed. and trans. from Arab.
Joseph Kafih, 6 vols. (Jerusalem, 1963–7)).

BT = Babylonian Talmud; JT = Jerusalem Talmud

A PORTRAIT OF THE ARTIST

THE PREMISE of Maimonides' code of law, *Mishneh torah*, is that a human being's purpose is to know God. It opens with the recognition of God's existence; it closes with Isaiah's messianic promise: 'For the earth shall be full of the knowledge of God as the waters cover the sea.'[1] That is the ultimate aim of all the ritual and civil laws that it prescribes. This book's theme is that *Mishneh torah*'s form is true to its aim; Maimonides shapes the law's prescriptions for action into an object of contemplation, a work of art itself designed to convey the knowledge of God.

Many have remarked on *Mishneh torah*'s artistic qualities; their views will be surveyed shortly. Such qualities have largely been seen, however, as an accident of the order and clarity that Maimonides produced out of the unruly mass of rabbinic legal literature in composing the first complete code of Jewish law. The contention in this study is that the art is of the essence, so that the code's form is a key to understanding it.

The Cosmic Model

Mishneh torah is one of the most closely scrutinized texts in the Jewish canon,[2] yet its most basic formal features have eluded explanation. Why does it have fourteen books? Why are the books ordered as they are?

---

[1] 'Laws of Kings and Their Wars', 12: 5, quoting Isa. 9: 9. In fact, Maimonides asserted early on in his career that the knowledge of God was the purpose of human life. In the introduction to the *Commentary on the Mishnah*, he states that human physical existence is meant to serve the development of the intellect, and that all intellectual disciplines serve the crowning purpose of acquiring knowledge of God (*Commentary on the Mishnah*, Order *Zera'im*, 22). What knowledge of God can consist of will be discussed in due course.

[2] *Mishneh torah* attracted intense scholarly and general interest as soon as it appeared, in late 1177 or early 1178 (see Davidson, *Moses Maimonides*, 203–6), and the intensity has never waned. On the phenomenon of its instant accession to canonic status, see Ben-Sasson, 'Canon Formation' (Heb.).

These features do seem to call for explanation, if only because of the way that the author draws attention to them. 'And I saw fit to divide this composition into fourteen books', he announces in his introduction to the work, prompting one to ask, 'Why that number and no other?' Did the commandments of the law just happen to fall into fourteen major categories, or was the number perhaps premeditated?

There follows a scheme of the fourteen books, with a synopsis of each. The scheme was not obvious. In the introduction to *The Book of the Commandments*, an annotated listing of the Torah's 613 commandments compiled in preparation for writing *Mishneh torah*,[3] Maimonides discusses his plans for a code, and confides: 'I turned over in my mind how this composition should be divided and how its sections should be ordered.' In the end, he tells us, he settled on a method of classification by topic. This is one respect in which Maimonides declared his model to be the Mishnah, yet his code deviates from the mishnaic order.[4] As we shall see later on, he read significance into that order, which makes it likely that his own is also significant.

Among less tangible reasons to wonder about form in *Mishneh torah* is its sheer elegance of expression and arrangement, giving the impression of an author fashioning his work with attention to every element, and indicating a sensibility that one is inclined to credit with awareness of form's possibilities. The credit is not misplaced. In fact, the questions about structure raised above, which might seem peripheral in comparison with *Mishneh torah*'s legal and historical importance, will turn out not to be peripheral at all: answering them can take us to the centre of Maimonides' vision.

Mishneh torah has the form of a microcosm. That proposition represents the backbone of this study. The form is a projection of the outline of the structure and dynamics of the universe found in chapters 2 to 4 of the work's first section, 'Laws of the Foundations of the Torah'. This cosmology is a

For summaries of contemporary responses to it, both adulatory and critical, see Twersky, *Introduction to the Code*, 102–8, 518–26; Davidson, *Moses Maimonides*, 263–85. The key to Frankel's edition of *Mishneh torah* lists some 1,600 works that comment upon or discuss it. The Halacha Brura and Birur Halacha Institute's 'Index to Commentaries on Rambam's Mishneh Torah' (<www.halachabrura.org/e-mavorambam.htm>) cites 'about 3,000 books'. These figures are only for the rabbinic works, and do not take into account the vast academic literature.

[3] By tradition the Torah contains 248 positive commandments and 365 negative ones, giving a total of 613—see BT *Mak.* 23*b*.

[4] Here I follow Shamma Friedman ('Organizational Pattern of Mishneh Torah' and '*Mishneh Torah*: The Great Composition'), who interprets Maimonides' remarks in the introduction to the *Book of the Commandments* on the organization of *Mishneh torah* as meaning that he adopted the method of the Mishnah, although not its actual order. See also Twersky, *Introduction to the Code*, 238–45.

blend of Aristotelian and Neoplatonic ideas deriving from the Islamic philosophers that Maimonides read and admired.[5] The ostensible reason for the outline is that Maimonides determines that there are commandments to love and fear God, and that the way to fulfil them is through studying God's works.[6] A concise (though, as we shall discover, very precise) account of God's works is therefore in order. But at the same time as it seeks to induce love and awe, and stimulate further study that will magnify those feelings, this account is also the blueprint for *Mishneh torah* itself.

The plan's proportions hinge on the numbers ten and four. The Maimonidean universe divides between what lies from the Moon upwards, and what lies below it. Below the Moon, in the centre, are the four forms, or elements, of matter (earth, water, air, and fire) that combine, separate, and recombine in various proportions, producing the variety of mineral, vegetable, and animal existence, in a perpetual process of generation and decay.[7] Surrounding this are nine nested spheres that carry the stars and planets, the Sun, and the Moon itself,[8] all composed of a fine substance not subject to change or decay.[9] More rarefied still are the angels, or separate intellects in philosophical language, which have no material substance at all. There are ten of these: nine cause the rotations of the spheres,[10] while the tenth and lowest-ranking, the *ishim*, also known as the agent intellect, projects forms onto earthly matter, each combination of elements being, as it were, stamped with the form it is capable of receiving,[11] and radiates theoretical knowledge, to be received by human minds primed to do so.[12] These two functions are essentially the same: what we have knowledge of is forms.

Correspondingly, *Mishneh torah* is divided between ten books that deal with commandments *bein adam lamakom* (between man and God), or ritual law, and four books that deal with commandments *bein adam lahavero* (between man and his fellow), or civil law.[13] The proposition is that the first

---

[5] For a brief account of this world picture, see Appendix II.

[6] 'Laws of the Foundations of the Torah', 2: 1–2.

[7] Ibid. 3: 10–4: 5.   [8] Ibid. 3: 1.   [9] Ibid. 2: 3.

[10] At least according to *Guide* ii. 10 (p. 271); in *Mishneh torah* itself only the rotation of the outermost sphere is mentioned as causing the motions of the rest of the system.

[11] 'Laws of the Foundations of the Torah', 4: 6.

[12] 'The tenth intellect is the Active Intellect, whose existence is indicated by the facts that our intellects pass from potentiality into actuality and that the forms of the existents that are subject to generation and corruption are actualized after they have been in their matter only in potential' (*Guide* ii. 4 (p. 257)). (The agent intellect is also known as the active intellect.) For an outline of the background to Maimonides' cosmology and his treatment of the agent intellect, see Appendix II.2.

[13] See Mishnah *Yoma* 8: 9.

ten books with their exalted themes are parallel to the ten orders of angels, or to the nine spheres plus the agent intellect, and, like them, are ordered hierarchically, while the more mundane last four books are parallel to the four elements of matter.

Clearly this needs considerable amplification and detailed proof, but it at least begins to look as though Maimonides designed *Mishneh torah* as a microcosm, so that 'Laws of the Foundations of the Torah' not only sets out the basic theological and moral principles underlying his code of law, but also contains the code's underlying principle of organization.

A principle of organization, though, does not make a work of art, or telephone directories would be masterpieces. What distinguishes art is that the principle (together with other formal aspects, such as, in the case of literary art, style and tone) contributes towards the work's meaning and embodies its values. Besides, in a writer of Maimonides' calibre, a mere numerical trick would be disappointing. The task therefore will be to demonstrate that the microcosmic structure is not just an antecedent principle, a frame onto which the books of *Mishneh torah* are bolted, and not merely decorative either, but that it grows from within, from Maimonides' conception of his subject, the commandments, so that the outward form is expressive of an inward significance.

The microcosmic form of *Mishneh torah* will be interpreted on two planes: a philosophical plane of ideas and an experiential plane.

Maimonides' universe has an Aristotelian superstructure and a Neoplatonic infrastructure. The same will be shown to apply to *Mishneh torah*. On the plane of ideas, this coherent architecture enables us to relate the parts to each other and to the whole, and thereby to apprehend links and patterns that may not be obvious in the halakhic material itself. In the most general terms, the relationship between *Mishneh torah*'s form and its content symbolizes the very relationship between philosophy and halakhah.

Philosophy, for these purposes, means physics and metaphysics. As far as Maimonides is concerned, these subjects are the content of Jewish esoteric lore. In his *Commentary on the Mishnah* he identifies one branch of that lore, *ma'aseh bereshit* (the account of the beginning),[14] with physics, and the other, *ma'aseh merkavah* (the account of the chariot),[15] with metaphysics.[16] In *Mishneh torah* the first two chapters of 'Laws of the Foundations of the

[14] i.e. the exposition of the Creation story in the opening chapters of Genesis.

[15] i.e. the exposition of the visions in Ezek. 1 and 10.

[16] The identification is made in the commentary on Mishnah Ḥag. 2: 1. This *mishnah* places restrictions on the teaching of *ma'aseh bereshit* and *ma'aseh merkavah*. See also *Guide* i, Introduction (p. 6).

Torah', concerning God and the angels, are summed up as being about *ma'aseh merkavah*,[17] while the next two chapters, concerning the heavenly spheres and the elements, are stated to be about *ma'aseh bereshit*.[18]

In 'Laws of the Foundations of the Torah', 4: 13, Maimonides describes the arcane, theoretical subjects of *ma'aseh bereshit* and *ma'aseh merkavah* (collectively known as *pardes*) as 'a great thing', and halakhah, the practical side of Torah which is understandable by all, as 'a small thing'.[19]

So *Mishneh torah's* microcosmic form is the 'great thing' encompassing and supporting the 'small thing', the details of halakhah that make up its content. Maimonides tells us explicitly that philosophy is nobler than halakhah, and that creating the conditions for philosophical enlightenment is the end of halakhah.[20] Through the structure of *Mishneh torah* he conveys an additional dimension of the relationship: philosophy emerges as the matrix of halakhah; in Aristotelian terms, its formal cause.

This inverts the accepted view of the order of priority between philosophy and halakhah in *Mishneh torah*. That the work has philosophical aspects is very clear. Maimonides himself draws attention to one radical philosophical assumption in it when he writes: 'you will always find that whenever, in what I have written in books of jurisprudence, I happen to mention the foundations and start upon establishing the existence of the deity, I establish it by discourses that adopt the way of the doctrine of the eternity of the world'.[21] That is to say, in setting out to prove the existence of God, even in a work of Jewish law, Maimonides starts from the philosophers' more problematic notion of a steady-state universe (in which he says he does not believe) rather than from the religious position that the universe was created, for if the proof stands for a steady-state universe, then it is all the more valid for a created one. The opening of his most important book of jurisprudence, *Mishneh torah*, duly refers to a First Being that 'brings into existence all that exists', not a God who created the world 'in the beginning'; there is no beginning here.[22]

---

[17] 'Laws of the Foundations of the Torah', 2: 11. Note that in the exposition of the vision of Ezekiel in *Guide* iii. 1–7 (pp. 417–30), *ma'aseh merkavah* seems more identified with superlunary physics than with metaphysics. See Freudenthal, 'Four Observations' (Heb.).

[18] 'Laws of the Foundations of the Torah', 4: 10.   [19] This is based on BT *Suk.* 28*a*.

[20] This is how Maimonides interprets the rabbinic dictum that 'God has nothing in this world except the four cubits of halakhah' (BT *Ber.* 8*a*) in the introduction to his *Commentary on the Mishnah* (Order *Zera'im*, 21–4). It is also the gist of 'Laws of the Foundations of the Torah', 4: 13, and the essence of Maimonides' conception of the days of the messiah in 'Laws of Kings and Their Wars', 12, and is stated clearly in *Guide* iii. 27.   [21] *Guide* i. 71 (p. 182).

[22] 'Laws of the Foundations of the Torah', 1: 1. On the duality of this opening, apparently making a religious statement while actually making a philosophical one, see Kellner, 'Literary Character'.

A little further on he argues for the existence of a God of limitless power on the grounds that 'the sphere revolves constantly',[23] without end, and again, apparently, without a beginning.

Maimonides' interpreters too have commented on *Mishneh torah*'s philosophical significance. But when Isadore Twersky, for example, describes it as a 'fusion of *halakhah* and philosophy',[24] he means that it constantly brings out the morally and intellectually elevating character of halakhah; in his reading, philosophy remains within the framework of halakhah, whereas the upshot of the formal analysis offered here is that the fusion ultimately takes place in the relationship between content and form, and from that point of view, the relationship is the other way round: *Mishneh torah* presents halakhah within a framework of philosophy, reflecting the Islamic philosophers' notion of religion as philosophy in popular form.[25]

This shift in perspective yields substantial gains. We shall find that it makes several puzzling features of *Mishneh torah* fall into place. It will also entail a rethinking of the relationship between *Mishneh torah* and *The Guide of the Perplexed*, Maimonides' other masterpiece. The greatest gain, though, is that the law is validated as it is explicated. The inference, via the ancient idea of man as microcosm, is that the commandments of the Torah are designed to perfect human beings by bringing the individual human personality, and the entire state, into line with the ideal order of the cosmos.[26] *Mishneh torah* offers something more than instrumental value, more than serving as a prelude to philosophy, as the commandments' purpose. It proposes that through fulfilment of the commandments we can join the great array of stars and spheres in the praise and glorification of God.

[23] 'Laws of the Foundations of the Torah', 1: 5.

[24] Twersky, *Maimonides Reader*, 18. See also id., *Introduction to the Code*, 48.

[25] See Berman, 'Ethical Views of Maimonides'; Pessin, 'Influence of Islamic Thought on Maimonides'.

[26] The idea of a parallel between nature and the commandments is to be distinguished from the idea of natural law. The latter is the notion that there is a law that is the product of universal, innate, practical human reason. The parallel suggested here implies rather the opposite: a law that is the product of supreme, and hard-won, understanding of physics and metaphysics, and with a transcendent aim. David Novak, who sees natural law as an element in Maimonides' legal method, ultimately concedes that 'despite the many specific things we can learn from Maimonides in connection with our search for natural law materials, I think his overall theory has insurmountable difficulties for us' (Novak, *Natural Law*, 137). See also Fox, 'Maimonides and Aquinas on Natural Law', and Hyman, 'Divine Law and Human Reason'. Hyman tends more towards the idea that Maimonides did countenance some kind of natural law. Hadad, 'Nature and Torah in Maimonides' (Heb.), makes a distinction similar to the one made here.

This is wonderful design. It proves to be a way of importing philosophical ideas into *Mishneh torah* without in the least disturbing the clear exposition of the law. It is not quite enough, however, to earn art's highest accolades. *Mishneh torah*'s true artistic quality lies beyond the encryption of ideas in formal patterns. Its meaning is something that cannot be stated, but only gestured towards.[27] It is the product of a mind fixed upon God and seeks to communicate the love of God. Just as, as a code of law, it is completed through action, as a work of art, it is completed in the imagination. *Mishneh torah* achieves more than the syncretic reconciliation of the Torah with the philosophy and science of a particular age. The artistic bonding of its form and content gives it the power to transcend the time and place of its creation, to effect not only an ordering of halakhah, but a reordering of the sensibilities of the reader, and to plant in him or her the germ of its inspiration.

Aggadah in *Mishneh Torah*

The Greeks and Arabs do not have *Mishneh torah*'s form all to themselves. In his introduction, Maimonides famously states: 'I have entitled this work *Mishneh torah*, for the reason that a person, who reads first the Written Law and then this compilation, will know from it the whole of the Oral Law, without having occasion to consult any other book between them.'[28]

It is mainly the second part of this statement, the claim that *Mishneh torah* renders study of the Talmud redundant, that has attracted attention—even hostile attention.[29] But it is also intriguing to ponder just what Maimonides meant by the first part. For while it is clearly desirable for a Jew to be

[27] Compare Halbertal's comment on the *Guide*: 'The distinction between political esotericism and essential esotericism engenders different understandings of the biblical text. Political-social esotericism understands Scriptural parables as allegory, whose hidden contents may be expressed in direct conceptual language. Essential esotericism sees the Scriptural parable as symbol rather than allegory. The symbol does not hide contents that could otherwise be expressed directly through concepts, but points and directs us to what cannot be expressed directly. Under this conception, the esoteric structure of language is not the result of a strategy adopted by philosophy in its relation toward society, but is part of the essence of the philosophical realm' (Halbertal, *Concealment and Revelation*, 57). See also Y. Lorberbaum, 'Maimonides' Conception of Parables' (Heb.).

[28] *Introduction* and *Book of Knowledge*, trans. Hyamson, 4*b*.

[29] Maimonides found himself forced to deny, in a letter to R. Pinhas the judge, that he really meant to eliminate study of the Talmud. See *Letters*, ed. Shailat (Heb.), 438–9. According to Ta-Shma, R. Pinhas had an Ashkenazi perspective, in which study of Talmud was central, whereas against the background of contemporary methods of study in Spain and in the East, which tended to focus on paraphrastic commentaries rather than on the Talmud itself, Maimonides' claim for *Mishneh torah* was not extraordinary—see Ta-Shma, 'Maimonides' Position on Talmud Study' (Heb.).

acquainted with the foundation document of Jewish nationhood, and by imbibing its wisdom to nurture his or her moral being, from the point of view of halakhah pure and simple, someone who 'reads first the Written Law' gains little. It is a standing joke that rabbinical scholars can cite references to biblical verses in the Talmud more readily than they can cite the Bible itself. To a practice-oriented, definitive recital of Jewish law according to the rabbinic tradition, the Bible is no more than scenery. Yet Maimonides refuses to perform without the scenery. The implication is that full appreciation of *Mishneh torah* requires familiarity with the Written Law. Nor is the Written Law only background; *Mishneh torah* abounds in direct citations of, and indirect allusions to, the Bible.[30]

All this may be contrasted with a later code, the *Shulḥan arukh* of R. Joseph Karo (1488–1575), in which biblical references are much less frequent. As I have noted, Maimonides prepared for writing *Mishneh torah* by compiling *The Book of the Commandments*, listing the 613 commandments of the Torah. R. Karo's path to writing the *Shulḥan arukh* lay through his *Beit yosef*, which sifts and weighs talmudic discussions and states rulings. It is not just that Maimonides concealed that process while R. Karo laid it bare. *Mishneh torah* sinks its foundations in the Torah as the *Shulḥan arukh* does not. The biblical commandment is the basic unit from which *Mishneh torah* is built. Having compiled his definitive listing of the 613 commandments, and having asserted that the Oral Law given to Moses was transmitted intact down the generations, without omission or controversy, Maimonides was in a position to give an account of the Oral Law structured upon the Written Law, without referring to talmudic disputations that, according to him, never arose out of uncertainty about the Mosaic legislation.[31]

Mishneh torah is not only technically based upon the Bible; it is in constant dialogue with it in ways that go well beyond the strict requirements of establishing halakhah. The Bible is not scenery, but one of the main actors. This feature has been described by Twersky.[32] Discussing what he terms 'Exceptions to the Austere Codificatory Form' in *Mishneh torah*, he writes:

The most significant category, which by itself would necessitate a redefinition of the codificatory form, is the colourful spectrum of expository-exegetical material which imperceptibly but irreversibly converts the *Mishneh Torah* into a compendium that

---

[30] See Greenberg, 'Bible Interpretation'.

[31] See *Commentary on the Mishnah*, Introduction (Order *Zera'im*, 3).

[32] See in general Twersky, *Introduction to the Code*, 143–54, and the same author's 'Non-Halakic Aspects' and 'Clarification of "Laws of Trespass", 8: 8' (Heb.).

teaches and not only guides, that instructs while it directs. In many respects it turns out to be a suggestive and selective commentary cast as a code. The expository-exegetical range is wide and varied, including many levels of explication and even rationalization, Scriptural exegesis, aggadic commentary and halakic investigation, counsel and exhortation, even the cultivation of ontological perceptions and teleological awareness—all these definitely transcend the needs of apodictic summary and serve a primarily informative-academic-edifying purpose.[33]

In other words, *Mishneh torah* combines many elements, including scriptural exegesis and aggadah, to create a work the effects of which go far beyond inculcating knowledge of the dos and don'ts.

To this must be added the part played by Midrash. On its role in *Mishneh torah*, Twersky comments:

Maimonides, who had a sustained and life-long interest in Midrash, its hermeneutic problematics as well as its ideational potential, freely and effectively utilized non-halakic materials throughout the *Mishneh Torah*. Aggadah and halakah had a synchronic relationship; the tendency to separate completely these two cognate areas, which often merged, should not obscure the literary-conceptual reality of Maimonides' work, or indeed of his age as a whole.[34]

Allusion to the Bible and Midrash is, then, one way in which Maimonides weaves into *Mishneh torah* strands of meaning that are not part of the warp and weft of halakhah. Combined with the structural features, it creates an original pattern of aggadah.[35]

Twersky includes in *Mishneh torah*'s 'expository-exegetical range' 'the cultivation of ontological perceptions and teleological awareness'. To appreciate this fully, we need to understand what aggadah meant to Maimonides. He believed that the truths perceived by Aristotle, for example, were known to the prophets and sages of Israel, and were transmitted by them in visions and *midrashim*, so that by interpreting these esoteric communications as parables of the way the universe works, as he did in the *Guide*, he saw himself as recovering Judaism's original philosophical patrimony, which time and troubles had eroded.[36] He went to the philosophers to find materials to restore

---

[33] Twersky, *Introduction to the Code*, 143.　　　　　[34] Ibid. 150.

[35] Maimonides stresses the importance of aggadah in the introduction to his *Commentary on the Mishnah* (Order *Zera'im*, 19–24). According to Hartman, Maimonides placed aggadah above halakhah. See Hartman, *Maimonides: Torah and Philosophic Quest*, 179.

[36] See *Guide* i. 71 (p. 175); ii. 11 (p. 276). Davidson finds Maimonides perfectly sincere in his view of the sages as philosophers—see Davidson, *Moses Maimonides*, 246–7. Davidson also cites Twersky, *Introduction to the Code*, 215 and 218. This does not mean that Maimonides considered all of rabbinical aggadah to be philosophically valuable—see Breuer, 'Maimonides and Aggadah'.

Judaism's more resplendent intellectual edifice, to understand the physics and metaphysics encoded in *ma'aseh bereshit* and *ma'aseh merkavah*.

Casting *Mishneh torah* in microcosmic form was one way of restoring Torah to its original wholeness; its aggadic stratum is another. It will frequently be found that Maimonides adapts aggadah in such a way as to mediate between halakhah and ontology, between the 'small thing' and the 'great thing'.

Teleology

As far as teleological awareness is concerned, this is not just a matter of sporadic allusions to aggadah; *Mishneh torah* has a teleological bearing built into its form.

A glance reveals that *Mishneh torah* has a narrative shape, a beginning, a middle, and an end.[37] It begins with the commandment to know God's existence, ends with that knowledge become universal in the age of the messiah, and in the middle presents, in an ever-widening circle, the commandments designed to infuse the knowledge of God into all aspects of individual and social existence. The stages of this process can be seen as corresponding in a very general way to the narrative of the Torah. For example, the idea of gathering together doctrinal material in a first, introductory book to a code of law is said to have been taken from the Hadith,[38] but might it not also be that *Mishneh torah* begins with *ma'aseh bereshit* because that is how the Bible begins, except that Maimonides transposes *ma'aseh bereshit* into the key of philosophy?[39] The main stations of Jewish history are mentioned: Abraham discovers God and leaves Haran;[40] Moses rescues the people from Egyptian degradation and corruption;[41] ultimately the messiah redeems and restores.[42] The commandments in the first three books of *Mishneh torah* are meant to

---

[37] 'A whole is that which has beginning, middle, and end' (Aristotle, *Poetics*, 1450*b*, 26).

[38] See B. Cohen, 'Classification of the Law', discussed further below.

[39] Warren Zev Harvey does see it this way in his 'Aggadah in *Mishneh Torah*'. Note Maimonides' comment in *Guide* i, Introduction (pp. 8–9) on the reason for the Torah beginning with *ma'aseh bereshit*: 'Do you not see the following fact? God, may His mention be exalted, wished us to be perfected and the state of our societies to be improved by His laws regarding actions. Now this can come about only after the adoption of intellectual beliefs, the first of which being His apprehension, may He be exalted, according to our capacity. This, in its turn, cannot come about except through divine science and this divine science cannot become actual except after a study of natural science . . . Hence God, may He be exalted, caused His book to open with the 'Account of the Beginning', which, as we have made clear, is natural science.'

[40] 'Laws of Idolatry', 1: 3.

[41] Ibid.

[42] 'Laws of Kings and Their Wars', chs. 11–12.

instil the foundational ideas of monotheism, which are associated with the patriarchs, whose lives are the main subject of Genesis. The Temple and its ritual occupy the central part of *Mishneh torah* just as the Tabernacle occupies the central part of the Torah, stretching from chapter 25 of Exodus, through Leviticus, to chapter 10 of Numbers. Moreover, the key concept of the Torah's middle book, Leviticus, is holiness, and holiness in its most recognizable aspects—the dedication of a certain space, as just mentioned, but also restraint of bodily desire—is also the keynote of the middle portion of *Mishneh torah*, starting in the *Book of Women*, clearly expressed in the *Book of Holiness*, and continuing through to the *Book of Sacrifices* (although we shall see later on that holiness is the overarching concept of all the first ten books of *Mishneh torah* taken as a unit). The last part of the Torah is largely concerned with political institutions, and with preparation for entry into Canaan and the formation of the first Jewish Commonwealth; the last part of *Mishneh torah* is concerned with the institutions of civil law and anticipates the restoration of that Commonwealth, to be accompanied by the recognition of the one God throughout the world. This is not to argue that the structure of *Mishneh torah* is based on the Torah, but only that the storylines are similar, making this one way in which it justifies its title, 'a duplicate Torah'.

The function of the commandments in this dimension, as we traverse from the origins of the Jewish people to the messiah, is as a vessel to preserve the knowledge of God in the interim, and eventually to carry it far and wide. But *Mishneh torah* does more than describe the arc of Jewish (indeed universal) history and destiny; a teleological intent seeps deeply into its structures, linking the personal to the national quest. The knowledge of God at the end of it is not the same as the knowledge of God at the beginning. Just as, at the close of a piece of music, a reference to the opening theme may mark the emotional distance travelled, so too the reference at the end of *Mishneh torah* to the idea of knowledge of God with which it began is a measure of how far we have come. Among other things, the historical strand has been added. We shall need to ask how the transition is made between the timeless assertion of God's existence with which *Mishneh torah* begins and the fulfilment in time on which it ends, or, to put it another way, to find where the ontological and teleological axes of *Mishneh torah*'s structure meet. The answer, it will be suggested, lies in Maimonides' theory of prophecy. This in turn raises a further question: does *Mishneh torah* itself have pretensions to prophecy?

These are the main lines of argument that this study will take up. By way of further introduction, I shall briefly survey earlier assessments of the artistic merit of *Mishneh torah*, and then take a step back to look at what might have motivated Maimonides to cast his code of law in artistic form: his predisposition to poetic expression, and the conflicting forces acting upon him that called for artistic resolution. I also look at the basis in literary theory from Plato through to the Islamic philosophers for the approach to *Mishneh torah* I have adopted, before describing the particular Hebrew literary tradition to which I believe it belongs, which is the key to much of what follows. Finally comes a survey of the various ways of arranging the commandments found in Maimonides' writings, and of previous explanations for *Mishneh torah*'s distinctive structure.

Mishneh Torah as Art: The History of an Idea

As far as I have been able to ascertain, the first to label *Mishneh torah* a work of art was the historian Heinrich Graetz, who wrote of Maimonides' achievement:

It is impossible to give the uninitiated an idea of this gigantic work, in which he collected the remotest things from the vast mine of the Talmud, extracting the fine metal from the dross, classifying all details under their appropriate heads, showing how the Talmud was based on the Bible, bringing its details under general rules, combining apparently unconnected parts into one organized whole, and cementing it into a work of art.[43]

Subsequent writers have also called attention to the code's aesthetic appeal. 'Through *Hayad haḥazakah*, Maimonides brought the beauty of Japheth, the artistic symmetry so characteristic of Greek philosophy, into the Holy of Holies of the people of Israel', wrote R. Isaac Herzog.[44] In his *Introduction to the Code of Maimonides*, Twersky refers to Maimonides as 'the author-artist',[45] and although he stops short of calling *Mishneh torah* a work of

---

[43] Graetz, *History*, 466.

[44] Herzog, 'Order of Books in Mishneh Torah' (Heb.), my translation. *Mishneh torah* became known as *Hayad haḥazakah* ('the mighty hand', from Deut. 34: 12) after Maimonides' death—he himself never gave it that title. It refers to *Mishneh torah*'s fourteen books, the numerical value of the Hebrew word *yad* ('hand'), under the system whereby Hebrew letters also stand for numbers, being 14. Twersky maintains that the alternative title arose from discomfort with the pretension of the original one—see *Introduction to the Code*, 105 and references there. Davidson (*Moses Maimonides*, 214) regards it more as an expression of admiration. Japheth was the youngest son of Noah and the father of Javan, who is identified with Greece, giving rise to the Hebrew name for that country. Behind Rabbi Herzog's comment is the verse 'God shall enlarge Japheth, and he shall dwell in the tents of Shem' (Gen. 9: 27).   [45] Twersky, *Introduction to the Code*, 17.

art, his book, which he himself styles 'a literary-historical study', is saturated with awareness of Maimonides' artistic sensibility and literary craft.[46]

Twersky repeatedly points out touches whereby Maimonides presents the commandments as motivators of moral behaviour, and as designed to sensitize, refine, and spiritualize character. This is also an aspect of the art with which *Mishneh torah* is composed, a most important one, and it should not be lost sight of in exploring the more abstract, formal aspects—although, in the end, one thing that makes *Mishneh torah* so compelling is the continuity from the apprehension of the movements of the stars to, say, the consideration owed to the poor and lonely on festivals (to take just one example of the kind of subtle moral urging that Twersky highlights), a continuity captured by *Mishneh torah*'s form.

Haym Soloveitchik regards *Mishneh torah*'s artistic perfection as its undoing. He maintains that it resisted adaptation to the ethos of the Ashkenazi community and has not been applied to the changing needs of Jewish jurisprudence because it is a work of art that cannot be continued or translated, but only interpreted in its own terms.[47] It thus failed to become the standard code among Jewish communities that Maimonides hoped it would be,[48] whereas R. Karo's *Shulḥan arukh*, being less artistically remote, succeeded in acquiring that status. Soloveitchik shows how some of the structural peculiarities of *Mishneh torah* can be explained once its rhetorical purposes and artistic mode are understood. For example, he interprets the apparently illogical arrangement of the section 'Laws of the Sabbath' as a way of conveying an anti-Karaite polemic.[49]

Soloveitchik's essay is further evidence that *Mishneh torah* possesses a mystique that prompts those who consider it closely to reach for the word 'art'. The findings of this study are absolutely in harmony with his assessments that *Mishneh torah* is 'an organic form that unfolds from within, according to laws derivable from its own essence', and that it is deep and complex enough for

---

[46] Some references from the chapter 'Language and Style': 'The massive erudition is ennobled by linguistic virtuosity and poetic prowess' (p. 346); 'The ethical interpretations and philosophical insights generally also have a stylistic-literary effect in that this material loosens what would otherwise have to be relentlessly austere prose. The impression of a conscious artist at work, ever mindful of form and symmetry, is greatly strengthened by these features' (p. 350); 'The unity of content and form ... is thus an impressive accomplishment' (p. 355).

[47] H. Soloveitchik, '*Mishneh Torah:* Polemic and Art'.

[48] A hope expressed in the 'Letters to R. Joseph Concerning the Dispute with the Head of the Academy', *Letters*, ed. Shailat (Heb.), 285.

[49] In this respect Soloveitchik resolves some of the cruxes he himself raised in his earlier 'Thoughts on Maimonides' Categorization'.

people to 'find themselves reflected in it'. In his account there is, however, a disjunction between *Mishneh torah*'s art and its purpose, and an implication in his verdict that it was written 'too well', that its author did not quite know his own artistic strength, which would really deny him full artistic credentials. That description arises from the assumption that promulgating a standard code was Maimonides' main aim. (The historical accuracy or otherwise of the claim that its literary quality is what prevented *Mishneh torah* from achieving that aim is not the issue here.) It does hint that he might have had other aims as well, but besides remarking, movingly, on the work's 'creative ambiguity', Soloveitchik does not define such aims.

Of Maimonides' ability to introduce such creative ambiguity into *Mishneh torah* without disturbing its surface serenity, Soloveitchik writes: 'His achievement is obvious; how he achieved it eludes me to this day.' In the reading offered here, the ambiguities are the surface signs of underlying general structures through which we can start to apprehend Maimonides' trans-halakhic aims. I suggest that *Mishneh torah* owes its taut surface, which resists manipulation and continuity, and its seemingly unending resonances, to its being stretched tight over the framework of Maimonides' physics and metaphysics. There is no need to resort to a paradoxical notion of overabundant artistry. Maimonides matched ends and means precisely. He brought his artistic strength to bear quite consciously on the task of presenting not just halakhah, but Torah in its entirety, of which the subjectivity released by Soloveitchik's ambiguities is part. *Mishneh torah*'s artistic perfection did not defeat its object; it was one of its objects.

When Maimonides came to recognize that his omission of rabbinical sources from *Mishneh torah* was impeding its acceptance, the solution he proposed was a companion volume—he did not wish to clutter the text with notes.[50] This, together with his refusal to translate *Mishneh torah* into Arabic, which will be discussed below, appears to indicate that, even at the price of diminished popularity, Maimonides was not prepared to compromise *Mishneh torah*'s poetic self-containment, or dull the polished finish on which, according to Soloveitchik, derivative commentary, as opposed to the interpretative kind, could not gain purchase. He must have had his reasons.

At any rate, there is certainly a history to the view that *Mishneh torah* is the product of an artistic mind, and that its form can be at least locally meaningful. The scholars cited do not follow up the full implications of artistic status, but they do provide some pointers to the directions further exploration might

---

[50] Letter to R. Pinhas the judge, *Letters*, ed. Shailat (Heb.), 444–5.

take. Herzog's account, which conveys strongly the work's momentum and pedagogic drive, and points out how the ending is a culmination of the opening theme, does treat *Mishneh torah* as a book to be read, and not just as a work of reference; Soloveitchik, as noted, finds it to be organic in form and multi-layered in meaning; and although Twersky refrains from describing *Mishneh torah* outright as a transcendent work of art, his comment on Maimonides' holistic approach to the commandments, that 'Holism is another aspect of making the "Torah great and glorious," commodious and comprehensive—it helps transcend functionality',[51] hints at the possibilities. It will be argued that the comprehensiveness of *Mishneh torah* (a feature Twersky continually stresses) is reflected in the work's form as well, and that this contributes both to integration on an artistic level and to significance on a philosophical level. For Maimonides brought into the Holy of Holies not just the symmetry of Greek philosophy, but, through that symmetry, in a thorough and systematic way, philosophy itself.

All in all, scholarship up to now has treated *Mishneh torah* as a work of halakhah that happens to be a work of art. The claim here is that it had to be a work of art.

Defining Art

If it is to be argued that *Mishneh torah* is a work of art, one ought perhaps first to define art, and then demonstrate that *Mishneh torah* meets the definition. Unfortunately, art has no widely accepted, universal definition, and may not be definable at all.[52] After all, art, at least in a modern notion of it, is about things in their indefinability, eluding universals and freed from instrumentality.

It would only be a distraction to try to develop a definition from first principles. The method is therefore to borrow as needed; to show that *Mishneh torah* has affinities with theories of art from the classical, medieval, and modern periods, and with notions that will be assumed to be common to most people's experience of art, the point being not an exercise in definition, but the insights that treating *Mishneh torah* as a work of art can yield. So the short answer to the definition question is that 'the tree beareth her fruit' (Joel 2: 22).

All the same, it would be as well to provide some kind of orientation. *Mishneh torah* is not a work of literary art in the same way as, say, *Hamlet*. The

---

[51] Twersky, *Introduction to the Code*, 187.
[52] See Davies, *Definitions of Art*, 5–22; Adajian, 'Definition of Art'.

contract with the reader/audience is quite different. *Hamlet* has no viable existence unless it entertains, and provokes admiration for the dramaturgical and poetic skill it displays; *Mishneh torah* has a viable and important existence even when its artistry goes unrecognized. Art for art's sake would be anathema to Maimonides; everything is for God's sake.[53] Yet the artistry is not incidental but, as has already been stressed, central to *Mishneh torah*'s meaning.

The appreciation of *Mishneh torah*'s value as art must therefore proceed in stages. Rather than a rationalization of the sensory and emotional *coup* delivered by a work the artistic status of which is its primary *raison d'être*, it must be a matter of a gradual climb, keeping content and form in step with each other, so that the vista steadily broadens.

Keeping content and form in step means that the interpretation of form should be in accordance with signposts in the content. This is not unlike the guidance Maimonides himself gives on the interpretation of a parable, using the biblical image of 'apples of gold in settings of silver',[54] that 'Its external meaning also ought to contain in it something that indicates to someone considering it what is to be found in its internal meaning.'[55] This is also a good point to state that I detect no sign of the form subverting the content.[56] The relationship is sometimes one of harmony, sometimes of counterpoint, but never of sustained discord.

Mishneh torah as art will unfold gradually, but it is possible to give a preview of what we shall see, and to indicate some of the ways in which the term 'art' as it is widely understood fits *Mishneh torah*.

On the whole, the approach is formalistic. It is summed up by Clive Bell's assertion that what works of art have in common is 'significant form',[57] or to cite Arthur C. Danto's more rigorous formulation, 'works of art, in categorical contrast with mere representations, use the means of representation in a way that is not exhaustively specified when one has exhaustively specified what is being represented'.[58] The form is pleasing in itself, and it expresses

---

[53] He himself said of *Mishneh torah*, 'I did what I did for the sake of God alone' (*Letters*, ed. Shailat (Heb.), 301).   [54] Prov. 25: 11.

[55] *Guide* i, Introduction (p. 12). The applicability of Maimonides' approach to parables to his own writing is explored more fully in Chapter 6.

[56] There is no suggestion in Maimonides' work, or for that matter in his life, of anything less than complete commitment to rabbinic Judaism; see Davidson, *Moses Maimonides*, 542–5.

[57] 'What quality is common to Sta. Sophia and the windows at Chartres, Mexican sculpture, a Persian bowl, Chinese carpets, Giotto's frescoes at Padua, and the masterpieces of Poussin, Piero della Francesca, and Cezanne? Only one answer seems possible—significant form' (Bell, *Art*, 17). One significance of form is that it 'conveys to us an emotion felt by its creator' (ibid. 43). Bell wrote about the visual arts, but his 'one answer' can equally be applied to literature.

[58] Danto, *Transfiguration*, 147–8.

something about the content. Applied to *Mishneh torah*, this means that the way the work is composed has a surplus value not accounted for by the halakhah ('what is being represented'), or even by the classification of halakhah.

The idea of significant form can even be derived from Maimonides himself. In 'Laws of the Foundations of the Torah', 4: 8, and in the first chapter of the *Guide*, he distinguishes between form in the sense of shape and appearance, and form in the sense of the essence of something, that which makes it what it is. In *Guide* i. 1, he also distinguishes between natural objects and artificial objects in this respect. In the case of a natural object, form has the meaning of essence. People, for example, come in many shapes, sizes, and colours, but that does not impinge upon their humanity, which is a matter of their common possession of an intellect, which is the form of a human being.[59] By contrast, in the case of an artificial object, form means shape.[60] A work of art could be said to be an artificial object that aspires to the condition of a natural object, so the two senses of form coincide, and shape becomes essential.

Though the approach is formalistic, it is not meant to divorce form from content. As Ismail Dahiyat puts it in relation to a comparison drawn by Aristotle between the process of memory and the process of artistic perception, 'there is no necessary contradiction between a formalistic and a mimetic view of an art form: it is both presentational, i.e., an object of contemplation, and representational, i.e., an analogue of reality'.[61] In looking at a portrait, for example, we can focus on line and colour abstracted from the subject, or on the idea of the person represented. The oscillation of the mind between the equal fascination of both gives the sense that the picture dissolves and reforms before our eyes, and hence the illusion of life. Similarly, in considering *Mishneh torah* we can focus upon its form as a set of abstract relations, or upon its legal and political content as it relates to the reality of life in the past and the present. Simultaneous awareness of these two aspects encourages the formation of a state of mind that will embrace them both, one unique to every reader and subtly different at every encounter. This active participation in

[59] 'Laws of the Foundations of the Torah', 4: 8.

[60] See also the discussion on artificial and natural form in chapter 9 of the *Treatise on Logic* (pp. 49–50), on which see further Kasher, 'On the Form of the "Images"' (Heb.). Davidson argues, forcefully, that Maimonides was not the author of the *Treatise on Logic*—see Davidson, *Moses Maimonides*, 313–22. That view has not caught on, and this study will proceed on the basis of the consensus that the attribution to Maimonides is correct, especially as some of its findings, such as on the reason for the frequency of the number fourteen as an organizing principle in Maimonides' works (the *Treatise* has fourteen chapters), tend to support the case for authenticity—see below, pp. 192–4.

[61] Dahiyat, *Avicenna's Commentary on the* Poetics, 42 n. 1.

recomposing the work makes for an impression of vitality.[62] (This approach would have to be modified to accommodate non-representational art, but since *Mishneh torah* is representational, that need not concern us.)

Another notion of art relevant to the case is that the experience of art is the apprehension by one mind of another through a medium.[63] Consider Tolstoy's definition of art, which he arrives at after dismissing idealist notions of beauty: 'Art is a human activity consisting in this, that one man consciously, by means of certain external signs, hands on to others feelings he has lived through, and that other people are infected by these feelings and also experience them.'[64] Consider also T. S. Eliot's contention that 'The only way of expressing emotion in the form of art is by finding an "objective correlative"; in other words, a set of objects, a situation, a chain of events which shall be the formula of that particular emotion; such that when the external facts, which must terminate in sensory experience, are given, the emotion is immediately evoked.'[65]

In a way, creation itself is the objective correlative of God's wisdom.[66] Being patterned on creation, *Mishneh torah* is an objective correlative of Maimonides' love of God.

Lastly, and in many ways this sums up the discussion, *Mishneh torah* meets Aquinas's three criteria of beauty: *integritas*, *consonantia*, and *claritas*. Its cosmic form bestows *integritas* in that it makes the work graspable as a single, complete, bounded whole. With *consonantia*, we move from the whole to the parts. *Consonantia* is evident in the effect of the form already discussed, that it brings the parts into meaningful relationship with one another, ordering, balancing, and harmonizing them. This phase of *Mishneh torah*'s aesthetic appeal was noted by Graetz, as we saw above, in considering the work purely as a code of law, when he wrote of Maimonides 'combining apparently unconnected parts into one organized whole'. The cosmic form elevates this inter-

---

[62] The fact that the content is practical in nature is not an impediment to this effect. Even in classical or idealist theory, having practical application need not in itself exclude a work from being considered art—see Schelling's remarks on architecture in *Philosophy of Art*, 168–80. Without intending any direct comparison with *Mishneh torah*, it may be pointed out that, within the classical tradition, there exists the genre of didactic poetry, exemplified by Virgil's *Georgics*, a poem about the pastoral ideal that apparently did influence farming practice for a long time—see de Bruyn, 'Reading Virgil's "Georgics" as a Scientific Text'.   [63] I owe this formulation to Dr Francis Warner.

[64] Tolstoy, *What Is Art?*, 45.   [65] Eliot, *The Sacred Wood*, 100.

[66] Lenn Goodman seems to me to indicate as much when he writes, 'the derived reality of all contingent beings is rationality objectified, refracted into specificity in their natural forms, and rendered subjective once again in the rational intelligence that makes us human' (Goodman, 'God and the Good Life', 124–5).

connectedness from the plane of legal coherence to the plane of philosophical coherence. In short, *consonantia*, as it applies to *Mishneh torah*, corresponds to the interpretation of its form on the level of ideas. *Claritas* corresponds to the second level of interpretation outlined above, that of inspiration. Umberto Eco explains Aquinas's concept as follows:

claritas refers to the expressive capacity of organisms. It is, as someone put it, the radioactivity of the form of things . . . An organism which is fully perceived and grasped reveals its organic nature, and the intellect can enjoy the beauty of its discipline and order. This ontological expressiveness is not something that exists even when it is not an object of knowledge; rather it becomes real and manifest when the *visio* focuses upon it, a form of disinterested observation which regards the object under the aspect of its formal cause . . . Ontologically, *claritas* is clarity in itself, and it becomes aesthetic clarity or clarity 'for us' in a specific perception of it.

It follows that the aesthetic *visio* is for Aquinas *an act of judgment*. It entails activities of collocating and distinguishing, the mensuration of parts with respect to the whole, studies of how the matter lends itself to the form, an awareness of purposes and of how adequately they are fulfilled. Aesthetic perception is not an instantaneous intuition, but a dialogue with its object. The dynamism of the act of judgment corresponds to the dynamism of the act of organised existence which is the object of judgment . . . Beauty is what pleases when it is seen, not because it is intuited without effort, but because it is through effort that it is won, and when the effort is successful it is enjoyed. We take pleasure in knowledge which has overcome the obstacles in its path and so brought about the quiescence of desire.[67]

This amounts to a fair description of what will be attempted in this study. The expressive capacity of *Mishneh torah* can be appreciated once we have undertaken the activities Eco lists. Through the art of *Mishneh torah*, Maimonides gives his perception of the *claritas* of the commandments, the manifestation of their organic nature, discipline, and order when they are regarded under their formal cause.

So *Mishneh torah*'s beauty is a discovered beauty, requiring a dynamic response on the reader's part corresponding to the dynamism of its act of organized existence.[68] It is itself a description of the overcoming of the obstacles in the path to knowledge, and a model of that process. By becoming involved with it on a literary level (as opposed to the religiously observant level, which must not be forgotten), which we can only do by the active exploration

---

[67] Eco, *Art and Beauty*, 82. The way Aquinas's tripartite definition of beauty is presented here also derives from Collinson, 'The Aesthetic Theory of Stephen Dedalus'.

[68] Eco does concede that 'nothing could be further from certain modern theories of aesthetic intuition' (*Art and Beauty*, 83).

of its *integritas* and *consonantia*, we can win through to appreciation of its *claritas*.

There must of course be some ambivalence about applying Aquinas's definition to *Mishneh torah*. On the one hand, it has appropriately Platonic, Aristotelian, and Neoplatonic roots; on the other hand, it is also rooted in Aquinas's doctrine of the Trinity.[69] One could resort to Maimonides' own saw, 'Hear the truth from whoever says it',[70] or simply observe that the two thinkers' approaches are ideologically different but functionally similar. In the end, however, Maimonides' different ontology and theology may well dictate a different aesthetic. The present study is exegetical rather than comparative, invoking classical and medieval aesthetics and literary theory only insofar as they help to elucidate *Mishneh torah*. It does not examine the place of Maimonides' aesthetic as such in the history of ideas, though it is to be hoped that it will provide materials for that broader enquiry.[71]

The Poet in Maimonides' Republic

The Andalusian Heritage

From the idea of art in general we now turn to an examination of what it was that demanded artistic creativity in the composition of *Mishneh torah*. The first step is to establish that Maimonides had a poetic bent at all, for some would find it hard to see in him any disposition to conceive of his code of law as an artistic project. He has come to be regarded as indifferent to the arts, and disapproving of poetry of any sort, as though this were the one part of his Andalusian heritage that he disowned,[72] giving rise to the following kind of

---

[69] See Eco, *Art and Beauty*, 101; Gallagher, 'Hybridity of Aquinas's Aesthetic Theory'.

[70] 'Eight Chapters', Preface (*Ethical Writings*, ed. Weiss and Butterworth, 60).

[71] On Maimonidean aesthetics in historical context see Bland, 'Medieval Jewish Aesthetics' and 'Beauty, Maimonides, and Cultural Relativism'. Bland places Maimonides in the Aquinian naturist camp, as opposed to the Augustinian symbolist camp (p. 537), but points out that he did not ascribe transcendental value to beauty, whereas Aquinas did. But see Lobel, 'Being and the Good'. I tend more towards Bland's view on this question; I am not sure that Lobel does not place more weight than it will bear on the remark in *Guide* i. 59 (p. 139): 'Thus all the philosophers say: We are dazzled by His beauty.' Is what all the philosophers say necessarily what Maimonides would say? Bland sees Maimonides as being critical of the philosophers here rather than concurring with them—see *Artless Jew*, 101. Note 'Laws of Repentance', 8: 2, where the rabbinical phrase *ziv hashekhinah*, 'the radiance of the divine presence' (BT *Ber.* 17*a*), is interpreted as signifying not an attribute of God, but the acquired intellect's enhanced understanding of God after death and the release from the trammels of bodily existence. See also Eco, *Art and Beauty*, 26. Bland's comments on Maimonides and symbolism are discussed below.

[72] For a general description of the cultural milieu in which Maimonides grew up, see J. L. Kraemer, *Maimonides*, 42–54.

assessment: 'But there is one hat Rambam did not wear. Rambam was not a poet. Unlike the popular pursuit of his kinsmen during that period, Rambam disliked poetry—even religious poetry whether in Arabic or Hebrew.'[73]

In Maimonides' writings there is no shortage of apparent support for this conclusion. Here, for example, is how he describes those who read Scripture as they would other works of literature:

O you who engage in theoretical speculation using the first notions that may occur to you and come to your mind and who consider withal that you understand a book that is the guide of the first and last men while glancing through it as you would glance through a historical work or a piece of poetry—when in some of your hours of leisure you leave off drinking and copulating.[74]

Associating history and poetry with drinking and sex is about as scathing as Maimonides could get.[75] It is also true that he disapproved of liturgical poetry in the synagogue, partly because it transgressed the prohibition against multiplying praises and attributes of God.[76] In the 'Introduction to *Perek ḥelek*', just before the enunciation of his famous thirteen doctrinal principles, and apropos R. Akiva's exclusion of those who read 'external books' from the world to come, Maimonides counts books of poetry among those that 'contain neither wisdom nor material utility and are a mere waste of time'.[77]

A more generous assessment of the arts, including the art of gardening, comes in 'Eight Chapters' 5, where Maimonides assigns them therapeutic value:

Similarly, if the humor of black bile agitates him, he should make it cease by listening to songs and various kinds of melodies, by walking in gardens and fine buildings, by sitting before beautiful forms, and by things like this which delight the soul and make the disturbance of black bile disappear from it.[78]

And again:

For the soul becomes weary and the mind dull by continuous reflection upon difficult matters, just as the body becomes exhausted from undertaking toilsome occupations until it relaxes and rests and then returns to equilibrium. In a similar manner, the soul

---

[73] Birnbaum, 'Maimonides, Then and Now'. Twersky states that Maimonides 'had little use for poetry of any kind, even liturgical and hymnal', but concedes, in a footnote to that remark, that 'Actually, Maimonides evaluated poetry in the light of the criterion which he applied to all human discourse: the extent to which it contributed to the attainment of the goal of perfection' (*Introduction to the Code*, 250). [74] *Guide* i. 2 (p. 24).

[75] For Maimonides' low view of sexual intercourse, see *Guide* iii. 8 (p. 432).

[76] *Guide* i. 59 (p. 141). [77] *Commentary on the Mishnah*, Order *Nezikin*, 140–1.

[78] *Ethical Writings*, ed. Weiss and Butterworth, 75. Black bile means melancholia or depression.

needs to rest and to do what relaxes the senses, such as looking at beautiful decorations and objects so that weariness be removed from it.[79]

This is part of a general theme in 'Eight Chapters' of wisdom and virtue as medicine for the soul, a theme that returns in *Mishneh torah* in 'Laws of Ethical Qualities', 2: 1. That being so, the welcome given to the arts in these passages is perhaps less qualified than at first appears. To suggest that physic for the senses can be physic for the soul is not the sentiment of someone deaf to poetry. Moreover, even though Maimonides states quite explicitly that the fine arts are means to an end, and makes no suggestion that aesthetic pleasure can be inspirational or in itself convey truth, they are means to a very high end. The first passage quoted above continues: 'In all this he should aim at making his body healthy, the goal of his body's health being that he attain knowledge.'[80]

The idea of art as therapy provides at least one reason for supposing that form in *Mishneh torah* is significant beyond cataloguing content. It may well be that Maimonides took such evident pains over the style of his code because, apart from considerations of clarity and brevity, he applied the remedy prescribed in 'Eight Chapters' for the weariness that comes with studying difficult and obscure material, and sought to refresh the mind of *Mishneh torah*'s reader, grappling with the intricacies of halakhah, through the elegance of his prose.

Did his aesthetic sensibility go further than this? To begin with, for someone supposedly inimical to poetry, he wrote rather a lot of it, showing no little skill.[81] He composed a prologue to his *Commentary on the Mishnah*, an epilogue to *Mishneh torah*, and a prologue and epilogue to the *Guide*, all in Hebrew verse or rhymed prose.[82] A verse letter to R. Anatoly the Judge is even based on an erotic conceit.[83] Maimonides does conclude the rhyming preamble to the letter to R. Jonathan of Lunel and his colleagues[84] with an expression of relief at having done his duty by a rather tired etiquette, but only after many well-wrought lines richly embroidered with biblical allusion in the best Andalusian style.[85]

[79] *Ethical Writings*, ed. Weiss and Butterworth, 77.   [80] Ibid. 75.

[81] For an appraisal of poems attributed to Maimonides, as well as of his attitude to poetry, see Schirmann, 'Maimonides and Hebrew Poetry' (Heb.).

[82] The biblical allusions in the prologue and epilogue to the *Guide* are analysed by David Tzri in Maimonides, *Guide* (Heb. trans. Schwarz), 767–9. Yosef Yahalom comments on the prologues to the *Commentary on the Mishnah* and the *Guide* and on the epilogue to *Mishneh torah*: 'Maimonides performed wonderfully well in this genre too' ('Maimonides and Hebrew Poetic Language' (Heb.), 15).

[83] *Letters*, ed. Shailat (Heb.), 468.

[84] Ibid. 499.   [85] On that style, see J. L. Kraemer, *Maimonides*, 51.

The key to this apparent duality is not difficult. Maimonides did like poetry, as long as its content was worthy, and appropriate to the arena in which it was performed. He was of course aware that much of Scripture *is* poetry. There is some irony when in *Guide* i. 59 he invokes Psalm 65: 2, 'Silence is praise to thee', in arguing against positive descriptions of God, and in favour of pure cerebration—if that were applied literally, there would be no psalms. He complains of 'poets and preachers or such as think that what they speak is poetry' who use the surface meaning of prophetic texts as a starting point for elaborate, concrete descriptions of God.[86] This at least hints at the possibility of genuine poetry that, like the prophets and the psalmist, will communicate correct doctrine, even if necessarily through concrete imagery. The objection is not so much to poetry as to what by Maimonides' lights was bad poetry. His castigation of those who treat Scripture like poetry aims at their casual manner. He seems to have had in mind the kind of poetry he outlawed in a response he gave to a question whether it was permissible to listen to Arabic song.[87] That response shows that he was not insensible of the charm and uplifting power of poetry. His objections are mainly to the context of the songs (drinking parties), their licentious content, and their musical accompaniment, all of which, besides other transgressions that they involve, lead to arousal of desire and distancing from holiness and perfection.[88] 'And we should not regard the exceptional, rare individual', the letter says, 'whom this [poetry and music] will lead to care of the soul and zeal in apprehending a concept, or submission to the commandments of religion, for the Torah's laws are indeed written according to the majority and what is common, "for the sages spoke about what is usual".'

Music and song are thus sometimes conducive to virtue, but are forbidden because they are in general undesirable.[89] As far as liturgical poetry was concerned, Maimonides approved the extra prayers found in the prayer book of Sa'adyah Gaon, which include poetry, as a means of arousing devotion, but wrote that they should preferably be recited at home, because in the synagogue they prolonged the service beyond the endurance of the aged and infirm.[90] In a responsum on the permissibility of inserting *piyutim* into the

[86] *Guide* i. 59 (p. 141). [87] *Letters*, ed. Shailat (Heb.), 428.

[88] 'It is thus quite clear that the strict view adopted by Maimonides in going so far as he could in proscribing music was not merely because he took a mere legal view of the matter, but because in the Orient music was furnished largely by women, and the songs were often too prone to kindle the passions' (B. Cohen, 'Responsum Concerning Music', 176).

[89] For more on this point, see Rosner, 'Maimonides on Music'.

[90] *Letters*, ed. Shailat (Heb.), 589.

Shema recital,[91] Maimonides ruled in the negative on two grounds. The first is that such *piyutim* lead to a loss of devotion in prayer and a hubbub in the synagogue because the congregation knows that they are not really part of the service. The second is that the composers of such *piyutim* are not all of the right moral and intellectual standing. These objections can be taken at face value, since Maimonides proposed abolishing the cantor's repetition of the Amidah prayer, a matter that has nothing to do with poetry, on similar grounds of loss of decorum when the congregation fails to take it seriously,[92] and concluded the responsum by saying that *paytanim* of the rank of the prophets, meaning, presumably, morally and intellectually worthy, deserved peace and God's goodwill. Perhaps he had Sa'adyah in mind. In his commentary on Mishnah *Avot* 1: 16, Maimonides divides discourse into five categories: mandatory (such as study of Torah); forbidden (such as bearing false witness); vile (empty prattle); desirable (praise of virtue and condemnation of vice); and permissible (as in commerce). Under the category of desirable discourse, he goes so far as to include 'awakening the soul to virtue through stories and poems, and making it shun vice by the same means', and goes on to stress that poetry is to be evaluated according to its content.

In short, where Maimonides expresses a negative attitude to poetry, our judgement of his motives should be governed by the things he actually says and the contexts in which he says them; we should not necessarily infer a general distaste.[93] From what we have seen so far, he views aesthetics as part of ethics. Like bodily appetites,[94] the desire for beauty should be indulged in moderation, to the degree required for psychological well-being, and as for poetry, it is permissible if its content arouses virtuous thoughts, helping to develop the moral disposition required as a basis for intellectual activity. As Warren Zev Harvey puts it, 'The aesthetics which follows from Maimonides' intellectualistic teleology is no surprise. A good work of art is one that assists us in our pursuit of intellectual knowledge.'[95]

Harvey goes on to state that 'Maimonides did not think that art *per se* imparts knowledge',[96] although he acknowledges that Maimonides assigns art heuristic value, in biblical parables, for example, and also political value. This

---

[91] *Letters*, ed. Shailat (Heb.), 591.   [92] Ibid. 568.

[93] Joel Kraemer, in 'Maimonides and the Spanish Aristotelian School', comes to a similar conclusion. See also Shiloah, 'Maïmonide et la musique'. Shiloah points out that, unlike other authorities, Maimonides did not impose a blanket ban on enjoyment of music as a sign of mourning for the destruction of the Temple.   [94] See 'Laws of Ethical Qualities', 3: 1.

[95] W. Z. Harvey, 'Ethics and Meta-Ethics', 134.   [96] Ibid. 135.

study will probe the idea that actually both ethics and art can have cognitive value for Maimonides.

So much for Maimonides' public pronouncements on art and poetry. In private, he seems to have been more relaxed. Yahalom goes so far as to suggest that it was Maimonides' susceptibility to the charm of poetry that enabled Joseph ben Judah ibn Shimon to gain entrée to him and become the favourite pupil to whom the *Guide* would eventually be addressed.[97] Writing to Maimonides (who was in Fostat) from Alexandria, Joseph ben Judah expressed his desire to study with him in an elaborate allegory, partly in verse, and having a definite erotic component. In the introduction to the *Guide*, Maimonides commends Ben Judah's verses: they persuaded him of the would-be student's desire to learn, if not necessarily of his ability.

Considering the unromantic attitude to sexuality expressed in *Mishneh torah*[98] and the *Guide*,[99] and the kind of poetry and song he condemns in his responsum to Aleppo and his commentary on *Avot* 1: 16, this aspect of Maimonides' correspondence might seem to call for explanation. But it is a reminder that literary convention and invention can be a long way from real life and real attitudes, and in any case, Maimonides knew how to judge his reader and his occasion. We should bear in mind also that his calls for sexual sublimation are very frank.[100] He stood in the Andalusian tradition of Hebrew poetry in which the erotic motif, whether literal or allegorical, is prominent, if modest in comparison with the Hebrew poets' Arabic models.[101] The great precedent for the allegorization of erotic love in Hebrew poetry is Song of Songs, interpreted in *Mishneh torah*[102] and the *Guide*[103] as an allegory of the relationship between God and the individual soul, and in the 'Epistle to Yemen' as an allegory of the relationship between God and the Jewish people.[104]

The Logic of Poetry

The philosophers whom Maimonides held in highest regard had a high regard for poetry and theorized about it at length, which of course is not to say that he agreed with them on all points.[105] The relevance to *Mishneh torah*

---

[97] See Yahalom, 'Maimonides and Hebrew Poetic Language' (Heb.).

[98] 'Laws of Ethical Qualities', 4: 19; 5: 4.   [99] *Guide* iii. 8 (p. 432).

[100] See 'Laws of Repentance', 10: 3; 'Laws of Forbidden Intercourse', 21: 19 and 22: 21.

[101] See Tobi, 'Hebrew and Arabic Poetry' (Heb.), 53.   [102] 'Laws of Repentance', 10: 3.

[103] *Guide* iii. 51 (pp. 623–4).   [104] *Epistles*, ed. Halkin and Hartman, 104.

[105] This discussion is mainly based upon Black, *Logic and Aristotle's* Rhetoric *and* Poetics; Dahiyat, *Avicenna's Commentary on the* Poetics; Kemal, *Poetics of Alfarabi and Avicenna*; Kemal, 'Aesthetics'; Leaman, 'Poetry and the Emotions in Islamic Philosophy'.

of the aesthetic theory of Aristotle, whom Maimonides considered little lower than the prophets,[106] will be discussed below. Alfarabi, who was apparently next after Aristotle in Maimonides' estimation,[107] wrote a *Canons of Poetry*, and poetry is a recurring subject in his other works as well.

Alfarabi subscribed to the 'context theory', as did Avicenna after him. This was the grouping of Aristotle's *Rhetoric* and *Poetics* with his works on logic, expressing the view that rhetoric and poetry are forms of syllogistic argument, albeit at a lower level than demonstrative and dialectical syllogism, a view that Alfarabi worked out in detail in his own writing on poetry.

In the eighth chapter of the *Treatise on Logic*, Maimonides lists the various kinds of syllogism, from demonstrative syllogism downwards. Last in the list is the poetic syllogism, which is characterized by its premises being imitative or imaginary.[108] Maimonides' account reads like a condensation of Alfarabi and Avicenna's view, as expressed by Kemal, that 'poetic utterances have a logical form which follows the pattern of demonstrative reasoning'[109] even though what they assert is only metaphorically true and not literally true.

Perhaps it is far-fetched to suppose that, when he recommended Alfarabi's works on logic in his letter to Samuel ibn Tibbon,[110] one of the works Maimonides had in mind was the *Canons of Poetry*, even if context theory implies that it comes into that category, but, as mentioned, Alfarabi's thoughts on the subject are not confined to that work, and appear in, among other places, his *Fusul al-Madani*, of which Maimonides definitely did take note.[111]

It might be thought that Maimonides' inclusion of the poetic syllogism in his list of syllogisms has no significance beyond making his summary of

---

[106] 'The mind of Aristotle represents the ultimate that the human mind can reach, apart from those to whom the divine superabundance flows so that they attain the rank of prophecy, than which there is no higher rank' (*Letters*, ed. Shailat (Heb.), 553).

[107] See ibid. 552–3. 'After Aristotle, al-Farabi is the philosopher whom, judging by the letter to Ibn Tibbon, Maimonides held in the highest esteem' (Pines, 'Philosophic Sources', p. lxxviii).

[108] 'Then there are some who praise and blame things in no other way than by means of imitation, and any syllogism whose premise is used in this way of imitation we call a poetic syllogism, and the art which deals with such syllogisms and explains the ways of imitations is called the art of poetry' (Maimonides, *Treatise on Logic*, 49).

[109] Kemal, *Poetics of Alfarabi and Avicenna*, 171. Leaman sums it up thus: 'An idea is produced as a premise, and then we work out the implications of that premise. Finally we arrive at some proposition, or an emotion (the *falasifa* differed on this issue) that represents a reasonable conclusion. What is it a conclusion to? It is a conclusion to the ideas that were set in motion, as it were, by the poem, and it can represent our sense that we now grasp the various links between those ideas and have pulled them together. It could also be an emotion, something that has been inspired in us by the poem' ('Poetry and the Emotions in Islamic Philosophy', 140).

[110] *Letters*, ed. Shailat (Heb.), 552–3.   [111] See Davidson, 'Maimonides' *Shemonah Peraqim*'.

logical terms complete. In fact, I will argue, recognition of the poetic syllogism is crucial for understanding Maimonides' technique in *Mishneh torah*. In outline, the microcosmic form of *Mishneh torah* functions just as poetry functions in Alfarabi's and Avicenna's accounts of it: it carries the argument in a way that wins imaginative assent, via a double-layered metaphor in which both man and the commandments are compared to the cosmos (which is itself not something about which we have demonstrative knowledge).[112] The art of *Mishneh torah*, in its formal aspect, thus does not directly give us information about the world, but nor is it merely ornamental. It forms the inner logic of a sophisticated fiction that the reader must process in order to extract a deeper truth.

Symbolism

The work of Kalman Bland on Maimonidean aesthetics ostensibly supports the view I have been trying to develop of a Maimonides friendlier to the arts than in some portrayals. As part of his general concern to demonstrate that Jews in the medieval period had a keen visual sense, and to counter the notion of Judaism as a religion of sound rather than sight, which he considers a nineteenth- and twentieth-century distortion, Bland contends that Maimonides allowed free enjoyment of the visual arts, and refers to the passages quoted above from 'Eight Chapters' about their therapeutic value as evidence. Anything that expands Maimonides' aesthetic range would seem to be supportive of my thesis, which demands a Maimonides possessed of a developed aesthetic sensibility, but elements of Bland's approach run directly counter to that thesis, and with those I must take issue.[113]

According to Bland, Maimonides classed enjoyment of the visual arts as somatic rather than rational, and therefore developed no rational critique of beauty. Beauty cannot be predicated of God any more than any other attribute, and so the beautiful cannot be thought of as a reflection of the divine. The strict denial that human concepts can have any application to God leads Maimonides to distrust symbolism, for symbolism implies similitude between things below and things above.

I agree with this as far as it goes, but Bland goes further, for in trying to present a Maimonides free of symbolism, he shunts aside the idea of man as microcosm as developed in *Guide* i. 72. In that chapter, the relationship between mind and body is at first compared to the relationship between God and the world, but at the end of it that view is modified: 'Know that it

---

[112] See *Guide* ii. 24 (p. 327); Kellner, *Maimonides on Judaism*; Stern, 'The Enigma of Guide i. 68' (Heb.).   [113] For a more general critique of Bland's ideas, see Blidstein, 'Art and the Jew'.

behooved us to compare the relation obtaining between God, may He be exalted, and the world to that obtaining between the acquired intellect and man . . . We should have compared, on the other hand, the rational faculty to the intellects of the heavens, which are in bodies.'[114] Bland comments: 'Of all the rich implications of the microcosm metaphor, only one remains standing after this Maimonidean critique: a drastically attenuated and obscure similarity between the perfected human intellect and the mysterious cognitive entities which cause the celestial bodies to move.'[115]

This strikes at the root of my argument. I find the microcosm metaphor to be a mainstay of *Mishneh torah*'s form, and, by implication, of Maimonides' thought, and intend to demonstrate that, far from being attenuated and obscure, the similarity between the human intellect and the separate intellects suggested in *Mishneh torah* is full, precise, and clear.

As far as I can see, Bland misrepresents the conclusion of *Guide* i. 72. It is not the perfected intellect that is compared to the cognitive entities which cause the celestial bodies to move, but the undeveloped hylic intellect. This suggests something perfunctory in Bland's dismissal of what is as wonderful and subtle a chapter of the *Guide* as any.

But the fundamental difference between the position advanced here and that of Bland lies in the assessment of Maimonides' attitude to symbolism. While it is true that he generally avoids symbolic explanations for individual commandments, he does use symbolism to convey the function of the system of the commandments as a whole, making powerful use of the microcosm idea in doing so. Moreover, whereas Bland denies that, for Maimonides, aesthetic experience has anything to do with the spiritual, writing: 'One prepares for the other, one superficially resembles the other, but the two have nothing else in common',[116] I shall argue that the way in which the microcosm idea's symbolic possibilities are exploited turns *Mishneh torah* into an aesthetic object of great spiritual potential.

Bland is probably right in suggesting that Maimonides considered Ibn Gabirol's poem *Keter malkhut* theologically unsound in its portrayal of a divine realm of resplendent beauty, but it is not impossible that he drew inspiration from its description of the cosmic order in devising his own more indirect evocation of the beauty of the cosmos, the true discovery of which is a matter of moral and intellectual striving, of becoming that beauty, and not merely being awestruck by it.[117]

---

[114] *Guide* i. 72 (p. 193), as cited by Bland.   [115] Bland, *Artless Jew*, 81.   [116] Ibid.
[117] This is to give a Plotinian colour to Maimonides' aesthetic ambition in *Mishneh torah*. See

It seems to me that Bland unreasonably stifles Maimonides' symbolism in order to keep literary art and visual art on the same plane in Maimonidean aesthetics. If there is no symbolic value in the latter, then there shall be none in the former. Actually, however, the dichotomy between sight and sound, which Bland sees as a retrospective imposition on a medieval Jewish sensibility that gave both free play, does seem to have been very much a part of Maimonides' outlook, and part of a tendency, for both theological and practical reasons, to invest spiritual wealth in the digital, portable, acoustic word rather than in the visual, fixed, analogue cathedral or mosque. The consolation must be that, just as Heschel called the sabbaths 'our great cathedrals',[118] in *Mishneh torah* Maimonides produced out of his digital medium an analogue capacious and beautiful enough to rank with any medieval monument.

All in all, then, we can compare Maimonides' public attitude to poetry to that of Plato.[119] He would banish poetry that is liable to corrupt morals or that anthropomorphizes the deity, but poetry that is uplifting and theologically correct is welcome on the right occasion and in the right place.[120] Poetry as such, although it was within his competence, was not his real medium, but, like Plato, he was someone with a critical stance towards myth-making and literary art who had a penchant for both.[121] His response to Joseph ben Judah's literary tribute shows a predilection for poetry sufficient for him to be persuaded that someone with poetic sensibility was probably talent he could work with. It seems not unreasonable to look for similar sensibility in his own magnum opus, for an aesthetic as well as a philosophical synthesis of the different streams of thought it unites, especially bearing in mind his adoption of the view of poetry as a form of logic. With that as an interim, impressionistic conclusion, we can start to explore deeper motivations for *Mishneh torah* being a work of art.

Necessities and Literary Invention

What were the forces acting on the author of *Mishneh torah* that elicited an artistic response? Essentially, they arose from the fact that he set out not just

O'Meara, *Plotinus*, 88–99. Further comparison of Maimonides' literary practice with the aesthetic theory of the Neoplatonists is made below.

[118] Heschel, *The Sabbath*, 8.

[119] See Murray and Dorsch, *Classical Literary Criticism*, pp. xxiii–xxix. This comparison is of course based on a simplification, for, as Murray remarks, 'Plato's attitude to poetry is neither simple nor consistent' (ibid., p. xxix).

[120] Faur, however, sees Maimonides as objecting to poetic form as well as to unedifying content. See Faur, 'Maimonides on Imagination', 97.

[121] See Hughes, '"The Torah speaks in the language of humans"'.

to codify halakhah, but to encompass Torah in all its dimensions: philosophical and historical as well as legal. This engendered tensions that called for creative resolution.

Esotericism

The first difficulty was the practical constraint that it was simply not convenient to include a full explication of *ma'aseh bereshit* and *ma'aseh merkavah* in what was supposed to be a practical work of reference. It would have made *Mishneh torah* top-heavy with philosophy. Moreover, such explication was forbidden. At the same time, to exclude that material would be to distort Torah. In the *Guide*, introducing his interpretation of the *merkavah* vision of Ezekiel, Maimonides put the dilemma thus:

if I had omitted setting down something of that which has appeared to me as clear, so that that knowledge would perish when I perish, as is inevitable, I should have considered that conduct as extremely cowardly with regard to you and everyone who is perplexed. It would have been, as it were, robbing one who deserves the truth of the truth, or begrudging an heir his inheritance. On the other hand, as has been stated before, an explicit exposition of this knowledge is denied by a legal prohibition, in addition to that which is imposed by judgment.[122]

The prohibition imposed by judgement is that discussing certain things openly before people who have not undergone the requisite training can cause actual harm.[123] The answer in the *Guide* is to create a puzzle:

I shall interpret to you that which was said by *Ezekiel the prophet*, peace be on him, in such a way that anyone who heard that interpretation would think that I do not say anything over and beyond what is indicated by the text, but that it is as if I translated words from one language to another or summarized the meaning of the external sense of the speech. On the other hand, if that interpretation is examined with a perfect care by him for whom this Treatise is composed and who has understood all its chapters— every chapter in its turn—the whole matter, which has become clear and manifest to me, will become clear to him so that nothing in it will remain hidden from him.[124]

We understand from this, and from the *Guide*'s general introduction, that most people will not even perceive that the puzzles exist, never mind be

---

[122] *Guide* iii, Introduction (pp. 415–16).

[123] See *Commentary on the Mishnah*, Ḥag. 2: 1; *Guide* i. 34 (pp. 72–9).

[124] *Guide* iii, Introduction (p. 416) The italics are original. The preface to Pines and Strauss's English edition of the *Guide* states, 'Italic type in the text has been reserved to indicate Maimonides' use of words that are clearly identifiable as being Hebrew or Aramaic', that is to say, not Arabic. This usage has been preserved throughout.

capable of solving them. They arise from deliberate contradictions, or from material germane to a certain question being scattered in different parts of the book.

A puzzle has a definite solution, and this is generally the way the *Guide's* difficulties are approached, as though a question such as 'What was Maimonides' true position on creation in the *Guide*?' is answerable, even if there is disagreement about what the answer is (although not everyone agrees with that approach, and the nature and extent of the *Guide's* esotericism are hotly debated questions).[125] *Mishneh torah*, at any rate, is not a puzzle, but a mystery. It has been shown to work on more than one level, addressing both the pure talmudist and the philosophically aware reader,[126] but its deeper esotericism consists of an endlessly suggestive symbolic form. In *Mishneh torah*, it is through the artistic combination of content and form that Maimonides solves both his practical and his political problem.

What Time Is It in *Mishneh Torah*?

Mishneh torah seeks to present Torah as a perfect, seamless, timeless whole, but, in practice, halakhah varies with time and place. Certain commandments apply only in the Land of Israel; others apply only in the messianic era. How to give an impression of Torah as fully integrated and eternally valid, and at the same time accommodate both a pre- and a post-messiah world? Or to put the question another way, what time is it in *Mishneh torah*? No definite answer can be given. The work inhabits both the timeless world of the spheres and the time-bound sublunary world; both the ideal, redeemed, post-messianic world, and the real, unredeemed present.

This stands out in the books on the Temple and its ritual. 'Laws of the Temple' begins thus: 'It is a positive commandment to make a house for the Lord, suitable for bringing sacrifices.' When? Now? From what is said in 'Laws of Kings and Their Wars', it would seem not—rebuilding the Temple is a task for the King Messiah[127]—but you would not know this from 'Laws of

---

[125] For example, Kenneth Seeskin contends that the *Guide* does not contain a single, true teaching, and writes, *contra* esotericist Leo Strauss, 'It is esoteric because it is difficult to achieve certainty in a field where all we have are brief glimpses of the truth; but there are no booby traps, and the *Guide* is not a book with seven seals' (*Searching for a Distant God*, 180). Faur describes the *Guide* as a puzzle, but as one in which readers find themselves, rather than an objective solution (Faur, *Homo Mysticus*, p. xi). For a (sceptical) review of 'The Esoteric Issue' see Davidson, *Moses Maimonides*, 387–402.

[126] See above, n. 22.

[127] 'Laws of Kings and Their Wars', 11: 4. 'Laws of the Temple', 1: 1, has been taken by some as implying that building the Temple is actually not dependent on the messiah. See Inbari, *Jewish Fundamentalism and the Temple Mount*, 111–14.

the Temple'. To say that this is obvious is to miss the point. We need to forget
what we know and attend to Maimonides' presentation. In his presentation
of the laws of the Temple, the messiah is present, even past, or rather the
commandment is ever present, waiting to be actualized.

There are parts of *Mishneh torah* in which orientation in time is not simple.
The *Book of Agriculture* presents the agricultural laws as though they apply at
all times everywhere. One has to pay careful attention to understand which
laws apply where, and when. In the *Book of Love* there is a particularly interesting example of the dual time track, one that gave rise to controversy. 'Laws of
Fringes' states that the *ḥilazon*, the mollusc from the blood of which the dye
for the sky-blue thread in the fringes to be placed on a four-cornered garment
is meant to be produced, is found in the Mediterranean, and gives a detailed
account of the dyeing process.[128] But in his *Commentary on the Mishnah*,
Maimonides writes that the correct dye is not currently available and that the
commandment of the sky-blue thread is consequently in abeyance.[129] The
inconsistency led R. Gershon Hanokh Lainer (who, in the nineteenth century, sought to reinstitute the sky-blue thread) to conclude that, in between
writing the *Commentary on the Mishnah* and writing *Mishneh torah*, Maimonides rediscovered the *ḥilazon*. It appears more likely that he did not have the
ḥilazon at any time,[130] and that in *Mishneh torah* he wrote both for the ideal
circumstances in which the *ḥilazon* would be available and for the reality in
which it was not, without distinguishing clearly between the two. That might
seem a very odd proceeding in what is supposed to be a practical manual of
law, but the many examples lead to the conclusion that it is deliberate, part
of the merging of time frames, which is in turn part of *Mishneh torah*'s
comprehensiveness.

It is not that a historical perspective is lacking in *Mishneh torah*. It gives
historical accounts of, for example, the rise of idolatry,[131] the institution of
fixed prayer,[132] and the institution of marriage.[133] The historical perspective,
however, is contained within a larger, timeless perspective.

Action versus Contemplation

The premise of *Mishneh torah* seems at odds with the body of the work, for to
know God is an intellectual task, but *Mishneh torah* is about commandments

---

[128] 'Laws of Fringes', 2: 2.   [129] On Mishnah *Men.* 4: 1.
[130] See 'Laws of Fringes', 1: 9 and *Rambam la'am* note to 'Laws of Fringes', 2: 9.
[131] 'Laws of Idolatry', 1.   [132] 'Laws of Prayer and the Priestly Blessing', 1: 4.
[133] 'Laws of Marriage', 1: 1.

that enjoin physical action. If knowing God means acquiring knowledge of God's works, with such knowledge engendering love and love inspiring desire for knowledge in a virtuous circle,[134] why are Jews burdened with such things as building a *sukah*, and why do they spend hours in the synagogue, when they would be better off devoting the time and effort to the study of biology or astrophysics?

The *Shulḥan arukh* presupposes that a human being's purpose is to serve God. It begins: 'A person should rise in the morning as mightily as a lion for the service of his creator, so that it is he who awakens the dawn.' This is clearly consonant with a religion that consists of divine commandments. But if the object is knowledge rather than service, the commandments present a problem.

Maimonides has solutions. He believed that part of the point of the Mosaic legislation was to reduce the burden of incessant ritual imposed by pagan religion, and for the very reason that the latter left no time to think.[135] Compared with paganism, therefore, Judaism is conducive to the cultivation of knowledge. It could not go all the way and abolish ritual because that would have been too sharp a rupture with convention. In the *Guide*, the commandments themselves are presented as instrumental rather than inherently valuable, designed to inculcate a modicum of knowledge, and to ensure individual morality and social stability, as a platform for the pursuit of philosophical speculation. The problem of the *ḥukim*, the non-rational commandments, such as the prohibition against wearing a wool and linen blend, is tackled in the *Guide* by tracing their origins to the rejection of idolatrous practices.[136] For the more advanced, the commandments are spiritual exercises, a course of training in detachment from worldly affairs, since conscientious observance of the commandments requires one to direct one's mind towards God

---

[134] This is putting together 'Laws of the Foundations of the Torah', 2: 2 and 'Laws of Repentance', 10: 6.

[135] See *Guide* iii. 30 (p. 523): 'God, may He be exalted, wished in His pity for us to efface this error from our minds and to take away fatigue from our bodies through the abolition of these tiring and useless practices', and iii. 47 (p. 592): 'I shall then say that this Law of God . . . came to facilitate the actions of worship and to lighten the burden. All the things in it that you may perhaps imagine to involve unpleasantness or a heavy burden appear so to you only because you do not know the usages and teachings that existed in those days.' Clearly, people constantly having to observe ceremonies and restrictions supposedly enjoined by many deities have no time to think about the fraud being perpetrated on them, let alone to contemplate the truth. Hence even in Judaism ritual is a two-edged sword, valuable only insofar as it is conducive to social harmony and to true understanding. As soon as it is seen as an object in itself, it actually becomes harmful; see e.g. 'Laws of Slaughter', 14: 16. This does not mean that the commandments may be taken lightly—on the contrary, as the *halakhah* just cited stresses, performance of the commandments in a respectful and conscientious manner demonstrates awareness of their source.　　　　　　　　　[136] *Guide* iii. 37 (p. 544).

without distraction.[137] Moreover, Maimonides builds *pardes*, which, as we saw above, he equates with physics and metaphysics, or science and philosophy, into the curriculum mandated by the commandment to study Torah.[138]

All these are solutions in practice, but not in principle. It remains the case that a religion in which the ideal is uninterrupted contemplation of the divine consists of commandments, that is, action.

This problem of philosophy versus religion can be expressed in aesthetic terms. Great art transcends the condition of its medium. If architecture is frozen music,[139] by the same token, music could be called fluid architecture, giving apparent shape to a succession of sounds. In *Mishneh torah*, Maimonides is constrained by his medium to relay the commandments successively, while the commandments themselves, insofar as they prescribe actions, are kinetic. But by constructing it on the plan of the cosmos, he gives *Mishneh torah* an architecture that creates an impression of simultaneity. He makes the commandments stand still. The contradiction between an ideal of contemplation and a religion of action forced Maimonides into a procedure that is quintessentially artistic: the transformation of *kinesis* into *stasis*.[140]

This is different from the notion that the practical commandments are training for a life of contemplation, which is the more prosaic way of reconciling the two modes. It captures an unending process, a constant relation of being to becoming, the radiation of divine permanence into the flux of life.

As well as contemplation versus action, the strain between philosophy and religion can also be seen as a conflict between the individual and the collective. The law is addressed to the collective, whereas the pursuit of the knowledge of God is an individual quest.[141] In Chapter 4 it will be shown that, through its form, *Mishneh torah* is bidirectional, that it incorporates both the flow of law from God via the prophet to the state, and the individual quest for God. Again, the containment of movement and counter-movement in a single work is an artistic endeavour, an exploitation of the capacity of art that

---

[137] *Guide* iii. 51 (pp. 622–3). Twersky refers to the *Guide*'s rationalization of the law as helping to 'bridge the gap between traditional religion, with its insistence upon the necessity and value of action, and philosophy, with its insistence upon the excellence and superiority of contemplation' (*Introduction to the Code*, 406). I shall argue in effect that, while the *Guide* bridges the gap, *Mishneh torah* poetically closes it.

[138] 'Laws of Torah Study', 1: 12. See Kasher, 'The Study of Torah' (Heb.) and 'Maimonides' Philosophical Division' (Heb.).

[139] The idea is generally attributed to Goethe, but the credit should probably go to Schelling, who wrote, 'Architecture, however, is a form of the plastic arts, and if it is music, then it is *concrete* music' (*Philosophy of Art*, 166).   [140] See Collinson, 'Aesthetic Theory of Stephen Dedalus'.

[141] See Ravitzky, 'Philosophy and Leadership in Maimonides'.

is perhaps one of its essential characteristics, to do more than one thing at once.

For all these reasons, the artistic aspects of *Mishneh torah* are compelled by the very nature of the enterprise. Only through supreme creative exertion was Maimonides able to incorporate and transcend the tensions, even contradictions, between religion and philosophy.

Art as *Imitatio Dei* [142]

Thus far, the description of the motivations for *Mishneh torah* being a work of art rests on the idea that a contradiction between two valid impulses or ideas stimulates the invention of a third entity, a greater whole that will contain them. But there is also another kind of motivation for artistic expression at work in *Mishneh torah*, giving rise to a response that is actually more consonant with classical and medieval notions of art: not invention, but imitation. [143]

Torah works through imitation. The primary commandment of 'Laws of Ethical Qualities' is to become like God. [144] The goal of ethics is to become fit to cultivate the love and knowledge of God, itself a kind of imitation, since through the pursuit of knowledge human beings fulfil the potential of their likeness to God, which lies in the possession of intellect. In other words, both of the twin goals of the law, the welfare of the body (which covers personal and social ethics) and the welfare of the soul, are attained through processes of imitation. The consequence of observance of Torah is also imitation, in that the ideal person sanctifies the name of God by becoming an object of love to be emulated. [145] That is the ultimate *imitatio*; to be so perfectly like the cosmos as to inspire in others the love and fear of God, and the desire for knowledge, that contemplation of the cosmos itself inspires. [146]

If it is to live up to its creed, *Mishneh torah* ought to do no less. After all, ethical behaviour means that one's every deed is directed to the knowledge of God, [147] and *Mishneh torah* was Maimonides' greatest deed. How can a code of law be imitative, so that it will set an example to be imitated and to inspire? For that, it must somehow embody the values that its content propounds, values that, in the case of *Mishneh torah*, are rooted in *imitatio Dei*. This *Mishneh torah* does in its artistic form. *Imitatio Dei* by a person is ethical; *imitatio Dei* by a book is aesthetic.

---

[142] The following discussion is largely based on Coulter, *Literary Microcosm*. Specific references to that monograph are given as appropriate.   [143] See Abrams, *The Mirror and the Lamp*, 8–14.

[144] 'Laws of Ethical Qualities', 1: 5.   [145] 'Laws of the Foundations of the Torah', 5: 11.

[146] Ibid. 2: 2. See also below, Ch. 1, under 'Portrait of Perfection'.

[147] 'Laws of Ethical Qualities', 3: 3.

Over the coming chapters it will be demonstrated that *Mishneh torah* indeed performs this feat of matching ethics with aesthetics. Observing its microcosmic structure is only the beginning of the exploration of a profound kind of mimesis; were it not so, that structure would be in danger of being regarded as a sort of pastiche. For now, the intention is to provide a theoretical grounding, and to look at the tripartite relationship between ontology, ethics, and aesthetics in classical and medieval literary theory as it bears on Maimonides' practice, with the aim of rendering this account of his practice more probable.

Law as Art Form

The idea that the relationship between religion and philosophy can be thought of as aesthetic mimesis is to be found in the medieval Islamic philosophers:

Religion is a reflection of and handmaiden to philosophy, dependent upon philosophy as a copy is dependent upon its original. In understanding religion as an imitation of philosophy, the Islamic philosophers were consciously evoking the background of Aristotle's *Poetics* and Plato's *Republic* and the aesthetic theories which they developed through a creative blending of the respective views of their two ancient sources on the nature of imitation.[148]

Maimonides does not present us with a general theory of imitation in art. In at least one place, however, he does drop a hint that the perfection of the Torah can be seen in aesthetic terms. In the *Guide*, he compares plagiarizers of prophecy with plagiarizers of poetry, as follows:

For among the people there are men who admire a certain perfection, take pleasure in it, have a passion for it, and wish that people should imagine that this perfection belongs to them, though they know that they possess no perfection. Thus you see that there are many who lay a claim to, and give out as their own, the poetry of someone else . . . This has also happened with regard to the prophetic perfection.[149]

That poetry and prophecy can live on the same page may be taken as

---

[148] Black, 'Aesthetics in Islamic Philosophy'. It is true that, in his letter to R. Jonathan of Lunel and his colleagues, Maimonides uses the handmaiden metaphor the other way round, and describes philosophy as the handmaiden of Torah who, in his own studies, usurped her mistress (*Letters*, ed. Shailat (Heb.), 502), but, even taking this at face value, we must distinguish between philosophy, which, as the 'great thing', is indeed prior to religion, and the philosophers, to whom Maimonides refers in the letter, and by means of whom he sought to reconstruct the original philosophical content of Torah. See also Pines, 'Philosophic Sources', p. xc, and his note 57 on mimesis in prophecy and poetry.

[149] *Guide* ii. 40 (p. 382).

further evidence of a warmer attitude to poetry on Maimonides' part than some attribute to him. This passage, though, at least hints at something more far-reaching. The context of the passage is a discussion of codes of law, such as the Torah, that are the product of prophetic perfection, versus ersatz codes that have no true prophetic inspiration. The implication, perhaps, is that the perfection of the Torah and the perfection of poetry are somehow comparable.

It is a pretty slender hint. To fill it out, we need to look more closely at how Maimonides defines the perfection of the Torah, in order to see what similarity it might bear to the perfection of poetry.

A primary source for law (religion being divine law) as an aesthetic imitation of philosophy is in Plato's *Laws*, in the response that the Athenian, engaged in formulating the laws of an ideal state, imagines making to an application by the tragedians, the best of the poets, for admission to that state:

Most honoured guests, we're tragedians ourselves, and our tragedy is the finest and best we can create. At any rate, our entire state has been constructed so as to be a 'representation' of the finest and noblest life—the very thing we maintain is most genuinely a tragedy. So we are poets like yourselves, composing in the same *genre*, and your competitors as artists and actors in the finest drama, which true law alone has the power to 'produce' to perfection.[150]

This is actually part of an argument for censorship: the Athenian goes on to say that, since the laws of the state are the best imitation of the ideal order, the poets, with their inferior imitations, cannot be allowed to undermine them. But neither poetry nor law is a positive creation. Imitation is the basis of both.

In a way, though, this is a bad example, in that it downgrades literary imitation. It is true that both Maimonides and Plato posit transcendent objects of imitation: God in Maimonides' case, the Forms in Plato's. For Plato, this relegates art to the status of a copy of a copy: nature copies the Forms, and art copies nature. Hence the questionable value of art, since the human goal is to know the Forms, and art is at an extra remove from them. But as far as Maimonides is concerned, all that we can know, and therefore all that we can imitate, is God as manifest in creation,[151] which puts ethics and art on a more level footing: both imitate nature. Much closer to Maimonides than Plato in this respect is Aristotle.

---

[150] Plato, *Laws*, VII. 817.
[151] 'Laws of Ethical Qualities', 1: 6; *Guide* i. 54 (pp. 123–8).

The Imitation of Nature

"'Art imitates nature,'" . . . says Aristotle.'[152] According to Maimonides, so does the Torah. We should first of all note that by the imitation of nature Aristotle means something more subtle than painting trees or otherwise reproducing natural objects:

nature in Aristotle is not the outward world of created things; it is the creative force, the productive principle of the universe . . . in the *Physics* the point of the comparison is that alike in art and in nature there is the union of matter . . . with constitutive form . . . and that the knowledge of both elements is requisite for the natural philosopher as for the physician and the architect . . . Art in its widest acceptance has, like nature, certain ends in view, and in the adaptation of means to ends catches hints from nature who is already in some sort an unconscious artist.[153]

Somewhat similarly, moral virtue in Maimonides consists in discerning forms of natural phenomena and adopting them as the forms of one's own actions. This is how *imitatio Dei* is to be pursued: 'Just as he is called gracious, so should you be gracious; just as he is called merciful, so should you be merciful', we are told in 'Laws of Ethical Qualities',[154] which is glossed in the *Guide* to mean the imitation of phenomena in nature that would be ascribed to these qualities, or forms, if they proceeded from a human being.[155] Maimonides insists that the Torah has intelligible ends in view, and in that respect reflects the purposiveness of God's actions in nature, adapting to its ends the means available.[156] The relationship of Torah to nature thus has similarities to the relationship between art and nature as described above.

What is it that connects nature, art, and Torah? The answer is the doctrine of the middle path, or the mean. The way that Maimonides recommends for arriving at moral virtue is to cultivate the mean between extremes of temperament. In 'Laws of Ethical Qualities', it is not quite clear how *imitatio Dei*, the commandment on which the section is based, connects to the doctrine of the mean. The bare statement 'We are bidden to walk in the middle paths which are the right and proper ways, as it is said "and thou shalt walk in His ways"'[157] skates over this point.

The missing link is to be found in Aristotle:

If it is thus, then, that every art does its work well—by looking to the intermediate and judging its works by this standard (so that we often say of good works of art that it is

---

[152] Butcher, *Aristotle's Theory of Poetry*, 116.
[153] Ibid. 116–17.   [154] i: 6.   [155] See *Guide* i. 54 (pp. 125–6).
[156] See *Guide* iii. 26 (pp. 506–7).   [157] 'Laws of Ethical Qualities', i: 5.

not possible either to take away or to add anything, implying that excess and defect destroy the goodness of works of art, while the mean preserves it; and good artists, as we say, look to this in their work), and if, further, virtue is more exact and better than any art, as nature also is, then virtue must have the quality of aiming at the intermediate.[158]

The mean is not an average but an excellence, a perfection: the perfection of nature, and, by derivation, the perfection of art and of morals. The virtuous person is not cautiously avoiding extremes, but triangulating from undesirable extremes to find the good. Hence Maimonides can identify the mean with God's actions in nature. The commandments of the Torah are also based upon the mean, as the translation of the perfection of nature, the precise balance of its processes, into norms of human behaviour that avoid excess or deficiency. This is made explicit in 'Eight Chapters' 4, where the commandments are described as embodying the mean, as well as counteracting the human tendency to veer from the mean in one direction or the other.[159]

Most interestingly for the present discussion, Aristotle builds the understanding of ethics upon aesthetics, in that he proposes 'good works of art' as a readily graspable example of a principle that he finds in ethics and in nature too, namely, that perfection consists in a mean to which nothing can be added and from which nothing can be taken away. For Aristotle there is continuity between nature, ethics, and art in this respect (even if something remains here of the Platonic deprecation of art, virtue and nature being 'more exact and better').

In the *Guide*, Maimonides adopts this definition of perfection for both

[158] Aristotle, *Nicomachean Ethics*, 1106b, 7 ff.; Barnes, *Complete Works of Aristotle*, 1106b, 7 ff. For a general account of Maimonides' indebtedness to Aristotle see Pines, 'Philosophic Sources'. Davidson, usually conservative in these matters, opines that Maimonides had direct knowledge of the *Nicomachean Ethics* (*Moses Maimonides*, 99), and in fact finds a reference to that work in *Guide* ii. 40, cited above (*Moses Maimonides*, 101 n. 38), which altogether maintains a close dialogue with Aristotle both explicitly and implicitly. It starts with the Aristotelian notion of man as 'political by nature', which is to be found in the *Nicomachean Ethics*, among other places (see Mulgan, 'Aristotle's Doctrine'), and goes on to state that society is to be perfected by a ruler 'perfecting that which is deficient and reducing that which is excessive' in the individuals that make it up.

[159] Fox argues that Maimonides accepts Aristotle's derivation from nature of the idea of perfection as a mean between extremes, but that while Aristotle finds the reference point for applying the idea of the mean to human behaviour in social convention, Maimonides finds it in the commandments of the Torah—see Fox, 'Doctrine of the Mean'. Fox notes the importance of the medical analogy in Aristotle's discussion of the doctrine of the mean, which is carried through into Maimonides' version of the doctrine, as in the curative function of the commandments in 'Eight Chapters', the diagnosis of deviation from the mean as a sickness of the soul in 'Laws of Ethical Qualities', 2, and the prescriptions for physical health in 'Laws of Ethical Qualities', 4.

nature and Torah.[160] The perfection of nature is defined in *Guide* ii. 28 thus:

On the other hand, *Solomon* himself has likewise stated that these works of the deity— I mean the world and what is in it—even though they are made, are permanently established according to their nature for ever. For he says: *That whatsoever God doeth, it shall be for ever; nothing can be added to it, nor any thing taken from it* (Eccles. 3: 14) ... As for his mention of the perfection of the acts of the deity and of its being impossible to add or to take away from them, the Master of those who know had already clearly stated this, saying: *The Rock, His work is perfect* (Deut. 32: 4). He means that all His works—I mean to say all His creatures—are most perfect, that no deficiency at all is commingled with them, that there is no superfluity in them and nothing that is not needed.[161]

With regard to the perfection and supremacy of the law of Moses, in *Guide* ii. 39, Maimonides makes a direct comparison to this property of nature:

We likewise believe that things will always be this way. As it says: *It is not in heaven, and so on; for us and for our children for ever.* And that is as it ought to be; for when a thing is as perfect as it is possible to be within its species, it is impossible that within that species there should be found another thing that does not fall short of that perfection either because of excess or deficiency. Thus in comparison with a temperament whose composition is of the greatest equibalance possible in the species in question, all other temperaments are not composed in accordance with this equibalance because of either deficiency or excess. Things are similar with regard to this Law, as is clear from its equibalance ... For this reason it is said with reference to them: *The Law of the Lord is perfect.*[162]

The permanence of the law, like the permanence of the universe,[163] is thus guaranteed by its biblically warranted perfection (and in passing we also have a reference here to the perfect temperament).

---

[160] The parallel is noted by Eliezer Berkovits in 'Torah and Nature' (Heb.), 12.

[161] *Guide* ii. 28 (pp. 335–6).

[162] p. 380. The closing quotation is from Ps. 19: 8. In *Guide* iii. 26 (p. 507), in discussing the law's wisdom, Maimonides cites verse 10 of the same psalm: 'The judgments of the Lord are true, they are righteous altogether.'

[163] Permanence here does not mean lasting for ever, but that the laws of nature are permanent as long as the universe does last. See Ravitzky, 'God and Nature' (Heb.). In *Guide* ii. 27 (p. 333) Maimonides states that both positions—that the universe is eternal post-Creation and that it will end—are compatible with the law, but that 'Speculation obliges us to affirm that the passing-away of the world need not necessarily follow'. For differing interpretations, see R. Weiss, 'Maimonides on the End of the World'; Feldman, 'End of the Universe'.

In *Guide* iii. 49,[164] nature and the commandments are again directly compared in respect of their perfection, via the same verse from Deuteronomy cited in *Guide* ii. 28:

Marvel exceedingly at the wisdom of His commandments, may He be exalted, just as you should marvel at the wisdom manifested in the things He had made. It says: *The Rock, His work is perfect; for all His ways are judgment*. It says that just as the things made by him are consummately perfect, so are his commandments consummately just.

The moderate interpretation of this comparison would be that it is a comparison of magnitude: God's commandments are as just as his works are perfect. A more radical interpretation, but more consonant with everything else that has been cited here, and certainly with the symbolic structure of *Mishneh torah*, is that it is a comparison of substance: the moral order is implicit in the natural order (which it must be if God created the world).[165] In fact, in *Guide* iii. 12, 'for all His ways are judgment' is taken to mean exactly that: creation embodies God's goodness and mercy.[166] God's ways can thus equally mean nature and the commandments, and the definition of their perfection is the same as Aristotle's definition of artistic perfection: nothing can be added or taken away.

Actually, we do not need to go to the *Guide* for the application of that definition of perfection to the Torah; it is to be found in *Mishneh torah* itself: 'It is clearly and explicitly set forth in the Torah that its ordinances will endure for ever without variation, diminution, or addition; as it is said, "All this word which I command you, that shall ye observe to do; thou shalt not add to it, nor take away from it" (Deut. 13: 1).'[167]

The verse intends 'Thou shalt not add to it, nor take away from it' as a prescriptive statement, meaning 'do not add to or take away from the Torah', but in this *halakhah* Maimonides treats it as descriptive, as meaning that nothing can, or nothing will, be added to or taken away from the Torah.[168] This is an instance on the micro-scale of the transformation of *kinesis* into *stasis*. The upshot is that the Torah is perfect, and its perfection coincides with aesthetic perfection.

In none of these places where he discusses perfection as the absence of excess or deficiency is Maimonides concerned with aesthetics. His concern

---

[164] pp. 605–6.

[165] Hadad, 'Nature and Torah in Maimonides' (Heb.), explores this idea in depth.

[166] *Guide* iii. 12 (p. 448). 'The Rock his work is perfect' is also cited in *Guide* iii. 25 (p. 506).

[167] 'Laws of the Foundations of the Torah', 9: 1.

[168] The prescriptive aspect is dealt with separately, in 'Laws of the Rebellious Elder', 2: 9.

is rather with the doctrines of creation, the permanence of nature, and the permanence of the commandments, which 'The Rock, his work is perfect' encapsulates. Perfection for Maimonides entails permanence, for if something is perfect, there is no possibility of change in it,[169] while 'rock', when it designates God, is defined in the *Guide* as meaning God as 'the principle and the efficient cause of all things other than Himself'.[170] Nevertheless, the similarity between Aristotle's definition of artistic perfection, on the one hand, and Maimonides' definition of natural perfection and the perfection of the Torah on the other, opens up the possibility that the latter could conceive of the reproduction of the Torah's perfection, such as he attempted in *Mishneh torah*, as an aesthetic mission. Haym Soloveitchik's perception of *Mishneh torah*'s artistic quality as lying in the impossibility of adding to it perhaps detects this, again, irrespective of the merits of his argument about *Mishneh torah*'s acceptance history.

Ontology and Aesthetics

The continuity between ontology, ethics, and aesthetics observed in Aristotle is not exceptional among classical and medieval thinkers. Notions of artistic worth tend to flow from notions of God's relationship to the world, with its consequences for ideas of human perfection and hence of artistic perfection.

In the creation myth recounted in the *Timaeus*, Plato posits a Demiurge that makes the world by imitating pre-existing Forms. As mentioned already, man's highest good is to perceive the Forms, the highest reality. Just as nature exists in relation to the perfection of the Forms, so art too is subject to criteria of excellence outside itself. Art is worthy insofar as it provides an uplifting example, promoting the good of the state, and ultimately the highest good.

By contrast, Aristotle, who saw form as immanent in, that is, inseparable from, nature, judged art according to how well it exemplified its form. A tragic play, for example, is good insofar as it realizes the characteristics of tragedy, and not necessarily insofar as it inspires noble behaviour. In nature, perfection, including human perfection, lies in being as perfect an example as possible of the genus; in art, it lies in being as perfect an example as possible of the genre.

Plato, then, is an ethical critic, while Aristotle is a genre critic. It should not be thought that ethical criticism relates solely to content; style, considered as a form of behaviour, also sets either a good or bad moral tone,[171] but,

---

[169] *Guide* ii. 28 (p. 335).   [170] *Guide* i. 16 (p. 42).

[171] See Plato, *Republic* 400d–401c, on which passage Coulter comments that it indicates the belief that 'the reader is as deeply influenced by exposure to varying kinds of literary behaviour, among

on the whole, for an ethical critic, questions of content, such as whether the characters in a play present edifying examples, are the main focus.

Just as the general metaphysics that Maimonides inherited was a Neo-platonized Aristotelianism, so his literary theory and practice exhibit a similar hybridity. His idea of the perfection of man is nearer to that of Plato than to that of Aristotle, in that he sees man's purpose as being to know God, who is external to nature. Correspondingly, he applies criteria to poetry external to it: poetry that degrades the moral perfection that is a necessary prelude to intellectual perfection, and that distracts from the awareness of God, is frowned upon. It is also not impossible that Maimonides saw an ethical as well as a therapeutic dimension to the cultivation of a clear and precise style.[172] To that extent, he, like Plato, is an ethical critic. Since, however, he regards God in himself as unknowable, the imperative to know God can be fulfilled only by knowing his works, and when it comes to those works, leaving the vexed question of origin aside, Maimonides is an Aristotelian. Like Aristotle, he defines perfection in nature as the best exemplification of a species.[173] Similarly, he is aware of genre in literature. In the introduction to Part I of the *Guide*, he distinguishes two types of parable: those that are significant only in outline, and those that are significant in their every detail.[174] As an example of the first type, he cites the parable of the temptress in Proverbs 7, interpreting it as a warning against surrender to physical desires, while the second type is represented by Jacob's dream of the ladder with angels ascending and descending, from Genesis 28. But of course these texts are not labelled; it takes sensitivity to tone and style to know which will bear exhaustive allegori-cal interpretation and which will not. Interpretation of a biblical text must not only serve truth in an ethical/philosophical way, it must also be true to the text itself, in an aesthetic way.[175] Hence Maimonides' restrictive public stance on poetry is compatible with his capacity to be affected by the versified wooing of an admirer. In sum, he demonstrates an ethical approach together with a

these stylistic behaviour, as he is by that of human beings in ordinary, non-literary contexts' (*Literary Microcosm*, 15). According to Janaway, as far as Plato is concerned, '*nothing* about an artistic product can be discounted as ethically or politically neutral' (*Images of Excellence*, 80).

[172] His explicit remarks on language and morality have to do with brevity and chastity. See *Guide* iii. 8 (pp. 435–6), and below, Ch. 1, n. 19.

[173] *Guide* iii. 13 (p. 450).   [174] *Guide* i, Introduction (pp. 12–13).

[175] Mordechai Z. Cohen, too, notes that, under Maimonides' method of interpretation, 'Discovering the intent of the biblical authors requires understanding of the literary principles that guided them', and contrasts this with the midrashic method (*Three Approaches to Biblical Metaphor*, 184). See also below, Ch. 5. Maimonides harmonizes the midrashic method with his own by treating Midrash as figurative—as Cohen also notes (ibid., nn. 19–20).

respect for genre. This may be compared with his approach to ethics as such. The notorious difficulties of 'Laws of Ethical Qualities' arise in part from the way in which it combines the Aristotelian doctrine of the mean, according to which the criteria of moral virtue are innate, with the doctrine of *imitatio Dei*, according to which the criteria of moral virtue are external.[176] Had Maimonides written a 'Laws of Aesthetic Qualities', it would probably have been no less complicated.

At any rate, we have seen that there is a basis on which Maimonides could transpose ethical perfection into aesthetic perfection, since the perfections of Torah, of the ethical personality, and of a work of art all embody the same idea of the mean, and all three are modes of imitation.

Neoplatonic Aesthetics and the Literary Microcosm

From Aristotle, let us now turn to the Neoplatonists, and the specific idea of microcosmic form. Although the resemblances between Neoplatonic literary theory and Maimonides' practice are striking, the channels of influence, if any, are less easy to trace than in the case of Aristotle. Those parts of the *Enneads* in which Plotinus discusses his ideas of sensible and intelligible beauty were available to the Islamic philosophers in *The Theology of Aristotle*,[177] one of the Arabic versions of the *Enneads* that circulated in the medieval period, and found expression in their own aesthetic theories.[178] Whether Maimonides had first-hand acquaintance with *The Theology of Aristotle* is not certain,[179] but in any case the focus here is not on beauty as such, but rather on the specific idea of literature as microcosm. That is to be found in the later Neoplatonists, and in their case there is even less of a trail to Maimonides.[180] For the time being, it must remain an open question whether there are direct or indirect links, or whether the resemblances are a matter of great minds of a similar cast finding similar solutions to similar problems.[181] Whichever way, the comparison is instructive.

[176] This problem, formulated as command ethics versus virtue ethics, is revisited in the next chapter.
[177] See O'Meara, *Plotinus*, 88–99.   [178] See Black, 'Aesthetics in Islamic Philosophy'.
[179] For estimates of Maimonides' degree of acquaintance with the *Enneads*, see Appendix II.2.
[180] S. Harvey, 'Greek Library of the Medieval Jewish Philosophers' covers only the works of Plato and Aristotle. On the availability in Arabic of the works of Proclus, a main source for Coulter's account of Neoplatonic literary theory, see Dodge, *Fihrist*, 608; D'Ancona, 'Greek into Arabic'; Endress, *Proclus Arabus*, 14–30; Zimmermann, 'Proclus Arabus Rides Again'. I have found no entry for Proclus, or for any other Neoplatonic author, in the index of Allony's *The Jewish Library in the Middle Ages*.
[181] A similar approach has been taken to comparing Iamblichus and Ibn Gabirol—see Mathis, 'Parallel Structures'.

These later Neoplatonic writers found themselves in a bind. Their reverence for Plato was almost matched by their reverence for Homer and Hesiod. How is appreciation of the poets to be reconciled with Plato's suspicion of poetry, especially in the case of poets whose characters, both human and divine, often behave in ways that are not in the least edifying? In addition, there was the problem of understanding Plato's own myths.

The way out was via allegory and symbolism, an approach facilitated by Platonic dualism. If the visible world presents shadows of a transcendent reality, so may a poem or myth.

Allegory is a more or less one-to-one correspondence between concept and representation. Symbolism is more elusive, hinting secretly at what it represents, but also hiding. The late Neoplatonic thinker Proclus distinguished three levels of myth: the demonic, or surface level, the eiconic level, which covers allegory, and the entheastic or inspired level, which operates more through symbolism. This three-tiered literary hierarchy parallels Proclus's version of the Neoplatonic ontological hierarchy of Soul, Intelligence, and the One.

A characteristic of entheastic myth is its comprehensiveness: 'The purpose of the latter is to fashion representatives of the whole of reality from its lowest material representations to its highest unity.'[182] For the receptive reader, the surface level of myth becomes symbol, 'awakening at the same time in the spirit of the reader a vivid desire to comprehend this reality'.[183]

The supreme value in Neoplatonic literary appreciation is unity. This derives partly from the Platonic idea of the role of the Demiurge in the creation of the cosmos, which is seen as a great living organism, and the parallel role of the artist, whose directing consciousness endows the artefact with organic unity. It also reflects the fundamental Neoplatonic doctrine of the All deriving from the One and One being in the All.

The relation of unity, viewed as controlling intention, to surface multiplicity—what we might call the intentional or teleological analysis of literary detail—is a paramount preoccupation of the Neoplatonic exegetes. If a work did not have oneness in this literally transcendental sense, if its details were not, all of them, rooted in the primal unity of the author's mind, it could not be intelligible or, what was for the Neoplatonists the same thing, beautiful.[184]

The parallel between artist and originator of the universe, however conceived, brings us to the ancient notion of the artefact as microcosm,[185]

---

[182] Coulter, *Literary Microcosm*, 49.   [183] Ibid. 53.   [184] Ibid. 78.
[185] Coulter traces the idea from Empedocles through to Plato, Cicero, and Seneca. He also finds

although this has of course been more or less implicit in everything that has gone before. According to Coulter, the special contribution of the Neoplatonists was in the application of this notion to literature: 'The consequence of this was a systematic elaboration of the notion that a work of literature organically conceived should also be viewed as a microcosmic organism, and, as a corollary, its creator as a microcosmic demiurge.'[186] Coulter goes on to state that, as far as the Neoplatonists were concerned, 'If the cosmos possesses form, matter, etc. it must also be true that literary compositions ... are made up of the same elements as the macrocosm itself.'[187]

In his twin commitments to rational, philosophical enquiry and to the truth of Scripture, Maimonides was in a similar bind to that in which the Neoplatonists found themselves in relation to Plato and the poets, and his solution was similar to theirs. Where the surface meaning of the biblical text conflicted with scientific truth, or seemed trivial or unintelligible, the text had to be interpreted in some non-literal way, allegory being one possibility.[188]

Maimonides does not allow allegorical interpretations to be made indiscriminately; some texts allow 'the intentional or teleological analysis of literary detail' more than others. The more a text does allow such analysis, that is, the more its details grow out of a single guiding concept and are not arbitrary, the greater its artistic unity and therefore, in Neoplatonic terms, the greater its value. Having established his two archetypes of parables, that of the temptress and that of Jacob's dream of the ladder, Maimonides goes on in the *Guide* to ascribe profound, indeed cosmic, significance to every element in Jacob's dream,[189] while the temptress simply stands for the waywardness of matter in general terms.[190]

---

that it 'emerges with special clarity in a passage of Philo. In the second book (135) of his *Life of Moses*, Philo is describing the High Priest's robe, and interprets it allegorically, as a "likeness and representation of the Universe". When the High Priest wears this garment, he should strive to be worthy of it and become in this way, himself, a "little cosmos" in imitation of the robe he wears as the sign of his office' (*Literary Microcosm*, 101). According to Conger, it is in Philo we find the first explicit formulation of the microcosm/macrocosm idea in general. See *Theories of Macrocosms and Microcosms*, 16.

[186] Coulter, *Literary Microcosm*, 102.   [187] Ibid.

[188] See W. Z. Harvey, 'Maimonides' Allegorical Readings'. Harvey sees Averroës as a possible influence on Maimonides' approach to allegory in the *Guide*, but notes that they may have drawn on common sources.   [189] This is analysed in Chapter 4—see pp. 272–4.

[190] See *Guide* iii. 8 (p. 431). This is not to denigrate parables of the second, temptress type. Within the parable all the elements make sense and contribute to the story's atmosphere, only they do not separately refer to anything outside the story. As Mordechai Z. Cohen points out, a book such as Song of Songs gains emotional impact from Maimonides' treatment of it as a meaningful whole rather than as an assembly of allegorical parts. See M. Z. Cohen, *Three Approaches to Biblical Metaphor*, 186–8.

It was suggested above that *Mishneh torah*'s form can be interpreted on the levels of ideas and inspiration. If we add to that its surface meaning, we have a triple-layered exegesis corresponding to Proclus's demonic, eiconic, and entheastic levels of myth. We have seen that entheastic myth is characterized by comprehensiveness. *Mishneh torah* certainly satisfies that condition, in more than one way. Its comprehensiveness is both actual, in that it covers the whole of the Torah, which governs the whole of human life from the highest intellectual aspiration to the lowest bodily function, and symbolic, in its microcosmic form. The aim of entheastic myth, of awakening in the spirit of the reader a desire to comprehend the whole of reality, is highly reminiscent of the person who gazes at creation and is filled with desire for the knowledge of God in 'Laws of the Foundations of the Torah', 2: 2. *Mishneh torah* itself, viewed as a whole, seeks to arouse, capture, enhance, and channel that desire, which is fulfilled by the prophet 'contemplating the whole wisdom of God as displayed in His creatures, from the first form to the very centre of the earth'.[191]

The idea of the cosmos as literary model in Neoplatonic literary theory, applied with care, can thus help us to understand Maimonides' use of microcosmic form. Form and matter are relative terms in Neoplatonic thought. Each level in the ontological hierarchy is as matter to the level above it, and as form to the level below it.[192] What is more, the parallel between author and Demiurge justifies a parallel between form in the literary, artistic sense and form in the philosophical sense. As suggested above, it is practically a definition of art to say that, in art, form in the aesthetic sense of shape and form in the philosophical sense of essence coalesce. With this in mind, the hierarchy of form and matter can be applied to *Mishneh torah*, substituting for 'matter' the word 'content': God, the form of forms, is the form of the cosmos, the content of which becomes the form of *Mishneh torah*, the content of which, the commandments, becomes in turn the form of certain actions.

The most important insight to be gained from comparison of Maimonides with the Neoplatonists is that the supreme philosophical/theological value of unity is the basis of aesthetic value as well.[193] The knowledge of God's unity is the third commandment in *Mishneh torah*, after the knowledge of

---

[191] 'Laws of the Foundations of the Torah', 7: 1.

[192] See also the *Treatise on Logic* 9: 'For, some of the four causes are proximate and some remote . . . One may follow their example in regard to form and purpose until one can differentiate the proximate from the remote purpose, and the first from the last form' (Maimonides, *Treatise on Logic*, 50–1).

[193] On unity as an ideal common to different doctrines of art and criticism, see McKeon, 'Philosophic Bases of Art', 82–3.

God's existence and uniqueness. This unity is ultimately incomprehensible, yet, as will be argued in the next chapter, the perfection of a human being is to come as close to it as possible. The organic unity of *Mishneh torah*, the way all of its details are connected to the single, central idea of the knowledge of God, makes it the aesthetic equivalent of the ethical and intellectual ideal that it propounds. Of the knowledge of God, Maimonides states, 'There is no way to apprehend Him except it be through the things he has made.' Perception of the oneness of nature in universal scientific laws is our only way of grasping some notion of the transcendent oneness of God, although it will always pass our understanding. By replicating nature in the laws governing *Mishneh torah*'s form, Maimonides brings his reader closer to the apprehension of God, through the thing he has made.

Maimonides and Modern Literary Theory

The idea of there being anything God-like about authorship is out of fashion. 'We now know that a text is not a line of words releasing a single "theological" meaning (the "message" of the Author-God) but a multidimensional space in which a variety of writings, none of them original, blend and clash', Roland Barthes declared.[194] By analogy to, or extension of, the linguistics of Ferdinand de Saussure, according to whom words have no fixed connection to concepts but are meaningful only in relation to other words in a language, literary theorists argue that texts are meaningful only in relation to other texts. By their lights, originality is no criterion of excellence—the term is almost meaningless—and authorial intention cannot be the guide or the goal of interpretation.

Perhaps one reason that modern literary theorists have sought to dethrone the God-like author is that for them there is no God for the author to be like. Barthes almost says as much:

Once the Author is removed, the claim to decipher a text becomes quite futile . . . literature (it would be better from now on to say writing), by refusing to assign a 'secret', an ultimate meaning, to the text (and to the world as text), liberates what may be called an anti-theological activity, an activity that is truly revolutionary since to refuse to fix meaning is, in the end, to refuse God and his hypostases—reason, science, law.

It seems that the link between ontology and aesthetics still holds.

---

[194] Barthes, *Image—Music—Text*, 146–7, cited in Allen, *Intertextuality*, 13.

On the face of it, nothing could be less like Maimonides, who is devoted to God, reason, science, and law. At the same time, it is not clear that there is a real clash, for it is open to doubt whether Barthes and Maimonides have the same concept in mind when they use the word 'God'. This God of Barthes sounds like a stage God, compared with the unknowable God of Maimonides, shorn of myth, of whom nothing can be predicated, and who has no hypostases. One might ask how such a God, whose meaning cannot be fixed, fixes meaning.[195] At any rate, although it involves some deciphering on the level of ideas, the ultimate aim of this study is to go beyond *Mishneh torah* as what Barthes calls a 'readerly' text, in which the reader finds 'ready-made meaning', and to nudge it towards the status of a 'writerly' text, in which the reader is 'no longer a consumer but a producer of the text'.

It is not proposed to attempt to fathom what literary theory might make of *Mishneh torah*, but the juxtaposition may be helpful in clarifying a few points:

1. For Maimonides, *imitatio Dei* is not a metaphor, but an urgent quest. Human likeness to God lies in possession of an intellect, but this is only a potential. Human actions are, or should be, a striving to realize this potential, but even once realized, the likeness is really only by way of analogy, for the most developed human intellect, that of Moses, still fell short of the divine intellect. Applied to writing, *imitatio Dei* is an aspiration, a response to the distance felt between man and God, not a reflection of authorial omniscience.

2. The notion of intertextuality, one of theory's key ideas,[196] is superfluous as far as *Mishneh torah* is concerned. It clearly only exists in relation to previous texts. In fact, from the point of view of theory, it could be considered an inverted text. In contrast to modern works of literature, in which originality is a quality most prized, and one that literary theory re-examines, *Mishneh torah* belongs to a genre in which originality is most to be deplored. It pursues accuracy and authenticity in relation to the sources of law and lore—on a plain reading, hardly anything in it is Maimonides' own contribution. Its style too is consciously derivative. The use of mishnaic Hebrew laced with biblical and talmudic reference and allusion makes it a kind of core sample of the Jewish literary past. Awareness of this dimension greatly adds to the enjoyment and interest it bears for the knowledgeable reader, and can at times be crucial for understanding its meaning. Much the same applies to its philosophical heritage. Of course this argument is a little disingenuous, since, at

---

[195] 'It is well known among all people engaged in speculation, who understand what they say, that God cannot be defined' (*Guide* i. 52 (p. 115)).   [196] See Allen, *Intertextuality*.

least for some exponents of theory, intertextuality is not synonymous with the sources and influences manifest in a work. Nevertheless, it can still be said that *Mishneh torah* wears its intertextuality on its sleeve; the task of criticism is to uncover its originality.

3. Maimonides is so authorial, so deliberate, so very much present in his work, even seeking to control the terms on which it should be appreciated, that he rather resists being displaced by the cry that the author is dead.[197] We are probably still very far from exhausting the intentionality of his work, and, on the level of ideas, the question 'What did he mean?', whether about content or form or both together, remains a valid one. The purpose of this study is to reveal certain symbolic and metaphorical workings in *Mishneh torah*. Before they have been revealed, their significance, intentional or otherwise, cannot be discussed. *Mishneh torah* has to be constructed before it can be deconstructed.

Literary Models: Hebrew as Genre

The sure and pleasing handling of a medium is one of the first things to awaken the peculiar respect we pay to what we decide is art. *Mishneh torah* is by common consent a pearl of Hebrew literature: elegant, clear, systematic and precise, richly allusive, at times lyrical, even dramatic.

Much of Maimonides' linguistic prowess is lost in translation, but to give a taste of his expressive power, here is a passage from a *halakhah* that will be referred to several times in the course of this study, describing the arduous path to becoming a prophet:

When one, abundantly endowed with these qualities and physically sound, enters *pardes* and continuously dwells upon those great and abstruse themes, having the right mind capable of comprehending and grasping them; sanctifying himself, withdrawing from the ways of the ordinary run of men who walk in the obscurities of the times, zealously training himself not to have a single thought of the vanities of the age and its intrigues, but keeping his mind directed upwards as though bound beneath the Celestial Throne, so as to comprehend the pure and holy forms and contemplating the whole of the wisdom of God as displayed in His creatures, from the first form to

---

[197] Compare Harold Bloom's verdict on Emerson in this respect: 'Deconstructing Emerson is of course impossible, since no discourse ever has been so overtly aware of its own status as rhetoricity' (Bloom, *Wallace Stevens*, 12, quoted in Norris, *Deconstruction*, 120). See also the remarks on intention in J. L. Kraemer, 'How (Not) to Read the *Guide*', 387–9.

the very centre of the earth, learning thence to realize His greatness—on such a man the Holy Spirit will promptly descend.[198]

This passage has a poetic cadence. It is a single, long sentence that dramatizes its meaning, embodying the long, hard struggle for moral and intellectual perfection, followed by the sudden precipitation of the prophetic gift. In the original, rhythm, weight, sound, and association are all brought to bear to support the meaning. We are supposed to feel the ascent to prophecy as well as be informed about it.

Such lyricism can be taken as a small pledge of *Mishneh torah*'s mimetic intent. But it also points towards a new answer to an old question: Why did Maimonides write *Mishneh torah* in Hebrew at all? It was by no means an obvious decision. All his previous important works were in Arabic, and they include books bearing on Jewish law: the *Commentary on the Mishnah*, and the *Book of the Commandments*. Most previous attempts at codification of hala-khah, notably by Sa'adyah Gaon and Samuel ben Hofni, were in Arabic too. Robert Brody mentions the use of Hebrew as one of three innovations of *Mishneh torah* in comparison with previous codes (the other two being its comprehensiveness and its omission of talmudic sources).[199]

So it was not the halakhic subject matter that compelled the switch to another language. Moreover, Hebrew was a difficult option. Maimonides decided to write *Mishneh torah* in 'the language of the Mishnah';[200] there was no adequate current Hebrew available to him, and Twersky testifies to the pains that the choice cost.[201]

Maimonides seems to have perceived that the hegemony of Arabic in Jew-ish scholarship was on the wane, and that *Mishneh torah* had to be in Hebrew in order to gain wide dissemination among the Jewish people beyond the Arabic-speaking world and to become accepted as authoritative.[202] Good evidence for this is a letter in which he expressed regret that he had written the *Book of the Commandments* in Arabic rather than Hebrew, since 'everyone

[198] 'Laws of the Foundations of the Torah', 7: 1.

[199] Brody, 'The Influence of Sa'adyah Gaon on *Mishneh Torah*' (Heb.).

[200] *The Book of the Commandments*, Introduction. In discussing his choice of language for *Mishneh torah*, Maimonides did not consider Arabic, but only which style of Hebrew (or possibly Aramaic) to use.

[201] 'Maimonides took great pains with his style; his use of Hebrew and his development of a rich, flexible style that enabled him to write with precision, brevity, and elegance were exacting, novel undertakings, for we know from the plaintive testimony of such writers as Judah ha-Levi and Moses ibn Ezra that contemporary Hebrew was in a sad state' (Twersky, *Maimonides Reader*, 17).

[202] See Twersky, *Introduction to the Code*, 336.

ought to read it'.[203] To these considerations Brody adds that Maimonides wished keep as closely as possible to the model of the Mishnah.[204]

These are plausible answers to our question, but there is another possibility. A general feature of Maimonides' career as a poet is that the verse prologues and epilogues even to his Arabic works are in Hebrew. This division of labour—Arabic for prose, Hebrew for poetry—has a history. Rina Drory describes how, for Jewish writers of the tenth century, Hebrew began to play the role in their literary conventions that classical Arabic played for Muslim writers.[205] Classical Arabic was the language of courtly and festive poetry, a kind of writing that did not refer to everyday reality and in which attention was paid to elegance and sophisticated imagery. For Jewish writers, Hebrew fitted the same bill. In general, Drory writes, 'The purpose of writing in Hebrew was to prove command of the language and to provide a text that would arouse admiration at its beauty and elegance; while writing in Arabic was intended to produce a clear and understandable text.'[206]

Maimonides' verses are exercises in virtuosity, particularly cunning in the way they give topical point to biblical references, and as such, in relation to the Arabic texts they accompany, they conform exactly to this description. *Mishneh torah*, however, is a different matter. Ostensibly, its whole point is to be 'a clear and understandable text'. This could mean that, in writing it in Hebrew, Maimonides broke with convention. Or perhaps he was hardly aware of the convention. It could be, however, that he maintained the convention, that the lyricism of the passage about the prophet is a trustworthy clue, and that *Mishneh torah* only looks like 'a clear and understandable text', while in reality it is a poetic text.

Clearly the whole tendency of what has been said so far points to this last possibility, which is that *Mishneh torah* is a highly sophisticated spiritual epic of surpassing beauty and elegance. The point, though, is that, insofar as what Drory calls the 'Jewish Literary System' is applicable to Maimonides, the literary quality of *Mishneh torah* is not an isolated flash, but can be seen in the steady light of a tradition, of which it is one of the most magnificent expressions. What made Maimonides consider Hebrew appropriate for *Mishneh torah*, and induced him to go to the effort of forging a Hebrew adequate to the task, was that his code, although not in verse form, would have a poetic, symbolic dimension for which Hebrew was the accepted medium. This puts

---

[203] *Letters* ed. Shailat (Heb.), 223.

[204] Brody, 'The Influence of Sa'adyah Gaon on *Mishneh Torah*' (Heb.), 216.

[205] Drory, *Models and Contacts*. I am indebted to Dr Moshe Lavee for putting Drory's book into my hands.   [206] Ibid. 179.

the kind of treatment of *Mishneh torah* offered here on a much sounder footing, while the light of the tradition also has the potential to illuminate the relationship between *Mishneh torah* and the Arabic-written *Guide of the Perplexed*, for the corollary of the suggestion that Maimonides wrote *Mishneh torah* in Hebrew because of his artistic aims is that he reverted to Arabic for the *Guide* because he had different artistic aims, calling for expression in prose rather than poetry. In other words, the difference between them is a literary one, a question of form. This is not how their relationship has been discussed hitherto, and so a brief history of that discussion is now in order.

Joining what Strauss Put Asunder

The relationship between Maimonides' two masterworks is a central topic in Maimonidean studies. To some, they appear utterly different in spirit—the one decidedly religious, presenting the commandments as decrees; the other ranging in foreign fields of philosophy and relativizing the commandments. The best-known case in point is the institution of sacrifices, treated in *Mishneh torah* as of eternal validity and in the *Guide* as a concession to a convention of worship that became obsolete.[207] R. Jacob Emden (1697–1776) found the contradiction so stark, and the position of the *Guide* so heretical, that he eventually concluded that the *Guide* must be spurious.[208]

Leo Strauss expounded a dichotomous view, in which the *Guide* is an esoteric book about the mysteries of the law, while *Mishneh torah* is an exoteric book about the practice of the law. Of *Mishneh torah*, Strauss wrote:

There can be no doubt that the code reproduces the Torah according to its external proportions only. For the Torah consists of true 'opinions' and of 'actions', and whereas the 'actions' are determined by it with extreme precision, the true 'opinions' are indicated only in bare outline . . . the Mishneh Torah deals in the most detailed fashion with 'actions' but speaks of the basic truths only briefly and allusively . . . and by haphazard.[209]

[207] The particular problem of sacrifices is discussed further in Chapter 3 (see pp. 260–2 below).

[208] 'And how is it possible to imagine that both these compositions (I mean *Yad haḥazakah* and the *Guide of the Perplexed*) issued from the hand of one author?' (Emden, *Mitpaḥat sefarim*, 61 (pt. 2, ch. 8)). See Schacter, 'Emden and Maimonides'. On R. Emden and others who found *Mishneh torah* and the *Guide* incompatible, see Davidson, *Moses Maimonides*, 418–25.

[209] Strauss, 'The Literary Character of the *Guide*', 83. It should be pointed out that elsewhere Strauss does give greater recognition to the philosophical aspect of *Mishneh torah*. In 'Notes on Maimonides' Book of Knowledge' he writes, 'To begin with philosophy (although not *eo nomine*) and to turn almost at once to the Torah may be said to be the law governing the *Mishneh torah* as a whole.' More trenchantly, Pines wrote in 1986 that 'the somewhat facile assumption which has been rather frequently made that Maimonides' halachic works are less "philosophical" or "Aristotelian" than the *Guide* is by no means true, indeed a close examination of some of the texts in question

Strauss even uses the terms 'great thing' and 'small thing' to distinguish *Mishneh torah* and the *Guide*: 'the chief subject of the Guide is ma'aseh merkabah, which is "a great thing," while the chief subject of the Mishneh Torah is the precepts, which are "a small thing".'[210] He divides the two works on the question of halakhah and aggadah too: 'If it is true that the Mishneh Torah is but the greatest post-talmudic contribution to the oral discussions of the halakhah, then it may be asserted with equal right that Maimonides, while writing the Guide, continued the aggadic discussions of the Talmud.'[211] His conclusion is that 'The Mishneh Torah is primarily addressed to the general run of men, while the Guide is addressed to the small number of people who are able to understand by themselves.'[212] The view of *Mishneh torah* and the *Guide* as existing on different planes is part of the general view implicit in Strauss of Maimonides as a secret antinomian for whom the law is a means of making the world safe for philosophers, who keep to it only as a matter of policy.

It is fair to say that, on the whole, the trend in Maimonidean studies over the past fifty years has been steadily to replace Leo Strauss's dual Maimonides with a unified one. Twersky contested Strauss's way of reading *Mishneh torah* by pointing out how it constantly gives the law an intellectual dimension, or, to use Straussian terms, transmutes 'action' into 'opinion'.[213] Hartman took issue with Strauss's aggadah–halakhah dichotomy, writing, 'To claim, as Strauss does, that Torah has significance for Maimonides solely in terms of political categories, as an instrument of social order, is to miss the point of Maimonides' constant stress upon the importance of Aggadah for Halakhah.'[214]

Further eroding the Straussian position, Menachem Kellner has demonstrated, in selected passages from *Mishneh torah*, Maimonides' art of writing simultaneously for the sophisticated reader versed in physics and metaphysics and for the talmudist ignorant of those disciplines, without the latter's composure being disturbed.[215] David Henshke, addressing the sacrifices problem, similarly treats Maimonides' writing in *Mishneh torah* as multi-dimensional,[216] while Warren Zev Harvey finds *Mishneh torah* sufficiently sophisticated to be used to resolve apparently unresolved matters in the *Guide*.[217] Over twenty

suggests that the diametrically opposite conclusion may come nearer to the truth of the matter' (Pines, 'Philosophical Purport', 2). Pines's point, however, is that, in the *Guide*, Maimonides abandoned the philosophy of *Mishneh torah*.

[210] Strauss, 'The Literary Character of the *Guide*', 89.
[211] Ibid. 47.　　　　　[212] Ibid. 91.　　　　　[213] Twersky, 'Some Non-Halakic Aspects'.
[214] Hartman, *Maimonides: Torah and Philosophic Quest*, 54.
[215] Kellner, 'The Literary Character of *Mishneh Torah*'.
[216] Henshke, 'Unity in Maimonides' Thought' (Heb.).
[217] W. Z. Harvey, '*Mishneh Torah* as a Key to the *Guide*'.

years ago, Gerald Blidstein gave the following assessment: 'The fact that the Code is studded with a variety of non-halakhic materials is by now well appreciated . . . We also see a narrowing of the gap between the philosopher's Guide and the legalist's Code, as it has been shown that Maimonides reveals many of his disconcerting doctrines in the Code.'[218]

Twersky's reading mostly depends on undisguised, albeit delicate, references in the text. Henshke and Kellner rely on more subtle hints and ambiguities. My own thesis is that the esotericism, if it may be called that, of *Mishneh torah* is formal as much as textual, that form is a hitherto unmined seam of 'opinion' in that work. It was asserted above that *Mishneh torah* encompasses the 'great thing' as much as the 'small thing', that it is a work of aggadah as much as of halakhah. Moreover, the reason that philosophy is conveyed through form in that work has much to do with a reason Strauss himself suggested for the esotericism he found in the *Guide*, namely, that 'the explanation of secrets is . . . not only forbidden by law, but also impossible by nature'.[219]

This study has pretensions of following Strauss's method of close attention to literary structure, and to numerical patterns in particular, but for now the aim is to complete the bridging of the Straussian gap, and to argue that the difference between *Mishneh torah* and the *Guide* is not a matter of degree of philosophical sophistication or target readership, but of literary genre.

Translation

'Poetry', Robert Frost is said to have said, 'is what is lost in translation.'[220] One indication that, whatever other reasons there may have been for it, the choice of Hebrew for *Mishneh torah* was intended to place that work on the poetic side of the conventional Hebrew–Arabic, poetic text–clear text divide, while the *Guide* is on the other,[221] is the different attitude Maimonides displayed towards translation in the case of each work.

[218] Blidstein, 'Where Do We Stand?', 3. On the relationship between form and content in *Mishneh torah*, he writes: 'The theoretical function conflicts but rarely with the legal; rather, the theory usually provides the form into which the legal materials are poured and of course shaped. The Maimonidean achievement rests in the quiet synthesis thus accomplished' (ibid.). This clearly anticipates the trend of the present study.

[219] Strauss, 'The Literary Character of the *Guide*', 55. See also above, n. 27.

[220] The sentiment has been traced to Dante: 'And therefore everyone should know that nothing harmonized through a musical bond can be translated from one tongue into another without breaking and destroying all sweetness and harmony'—see Satterlee, 'Robert Frost's Views on Translation'.

[221] It will come as news to many people that the *Guide of the Perplexed* is a clear text, but at any rate its complexities are of a different kind from those of *Mishneh torah*, of the puzzle rather than the mystery variety, as discussed above.

In 1191 or 1192, he wrote a letter to Joseph ibn Jaber, a devotee of his in Baghdad,[222] in reply to a non-extant letter in which Ibn Jaber apparently expressed regret at his lack of learning and his poor knowledge of Hebrew, and requested that *Mishneh torah* should be translated into Arabic. Ibn Jaber also raised queries he had heard about certain rulings by Maimonides in halakhah, and seems to have mentioned his attempts to defend Maimonides' honour against personal attacks made on him in Baghdad, which was the seat of the gaonate, and a place where *Mishneh torah* was regarded by some as the precocious brainchild of an upstart.

Maimonides' letter is gracious and sympathetic, and full of encouragement. He assures Ibn Jaber that what counts is not what he knows but his efforts to learn, gives detailed responses to the queries raised, and seeks to dissuade Ibn Jaber from being provoked by the gainsayers into taking any risk on his behalf. On one point, though, Maimonides is adamant: he will not countenance the translation of *Mishneh torah* into Arabic. In encouraging Ibn Jaber to persist in studying it in Hebrew, this is what he writes: 'If you want to study my work you will have to learn Hebrew little by little . . . I do not intend, however, to produce an Arabic edition as you suggest; the work would lose its specific colour. How could I do this, when I should like to translate my Arabic writings into the holy language!'[223]

This is a strange response. If the motive for adopting Hebrew as the language of *Mishneh torah* was the utilitarian one of ensuring that non-Arabic speakers could read it, what was wrong with the idea of translating it into Arabic so that it might be read as widely as possible within the Arabic-speaking world? Surely that could only have furthered Maimonides' ambition for it to become a standard code?

Moreover, why was he only worried about loss of nuance in translation in one direction, so that 'to translate my Arabic writings into the holy language' was even desirable? What was special about *Mishneh torah*, and about Hebrew in general? When the community of Lunel requested that the *Guide* should be translated from Arabic into Hebrew, Maimonides responded positively, and supported Samuel ibn Tibbon's translation effort.[224] Why were the Provençal rabbis indulged while poor, loyal Ibn Jaber in Baghdad was told to go and study?

[222] *Letters*, ed. Shailat (Heb.), 402.
[223] Translation from Twersky, *Maimonides Reader*, 479. Shailat (*Letters* (Heb.), 409 n. 23) points out that most of this excerpt is not in the extant Arabic manuscript of the letter, but only in Hebrew versions. He does not on that account cast doubt on its authenticity. For Shailat's review of the manuscripts, see *Letters*, 402–3.   [224] *Letters*, ed. Shailat (Heb.), 555.

We should not be misled by the expression 'the holy tongue'. It is highly unlikely that it was a religious scruple that made Maimonides unwilling to translate *Mishneh torah*. His general view is that language is conventional,[225] and that Hebrew is no different in this respect from any other language. It is sacred because it contains no direct words for certain bodily functions,[226] but not because it has any special ontological status.[227] In the letter to Ibn Jaber, Maimonides reiterates his position that in any discourse it is the content that is important, not the language in which it is expressed, citing the ruling that the Shema may be recited in any language.[228] Ibn Jaber might have been forgiven if he was confused. Almost in the same breath he is told that language is of no account, and then that if *Mishneh torah* were to be translated it would not be the same.

On the other hand, although as a philosopher Maimonides awards Hebrew no special status, there are places where he exhibits a prejudice in favour of it. In the letter to Lunel, he refers to Arabic as 'the language of Kedar whose sun has darkened, for I have dwelt in their tents, and it would be a great joy for me to remove the precious thing from its devourer and restore what is lost to its owner'—remarks that have a nationalist overtone—while in a letter to Samuel ibn Tibbon he goes so far as to say that Arabic is 'certainly Hebrew that became somewhat debased'.[229] Even after allowance is made for Maimonides tailoring his attitude to suit his correspondent, a preference for Hebrew emerges. Moreover, since the Hebrew of *Mishneh torah* cost Maimonides such great pains, it is understandable that he would not wish to see it mangled.

That said, it is still hard to believe that a sufficiently responsible translator (an Ibn Tibbon?) could not have been found to render *Mishneh torah* into Arabic. After all, it was supposed to be a practical manual of Jewish law, and a response to a crisis in Jewish learning. Was Maimonides really prepared to sacrifice the needs of people like Joseph ibn Jaber for the sake of the charm of *Mishneh torah*'s style?

There is also the question why 'the language of Kedar' was good enough for the *Guide*. We gather from the foregoing that Maimonides regretted

---

[225] 'Languages are conventional and not natural' (*Guide* ii. 30 (p. 358)). See Septimus, 'Maimonides on Language'.

[226] 'For in this holy language no word at all has been laid down in order to designate either the male or the female organ of copulation, nor are there words designating the act itself that brings about generation, the sperm, the urine, or the excrements' (*Guide* iii. 8 (p. 435)).

[227] See Kellner, *Maimonides' Confrontation with Mysticism*, 155–78.

[228] See also 'Laws of Recitation of the Shema', 2: 10.   [229] *Letters*, ed. Shailat (Heb.), 531.

writing earlier works in Arabic and wanted them to appear in Hebrew, and
also that he had a sentimental preference for that language. Having discovered that Hebrew was the coming lingua franca of Jewish scholarship, and
having conquered it as a literary medium in *Mishneh torah*, he then reverted
to Arabic. What is more, the letter to Lunel describes a decline of learning in
the strongholds of Judaeo-Arabic in both the East and the West and a shift
in the centre of gravity to Christian Europe.[230] Maimonides as much as says in
the letter that, besides a few places in Palestine and Yemen, and Aleppo
(which is where Joseph ben Judah, the nominal addressee of the *Guide*, lived),
Provence was the only region where his writings could be properly appreciated. He might as well have written the *Guide* in Hebrew in the first place.
Was it only Hebrew's supposed deficiency in philosophical vocabulary that
prevented him from doing so?

A further dimension of Maimonides' language choices is hinted at in
the nationalist tone noted in the letter to Lunel. That tone fits Maimonides'
description of his motives for writing *Mishneh torah* given in another letter, to
Joseph ben Judah:

> Indeed I composed it—and God knows this—for myself in the first place, for ease of
> reference in searching for what might be needed, and for old age, and for the sake
> of God may he be exalted, because I—as God lives—was jealous for the Lord God of
> Israel, when I saw a nation without a genuinely comprehensive code of law, and with-
> out true and exact doctrines, and I did what I did for the sake of God alone.[231]

Twersky comments on this passage: 'A code for the entire nation, rather than
for its Arabic-speaking segment, had to be in Hebrew.'[232] Earlier, commenting on the rejection of Arabic as the language of *Mishneh torah*, he writes,
'Maimonides never tired of emphasizing that the major determinant in study
and writing . . . was the subject matter; language was ancillary to the contents.
No "metaphysical pathos" or imperialistic flavor attached to Hebrew in the
Maimonidean scheme.'[233]

There are two assumptions here. One is that by 'a nation', Maimonides
meant Jews as individuals, some of whom understood Arabic and some of
whom did not. The choice of Hebrew was, then, a utilitarian one, aimed at

---

[230] In the case of the Jewish civilization of Andalusia, the agent of this breakdown is generally held
to have been persecution under the fanatically Islamic Almohad dynasty, which ruled Moorish Spain
in the latter part of the twelfth century. This is what is presumed to have led Maimonides' family to
leave his birthplace, Córdoba, although Davidson denies the existence of any reliable evidence of
such persecution (*Moses Maimonides*, 9–30). At any rate, in 1236, thirty-two years after Maimonides'
death, Córdoba fell to Christian armies.

[231] *Letters*, ed. Shailat (Heb.), 300–1.   [232] *Introduction to the Code*, 336.   [233] Ibid. 334.

the greatest comprehension by the greatest number. The other assumption is
that his emphasis on content means that language is neutral, transparent. We
are not forced to make either assumption. When Maimonides talks about a
nation without a comprehensive code of law, the meaning is probably not that
every Jewish home should have one; more likely, he intends the Jewish people
as a collective, and his code as a national possession. There might then be
some 'imperialistic flavor' attached to the choice of Hebrew. After all, if that
choice was entirely utilitarian, and if language is entirely neutral, a translation
for the nation's Arabic-speaking segment should not be precluded. Yet Maimonides precluded it. Moreover, as we have seen, he was both a genre critic
and an ethical critic. It was as an ethical critic that he emphasized subject matter as the major determinant in writing. As a genre critic, he was sensitive to
medium as well as to message. In the Jewish literary tradition that Drory
describes, language was not ancillary to content, not neutral: it determined,
shaped, and coloured content. If Maimonides saw himself as continuing the
tradition, then, whatever other considerations he may have had, by opting
for Hebrew as the language of *Mishneh torah*, he was opting for a certain
genre. Hebrew had for him at least a literary flavour, if no other.

The answer that fits all our questions is that Maimonides was following a
convention in which Hebrew was the language of untranslatable poetry, and
Mishneh torah was a nationalist (in a good sense) poetic work, while the *Guide*
was a universalist, discursive, prose work of philosophy, and therefore written
in eminently translatable Arabic.

Support for this thesis can be found in Drory's research on the phenomenon of texts that were written by their authors in both Hebrew and Arabic.
Both versions were for the *same readership*—it was not a matter of some
people understanding one language and some the other. Rather, these were
two distinct kinds of literary performance.

As an example, Drory examines the Hebrew and Arabic introductions to
Sa'adyah Gaon's *Sefer ha'egron*, his book on Hebrew poetics. In both introductions, Sa'adyah is concerned to account for the decline of Hebrew, and
calls for its restoration.

Drory analyses certain variables in each of the two introductions to bring
out their different orientations. To take, for example, the stance of the
speaker and the projected readership: in the Arabic introduction the speaker
is generally in the first person singular, and the readership addressed in the
first place is scholars, only secondarily 'the nation', whereas in the Hebrew
introduction, the speaker is a representative of the Jewish people, sometimes

in the third person, and the readership is the entire nation. The speaker is not a scholar talking to scholars. 'He adopts, rather, the mantle of a leader, even a prophet, who has come forth at a moment of crisis and is arousing the people to return to the straight path for the sake of God; in this case, the program for the revival of Hebrew.'[234]

In the Arabic version, the time covered is the history of *piyut*. As opposed to this, 'The time span covered in the Hebrew introduction is immense, embracing past, present, and future. The range of time extends from the creation of the world to the very days of Sa'adyah Gaon and further on to the time when Hebrew will again become the sole language spoken on earth.'[235] Time in this version is 'indistinct and unbounded'.

In another contrast, Drory finds that 'the framework of discourse' in the Arabic version is a philosophical-philological one, and not specifically Jewish, whereas in the Hebrew introduction, the framework is 'the Biblical crime and punishment narrative'.[236] Revival of Hebrew is part of the effort to achieve redemption from the long punishment of exile.

Further, while the Arabic introduction is respectful towards the surrounding Arabic culture, seeing Hebrew and Arabic as suffering from similar neglect and for similar reasons, the Hebrew introduction ignores the Arabic context.

Drory notes that the Arabic introduction uses quotations from Proverbs, to which Sa'adyah relates as wisdom literature, 'the least national literary genre in the Bible'. The quotations do not inject Jewish content into the philosophical framework of the discussion. 'On the contrary, connecting philosophical ideas to the biblical verses and thus interpreting them in a non-traditional philosophical spirit was a departure from the conventions of Rabbinic interpretation of the Bible as reflected in the Midrash.'[237]

One cannot help but be struck by the exactness with which some of these distinctions apply to Maimonides' *Mishneh torah* and *Guide of the Perplexed*. The subject matter is different, of course: Maimonides' subject is the law, not the Hebrew language. But, *mutatis mutandis*, the differences in orientation and ambiance between those two books are remarkably like the differences Drory describes. Maimonides' pose in the introduction to *Mishneh torah* is very much that of the leader coming to the rescue in a time of national crisis, a time when dispersion and the instability caused by wars are liable to disrupt transmission of the law. In this respect, he presents himself as taking on the mantle of R. Judah the Prince, who permitted himself to record the Oral Law

[234] Drory, *Models and Contacts*, 188.   [235] Ibid.   [236] Ibid. 189.   [237] Ibid. 185.

(which was never supposed to be written down) because of similar threats.[238] Invoking authority bordering on that of a prophet, who can suspend the law in an emergency, Maimonides, like R. Judah, broke with tradition in order to save the tradition. There is also the further point that clothing his book in R. Judah the Prince's language was a way of assuming R. Judah the Prince's role.

The crisis that occasions the *Guide* is personal rather than national.[239] The book is dramatized as a treatise addressed to a single student who finds it difficult to reconcile parts of the Bible with philosophical truth. Hence, although Maimonides does not of course confine himself to quotations from Proverbs, 'connecting philosophical ideas to the biblical verses' is a central activity in the *Guide*.

As we have seen, the historical sweep of *Mishneh torah* is from creation to redemption, and within that comprehensive timeframe, actual time seems indeterminate. The time setting in the *Guide* is the present, while its historical excursions are localized, for example in the historical explanations of the commandments.

The distinction between the philosophical nature of the discourse in Arabic and its non-philosophical nature in Hebrew clearly applies, at least on the face of it, to the *Guide* and *Mishneh torah*.

In *Mishneh torah*, divine law means Torah; even the seven Noahide laws that apply to non-Jews derive their authority from the Torah. In the *Guide*, Maimonides describes the characteristics of a divine law as a class of law,[240] leaving open the possibility of other divine laws besides Torah (even if the Torah may happen to be the only member of its class).[241] This is a similar

[238] On the historicity of Maimonides' characterizations of R. Judah the Prince, his times, and the Mishnah itself, and what motivated those characterizations, see the discussion and references in Halbertal, 'What Is *Mishneh Torah*?' Menahem Ben-Sasson treats the stress on the timeliness of *Mishneh torah* as a marketing ploy—see his 'Canon Formation' (Heb.), 145–7. For the view that Maimonides portrays R. Judah as a prophet, with clear implications for his own status, see Kreisel, *Maimonides' Political Thought*, 27. The possibility that *Mishneh torah* should be considered as prophecy is discussed below on pp. 359–66.

[239] Maimonides invokes Ps. 119: 126: 'It is time to do something for the Lord, and so on' (*Guide* i, Introduction (p. 16)), the continuation of the verse being 'for they have infringed Thy Law', as Pines points out. This is to justify writing down esoteric knowledge that had up to then been transmitted orally, against the background of Mishnah *Ber.* 9: 5 and BT *Ber.* 63a, where the verse is cited in the context of permitting something that would ordinarily be forbidden, because of overriding circumstances. (Although, as noted at BT *Ber.* 63a, the verse can also be interpreted as meaning 'It is time for the Lord to act', which is how the Revised Version translates.) The action that Maimonides seeks to justify is therefore similar to his action in composing *Mishneh torah*, but for an individual rather than for the nation. [240] *Guide* ii. 40 (p. 384).

[241] *Guide* ii. 39 (pp. 378–81). Pines notes a 'slight discrepancy' between *Guide* ii. 39 and *Guide* ii. 40 on whether there may be more than one divine law or whether the Torah is unique ('Philosophic

contrast to that between Hebrew as God's language in the Hebrew introduction to *Sefer ha'egron*, and Hebrew as a language with characteristics similar to those of other languages in the Arabic introduction.[242]

Drory sums up Sa'adyah's bicultural exercise thus:

An analysis of the introductions shows that even when the two texts are aimed at the same target audience—an educated Jewish public interested in the Hebrew language, the Bible, and the piyut—his choice of language caused Sa'adya Gaon to imagine in each case two completely different audiences, to project two distinct identity models on them, to address the two implicit audiences through dissimilar conceptual systems and means of persuasion, and to construct two different images of his role vis-à-vis the audience.[243]

This is almost uncannily appropriate to Maimonides as author of both *Mishneh torah* and the *Guide*. If it can be projected onto those two works, it means that they were not written for different readerships, but for the same elite readership, with Maimonides playing different roles in each, and masking his true intentions from the masses to the same extent, though in different ways.

Drory's study focuses on the tenth century. Tracing, across two centuries, cultural links that might confirm the legitimacy of superimposing Drory's Jewish Literary System on *Mishneh torah* and the *Guide* is a matter for separate research. The idea is therefore something of a speculative hypothesis, but it is one that seems to be supported by the *prima facie* evidence outlined above, both circumstantial (the letter to Ibn Jaber) and internal (the different orientations of *Mishneh torah* and the *Guide*), and it will be found to have considerable explanatory power, for example in resolving the apparent contradiction between the treatment of sacrifices in the *Guide* as a temporary

---

Sources', p. xc). What is perhaps most important in this context is that *Guide* ii. 39 gives philosophical grounds for the Torah's uniqueness—that there can be only one perfect thing within a species—rather than historical grounds, or the grounds of the Jewish people's election. Moreover, it attributes the Torah's perfection to Moses' perfection as a prophet. This is in contrast to the end of 'Laws of Idolatry', 1: 3, where the giving of the Torah has a historical context, where the election of the Jewish people is mentioned as a factor in it, and where Moses is more instrument than agent.

[242] Just to be absolutely clear, the parallel is valid notwithstanding that Maimonides' view of Hebrew was very different from the view Sa'adyah expressed in the Hebrew introduction to *Sefer ha'egron*. Maimonides would not have tolerated the idea of God using any language at all (see *Guide* i. 65 (pp. 158–60)). But Maimonides' and Sa'adyah's texts are being compared for their meta-characteristics, not their content, for the way the two writers write in Hebrew, not for what they write about Hebrew. For the purposes of this argument, therefore, *Sefer ha'egron*'s subject being the Hebrew language is coincidental.   [243] Drory, *Models and Contacts*, 181.

historical necessity and in *Mishneh torah* as an eternal institution temporarily in suspense, a subject that will be dealt with in Chapter 3.

The suggestion, then, is that Maimonides' choice of Hebrew as opposed to Arabic for *Mishneh torah* was determined by cultural as much as utilitarian considerations, arising from the conventions that governed the use of Hebrew and Arabic for Jewish writers. In his Hebrew work, Maimonides projects the law, as in his Hebrew introduction Sa'adyah projects the Hebrew language, beyond everyday reality into a metaphysical dimension. Direct imitation of *Sefer ha'egron*, conscious or otherwise, cannot be ruled out.[244] In Drory's system, *Mishneh torah* occupies the timeless, poetic-symbolic position, while the *Guide* occupies the contemporary, discursive position. The point is not to deny artistic quality to the *Guide*, but to reinforce the idea that the key difference between it and *Mishneh torah* is not one of subject matter or of intended readership, but of literary genre.

For the reader who understood the conventions, the fact of *Mishneh torah* being in Hebrew would have aroused certain expectations. It remains to demonstrate that these expectations would have been fulfilled, but, time and again, ideas discussed explicitly in the *Guide* will be found expressed in *Mishneh torah* symbolically, that is to say, poetically, through its form (the concept of macrocosm and microcosm being a prominent case in point: it is discussed at some length in the *Guide*,[245] but there is no explicit mention of it in *Mishneh torah*).

The ultimate claim made above for *Mishneh torah* as a work of art is that it is designed to be a transformative book: the experience of reading it is meant to move the reader closer to the knowledge of God. Such claims have already been made for the *Guide*.[246] This transformative effect operates in different ways in the two books. As a work of discursive prose, the *Guide* progressively dismantles false notions of God and enables a true understanding to take

---

[244] Other parallels that spring to mind are Ibn Gabirol's Hebrew poem *Keter malkhut* and Arabic treatise *Fons Vitae*, and Judah Halevi's Hebrew poetry and Arabic *Kuzari*.   [245] i. 72.

[246] See the remarks on the *Guide* by J. L. Kraemer, 'Naturalism and Universalism', 66:

The reader's attention should be drawn to the term *tanbih* ('arousal', 'stimulus'). It is a pivotal term throughout the *Guide*, and indicates that the treatise is, inter alia, a protreptic work—a stimulus to pursue philosophical knowledge. The law does not contain knowledge of being in its true form. It *arouses* and *directs attention* as a propaideutic to philosophical understanding.

Jon Whitman writes of the twists and turns in interpreting Scripture in the *Guide*: 'As the semiotic transfers he describes cannot exactly reach their divine object, Maimonides seeks to make them a means of transfiguring the human subject, whose very reading of the *Guide* is to be a way of proceeding toward God' ('Antiquity to the Late Middle Ages', 51). Kellner also argues for the *Guide* to be read as a transformative book, in *Maimonides on Human Perfection*.

shape, so that the reader should be different at the end from what he or she was at the beginning. There is a progressive element to the reading of *Mishneh torah* too, but its inspirational effect really derives from the synoptic perception of its wholeness and of the intricate interconnection of its parts. Where the *Guide* works dialectically, *Mishneh torah* works poetically. In a sense, Maimonides did translate *Mishneh torah* into Arabic, but translation involved more than linguistic substitution, and the result was the *Guide*.[247] This is not meant to suggest that all tensions in Maimonides' thought necessarily disappear, or that there was no development between *Mishneh torah* and the *Guide*. It does mean that, in considering such questions, a very high degree of literary sophistication must be taken into account. The fundamental distinguishing feature, as it were the chromosome that determines basic genre, is language.

Islamic Models

On the specific question of Islamic models for Maimonides' literary method, two studies, one by Tzvi Langermann,[248] the other by Oliver Leaman,[249] point in opposite directions: the first fragments while the second seeks to integrate, or rather, the first looks at origins and the second at goals.

Langermann compares *Mishneh torah* and the *Guide* (in fact the article is mainly about the *Guide*) with Maimonides' compilation of medical aphorisms, *Fusul musa* (*Pirkei mosheh*), and suggests that they were composed in similar ways, namely, from *fusul*, or short chapters, each summarizing a topic, and composed over a long period of time. In this, Langermann argues, he was following an Arab model, particularly Alfarabi. The introduction to *Fusul musa*, in which Maimonides gives an account of how the work was composed, is, according to Langermann, indicative of his method of composition in general. *Fusul musa* is a collection of paraphrases, epitomes, and citations from Galen; similarly, *Mishneh torah* paraphrases, summarizes, and reproduces material from the Jewish legal sources. And although Langermann does not cite it, the description Maimonides gives of *Fusul musa* as an *aide mémoire* fits the account he gives of *Mishneh torah* in the letter to his favourite pupil Joseph ben Judah quoted above.

The *fusul* model seems to stress subservience to the sources on which

---

[247] Note that the detail of halakhah is supplied in the *Guide* by, as it were, plugging in *Mishneh torah* through the cross-references to it in the *Guide*'s account of the commandments (*Guide* iii. 36–49).

[248] Langermann, 'Fusul Musa'.

[249] Leaman, 'Maimonides and the Development of Jewish Thought'.

the *fuṣul* are based. Leaman seeks to emphasize the potential for originality in the Islamic form of the summary:

But is not a summary merely a shorter version of something else? In art, not necessarily; a summary is a specific form of representation that has its own logic and metaphysics. Its structure is based on a set of ideas and presuppositions which might be very different from those employed by someone else trying to describe the same situation.[250]

In the organization of *Mishneh torah*, Leaman sees Maimonides as responding to Islamic jurisprudence, in which distinctions are made between the basic principles of the law and the details that branch from those principles.

Maimonides was not just giving his take on the law, he was doing more than that. He was giving his view of what the law, and Judaism, is all about. He set out to describe the essence of the law, and the essence of religion, in a way that gives the reader a grasp of how it operates as a whole. That is why it is wrong to criticize him for not giving his sources or entering into the Talmudic fray, his purpose was not to add to the discussion but to summarize it. What we should concentrate on is not the content of the *Mishneh Torah* and Maimonides' other halakhic works, but their design.[251]

That is a challenge that this study attempts to take up.

Structures of the Commandments

I have said that understanding the structure of *Mishneh torah* is a key to appreciating it as a work of art. That structure arises from the way the commandments are classified. But we encounter other arrangements of the commandments in Maimonides' works, and there is also the precedent in the structure of the Mishnah to consider. A brief survey comparing and contrasting *Mishneh torah*'s structure with these others will help in perceiving its special character. This will also present an opportunity to look at some explanations of its structure that scholars have offered, and to indicate the ways in which this study's approach will differ from theirs.

The Structure of *Mishneh Torah* and the Structure of the Mishnah

Let us start with the background. Although Maimonides' mission was to codify Jewish law, he did not find the law entirely without system. The Mishnah, the first redaction of the Oral Law, though prone to digress, does classify the laws under major categories, the 'six orders of the Mishnah'

---

[250] Ibid. 188.   [251] Ibid. 194.

Table 1. The books of *Mishneh torah* and the corresponding orders of the Mishnah

Mishneh torah			**Mishnah Order**	
1	*Knowledge*	Theology; ethics; study; idolatry; repentance	4	No real parallel
2	*Love*	Prayer; blessings; circumcision	1	*Zera'im*
3	*Seasons*	Sabbath and festivals	2	*Mo'ed*
4	*Women*	Marriage and divorce	3	*Nashim*
5	*Holiness*	Forbidden intercourse; forbidden food	6, 5	*Tohorot, Kodashim*
6	*Asseverations*	Vows of abstinence	3, 4	*Nashim, Nezikin*
7	*Agriculture*	Forbidden agricultural practices; charity; tithes; sabbatical years	1	*Zera'im*
8	*Temple Service*	Temple building, public sacrifices	5	*Kodashim*
9	*Offerings*	Private sacrifices	5	*Kodashim*
10	*Purity*	Ritual impurity and purification	6	*Tohorot*
11	*Torts*	Tort; theft; injury; murder	4	*Nezikin*
12	*Acquisition*	Sale; gifts; partnerships; slaves	4	*Nezikin*
13	*Civil Laws*	Hire; deposit; loans; inheritance	4	*Nezikin*
14	*Judges*	Justice system; constitution; mourning; the messiah	4	*Nezikin*

(*Zera'im*, *Mo'ed*, *Nashim*, *Nezikin*, *Kodashim*, *Tohorot*), and sub-categories, namely the *masekhtot*, or tractates, within each order.

It has been suggested that the structure of *Mishneh torah* is actually based upon that of the Mishnah.[252] It is true that, in composing it, Maimonides adopted the Mishnah's topical method of arrangement,[253] and to a large extent he did follow the mishnaic structure, but it is precisely this closeness that makes the deviations stand out and call for explanation, as Table 1 indicates.[254] The most extreme deviations are the excision of the civil laws in Order *Nezikin* from their place at number four in the mishnaic sequence and their placement in four books at the end of *Mishneh torah*, and the splitting of the material of the final order of the Mishnah, *Tohorot*, into two books placed much earlier in Maimonides' sequence, in book number 5, the *Book of Holi-*

---

[252] Tabory, 'The Structure of the Mishnah versus *Mishneh Torah*' (Heb.).

[253] See *The Book of the Commandments*, Introduction, and above, n. 4.

[254] The correspondences shown with the mishnaic orders are fairly rough because the laws Maimonides presents in any one book may be culled from many places in the Mishnah and Gemara, and indeed from other sources altogether.

ness, and just before the subject matter of *Nezikin*, in book number 10, the *Book of Purity*. The *Book of Knowledge* also stands out: as a unit, it has no mishnaic equivalent at all. What is more, we have considered only the larger units. A more detailed table would reveal that even when a book or group of books in *Mishneh torah* appears to correspond to one of the orders of the Mishnah, the internal arrangement is sometimes very different. Twersky remarks of books 11 to 13, 'None of these three books has even an approximate parallel in any single order of the Mishnah.'[255] These differences are material enough to render implausible a theory that the Mishnah served as a structural model for *Mishneh torah*. Maimonides indeed adopted the method of the Mishnah but not its order.

The relationship of *Mishneh torah* to the Mishnah is actually triple-layered: there is the Mishnah itself; Maimonides' explanation for the structure of the Mishnah in his own *Introduction to the Mishnah*; and *Mishneh torah*. It would be a subject for a separate study to examine in detail what bearing the second layer, Maimonides' own account of the Mishnah, has on the third, the structure of *Mishneh torah*.[256] For present purposes, a few examples will suffice to illustrate some general points.

Maimonides' default explanation for sequences of topics in the Mishnah is the sequence in the Torah. In Order *Nashim*, for instance, the tractate *Gitin* (Divorce) precedes *Kidushin* (Marriage) because, according to Maimonides, the editor of the Mishnah wished to follow the sequence of events described in Deuteronomy 24: 1–2: 'then let him write her a bill of divorcement, and give it in her hand, and send her out of his house. And when she is departed out of his house, she may go and be another man's wife.' Maimonides refers us to a talmudic discussion on the significance of these verses.[257] In his own *Book of Women*, however, he follows the logical order, and the laws of marriage precede the laws of divorce.

But this is by no means the only kind of explanation proffered. The reason given for Order *Zera'im* (Seeds) being placed first in the six orders of the Mishnah is that it deals with the most basic need of all living creatures, which is to derive sustenance from the earth, without which there can be no service of God. Similarly, when he comes to consider the sequence of tractates within *Zera'im*, Maimonides explains that the tractate *Berakhot* (Blessings) comes first because, just as the first thing a physician needs to mend is

---

[255] Twersky, *Introduction to the Code*, 271.
[256] Tabory does go into this question to some extent. See also Twersky, *Introduction to the Code*, 242–5.
[257] BT *Kid. 5a*.

the patient's diet, so the blessings mend our diet in that they enable us to eat at all, since it is forbidden to enjoy food without first making the appropriate blessing. Maimonides goes on to say that, since it needs to cover blessings over food, the first tractate of *Zera'im* also takes in blessings and prayer generally, while the remaining tractates in this first order of the Mishnah deal with laws pertaining to agriculture as such.

Notwithstanding this rationale, when it comes to *Mishneh torah*, Maimonides unbundles prayer and agriculture. Blessings and prayer are dealt with in book 2, the *Book of Love*, while the agricultural laws, despite being so basic, are not dealt with until book 7, the *Book of Agriculture*.[258]

Where he can, Maimonides introduces a didactic or spiritual element into his account of the structure of the Mishnah. He sees the sequence of Order *Nezikin*, for example, as presenting the stages by which a wise judge brings order to society. Yet, as I have already noted, in the three books of *Mishneh torah* that cover the same material (*Torts*, *Acquisition*, and *Civil Laws*), he considerably modifies the mishnaic arrangement.

All this is made the more significant, and even poignant, by the fact that the consensus among scholars is that, within any mishnaic order, the sequence of tractates as we have it is determined, on the whole, simply by the number of chapters in each.[259] In the case of the above example, *Gitin* happens to have nine chapters, while *Kidushin* has only four, so *Gitin* comes first. It is unlikely that Maimonides would have overlooked this, but he was clearly unsatisfied with it as an explanation.

We may draw certain conclusions. Firstly, Maimonides saw structure as important. He believed that it should be based on some non-arbitrary principle (say, the order of the Torah), and that it ought preferably to be meaningful (as in the political significance of the sequence in *Nezikin*).

---

[258] The book's Hebrew title is *Zera'im*, reflecting the name of the mishnaic order. The comparison between blessings and a healthy diet may seem not quite symmetrical, until we remember that, as stated later on in the *Commentary on the Mishnah* (in 'Eight Chapters', 5—discussed on pp. 135–6 below), mending the diet essentially means establishing control of the intellect over the appetite, which is what distinguishes human beings from beasts, so that 'the art of medicine is given a very large role with respect to the virtues, the knowledge of God, and attaining true happiness'. Blessings over food are in part a matter of establishing the priority of awareness of God over the satisfaction of appetites, of heeding the inward representative of the divine, which is the intellect (see *Guide* iii. 52), through which 'man is man' (*Guide* iii 54 (p. 635)). Maimonides' understanding of the very start of the Mishnah thus displays the single concept underlying his three roles, as rabbi, philosopher, and physician.

[259] See Epstein, *Introduction to Mishnaic Text* (Heb.), 985–7. The exception to this rule is the first half of Order *Zera'im*.

Secondly, he must have had very good reason for deviating from the sequence of the laws as found in the Mishnah, when he had elucidated the mishnaic sequence in such depth, and when he would have regarded that sequence as in some measure authoritative.[260]

These considerations reinforce the hypothesis that it is worth looking for an organizing principle that will explain the structure of *Mishneh torah*. Such questions as why *Mishneh torah* does not open like the Mishnah with the Shema recital, which, with its declaration of God's existence and unity, would have provided an excellent occasion for the kind of disquisition on fundamental principles we find in 'Laws of the Foundations of the Torah', and why agriculture is dealt with only halfway through, demand answers that flow from a general concept that justifies a radical reorientation of the mishnaic material.

The reshuffling of Order *Nezikin* is a different case. Far from abandoning the rationale of his *Introduction to the Mishnah*, it will be found that Maimonides applies it even more thoroughly. The last four books of *Mishneh torah* progress from utter chaos to perfect order. This is an example of a point that will recur several times in this study: the reinforcement in *Mishneh torah* of a trend that Maimonides has identified in his rabbinic source.

From the *Book of the Commandments* to *Mishneh Torah*

The *Book of the Commandments* lists all 613 Torah commandments, dividing them into 248 positive commandments and 365 negative ones. Within those categories, the arrangement is topical, but it is not the same as in *Mishneh torah*. The separate listing of positive and negative commandments was clearly inappropriate for that work, but within those major categories, we find in the *Book of the Commandments* perfectly logical groupings that are not carried over.

---

[260] There is evidence of other arrangements of the Mishnah besides the standard *ZeMaN NaKaT*, notably of an arrangement that put Order *Nezikin* as the last of the six orders (and of course this material is placed last in *Mishneh torah*). See Epstein, *Introduction to Mishnaic Text* (Heb.), 980–1. There were also different arrangements of the tractates within the orders. It is clear, however, from his introduction to the *Commentary on the Mishnah* that Maimonides had the now standard arrangement in front of him. His explanation of the sequence of the orders and tractates presents them in almost exactly the same order as we have them. The sole exception is that in Order *Nashim* he reverses the standard order of tractates *Sotah* and *Gitin*, putting *Gitin* first. This was a known variation (see Epstein, *Introduction to Mishnaic Text* (Heb.), 986), explicable according to the numerical theory of the order of tractates by the fact that *Sotah* and *Gitin* both have nine chapters. It is possible, though, that Maimonides saw in the recorded variations a kind of licence to deviate from the standard arrangement when he came to compose *Mishneh torah*. I thank Dr Hillel Newman for directing me to the references here.

For example, in the *Book of the Commandments*, the prohibitions concerning food[261] (except those related to tithes and the Temple[262]) are brought
together, whether the prohibition is due to something inherent in the food
itself, as in the case of the flesh of one of the animals one may not eat, or
whether it derives from some external circumstance, such as time, as in the
case of the ban on eating leaven on Passover[263] or on eating at all on Yom
Kippur.[264] In *Mishneh torah*, the former type of prohibition is found in the
Book of Holiness, while the latter is found in the *Book of Seasons*.

This alteration between the *Book of the Commandments* and *Mishneh torah*
may well have arisen in part from a change of mind about where certain
laws might be more conveniently found. The abandonment of the division
between positive and negative commandments is also clearly a factor, for if
the positive commandments associated with Passover[265] are not available as a
hook, it is hard to find anywhere to hang such commandments as not to
eat leaven during Passover, other than on the topic of food.[266] But the change
is much more powerfully motivated than this. To anticipate somewhat the
discussion in Chapter 3, the Neoplatonic concept of emanation, acting as a
principle of organization in *Mishneh torah*, entails that commandments determined by time belong further up the scale of value than commandments
associated with grosser physical properties. It is this principle, allied to the
mishnaic conceptual method of classification, that splits the general dietary
laws and those associated with particular periods, and causes the latter to be
placed earlier, or higher, than the former. Similar considerations apply to
other differences between the way the commandments are grouped in the
Book of the Commandments and the way they are grouped in *Mishneh torah*.

From *Mishneh Torah* to the *Guide*

Yet another taxonomy of the commandments is to be found in the *Guide of the
Perplexed*. In Part III of the *Guide* Maimonides sets out to explain the reasons
for the commandments. To facilitate his discussion, he divides the commandments into fourteen classes. It could almost be seen as provocative that these

---

[261] Negative commandments 172–206.

[262] Negative commandments 125–51.

[263] Negative commandments 197–9.

[264] Negative commandment 196.

[265] Positive commandments 156–60.

[266] The negative commandments concerning the paschal sacrifice (115–28) are not really an appropriate hook, since their context is the Temple ritual, although commandments 115 (not to perform
the paschal sacrifice whilst in possession of leaven) and 199 (not to consume leaven after midday on
Passover eve) provide links that might possibly have been exploited. The negative commandments
concerning labour on Passover (323–4) provide another possible location, but again, they are in a
certain context, namely, prohibitions on labour on the sabbath and festivals generally (320–8).

Table 2. The classes of the commandments in *The Guide of the Perplexed* iii. 35 and the corresponding books of *Mishneh torah*

Class	Content		*Mishneh torah* corresponding book
1	Fundamental opinions	1	Knowledge
2	Idolatry	1	Knowledge
3	Ethical qualities	1	Knowledge
4	Alms, lending, gifts	7	Agriculture
5	Wrongdoing and aggression	11	Torts
6	Punishments	14	Judges
7	Property	12, 13	Acquisition, Civil Laws
8	Sabbaths and festivals	3	Seasons
9	Prayer	2	Love
10	Temple	8	Temple Service
11	Sacrifices	8, 9	Temple Service, Offerings
12	Clean and unclean	10	Purity
13	Prohibited foods	5, 6	Holiness, Asseverations
14	Prohibited sexual unions	4, 5	Women, Holiness

fourteen classes do not correspond to the fourteen books of *Mishneh torah*.[267] The chief differences can be seen in Table 2.

This table is schematic; some significant differences between the *Guide* and *Mishneh torah* are apparent only at a greater level of detail, such as the fact that circumcision is dealt with in the *Book of Love* in *Mishneh torah*, but in class number 14 in the *Guide*'s classification, rather than in class number 9—a change to which Maimonides calls attention, and which will be important later on. Nevertheless, the chief variations between the two works can be seen here. The most prominent one is that the man–man commandments and the commandments concerning restraint of physical appetites swap positions. The former are in books 11–14 of *Mishneh torah*, but in classes 5–7 in the *Guide*, while the latter are in books 4–6 in *Mishneh torah*, but in the *Guide* are in last position, forming classes 13–14.

The changes in the ordering of the commandments between the *Book of*

---

[267] Berman finds the number fourteen significant in the arrangement of the commandments in the *Book of the Commandments* too, for he divides each half of the listing, the positive and negative commandments, into fourteen groups. See 'Structure of the Commandments', 52, and references there. As it happens, the sums of the digits of the totals of the positive and negative commandments, 248 and 365 (when written in Arabic numerals, rather than using the numerical values of Hebrew letters) are both 14, but it is hard to know whether Maimonides would have been impressed by that coincidence.

the Commandments and *Mishneh torah* can perhaps be explained by the notion that Maimonides was feeling his way towards a satisfactory classification, and in the earlier work had not yet hit upon the idea of a cosmological scheme, but what can explain him going to the trouble of devising another arrangement for the *Guide*, yet within the same fourteen-section format? It does not appear that he abandoned the *Mishneh torah* classification as unsatisfactory, for throughout the relevant section of the *Guide* he provides cross-references back to it, to the extent that producing Table 2 took no effort: all the correspondences shown in columns three and four are taken from the *Guide* itself. Rather, the two classifications seem intended to serve two different purposes.

Theories of *Mishneh Torah*'s Structure

This is an appropriate point at which to survey earlier theories of *Mishneh torah*'s structure (besides the theory that it is based on the Mishnah, discussed above), since in their discussions of the subject scholars have tended to occupy themselves with just this question of the altered classification in the *Guide*, and are thereby led to attempt to characterize the orientations of the two works.

Boaz Cohen finds two main principles at work in *Mishneh torah*: firstly, a distinction between those commandments that are currently applicable and those, such as commandments appertaining to the Temple, that are not; and secondly, a division of the commandments into the categories of ritual, purity, and civil law.[268] This second principle, says Cohen, is suggested in Maimonides' introduction to *Mishneh torah*, and is based on the amoraic division between the areas of ceremonial (*issura*), impurity (*tuma*), and jurisprudence (*mamona*), itself a development of the distinction made by R. Eleazar ben Azariah in the last *mishnah* of tractate *Yoma* between commandments governing the relationship between man and God (*bein adam lamakom*) and those governing relationships between man and man (*bein adam laḥavero*).

Cohen summarizes the arrangement of *Mishneh torah* as follows: '(1) The Ritual, which is still in force, is treated in books II–VI, the obsolete rules in books VII–IX; (2) Laws of Purity, the bulk of which was obsolete, in book X; (3) Civil Law that is in vogue is dealt with in books XI–XIII, while that branch which was no longer in operation, in book XIV.'

As for the *Book of Knowledge*, which deals with theological and ethical principles and corresponds to none of the above categories, Cohen says that its

---

[268] B. Cohen, 'Classification of the Law'. An analysis similarly based on practicality and applicability is given in Ziemlich, 'Plan und Anlage'.

composition and placing as book 1 show Islamic influence on Maimonides' method: 'The idea of writing such a prolegomenon was suggested to him undoubtedly by the Hadith.'

Berman finds a primary distinction between theoretical commandments and practical commandments, with the theoretical being treated in book 1, while the practical are treated in books 2–14.[269] He divides the practical commandments in turn between man–God commandments (books 2–10), and man-man commandments (books 11–14).

Berman describes books 2–10 as being keyed to three of the five sections of book 1: books 2 and 3 to 'Basic Principles' ('Laws of the Foundations of the Torah'); books 4 to 6 to 'Ethical Qualities'; and books 7 to 10 to 'Idolatry'.

The broad division that both Cohen and Berman make between the books on man–God commandments and those on man–man commandments is also the basis for my own structural analysis. Cohen's further division of the man–God books between *issura* and *tuma* also seems accurate, and there is no disputing both scholars' observation that book 1, the *Book of Knowledge*, fits no traditional grouping. Cohen, however, sees that book as a prolegomenon, while Berman sees it as integrated into the general structure, and indeed as holding the key to it. The argument that will be developed here about the way in which the first book informs both the content and the structure of the rest of the work is very much in line with Berman's approach, in principle, and to a large extent also in detail.

As for Cohen's distinction between current and obsolete legislation, this is effectively disposed of by Twersky, who points out that it is vitiated by too many instances in which, within the different books, both kinds of laws are treated side by side. In any case, Twersky finds this approach simply too tame, not consonant with Maimonides' deeply considered and daring conceptualization of the commandments, and his comprehensive, holistic treatment of them.[270]

In comparing the classification of the commandments in *Mishneh torah* with that in *Guide* iii. 35, Berman continues with the idea that the discussion of the practical commandments is keyed to the theoretical commandments, arguing, for example, that because, in the *Guide*, the commandments to do with idolatry and ethical qualities switch places, the ordering of the practical commandments keyed to these theoretical topics is also switched.

More generally, Berman finds that the man–God/man–man distinction in

[269] Berman, 'Structure of the Commandments'.
[270] Twersky, *Introduction to the Code*, 297–308.

Mishneh torah disappears in the *Guide*—as noted above, the man–man commandments are placed in the middle of the later classification, instead of being isolated at the end as in the earlier one. He attributes the different structures of the commandments in the two books to the different roles Maimonides plays in each: jurisprudent in the former, seeking to 'follow the guidelines laid down by the first legislator and interpreted by his followers, the rabbis'; theologian in the latter, seeking to demonstrate the philosophical viability of the Torah.

Berman sees the structure of the commandments in the *Guide* as representing a more advanced stage in Maimonides' thought, going so far as to suggest that *Mishneh torah* might have been structured differently had it been written after the *Guide*: 'In fact, *The Book of Commandments*, the *Mishneh torah*, and the scheme of Part III, chapter 35 of the *Guide* may be considered closer and closer approximations to the deep structure of the commandments of the law.'

Twersky rejects this evolutionary approach, and firmly asserts that the different classifications reflect the different emphases of each work. According to him, the categorization in *Mishneh torah* is topical-conceptual, while in the *Guide* it is philosophical-teleological, in line with the twofold purpose of the commandments described there, namely, the welfare of the soul and the welfare of the body. He mentions the point noted above that Maimonides is quite open about the different categorizations, and he leaves no room for the idea that the categorization in *Mishneh torah* is a station on the road to the *Guide*.

This is a crucial point for the thesis I intend to put forward, for interpreting the structure of *Mishneh torah* will play an important part in presenting it as a fully fledged work of art. If the categorization of the commandments there is regarded as undeveloped in relation to the categorization in the *Guide*, this will diminish its interest and limit its significance. But here, Berman seems to me unclear and inconsistent. First of all there is the question of what he means by 'the deep structure of the commandments'. Is he suggesting something inherent in the commandments that Maimonides is in the process of discovering, and that the categorizations Maimonides uses are not constructs? That would be a far-reaching claim. Or does he mean that Maimonides came nearer and nearer to moulding what he, subjectively, considered a satisfactory structure?

In the final paragraph of his article, Berman seems to backtrack somewhat:

Do the differences in structure which have been pointed out between the *Mishneh*

Torah and the *Guide* represent substantive changes in Maimonides' general concept of the commandments and their relative value? Spinoza and Moses Mendelssohn would most probably have understood them as substantive changes; others of a more traditional mold as but tactical changes. In any event, the two different points of view which the *Mishneh Torah* and the *Guide* represent are clear enough. We do not, of course, have here two different authors as Jacob Emden claimed, but we certainly do have two very different views on the nature of the commandments of the Torah.

This is puzzling. Are there 'two very different views', or a gradual discovery/ formulation of a single deep structure? Actually, neither conjecture is necessitated by Berman's analysis of the categorizations in each work. As mentioned, Maimonides is quite explicit about his intentions in the *Guide* and the many cross-references to the relevant books of *Mishneh torah* suggest that he did not regard the categorization in the earlier work as superseded. On the contrary, he seems to be signalling that each scheme is valid in context.

Since the different schemes in *Mishneh torah* and the *Guide* can be accounted for without resort to notions of evolution or shift, and since such notions go against the grain of Maimonides' own comments, there is no reason for adopting them. In other words, there seem to be no grounds for supposing that the structure of *Mishneh torah* would have been substantially different had it been written after the *Guide* instead of before. *Mishneh torah* is a mature work of art with its own perfection, in which the structure contributes to, indeed is inseparable from, the exposition of its themes and the impression sought on the reader.

Berman and Twersky agree, however, in their general characterizations of *Mishneh torah*'s classification of the commandments as exhibiting a jurisprudential approach, in contrast to a theological-philosophical approach in the *Guide*. Both explicitly rule out the possibility of a philosophical basis for *Mishneh torah*'s structure. Berman asserts that 'the commandments in the *Guide* are ordered hierarchically according to a philosophical scale of values, which is not the case in the *Mishneh Torah*';[271] and Twersky comments,

While the *Mishneh Torah* classification is sustained by a philosophical as well as a juridical sensibility, the former is clearly and appropriately subservient to the latter … while the *Mishneh Torah* has an unmistakable philosophic flavour, contains original explanations of laws stemming from philosophical or medical conceptions, and even formulates laws because of certain philosophical emphases, the latter did not impinge on the book's classification.[272]

---

[271] Berman, 'The Structure of the Commandments', 61.

[272] *Introduction to the Code*, 307–8. Despite his sensitivity to Maimonides' literary art, and although

Eliezer Hadad develops Berman's approach in that he too sees the structure of *Mishneh torah* as keyed to the *Book of Knowledge*; he gives a detailed account of how each of the subsequent books is linked to the first.[273] That account is an outcome of Hadad's study of the relationship between law and nature in Maimonides, a subject that is also an underlying theme of the present study. He sets out to show how the operation of the law reflects God's *modus operandi* in earthly creation. One aspect of this is the purposefulness of God's actions in the sublunary world. It is in terms of their purposes that Hadad explains the way the commandments are structured in both *Mishneh torah* and the *Guide*. He asserts that, once this basis of categorization is understood, the differences between the structures in the two books are not substantial and can be accounted for.

We have, then, two views of the relationship between *Mishneh torah* and the *Guide* in respect of their classification of the commandments. Twersky and Berman see the two classifications as sharply contrasting, and as representing jurisprudence versus philosophy. Hadad on the other hand sees them as essentially similar, both reflecting the idea of purpose in creation.

My own approach agrees with neither view. Against Berman and Twersky, I shall argue that a hierarchic arrangement according to a philosophical scale of values is precisely what *Mishneh torah*'s structure exhibits, revealing that work to be every bit as philosophical as the *Guide*; philosophical to its core, and not just as added flavour. The philosophical dimension, the 'great thing', very much impinges on the book's classification—it is in fact the ultimate determinant of it. The 'original explanations' that Twersky notes are outcrops of deep formations.

At the same time, against Hadad, I shall argue that the two classification schemes cannot be boiled down to the same philosophical idea. Hadad first devises a theory of the relationship between the law and nature in Maimonides, in which the nature side is restricted to sublunary nature, and then applies his conclusions to *Mishneh torah*'s structure. My approach is the

---

he discusses the structures of the individual books, Twerksy offers no explanation of the structure of *Mishneh torah* as a whole, but only criticizes theories of previous scholars, notably those of Ziemlich and of Boaz Cohen. It is possible that this is because, for all his insight into the non-halakhic aspects of *Mishneh torah*, Twersky sought to preserve the status and integrity of the halakhic method, independently of philosophy, and so any theory of *Mishneh torah*'s structure beyond the mechanical would have involved him in self-contradiction—hence his insistence on the subservience of the philosophical to the juridical sensibility in the *Mishneh torah* classification. Actually, Maimonides' art respects the integrity of halakhah; further on this see below, p. 381.

[273] Hadad, 'Nature and Torah in Maimonides' (Heb.), 260–95.

reverse: first to describe the structure, and then, having determined that it reflects Maimonides' cosmology, to examine its implications for the relationship between the law and nature, with the consequence that the relationship is seen as embracing superlunary nature as well. It is entirely possible that the two approaches are reconcilable, for Hadad is concerned with the law in action, whereas my emphasis is on the law as a form of knowledge. The law in action does belong to the sublunary world,[274] but the law as object of contemplation extends the diapason to the heavens. Moreover, Hadad's analysis of Torah in Maimonides' view as a means of replicating the constitution of the cosmos in the constitution of the state bears strong similarity to the view taken here of *Mishneh torah* as a microcosm. Nevertheless, while purpose seems an appropriate basis for explaining the structure of the commandments in the *Guide*, it is less clear that it is appropriate for *Mishneh torah*.

My own account of the two classifications will embrace the tension between the consistency of the number fourteen and the inconsistency of the arrangement within that number. The basis of it will be the distinction between Arabic and Hebrew genres discussed above, for I shall argue that each genre involves its own logical method, and that the classification in the *Guide* can actually be seen as a reversion to the method of *The Book of the Commandments*. For the present, suffice to say that the classification in the *Guide* is meant to bear out Maimonides' argument that 'The Law aims at two things, the welfare of the soul and the welfare of the body', but that although the welfare of the soul is 'indubitably greater in nobility', the welfare of the body is 'prior in nature and time'.[275] After commandments establishing certain essential beliefs, the classification broadly follows this order of priorities, and it ends with commandments to do with a third aim that Maimonides sets out in the chapters that introduce his classification, namely, the 'restraint of desires'.[276] This scheme is part of his effort to persuade us that the purpose of the commandments is to establish a harmonious society made up of enlightened, moral individuals.

If we compare this with the classification in *Mishneh torah*, we can say, very broadly speaking, that whereas the *Guide* places civil society first, *Mishneh torah* places the individual and ritual first. We might have expected

---

[274] Note the similarity of language between 'Laws of the Foundations of the Torah', 3: 11, where Maimonides describes the general comprehensibility of the four sublunary elements, 'the power of which, old and young constantly perceive', and 'Laws of the Foundations of the Torah', 4: 13, where he describes the general comprehensibility of the practical commandments, the 'small thing': 'the knowledge of them is within the reach of all, young and old, men and women'.

[275] *Guide* iii. 27 (p. 510).   [276] *Guide* iii. 33 (p. 532).

Mishneh torah, if it is supposed to be a practical code of law, to deal first with those matters that Maimonides says are 'prior in nature and time', that is, the establishment of a social and moral framework, and then to give us the content, the laws that reinforce correct opinions. Instead, as we have seen, Maimonides saves the four books of *Mishneh torah* that deal with social laws until last.

We could rest content with saying that, since in *Mishneh torah* Maimonides was providing a reference work, rather than constructing an argument as he is in the *Guide*, he could afford to place first those matters that are 'indubitably greater in nobility': if we need to look up the social laws, we know where to find them. There is, however, another possibility, which is that Maimonides does construct an argument in *Mishneh torah*, but a different argument.

Summary: Philosopher, Statesman, Artist

Maimonides applied the highest literary art to the highest of tasks: to bequeath, as philosopher-statesman,[277] a law that would regulate the life of the individual and of society and move people closer to the knowledge of God. The result of that art is a book to be read and experienced, not just consulted.

The central feature of *Mishneh torah* as a work of art is the casting of the commandments of the law in the form of the cosmos. The microcosmic form suggests, in the first place, that studying *Mishneh torah*, like the study of the universe, can be a way to the knowledge and love of God. On the plane of ideas, this form embodies the relationship between the 'small thing' and the 'great thing', between halakhah, on the one hand, and physics and metaphysics on the other. It depicts philosophy as the matrix of halakhah, reflecting the view of the relationship between philosophy and religion in the Islamic philosophers.

Moses, the greatest philosopher-statesman, produced the perfection of Torah, which Maimonides describes in the same terms as the perfection of nature. *Mishneh torah*, in its mimesis of nature's perfection, fulfils the ideal of *imitatio Dei*, and can therefore transmit this ideal.

The fact that *Mishneh torah* is written in Hebrew, against the background of medieval Jewish literary convention, signals its poetic intent. It also marks the chief difference between *Mishneh torah* and the *Guide of the Perplexed*,

[277] For the idea of the statesman as Maimonides inherited it, see Berman, 'Maimonides the Disciple of Alfarabi'.

which is not a matter of philosophical depth or of target readership, but of literary genre. The idea of the microcosmic form too resonates in a tradition, the literary theory of the late Neoplatonists.

Poetry was not Maimonides' real medium. He was, however, sufficiently possessed of poetic sensibility and plastic imagination that the welling love of God could combine in him with philosophical and legal rigour to shape the material of halakhah into a work that embodies an entire vision, with the complexity-in-simplicity of a true poem. It is time to turn to the direct evidence for this assertion.

CHAPTER ONE

IN GOD'S IMAGE

G OD'S MANIFESTO in Genesis for the creation of humankind, 'Let us
make man in our image, after our likeness',[1] presents Maimonides with a
special challenge. Biblical expressions that appear to undermine his doctrine
of God's non-physicality,[2] such as 'beneath his feet'[3] and 'written with the
finger of God',[4] can generally be neutralized by treating them as concessions
to the inescapable concreteness of everyday language: 'All these expressions
are adapted to the mental capacity of mankind, who have a clear perception of
physical bodies only. The Torah speaks in the language of men. All these
phrases are metaphorical.'[5] Not so 'Let us make man in our image, after our
likeness'. This verse needs to be defused much more carefully, for it is not
reducible to metaphor. Even after we explain that the image and likeness in
question are not physical, it still asserts what Maimonides denies: 'there is
absolutely no likeness in any respect whatever between Him and the things
created by Him', he states in the *Guide*, meaning no likeness of any kind,
physical or non-physical.[6]

At the same time, the love of God and the consequent desire to be like him
drive Maimonides' entire system. On the cosmic plane, these longings are the
motive forces that make the spheres revolve, as we shall shortly see. On the
human plane, likeness to God underlies human perfection, being the basis of

---

[1] Gen. 1: 26.

[2] 'Introduction to *Perek ḥelek*', third fundamental principle (*Commentary on the Mishnah*, Order
Nezikin, 141); 'Laws of the Foundations of the Torah', 1: 5–12.   [3] Exod. 24: 10.   [4] Exod. 31: 18.

[5] 'Laws of the Foundations of the Torah', 1: 9. 'In our image, after our likeness' is not among the
expressions to which this generalization is applied in this *halakhah* and in 'Laws of the Foundations of
the Torah', 1: 12, but it is dealt with separately, in 'Laws of the Foundations of the Torah', 4: 8, which
is examined below.

[6] *Guide* i. 35 (p. 80). See also 'Laws of the Foundations of the Torah', 1: 8: 'and again it is said, "To
whom will Ye liken me, or shall I be equal" [Isa. 40: 25]. If He were a body, He would be like other
bodies.' The same verse is cited in *Guide* i. 55 (p. 128) in support of the assertion that 'One must likewise of necessity deny, with reference to Him, His being similar to any existing thing.'

both intellectual virtue and moral virtue in Maimonides' version of these Aristotelian categories.[7]

As far as intellectual virtue is concerned, the ultimate aim of all intellectual activity is the knowledge of God.[8] Knowledge, in Aristotelian psychology, is a matter of likeness, for the act of cognition consists of the mind abstracting the form of the object that it contemplates and merging with that form.[9] 'Whenever intellect exists *in actu*, it is identical with the intellectually cognized thing' is how this is put in the *Guide*.[10] Knowledge of God would therefore appear to entail some kind of likeness to God.

Moral virtue is even more clearly associated with likeness to God, for the governing commandment of 'Laws of Ethical Qualities', where moral virtue is explained, is precisely to become like God.

Both these virtues are means to the love of God: moral virtue is a prerequisite for acquiring intellectual virtue, and intellectual virtue engenders love, for 'according to the knowledge shall be the love, if little, little, if much, much'.[11] Love in turn spurs the desire for greater knowledge, in a virtuous circle.

The Maimonidean values of love and knowledge are thus intertwined with the notion of likeness. Our verse must therefore be handled with double care: its destructive potential must be disarmed while its positive force is released. It is no coincidence that 'in the image of God' is the subject of the *Guide*'s very first chapter. This suspected anthropomorphism is not first in line just because it occurs early in Genesis. The whole enterprise of the *Guide* could be said to be the replacement of an erroneous reading of this verse with a true one, which means dismantling a misconception that is really God in the image of man, and building a framework in which man can truly be in the image of God, yet without violating cardinal principles. A way must be found in which human beings are like God, yet not like God.

Maimonides is well aware of the seeming incompatibility of his doctrine of a deity beyond our intellectual horizon, utterly removed from all human concepts and categories and unlike anything in the universe, with the imperatives to know God and become like him. We shall look presently at the solutions that he offers. Our subject, however, is the form of *Mishneh torah*,

---

[7] The categories are taken from Aristotle's *Nicomachean Ethics*. In 'Eight Chapters', 2 (part of the *Commentary on the Mishnah*, which pre-dates *Mishneh torah*) Maimonides sums them up as follows: 'Now as for the virtues, they are of two kinds, moral and intellectual, with the corresponding two classes of vices.'

[8] See above, Introduction, n. 1.   [9] This is explained more fully below and in Appendix II.2.

[10] *Guide* i. 68 (p. 164).   [11] 'Laws of Repentance', 10: 6.

and the theme of this chapter will be the way in which form bears on the problem.

The discussion will focus on a certain structural parallel between 'Laws of the Foundations of the Torah' and 'Laws of Ethical Qualities', the opening sections of the first book of *Mishneh torah*, the *Book of Knowledge*. These two sections have quite different orientations. 'Laws of the Foundations of the Torah' looks to the divine. It lays down doctrines: what we must know about God, creation, and prophecy. 'Laws of Ethical Qualities' looks towards the human condition, and is about morality, both individual and social. This division broadly corresponds to the two purposes that Maimonides assigns to the law in the *Guide*: the welfare of the soul, and the welfare of the body (which includes the body politic).[12] In Aristotelian terms, 'Laws of the Foundations of the Torah' is about intellectual virtue, while 'Laws of Ethical Qualities' is about moral virtue.

Formal analysis, however, will reveal that, underneath the differences in their contents, the two sections exhibit close structural similarity. The second section will be shown to be modelled on the first, in a microcosm–macrocosm pattern. 'Laws of Ethical Qualities' can be said to be 'in the image' of 'Laws of the Foundations of the Torah'. Latent in this pattern are ideas that supplement the explicit solutions that Maimonides provides to the problem of human likeness to God, giving access to a deeper understanding than was sketched above of the relationship between the moral and intellectual applications of being created in God's image. This involves a departure from the Aristotelian model, and an altogether more holistic notion of human perfection.[13]

We shall begin our exploration of the formal pattern with an intriguing repetition.

Two Scholars

In chapter 5 of 'Laws of Ethical Qualities', Maimonides does something uncharacteristic and strange: he repeats an entire topic. As I have said, the

---

[12] *Guide* iii. 27 (p. 510).

[13] In an unpublished paper by the late Professor Joseph M. Yoffey entitled 'Rambam as Physician', Maimonides emerges as having a holistic approach to medicine too, an approach that Professor Yoffey characterizes as ahead of its time: 'He regarded body and mind as inseparable in the treatment of disease, and it followed therefore that the hygiene of the mind was just as important as that of the body.' This, of course, is reflected in the comparison between diseases of the soul and diseases of the body in 'Laws of Ethical Qualities', 2: 1, and in the inclusion in chapter 4 of that section of prescriptions for physical health. My late aunt Mrs Betty Yoffey kindly gave me access to the paper.

subject of 'Laws of Ethical Qualities' in general is moral virtue. This finds expression in a well-tempered personality, the control of physical appetites, and the maintenance of a healthy body. The fifth chapter of this section portrays the *talmid ḥakham*, the scholar, who embodies, and even exceeds, all the virtues propounded in chapters 1 to 4.

But Maimonides has already presented his model scholar once before, if much more briefly, in chapter 5 of the previous section, 'Laws of the Foundations of the Torah', which focuses on intellectual virtue. The chapter's subject is *kidush hashem*, the sanctification of God's name, the duty to attest to the truth of God's existence. Most of that chapter deals with the (strictly limited) circumstances in which a Jew is called upon to sanctify the name through martyrdom. The final *halakhah*,[14] however, treats *kidush hashem* more broadly, as an attribute of the daily behaviour of the sage or scholar, to whom the masses look as an exemplar of the religious life, and whose every deed may therefore either enhance their faith and their respect for religion, or bring religion into disrepute.[15]

It is not just that the subject matter of the model scholar is repeated; the final *halakhot* of 'Laws of the Foundations of the Torah', chapter 5, and of 'Laws of Ethical Qualities', chapter 5,[16] are similar in their details and in their very language. First, here is 'Laws of the Foundations of the Torah', 5: 11:

There are other things that are a profanation of the Name of God. When a man, great in knowledge of the Torah and reputed for his piety, does things which cause people to talk about him, even if the acts are not express violations, he profanes the Name of God. For example, if such a person makes a purchase and does not pay promptly, provided that he has means and the creditors ask for payment and he puts them off; or if he indulges immoderately in jesting, eating, or drinking when he is staying with

---

[14] *Halakhah* 11.

[15] Sanctification of the name belongs with intellectual virtue because it is a matter of bearing witness to the truth, and is separate from the actions it may involve. This is demonstrated by the fact that, in the case of the generality of commandments, unless there is a state-instigated attempt to wipe out Jewish practice, one should prefer martyrdom to transgression only if the oppressor demands transgression for its own sake and not for his material benefit, and if the transgression is in public ('Laws of Foundations of the Torah', 5: 2). In other words, what counts is not the act itself but the impression it makes. Even in the case of idolatry, murder, and forbidden sexual relations, where the profanation of God's name is considered to be inherent in the act, and where one should prefer martyrdom to transgression in all circumstances, anyone who chooses to transgress and live has failed to sanctify God's name, and has even profaned it, but he or she is not liable for the act itself, because it was committed under duress ('Laws of Foundations of the Torah', 5: 4). On the question of duress, see also *The Epistle on Martyrdom* (*Epistles*, ed. Halkin and Hartman, 15–45), where Maimonides objects to the notion that a forced profession of faith in Islam disqualifies a person as a Jew. Davidson doubts Maimonides' authorship of this epistle—see *Moses Maimonides*, 501–9.   [16] *Halakhah* 13.

ignorant people or living among them; or if his mode of addressing people is not gentle, or he does not receive people affably, but is quarrelsome and irascible. The greater a man is the more scrupulous should he be in all things, and do more than the strict letter of the law requires.

And if a man has been scrupulous in his conduct, gentle in his conversation, pleasant towards his fellow-creatures, affable in manner when receiving them, affronted by them and not offering affront, but showing courtesy to all, even to those who treat him with disdain, conducting his commercial affairs with integrity, not readily accepting the hospitality of the ignorant nor frequenting their company, not seen at all times, but devoting himself to the study of Torah, wrapped in *talit*, and crowned in phylacteries, and doing more than his duty in all things, avoiding however extremes and exaggerations, to the point where everyone praises him, and loves him, and desires to emulate his deeds—such a man has sanctified God, and concerning him Scripture says, 'And He said to me, You are my servant Israel, in whom I will be glorified' (Isa. 49: 3).

Now 'Laws of Ethical Qualities', 5: 13:

The scholar conducts his business affairs honestly and in good faith. His nay is nay; his yea, yea. In his accounts, he is strict (in meeting his obligations). At the same time, when buying, he is liberal and does not drive a hard bargain. He pays promptly for his purchases. He declines to act as a surety or trustee; nor will he accept a power of attorney.

In commercial matters, he acknowledges liability even where the law would not hold him liable; his principle being to keep his word and not change it. If others have been adjudged liable to him, he is considerate, and even forgives them the amount due. He grants benevolent loans and does favours. He will not encroach on another man's business, and throughout his life he will not vex a human being.

In short, he belongs to the class of those who are persecuted but do not persecute, who are affronted but do not offer affront. A man who does all these things and their like, concerning him Scripture says, 'And He said to me, You are my servant Israel, in whom I will be glorified.'

It is true that these two *halakhot* have different emphases. In keeping with the theme of sanctification of God's name, the first presents the scholar as exemplar to others, while the second, in line with the theme of 'Laws of Ethical Qualities' of the balanced and ethical personality, presents him more as he is in himself.[17] Nevertheless, the similarities are inescapable. Both *halakhot*

---

[17] Even so, the two themes are not kept entirely separate. In 'Laws of Foundations of the Torah', 5: 11, the proviso about the scholar 'avoiding however extremes and exaggerations' (the Hebrew *vehu shelo yitraḥek velo yishtomem* could also be translated as something like 'provided that he does not

portray a person who is punctilious in fulfilling his obligations but lenient towards others, gracious in his manner, and prepared to suffer indignity without offering any—in short, a person of surpassing nobility of character. The second *halakhah* even echoes the first's phraseology.[18] Then, as though to make absolutely sure that the echo is not missed, Maimonides seals each *halakhah* with the same quotation from Isaiah: 'You are my servant, Israel, in whom I will be glorified.'

All in all, these two passages could, on the face of it, swap places almost without the switch being noticed. Such blatant repetition by so careful and economical an author[19] deserves investigation.[20]

We should be clear, though, about what it is that we are investigating. It is not the mere fact of repetition. *Mishneh torah*'s topical arrangement makes

become very aloof and unsocial—see the use of *yitraḥek* in 'Laws of Ethical Qualities', 5: 6 and 7—but the basic sense of not overdoing things would be the same) anticipates the doctrine of the golden mean discussed in 'Laws of Ethical Qualities', while in chapter 5 of the same section Maimonides is clearly still conscious of the scholar as exemplar, saying of him in *halakhah* 3: 'and if he becomes drunk in front of the ordinary people he desecrates the name of God'.

[18] Rawidowicz notes the parallels, and remarks that they indicate the close connection Maimonides saw between moral virtue and the sanctification of God's name ('The Opening Book of *Mishneh Torah*' (Heb.), 417).

[19] In 'Laws of Ethical Qualities', 2: 4 Maimonides commends parsimony with words even in matters of Torah and science. In the *Guide* he protests his care over language: 'the diction of this Treatise has not been chosen at haphazard, but with great exactness and exceeding precision' (*Guide* i, Introduction (p. 15)), while in the *Essay on Resurrection* he declares, 'If I could squeeze the entire Law of the Torah into one chapter, I would not write two chapters for it' (*Epistles*, 225). On Maimonides' commitment to brevity, and reasons for his occasional breach of that commitment, see Twersky, *Introduction to the Code*, 337–46.

[20] The chances that the repetition of the content is not deliberate are very low. The Oxford Huntington 80 manuscript copy of the first two books of *Mishneh torah*, *Book of Knowledge* and *Book of Love*, bearing the author's certification and signature, shows no sign of an attempt to correct this feature—see '*Authorized Version of the Code*'. Nor is the verse that draws attention to the repetition a particular favourite of the author's. According to Kafih (*The Hebrew Bible in Maimonides* (Heb.)), the only other place in which it appears in all of Maimonides' writings is in the *Epistle on Martyrdom*. In general, Maimonides does not make a habit of citing the same verse in more than one place. The Or Vishua edition of *Mishneh torah* lists about 2,000 verses quoted in the work, and states that there are about 4,000 references to these verses. But many verses recur because they are cited in the list of the commandments in the introduction, or because they happen to be in the prayer book or the Haggadah (the texts of which Maimonides provides), as well as in the body of the work, or because the same verse is cited several times in the course of discussion of a single matter. Of seventy-six verses from Isaiah quoted in *Mishneh torah* (twelve of which are in the prayer book), seven appear more than once. As far as I am aware, the only other verse used to make exactly the same point in two places in *Mishneh torah* is Hos. 9: 4, in 'Laws of Resting on Festivals', 6: 18, and 'Laws of Festal Offering', 2: 14, but these *halakhot* are spaced widely apart. In short, the way that the quotation in our passages is repeated is deliberate and unique.

some repetition inevitable, since one law or set of laws may straddle more than one topic. To take just one example: it is forbidden to sow a vineyard with any other kind of produce; nor may one eat, or derive any other benefit from, either produce or grapes when they grow together.[21] These prohibitions belong partly under the category of agricultural laws and partly under the category of dietary laws, and for the dietary aspect to be comprehensible, the agricultural aspect really needs to be explained first. In *Mishneh torah*, however, 'Laws of Forbidden Foods' is in the *Book of Holiness*, which comes before the *Book of Agriculture*.

To overcome the difficulty, Maimonides resorts to repetition.[22] In 'Laws of Forbidden Foods', 10: 6, he gives a very brief account of the prohibition against sowing a vineyard with produce other than grapes, before going on to discuss the prohibition against eating what grows in such a vineyard. The full details of the prohibition against sowing are given later, in 'Laws of Diverse Kinds'. In fact, chapter 10 of 'Laws of Forbidden Foods' brings together various additional dietary laws that have more than one aspect. It also mentions very briefly some that are not general but have to do with tithes and Temple sacrifices, or that apply to a special person or on a special occasion, such as the prohibition against eating leaven on Passover, stating that each has been, or will be, dealt with in the appropriate place.[23] In other words, the method of classification in *Mishneh torah* entails a certain amount of repetition when classifications overlap, and a great deal of the kind of 'see under' reference to be found in any classified work.[24]

In part, the repetition about the scholar derives from the same cause: different aspects of the same topic are dealt with in the appropriate places, with some inevitable overlap. The behaviour expected of the scholar is mentioned briefly in 'Laws of the Foundations of the Torah', chapter 5, in the context of

[21] For Maimonides' rationalization of these laws as a repudiation of pagan practices, see *Guide* iii. 37 (p. 549); and below, p. 255.

[22] He is not always so helpful. Haym Soloveitchik points out an instance in 'Laws of the Sabbath' where repetition would have been desirable and where the lack of it actually proved confusing ('Thoughts on Maimonides' Categorization', 114–15).

[23] As noted above, in the *Book of the Commandments* most of the prohibitions concerning eating, whether arising from the food itself or from the circumstances in which it is eaten, are grouped together, in negative commandments 172 to 206. The prohibition against eating grapes or produce from a vineyard sown with diverse kinds is no. 193, while the prohibition against sowing produce in a vineyard is no. 216.

[24] *Mishneh torah* is laced with such cross-references, far too numerous to list, but for examples of hubs providing clear cross-references to several overlapping topics, see 'Laws of First Fruits and other Priestly Offerings', 1: 16, and 'Laws of Passover Offering', 8: 15. On cross-references in *Mishneh torah* generally, see Twersky, *Introduction to the Code*, 276–81.

sanctification of God's name, to make the point that moral or immoral conduct by a religious luminary can sanctify or desecrate the name. 'Laws of the
Foundations of the Torah', however, concerned as it is with correct doctrines,
or intellectual virtue as it was put above, is not the place for discussing such
conduct in detail. That discussion belongs in 'Laws of Ethical Qualities',
where the subject is moral virtue: hence the expanded prescription for the
behaviour of a scholar in 'Laws of Ethical Qualities', chapter 5, of which the
halakhah cited is only the conclusion. The matter could be left at that, were it
not for clear indications that more is at stake.

Firstly, while eloquent codas to chapters and sections expressing moral
rather than strictly halakhic ideas are a feature of *Mishneh torah* throughout,[25]
that Maimonides should twice wax lyrical about the same subject in such similar terms and within such a short space, as he does in the passages quoted
above, seems excessive. 'Laws of the Foundations of the Torah' and 'Laws of
Ethical Qualities' are in a different register from that of 'Laws of Forbidden
Foods' and 'Laws of Diverse Kinds', and of most other sections of *Mishneh
torah*. These first two sections deal directly with the elevated subject of the
relationship between man and God, making their atmosphere more rarefied
and more charged. Nuances come under extra scrutiny for their philosophical as well as their halakhic significance. The excess is therefore all the more
striking.

Two formal features that call attention to the repetition are also notable.
The first is that it occurs in the same position, at the end of the fifth chapter,
in each section, the end of a chapter being, of course, a prominent place. The
other feature, already mentioned, is the repeated quotation from Isaiah. Generally, related passages in *Mishneh torah* are supplied with a cross-reference
using phrases such as 'as was explained in' or 'as will be explained in'. The
linkage of our two *halakhot* by a biblical verse adds a touch of mystery.[26]

Manipulated Sources

The mystery intensifies if we look more closely at how the biblical reference
is deployed. It turns out to be a fine example of Maimonides' skill in manipulating his sources to achieve an effect.

[25] Oft-cited examples are 'Laws of Megilah and Hanukah', 4: 14; 'Laws of Forbidden Intercourse',
22: 21; 'Laws of Slaughter', 14: 16; 'Laws of Sabbatical and Jubilee Years', 13: 13; 'Laws of Trespass',
8: 8; 'Laws of Substituted Offerings', 4: 13; 'Laws of Immersion Pools', 11: 12; 'Laws of Slaves', 9: 8;
and of course the conclusion to the whole work, 'Laws of Kings and Their Wars', 12: 5.

[26] Buchman, '*Mishneh Torah*: Science and Art', 218–19, also calls attention to the poetic dimension
of this repetition.

Each of the *halakhot* under discussion is a blend of several talmudic and midrashic passages, but the main sources of the material they have in common are a discussion in BT *Yoma* of the way a scholar can profane or sanctify the name of God, and a passage about long-suffering (not necessarily of a scholar) that occurs in several places.

The relevant passage in *Yoma* is as follows:

What constitutes profanation of the Name? Rab said: If, e.g., I take meat from the butcher and do not pay him at once. Abaye said: That we have learnt [to regard as profanation] only in a place wherein one does not go out to collect payment, but in a place where one does go out to collect, there is no harm in it [not paying at once] . . . R. Johanan said: In my case [it is a profanation if] I walk four cubits without [uttering words of] Torah or [wearing] *tefilin*.

Isaac, of the school of R. Jannai, said: If one's colleagues are ashamed of his reputation, that constitutes a profanation of the Name. R. Nahman b. Isaac commented: e.g., if people say, May the Lord forgive so-and-so. Abaye explained: As it was taught: And thou shalt love the Lord thy God, i.e., that the Name of Heaven be beloved because of you. If someone studies Scripture and Mishnah, and attends on the disciples of the wise, is honest in business, and speaks pleasantly to persons, what do people then say concerning him? 'Happy the father who taught him Torah, happy the teacher who taught him Torah; woe unto people who have not studied the Torah; for this man has studied the Torah—look how fine his ways are, how righteous his deeds!'

Of him does Scripture say: And He said unto me: Thou art My servant, Israel, in whom I will be glorified.[27]

The second passage is as follows: 'Our rabbis taught: Those who are affronted but do not give affront, hear themselves reviled without answering, act through love and rejoice in suffering, of them Scripture says, But they who love Him are as the sun when he goeth forth in his might' (Judg. 5: 31).[28]

In 'Laws of the Foundations of the Torah', 5: 11, the sentence leading up to the quotation from Isaiah 'Thou art my servant, Israel' reflects the *baraita* quoted by Abaye in *Yoma* about the admiration aroused by the gentle scholar, and so the quotation follows naturally. In 'Laws of Ethical Qualities', 5: 13, on the other hand, the immediate lead up to the quotation is about patience in the face of provocation: 'In short, he belongs to the class of those who are persecuted but do not persecute, who are affronted but do not offer affront. A man who does all these things and their like, concerning him Scripture

---

[27] BT *Yoma* 86a.

[28] BT *Shab.* 88b. Similar passages are to be found at BT *Yoma* 23a; BT *Git.* 36b; *Derekh erets*, *halakhah* 13.

says . . .'. This closely echoes the second talmudic passage,[29] and the reader familiar with that passage would expect 'concerning him Scripture says' to introduce the verse from Judges ('But they who love him') as cited there, but Maimonides defeats expectation by reverting to the verse from Isaiah cited in *Yoma*.[30] Source A ends with verse a, and source B with verse b, but Maimonides uses source B with verse a.

Could he perhaps have made a mistake? That possibility appears to be ruled out by the fact that, only three chapters earlier, in 'Laws of Ethical Qualities', 2: 3, he gives a preview of the ideal of restraint in the face of provocation based on the very same talmudic source, but with the original reference to Judges intact.

In short, at the ends of the fifth chapters of 'Laws of the Foundations of the Torah' and of 'Laws of Ethical Qualities', Maimonides deliberately repeats a biblical quotation even though it does not really belong the second time around. The use of the unexpected[31] quotation in 'Laws of Ethical Qualities', 5: 13, emerges fairly clearly as a way of establishing a formal link, and of making the reader pause and think back.

Altogether, the repetition of the material about the scholar is not, or is not wholly, necessitated by the exigencies of Maimonides' method of classification. The intensity of the material itself, the way it is moulded from the sources, and the use of formal devices instead of conventional cross-references to signal the repetition, invite us to look for some greater significance. 'Laws of the Foundations of the Torah' and 'Laws of Ethical Qualities' converge upon the representation of an ideal. What is this meant to convey?

---

[29] In two of the places in the Talmud where this passage occurs (BT *Shab.* and BT *Git.*—see previous note) the context is God's continued love for Israel despite the insult of the golden calf, which would imply that to bear insult patiently is *imitatio Dei*. It is possible that this is why Maimonides chose to end 'Laws of Ethical Qualities', chapter 5, with an allusion to this passage, *imitatio Dei* being the keynote of 'Laws of Ethical Qualities'.

[30] Of course, *Mishneh torah* is ostensibly for people who are not thoroughly conversant with the Talmud, and it is meant to save them having to become so. Here is a further small piece of evidence that, as aggadah, *Mishneh torah* is written on more than one level. The reader who does not recognize the talmudic reference will simply note the repeated quotation; the reader who does will find it doubly intriguing.

[31] Unexpected, but not wrong, for the way the quotation is introduced, 'A man who does all these things and their like, concerning him Scripture says', indicates that it applies to someone with all the qualities discussed in 'Laws of Ethical Qualities', chapter 5, and not just the last one mentioned; that is to say, there is no pretence of direct, complete citation of the talmudic passage. Nevertheless, since being affronted without offering affront is presented as a *summary* of all those qualities (*kelalo shel davar*, rendered in the translation as 'in short'), one should expect the appropriate quotation to follow.

Descent and Ascent

One approach to an answer, after the similarities between the two *halakhot* in question have been noted, is to think about the differences between them.

I have said that 'Laws of the Foundations of the Torah' is about intellectual virtue, while 'Laws of Ethical Qualities' is about moral virtue, and that the earlier section has a divine orientation, while the later one has a human orientation. The difference is felt in their styles. The chapters of 'Laws of the Foundations of the Torah' tend to begin with axioms, for example: 'The foundation of foundations and the pillar of sciences is to know that there is a primary existence';[32] 'It is among the fundamentals of religion to recognize that God bestows the power of prophecy on men.'[33] The chapters of 'Laws of Ethical Qualities' on the other hand mostly open with empirical observation, for example, 'There are many dispositions in human beings';[34] 'It is in the nature of man to be influenced by neighbours and friends.'[35]

This is not just a difference in tone, as Maimonides switches from theologian to psychologist. The change reflects the discontinuity, at least from our perspective, between the single, invisible, indivisible, invariable God, and the multiple, sensible, compound, changing world.

The different emphases of 'Laws of the Foundations of the Torah', 5: 11, and 'Laws of Ethical Qualities', 5: 13, the one presenting the scholar as exemplar and the other presenting him more from the point of view of his inward qualities, turn out to reflect the general difference in approach between the two sections. In 'Laws of the Foundations of the Torah' we move from the divine and absolute to the human and contingent, whereas in 'Laws of Ethical Qualities' the movement tends to be the other way. The contrast may be summed up as descent versus ascent, as being versus becoming, and as unity versus multiplicity.

Thus we find that, in 'Laws of the Foundations of the Torah', man is made in the image of God—this is a given—while in 'Laws of Ethical Qualities', man is commanded to become like God—this is a process. Man is made in the image of God in respect of the possession of an intellect: 'The vital principle of all flesh is the form which God has given it. The superior intelligence in the human soul is the specific form of the mentally normal human being. To this form, the Torah refers in the text, "Let us make man in our image, after our likeness".'[36] We are still far from deciphering exactly what this means, but

---

[32] 'Laws of the Foundations of the Torah', 1: 1.   [33] Ibid. 7: 1.

[34] 'Laws of Ethical Qualities', 1: 1.

[35] Ibid. 6: 1.   [36] 'Laws of the Foundations of the Torah', 4: 8.

we can say that the way matters are presented here (and in the consideration of literary form, presentation is all), man's intellect is a form that descends from God,[37] while becoming like God is an ascent from matter.[38]

Just so, the scholar of 'Laws of the Foundations of the Torah' is depicted objectively. He arrives on the scene fully fledged. In his perfection, he stands for God in this world, for everyone 'desires to emulate his deeds', just as, in 'Laws of Ethical Qualities', everyone is supposed to emulate God's deeds.

The scholar of 'Laws of Ethical Qualities' 5 is also at first presented by way of his outward distinguishing marks. But then we follow him through thirteen *halakhot* in the process of acquiring that distinction, as he shapes his traits and habits into virtue, a process we understand from the inside because we have been instructed in it in the preceding four chapters. We gain a sense of the scholar as someone who actively makes room for God in this world. By carrying out the imperatives of 'Laws of Ethical Qualities' to imitate God's actions and to make all actions for the sake of God, he acquires the integrity of the scholar of 'Laws of the Foundations of the Torah', whom people imitate. The repeated verse from Isaiah, 'You are my servant Israel, in whom I will be glorified', forms an interface between the scholar's subjective striving and his objective role.[39] The formal convergence on this point represents the drama of the inner versus the outer person, and the final merger of our two scholars into one.

[37] The actual bestower of form in Maimonides' system is the agent intellect (see above, Introduction, nn. 11, 12), but at this point the precise mechanism is not important.

[38] In 'Laws of the Foundations of the Torah', thought is prior to action (as it is in 'Laws of Torah Study': 'for study leads to performance [of the commandments]. Therefore study takes priority over performance everywhere' ('Laws of Torah Study', 3: 3)). Such action as there is, in the form of committing oneself to martyrdom, is, in the first place, really more passive than active, and, secondly, derived from and expressive of thought rather than concerned with matter, being testimony to belief in the one God. In 'Laws of Ethical Qualities', action is sometimes prior to thought, for if the personality goes into imbalance, no amount of thinking will cure the fault but only repeated action opposite to the extreme to which a person has deviated—see 'Laws of Ethical Qualities', 2: 2. This kind of action is not expressive of an idea; rather, it moulds the 'matter' of a human being's emotions and desires to make him or her receptive to the form of intellect. Note that a degenerate person may be incapable of self-direction and needs to consult a sage, thought having become inoperative—see 'Laws of Ethical Qualities', 2: 1. Such a person has been ensnared by his or her material nature, and has therefore become more like sublunary matter, which is distinguished from heavenly matter by its lack of consciousness—see 'Laws of the Foundations of the Torah', 3: 11.

[39] Maimonides actually distinguishes between the scholar of 'Laws of the Foundations of the Torah' and the scholar of 'Laws of Ethical Qualities' by calling the first *ḥakham*, literally meaning a wise person, that is, a scholar or sage, while the second is called *talmid ḥakhamim*, literally a student of the wise, although the term *talmid ḥakham* is generally used simply to mean a scholar. This, of course, reinforces the point about being versus becoming.

After this convergence, 'Laws of the Foundations of the Torah' and 'Laws of Ethical Qualities' go their respective ways, but in doing so they follow similar patterns, a widening from the private to the public sphere. Chapters 1 to 5 of each section are about individual virtue, while the remaining chapters are social and institutional in their orientation. The first five chapters of 'Laws of the Foundations of the Torah' deal with commandments concerning inward conviction about God: to know, to love, to fear, to sanctify. Chapter 6 is about physical objects: the written name of God, holy writings, the Temple, while chapters 7 to 10, although they do contain a description of the process of becoming a prophet,[40] chiefly concern prophecy as an institution: the relevant commandments are to obey the prophet and not to put him to the test, commandments addressed to the collective that establish the prophet in the public, political role of lawgiver.

In 'Laws of Ethical Qualities', chapters 1 to 5 all come under the rubric of the commandment to imitate God's ways, which is an inward process of character development. Chapter 6 then takes us into the social sphere, with the interpretation of the commandment to cleave to God as meaning that one should associate with scholars[41]—since one's character is affected by the company one keeps[42]—followed by a series of essentially social commandments in the rest of chapter 6 and in chapter 7. What is more, chapter 6 of 'Laws of the Foundations of the Torah' is about destruction, in the shape of the erasure of God's name, symbolic, perhaps, of the undermining of the doctrines in the previous five chapters.[43] Similarly, chapter 6 of 'Laws of Ethical Qualities' is about the risks to virtue of living in society; it urges us to seek the society of the righteous, for otherwise we will be corrupted. Actually, Maimonides expresses despair of the possibility of finding a just state in which to live, and a preference for isolation, so the perils of social existence were clearly very real to him.[44]

---

[40] 'Laws of the Foundations of the Torah', 7: 1 (cited above as an example of Maimonides' skill at dramatization).   [41] 'Laws of Ethical Qualities', 6: 2.

[42] This is also a further application of being versus becoming: in 'Laws of Foundations of the Torah', the scholar is an exemplar; in 'Laws of Ethical Qualities', we are commanded to make him our exemplar. We may be inspired to the love of God by looking at the stars, but we will be influenced at least as much, for better or worse, by looking at the neighbours.

[43] This is explored at greater length in Chapter 4 (see pp. 285–7 below).

[44] 'Laws of Ethical Qualities', 4: 1. Note how Maimonides appears to identify with the prophet Jeremiah in this *halakhah*, with quotations from Jeremiah and from Lamentations. There is also a hint of such identification in an allusion to Jer. 1: 5 in the rhymed-prose salutation that opens the letter to R. Jonathan of Lunel and his colleagues (*Letters*, ed. Shailat (Heb.), 502, line 10). Jeremiah is the first scriptural book cited in *Mishneh torah* ('Laws of the Foundations of the Torah', 1: 4), and, excluding

In both 'Laws of the Foundations of the Torah' and 'Laws of Ethical Qualities', then, the fifth chapter is on the cusp, representing the point at which the inward virtues go public, as it were. Hence the convergence of the two sections at that point.

Man as Microcosm

Taking our cue from this, let us trace in more detail how we arrive at the point of convergence in each section.

Chapter 1 of 'Laws of the Foundations of the Torah' deals with the command to know that God exists, and with God's unity and incorporeality. Any possible relation to our familiar, physical world is excluded. As we have seen, the anthropomorphic descriptions of God in the Bible are explained as owing to the fact that 'the Torah speaks in the language of men';[45] they are in no way to be taken literally. The unity of God has nothing to do with our normal concept of unity, that is, a whole that subsumes many parts, but is 'a unity like which there is no other unity in the world'.[46] In this chapter we are at the very edge of the knowable, at the highest level of intellectual abstraction, as we attempt to grapple with divine science, the idea of God as he is in himself.

In chapter 2 we descend a rung in the ladder of abstraction. After the commandment in chapter 1 to know that God exists, which is performed purely intellectually, the commandments under discussion in this chapter are to love God and to be in awe of him. The love of God is a refined, intellectualized kind of love, consisting, as we shall see, mainly in the desire for knowledge, but it cannot be divorced from an emotional component. After all, Maimonides compares the required intensity of the love of God to obsessional love of a man for a woman.[47] Along with this less purely cerebral relation to God, Maimonides begins to introduce the sensible world, for the way to attain love and awe is to contemplate God's works.[48] Hence we are given an account of the cosmos, and at the same time, the description of God changes from the purely philosophically conceived primary existence of chapter 1 to a

---

the epilogue, the last cited in the *Guide* (i. 54 (p. 637)). It may or may not be significant that Jeremiah, like Maimonides, had to leave the Land of Israel for Egypt (Jer. 43). Compare also *Guide* iii. 51 (pp. 618–28), termed by Efodi (ad loc.) *perek hamitboded*, 'the chapter of the solitary'. On solitude versus social responsibility in Maimonides, see references in Ch. 4, n. 23 below.

[45] 'Laws of Foundations of the Torah', 1: 9.   [46] Ibid. 1: 7.

[47] 'Laws of Repentance', 10: 3. Rabinovitch, *Yad peshutah*, ad loc., points out the allusions in this *halakhah* to Song of Songs and Proverbs, besides the explicit citation of Song of Songs on which it ends. See also below.   [48] 'Laws of Foundations of the Torah', 2: 2.

more religiously conceived, more familiarly biblical, more anthropomorphic in fact, creator:[49] 'Everything that the holy one blessed be he created in his world is divided into three parts.'[50]

The three parts comprise creatures consisting of form and matter that degenerate, that is, the entire sublunar animal, vegetable, and mineral world, including man; creatures consisting of form and matter that do not degenerate, namely, the stars and spheres, which are made of a different kind of matter from that found on Earth; and lastly, creatures consisting of pure form without matter, which are the angels, or separate intellects.[51]

Maimonides then proceeds to deal with each of these three parts of creation in reverse order. The remainder of chapter 2 is an account of the ten orders of angels, in the course of which we find a discussion of God's unique way of knowing: rather than assimilating knowledge of things outside himself (which would imply a division in God between knower and known, and thus violate his unity), God knows all things through himself.[52]

After this summary of *ma'aseh merkavah*, chapters 3 and 4 deal with *ma'aseh bereshit*. Chapter 3 describes the system of the spheres, and then introduces matter and its four elements of earth, air, fire, and water. Chapter 4 describes the vegetable and animal realms and man, explaining, as we have seen, that man is distinguished by his intellect. It closes with a warning about the esoteric nature of *ma'aseh merkavah* and, to a lesser extent, of *ma'aseh bereshit*; a repetition of the idea that knowledge of these things is conducive to the love of God (which is ostensibly why Maimonides discusses them at all); and the assertion that *ma'aseh merkavah* and *ma'aseh bereshit* are greater subjects than the commandments, even though the latter are first in practical importance.

Chapter 5 then introduces the first practical commandment in *Mishneh torah*, namely, the Jew's obligation, in certain circumstances, to sacrifice his or her life rather than be forced to transgress other commandments. Finally, as

---

[49] On the implications of Maimonides' use of the terms 'create' and 'creator' in the *Guide*, see Klein-Braslavy, 'Creation of the World'; Nuriel, *Concealed and Revealed* (Heb.), 25–40.

[50] 'Laws of the Foundations of the Torah', 2: 3.

[51] The idea of a non-material created entity may be hard to grasp, but one way of thinking of angels is as forces of nature endowed with consciousness. In *Guide* ii. 6 Maimonides explicitly identifies angels with natural forces. Forces associated with perishable matter are themselves perishable. Forces associated with permanent bodies such as the spheres are permanent, hence the fixed list of ten angels in 'Laws of the Foundations of the Torah', 2: 7. The last of the list, the *ishim* (agent intellect), does not govern a sphere but sublunary matter; it is associated not with permanence of substance but with permanent processes of generation and decay. This conception of natural forces as pure forms without material carriers is probably not compatible with modern physics.   [52] Ibid. 2: 10.

we have seen, chapter 5 describes the sanctification of God's name as a potential attribute of all human action, action exemplifying an idea, bearing witness to the truths elucidated up to this point.

To sum up, the sequence of topics in chapters 1 to 5 of 'Laws of the Foundations of the Torah' is the divine, followed by the angels, then the spheres and stars, then sublunary matter, then action. If we abstract from this further, remembering that the spheres and stars are made of a special kind of everlasting material and possess consciousness, we find the sequence non-physical–non-physical/material–material–action. Human beings, it should be noted at this point, do not fit into any of these categories, and in fact show aspects of all four.

Now let us map 'Laws of Ethical Qualities' in a similar way. Whereas the first chapter of 'Laws of the Foundations of the Torah' is about God, the first chapter of 'Laws of Ethical Qualities' is about the imitation of God. The intellect that looks outwards at creation in 'Laws of the Foundations of the Torah' now looks inwards, applying the discernment of the attributes of God's actions to the scrutiny and control of the emotions and appetites, thereby regulating action.[53]

Chapters 2 and 3 bring us into closer contact with those emotions and appetites themselves, and deal with the ways of gauging and tempering them, with emotional drives and moral integrity being the subject of chapter 2, and appetites the subject of chapter 3. Here we are intermediate between intellect and body.[54]

Chapter 4 presents recommendations for bodily health.

Chapter 5, as we have seen, is about the ideal temperament, bearing, manners, and behaviour of the scholar.

From this outline we can see that the sequence of themes in 'Laws of the Foundations of the Torah' is repeated in 'Laws of Ethical Qualities', for from the sequence mind–emotions/appetites–body–behaviour, we can abstract the same hierarchy as emerged in the earlier section. The sequence also corresponds to the make-up of human beings as set out in 'Laws of the Foundations of the Torah', 4: 9, namely, intellect–life force–body.

---

[53] The role of intellect, implicit in 'Laws of Ethical Qualities', chapter 1, actually emerges more clearly in 'Eight Chapters'. 'Eight Chapters', 4, is about the middle way, the attainment of which is summed up thus at the beginning of ch. 5: 'Man needs to subordinate all his soul's powers to thought, in the way we set forth in the previous chapter' (*Ethical Writings*, 75).

[54] This is in line with Septimus's definition of *de'ot*: '*de'ot* straddle the mind–body divide—though manifest in conduct, they are psychic in essence. The term *de'ot* (singular *de'ah*), underscores their relationship to *madda* (= "mind", "psyche")' ('What Did Maimonides Mean by *Madda*?', 98).

Table 3 Parallel structures of 'Laws of the Foundations of the Torah' and 'Laws of Ethical Qualities'

Chapter	'Foundations of Torah'	'Ethical Qualities'	Theme
1	God (*de'ah*)	Imitation of God/Intellect (*de'ah*)	Non-physical
2–3	Angels, spheres, stars (*de'ot*/*ba'alei de'ah*)	Emotions, appetites (*de'ot*)	Non-physical/ physical
3–4	Sublunary matter	Body	Physical
5	Behaviour	Behaviour	Action

The parallel is reinforced by Maimonides' nomenclature.[55] Man's intellect is his *da'at* or *de'ah*; man is in God's image in respect of *de'ah*, while God himself *is de'ah*, according to the Aristotelian definition that Maimonides adopts of intellect intellecting itself.[56] The term for human character traits, emotions, and appetites is the plural of *de'ah*, *de'ot*. The English title 'Laws of Ethical Qualities' translates *Hilkhot de'ot*. The same term, *de'ot*, is used of the angels,[57] while the spheres and stars are said to be *ba'alei de'ah* (possessed of intellect).[58]

The parallels between 'Laws of the Foundations of the Torah', 1–5, and 'Laws of Ethical Qualities', 1–5, are summarized in Table 3.[59]

'Laws of the Foundations of the Torah' and 'Laws of Ethical Qualities' thus exhibit corresponding sequences. The quotation from Isaiah that closes the fifth chapter of each section serves as an axis of symmetry between the two.

The picture that emerges from these parallel structures is of the human being as a microcosm. In itself, this concept is scarcely a novelty; it is a com-

[55] Davidson notes, 'Greek and Arabic do not have separate terms for intellect and intelligence' (*Alfarabi, Avicenna and Averroes on Intellect*, 6). In his translation of 'Eight Chapters', Ibn Tibbon gives *sekhel* for intellect, but in *Mishneh torah* Maimonides prefers *de'ah*. On the various meanings of *de'ah* or *da'at* in Maimonides, see Baneth, 'On the Philosophic Terminology of Maimonides' (Heb.), 16–18.

[56] 'Laws of the Foundations of the Torah', 2: 10; *Guide* i. 68 (p. 165).

[57] 'Laws of the Foundations of the Torah', 4: 8. Here the angels are classed as *de'ot she'ein lahem golem*, 'intellects without matter'. In 'Laws of the Foundations of the Torah', 2: 3 they are described as *tsurah belo golem*, 'form without matter', and as *tsurot nifradot*, 'separate forms'.

[58] 'Laws of the Foundations of the Torah', 3: 9: 'Every star and sphere has a soul and is endowed with knowledge and intelligence.'

[59] Subjects are not allotted to chapters as neatly as the table would indicate—there are overspills here and there—but what is important is the general sequence.

monplace of late classical and medieval thought.[60] What matters is what Maimonides does with it. We shall find that, in his hands, it becomes a most powerful device for conveying ideas about the relationship of God to human beings and the role of the commandments in that relationship.

Man as Microcosm in the *Guide of the Perplexed*

Our confidence that the patterns detected in 'Laws of the Foundations of the Torah' and 'Laws of Ethical Qualities' represent man as microcosm is reinforced when we look at the *Guide* and find that the idea is treated there explicitly, in Part I, chapter 72.

The discussion in that chapter progresses through various stages. At first, the comparison between a human being and the universe is used to illustrate the idea that the universe possesses unity in its diversity. Just as a human being has many limbs yet is regarded as a single entity, so the universe is a single entity though made up of many spheres, stars, and elements.

The comparison is then extended to the relationships between the parts and the whole. The Earth is at the centre of the system of spheres. Immediately surrounding it, in ascending order, are the spheres of water, air, and fire. The rotation of the fifth body, that is, the system of spheres that surrounds fire, induces movement in the four spheres below it. This latter motion is not rotation, but vertical movement of fire, air, and water towards or away from Earth. This movement causes mixture and separation of the four elements, which is the cause of generation and corruption of animals, plants, and minerals on Earth.

The heart of a human being is likened to the fifth body. The motion of the heart sends to the rest of the body the forces the body parts require in order to function. So the fifth body is to what is below it as the heart is to the body: it is a relationship of ruler and ruled.

Maimonides then points out that, as it has been described so far, the microcosm–macrocosm idea would apply to any living creature. Every creature has four faculties: 'the attractive faculty, the retentive faculty, the digestive faculty, and the repellent faculty',[61] with the heart governing them. What really makes a human being a microcosm is a fifth faculty, the intellect,

---

[60] Altmann, in 'Delphic Maxim', briefly traces the history of the idea from classical Greek thought through to medieval Jewish writers. This essay is discussed more fully below. See also Conger, *Theories of Macrocosms and Microcosms*. For a general account of the grip that 'the Model' held on the medieval literary imagination, see Lewis, *The Discarded Image*.   [61] *Guide* i. 72 (p. 189).

without which human beings would not be human, just as the universe cannot be imagined to exist without God.

But then Maimonides corrects himself, saying that the intellect is different in its relationship to the body from God in his relationship to the universe, since God exists separately from the universe whereas the intellect is not separable from the body. He therefore modifies the comparison slightly, substituting for the intellect the acquired (or developed) intellect. After describing how God is separate from the universe yet influences everything in it, Maimonides writes,

> Know that it behooved us to compare the relation obtaining between God, may He be exalted, and the world to that obtaining between the acquired intellect and man; this intellect is not a faculty in the body but is truly separate from the organic body and overflows toward it. We should have compared, on the other hand, the rational faculty to the intellects of the heavens, which are in bodies.[62]

To summarize, the argument has four stages. In the first two, the idea of man as microcosm is purely illustrative. The physical structure of a human being is used as a simile to explain the unity in diversity of the universe, and then the psychological/physiological structure of a human being is used as a simile to explain how changes in the elements are controlled by the fifth sphere. In the next stage, the ultimate ruler of the universe is compared to the intellect in man. Finally, this idea is modified so that the equivalent to God in man is not the rational faculty, or hylic intellect, but that faculty in its realized state as the acquired intellect, having gained knowledge of the intelligibles, making it separable from the body and potentially immortal.[63] We have come some way from the rather static idea of the unity in complexity of the cosmos being comparable to the unity in complexity of a human being. The comparison now works the other way: a human being has the potential to become a microcosm in the most complete sense by realizing his or her intellectual capacity.

It is now possible to explain why it is over five chapters that the structures of 'Laws of the Foundations of the Torah' and 'Laws of Ethical Qualities' run in parallel. Five is the number of the cosmos: the four elements, plus the fifth

---

[62] *Guide* i. 72 (p. 193). On the different states of the human intellect, see Appendix II.2.

[63] The modification does not entirely disqualify the first comparison; if it did, Maimonides would presumably not have taken his discussion via that route but would have proceeded directly to his conclusion. The switch from comparing God to the hylic intellect to comparing him to the acquired intellect corresponds to the difference between man in God's image and man after God's likeness, as is discussed later in this chapter.

body, the rarefied substance not subject to generation and decay, of which everything above the earth is composed. Man is a material creature made up of the four elements, and he has the four faculties belonging to any animal, but he also has an intellect, which, because of its rarefied nature, is to the human body as the fifth body is to the four elements, so five is man's number too.[64] By virtue of their intellectual capacity, therefore, human beings share a dynamic with the spheres.[65]

From this excursus to the *Guide* we learn that the microcosm–macrocosm theory is certainly part of Maimonides' thought. We shall need to bear in mind the details of his exposition for later, but for now, the issue is a general one. Why is the theory embedded in a formal pattern in the *Book of Knowledge*, rather than being mentioned there explicitly? A discussion at the length of *Guide* i. 72 would have been overdoing it in a code of law, but in the course of the description of the universe and all its parts in 'Laws of the Foundations of the Torah' the idea could have been conveyed in a sentence, and without upsetting the non-philosophical readership to which *Mishneh torah* is

[64] The cosmic significance of the numbers four and five is discussed further in *Guide* ii. 9–10 (pp. 268–73). It is not clear whether the model developed there can be applied to the *Book of Knowledge*. That model, a particular variant of the system of nested revolving spheres with Earth at the centre that made up the classical and medieval picture of the universe, depends upon the spheres of the planets being counted as one, to give four 'informed' spheres, of the Moon, Sun, planets, and fixed stars, plus the diurnal 'uninformed' outer sphere, to make five. ('Informed' means star-bearing, for 'the ancients called the stars forms' (*Guide* ii. 9 (p. 269), all heavenly bodies, including the Moon and planets, being stars for this purpose.) This in turn depends upon the spheres of the planets being contiguous, which in 'Laws of the Foundations of the Torah', 3: 1 they are not. There, Maimonides follows Ptolemy in putting Venus and Mercury below the Sun, and Mars, Saturn, and Jupiter above it. In *Guide* ii. 9 (pp. 268–9) he argues for preferring the opinion of 'all the early mathematicians', who put Venus and Mercury above the Sun, which enables him to go on in *Guide* ii. 10 (pp. 269–73) to set out his theory of the number four as the 'wondrous' number that connects all the systems and processes in the universe. See Freudenthal, 'Four Observations' (Heb.).

It is, however, possible that, in 'Laws of the Foundations of the Torah', Maimonides set out the more conventional Ptolemaic system in the text to save having to explain himself, while suggesting the other system through the structure. Even if that is disallowed, enough of the 'four plus one' pattern remains for the number of chapters over which the structures of 'Laws of the Foundations of the Torah' and 'Laws of Ethical Qualities' correspond to be seen as significant.

The various ways in which Maimonides counted the spheres are discussed more fully in later chapters, as is the possible significance of the number of chapters in each section of the *Book of Knowledge*.

[65] The intellectualism and dynamism of Maimonides' approach to the microcosm–macrocosm idea is to be contrasted with the pagan approach, which, as he describes it, 'consisted in imagining that God was the spirit of the sphere and that the sphere and the stars are a body of which the deity, may He be exalted, is its spirit' (*Guide* iii. 29 (p. 515)). Abraham's great realization was that God 'is neither a body nor a force in a body' (*Guide* iii. 29 (p. 516)). On other ways in which Maimonides' presentation of the microcosm–macrocosm theory counters pagan ideas, see Langermann, 'Maimonides' Repudiation of Astrology', 144.

supposedly addressed, for, as mentioned, it was commonplace, as indeed Maimonides acknowledges.[66] The conclusion must be that it is not the idea as such that is important in *Mishneh torah*; we must ask what specific function it has there.

That question will occupy us for the rest of this chapter and for the bulk of the next three. On the plane of ideas, it will be a means of exploring the relationship between Maimonides' view of the cosmos and his view of the commandments of the law, their significance and their authority. On the aesthetic plane, it will provide insight into how Maimonides gave *Mishneh torah* artistic unity, and turned a code of law into a self-sustaining web of thought and feeling. This is on the large scale. The immediate function of the microcosm idea as represented in the structures of 'Laws of the Foundations of the Torah' and 'Laws of Ethical Qualities', it will be argued, is to give an extra dimension to the relationship between intellectual virtue and moral virtue. If the content of 'Laws of Ethical Qualities' offers a version of Aristotelian ethics, based upon habituating oneself to the middle way between extremes of character and behaviour, so that moral virtue is a matter of character training in preparation for the higher task of acquiring intellectual virtue, the microcosmic form suggests a contrary, Neoplatonic approach, in which moral virtue flows from intellectual enlightenment. This will serve as an initial example of the general point that, throughout *Mishneh torah*, Maimonides uses the relationship between form and content to combine, with high artistic skill, Aristotelian and Neoplatonic models for his philosophy of the commandments. Answering this question of microcosm–macrocosm theory's function in *Mishneh torah* will also provide an opportunity to test the boundaries of Maimonides' Neoplatonism.

Intellectual Virtue and Moral Virtue

What should be the relationship, if any, between morality and intellect or knowledge? We might not find this question easy to answer. For his part, Maimonides earnestly believed that, without a sound moral foundation, intellectual enquiry is confusing and corrupting rather than enlightening.[67] He also believed that, matter and intellect being opposites, intellectual attainment is proportionate to the degree of restraint of our material nature,[68]

---

[66] 'You never hear that one of the ancients has said that an ass or a horse is a small world. This has only been said about man' (*Guide* i. 72 (p. 190)).

[67] See *Commentary on the Mishnah, Ḥag.* 2: 1, and *Guide* i. 34–5 (pp. 72–81).

[68] See *Guide* iii. 9 (pp. 436–7).

and that, as we have seen, both moral and intellectual virtue involve likeness to God. This makes morality and intellect closely connected, but the relationship is still not entirely straightforward. Questions arise such as: Is moral virtue only a condition of intellectual virtue, or does it have intrinsic value? What are the criteria of moral virtue? How close is Maimonides to Aristotle on the relationship between the two virtues? Above all, there is the question with which this chapter began: What exactly is likeness to God?

Maimonides' interpreters differ in their views of where he stood on these questions, and some see changes in his approach between *Mishneh torah* and the *Guide*. My general contention is that the sophistication of *Mishneh torah* in this connection has been underestimated, so that the gap between it and the *Guide* has been exaggerated. The consideration of form, and appreciation of the literary plane on which each work operates, can solve many of the difficulties.

Intellectual virtue in a Maimonidean context is knowledge of God, as will straightaway become clear if it is not so already. Moral virtue is a person's governance of themselves and their social relations. As mentioned above, these two virtues correspond to the dual purpose of the commandments as set out in *Guide* iii. 27:

The Law as a whole aims at two things: the welfare of the soul and the welfare of the body. As for the welfare of the soul, it consists in the multitude's acquiring correct opinions according to their respective capacity . . . As for the welfare of the body, it comes about by the improvement of their ways of living with one another.

As we saw in the previous chapter, Maimonides stresses that, although intellectual virtue is the higher of the two virtues, in practice, moral virtue must come first: 'Know that as between these two aims, one is indubitably greater in nobility, namely, the welfare of the soul—I mean the procuring of correct opinions—while the second aim—I mean the welfare of the body—is prior in nature and time.'

In this chapter of the *Guide*, the emphasis is on the social aspect of moral virtue, and the reason given for the welfare of the body taking priority is that unless the city is peaceful and stable and organized to provide for each person's physical needs, the individual cannot undertake the pursuit of intellectual perfection, which is 'to have an intellect *in actu*', consisting of 'knowing everything concerning all the beings that it is within the capacity of man to know'. Elsewhere, the priority of moral virtue is treated as applying within the individual: 'For it has been explained, or rather demonstrated, that the moral virtues are a preparation for the rational virtues, it being impossible to achieve true, rational things—I mean perfect rationality—unless it be by a man thoroughly trained with the qualities of tranquillity and quiet.'[69]

Either way, intellectual virtue remains the ultimate perfection. In summing up the hierarchy of the four perfections—wealth, physical prowess, moral virtue, and intellectual virtue—the final chapter of the *Guide* states: 'neither the perfection of possession nor the perfection of health nor the perfection of moral habits is a perfection of which one should be proud or that one should desire; the perfection of which one should be proud and that one should desire is knowledge of Him, may He be exalted, which is the true science.'[70]

Thus far things seem clear: intellectual virtue is the highest end, but a prerequisite for that individual pursuit is moral virtue, in the individual and in society alike. The final twist in the *Guide*, however, is that intellectual virtue is not the end. Maimonides' main text in this closing chapter of the *Guide* is Jeremiah 9: 23: 'But let him that glorieth glory in this, that he understandeth and knoweth me, that I am the Lord which exercise loving-kindness, judgment, and righteousness, in the earth: for in these things I delight, saith the Lord.' Had intellectual virtue been the ultimate perfection, Maimonides points out, the verse would have stopped after 'knoweth me'. The way it carries on indicates that there is something else: 'He means that it is My purpose that there should come from you *loving-kindness, judgment, and righteousness, in the earth* in the way we have explained with regard to the thirteen attributes: namely, that the purpose should be assimilation to them and that this should be our way of life.'[71]

Pines provides a cross-reference to *Guide* i. 54, which discusses the imitation of the thirteen attributes of God's actions as revealed to Moses: 'The Lord, the Lord, mighty, merciful, and gracious, longsuffering, and abundant in goodness and truth',[72] and so on, but of course the thought, and the language, are also reminiscent of 'Laws of Ethical Qualities', 1: 6, which, like *Guide* i. 54, cites *Sifrei*: 'He is gracious, so be you also gracious; He is merciful, so be you also merciful.' The order of things in *Guide* iii. 54, though, is different:

---

[69] *Guide* i. 34 (p. 77). I have provided the literal translation 'true, rational things' mentioned by Pines in his note (p. 77, n. 20) rather than 'true, rational acts' as given in his text. In *Guide* i. 34 and 35 we find that there are people whose moral being will never be adapted for intellectual pursuits, whereas in 'Laws of Ethical Qualities' moral virtue seems attainable by anyone who will strive for it. See Freudenthal, 'Biological Limitations'.

[70] *Guide* iii. 54 (p. 636).   [71] Ibid. (p. 637).   [72] Exod. 34: 6.

It is clear that the perfection of man that may truly be gloried in is the one acquired by him who has achieved, in a measure corresponding to his capacity, apprehension of Him, may He be exalted, and who knows His providence extending over His creatures as manifested in the act of bringing them into being and in their governance as it is. The way of life of such an individual, after he has achieved this apprehension, will always have in view *loving-kindness*, *righteousness*, and *judgment*, through assimilation to His actions, may he be exalted, just as we have explained several times in this Treatise.

Rather than being a platform for the pursuit of intellectual virtue, moral virtue is now a consequence of intellectual virtue. The imitation of the attributes of God's actions that constitutes moral virtue now comes almost naturally, instead of through the careful calibration of one's temperament required in 'Laws of Ethical Qualities'. This makes sense: the intellectually perfected person is closely attuned to those actions and their attributes.

Virtue is thus a kind of water cycle: moral virtue rises to become intellectual virtue, which is then precipitated as moral virtue. The constant is *imitatio Dei*. Moral virtue is the imitation, deliberate or intuitive, of God's actions in nature. Intellectual virtue is the imitation of God as intellect. It is also an analogy of God's relationship to the world, for the criterion of perfection in *Guide* iii. 54 is self-sufficiency: intellectual perfection is the highest of the perfections because it is completely intrinsic, whereas the inferior perfections rely on external things or on other people. This means, although Maimonides does not spell it out, that the intellectually perfected person comes as close as is possible to a condition analogous to God's non-contingency.[73] Out of this God-like suspension from the material world, this moment of unimpeded intellect contemplating, as far as a human being may, pure form, flows constant devotion to the practical replication of God's governance as loving-kindness, righteousness, and judgement, just as out of God's total self-containment flows that very goodness, giving rise to existence itself.[74]

To sum up, the *Guide* describes two phases of moral virtue: as preparatory to intellectual virtue, and as consequent upon intellectual virtue. It has been

[73] The parallel is noted by Shatz, 'Maimonides' Moral Theory', 167. This is contrary to Kellner's position that 'Maimonides sees *imitatio Dei* not in terms of our actually becoming like God, but in terms of our patterning our actions after God's actions' (*Maimonides on Human Perfection*, 63). Kellner traces the tradition of *imitatio Dei* as meaning to become like God to Plato (*Maimonides on Human Perfection*, 41). Here, and in the analysis of *imitatio Dei* in *Mishneh torah* that follows, I do find a Platonic undertone to Maimonides' treatment of the subject. On Plato and becoming like God, see Annas, *Platonic Ethics*, 52–71.

[74] See also *Guide* iii. 11 (pp. 440–1) on the idea that wrongdoing proceeds from ignorance.

argued that this marks a radical difference between the views taken in the *Guide* and *Mishneh torah* of the nature of moral virtue. According to Davidson, 'Eight Chapters' and 'Laws of Ethical Qualities' present moral virtue as applying to character traits, with actions being secondary, their importance lying in their tendency to improve or corrupt character.[75] *Imitatio Dei* in that case is an inward state, a matter of internalizing the attributes of God's actions. In the *Guide*, by contrast, the model is not the attributes of God's actions, but God as he is in himself, that is, without attributes. Correspondingly, the *Guide*'s ideal is not the balanced temperament, but no temperament at all, that is, complete impassivity, just as God is impassive. This is a different emphasis from the idea of an analogy to God's separateness just outlined.[76] Davidson sees moral virtue in the *Guide* as applying to actions only, not to the inner self, and as having social rather than personal value.

Kreisel, with acknowledgement to Davidson, takes this line further:

In his legal writings[77] the commandment to imitate God is described with no explicit reference to theoretical perfection. Only one's conformity to a certain type of activity and the training of one's soul to attain certain character traits ensuring this activity are demanded. This ethical approach to *imitatio Dei* is appropriate for works aimed at the entire Jewish people. It is the highest level of perfection possible for the masses, though few may in fact attain it. The end of the *Guide*, on the other hand, describes the form of *imitatio Dei* characterizing the perfect. This is practical activity which follows perfection inasmuch as it is determined purely by reason rather than any character traits of the soul.[78]

Consideration of form in *Mishneh torah* is capable of reversing these assessments, and of finding greater correspondence between *Mishneh torah* and the *Guide* on the question of the relation between moral virtue and intellectual virtue. It is not the intention here to decide just what form of activity Maimonides meant the perfected person to engage in at the end of the *Guide*,[79] or to discuss Davidson's view of moral virtue in the *Guide* as such. What matters for present purposes is not so much the content as the move-

---

[75] Davidson, 'Middle Way'.

[76] Further on analogy to God, see later in this chapter.   [77] i.e. Maimonides' legal writings.

[78] Kreisel, '*Imitatio Dei* in "Guide"', 191 n. 53. Kreisel stresses the holistic approach to *imitatio Dei* in the *Guide*, and his comments to that effect are cited more fully in Chapter 6, n. 15, below, but in my view he underestimates the degree of integration of moral and theoretical virtue in *Mishneh torah*.

[79] Kellner maps the controversy over this as a three-cornered affair between those who see the practical manifestation of perfection according to Maimonides as political activity, those who see it as morality, and those who, like him, see it as fulfilment of the commandments (*Maimonides on Human Perfection*, 8–11). See Altmann, 'Maimonides' "Four Perfections"'; Berman, 'Political Interpretation';

ment of ascent and descent that the last chapter of the *Guide* displays. I shall argue, via the microcosm–macrocosm pattern (taking some imaginative licence' from its symbolism, but within the bounds set by Maimonides' explicit statements), that that movement, and the two kinds of *imitatio Dei* that Kreisel describes, are also present in 'Laws of the Foundations of the Torah' and 'Laws of Ethical Qualities', and thereby contest the view that the account of *imitatio Dei* presented in *Mishneh torah* is only aimed at the masses. The form of the first two sections of the *Book of Knowledge* suggests both the pre- and post-enlightenment phases of moral virtue, and even points to a third possibility, which is that moral virtue is itself a kind of knowledge of God.

Moral Virtue's Two Phases in *Mishneh Torah*

Preparation for Intellectual Virtue

No more than the *Guide* does *Mishneh torah* advocate moral virtue as an ultimate perfection, an end in itself. For Maimonides, the great sin is always to take means for ends or the part for the whole. For example, chapter 4 of 'Laws of Ethical Qualities' is entirely devoted to physical health, but we are cautioned that a healthy body is not to be cultivated for its own sake: one needs to be healthy only in order to avoid distraction from the quest for knowledge of God.[80] The same applies to 'Laws of Ethical Qualities' as a whole: the ethical personality is not something to be cultivated for its own sake. In the first two chapters, which deal with temperament, and which could be seen as allowing moral virtue value in its own right because of the importation of the Aristotelian ideal of the middle path, the ultimate value of knowledge of God is not far beneath the surface, and breaks through in the strictures about pride and anger, which lead to forgetfulness of God and loss of wisdom, and are therefore to be suppressed altogether.[81] Chapter 3, which introduces the subject of bodily appetites, is clear that restraint is not an end in itself, and indeed condemns asceticism, for 'a man should direct all his actions to the knowledge of God alone',[82] whereas asceticism is a constant battle with desire, rather than a quietening of desire that frees the mind to concentrate on higher things. Appropriately, then, the section following

---

Kreisel, '*Imitatio Dei* in "*Guide*"'; Pines, 'Limitations of Human Knowledge'; Schwarzschild, 'Moral Radicalism'.

[80] 'Laws of Ethical Qualities', 3: 3.   [81] Ibid. 2: 3.   [82] Ibid. 3: 2.

'Laws of Ethical Qualities' is 'Laws of Torah Study'. The acme of Torah study is *pardes*,[83] that is, the physics and metaphysics outlined in 'Laws of the Foundations of the Torah'. The purpose of ethics is the establishment of a stable personality and a stable society as a basis for intellectual development to the highest possible level, and 'Laws of Torah Study' in fact reminds us that a would-be student must exhibit moral virtue.[84]

Even in this phase, the microcosm–macrocosm pattern may have a role to play, deepening our understanding of how moral virtue does prepare for intellectual virtue, for it perhaps suggests that someone who inwardly reflects the harmony of the cosmos will better be able to understand the cosmos.[85]

To put it more scientifically, everything in the sublunary world receives the form appropriate to the mixture of matter that it contains.[86] Maimonides' view of moral virtue can be interpreted thus: human beings are uniquely able to affect the mixture of matter in themselves, the make-up of their material souls, and if they do so in accordance with the prescriptions of 'Laws of Ethical Qualities', the soul will be prepared to receive form in the guise of thought from the agent intellect. The scholar of 'Laws of Ethical Qualities' then becomes the scholar of 'Laws of the Foundations of the Torah'.

Consequence of Intellectual Virtue

This brings us to the second phase, in which moral virtue flows from intellectual virtue. The lack of explicit reference to it in *Mishneh torah* must be admitted, but the idea is strongly implied. Intellectual virtue begins in *Mishneh torah* with a person contemplating the wisdom in creation and being seized with love of the creator, a love that leads to intense desire for knowledge.[87] In other words, the study of physics stimulates a desire for the study of metaphysics. Will it not also stimulate a desire to study ethics? The microcosm–macrocosm pattern suggests that it should, because the person who gazes at the universe sees in God's wonderful handiwork an image of what they themselves ought to be.[88]

[83] 'Laws of Torah Study', 1: 12.   [84] Ibid. 3: 9; 4: 1.

[85] This echoes the Empedoclean notion that like perceives like (see Parry, 'Empedocles'), but it also has a nearer source: 'through the mediation of Alfarabi, Maimonides is indebted to Plato for the view that the purification of one's character is a prerequisite for the contemplative life. Alfarabi traces this view to Plato's statement in the *Phaedo* that "whoever is not completely pure is unable to approach that which is completely pure"' (R. L. Weiss, *Maimonides' Ethics*, 177).

[86] See above, Introduction, n. 11.   [87] 'Laws of the Foundations of the Torah', 2: 2.

[88] Compare *Timaeus* 47b–c: 'the god invented and gave us vision in order that we might observe the circuits of intelligence in the heaven and profit by them for the revolutions of our own thought, which are akin to them, though ours be troubled and they are unperturbed; and that by learning to know

This person will wonder what makes the spheres go round, and discover that it is the desire to become like God:

> the sphere has a desire for that which it represents to itself and which is the beloved object: namely the deity, may His name be exalted. He [Aristotle] says that it is in this manner that the deity causes the sphere to move, I mean to say through the fact that the sphere desires to come to be like that which it apprehends.[89]

By means of this idea that heavenly bodies possess consciousness and are in love with God, Maimonides and his contemporaries explained the movements of the stars. The sphere that contains them has a soul that loves God and therefore desires to become like him, and this constant yearning causes constant circular movement. This also explains how God is the cause of the motions of the heavens without any mechanical connection to them. So the spheres are motivated by *imitatio Dei*, exactly the motivation we are told to adopt in 'Laws of Ethical Qualities'. Note too the close similarity between this passage from the *Guide*: 'Consequently He, may He be exalted, is the ultimate end of everything; and the end of the universe is similarly a seeking to be like unto His perfection as far as is in its capacity,'[90] and the way the commandment of *imitatio Dei* is phrased in *Mishneh torah*: 'Thus too the prophets described the Almighty by all the various attributes . . . to teach us that these qualities are good and right and that a human being should cultivate them, and thus imitate God, as far as he can.'[91]

Both human beings and the heavenly bodies perceive God's perfection; both seek to imitate it; and both are limited in their capacity to do so, being physical entities, albeit of different composition. They differ in two ways. The first is that 'the sphere desires to come to be like that which it apprehends' spontaneously, unchangingly, and everlastingly, whereas a human being is under a commandment to arouse that desire in himself. The opposition of the heavens and human beings is the opposition of is and ought—being and becoming.

The other difference is in the faculties involved. The qualities that are 'good and right' are the qualities perceived in God's actions in the sublunary world of matter. On a plain reading, and considered by itself, 'Laws of Ethical Qualities' concerns that world only. Moral virtue is then confined to the

them and acquiring the power to compute them rightly according to nature, we might reproduce the perfectly unerring revolutions of the god and reduce to settled order the wandering motions in ourselves' (Cornford, *Plato's Cosmology*, 158).

[89] *Guide* ii. 4 (p. 256).   [90] *Guide* i. 69 (p. 170).   [91] 'Laws of Ethical Qualities', 1: 6.

narrow band of personal and social ethics, which means training in self-restraint. Such a reading is in line with the division of the soul in 'Eight Chapters', 1, into five parts: 'nutritive, sentient, imaginative, appetitive, and rational',[92] and the assertion in 'Eight Chapters', 2, that 'the moral virtues are found only in the appetitive part',[93] which spheres, of course, lack.

The microcosm–macrocosm pattern changes the perspective. It brings all of the soul into play. The five parts of the soul now appear capable of receiving the regularity of the movements and interrelations of the five spheres, both systems being described, to remind ourselves once more, over five chapters.

The simple fact that 'Laws of Ethical Qualities' follows 'Laws of the Foundations of the Torah' is enough to hint at the idea of moral perfection following on from theoretical perfection. The replication of the structure of 'Laws of the Foundations of the Torah' in 'Laws of Ethical Qualities' looks like confirmation of the hint. The pattern of the latter flows from that of the former, giving the sense that its content flows from there too; that is to say, moral virtue flows from intellectual virtue. Knowledge of the spheres endows us with knowledge of how to be, and consequently of how to behave.

The *imitatio Dei* consisting in the imitation of the attributes of God's actions is limited to the sublunary level and entails a projection of human feelings onto nature.[94] God is beyond qualities such as mercy and compassion, but we observe how, for example, creatures are born and cared for in a way that, were it to proceed from us, we should call it merciful and compassionate, and in adopting this as a model, we say that we are imitating God's ways. The person with theoretical knowledge, however, who understands how God's sublunary actions are the product of the motions of the spheres transmitted to the four elements, replicates the cosmic order in himself or herself by a sort of reverse engineering—because knowledge is likeness. His or her *imitatio Dei* then becomes like that of the spheres, a purely intellectual activity (there being no moral choices above the planet Earth), which entails understanding nature's laws rather than merely observing natural phenomena. The result is a reversal of the fall of Adam, from perception of good and bad back to perception of true and false.[95] From there, moral behaviour will become a dictate of reason, as at the end of the *Guide*.[96]

---

[92] *Ethical Writings*, ed. Weiss and Butterworth, 61.   [93] Ibid. 65.

[94] See *Guide* i. 54 (pp. 124–7).   [95] See *Guide* i. 2 (pp. 23–6).

[96] Compare Plato's *Republic* 500c: 'Then the philosopher, by consorting with what is ordered and divine . . . himself becomes as divine and ordered as a human being can' (cited in Seeskin, *Searching for*

Guide i. 72 does use the man-as-microcosm idea specifically to connect ethics and theory, for a person's governance of him- or herself and the governance of the state are compared to God's governance of the universe. As we have seen, this comparison is modified at the end of the chapter, but perhaps the two versions reflect the two phases of the relationship between ethics and theory, justifying the use of the microcosm–macrocosm pattern to represent both moral virtue as preparation for intellectual virtue and moral virtue consequent on intellectual virtue. In the first phase, the operation of the hylic intellect on a person's ethical qualities, bringing them to the mean, is comparable to the relationship between the intellect of a sphere and the sphere, and confers the kind, though not the degree, of knowledge that a sphere possesses. In the second phase, the human intellect conjoins with the agent intellect and attains angelic knowledge. Once that is achieved, a person's self-governance is comparable to God's governance of the cosmos. That relationship is one of a spontaneous, infinite, indiscriminate flow of goodness from God to creation.[97]

The descent of form onto matter in the ontological sense is reflected in the descent of the literary form of 'Laws of the Foundations of the Torah' onto 'Laws of Ethical Qualities'. The relationship of form to content in these two sections becomes a poetic representation of the two-phase cycle of moral virtue and intellectual virtue described in the *Guide*.

In sum, 'Laws of the Foundations of the Torah' and 'Laws of Ethical Qualities' are not just placed side by side. The former, in every sense, informs the latter. Through the interplay of form and content, Maimonides has it both ways. He presents morality as a separate, Aristotelian category, something attained through adherence to the mean and understood as providing the inward psychic conditions and the outward social conditions for the pursuit of intellectual virtue; yet at the same time he presents it as a Neoplatonic outflow from knowledge.[98]

---

a Distant God, 99). Further on Plato's view of contemplation of the universe as a means of restoring an original rationality in man, see Carone, *Plato's Cosmology*, 77–8.

[97] *Guide* ii. 11 (p. 275).

[98] This conclusion is *contra* Shatz, who, apropos Davidson's theory that moral virtue in the *Guide* consists in the extirpation of emotion, writes: 'Theoretically one could view the legal writings' account as referring to propaedeutic morality and the *Guide*'s as referring to consequent morality, and insist that there is no formal contradiction between the psychological states required by one and the absence of such states in the other. But the lack of reference in the legal writings to anything resembling the 'consequent' morality is striking and would suggest that Maimonides came to the idea of emotionless perfection late in his career' ('Maimonides' Moral Theory', 188).

Self-Knowledge and the Knowledge of God

The general meaning derived so far from the microcosm–macrocosm pattern in 'Laws of the Foundations of the Torah' and 'Laws of Ethical Qualities' is that the virtuous personality reproduces the harmony of the cosmos.

I suggest, somewhat speculatively, that the implications go further, and that the pattern implies that moral virtue actually is a form of knowledge of God. The logic is clear: if knowledge of God is attained through knowledge of the world, and a human being is a small world, then it follows that a human being's knowledge of self, gained through bringing that inner world under the control of the intellect, should confer knowledge of God. What appear to be logical steps may well lead us astray, however, without a wider orientation. As far as I am aware, Maimonides nowhere discusses this idea explicitly, and although it was current in his time and has a respectable history, he has not been considered part of that history.[99] Nevertheless, I wish to probe the proposition that, in a sense special to Maimonides, but deriving from the Neoplatonists and possibly influenced by Alghazali, moral self-perfection is equivalent to a kind of knowledge of God. At any rate, much of the history of the idea, in which microcosm–macrocosm theory plays an important part, will be found to resonate in Maimonides too.

A key to this is a modification Maimonides made to the Aristotelian categories of moral and intellectual virtue. For both Aristotle and Maimonides, perfection means resembling God as closely as possible. Aristotle, however, applies this only to intellectual virtue. The gods must be supposed perfectly happy, so their sole activity must be contemplation, as no action could improve their lot. Human beings who seek happiness are best advised to cultivate the divine in themselves, that is, the intellect, and to prefer a life of contemplation to one of action.[100] Aristotle does not associate moral virtue with *imitatio Dei*.[101] He conceives of it as the excellence of a thing as it is in itself, which only secondarily finds practical and social expression.[102]

---

[99] See Altmann, 'Delphic Maxim'.

[100] See also Pines, 'Philosophic Sources', pp. lxvi–lxvii; Shatz, 'Maimonides' Moral Theory'.

[101] On differences between Aristotle's and Maimonides' concepts of moral virtue, see Fox, 'Doctrine of the Mean'.

[102] 'The excellence of the horse makes a horse both good in itself and good at running and at carrying its rider and at awaiting the attack of the enemy. Therefore, if this is true in every case, the virtue of man also will be the state of character which makes a man good and which makes him do his own work well' (Aristotle, *Nicomachean Ethics*, 1106a). Possibly the nearest equivalent within the Jewish tradition is Mishnah *Avot* 2: 1: 'R. Judah the Prince said: Which is the proper course that a man should

For Maimonides, as we have seen, there is no such thing as virtue for its own sake: everything, including moral virtue, is for the sake of the love and knowledge of God. Moreover, while for him as for Aristotle the intellect is the divine element in man, he makes *imitatio Dei* the basis of moral virtue as well. Stretching *imitatio Dei* to cover moral virtue as well as intellectual virtue creates considerable mobility between the two. Underlying this is a more fundamental difference between Maimonides and Aristotle: the latter sees the intellect as grafted upon an animal soul; the former sees all the faculties of the human soul, its nutritive, appetitive, sentient, and imaginative parts as well as its intellectual part, as distinctively human.[103] The question is, how far does this integrative view of human nature go? Is moral virtue conceived of as *imitatio Dei* only a way of making a person fit to pursue intellectual virtue, or does it bring with it knowledge?

Image and Likeness

In order to decide whether moral virtue can constitute knowledge of God, we must finally confront the problem set out at the beginning of this discussion. We need a precise notion of what knowledge of God means, and, since knowledge is a kind of likeness, we must be able to define likeness to God.

So far, it has been somewhat glibly asserted that the intellect is the divine part of man, as though that should solve matters, when we were aware from the start that the lack of commonality between God and creation applies to intangible qualities just as much as to tangible ones. It follows from God's incorporeality that he is a unity, but this unity 'is such that there is no other unity like it in the world'.[104] God must have knowledge, but his knowledge is not the same as human knowledge:

The Holy One, blessed be He, realizes His true being, and knows it as it is, not with a knowledge external to himself, as is our knowledge. For our knowledge and ourselves are separate. But as for the Creator, His knowledge and His life are One, in all aspects, from every point of view . . . Hence the conclusion that God is the One who knows, is known, and is the knowledge—all these being One. This is beyond the

choose for himself? That which is an honour to him and elicits honour from his fellow men.' True enough, Maimonides, ad loc., identifies this with the Aristotelian doctrine of the golden mean.

[103] See 'Eight Chapters', 1, and Frank, 'The Moral Psychology of *Shemonah Peraqim*'. Frank stresses Maimonides' holistic view of human nature, his inclusion of all man's psychic powers as part of the human essence, and 'the actualization of them all as necessary conditions for attaining knowledge of God, the human goal' (ibid. 31).   [104] 'Laws of the Foundations of the Torah', 1: 7.

power of speech to express, beyond the capacity of the ear to hear, and of the human mind to apprehend clearly.[105]

In other words, the intellect may in some way be the divine part of man, but human intellect and divine intellect are not the same. Our understanding of 'in our image, after our likeness' therefore needs to be refined.

In *Mishneh torah*, in chapter 4 of 'Laws of the Foundations of the Torah', the problem is addressed in the following way:

The vital principle of all flesh is the form which God has given it. The superior intelligence in the human soul is the specific form of the mentally normal human being. To this form, the Torah refers in the text, 'Let us make man in our image, after our likeness'. This means that man should have a form that knows and apprehends idealistic beings that are devoid of matter, such as the angels which are forms without substance, so that (intellectually) man is like the angels. It does not refer to the visible features—the mouth, nose, cheeks, and other distinguishing bodily marks. These are comprehended in the nomenclature 'feature'. Nor does it refer to the vital principle in every animal by which it eats, drinks, reproduces, feels and broods. It is the intellect which is the soul's specific form. And to this specific form of the soul, the Scriptural phrase 'in our image, after our likeness' alludes.[106]

Having asserted that being in the image and likeness of God is not in respect of physical resemblance but in respect of possession of an intellect, Maimonides goes on to promise this intellect immortality:

This form of the Soul is not compounded of elements into which it would again dissolve . . . But it comes from God, from Heaven. Hence, when the material portion of our being dissolves into its component elements, and physical life perishes . . . this form of the Soul is not destroyed, as it does not require physical life for its activities. It knows and apprehends the Intelligences that exist without material substance; it knows the Creator of All things; and it endures for ever.[107]

At first sight, this is splendid. What makes human beings unique is that God gives them a specific form that is an intellect with the power to perceive nonphysical entities, and this intellect is immortal. A more alert reading, however, is liable to leave us feeling short-changed. There is actually no explanation at all of how exactly, in the face of the negation of similarity between human and divine knowledge we have just seen, having an intellect makes us like God. In fact, the only similarity we attain here is to the angels (otherwise known as intelligences or separate intellects), which is less than we

---

[105] 'Laws of the Foundations of the Torah', 2: 10.   [106] Ibid. 4: 8.   [107] Ibid. 4: 9.

were led to expect. It seems that there are some steps missing from these *halakhot*, which perhaps the *Guide* will be able to supply.

The explanation of 'in our image, after our likeness' in the *Guide*'s first chapter largely parallels the one in 'Laws of the Foundations of the Torah'. The same distinction is made between image (*tselem*) and feature (*to'ar*) to argue that image does not mean physical resemblance but form, which in the case of a natural object means its specific form, that which makes it what it is, its essential characteristic.[108] What makes human beings human and differentiates them from other sentient creatures is the possession of intellect. It is 'because of the divine intellect conjoined with man, that it is said of the latter that he is "in the image of God and in His likeness"'.[109]

This first chapter of the *Guide*, however, distinguishes between image and likeness. If image is form rather than physical shape, 'likeness' refers not to appearance, but to 'likeness in respect of a notion'. The notion in respect of which human beings bear a likeness to God is that human intellectual apprehension, like God's, is non-physical:

In the exercise of this, no sense, no part of the body, none of the extremities are used; and therefore this apprehension was likened unto the apprehension of the deity, which does not require an instrument, although in reality it is not like the latter apprehension, but only appears so to the first stirrings of opinion.[110]

Human apprehension, then, is not the same as divine apprehension, but it is analogous to it in that it is non-physical.[111]

This provides a platform for more detailed explanation further on in the *Guide* of how the intellect is like God, which it might be as well to preface with a summary of Maimonides' theory of intellectual apprehension.

If you are carrying a basket of apples, you, the basket, and the apples are separately identifiable, even though all move as one. In particular, the basket can be considered separately from its present use as a convenient container of apples. Something similar applies if you are not carrying the apples, but only

---

[108] Warren Zev Harvey argues that Maimonides intimates in the course of the chapter that the distinction between *tselem* and *to'ar* may not be tenable, and that the interpretation of *tselem* in the story of the creation of Adam to mean form in the Aristotelian sense is really a philosophical overlay, not necessarily derivable from the meaning of the word itself. ('How to Begin to Study *Guide* i. 1' (Heb.)). I do not believe that this affects the argument advanced here.   [109] *Guide* i. 1 (p. 23).   [110] Ibid.

[111] Later, in *Guide* i. 56, the subject of which is likeness, Maimonides may appear to undercut this explanation, for there he disallows even a 'likeness in respect of a notion' between human beings and God. However, since the likeness in *Guide* i. 1 is expressed negatively, it qualifies as a negative attribute 'used in order to conduct the mind toward that which must be believed with regard to Him' (*Guide* i. 58 (p. 135)).

looking at them. You receive a sense impression of the apples, which you can carry in your mind, but you and this sense impression that your mind contains remain separable. Maimonides terms the mental faculty that receives and stores sense impressions 'imagination'. The imagination can also manipulate sense impressions to produce both realistic and absurd images. None of this involves the intellect: 'I do not consider that you might confuse intellectual representation with imagination and with the reception of an image of a sense object by the imaginative faculty.'[112]

The function of the intellect is to conceptualize, or, in Maimonides' language, apprehend, forms. From your sense impressions of apples your intellect can extract an idea of 'appleness', which is a form that all apples, green and red, large and small, share.

The key point is that the intellect is not like a basket. As Maimonides emphasizes in *Guide* i. 68, thought and the content of thought are inseparable: 'You should not then think that the intellect *in actu* is a certain thing existing by itself apart from apprehension and that apprehension is something else subsisting in that intellect. For the very being and true reality of the intellect is apprehension.'[113] When the intellect is inactive, it is only a potential. When it is active, it *is* the thought that it is thinking—in the case of our example, it *is* 'appleness'. Maimonides assumes that it is possible to think of such a form in the abstract, without visualizing anything, an assumption perhaps more understandable (though still debatable) if we take forms to be laws of nature, such as 'a body remains at rest or in constant motion unless acted upon by a force', abstracted from observation of material objects, or at least tested against such observation. Whenever the intellect thinks of such a form, it and the form are a unity.

Furthermore, the thinking subject is also united with its thought. This might be phrased in the following way. The intellect is the form of man, that which makes human beings human, their essence. But we have just said that the intellect is identical with what it thinks about. When someone's intellect is active, therefore, their form and the form they perceive merge, or, as Maimonides puts it, 'the intellect, the intellectually cognizing subject, and the intellectually cognized object are always one and the same thing in the case of everything that is cognized *in actu*'.[114] You are what you are thinking. When

---

[112] *Guide* i. 68 (p. 166).　　　　　　　　　　　　　　　　　[113] p. 164.

[114] See 'Laws of the Foundations of the Torah', 4: 7. See also n. 9 above and Appendix II.2. Maimonides' identification of angels with forces of nature (see n. 51 above) brings us very close to the idea that to have an angel as the object of one's intellect means to understand a law of nature.

you stop thinking, the components—you, your intellect, and the object of your thought—separate out again.

Human beings are capable of thinking about more than apples or laws of motion. They can progress from physical to metaphysical knowledge, for just as the intellect can distinguish form from matter, it can also apprehend entities that are form only, such as the agent intellect.[115] This can be put either negatively or positively. Once you have gained all the physical knowledge of which you are capable, you can then conceive of what lies beyond the physical. Or, to put it positively, if you understand all natural forms, you become like, and thus know, the agent intellect, which contains all those forms. Having no material side, an entity such as the agent intellect can be grasped by the intellect in its entirety. Such entities are therefore known as intelligibles.

Knowledge of an intelligible like the agent intellect is termed in Aristotelian philosophy 'the acquired intellect'.[116] The acquired intellect is immortal as the agent intellect is immortal. In other words, if you fully realize your intellectual potential, you will forever be what you know.[117]

God's intellect is not a potentiality, but perpetually active. To say otherwise would imply change in him, and God is unchanging. Nor can God's thoughts be abstractions like ours, for that would imply the kind of division that exists in our minds between intellect and imagination, in violation of the doctrine of God's unity; nor can they be stimulated by external objects, for he is unaffected by anything outside himself. In fact, we cannot speak at all about 'God's intellect' or 'God's thoughts', as though God existed separately from stored thoughts. We must therefore say that God is 'thought thinking itself', in a kind of absolute unity that, as we saw above, Maimonides acknowledges to be beyond human comprehension.[118]

Nonetheless, despite this unbridgeable, incomprehensible gap, when your intellect is active, your subjective self, your intellect, and the thought you are

---

[115] *Guide* i. 68 (pp. 164–5).

[116] On the concept of the acquired intellect in Maimonides, see Kellner, *Maimonides on Judaism*, 9–15; Davidson, *Alfarabi, Avicenna and Averroes on Intellect*, 197–203.

[117] 'For Maimonides as for Al-Farabi knowledge was a grasp of the object itself, which leads to an identification between the intellecting subject and the intellected object. When the subject intellects a material and perishable object it becomes perishable like the object. On the other hand, when the subject intellects an eternal object it becomes thereby eternal' (Sirat, *History of Jewish Philosophy*, 287).

[118] See also *Guide* i. 57 (p. 132): 'Now to ascribe to Him—whose existence is necessary, who is truly simple, to whom composition cannot attach in any way—the accident of oneness is just as absurd as to ascribe to Him the accident of multiplicity. I mean to say that oneness is not a notion that is superadded to His essence, but that He is one not through oneness.' Even this, Maimonides admits, involves us in 'a certain looseness of expression' (ibid. (p. 133)).

thinking are in a state of unity analogous to the unity that is God, and in that sense you are in God's likeness.

With this in mind, we can now see how Maimonides himself sums up the similarity and difference between human beings and God in respect of apprehension, in the passage from which the above quotation is taken:

Accordingly He is always the intellect as well as the intellectually cognizing subject and the intellectually cognized object. It is accordingly also clear that the numerical unity of the intellect, the intellectually cognizing subject, and the intellectually cognized object, does not hold good with reference to the Creator only, but also with reference to every intellect. Thus in us too, the intellectually cognizing subject, the intellect, and the intellectually cognized object, are one and the same thing wherever we have an intellect *in actu*. We, however, pass from potentiality to actuality only from time to time.[119]

When the human intellect is not active, when it goes off the boil, as it were, the state of separation resumes. The human intellect reverts to being

[119] *Guide* i. 68 (p. 165). According to Pines, this parallel is original to Maimonides—see 'Philosophic Sources', p. xcviii. Even a separate intellect's activity is subject to disturbance, and therefore not the same as God's intellection (ibid. (p. 166)). In his 'Translator's Introduction to the *Guide of the Perplexed*' (p. xcviii), Pines identified a contradiction between the Aristotelian definition of God as intellect intellecting itself, a positive description, and the doctrine of negative attributes, which forbids any such positive description of God. He also pointed out that Maimonides' comparison of human intellect to divine intellect implies that God has knowledge not just of his own essence, but also of forms and natural laws. Since such knowledge involves an identity between intellecting subject, intellect, and intellected object, this brings us 'perilously close' to Spinoza's idea of God coeval with nature. Later Pines changed his view and decided that the comparison between human intellect and divine intellect in *Guide* i. 68 was of theological but not philosophical import, and that the Maimonides of the *Guide* did not believe in the possibility of human apprehension of a separate intellect and considered the very existence of separate intellects as 'merely probable' ('Limitations of Human Knowledge', 94). In a subsequent article he divorced *Mishneh torah* and the *Guide* even more firmly:

in the interval of time which elapsed between the writing of the *Mishneh torah* and the composition of the *Guide*, Maimonides had completely revised his view of the 'Aristotelian' verities, that he no longer gave credence—as far as metaphysics and extraterrestrial physics were concerned—to the claims of the *falasifa* (whose system he had taken over in the *Book of Knowledge*) according to which their coherent systems corresponded to the true reality and could be regarded as certain. ('Philosophical Purport', 10)

This reversal by Pines is perhaps the most noted development in modern Maimonidean studies. It is rehearsed here because my argument assumes, *contra* the later Pines, that *Mishneh torah* and the *Guide* are doctrinally harmonious and may be used to comment on each other on the question of the likeness of man to God. I rely on the general assertion that differences between them are a matter of genre rather than substance, and, in this particular case, on Stern, 'The Enigma of *Guide* i. 68' (Heb.). Stern reads *Guide* i. 68 as expressing the ineffability of God's mode of intellection rather than any kinship with human intellection, and finds complementarity between the *Guide* and the *Book of Knowledge* in this respect.

part of the human soul, which is a soul similar to those of animals except that it possesses this intellectual potential. The analogy to God then ceases to apply.

This clarifies the statement quoted above from *Guide* i. 1: 'In the exercise of this, no sense, no part of the body, none of the extremities are used; and therefore this apprehension was likened unto the apprehension of the deity.' The point of comparison lies in the exercise, not the mere possession, of intellect; in the function, not the thing. Maimonides troubles to mention that the derivation of the Hebrew for likeness is from a verb: 'As for the term *likeness* [*demuth*], it is a noun derived from the verb *damoh* [*to be like*]'.

In short, human beings have a likeness to God when their intellects are active, but this happens only intermittently, and the likeness is not a matter of identity but of analogy.[120]

The philosophically trained reader can close the apparent gap between this and 'Laws of the Foundations of the Torah', 4: 8–9, by reading the latter as conditional rather than indicative, and filling in the missing links. These *halakhot* then turn out to be formulated with great precision. When you exploit your intellectual potential, you become analogous to God in the unity

---

[120] Julia Annas refers to Plotinus's solution to the problem of likeness to God:

The problem of becoming like God is solved by distinguishing two kinds of likeness: that of one copy to another copy, where they are the same kind of thing, and that of copy to original, where this may not be true. Two houses, for example, can be like each other, being the same kind of thing. But a house can also be like the blueprint (and one house can be more like the blueprint than another) even though a house is not the kind of thing to be a blueprint—it is a different kind of thing altogether. So, Plotinus comments, there is no paradox in our becoming like God, although God is something completely different from us. (*Platonic Ethics*, 67)

The likeness of one house to another is a likeness of identity, where identity means direct similarity, having a quality in common, not necessarily complete congruence. The likeness of a house to a blueprint is a likeness of analogy.

Hannah Kasher, writing on the general tension in Maimonides between the Aristotelian, positive conception of God as intellect intellecting itself, and the Neoplatonic idea that the One is utterly separate from the world and indescribable in any positive terms, comments on the comparison of the unity of human intellection to the unity of divine intellection in *Guide* i. 68 as follows: 'The similarity is purely theoretical, however, as living people are never an actualized intellect: "We, however, pass from potentiality to actuality only from time to time." Hence Maimonides' characterization of God as intellect cognizing itself, by analogy with rational humanity, is only a positive statement on first sight' ('Self-Cognizing Intellect', 465, criticized in Stern, 'The Enigma of *Guide* i. 68' (Heb.), 439 n. 6). From the point of view of the current argument, the key word here is 'analogy'.

The specific question of God's unity and the unity of human apprehension is discussed in Lahey, 'Maimonides and Analogy'. On analogical thinking in Maimonides, see Schwartz, 'Maimonides' Philosophical Methodology' (Heb.). Schwartz argues that the importance of analogy for Maimonides' science and hermeneutics has been underestimated. More generally on analogy in discourse about God, see Mascall, 'Doctrine of Analogy'.

of you as intellecting subject, your intellect, and the intellected object. If this potential is exploited to apprehend beings devoid of matter, such as the agent intellect, that is, the *ishim*, the lowest angel, then, having this immortal entity as the object of your thought, you become identical with it and thus immortal like it as an acquired intellect;[121] otherwise, your intellect will perish with your animal soul and your body, just as the forms of all other material entities perish when the matter decays.

The disappointment registered above at 'Laws of the Foundations of the Torah', 4: 8, can thus be dispelled by the realization that two kinds of likeness are spoken of: analogy and identity. We arrive at the following formula: the *operation* of human intellect is God-like by analogy; the *product* of that operation, at its highest level, is angel-like by identity.

This is reflected in the language used in 'Laws of the Foundations of the Torah', 4: 9, for knowledge of God and knowledge of the angels. The intellect 'knows and apprehends the Intelligences that exist without material substance; it knows the Creator of all things; and it endures for ever', meaning that God is known through what he has created, not in himself; and, unlike the intelligences, he is only known, not apprehended, that is, not fully grasped, since 'God's essence as it really is, the human mind does not understand and is incapable of grasping or investigating'.[122]

Having used the *Guide* to elucidate 'Laws of the Foundations of the Torah', 4: 8, we are now in a position to compare the ways in which the *Guide*

[121] Kreisel similarly construes these passages as referring to the acquired intellect ('*Imitatio Dei* in "Guide"', 188). Pines ('Limitations of Human Knowledge') found that Maimonides denies the possibility of direct knowledge of the agent intellect (see above, n. 119), a view countered by Davidson ('Maimonides on Metaphysical Knowledge'). For differences between Alfarabi and Avicenna on whether having the agent intellect as an object of knowledge entails identity with it, see Davidson, 'Maimonides on Metaphysical Knowledge', 69. The language of 'Laws of the Foundations of the Torah', 4: 8 seems to imply identity.

[122] 'Laws of the Foundations of the Torah', 1: 9. The distinction is made by careful deployment of the verbs *lada'at*, 'to know', and *lehasig*, 'to apprehend' or 'to grasp'. See also 'Laws of Idolatry', 1: 3, where Abraham's knowledge of God's existence (*veyada*) follows from what he has managed to apprehend (*shehisig*) of natural phenomena, or of the right way of thinking about natural phenomena—the phrase is *shehisig derekh ha'emet*, 'he apprehended the way of truth'. At the end of *Mishneh torah* knowledge and apprehension come together in relation to God, in the phrase *veyasigu da'at boram kefi koḥam*, 'and they will apprehend the knowledge of their creator according to their capacity' ('Laws of Kings and Their Wars', 12: 12). However, *lehasig* is still not applied directly to God, but only to such knowledge of him as humans are capable of, while he is in any case referred to here as creator, again implying knowing God through the things he has made, not in himself.

These remarks are restricted to the local context, and do not pretend to be valid for all of Maimonides' writings. On different terms for different grades of knowledge in Maimonides, see Manekin, 'Limitations of Human Knowledge' (Heb.).

and *Mishneh torah* tackle the problem of man's likeness to God. In the *Guide*, there is a progressive discussion, in which Part I, chapter 68 is a refinement of Part I, chapter 1. The conclusion could be that the difference between that and *Mishneh torah* is that the latter is no place for such a discussion, which will in any case be lost on most of its readers, and so the matter is dealt with summarily, with a nod in the direction of the advanced reader. *Mishneh torah* does not deal in elusive analogies, and, as we have seen, rather stresses the chasm between human knowledge and divine knowledge.

The alternative conclusion is that *Mishneh torah* very much deals in analogies, but does so symbolically, so that the structural correspondence between 'Laws of the Foundations of the Torah' and 'Laws of Ethical Qualities' is an analogical model of likeness to God. This will be developed as we move from discussing likeness to God to answering the further question of how human beings can be said to have knowledge of God.

From Likeness to Knowledge

Let us ask that question again at the most basic level. It was stated at the outset that the premise of *Mishneh torah* is that man's purpose is to know God, but, as defined by Maimonides, God is unknowable. We have seen that even in respect of such abstract notions as knowledge and unity, the human conception and the divine reality have only the name in common. How is it possible to know an entity that has no characteristic with which we can identify?

Maimonides presents three answers. The first is readily gleaned from *Mishneh torah*; the second takes us to the *Guide*, while the third solution proposed here, of knowledge of God through the self, returns us to *Mishneh torah*, but this time in a reading that looks at form as much as content.

The first solution offered in *Mishneh torah* is that, while there is no crossing the great divide between man and God, God is represented on this side of the divide by his works. The contemplation of creation inspires love (and awe), which gives rise to an intense desire to know the Creator.[123] This desire is satisfied through scientific study,[124] which in turn reinforces the response of love.[125] Living in this virtuous circle is what is meant by knowledge of God.

In the *Guide*, we find a different approach, presented in response to a

---

[123] 'Laws of the Foundations of the Torah', 2: 2.

[124] What Maimonides meant by science is clearly not the same as what we mean by it. He accepted the authority of Aristotle on sublunary phenomena, though he was sceptical about the possibility of real knowledge of the spheres and stars. At any rate, his was not the method of theorizing and experiment that we know today. On Maimonides as scientist and his attitude to Aristotle, see Kellner, 'Astronomy and Physics in Maimonides'. [125] 'Laws of Repentance', 10: 6.

further difficulty that God's unknowability raises. Having asserted that no direct, positive knowledge of God is to be obtained,[126] Maimonides acknowledges that this apparently rules out any gradations in knowledge.[127] Of that which cannot be known, all are equally ignorant. In that case, how is it that we ascribe greater knowledge to such figures as Moses and Solomon?

The answer is that the very understanding of God's unknowability amounts to a kind of knowledge. That is to say, the more we manage to purge our notion of God of any physical connotation, the clearer and more exact that notion becomes. From this point of view, the advantage of science is that it gives a more precise idea of what God is not.[128] This negation is a lifetime's work, in which some progress further than others.[129]

Those are Maimonides' explicit solutions to our problem. We shall now examine whether the form of *Mishneh torah* can enlighten us further.

As we saw above, in the Aristotelian system, to know something is to be like it in the sense that the mind of the perceiver becomes identical with the form of the perceived object. It should follow that, for an intelligent being, to be like something, that is, to adopt its form, is to know it. In 'Laws of Ethical Qualities', moral virtue is grounded in *imitatio Dei*. This means not just imitating the attributes of God's actions, but, mainly, developing the qualities that those actions imply, so that moral virtue is an inward state of being like God.[130] In that case, on the basis of the equivalence of similarity and knowledge, moral virtue can actually constitute knowledge of God.

It would be useful to find a foothold for this argument in the text itself. It is possible that one can be found in the attributes of God which Maimonides

---

[126] *Guide* i. 58 (pp. 134–7).   [127] *Guide* i. 59 (pp. 137–8).

[128] 'It has accordingly become manifest to you that in every case in which the demonstration that a certain thing should be negated with reference to Him becomes clear to you, you become more perfect, and that in every case in which you affirm of Him an additional thing, you become one who likens Him to other things and you get further away from the knowledge of his true reality' (*Guide* i. 59 (p. 139)). See also the moral of the *Guide*'s parable of the ship: 'For on every occasion on which it becomes clear to you by means of demonstration that a thing whose existence is thought to pertain to Him, may He be exalted, should rather be negated with reference to Him, you undoubtedly come nearer to Him by one degree' (*Guide* i. 60 (p. 144)). On this see Davidson, 'Maimonides on Metaphysical Knowledge', 94.

The whole of Part I of the *Guide* plays out just such a process of purgation, as one by one the biblical anthropomorphic descriptions of God are interpreted away, allowing a true philosophical understanding to take shape. Compare also 'Laws of the Foundations of the Torah', 1: 10.

[129] Ivry sees this approach to the knowledge of God as of Neoplatonic origin. See 'Neoplatonic Currents in Maimonides', 133.

[130] See Davidson, 'Middle Way'. For a different view of the way in which man assimilates himself to God in 'Laws of Ethical Qualities', see Frank, 'Anger as a Vice'. Both articles are further discussed below.

states we are required to imitate: 'Thus they taught this commandment explicitly: Just as he is called gracious, so should you be gracious; just as he is called merciful, so should you be merciful; just as he is called holy, so should you be holy.'[131] As will be discussed in some detail in Chapter 3,[132] although this passage is based on a talmudic source, there appears to be no source for the last in the trio of virtues that it presents: 'just as he is called holy, so should you be holy'. Why did Maimonides add it?

Kellner suggests that, by introducing it here, 'Maimonides emphasizes the non-ontological character of holiness. Just as mercy and graciousness are matters of action and character, so also is holiness.'[133] I should like to stress the difference between holiness and the other two virtues rather than the similarities. The theory of the middle way is that the ideal temperament is a midpoint between two extremes; mercy, for example, being midway between laxity and cruelty. It is associated with *imitatio Dei* because we learn desirable traits by observing the attributes of God's actions in nature. As we have seen, when qualities such as grace and mercy are attributed to God, the meaning is that God's actions in nature are such that, were they predicated of human beings, we should call them gracious, merciful, and so on. Hence the circumlocution of 'Laws of Ethical Qualities', 1: 6: not 'as he is merciful, so should you be merciful', but 'as he is *called* merciful, so should you etc. But what can be seen in nature that, were it the action of a human being, we should call it holy? Whatever it means, to call God holy seems to be a description not of God's actions, but rather of God as he is in himself.

The essential meaning of the Hebrew for holy, *kadosh*, is 'separate' or 'set apart'. Applied to God, it refers to his utter separateness from matter. From God's absolute non-materiality flows the concept of his oneness, both in the sense of uniqueness and in the sense of unity.[134] In other words, holiness is not an attribute of God's actions within nature, but a way of expressing the idea of God apart from nature, standing in relation (if that loose expression may be pardoned) to nature as a whole, rather than being manifest in some particular aspect of nature. In fact, it is just after he has set forth the doctrines of God's non-materiality and oneness that Maimonides starts to call God by the name *hakadosh barukh hu* ('the holy one blessed be he').[135] It is using this name that Maimonides describes the aspiration of Moses to understand the notion of

---

[131] 'Laws of Ethical Qualities', 1: 6.   [132] Full references are provided in that chapter.
[133] Kellner, *Maimonides' Confrontation with Mysticism*, 101. See also Kreisel, *Maimonides' Political Thought*, 154.   [134] 'Laws of the Foundations of the Torah', 1: 7.   [135] Ibid. 1: 8.

God as distinct and separate from everything else that exists,[136] and he employs the same name again, after an interval of referring to God as *habore* ('the creator'), when he comes to describe how God's knowledge is self-knowledge.[137]

The name, however, is of secondary importance;[138] what matters is the concept, the ways in which God is defined as distinct from nature, or holy. On that basis, to be holy as God is called holy means that, within the limitations imposed by their material condition, human beings should be separate, unified, and possessed of knowledge through self-knowledge as continuously as possible, and not just at those times when they have an intellect *in actu*.

This is what the form of the *Book of Knowledge* seems to model. Just as 'Laws of Ethical Qualities' is created in the literary image of 'Laws of the Foundations of the Torah', man fulfils the challenge of being created in the image of God in respect of his ontological form, his intellect, by establishing the rule of intellect over all his faculties, making unity out of multiplicity, thus reflecting the unity in multiplicity of the cosmos. Being 'in our likeness' (*kidmutenu*), or potentially holy, is answered by 'to become like' (*lehidamot*), or actually holy.[139]

Or to follow another verbal thread, and to sum up this stage of the argument, the microcosm–macrocosm pattern leads to the conclusion that the more a human being brings his plural *de'ot* within the ambit of his single *da'at*, the more separate he is from matter, and the more closely he approximates

---

[136] 'Laws of the Foundations of the Torah', 1: 10.   [137] Ibid. 2: 10.

[138] 'Laws of the Foundations of the Torah', 2: 3, for example, begins, 'All that the Holy One, blessed be He, created in His universe', which could be seen as confusing the issue. It can at least be said that there is a tendency for Maimonides to think of God under the name 'the Holy One' when he considers God's separateness, even if there is no hard and fast rule. A small hint in that direction can be derived from *Guide* i. 61 (p. 149) (part of the discussion of the names of God that extends from *Guide* i. 61 to 64): 'In the *Chapters of Rabbi Eliezer* they have said: *Before the world was created, there were only the Holy One, blessed be He, and His name*. Consider now how this dictum states clearly that all the derivative names have come into being after the world has come into being.'

[139] In Hebrew the forms of the verb *damoh* that can mean 'to resemble' (*kal* and *nifal* constructions), and the form that means 'to come to resemble', 'to become like' (*hitpa'el* construction), are indistinguishable in the future third person masculine singular, the part of the verb that Maimonides uses in 'Laws of the Foundations of the Torah', 4: 8, and in the infinitive, the part he uses in the preamble to 'Laws of Ethical Qualities', certainly without vocalization. In 'Laws of the Foundations of the Torah', 4: 8, following the Huntington manuscript, Hyamson reads *sheyidameh* (p. 39*a*), which he parses as *hitpa'el* (note on p. viii). The Or Vishua edition gives *sheyidmeh* (*kal*), which is more consonant with my interpretation. I take the commandment *lehidamot bidrakhav* that heads 'Laws of Ethical Qualities' to mean 'to become like his ways' (*hitpa'el*). This is not incontestable, but even if the commandment is 'to resemble his ways' (*nifal*), the body of 'Laws of Ethical Qualities' is about working on one's character, that is to say, becoming like God's ways.

the condition of the one who possesses a unity that passes understanding and for whom all knowledge is self-knowledge.[140] That approximation is perhaps as much knowledge of God as is to be had.

In this latter respect, a human being comes to resemble a heavenly sphere in its knowledge of God:

> Every star and sphere has a soul and is endowed with knowledge and intelligence. They are living beings who apprehend 'Him who spake and the world was'. They praise and glorify their Creator, just as the angels do, each according to its greatness and degree. And as they apprehend God, so are they conscious of themselves and of the angels above them. The knowledge possessed by the stars and spheres, is less than that of angels, more than that of human beings.[141]

For a sphere, the desire to be like God and the apprehension of God are scarcely distinguishable, and its apprehension is simultaneous with its consciousness of itself. Compare this with the apprehension of human beings as described in 'Laws of the Foundations of the Torah', 2: 2:

> And what is the way that will lead to the love of Him and the fear of Him? When a person contemplates His great and wondrous works and creatures and from them obtains a glimpse of His wisdom which is incomparable and infinite, he will straightway love Him, praise Him, glorify Him, and long with an exceeding longing to know His great Name.... And when he ponders these matters, he will recoil affrighted, and realize that he is a small creature, lowly and obscure, endowed with slight and slender intelligence, standing in the presence of Him who is perfect in knowledge.

The structure of human consciousness is the same as that of the sphere's consciousness: awareness of God and awareness of self. The difference is that a sphere is serenely aware of itself as a permanent, unchanging being in no danger of being corrupted by the stuff of which it is made, and therefore with nothing to be ashamed of or to fear, whereas a human being is aware of himself as a low, material, mortal creature, of negligible intelligence, liable to be submerged in materiality.[142] This rightly manifests itself as awe, a proper fear. The transition from 'Laws of the Foundations of the Torah' to 'Laws of Ethical Qualities', where the human creature grapples with his material condition, follows this structure of consciousness, and is a transition from love to

---

[140] It should be made clear that this relates only to Maimonides' mode of presentation in 'Laws of the Foundations of the Torah' and 'Laws of Ethical Qualities', and is not meant to capture all the ramifications of man in the image of God and *imitatio Dei* in his writings.

[141] 'Laws of the Foundations of the Torah', 3: 9.

[142] See also 'Laws of the Foundations of the Torah', 4: 12, where the shame of corporeal existence is conveyed even more strongly.

fear. Asserting the control of intellect works this self-consciousness into a more sphere-like self-knowledge,[143] and renews the possibility of knowledge of God.

Neat as these conclusions can be made to look, there may be some discomfort with them. They blur the boundary between moral virtue and intellectual virtue in a way that is not consonant with things that Maimonides says elsewhere,[144] and they may seem to flout the doctrine that there can be no positive knowledge of God. Let us, however, put off dealing with the apparent difficulties for a while, and place the idea of knowledge of God through knowledge of the self in a wider context.

'He Who Knows Himself Knows His Lord'

The idea might have reached Maimonides via the Neoplatonist Islamic philosophers. In general, knowledge of the supreme being through the self is an important theme in Neoplatonism, and it is based in that school precisely on the idea that the psychic structure of human beings corresponds to the cosmic hierarchy of hypostases: the One, Intelligence, and Soul.[145] A human being's highest goal is to achieve union with the One through renunciation of the material concerns of Soul and abolition of the differentiations of Intelligence.

In his essay 'The Delphic Maxim in Medieval Islam and Judaism', Alexander Altmann traces the history and influence of the knowledge-of-God-through-self idea, beginning from a saying attributed to Muhammad: 'He who knows himself knows his Lord', a saying that Altmann says is 'obviously based on the Delphic exhortation, "Know thyself"'.

Altmann barely mentions Maimonides in that essay, and clearly does not see him as a flag-bearer for his theme.[146] Yet, if it is accepted that the symbolic

[143] Kreisel arrives at a similar view of the fear of God in 'Laws of the Foundations of the Torah', 2: 2: 'the fear that Maimonides describes in the Laws of the Principles of the Torah designates a type of humbleness of spirit that belongs to the intellect. It is not an ethical trait or an emotional "feeling." This fear is reminiscent of the philosophic exhortation: "Know thyself"' (*Maimonides' Political Thought*, 265).

[144] e.g. the statement in 'Eight Chapters', 2, cited above: 'As for the virtues, there are two kinds: moral virtues and rational virtues . . . The moral virtues are found only in the appetitive part.'

[145] 'Just as each Intelligence contains the whole Intelligible world, so each soul contains all the principles operative within the psychical order (v.7.1.7.ff.); hence "we are each of us an intelligible cosmos" (iii.4.3.22, IV.7.10.32–7, cf. iii.8.6.40) and determine our destiny by choosing which of these principles shall rule our lives' (Wallis, *Neoplatonism*, 70). The references are to Plotinus, *Enneads*. See also Appendix II.1.

[146] In the forty pages of the essay there are four references to Maimonides, all of them more or less parenthetical.

structure described above is present in the *Book of Knowledge*, a case can be made that much of what Altmann says does apply to Maimonides.

Altmann identifies three elements in the idea of knowledge of God through self-knowledge, and surveys a series of Islamic and Jewish authors, each of whom uses one or more of these elements in his approach to the idea. The three elements are: the motif of the soul's 'likeness' to God; the microcosm motif; and soul and intellect, or the Neoplatonic approach.

It has already been established that the first two elements are very much present in the *Book of Knowledge*. We have seen how, in 'Laws of the Foundations of the Torah', the soul's likeness to God is what makes human beings human, the likeness being in respect of the intellect, which is the form of the soul,[147] and how the microcosm motif emerges from the parallel structures of the first five chapters of 'Laws of the Foundations of the Torah' and of 'Laws of Ethical Qualities'.

The third element, the Neoplatonic approach, branches into two main components in Altmann's account. The first is that the emanant knows itself when it looks back to its source. 'Thus, essentially, the soul knows itself by looking upward to Intellect, not by looking merely into itself . . . For Plotinus, "knowing God" . . . cannot be divorced from the self-possession of the soul in the pure act of intellect'.[148]

The other component is that of purification: 'The soul is capable of a true introversion only if it turns away from the things of the sentient, external world and, thus purified, rests entirely in the intellect from which it has its true being.'[149] In this context, Altmann cites the Hebrew Pseudo-Empedocles Fragments published by D. Kauffman,[150] the influence of which on Solomon Ibn Gabirol 'cannot be gainsaid'.[151] Among the Arab philosophers Altmann mentions Ibn Bajja as having 'succumbed to the spiritual temper of the Pseudo-Empedoclean tradition . . . In following the trend of the Neoplatonic emphasis on purification, he makes the attainment of self-knowledge and union dependent upon a conversion from the world of the senses to the pure intelligibles.'[152]

There is at least one place in *Mishneh torah* where these components come together most strikingly, and that is the well-known passage at the end of the *Book of Purity* where Maimonides makes the Jewish laws of purity symbolic of

---

[147] 'Laws of the Foundations of the Torah', 4: 8–9.
[148] Altmann, 'Delphic Maxim', 29–30. See also Armstrong, 'Apprehension of Divinity'.
[149] Altmann, 'Delphic Maxim', 31.
[150] *Studien über Salomon ibn Gabirol* (Budapest, 1899), 17–51—Altmann's citation.
[151] Altmann, 'Delphic Maxim', 34.   [152] Ibid. 35.

the purification of the soul, in what is possibly the most Neoplatonic moment in all of *Mishneh torah*:

It is plain and manifest that the laws about impurity and purity are decrees laid down by Scripture and not matters about which human understanding is capable of forming a judgment . . . Nevertheless, we may find some indication [for the moral basis] of this: just as one who sets his heart on becoming pure becomes pure as soon as he has immersed himself, although nothing new has befallen his body, so, too, one who sets his heart on purifying himself from the impurity that besets men's souls—namely wrongful thoughts and bad character traits—becomes clean as soon as he consents in his heart to shun those counsels and brings his soul into the waters of intellect [*da'at*]. Behold, Scripture says, 'And I will sprinkle pure water upon you and you shall be pure; from all your impurity and from all your idols will I purify you' (Ezek. 36: 25).[153]

The division of the human personality into 'soul' and 'intellect' is a remarkably clear reflection of the hierarchy that in Neoplatonic thought exists both in the cosmos and in man.[154] We may take it that by 'soul' and 'intellect' here Maimonides means the same as he does in 'Laws of the Foundations of the Torah', 4: 8, where the soul is what moves creatures to eat, drink, procreate, feel, and think, while the intellect is the uniquely human capacity for higher thought and apprehension of non-physical beings. But man's soul, though it performs the same functions as the souls of animals, remains different from theirs, uniquely human, taking its form, or at least capable of taking its form, from the intellect. The process described at the end of the *Book of Purity* sounds very like the soul turning away from the things of

---

[153] 'Laws of Immersion Pools', 11: 12. The Yale translation, by Danby, gives 'and false convictions' for the Hebrew *vede'ot hara'ot*. In other places in *Mishneh torah* where this phrase occurs, it is clear from the context that it refers to character and dispositions rather than beliefs (see 'Laws of Ethical Qualities', 2: 1; 'Laws of Repentance', 4: 5; 'Laws of Forbidden Foods', 16: 12; 'Laws of Sales', 15: 13). In *Guide* i. 2 (pp. 24–5) Maimonides himself states that the terms 'good' and 'bad' belong only in the realm of moral judgement, and not in the realm of intellectual apprehension, where true and false apply. On this basis, *ra* (bad) cannot qualify *de'ah* in the sense of opinion. Moreover, the word for 'soul' here, *nefesh*, is used in contradistinction to *da'at* meaning intellect, and it therefore seems that by 'soul' is meant the animal soul, the seat of the emotions and appetites that give rise to character traits—see 'Laws of the Foundations of the Torah', 4: 8. The translation of *vede'ot hara'ot* has therefore been emended to 'and bad character traits'. In 'Eight Chapters', 2, the rational part may bring about obedience and disobedience, but commandment and transgression do not apply: 'the moral virtues are to be found only in the appetitive part'. On the term *de'ot*, see Septimus, 'What Did Maimonides Mean by *Madda*?', 97–100, and Kreisel, '*Imitatio Dei* in "Guide"', 207 n. 90. Septimus points out that, in a letter to Ibn Tibbon, rather than using the word *de'ot*, Maimonides proposed *madaot mutot* for erroneous opinions ('What Did Maimonides Mean by *Madda*?', 92). More generally, see Nuriel, 'Maimonides' Epistemology', 42–3; Pines, 'Truth and Falsehood'. For a qualifying view, see Kellner, 'Virtue of Faith'.   [154] See also 'Eight Chapters', 1.

the sentient world and resting, purified, in the intellect. The closing quotation from Ezekiel both justifies the metaphor, since it associates purification through water with ideological purification, and also brings the entire process under the rubric of knowledge of God, purification from idols being an intellectual rather than a moral process, and meaning, ultimately, the divorcement of one's notion of God from any material connotation, which is the negative path to the knowledge of God discussed above.

This *halakhah* really offers a Neoplatonic alternative to 'Laws of Ethical Qualities' and 'Laws of Repentance', for it describes moral regeneration as something achieved instantly through the reunification of soul and intellect, without the process prescribed by the former of countering an undesirable extreme by going to the opposite extreme,[155] and without the process prescribed by the latter of reform, remorse, and confession,[156] at the same time implying that the ultimate source of purification is a flow from God. Of course one can try to reconcile matters by saying that 'Laws of Immersion Pools', 11: 12, sets us on the right course but leaves work to do. As ever, though, what is interesting is Maimonides' presentation, and in that respect this *halakhah* will be of key importance in later chapters when we come to consider Neoplatonic motifs in the structure of *Mishneh torah* as a whole. For the time being, it is sufficient to note that it provides the purification component of the Neoplatonic element that Altmann identifies as characterizing the medieval Islamic and Jewish interpretation of the *hadith* 'He who knows himself knows his Lord'. In this chapter, I shall concentrate on the first two elements.

Alghazali and Ibn Zadik

Taken separately, each of these two elements—man as microcosm and man in the image of God—is interesting and worthy, but somehow inert. Combined, they become explosive. This is what happens in perhaps the most subtle treatment of the knowledge-of-God-through-self idea that Altmann mentions, and the closest to Maimonides, namely, that of Alghazali.

Alghazali, Altmann finds, combined three elements of Islamic and Hellenic thought to create a coherent account of how knowledge of the self can confer knowledge of God. In the first place, there is the Delphic maxim itself. Secondly, there is the *hadith*, 'Allah created Adam in his image'. Thirdly, there is the idea of man as microcosm:

---

[155] 'Laws of Ethical Qualities', 2: 2.   [156] 'Laws of Repentance', 2: 2.

The microcosm motif is one which seems to have been very dear to al-Ghazali. We find it in the *Mizan al-Amal*: 'It is an effect of the mercy of God that man is a copy *en miniature* of the form of the universe; by contemplating it he comes to know God'. The *Imla* offers a detailed list of correspondences between man as a microcosm and the world at large. But it is hard to see how the knowledge of the macrocosm achieved by introspection can yield a knowledge of God. Al-Ghazali therefore adds that it is the soul which by virtue of her kinship with God leads us to the knowledge of the Creator. The soul, he says distinctly, and hereby reflects Plato's view, is the essence of man, and thus the *hadith* describing man as created in the image of God must be understood to refer to the soul of man. Hence, we conclude, only he who knows his soul knows his Lord.[157]

Altmann goes on to discuss Alghazali's treatment of this theme in the treatise *Mishkat al-Anwar*, where it apparently takes a more mystical turn. 'Man in the image of God here', Altmann writes, 'therefore, means the intellect as "a pattern of the attributes of Allah".'[158]

The ultimate application of man in the image of God is a mystical sense of unity with God: 'it is noteworthy that al-Ghazali considered, albeit for a fleeting moment and with great hesitation, the possibility of understanding the *hadith* about man being in the image of God and, obviously, also the *hadith* about self-knowledge, in terms of an ultimate identity'.[159]

How far down this road would Maimonides be prepared to travel? The answer could be, quite far. All the elements that make up Alghazali's teaching are present in 'Laws of the Foundations of the Torah' and 'Laws of Ethical Qualities': man as microcosm, represented symbolically, as we have seen; man created in the image of God in respect of his essence; contemplation of the universe as a route to the knowledge of God; and, in a modification of the formula quoted above, the attributes of God's actions as a pattern for man's character. In short, if we put all these elements together, we have a composite not unlike the formula of Alghazali as Altmann describes it. Through symbolic form, then, Maimonides becomes a subscriber to both phases of Alghazali's treatment of the microcosm idea: that it is because he is a microcosm that the contemplation of the universe can lead man to knowledge of God; and that in the correct alignment of his or her personality through the application of intellect, which I think is what Maimonides would understand by knowing one's soul, a human being attains that degree of the knowledge of God of which humans are capable.[160]

[157] Altmann, 'Delphic Maxim', 9.   [158] Ibid. 11.   [159] Ibid.
[160] Further on the relationship between Maimonides and Alghazali see Eran, 'Al-Ghazali and

A further possible influence on Maimonides in this regard is Joseph Ibn Zadik, who was a contemporary of Maimonides' father in Córdoba. Ibn Zadik himself, according to Altmann, was influenced by Isaac Israeli. Of Ibn Zadik's *Olam katan*, Altmann writes:

It quotes Israeli's definition of philosophy as self-knowledge by which man 'knows everything' . . . and adds: 'And this is the science of philosophy, which is the science of sciences and their final purpose, because it is the preliminary step (*madregah*) and road (*shebhil*) to the knowledge of the Creator and Initiator of everything, blessed and exalted be He'. In another passage, which once more quotes Israeli's definition of philosophy as self-knowledge, he adds: 'and he will thence reach the knowledge of his Creator, as it is written in Job (19: 26), "And from my flesh I shall behold God."'[161] This verse, we have already noted, represents the Jewish version, so to speak, of the *hadith* formula, 'He who knows himself, knows his Lord'. Joseph ibn Saddiq thus interprets this saying to mean that by knowing oneself as a microcosm one will eventually know God.[162]

It is true that, in his letter to Ibn Tibbon, Maimonides denied having seen Ibn Zadik's *Olam katan*.[163] Nevertheless, he expressed esteem for the man and his work, and it may reasonably be supposed that the ideas in *Olam katan* were discussed in his youthful milieu.

The point on this road at which Maimonides would definitely stop is where it takes a turn towards mystical union with God. This for Maimonides is anathema. Human beings cannot escape the material condition that places a barrier between them and the divine. The awe of God, which is induced by that condition, acts as a brake on the love of God that would seek union.[164] Even when it is a matter of a person's self-knowledge, the limitation that human knowledge and God's knowledge have only the word in common still applies, ruling out any possibility of merger.[165] In Maimonides, therefore, the idea of knowledge of God through knowledge of self must be interpreted as working strictly by analogy.

Maimonides on the World to Come', and S. Harvey, 'Alghazali and Maimonides and their Books of Knowledge'. Neither comments on the particular issue of knowledge of God through the self.

[161] It was also a locus for medieval Spanish Hebrew poetry on the theme of knowledge of God through self-knowledge—see Tanenbaum, *The Contemplative Soul*, 160–73.

[162] 'Delphic Maxim', 23. See also Ibn Zaddik, *Ha'olam hakatan*. The passages to which Altmann refers are on pp. 54 and 77 of Haberman's translation.   [163] *Letters*, ed. Shailat (Heb.), 552.

[164] Hartman puts it thus: 'For Maimonides, intellectual love of God does not lead to a condition of mystic union in which man transcends the awareness of his humanity. Yirah implies that man is conscious of himself as a creature even during moments of intellectual communion' (*Maimonides: Torah and Philosophic Quest*, 208). See also Kreisel, *Maimonides' Political Thought*, 265.

[165] *Guide* iii. 20 (pp. 481–2).

A Circle Completed

This brings us full circle. In trying to understand 'Laws of the Foundations of the Torah', 4: 8, we found that intellectual virtue meant a likeness to God by analogy to God's unity producing a likeness to the separate intellects through identity. In interpreting moral virtue as the knowledge of God through self-knowledge, we have found the reverse process: likeness by identity produces likeness by analogy, in that assimilation to the attributes of God's actions produces in a human being a simulacrum of God's unity.[166]

We thus have a solution to the problem with which we started, of how to fulfil the command to know a God who is unknowable, and without violating the doctrine of negative attributes. The virtuous person who inwardly replicates God's governance, who is to himself or herself as God is to the world, is in a state of knowledge, but can say nothing about that knowledge, for it lies in the unutterable whole that is greater than the sum of the analysable parts. God is known, but remains without attributes.

Absence in the *Guide*

This suggests two reasons why Maimonides should have conveyed the microcosm–macrocosm theory only indirectly in *Mishneh torah*, when there is nothing in the theory itself to which anyone would take exception. As expressed in the *Book of Knowledge*, the idea of knowledge of God through knowledge of the self that follows from the microcosm idea is very much Maimonides' own, its outline delimited by the framework of his theology. The risk that he might be misconstrued as implying something that breaches that framework and strays into mysticism would have been a strong incentive for him to keep his version of the idea well hidden.

A more profound reason may be precisely the ineffability of the experience: it is conveyed symbolically because it is something that cannot be said, but only shown.[167]

Of course the simplest reason for the idea of knowledge of God through self-knowledge not being obvious in *Mishneh torah* would be that it is not there. Two concrete objections that might be raised to the above analysis are the lack of any reference to the *locus classicus* for the idea in the Jewish tradi-

---

[166] Ivry has described the function of *imitatio Dei* in Maimonides in similar terms: '"assimilation" to God's ways, to his actions, is the highest form of conjunction with the divine, for it is identification with the totality of being, through an endorsement of the seemingly particular' ('Neoplatonic Currents in Maimonides', 134).   [167] See above, Introduction, n. 27.

tion, Job 19: 26, 'And from my flesh I shall behold God',[168] and the absence of the idea in the *Guide*. Maimonides' failure to allude to it in *Guide* i. 72, where he discusses the microcosm–macrocosm theory, is a particular embarrassment.

As far as Job 19: 26 is concerned, that verse tended to be a starting point for anthropomorphic and mystical versions of the idea, whereas, according to my reading, Maimonides presents a rational version that is very much his own; good enough reason for him to avoid Job.

As for the absence in the *Guide*, one explanation that offers itself is Davidson's thesis that Maimonides' view of *imitatio Dei* changed between *Mishneh torah* and the *Guide*, from seeing it as the inculcation of an inward state of moral virtue through the imitation of God's actions to seeing it as the imitation of God's impassivity, so that moral virtue applies to actions only, not to the inner self. The idea of knowledge of God through self depends upon moral virtue being, fundamentally, an inward quality, an ordering of the personality that, in my interpretation, reflects the structure of the cosmos. Once that inwardness is extracted from the formula, the knowledge-of-God-through-self effect disappears. This solution is highly advantageous, for demonstrating why the *Guide* is not a friendly environment for the idea serves to highlight why *Mishneh torah* is.

Unfortunately, as convenient as it appears to be, Davidson's thesis cannot be accepted as a ready-made solution to our problem without qualification. Davidson finds a three-phase process in the *Guide*. Moral virtue is a requisite for even starting on the path to intellectual virtue, and it takes a struggle to acquire it, but once a peak of intellectual virtue has been reached, moral virtue flows naturally. Davidson puts it thus:

Human perfection, by the higher standard of the *Guide*, contains three moments: the extirpation of all psychological characteristics, the acquisition of scientific knowledge culminating in knowledge of God, and the overflowing of man's knowledge of God into actions towards others which are modeled upon God's acts.[169]

In *Mishneh torah*, one can take it, Davidson sees only two moments: moral perfection, followed by intellectual perfection, for as he says, 'On one particular, Maimonides remained firm throughout his writings: The ultimate human perfection is knowledge of God.'[170] However, since it was argued above that, through its structure, the *Book of Knowledge* also conveys 'the

---

[168] Kafih (*The Hebrew Bible in Maimonides*) records no reference to this verse in any of Maimonides' writings.   [169] Davidson, 'Middle Way', 72.   [170] Ibid. 59.

overflowing of man's knowledge of God into action towards others which are modelled upon God's acts', that is to say, moral virtue consequent upon intellectual virtue as well as preparatory for it, the demarcation between *Mishneh torah* and the *Guide* has been blurred. Moreover, the very presence of the microcosm–macrocosm theory in the *Guide*, even if its scope there may be narrower than in *Mishneh torah*, contradicts the idea of *imitatio Dei* through the extirpation of feeling, for it places a positive value on human characteristics. If a human being's dispositions, emotions, and appetites constitute a small world, then he or she should maintain that world, just as God's existence maintains the universe. In short, the similarity we have found between *Mishneh torah* and the *Guide* on moral virtue, and the stress laid upon microcosm–macrocosm theory, make it difficult to adopt the solution to our problem offered by Davidson's thesis and remain consistent. Instead, we shall have recourse to the genre difference between *Mishneh torah* and the *Guide*.

To begin with, let us return to the problem of 'in our image, after our likeness'. As mentioned, it is discussed in the very first chapter of the *Guide*, but in *Mishneh torah* it does not appear until the fourth. Instead, *Mishneh torah* opens thus: 'The foundation of foundations and the pillar of the sciences is to know that there is a First Being who brought all existing things into being.'

This is a heroic opening. The setting of 'Laws of the Foundations of the Torah', 1: 1, is the cosmos; the setting of *Guide* i. 1, one could say, is the city[171]—perhaps a seminar room in the university in the city. No value judgement is implied by this. It is simply a way of stating, though the main evidence is yet to come, that *Mishneh torah* has the energy and tension of epic poetry, as opposed to the more urbane subtleties of the *Guide*—which is not to deny the *Guide* its urgency. In both cases, the theme introduced at the start is the connection between God and the human mind. In the *Guide*, the connection is made by interpreting a biblical expression about likeness to God as the workings of intellect, a likeness that is not a likeness. From there, the *Guide*, or at least the first part of it, is largely a process of emptying out, the dissociation of the divine from materially derived concepts and false ideas.[172] In *Mishneh torah*, by contrast, the human connection with the First Being is initially forged through a connection between knowledge as a commandment and 'all existing things', from which point it is a filling up of existence with the divine,

---

[171] Hence the parable of the palace in *Guide* iii. 51 (pp. 618–20). The subject of the city also includes the desire to escape the city into solitude. See S. Harvey, 'Maimonides in the Sultan's Palace'.

[172] Strauss characterizes Part I of the *Guide* as 'negative and pre-philosophic', while 'the Second and Third Parts are positive or edifying' ('How to Begin to Study *The Guide*', p. lii).

via the commandments.[173] In short, *Mishneh torah* goes from God to the world, while the *Guide* goes from the world, or even the word, to God.

Looked at this way, the idea of the human intellect as a gift from God, as expressed in 'Laws of the Foundations of the Torah', 4: 9, is not a simplification; it flows from God as the origin of all existing things, and the form of all forms; it is part of the onrush of the divine that is *Mishneh torah*'s poetic momentum.[174]

One instance that illustrates the genre difference very clearly is the different treatments of the laws of purity in *Mishneh torah* and the *Guide*. In *Mishneh torah*, as we have seen, these laws are given a symbolic significance, and signify the washing away of wrongful thoughts and bad character traits by the waters of intellect. No such significance for the laws of purity is to be found in the *Guide*. There, they are rationalized as being designed to prevent over-familiarity with the Temple, the impure being barred from entry there.[175] Does that mean that Maimonides decided he was mistaken to have thought of purification in symbolic terms? Not at all. In both cases, he avoids assigning intrinsic value to the laws of purity, but in *Mishneh torah* he gives a positive, transcendent, personal reason for them, while in the *Guide* he gives a negative, prosaic reason of policy.

What is true of the overt symbolism of *Mishneh torah*'s explanation for the laws of purity could easily be true of the covert symbolism of the parallel structures of 'Laws of the Foundations of the Torah' and 'Laws of Ethical Qualities': it represents man becoming in the image of God, and thereby arriving at the knowledge of God, in the fullness of his being. It has no place in the *Guide*, which drives towards closeness to God via negative cognition.[176]

---

[173] Fullness is, of course, the closing image in *Mishneh Torah*: 'For the earth shall be full of the knowledge of the Lord' ('Laws of Kings and Their Wars', 12: 5).

[174] On the subject of the point of origin, it is possible that the acrostic spelling out of the name of God that lurks in *Mishneh torah*'s first four words, and perhaps even the architectural metaphor of foundations and a pillar, indicate that our understanding of the connection between the human mind and God will develop through some kind of latent symbolism.   [175] See *Guide* iii. 47 (pp. 593–4).

[176] That said, the structure of the *Guide* may nevertheless be significant in this respect, for it can be analysed into the same sequence of themes as found in 'Laws of the Foundations of the Torah' and 'Laws of Ethical Qualities'. Chapters i. 1 to i. 68 of the *Guide* deal with theology; i. 69 is a kind of bridge. Chapters i. 70 to iii. 7 deal with the stars and spheres. This section is framed by the idea of the chariot. It begins with a lexicographical chapter on *rakhov*, 'to ride' (the root of *merkavah*, 'chariot'), that refers to various biblical passages about chariots, including a reference to 'the throne of glory' that 'was borne by four animals' (i.e. Ezek. 1), and purports to demonstrate that 'chariot' means four horses, a prelude to the expatiation on the cosmic significance of the number four in ii. 10. The section ends with the explication of Ezek. 1 and *ma'aseh hamerkavah* in iii. 1–7. Chapters iii. 8 to iii. 24 deal with sublunary matters; and chapters iii. 25 to the end deal with action, particularly the

The analysis of the structure of 'Laws of the Foundations of the Torah' and 'Laws of Ethical Qualities' as a microcosm–macrocosm pattern seems fairly certain, and it will receive reinforcement in the next chapter when we look at the structure of *Mishneh torah* as a whole. Interpretation is another matter, but the idea of knowledge of God through self-knowledge fits the pattern itself, as well as other motifs we have examined, and is in line with Maimonides' generally holistic approach to human perfection. I propose that in *Mishneh torah* he took the idea of knowledge of God through knowledge of self, rationalized it, and adapted it to his purposes, providing for a relationship between the whole person and God without violating philosophical principles.

In Maimonides' Workshop

'Laws of Ethical Qualities' is not Maimonides' first essay on moral virtue. In many ways, 'Eight Chapters' is an early draft. It will be interesting to examine at least some of the changes between the earlier treatment and the later one, with a view to determining whether there is a traceable line of development that might encourage us to believe that Maimonides was indeed tending towards the idea of knowledge of God through the self, rather than it being a sudden efflorescence in the *Book of Knowledge*.

One difference between 'Eight Chapters' and 'Laws of Ethical Qualities' lies in the ways in which Maimonides uses certain biblical and talmudic quotations. This affords an intriguing glimpse into his workshop. In particular, his varying treatment of the verse 'And thou shalt love the Lord thy God with

commandments. (Here the division coincides with that of Strauss. In Strauss's plan of the *Guide*, too, beginnings and ends of thematic sections do not necessarily coincide with the original division of the work into parts. R. Nissim ben Reuben of Gerona suggested a slightly different division of the *Guide* to the one put forward here, but based on a similar principle (see W. Z. Harvey, 'Maimonides' Critical Epistemology', 233 n. 46).) Most importantly, the *Guide*'s first chapter is about man in the image of God in the bare sense of man possessing intellect, while its final chapter is about man in the image of God in the full-blown sense of actualization of the intellect and the realization of *imitatio Dei*. The *Guide* may be regarded as a journey from the one to the other, thereby replicating in linear, discursive fashion the simultaneous, symbolic relationship between 'Laws of the Foundations of the Torah', 1–5, and 'Laws of Ethical Qualities', 1–5.

See also Rawidowicz, 'The Structure of the *Guide*' (Heb.). Rawidowicz treats each part of the *Guide* as a discrete unit, but he comments on *Guide* i. 1 to the effect that the beginning has the end in mind, in that, since in Part III it would explain the reasons for the commandments, it had to begin by clearing away error, of which misunderstanding of the idea of man in God's image was the source—see 'The Structure of the *Guide*' (Heb.), 243. It is as though Maimonides had to separate God and man conceptually before he could join them through a human being's imitation of God's actions.

all thy heart and with all thy soul and with all thy might'[177] in 'Eight Chapters' and the *Book of Knowledge*, and later on in the *Guide*, including one revealing oversight concerning his own oeuvre, enables us to follow some of the turns his thinking took, and also serves as a tracer of the development of his literary skill.

After a discussion in chapters 1 to 4 of the distinction between moral and intellectual virtue, the various faculties of the soul, and the doctrine of the mean, chapter 5 of 'Eight Chapters' opens as follows:

Man needs to subordinate all his soul's powers to thought, in the way we set forth in the previous chapter, and to set his sight on a single goal: the perception of God (may He be glorified and magnified), I mean knowledge of Him, in so far as that lies within man's power. He should direct all his actions, both when in motion and at rest, and all his conversation toward this goal so that none of his actions is in any way frivolous, I mean an action not leading to this goal. For example, he should make his aim only the health of his body when he eats, drinks, sleeps, has sexual intercourse, is awake, and is in motion or at rest. The purpose of his body's health is that the soul find its instruments healthy and sound in order that it can be directed toward the sciences and toward acquiring the moral and rational virtues, so that he might arrive at that goal.[178]

This depicts an instrumental relationship between moral virtue and intellectual virtue. Subordinating physical functions to the intellect means not letting appetite run amok to the detriment of one's health, for only a healthy body will allow the mind to pursue its proper function. Neither moral virtue nor intellectual virtue can begin until appetite is under control. A little later on in the same chapter, however, it emerges that the exercise of the intellect's control over the appetites is intrinsically worthwhile:[179]

On the basis of this reasoning, the art of medicine is given a very large role with respect to the virtues, the knowledge of God, and attaining true happiness. To study it diligently is among the greatest acts of worship. It is, then, not like weaving and carpentry, for it enables us to perform our actions so that they become human actions, leading to the virtues and the truths. For if a man sets out to eat appetizing food which is pleasant to the palate and which has an agreeable odor, but is harmful and could be the cause of grave illness or eventually of destruction, then this man and the beasts are alike. That is not the action of a man insofar as he is a man. Indeed it is the action of a man insofar as he is an animal: *He is like the beasts that perish* [Ps. 49: 13 and 21].

---

[177] Deut. 6: 5.   [178] *Ethical Writings*, ed. Weiss and Butterworth, 75.

[179] On the basis of Eliezer Hadad's analysis of actions that are purposeful, and to a good purpose, being reflective of God's actions in nature, the purposefulness called for in the first passage can also be seen as intrinsically valuable. (See Hadad, 'Nature and Torah in Maimonides' (Heb.), 19 ff.)

A human action [requires] taking only what is most useful: one sometimes leaves the most pleasant aside and eats what is most repugnant, with a view to seeking what is most useful. This is an action based upon thought and distinguishes man in his actions from what is unlike him.[180]

It is in respect of intellect, we should remind ourselves once more, that man has the form of man and is created in the image of God. We see in this passage that in the very exercise of intellect in governing appetite, a human being realizes his or her form and fulfils the meaning of man created in God's image, and that such discipline is not just preparatory.

Maimonides goes on to state that all activity, whether physical or intellectual, should have as its end attaining 'knowledge of the truth of the existence of God, blessed be he'.

At the end of chapter 5, this teleology of virtue is given intense expression:

This is what the Exalted requires that we make as our purpose when He says: *And you shall love the Lord your God with all your heart and with all your soul.* He means, set the same goal for all the parts of your soul, namely to love the Lord your God. The prophets, peace be upon them, have also urged this purpose. He [Solomon] said: *In all your ways know Him* [Prov. 3: 6]. The *sages* explained this and said: *Even with a transgression* [BT *Ber.* 63*a*]; i.e., you should make your goal the truth when doing such a thing, even if from a certain point of view you commit a transgression. The *sages*, peace be upon them, summarized this whole notion in the briefest possible words and encompassed the meaning with utmost perfection, so that if you were to consider the brevity of those words—how they express the greatness and magnificence of this notion in its entirety, about which so many works have been composed without being able to grasp it—then you would know it was undoubtedly spoken by divine power. This is what they say in one of their commands in this tractate: *Let all your deeds be for the sake of Heaven* (Mishnah *Avot* 4: 27).[181]

This is a level of spirituality which, a little earlier in the same chapter, Maimonides states is tantamount to prophecy, a state of suffusion of the entire personality with the love and knowledge of God. We have come a long way from the self-contained Aristotelian ideal, but we have also come closer to the idea of knowledge of God through the self.

In *Mishneh torah*, we find that the second and third proof-texts employed in this passage turn up again, in 'Laws of Ethical Qualities', 3: 3:

Even when he sleeps and seeks repose, to calm his mind and rest his body, so as not to fall sick and be incapacitated from serving God, his sleep is service of the Almighty. In

---

[180] *Ethical Writings*, ed. Weiss and Butterworth, 75–6.   [181] Ibid. 78.

this sense our wise men charged us, 'Let all your deeds be for the sake of heaven'. And Solomon in his wisdom said, 'In all thy ways acknowledge Him'.[182]

The texts are the same, but their order is reversed. The order in 'Eight Chapters' could be a matter of Maimonides respecting a traditional hierarchy: he first cites a text from the Torah, then one from Proverbs, and concludes with one from the Talmud. On the other hand, he presents the talmudic text as climactic: it is a summary expressing 'greatness and magnificence' and is 'said with divine power'. Either way, the order is not haphazard, and so its reversal in 'Laws of Ethical Qualities' calls for comment.

One effect of the reversal is that it creates an end-rhyme with the preceding chapter of 'Laws of Ethical Qualities', the final *halakhah* of which concludes:[183]

Thus our wise men said, 'Envy, lust and ambition take a man from the world'.[184] In fine, in every class of dispositions, a man should choose the mean so that all one's dispositions shall occupy the exact middle between the extremes. This is what Solomon expressed in the text, 'Let all thy ways be established'.[185]

These two passages have similar formats, each presenting a quotation from Mishnah *Avot*,[186] followed by one from Proverbs. In the Hebrew, the two quotations from Proverbs are even closer sounding than they are in translation: *vekhol derakhekha yikonu* ('Let all thy ways be established'); *bekhol derakhekha da'ehu* ('In all thy ways acknowledge Him'). The similarity serves to highlight the difference: the movement from attaining the mean to the purpose of attaining the mean. The transition involves a heightened degree of inwardness and intensity, and possibly even a move away from moral virtue as preparatory to knowledge of God to moral virtue as a consequence of such knowledge.

This point will become clearer if the two quotations from Proverbs are expanded. Here is the first in its context in Proverbs 4:

25. Let thine eyes look right on, and let thine eyelids look before thee. 26. Ponder the path of thy foot, and let all thy ways be established. 27. Turn not to the right nor to the left: remove thy foot from evil.

Here is the second, from Proverbs 3:

---

[182] In the Or Vishua edition this passage forms a separate paragraph.
[183] 'Laws of Ethical Qualities', 2: 7.   [184] Mishnah *Avot* 4: 27.   [185] Prov. 4: 26.
[186] The first part of 'Laws of Ethical Qualities', 2: 7, not cited here, contains an additional quotation from *Avot*.

5. Trust in the Lord with all thine heart and lean not unto thine own understanding. 6. In all thy ways acknowledge him, and he shall direct thy paths.[187]

There is no doubt that quoting from the first verse makes an appropriate conclusion to chapter 2 of 'Laws of Ethical Qualities', which is about directing one's temperament to the middle path, and turning 'not to the right nor to the left', while quoting from the second is appropriate to chapter 3, which is about dedicating all actions to the acquisition of knowledge. At the same time, it is possible to interpret the first verse as being about following the right path through deliberation and willpower, while the second is about following the right path intuitively because of closeness to, or knowledge of, God, since, for Maimonides, 'he shall direct thy paths' can only mean divine providence 'consequent upon the intellect' as per *Guide* iii. 17, or moral virtue consequent upon intellectual virtue, as per *Guide* iii. 54. Within 'Laws of Ethical Qualities' 3: 3 itself, the revised order of the quotations represents an intensification, a progression from moral virtue as instrumental, a preparation for acquiring knowledge of God, to moral virtue as being of intrinsic value. 'Let all your deeds be for the sake of heaven' implies separation between deeds and Heaven, as in sleeping in order to be refreshed for doing Heaven's work. '*In* all thy ways acknowledge Him' implies coalescence of ways and knowledge, a movement to moral virtue as an inward state. Placing this verse at the end of its chapter as a summarizing conclusion may be seen as a shorthand way of making the argument we saw in 'Eight Chapters', that control of the appetites is what makes human beings human, and of connecting such self-governance with the ultimate realization of the human form, the knowledge of God, not just as a means to that end, but as participating in it.

Perhaps this is to over-freight our texts, but the comparison with 'Eight Chapters' does give some confidence that Maimonides deliberately redeployed the references from the earlier work in order to bring out their potential significance, and that the nuances are not imaginary. What is certain is that, through the rearrangement of those references as much as anything else, the discussion in 'Eight Chapters' becomes in 'Laws of Ethical Qualities' something altogether more poetic: compact, cross-connected, rhythmic.

At any rate, conspicuous by its absence from 'Laws of Ethical Qualities' is the first reference from 'Eight Chapters' to 'And thou shalt love the Lord thy God with all thy heart and all thy soul and all thy might'. This absence could

---

[187] In 'Laws of Ethical Qualities', 2: 7, the Huntington MS gives the whole of Prov. 4: 26, whereas the Or Vishua edition gives only the latter half. Similarly, in 'Laws of Ethical Qualities', 3: 3, the Huntington MS gives the whole of Prov. 3: 6; the Or Vishua edition only the first half.

be seen as weakening the thesis being put forward here, for in *Mishneh torah* it is precisely this text that is associated with intellectual virtue. In both 'Laws of the Foundations of the Torah', 2: 1, and 'Laws of Repentance', 10: 2, where it is cited, love of God and knowledge of God are made almost equivalent. If Maimonides wanted to hint that moral virtue can constitute knowledge of God, should he not have carried over this text about love from 'Eight Chapters' to 'Laws of Ethical Qualities', chapter 3?

This is where Maimonides makes an interesting error, for when he wrote the *Guide* he apparently thought that he had done so. This is what he says about the verse in question in *Guide* i. 39:

As for the dictum of Scripture: *And thou shalt love the Lord thy God with all thy heart*—in my opinion its interpretation is: with all the forces of your heart; I mean to say, with all the forces of the body, for the principle of all of them derives from the heart. Accordingly the intended meaning is, as we have explained in the Commentary on the *Mishnah* and in *Mishneh torah*, that you should make His apprehension the end of all your actions.[188]

The reference to the *Commentary on the Mishnah* is correct, but in citing *Mishneh torah* as well, Maimonides does seem to betray imperfect recollection of his own work.[189] There, 'the dictum of Scripture' is not at all interpreted as meaning 'that you should make His apprehension the end of all your actions'. In 'Laws of the Foundations of the Torah', chapter 2, and 'Laws of Repentance', chapter 10, the context is knowledge leading to love, not actions imbued with love leading to knowledge (which is the context in 'Eight Chapters'), in fact not actions at all.[190]

---

[188] p. 89.

[189] It could be that there is no error, and that Maimonides is not saying that in *Mishneh torah* he interpreted the verse as meaning 'you should make His apprehension the end of all your actions', but only that in *Mishneh torah* (and in the *Commentary on the Mishnah*) he explained 'that you should make His apprehension the end of all your actions', and now, in the *Guide*, he associates that injunction with the verse 'And thou shalt love'. Professor Joseph Drory, whom I consulted on this point, and whom I thank for his assistance, gave as his opinion that the sense of the original Arabic is in accordance with the former reading.

[190] Schwarz gives a reference to 'Laws of the Foundations of the Torah', 2: 2, but that *halakhah* is clearly about knowledge leading to love, not the other way round, and is certainly not about actions. 'Laws of Repentance', 10: 6, might seem a candidate for Maimonides' reference the way that Hyamson translates it, but it seems to me that Hyamson parses the *halakhah* wrongly.

He gives: 'It is known and certain that the love of God does not become closely knit in a man's heart till he is continuously and thoroughly possessed by it and gives up everything else in the world for it; as God commanded us "with all thy heart and with all thy soul" (Deut. 6.5). One only knows God with the knowledge with which one knows Him. According to the knowledge will be the love.'

I would amend thus: 'It is known and certain that the love of God does not become closely knit in a

A possible explanation is that, between *The Commentary on the Mishnah* and *Mishneh torah*, Maimonides veered towards a stricter separation of moral virtue and intellectual virtue, and the migration of the verse 'And thou shalt love the Lord thy God' from the former to the latter is emblematic of that change of mind, only when he came to write the *Guide* he forgot what he had done, and put the verse back into the moral virtue field. It is also just possible that this verse is hinted at in 'Laws of Ethical Qualities' via a *midrash*, not in chapter 3 but in chapter 1, for *Sifrei* connects it to Genesis 18: 19 concerning Abraham, 'For I know him, that he will command his children and his household after him, and they shall keep the way of the Lord.' The latter verse is cited in 'Laws of Ethical Qualities', 1: 7, as proof that Abraham taught the doctrine of the middle path. This link may have caused the later Maimonides to make a mistaken association. But another possibility is that Maimonides' memory did not in fact let him down so badly, and that the verse 'And thou shalt love the Lord thy God' actually is meant to be present in 'Laws of Ethical Qualities' 3: 3; it is not written there, but it is projected by the structure. *Mishneh torah* separates out love and knowledge of God on the one hand, and the middle way in ethics and *imitatio Dei* on the other, allowing each realm to be developed powerfully in its own terms. In *Mishneh torah*, the love of God is a passion in its own right, not an adjunct of action, whether small or great. But the two realms are reconnected through the formal parallel between 'Laws of the Foundations of the Torah', chapters 1–5, and 'Laws of Ethical Qualities', chapters 1–5, which are like two transparencies that need to be placed one on top of the other and a light shone through for the whole picture to be seen at once in all its richness and detail. The result is a more sophisticated, more precise, and more profound version of the original message in 'Eight Chapters': the love of God is on a plane with intellectual virtue; it is a stimulus to knowledge and commensurate with knowledge, yet it is also involved in moral virtue, and how a person governs their little world has a bearing on their capacity to understand the governance of the great world and to expand their love. In both 'Eight Chapters' and 'Laws of Ethical Qualities', Aristotle's divine in man is realized on the moral as well as the

man's heart to the point that he is continuously and thoroughly possessed by it as he should be and gives up everything else in the world apart from it as God commanded us "with all thy heart and with all thy soul", unless it be through the knowledge with which one knows Him. According to the knowledge will be the love.' The language of this *halakhah* echoes that of the preceding *halakhah* 3; its message is that only knowledge can lead to the strength and constancy of love described in that *halakhah*. This is a different message from that of *Guide* i. 39. (*Yad peshutah* reads 'Laws of Repentance', 10: 6 in the same way as proposed here.)

intellectual plane. We are back to the cycle: love motivates moral actions for the purpose of acquiring knowledge that stimulates love that translates back into moral actions.

Further tracing of the use of the verse 'And thou shalt love the Lord thy God' in the *Guide* tends to confirm the validity of this approach. At first, Maimonides treats moral virtue in the *Guide* as at best a preparation for intellectual virtue, but separate from it, and inferior to it. In considering the obstacles to the higher reaches of knowledge, he writes:

> The fourth cause is to be found in the natural aptitudes. For it has been explained, or rather demonstrated, that the moral virtues are a preparation for the rational virtues, it being impossible to achieve true, rational acts—I mean perfect rationality—unless it be by a man thoroughly trained with respect to his morals and endowed with the qualities of tranquillity and quiet.[191]

Five chapters later we get the passage quoted above about every act being for the sake of the knowledge of God, where 'And thou shalt love the Lord thy God' is first cited.

In *Guide* iii. 28 Maimonides explains that, while the law commands 'correct opinions through which the ultimate perfection may be obtained', such as belief in God's existence and unity, it does not convey all the theoretical knowledge that supports those opinions. However, he goes on to say,

> With regard to all the other correct opinions concerning the whole of being—opinions that constitute the numerous kinds of all the theoretical sciences through which the opinions forming the ultimate end are validated—the Law, albeit it does not make a call to direct attention toward them in detail as it does with regard to [the opinions forming ultimate ends], does do this in summary fashion by saying: *To Love the Lord.*[192] You know how this is confirmed in the dictum regarding *love*: *With all thy heart, and with all thy soul, and with all thy might.* We have already explained in *Mishneh torah* that this love becomes valid only through the apprehension of the whole of being as it is and through the consideration of His wisdom as it is manifested in it.

Here, Maimonides reflects *Mishneh torah* more accurately—this passage is a fair paraphrase of what he says about love in 'Laws of the Foundations of the Torah', 2: 1–2. The commandment to love God 'with all thy heart, and with all thy soul, and with all thy might' is firmly associated with intellectual virtue, and is not an attribute of everyday behaviour.

The third citation of this verse occurs in *Guide* iii. 52. This chapter is explicitly about moral virtue flowing from intellectual virtue. The light of the

---

[191] *Guide* i. 34 (pp. 76–7).   [192] Deut. 11: 13 and 22; 19: 9; 30: 6, 16, and 20.

intellect is the light by which a person's conduct is examined at all times, and the awareness of this arouses the fear that induces moral virtue. This is not yet quite the unselfconscious outpouring of goodness from the person who has reached intellectual perfection at the very end of the *Guide*, but it is getting towards it. At the end of the chapter, Maimonides considers how love and fear are promoted by the Torah.

As for the opinions that the *Torah* teaches us—namely the apprehension of His being and His unity, may he be exalted—these opinions teach us love, as we have explained several times. You know to what extent the *Torah* lays stress upon love: *With all thy heart, and with all thy soul, and with all thy might.* For these two ends, namely, *love* and *fear*, are achieved through two things: *love* through the opinions taught by the Law, which include the apprehension of His being as He, may He be exalted, is in truth; while *fear* is achieved by means of all actions prescribed by the Law, as we have explained. Understand this summary.[193]

The orientation of the verse has changed again. In *Guide* iii. 28, the love of God was achieved 'through the apprehension of the whole of being as it is', while here in *Guide* iii. 52 it is achieved through 'the apprehension of His being as He, may He be exalted, is in truth'. There is literally a world of difference between 'being as it is' and 'His being as He is'. In Maimonides' deployment of the verse 'And thou shalt love the Lord thy God' in the *Guide* there is thus a progression from moral virtue to natural science to divine science. The same verse encompasses all three applications of intellect, meaning that all three are modes of the love of God. Love is both the stimulus to and the outcome of knowledge, in the virtuous circle that the *Book of Knowledge* describes.

The morphosis of the interpretation of 'And thou shalt love the Lord thy God' in the *Guide* is in line with Kellner's characterization of that work as a transformative book, aimed at replacing an Aristotelian concept of God with a Neoplatonic one, specifically of replacing the Aristotelian stratification of moral and intellectual virtue with a Neoplatonic flow of one from the other.[194] Again, what is conveyed through progressive argument in the *Guide* is conveyed through symbolic structure in *Mishneh torah*: it is a matter of rhetoric versus poetry.

So structure does for the *Book of Knowledge* what a repeated biblical quotation does for the *Guide*. But the *Book of Knowledge* has its own motifs as well, which complement the structural indications of love permeating all phases of

---

[193] *Guide* iii. 52 (p. 630).

[194] See above, Introduction, n. 246. For a reading of the *Guide* as pointing beyond both rational and imaginative conceptions of God, see Faur, *Homo Mysticus*.

intellect. While, as we have seen, the verse 'And thou shalt love the Lord thy God' is missing from 'Laws of Ethical Qualities', we do find in 'Laws of Ethical Qualities', 3: 2, an allusion to another part of the Shema: 'A man should direct all his thoughts and activities to the knowledge of God, alone. This should be his aim in sitting, rising, and conversation.' This echoes the verse 'and shalt speak of them when thou sittest in thine house and when thou walkest by the way, and when thou liest down, and when thou risest up'.[195] The same allusion is made again in 'Laws of Repentance', 10: 3:

> What is the love of God that is befitting? It is to love the Eternal with a great and exceeding love, so strong that one's soul shall be knit up with the love of God, and one should be continually enraptured by it, like a love-sick individual, whose mind is at no time free from his passion for a particular woman, the thought of her filling his heart at all times, when sitting down or rising up, when he is eating or drinking.

This passage is rich in biblical allusion, almost every word touching off some association. What is translated as 'a great and exceeding love' is in the original *ahavah gedolah yeterah azah ad me'od*, which echoes Song of Songs 8: 6, *azah kamavet ahavah* ('love is as strong as death'). The *Yad peshutah* commentary points out that *ahavah gedolah yeterah* also echoes the paragraph just before the Shema recital in the liturgy. 'One's soul shall be knit up', *nafsho keshurah* in the Hebrew, is from Judah's appeal to Pharaoh to release Benjamin, describing Jacob's love for his youngest son: *nafsho keshurah benafsho* ('his life is bound up in the lad's life');[196] 'and one should be continually enraptured by it', *shogeh bah tamid*, takes us to Proverbs 5: 19: *be'ahavatah tishgeh tamid* ('and be ravished always with her love'); 'like a love-sick individual', *ka'elu holei ahavah* in the original, recalls Song of Songs 2: 5: *ki holat ahavah ani* ('for I am sick with love').[197]

Maimonides' style generally is an allusive one, but the many allusions here create a heightened intensity of expression. They could be regarded as ornament, or as a pulling out of all the rhetorical stops as the *Book of Knowledge* ends with a crescendo of love. They do prepare the aware reader for the comparison of the love of God to the love of a woman. More subtly, they serve to convince the reader that the writer actually feels the kind of love he advocates and presents as a command. He preaches love, and his very language is informed by love. It is as though the *halakhah* has internalized its own message, giving it the authority to instruct. This takes great delicacy. Were it

---

[195] Deut. 6: 7. [196] Gen. 44: 30.
[197] Also S. of S. 5: 8. This reference is made explicit at the end of the *halakhah*.

overdone, it would degenerate into mere floridity, deadening rather than enlivening, and even betraying insincerity. As it is, literal meaning and allusion combine perfectly.

The *halakhah* concludes with explicit references to the Shema, and to the very verse from Song of Songs to which it has already alluded:

Even intenser should be the love of God in the hearts of those who love Him. And this love should continually possess them, even as he commanded us in the phrase, 'with all thy heart and with all thy soul'. This, Solomon expressed allegorically in the sentence, 'for I am sick with love'. The entire Song of Songs is indeed an allegory descriptive of this love.

Such sublimation can be felt in the very first passage in which Maimonides describes the love and awe of God, in 'Laws of the Foundations of the Torah', 2: 2, where a sense of wonder and desire is immediately undercut by an equal and opposite sense of unworthiness.[198] The comparison in 'Laws of Repentance' of the love of God with the love of a woman is not *ad hoc*; it is the surfacing of the deep stream of Maimonides' sense of his relationship to God.

Virtue Ethics and Command Ethics: Abraham and Moses

Maimonides and Aristotle may differ in their views of moral and intellectual virtue, but as one reads through 'Eight Chapters', the discrepancy between the autonomous, reason-based philosophical outlook and the heteronomous, commandment-based religious outlook is not strongly felt.[199] The commandments are presented as aids to keeping to the mean, but no commandment is

---

[198] A further example of sexual sublimation, outside the *Book of Knowledge*, is to be found at the end of 'Laws of Forbidden Intercourse':

A person should be wont to avoid frivolity and drunkenness and lewd talk, which are powerful stimuli and steps towards fornication. Nor should he remain without a wife, for this causes excessive purity. More than all this, they said: a person should devote himself and his thought to words of Torah and broaden his mind with wisdom. For the thought of fornication only holds sway in a heart detached from wisdom. And of wisdom he says: Let her be as the loving hind and pleasant roe; let her breasts satisfy thee at all times; and be thou ravished always with her love (Prov. 5: 19).

On Maimonides' view of sexuality, including discussion of the passages cited here, see Halbertal, *Maimonides* (Heb.), 38–9.

[199] Davidson ('Maimonides' *Shemonah Peraqim*') opines that, at least at the time when he wrote 'Eight Chapters', Maimonides probably did not know Aristotle's *Nicomachean Ethics* directly, but only Alfarabi's rendition of its ideas; Kaplan ('Introduction to "Eight Chapters"') finds evidence to the contrary. The contrast being made here, however, is between Maimonides and Aristotle at the conceptual level; precisely how the Aristotelian concept reached Maimonides is not the point at issue.

invoked enjoining the mean. One chapter follows another in a way that makes the doctrine of the mean as a basis for pursuing the knowledge of God seem a reasonable proposition.

'Laws of Ethical Qualities' brings matters to a head. At first, it follows the Aristotelian doctrine of the mean closely, and describes it empirically, but then it introduces the idea of the mean as a commandment of *imitatio Dei*.[200] Ethics is then no longer a matter of voluntarily seeking excellence according to inner criteria, but of seeking excellence according to external criteria, imposed externally.

Various explanations have been offered for this incongruity.[201] The tension between the autonomous and heteronomous aspects of Maimonides' ethics is nevertheless felt, and becomes acute when we move from the criteria of virtue to the purpose of virtue, which for Aristotle is excellence for its own sake and for Maimonides is pursuit of the knowledge of God, leading to what looks like a crisis, in which Maimonides abruptly abandons the mean, and announces that in the cases of pride and anger, because they cause forgetfulness of God, one should go to extremes of humility and impassivity, contradicting what he has said earlier about those traits.[202]

This is a much-discussed problem; the point here is to see whether the microcosm–macrocosm pattern helps to resolve it.[203]

Let us first observe that, besides that pattern, there is another structural correspondence between 'Laws of Ethical Qualities' and 'Laws of the Foundations of the Torah'. The first chapter of each section has a long lead-in to the commandment on which it hangs. 'Laws of the Foundations of the Torah' states God's existence and proves it from the constant motion of *hagalgal* ('the sphere'), before presenting the commandment 'I am the Lord thy God'. Similarly, 'Laws of Ethical Qualities' discusses the doctrine of the mean in empirical fashion, quite extensively, before introducing the commandment

---

[200] 'Laws of Ethical Qualities', 1: 5–6.

[201] D. S. Shapiro, for example, suggests that the attributes of God are the virtues that a person should cultivate, and the doctrine of the mean is the way of cultivating them and of arriving at the correct measure of each ('Doctrine of the Image of God', 62). One might, then, have expected the commandment of *imitatio Dei* to be mentioned first and the doctrine of the mean second, rather than the other way round. Fox argues that Maimonides and Aristotle both derive the idea of the mean from nature, and that both see the criteria of virtue as external, but that the first locates them in the Torah, and the second in social convention (Fox, 'Doctrine of the Mean').

[202] See 'Laws of Ethical Qualities', 2: 3.

[203] Besides the sources already cited, see Kampinsky, 'Saint and Sage' (Heb.); Kirschenbaum, '*Middat Hasidut*'; Kreisel, 'Asceticism in Ibn Paquda and Maimonides'; Shatz, 'Maimonides' Moral Theory'; Septimus, 'Literary Structure'; Frank, 'Anger as a Vice'; Davidson, 'Middle Way'. On heteronomy versus autonomy in Maimonides more generally, see Twersky, *Introduction to the Code*, 453–9.

'and thou shalt walk in his ways'. Both God's existence and the desirability of the mean were deducible from nature before they were formalized as commandments.[204]

This is brought home in the *Book of Knowledge* by the different roles played by Abraham and Moses.[205] Abraham, as presented by Maimonides, can be regarded as the Jewish Aristotle, a hero who found truth through his powers of speculation. At the close of chapter 1 of 'Laws of Ethical Qualities', he appears as the discoverer of the golden mean:

And as the creator is called by these attributes, which constitute the middle path in which we are to walk, this path is called the Way of God and this is what the patriarch Abraham taught his children, as it is said 'For I know him, that he will charge his children and his household after him, and they shall keep the way of the Lord' (Gen. 18: 19).[206]

The commandment to be like God is thus confirmation of a discovery made independently by Abraham and passed on to his descendants before the commandments were ever given.

In the first chapter of 'Laws of Idolatry', it is through observation of the motion of *hagalgal* that Abraham discovers God and rescues a world in thrall

---

[204] Septimus, in 'Literary Structure', uses this pattern to argue that the doctrine of the mean is the natural law embodied in a commandment of *imitatio Dei*, but that, since the purpose of this commandment, whether intrinsically or instrumentally, is the knowledge of God, then a kind of rabbinical ordinance intervenes in cases where the attempt to follow the mean is liable to defeat the purpose, hence the switch to an outright ban on pride and anger in 'Laws of Ethical Qualities', 2: 3. Precisely such precautionary grounds are given for deviation from the mean in 'Eight Chapters', 4.

This switch can also possibly be seen as reflecting the love–awe polarity. *Imitatio Dei* is a daring notion. It implies the capacity to understand God's ways in nature and to apply them to oneself. This is the confident, unselfconscious, outgoing mood of the initial encounter with nature. The eschewal of pride and anger reflects the sudden evaporation of this mood, followed by the access of fear, as love is overwhelmed by the sense of lowliness and inadequacy. (For an example of *Mishneh torah* presenting the Torah law and then countermanding it with a rabbinic enactment, see 'Laws of Robbery and Lost Property', 5: 5–6.) The upshot is that, contrary to the eradication of pride and anger being the acme of *imitatio Dei*, since God has no emotions, as has been argued (Frank, 'Anger as a Vice'), it is actually the suspension of *imitatio Dei*. The microcosm–macrocosm pattern itself validates emotions, since God sustains and controls the macrocosm rather than eradicating it. A difficulty with this view that must be acknowledged is that Maimonides concludes his discussion of anger not with a simple recommendation or ruling, but by citing a talmudic paean to the person who bears insult and slander without responding ('Laws of Ethical Qualities', 2: 3). The proud Aristotelian gentleman seems to have been completely supplanted as an ideal.

Septimus's article, which is about the importance of literary structure to understanding Maimonides in general, has also been published in a Hebrew version, 'Mivneh veti'un besefer hamada', that cites more examples.

[205] Generally on Abraham and Moses in Maimonides' legal writings see Hartman, *Maimonides: Torah and Philosophic Quest*, 57–65.   [206] 'Laws of Ethical Qualities', 1: 7.

to idolatry.[207] Only at the end of that chapter, after Abraham's descendants have relapsed into idolatry, does Moses appear with commandments that will uproot it.

Abraham features a third time in the *Book of Knowledge*, in 'Laws of Repentance', when he represents the service of God out of love:

This standard is indeed a very high one; not every sage attained to it. It was the standard of the patriarch Abraham whom God called His lover, because he served only out of love. It is the standard which God, through Moses, bids us achieve, as it is said, 'And thou shalt love the Lord thy God'. When one loves God with the right love, he will straightway observe all the commandments out of love.[208]

Once again we have Abraham before Moses—the principle discovered by speculation and later enjoined as a commandment. It should be stressed that this does not make Moses inferior to Abraham: on the contrary, Moses was the greater prophet. He attained superior understanding of nature and of God, and was able to transmit it in more durable form than Abraham's theoretical legacy, through the commandments of the Torah. All the same, he was the recipient of a tradition that Abraham originated. In 'Laws of the Foundations of the Torah', the first four chapters are about Abrahamic theory, while the last four are, largely, about the stature of Moses, but we only have the former thanks to the latter, since, according to the historical account at the beginning of 'Laws of Idolatry', the theory was in danger of being forgotten, and it took Moses to rescue it from oblivion through commandments about knowledge, unity, love, and fear of God that anchor it in a system of law.

At any rate, Abraham is a motif in the *Book of Knowledge* linking the different modes of intellect. After discovering moral science in 'Laws of Ethical Qualities' and natural science in 'Laws of Idolatry', he is presented in 'Laws of Repentance' as a master of divine science, having achieved the utmost in the knowledge of God, such that God calls him 'my lover'. One who reaches such a level will perform the commandments out of love alone. At the end of the *Book of Knowledge* we are in the same position as at the end of the *Guide*, with a portrayal of perfection as a spontaneous outpouring of goodness consequent upon knowledge of God.

It would be fair to say that, in the *Book of Knowledge*, Abraham represents love, in this passage explicitly, but also throughout, in that his intellectual striving is the way to the love of God, so that, by association with Abraham, love accompanies all the phases of virtue. The figure of Abraham thus

---

[207] 'Laws of Idolatry', 1: 3.   [208] 'Laws of Repentance', 10: 2.

performs the same function in the *Book of Knowledge* as the verse 'And thou shalt love the Lord thy God', with its changing interpretations, performs in the *Guide*.[209]

Such love as Abraham's understands the virtues from nature, and finds no tension between autonomous will and heteronomous commandment. The gap between virtue ethics and command ethics is finally closed, however, by the man-as-microcosm theory symbolized by the structural correspondence between 'Laws of the Foundations of the Torah' and 'Laws of Ethical Qualities'. Through it, inner and outer are reconciled, and through it, a human being can rise from the service out of fear of Mosaic law to service out of Abrahamic love. If man is a microcosm, then it is man's nature properly considered, his virtue in the Aristotelian sense, to govern himself in the way that the universe is governed. This can be understood in two, complementary, ways: in the way that Fox understood it, that for Maimonides, as for Aristotle, nature, which always tends towards the mean, provides the theoretical basis for taking the mean as the ideal (although from there Maimonides and Aristotle diverge, the latter seeing the criterion of the mean in social convention, the former in the commandments).[210] It can also be understood as reflecting the fact, already discussed, that 'and thou shalt walk in his ways', the commandment of *imitatio Dei*—which is the religious basis for adopting the mean—is also the motive power of the universe, the revolutions of the spheres being caused by their love of God and desire to become like him. In its explicit statements, in its allusions, in the character of its hero, and in the implications of its form, the *Book of Knowledge* is permeated by love.

So *imitatio Dei* is both a law of the Torah and a law of nature. Conger, who, although he traces its roots to Plato and Aristotle, attributes the first explicit formulation of the man-as-microcosm idea to Philo, comments: 'In general, it may be said that in the works of Philo the chief function of the theory was to help harmonize the Hebrew and Greek views of the world and of man. And

---

[209] Note that, in the *Book of the Commandments*, under positive commandment 3 ('And thou shalt love the Lord thy God'), the love of God is described both as a product of intellectual activity and as the motivation to bring others to God's service, and Abraham is mentioned there as the example of the latter. Bringing people to God's service is the activity Abraham is described as being engaged in in 'Laws of Idolatry', ch. 1. The same verse from Isaiah cited in 'Laws of Repentance', 10: 2, about Abraham as lover of God is cited in the *Book of the Commandments* in connection with that activity. This strengthens the hypothesis that Maimonides intends Abraham to represent the love of God in all his appearances in the *Book of Knowledge*.

See also the characterization of Abraham, in contrast with Balaam, in *Avot* 5: 17 (Order *Nezikin*, 303–4), which also cites the same verse, and Maimonides' commentary thereon.

[210] Fox, 'Doctrine of the Mean'.

linked in, as it were, between these two great bodies of thought, microcosmic theories remained in Jewish philosophy for centuries.'[211] Harmonization of the Hebrew and Greek views of the world and of man, insofar as those views are represented by command ethics and virtue ethics, is precisely the function that the theory performs in Maimonides' *Book of Knowledge.*

We must, however, return to the point where Maimonides has diverged from his supposed model. Once moral virtue is identified as 'the Way of God', it is no longer the genuine Aristotelian article. If God is both the way and the destination, then moral and intellectual virtue really are hardly distinct.

Although Maimonides couches his argument in the Aristotelian terms of the mean and of moral and intellectual virtue, what emerges is something that has at least as much to do with the Plato of the *Timaeus* as the Aristotle of the *Nicomachean Ethics.*[212] It may or may not be the case that, in the *Guide*, Maimonides secretly sides with the Platonic theory of creation out of pre-existent matter that he ostensibly rejects,[213] but it is certainly the case that, in 'Eight Chapters' and 'Laws of Ethical Qualities', man's reason has to contend with his pre-existent material condition, so that a human being plays out within himself the cosmic drama of Reason versus Necessity,[214] accommodating his

[211] Conger, *Theories of Macrocosms and Microcosms*, 19.

[212] Maimonides considered Plato inferior as a thinker to Aristotle, but nevertheless described his works to Samuel ibn Tibbon as 'deep, and in the form of parables' (*Letters*, ed. Shailat (Heb.), 553). If there is any influence from Plato in 'Laws of the Foundations of the Torah' and 'Laws of Ethical Qualities', it seems likely to have come from the *Timaeus*, in the light of Pines's finding that 'In the few passages in the *Guide* in which Plato is explicitly mentioned, the reference is to the *Timaeus* or to some paraphrase or doxographical summary of that dialogue' ('Philosophic Sources', p. lxxv). There is an explicit mention of the *Timaeus* in *Guide* ii. 13 (p. 283). See also Robinson, 'Some Remarks on the Source'. [213] Kraemer suggests, tentatively, that he did—see *Maimonides*, 383–7.

[214] Apropos the *Timaeus*, the expression used for the creator in the passage above about Abraham in 'Laws of Ethical Qualities', 1: 7, is *hayotser*. As far as I am aware, Maimonides uses this term to refer to God in only two other places in *Mishneh torah*. One of them is in 'Laws of the Foundations of the Torah', 1: 7, where he proves the unity of *hayotser* from the constancy of the motion of the diurnal sphere. It is the observation of this constant motion that, in 'Laws of Idolatry', 1: 3, stimulates Abraham to the realization that God is one. In 'Laws of Idolatry', Abraham is depicted as bequeathing metaphysical truth to his descendants, 'the way of truth', while in 'Laws of Ethical Qualities' he bequeaths moral truth, 'the way of God', but both have the same origin, in Abraham's contemplation of the cosmos. The other place is 'Laws of Repentance', 5: 4, where *hayotser* is described as willing free will, just as he willed the vertical motions of the elements and the circular motions of the spheres.

Elsewhere in *Mishneh torah* Maimonides uses *hayotser* to mean a craftsman ('Laws of Forbidden Foods', 16: 23; 'Laws of Sabbatical and Jubilee Years', 8: 5; 'Laws of Slaughter', 14: 11; 'Laws of Utensils', 18: 16; 'Laws of Creditor and Debtor', 9: 1). In neither sense is the word common in the mishnaic literature. My searches have found only one place in that literature where it refers to God (*Avot* 4: 28), besides in citations of Ps. 33: 15 (*RH* 1: 2; Tosefta *RH* 1: 11). Nor, as far as I am aware, is it commonly used as a name for God (as opposed to *yotser* as a description) in later literature. It refers to a craftsman in two places in the Mishnah (*Shevi.* 5: 7; *Shab.* 2: 4). In the light of all this, one cannot

material nature and imposing upon it a unity that is analogous to the incomprehensible unity of the divine.[215] From the point of view of this study, what is most interesting is not so much whose ideas Maimonides combined as the way in which he combined them, through interactions between content and form that result in something uniquely Maimonidean: not dead syncretism, but live art.

Portrait of Perfection

Before leaving the comparison between 'Laws of the Foundations of the Torah' and 'Laws of Ethical Qualities', it is worth taking a final look at the figure of the scholar, which gave rise to the discussion in the first place. Who is he, and what is he doing?

To begin with, although 'Laws of the Foundations of the Torah', 5: 11, and 'Laws of Ethical Qualities', 5: 13, the two *halakhot* cited above that describe the scholar, are collages carefully assembled from many sources, they flow perfectly smoothly. Their cadences and rhythm transmit a surge of feeling. Maimonides' ideal scholar is not just an abstract amalgamation of elevated qualities, but a living whole.[216] And it is possible to trace in his lineaments resemblances to the biblical figures of Abraham and Moses. He is in a way an everyday version of those historical heroes.

help wondering whether Plato's Demiurge, craftsman of the universe, is very far behind *hayotser* of 'Laws of the Foundations of the Torah', 1: 7, 'Laws of Ethical Qualities', 1: 7, and 'Laws of Repentance', 5: 4. See also *Guide* ii. 30 (p. 358), where the verb *yotser* is limited to 'shaping and forming a configuration or to one of the other accidents'. A nearer source for *hayotser* could however be the 99 names of God in the Islamic tradition, possibly *al-musawwir* (The Fashioner). At any rate, in his derivation of the doctrine of the mean from contemplation of the cosmos, Abraham could be thought of as the Jewish Aristotle and the Jewish Plato rolled into one.

We do not have to assume that Maimonides held a Platonic theory of the origin of the world in order to adapt his cosmology as a model of the workings of the soul. Neither Plato nor Maimonides claimed to have penetrated to the objective truth about the relationship of the divine to the world. Plato calls the myth of the Demiurge 'a likely story' (*Timaeus* 29d; Cornford, *Plato's Cosmology*, 23), while Maimonides says he accepts the scriptural account of creation *ex nihilo* and that nothing else is demonstrable, but admits that he has no true knowledge of how the spheres really are or of how God makes them move (*Guide* ii. 24). What is presupposed is that the cosmos does work by correspondences, and so even if any account of the macrocosm is mythical or provisional, insofar as it is coherent, it also provides insight into man's relationship with nature, including his own nature.

[215] 'Despite the fact that our sensible realm is one of multiplicity and in that sense departs from the unity of the Form, the closest approximation to the latter can be achieved by producing order in this multiplicity, making all its elements friendly and harmonious with each other' (Carone, *Plato's Cosmology*, 30).

[216] It is possible that Maimonides' scholar is his answer to Aristotle's encomium to the proud man in *Nicomachean Ethics* iv. 3 (1123a–1125a). At any rate, the comparison is interesting.

He has the Abrahamic trait of bringing people to recognition of the truth. In the source from BT *Yoma* for the *halakhot* about the scholar, we read, 'Abaye explained: As it was taught: "And thou shalt love the Lord thy God", that is, that the Name of Heaven be beloved because of you.' Curiously, in the descriptions of the scholar in our two *halakhot*, the love of God is not mentioned. What we see is the product of the love of God as per Abaye's explanation, namely, that the people love the scholar for his actions, which constitutes sanctification of the name.

It seems that in chapter 5 of 'Laws of the Foundations of the Torah' Maimonides wished to transfer the stress from love to sanctification or holiness, and on this there will be more to say in later chapters. In *The Book of the Commandments*, love is prominent in the exposition of the commandment of sanctification of the name: 'And this is the commandment of sanctification of the name about which all the children of Israel were commanded, meaning that we should surrender ourselves to death at the hands of the oppressor for the love of him may he be exalted and the belief in his uniqueness.'[217] By contrast, in 'Laws of the Foundations of the Torah' chapter 5, the love of God is mentioned directly only in the context of a discussion of transgressions permitted in medical emergencies.[218]

Yet love is perhaps the word heard the more loudly for being unspoken. The love of God lies behind the entire notion of the sanctification of the name. For Maimonides, 'the name' seems to stand for what is visible of God in creation. The account of creation in 'Laws of the Foundations of the Torah', chapters 1–4, is stimulated by the love aroused by the fresh encounter with the world that turns into desire 'to know the great name'.[219] In that respect chapter 5 repesents continuity. The name is visible in *ma'aseh bereshit* and *ma'aseh merkavah*, but for most people, for whom *ma'aseh bereshit* and *ma'aseh merkavah* will remain, and should remain, a closed book,[220] it is visible in the demeanour of the righteous. *The Book of the Commandments* cites *Sifrei* on the verse 'And thou shalt love the Lord thy God': 'Make him beloved by people as did Abraham your father.'[221] That is exactly what the scholar does.

Abraham was the discoverer and promulgator of 'the name'. He it was who found God in creation, and he was prepared to suffer martyrdom.[222] When he reached Canaan, 'he called on the name of the Lord, the everlasting

---

[217] *The Book of the Commandments*, positive commandment 9.
[218] 'Laws of the Foundations of the Torah', 5: 6.   [219] Ibid. 2: 2.   [220] See ibid. 2: 12 and 4: 13.
[221] *The Book of the Commandments*, positive commandment 3.   [222] 'Laws of Idolatry', 1: 3.

God'.[223] That of course is also the motto of both *Mishneh torah* and the *Guide*. Could that be a hint that those books are themselves meant to make God visible? That they carry the responsibility of the scholar, Maimonides would surely acknowledge, and insofar as, like the scholar, they embody the values they promote, both reach the heights of art. At any rate, the portrait of the scholar marks a literary advance, for instead of specifying the motivation of love as he did in *The Book of the Commandments*, Maimonides allows a character to represent it, thus engaging the imagination of the reader.

Maimonides' scholar is, then, a type of Abraham, the lover of God, but he is also a type of Moses. In 'Eight Chapters', 4, Maimonides attributes the downfall of Moses, in the incident in which he made a rock produce water by striking it rather than speaking to it as he had been commanded to do,[224] thereby forfeiting the privilege of leading the children of Israel into the Promised Land, to his outburst of anger. This divergence from the mean of patience, on the part of someone whose every action was scrutinized by the people for whom he was a model, constituted a desecration of God's name.[225]

The scholar of the *Book of Knowledge* resembles Moses both in his guise as the exemplar of 'Laws of the Foundations of the Torah', who brings about the sanctification or desecration of God's name, and in the guise of the embodiment of the middle way and *imitatio Dei* in 'Laws of Ethical Qualities'. Anger is the trait against which Maimonides cautions more than any other in 'Laws of Ethical Qualities',[226] so that Moses, whose downfall was caused by anger, can be sensed haunting this section. Furthermore, it was to Moses that the attributes of God's actions, the guides to moral virtue, were first revealed.[227] Anyone who aspires to know these attributes and apply them aspires to be like him.

In the *Guide*, Moses, along with the patriarchs, is presented as an example of the ideal personality, someone whose mind is constantly fixed on God even as he conducts his everyday affairs.[228] This is perhaps symbolized by the

---

[223] 'Laws of Idolatry', 1: 3. quoting Gen. 21: 33.   [224] Num. 20.

[225] Maimonides is not repeating a consensus view of wherein Moses sinned, but defiantly putting forward his own. He concludes his account with the words, 'Let what others have said be compared with our opinion and the truth will surely prevail' (Twersky, *Maimonides Reader*, 376). Nahmanides, in his commentary on the Torah, criticizes Maimonides' interpretation and quotes approvingly that of Rabbenu Hananel, to the effect that Moses and Aaron sinned by saying 'We will bring forth water for you' when they should have said 'God will bring forth water for you'. (See Mossad Harav Kook *Rambam la'am* edition, volume *Hakdamot*, 183 n. 5.) Maimonides makes the biblical episode consistent with his general views on virtue.   [226] 'Laws of Ethical Qualities', 2: 3.

[227] Exod. 34: 5–7; *Guide* i. 54.   [228] *Guide* iii. 51 (p. 623).

scholar's parallel existence on the divine and human planes in 'Laws of the Foundations of the Torah' and 'Laws of Ethical Qualities'.

The scholar of 'Laws of Ethical Qualities' is, at the outset, described as having achieved high intellectual status. His task is to ensure that even his most private activity reflects this:

Even as a sage is recognized by his wisdom and moral principles which distinguish him from the rest of the people, so ought he to be recognized in all his activities, in his food and drink, in the fulfilment of his marital obligations, in attention to excretory functions, in his talk, walk, dress, management of his affairs and business transactions.[229]

As we move through the ways of refining all these aspects of physical existence in 'Laws of Ethical Qualities', chapter 5, is the process not precisely that described in 'Laws of Immersion Pools', 11: 12,[230] namely, bringing the soul into the waters of pure reason, remembering that the soul is responsible for the functions listed above? The soul of the scholar of 'Laws of Ethical Qualities' seeks to reunite with the intellect of the scholar of 'Laws of the Foundations of the Torah'. The convergence on the verse from Isaiah symbolizes the achievement of this unity, while the content of the verse indicates its effect: the glorification of God.

The scholar is not content with achieving intellectual perfection, but nor do we see him engaged in performing the commandments. His defining characteristic is his preparedness to act *lifnim mishurat hadin*, to go beyond the letter of the law (literally 'short of the line of the law').

Only someone who already knows and fulfils the law can be said to be consciously acting beyond its requirements. In Maimonides' presentation of it, *lifnim mishurat hadin* does not describe particular acts but an attitude of mind on the part of someone who has internalized the law and come as close as possible to God both morally and intellectually.

Robert Eisen writes that, in his treatment of *lifnim mishurat hadin*, 'Maimonides has taken what is essentially a legal principle and converted it into a philosophical one'.[231] He further argues that *lifnim mishurat hadin* is a form of *imitatio Dei* in Maimonides' view, in that it is associated by him with the

---

[229] 'Laws of Ethical Qualities', 5: 1.

[230] See also 'Laws of Impurity of Foodstuffs', 16: 12, where a similar process of detachment from the common run of people and the adoption of standards beyond the strict requirements of the law purifies the body and its actions, which leads to sanctification of the soul, which in turn leads to assimilation to the divine. Here again, a physical ritual is transmuted into moral improvement and thence to intellectual perfection.   [231] Eisen, '*Lifnim Mi-Shurat ha-Din* in *Mishneh Torah*'.

suppression of anger, recalling the statement of R. Zutra bar Tuvia that God prays that his mercy should suppress his anger and that he should act *lifnim mishurat hadin*.[232] This line of argument could be taken further. It could be said that the scholar, beyond imitating one or other of God's attributes of action, is, in his excess of virtue, imitative of God's relationship to the world in general, which Maimonides describes as an overflow of good things.[233]

It is true that most of the descriptions of the scholar are negative; he is characterized largely by what he avoids. This makes him a somewhat attenuated version of the perfect person found at the conclusion of the *Guide*, who 'will always have in view loving-kindness, righteousness, and judgment'.[234] Nevertheless, this is a sophisticated portrait. Looking at the figure of the scholar, we see the depiction of a religious ideal to which any pious and learned Jew would consent. But as in Renaissance portraiture, where one must note not just the face, but also the posture, the clothes, the background, the shadows, the objects on the table, in order to appreciate all that is conveyed about the subject, so too the picture of Maimonides' scholar can only be fully appreciated if the extra dimensions conferred on him by the formal devices discussed here are taken into account. He realizes his potential to be in the image and likeness of God, and so emerges worthy of a place in the gallery of sketches for Maimonides' portrait of human perfection.

Summary

In dividing intellectual virtue and moral virtue, 'Laws of the Foundations of the Torah' and 'Laws of Ethical Qualities' present an Aristotelian structure. Underlying this division of content, however, is a formal pattern whereby 'Laws of the Foundations of the Torah' represents the macrocosm and 'Laws of Ethical Qualities' represents man as a microcosm. Supported by the idea of likeness to God common to both sections, this pattern implies a more holistic view of perfection, and is a way of introducing Platonic and Neoplatonic ideas. Both kinds of virtue emerge as ways in which a person becomes inwardly analogous to God, fulfilling the potential of being created in God's image. In the process, it was suggested, what is gained is not only virtue, but also knowledge.

The form of 'Laws of the Foundations of the Torah' and 'Laws of Ethical Qualities' is a representation of the ideal of man in the image of God; the contents of these sections are the means of realizing the ideal; and the scholar, who unites them, is the personification of the ideal.

---

[232] BT *Ber.* 7a.   [233] *Guide* ii. 11 (p. 275).   [234] *Guide* iii. 54 (p. 638).

The formal parallel between 'Laws of the Foundations of the Torah' and 'Laws of Ethical Qualities' provides a way of reconciling *Mishneh torah* and the *Guide* on the relationship between intellectual virtue and moral virtue. In the course of this reconciliation, the importance of the genre difference between the two works has also started to appear.

These same features, of microcosm and macrocosm, the integration of Aristotelian and Platonic/Neoplatonic ideas, and symbolic representation of discursive arguments of the *Guide*, will emerge again, amplified, in the coming chapters, as we widen the perspective to consider the form of *Mishneh torah* as a whole.

CHAPTER TWO

THE 'GREAT THING' AND THE 'SMALL THING'
Mishneh Torah as Microcosm

IT WAS ASSERTED in the Introduction that Maimonides based the design of *Mishneh torah* on the cosmology set out in 'Laws of the Foundations of the Torah'. To recapitulate, *Mishneh torah* comprises ten books on man–God commandments and four on man–man commandments. In the Maimonidean universe ten is the number of the orders of non-corporeal beings consisting of form only, the separate intellects, better known as angels, while four is the number of the elements of matter: fire, air, water, and earth. Ten is also the number of the nine spheres plus the lowest of the separate intellects, the agent intellect. The books on the man–God commandments correspond to the angels and spheres, while those on the man–man commandments correspond to the elements. This microcosmic form represents the 'great thing', physics and metaphysics, cradling the 'small thing', the practicalities of halakhah.

Here and in the following two chapters, this idea will be substantiated more fully. The aim will be to demonstrate in detail that *Mishneh torah* is shaped by the synthesis of Aristotelian and Neoplatonic physics and metaphysics that Maimonides inherited from the Islamic philosophers, chiefly Alfarabi and Avicenna. In conjunction with the idea of man as microcosm, with which we are already supplied, I will ponder what this means for the place of the commandments in Maimonides' scheme of things. The general idea, though, is the one broached in the Introduction: if, as argued in the previous chapter, a virtuous person aligns his or her personality with the perfect order of the cosmos, then the function of the commandments, the microcosmic design implies, is to bring about such an alignment.

Of course, *Mishneh torah* is not directed only at the individual. The welfare of the body also 'consists in the governance of the city and the well-being of the states of all its people according to their capacity'.[1] So while intellectual and moral virtue are the subjects of 'Laws of the Foundations of the Torah' and 'Laws of Ethical Qualities', the product of the comprehensive legislation in *Mishneh torah* as a whole is political virtue, that is, the ideal state, as conceived at the end of 'Laws of Kings and Their Wars'. The ideal state, no less than the ideal individual, is a microcosm. The idea goes back to Plato's *Republic*, and it was given clear expression by Alfarabi, whom Maimonides so much admired,[2] in his *Attainment of Happiness*:

political science is the knowledge of things by means of which the inhabitants of states in political association achieve happiness, each one in proportion to his natural capacity. It will become clear to him (i.e. the student) that the political group and the whole which comes to be as a result of the association of the citizens in the cities is similar to the association of bodies in the whole of the universe and it will become clear to him that everything which the state and the nation contains has its counterpart in what the entire universe contains.[3]

The microcosmic structure of *Mishneh torah* is, then, a symbolic representation of this concept of political science articulated by Alfarabi. Most importantly, though, the idea of the city as microcosm does not refer only to institutional political arrangements. As Kraemer comments on Alfarabi's *Opinions of the Virtuous City*:

His entire plan lays stress upon the hierarchy of existence, the great chain of being suspended from the First, which should be presented to the people of the virtuous city by political symbols, i.e., the hierarchy of rulers and ruled; for the imitation of cosmic order is what induces political order and stability in the city. The elementary knowledge of metaphysics and physics possessed by the people of the city has a political aim: the love, justice and harmony in the city flow from consciousness of the cosmic order.[4]

---

[1] *Guide* iii. 27 (p. 510).

[2] Maimonides wrote to Samuel ibn Tibbon, 'Do not bother with books on logic besides what the sage Abu Nasr Alfarabi composed alone.' See *Letters*, ed. Shailat (Heb.), 552–3; Pines, 'Philosophic Sources', pp. lxxviii–xcii; Berman, 'Maimonides the Disciple of Alfarabi'.

[3] Cited in Berman, 'Political Interpretation', 56. See also J. L. Kraemer, 'Alfarabi's *Opinions of the Virtuous City*'. Like 'Laws of the Foundations of the Torah', *Opinions of the Virtuous City* begins with discussion of God and the universe, and Kraemer traces the parallels in detail. Concerning another work of Alfarabi, Davidson notes, 'He [Maimonides] specifically recommends a book of Alfarabi's called the *Principles of Existent Beings*. The book in question—better known under the title of *al-Siyasa al-Madaniyya*, or *Political Government*—opens by sketching the structure of the universe very much as Maimonides was to do, whereupon it turns to political theory' (*Moses Maimonides*, 113). The recommendation is in the letter to Ibn Tibbon (see previous note).

[4] J. L. Kraemer, 'Alfarabi's *Opinions of the Virtuous City*', 135.

That is to say, the virtuous city comes about not just through the city reflecting the cosmic order in its constitution, but through that order being internalized by its citizens. This, *Mishneh torah*'s structure implies, is a function of the commandments, which mediate between the idea of man as microcosm and the state as microcosm. Thus Maimonides builds out from first principles towards the ideal state that comes about at the end of *Mishneh torah*, in the messianic age. Then, the cosmic order is realized in earthly society, and state and individual are in perfect harmony in the promotion and pursuit of the knowledge of God.[5]

As far as the content is concerned, after the exposition in the first four chapters of 'Laws of the Foundations of the Torah', the 'great thing' recedes into the background, while the foreground is taken up by the 'small thing', the detail of halakhah. The physics and metaphysics are like a subterranean spring, keeping halakhah well watered with philosophy through their silent, underlying presence in *Mishneh torah*'s form. The spring does resurface at certain strategic points, as will be shown later, when it will also become clear that the metaphor of water is used here advisedly.

The *Book of Knowledge* therefore has special status. It is the reservoir of the ideas that underlie the law and find expression in the commandments. It will also be found to be the font of *Mishneh torah*'s form, for certain structural features of the *Book of Knowledge* represent a pattern for *Mishneh torah* as a whole. In fact, the general structure grows out of the microstructure of the individual commandment, which, like all existing things, is composed of form and matter. The *Book of Knowledge* informs *Mishneh torah* in every sense.

The Divide in *Mishneh Torah*

The division of *Mishneh torah* into ten books dealing with man–God commandments and four dealing with man–man commandments was taken in the Introduction as self-evident. Since the theory of *Mishneh torah*'s form advanced here depends on this division, we should check that the work really does articulate at the end of book 10, and that the hinge can bear the weight we wish to place upon it. This means demonstrating, independently of the microcosm idea, that Maimonides did observe the sorting of the commandments into these two classes, that he partitioned his code accordingly, and that this partition marks its major structural divide. These propositions are not without apparent difficulties, and the ten–four division of *Mishneh torah* is not the only one that has been suggested.

---

[5] The messiah does have to apply some coercion at first—see 'Laws of Kings and Their Wars', 11: 4.

The primary evidence is from the introduction to *Mishneh torah*. In the synopsis of the fourteen books that he provides there, Maimonides distinguishes book 11 by stating: 'I will include in it commandments between man and his fellow'. Of book 13 he states: 'I will include in it commandments between man and his fellow concerning other laws that do not arise out of damage'. The discussion of this latter type of commandment (essentially law of contract) actually begins in book 12. We see, then, that the chief characteristic of books 11 to 13 as far as Maimonides is concerned is that they are about man–man commandments, in contradistinction to books 1 to 10. While it is true that book 14 steers back towards the man–God relationship (back to the home key, as it were), concluding as it does with the idea of universal knowledge of God, that book's main subjects are the judicial and executive organs of the state, still in the man–man domain. We thus have the main division of *Mishneh torah*: books 11 to 14 concern man–man commandments, and, by implication, books 1 to 10 concern man–God commandments.

This is, in fact, the only general distinction drawn in the introduction to *Mishneh torah* between different kinds of commandments, indicating that the transition from book 10 to book 11 does indeed mark the work's major divide.

Further support for this analysis may be found in *Guide* iii. 35, where Maimonides states that the two main purposes of the commandments, the welfare of the soul and the welfare of the body,[6] correspond to the classic division between man–God and man–man commandments. This confirms the importance of the distinction to him. Very usefully for present purposes, when in that chapter Maimonides sorts the commandments into classes as a preliminary to explaining the reasons for them, he indicates to which category, man–God or man–man, each class belongs, and also states to which part or parts of *Mishneh torah* each class corresponds. He puts 'the fifth, sixth, seventh, and a portion of the third' classes in the man–man category,[7] and associates the fifth, sixth, and seventh classes with books 11 to 14 of *Mishneh torah*.[8] Books 1 to 10 must therefore be in the man–God category.

This formal argument deriving from Maimonides' own statements is really conclusive, but, from a conceptual point of view, there are some seeming anomalies that are worth resolving because in the process we shall gain a preliminary idea of what Maimonides understood by a man–God or man–man commandment, which is necessary to the analysis of *Mishneh torah*'s form.

---

[6] See *Guide* iii. 27 (p. 510).   [7] *Guide* iii. 35 (p. 538).   [8] Ibid. (p. 536).

One anomaly is 'Laws of Gifts to the Poor', which might be considered a matter between people, but which appears in book 7, the *Book of Agriculture*, that is, in the man–God division. Maimonides' approach to these commandments, however, is to emphasize the way that they inculcate mercy, that is, promote the welfare of the soul,[9] although he does also of course recognize their social utility.[10] In 'Laws of Gifts to the Poor', 10: 1, charitableness is said to be a sign of descent from Abraham, with a citation of the same verse (Gen. 18: 19) as is cited in 'Laws of Ethical Qualities', 1: 7, to prove that the doctrine of the middle path, the basis of ethics, is part of Abraham's heritage. In *halakhah* 3 of the same chapter, ignoring the claims of charity is compared to idolatry.[11] In other words, in Maimonides' eyes, charity primarily has to do with one's personal ethics and belief system. On a more technical level, the contract in 'Laws of Gifts to the Poor', if any, is between the giver and God, not between giver and poor recipient, although it awards the poor enforceable rights as third-party beneficiaries.[12] All this puts charity in the domain of the welfare of the soul, or the man–God domain, so that its place within the man–God division is conceptually justified.

Another set of laws that might seem strange in that division is book 4, the *Book of Women*, on laws of marriage and divorce, especially since a large part of the book is about marital property. Formally speaking, since in *Guide* iii. 35[13] the commandments in the *Book of Women* are explicitly associated with the fourteenth class, which is not one of the designated man–man classes, we know that Maimonides put them in the man–God category. But there are also conceptual grounds for the man–God categorization of the *Book of Women*, conveyed via the brief historical preamble in the first *halakhah* of the opening section, 'Laws of Marriage', which relates that, before the Torah, sexual relations between men and women were purely a matter of consent, and that the Torah introduced the formality of marriage. This lends marriage its man–God dimension, a dimension of holiness, also implied in the general reason Maimonides gives for the fourteenth class of the commandments in the *Guide*, namely, the restraint of desire, which, as will be discussed in Chapter 3, is the core meaning of holiness as far as Maimonides is concerned. This moral purpose puts these laws in the man–God category, even though in *Guide* iii. 49, where the fourteenth class is treated at length, the emphasis is

---

[9] See *Guide* iii. 39 (pp. 550–1) and Twersky, *Introduction to the Code*, 265–6, 305.

[10] *Guide* iii. 35 (p. 536). On an organizational level, of course, these laws belong in the *Book of Agriculture* because, like most of the book, they largely have to do with harvesting and the disposal of the produce.   [11] On the basis of BT *BB* 10*a*.

[12] See 'Laws of Gifts to the Poor', 1: 8, and Twersky, *Introduction to the Code*, 433–4.   [13] p. 537.

on their social significance for, as stated there, 'every commandment . . . which only concerns the individual himself and his becoming more perfect, is called by them between man and God, even though in reality it may affect relations between man and his fellow man. But this happens only after many intermediate steps and through comprehensive considerations.'[14] The laws of marriage are not peculiar in this respect. The laws of the festivals are essentially of the man–God type, but they also promote social cohesion.[15]

This brings us to the difficulty that, according to *Guide* iii. 35, besides classes 5, 6 and 7, the man–man commandments are also in 'a portion of the third' class. In *Guide* iii. 38 we learn that the third class corresponds to 'Laws of Ethical Qualities', which is in the very first book of *Mishneh torah*, the *Book of Knowledge*, supposedly a man–God preserve. Does this not spoil the picture?

It does not, for at least two reasons. The first is, again, formal: we can fall back on the indications already cited, in the introduction to *Mishneh torah*, of the division between man–God and man–man books; Maimonides does not appear to have regarded the portion of 'Laws of Ethical Qualities' that treats man–man commandments as upsetting the general plan, for all his later remarks in the *Guide*. The statistics support this view: the portion of 'Laws of Ethical Qualities' to which Maimonides appears to refer is chapters 6 and 7 of that section, about the commandments to love one's fellow and to eschew grudges and vengeance, that is to say, two out of the total of forty-six chapters in the *Book of Knowledge*. That is not enough to deflect the book from its man–God orientation. Secondly, the commandments in chapters 6 and 7 of 'Laws of Ethical Qualities' are only embryonically of the man–man type. They are still in the moral sphere, connected to 'the welfare of the soul', and are not fully differentiated into the kind of transactional laws found in books 11 to 13 that fall squarely into the 'welfare of the body' category, although they certainly form the basis of the harmonious society those laws are intended to build, as will be discussed more fully later on.[16]

So the idea that *Mishneh torah* is divided between ten books on man–God commandments and four on man–man commandments emerges formally confirmed and conceptually intact. It is not just an impression; it is very much what Maimonides had in mind.

But is this the main division? Cohen and Berman see it as such, but Nachum Rabinovitch divides the fourteen books exactly in half, on the

---

[14] *Guide* iii. 35 (p. 538).   [15] See Guide iii. 43 (p. 570).
[16] On Maimonides' approach in *Mishneh torah* to the prohibition on vengeance as a law designed to cultivate moral perfection, see Twersky, *Introduction to the Code*, 441.

grounds that, up to and including book 7, *Mishneh torah* is concerned with the individual, and thereafter with the collective.[17] There certainly is a widening of the social sphere as the first nine books progress, a point that will be taken up in the next chapter, but a difficulty with Rabbi Rabinovitch's thesis is the position of the *Book of Purity* at number ten. Purity and impurity are matters for the individual—in fact, where the Jewish people as a collective is concerned, the laws of impurity are sometimes relaxed[18]—and at the end of the *Book of Purity*, where immersion in a *mikveh* is compared to purification of the soul, the focus is very much on the individual conscience.[19] I therefore prefer the classic division between man–God and man–man commandments, in line with Maimonides' explicit remarks, locating the caesura after book 10.

Ultimately in Maimonides the distinction falls away: all commandments in a divine law are man–God commandments; all the commandments contribute to knowledge of God. A divine law does not mean a *nomos*, an ordinary civic law, with a religious or philosophical topping. Divinity transfigures the entire law, permeating even its most mundane provisions, the whole of it conforming to God's governance of the world. The idea cited above from *Guide* iii. 35, that relations between man and God affect relations between man and man, is the Maimonidean ethos in a nutshell, as seen at the very end of the *Guide*, and as we shall see, 'after many intermediate steps and through comprehensive considerations', in *Mishneh torah* too.

How Many Spheres Make a Universe?

Maimonides identifies the angels with the separate intellects in the system of the Aristotelians.[20] In that system, there is an intelligence or separate intellect governing the motion of each of the nested spheres that contain the stars and planets. But how many spheres are there? Maimonides' attitude towards this interesting question provides further corroboration of the idea of a correspondence between the cosmology set out in 'Laws of the Foundations of the Torah' and the arrangement of the books of *Mishneh torah*.

Although he gives summary accounts of physics and metaphysics in both books, neither in *Mishneh torah* nor in the *Guide* does Maimonides set himself up as a scientist. In the *Guide*, he states that his purpose is not to describe the

---

[17] Rabinovitch, 'Sanctuary, Society, and History' (Heb.).

[18] See 'Laws of the Temple', 7: 23, and *Rambam la'am* edn., n. 115 thereto; 'Laws of Entrance into the Sanctuary', 4: 10–18; 'Laws of the Passover Offering', 7.

[19] 'Laws of Immersion Pools', 11: 12. This *halakhah* is discussed at greater length in the next two chapters.   [20] *Guide* ii. 3–6.

spheres and separate intellects and their number, but only to elucidate difficulties in the law.[21] That is to say, the cosmology he outlines there is really necessary only insofar as those sciences cast light on obscure matters in Scripture.[22] As pointed out in the Introduction, Maimonides was aware that the science of his day was flawed.[23] In particular, he is non-committal on the number of the spheres. When he first mentions the subject in the *Guide*, he says that the number is at least eighteen.[24] When he introduces his discussion of the question whether the world was created in time or not, he uses the number nine, but later in the same chapter we find that the universe can be described in terms of two, four, or five spheres.[25]

These numbers are not irreconcilable. The number eighteen arises because some spheres comprise more than one layer. We saw the numbers five and four in the previous chapter: five is a simplification of the system into diurnal sphere, fixed stars, planets, Sun, and Moon, while four arises by leaving out the diurnal sphere, which contains no stars or planets. Two refers to all the informed spheres (those containing stars or planets) as one, plus the diurnal sphere. In the *Guide* Maimonides uses different numbers in different contexts, without being inconsistent, and without asserting that any particular number represents verifiable physical fact.[26]

---

[21] *Guide* ii. 2 (p. 253).

[22] Dov Schwartz, however, finds that this declaration of Maimonides is a cover for his real intention. See Schwartz, 'Maimonides' Philosophical Methodology' (Heb.).

[23] *Guide* ii. 3 (p. 254); ii. 11 (pp. 273–4); ii. 24 (pp. 322–7). What Maimonides believed could be known about anything above the sphere of the Moon is a matter of controversy—see Langermann, 'Astronomical Problems in Maimonides' (Heb.) and 'The True Perplexity'; Pines, 'Limitations of Human Knowledge'; Freudenthal, 'Maimonides' Philosophy of Science'; Kellner, 'Astronomy and Physics in Maimonides'; Davidson, 'Maimonides on Metaphysical Knowledge'; W. Z. Harvey, 'Maimonides' Critical Epistemology'; Stern, 'The Knot That Never Was'; J. L. Kraemer, 'How (Not) to Read the *Guide*'. Langermann insists that the cosmology set out in 'Laws of the Foundations of the Torah', while it may be simplified, is not knowingly fictional ('Astronomical Problems in Maimonides' (Heb.), 113–18). On the vexed question of the interpretation of the disavowal of knowledge of the heavens at the close of *Guide* ii. 24 (pp. 326–7), and of the comments there about the proof of God's existence from heavenly movements, I accept Stern's solution that there was never really a problem, and that a distinction should be drawn between what can be deduced from a phenomenon, and explanatory knowledge of that phenomenon. Besides its inherent cogency, this solution has the advantage, it seems to me, of maintaining consistency between the *Guide* and *Mishneh torah*, by preserving the validity of such things in *Mishneh torah* as the account in 'Laws of Idolatry' of Abraham's discovery of God through observation of the motions of the heavens (an application of Occam's razor—we should not multiply Maimonides beyond necessity).

[24] *Guide* i. 72 (p. 185). [25] *Guide* ii. 9 (pp. 268–9).

[26] James Diamond concludes that Maimonides adapts cosmology as required for the purposes of symbolism and allegory (see Diamond, *Maimonides and the Hermeneutics of Concealment*, 112–14). It will be recalled that in the previous chapter the key number was five.

In *Guide* ii. 10, four turns out to be a favourite number for the spheres because it corresponds to so many things: to the number of the elements, to the number of forces that move each sphere, and to a number that crops up frequently in Scripture and Midrash. Again, it must be stressed that Maimonides' stated purpose in the part of the *Guide* under consideration here is not to write a textbook of science or philosophy, but to demonstrate that Jewish doctrine is not incompatible with science, and that what may seem obscure, trivial, or childish passages in Scripture and Midrash actually reflect what is at least a possible description of God's governance of the world.

Returning to *Mishneh torah*, we find that, after Maimonides has stated at the opening of chapter 3 of 'Laws of the Foundations of the Torah' that the spheres are nine in number, he goes on to explain that the full system of spheres is much more complicated, with eighteen spheres and eight epicycles.[27]

Two things emerge from all this. One is that the numbering of the spheres, while not arbitrary, is certainly flexible. The other is that Maimonides was very keen on numerical correspondences. Moreover, the idea of a numerical motif in the structure of his writings is by no means new: Strauss finds in the number seven a key to the structure of the *Guide*.[28] Therefore, when, in 'Laws of the Foundations of the Torah', Maimonides headlines the number nine for the number of the spheres, we should ask, why that particular number, and to what might it correspond?

Now these questions could be deflected by arguing that Maimonides only engages in a discussion of cosmology at all in *Mishneh torah* because he has prescribed science as a means to the love of God, and he promises no more than a very general introduction to the subject.[29] In this context, nine is a reasonable number, since it accounts for the main classes of heavenly bodies plus what moves them, and it seems to have been widely accepted.[30] The number eighteen is provided in order to indicate that there is more to cosmology than

[27] 'Laws of the Foundations of the Torah', 3: 2–5.

[28] Strauss, 'How to Begin to Study *The Guide*'. See also S. Harvey, 'Maimonides in the Sultan's Palace'. It is presumably not happenstance that *Mishneh torah* has precisely 1,000 chapters (see Appendix I), although that fact plays no part in the numerical scheme set forth here.

[29] 'Laws of the Foundations of the Torah', 2: 2. It is worth pointing out that the physics and metaphysics Maimonides does provide in that section are remarkably close to the syllabus prescribed by Avicenna as the minimum necessary for admission to the lowest grade of immortality (see Davidson, *Alfarabi, Avicenna and Averroes on Intellect*, 110), intellectual fulfilment being the only way immortality can be achieved. The good that the *Book of Knowledge* proposes at its end is *olam haba*, the world to come, and the book can be seen as a handbook for obtaining that good. Like a competent teacher, Maimonides takes care to ensure that even his less talented pupils will at least pass their examinations.

[30] *Guide* ii. 9 (p. 268) refers to 'those who in our time count nine spheres'.

that, and that anyone who wants to develop his or her knowledge (and hence love of God) further will study in more depth.[31]

This is fine, except that it ignores the fact that Maimonides' penchant for numbers is not like some preacher's fondness for *gematria*. What we see in *Guide* ii. 10 is a certain number, the number four, making everything—the heavens, the earth, Scripture—cohere. Therefore, the feeling returns that if Maimonides gives prominence to the number nine for the number of the spheres, yet a few lines later acknowledges that nine is not the true number, we should look for his reasons for doing so. The suggestion advanced here is that, in combination with the enumeration of ten orders of angels, he is referring to Alfarabian cosmology as the basis for the structure of his own work. Just as the number four binds the heavens and the earth and the Torah, the numbers ten and four bind the heavens and the earth and *Mishneh torah*.

The Spheres and the Commandments

With the numbers settled, we can now turn to the substance of the correspondences between angels, spheres, and elements on the one hand, and the man–God and man–man commandments on the other.

Maimonides establishes a hierarchy of existence based on the Aristotelian concepts of form and matter, dividing created existence into three parts: forms without matter (angels); permanent forms united with immutable matter (spheres and stars); and temporary forms united with mutating matter (sublunary entities).[32]

The imperishable, weightless, colourless material of which the spheres consist represents a halfway stage between the physical as we know it on Earth, and the non-physical.[33] As we saw in the previous chapter, the spheres possess consciousness. Their function, and that of the similarly conscious and imperishable stars they contain, is to praise and glorify God. They are governed by intelligences that have nothing material in their make-up at all, but are pure form.[34] The whole system forms a hierarchy leading up to the divine source.

The man–God commandments, like the spheres, are intermediate between the non-corporeal and the world of matter. To varying degrees they have material substrata, such as phylacteries and the *lulav*, but their purpose

---

[31] Maimonides' own full credentials as an astronomer are presented in 'Laws of Sanctification of the New Moon'.   [32] See 'Laws of the Foundations of the Torah', 2: 3.

[33] Maimonides confesses to a lack of understanding of what superlunary matter really is and how it might vary between the spheres—see *Guide* ii. 22 (p. 319).   [34] See Chapter 1, n. 51.

is not mainly material. These commandments aim at the spiritualization or intellectualization of earthly life, influencing our material existence as the stars and spheres influence matter. Maimonides sees a man–God commandment as a consciousness-raising exercise that makes a person self-reflective in the way that superlunary entities are, and the sublunary elements of matter are not.[35] In their ritual aspects, the man–God commandments provide a vehicle for man to praise and glorify the Creator, as do the stars and the spheres.

These commandments have a didactic purpose too. Maimonides explains many of them as demonstrative rejections of idolatrous superstition, intended to uphold monotheism. In this respect their function is partly reflexive and partly testamental. In general, though, just as the spheres lead from earth to the highest heaven, the man–God commandments represent, as it were, a ladder up to God.

The man–man commandments, on the other hand, govern our mundane affairs. They cover subjects found in any legal system: contract, torts, land law, criminal law, evidence and court procedure, and constitutional law. Ultimately they too have a spiritual purpose of course, in that the rule of law provides the stability people require in order to realize their spiritual potential, but, as was stressed above, their immediate province is unregenerate matter. The parallels between the ten books dealing with ritual law and the nine spheres plus the agent intellect, and between the four books dealing with civil law and the four elements, thus neatly symbolize the different orientations of these two main divisions of the law.

Among the spheres the outer, diurnal sphere is exceptional in that it contains no stars, but rather controls the motion of the others. *Mishneh torah* contains a similar exception, for although I have divided it into a group of ten books and a group of four, the first book, the *Book of Knowledge*, is really in a class of its own. As its name implies, the commandments it contains are conceptual rather than practical. They do not make use of physical objects or enjoin particular actions; they work in the mental rather than the physical realm. But just as the diurnal sphere imparts motion to the other spheres, the *Book of Knowledge* as it were imparts motion to the other books. It contains the ideas that underlie the rest of the commandments and that motivate their performance. 'Laws of the Foundations of the Torah' sets out the fundamentals of physics and metaphysics, without which the commandments are meaningless, and the notion of prophecy, without which they have no authority, since

---

[35] See 'Laws of the Foundations of the Torah', 3: 9–11.

it was the prophet Moses, uniquely combining the roles of prophet and law-giver, who transmitted them.[36] 'Laws of Ethical Qualities' aims to adjust the condition of the individual and of society to make performance of the commandments possible. 'Laws of Torah Study' instructs us on how to acquire knowledge of the law—no one who is ignorant of the commandments can possibly keep them. 'Laws of Idolatry' warns against the degeneration that follows from the neglect of the fundamental truths. 'Laws of Repentance' attaches to all the commandments in that it tells us how to repent of the breach of any of them, but, perhaps even more importantly, in its assertion that the world to come lies in store for those who fulfil the commandments, though they should ideally be obeyed out of disinterested love. As explained in the previous chapter, love as the motivator on the religious plane parallels love as the mover of the spheres on the cosmic plane.

The role of the *Book of Knowledge* in laying down principles on which the rest of the law is based can be illustrated by specific instances. For example, the twice-daily recital of the Shema is enjoined by 'Laws of Recitation of the Shema', the first section of the *Book of Love*. The essential part of the commandment is the recital of the verse 'Hear o Israel, the Lord our God, the Lord is one', which asserts the existence and unity of God. This cannot be conscientiously performed without some notion of what God's existence and unity mean. This is supplied by 'Laws of the Foundations of the Torah'.[37] A further example: the man–man commandments in the last four books of *Mishneh torah*, which are designed to ensure that civil society works properly so that individuals are secure enough to devote themselves to pursuing the knowledge of God, cannot be effective without a measure of self-restraint, the kind of character trait that 'Laws of Ethical Qualities' seeks to instil. 'Laws of Ethical Qualities' in fact ends on the subject of morality making civilization and commerce possible.

In outline, in the structure of *Mishneh torah*, the *Book of Knowledge* corresponds to the first part of existence; the following nine books to the second part, and the last four books to the third part.

It will be helpful to summarize the discussion so far by expanding the table presented in the previous chapter to a threefold structural parallel between the cosmos, *Mishneh torah*, and humankind (see Table 4).[38]

---

[36] It is, of course, fundamental that no prophet after Moses can, *qua* prophet, be a lawgiver, or even an interpreter of the law. See 'Laws of the Foundations of the Torah', 9.   [37] 1: 1–7.

[38] In Table 3 the human intellect is shown as corresponding to God, whereas in Table 4 the correspondence is to the highest order of angels, the *ḥayot*. There is no confusion. Chapter 1 of 'Laws of the Foundations of the Torah' is about God himself, and Table 3 reflects this. The *Book of Knowledge*,

Table 4 Parallel structures of cosmos, *Mishneh torah*, and humankind

Universe	*Mishneh torah*	Human being
First part: angels	*Book of Knowledge*	Intellect
Second part: nine spheres	Nine man–God books: *Book of Love* to *Book of Purity*—'welfare of the soul'	Emotions and appetites
Third part: four elements	Four man–man books: *Book of Torts* to *Book of Judges*—'welfare of the body'	Body

This is not the only hierarchy in Maimonides' cosmos. Within the first two parts there is another, based on the Neoplatonic concept of emanation. The double hierarchy is seen in a passage from 'Laws of the Foundations of the Torah' cited in the previous chapter in connection with the self-awareness of the sphere and its knowledge of God. Here it is again:

Every star and sphere has a soul and is endowed with knowledge and intelligence. They are living beings who apprehend 'Him who spake and the world was'. They praise and glorify their Creator, just as the angels do, each according to its greatness and degree. And as they apprehend God, so are they conscious of themselves and of the angels above them. The knowledge possessed by the stars and spheres, is less than that of angels, more than that of human beings.[39]

The division between the three parts of existence is presented in this passage on the basis of degrees of knowledge rather than on the mix of form and matter, but since matter is the inhibitor of knowledge,[40] it comes to the same thing. The second, internal kind of hierarchy is only within each of the first two parts; sublunary existence is excluded from it. Spheres praise the Creator 'each according to its greatness and degree', and so do angels.

Great and Glorious

Before we go on to interpret these features, it is worth stepping back to take in the sheer beauty of Maimonides' design, to marvel at its ingenuity, and,

taken as a whole, is about the knowledge of God, which the human intellect seeks to attain and which the *ḥayot* possess in the highest possible degree. This is reflected in Table 4.

[39] 'Laws of the Foundations of the Torah', 3: 9.

[40] See 'Laws of the Foundations of the Torah', 1: 10; *Guide* iii. 9 (pp. 436–7).

momentarily at least, to be rapt like him by a world of conscious orbs and stars moving in love, a love offered even to human beings through commandments that flow from the same superabundant goodness of God.

Twersky objects to what he calls the 'crushing literalism' of Maimonides' interpretation of the talmudic passage from which the notion of the 'great thing' and the 'small thing' originates.[41] 'Laws of the Foundations of the Torah', 4: 1, appears to indicate that the 'small thing' is so called because its status is indeed small, being accessible to all, and only a preparation for the 'great thing', which not everyone reaches. The symbolic projection of this relationship in *Mishneh torah*'s form suggests something quite otherwise. Far from being crushingly literal, Maimonides' reading, or deliberate mis-reading, of the Talmud opens the way to clothing the 'small thing' with time-less grandeur, 'making the "Torah great and glorious"', as Twersky himself remarks of *Mishneh torah*'s timeless scope.[42] The Torah is, as it were, God's other creation, designed to bring human beings to the perfection of the first creation, and Maimonides' artistry allows us to appreciate this.

It will be recalled that the first use Maimonides makes of the microcosm–macrocosm idea in *Guide* i. 72 is to convince us that, like the human body, the cosmos is one whole composed of many parts. Here, it is the cosmos that serves as the model. It is vast and intricate, but (in the Aristotelian conception of it) finite; by being modelled upon it, the vast and intricate law becomes graspable as one thing, distinct and bounded. In *Guide* i. 72 Maimonides goes on to describe how the relationships between the parts of the cosmos can be understood from the relationships between the parts of a human being. Again, in interpreting *Mishneh torah*'s form, matters are reversed: the cosmos is the model, and the way that the commandments interrelate will be inter-preted in terms of the relationships between its parts. These are the phases of *integritas* and *consonantia* in the Aquinian definition of beauty discussed in the Introduction.

The interpretations about to be offered do not pretend to be exhaustive. It is not just that the task is great; open-endedness is part of the artistic dimension that we are discovering. We are dealing with symbol, and the beauty of a symbol lies partly in the fact that its meaning need not be single or static. Interpretation must therefore avoid being confining. To use the Neo-platonic terminology that is perhaps appropriate here, interpretation is a descent from the level of Intellect, in which meanings are grasped intuitively

---

[41] Twersky, *Introduction to the Code*, 494.   [42] Ibid. 237.

and simultaneously, to the level of Soul, which employs discursive reasoning. And Soul, we know, yearns to be reunited with Intellect.

The remainder of this chapter will deal with the Aristotelian superstructure of *Mishneh torah*, and continue to pursue the correspondence between its arrangement into fourteen books and the simplified structure of the cosmos that Maimonides sets out in 'Laws of the Foundations of the Torah',[43] but with an emphasis on the first two parts of existence, pure forms and permanent bodies, and the first ten books. The next chapter will look at the Neoplatonic infrastructure, the internal hierarchies in the first two parts of existence and their reflection in the internal dynamics of *Mishneh torah*'s design, especially in the way that ideas developed in the *Book of Knowledge* translate into practical commandments in later books. The last part of existence, perishable matter that changes its forms, and the last four books of *Mishneh torah*, will be considered more fully in Chapter 4.

The Commandment as Form

The first enquiry is into the composition of the basic unit out of which the superstructure is built. What, for Maimonides, constitutes a commandment?

A way into this enquiry is via a possible objection to the general outline

[43] Within the fourteen classes of commandments listed in the *Guide*, the 10:4 ratio between man–God commandments and man–man commandments remains very nearly constant: 'Among the classes we have differentiated and enumerated, the fifth, sixth, seventh, and a portion of the third, belong to the group devoted to the relation *between man and his fellow man*, while all the other classes deal with the relation *between man and God*' (*Guide* iii. 35 (p. 538)), but since the correspondence is not exact, perhaps it ought not to be pushed too far.

Incidentally, the statement that a portion of the third class of commandments belongs in the man–man category presents some difficulty to the thesis that Maimonides switched from a view of moral virtue as an inward quality in *Mishneh torah* to a purely social view of moral virtue in the *Guide*. In *Guide* iii. 38 (p. 550), the very short chapter that deals with this third class, he essentially refers the reader to 'Laws of Ethical Qualities' for the details. If only a portion of the third class is stated to be in the man–man category, then this reference is intended to import all of 'Laws of Ethical Qualities' into the *Guide*, both the last two chapters, the portion which does indeed treat of social behaviour, and the first five, the portion which does not. It is true that *Guide* iii. 38 states, 'The utility of all of them', i.e. of all the commandments in 'Laws of Ethical Qualities', 'is clear and evident, for all concern moral qualities in virtue of which the association among people is in good condition', but that only means that a man–God commandment can have social utility as well, and Maimonides here is interested in the social, utilitarian aspect. The manifestly social laws in 'Laws of Ethical Qualities', such as the prohibition on taking revenge, depend on the inward quality of a balanced temperament, and so the doctrine of the mean too can be said to be socially useful. That does not derogate from its inward significance. In *Guide* iii. 43 the reasons assigned to the sabbath and festivals are very much a mix of the moral, social, and intellectual. In short, Maimonides appears to endorse 'Laws of Ethical Qualities' wholesale in the *Guide*, with no indication of a shift in his view of moral virtue.

given above of the parallel between *Mishneh torah* and the cosmos. It was stated that the *Book of Knowledge* exists entirely on the mental plane, but in fact that book does concern itself with particular acts in the physical world. Chapter 4 of 'Laws of the Foundations of the Torah' is about damaging sacred writings and the fabric of the Temple. The fourth chapter of 'Laws of Ethical Qualities' presents prescriptions for physical health, and the fifth describes in detail the behaviour expected of the scholar, down to the level of his sexual relationship with his wife, and even his bowel movements.[44] Similarly, the third chapter of 'Laws of Idolatry' proscribes many particular acts involving particular objects. So what is left of the proposition that the *Book of Knowledge* is conceptual rather than practical, other than the book's title?

This brings us to a most important general principle, one that governs all that follows about *Mishneh torah*'s structure: it is the title that counts. The characterization of any part of *Mishneh torah* will be according to the rubric under which the laws it contains are gathered, and not according to the details of those laws themselves, which must rather be considered in the light of the general characteristic of the book, section, or chapter in which they are found. This is not a rule of convenience designed to skirt awkward facts. It is in line with Maimonides' own statements about his method of enumerating and classifying the commandments, and goes to the heart of his conception of what a commandment is. To demonstrate this, it is necessary to turn from *Mishneh torah* to the work written in preparation for it, *The Book of the Commandments*.

In that work, Maimonides himself makes the distinction between practical and conceptual commandments. In his methodological introduction, where he lays down his fourteen criteria or principles for deciding which statements of the Torah should count as commandments, he divides the commandments into four areas: doctrines, acts, ethics, and speech. If we want to describe the *Book of Knowledge* as covering doctrines and ethics, while the other thirteen books cover acts and speech, we have Maimonidean authority for applying such categories. But what about the objection just raised, that acts and speech are to be found in the *Book of Knowledge* as well? They are, but only as consequences of the main ideas. In 'Laws of Ethical Qualities', for example, the main idea is *imitatio Dei*. This devolves onto particular areas of conduct, but those areas remain within the field of the governing idea. In 'Laws of Idolatry', the main idea is to avoid the conceptual error of attributing independent power to created beings and considering them worthy of worship. This is the

---

[44] 'Laws of Ethical Qualities', 5: 4–6.

burden of the historical introduction to that section. Again, this forms a field within which the particulars find their place and from which they derive their force.

This approach grows out of the fourteen roots, or principles for enumerating the commandments, set out in the introduction to *The Book of the Commandments*. The first two principles distinguish between Torah commandments and rabbinical commandments. The third distinguishes between permanent and ad hoc commandments. All the rest seek to decide which of the many hundreds of imperative statements in the Torah qualify as commandments to be included in the traditional total of 613. This is very largely a matter of distinguishing between generalities and specifics. Principle number 4 excludes statements that are too general. The others, apart from number 8, which turns on a point of language, serve to distinguish between main headings and subordinate or accompanying details. Of especial interest in our context are two principles. The first of them is number 9:

> It is not admissible to include in this Classification (as distinct and independent commandments) the (Scriptural) statements (severally) embodying a given negative commandment or a given positive commandment; it is the (essential object or) act which these statements prohibit or command (irrespective of the number of times it is repeated in Scripture that should be included in the Taryag-Classification).[45]

It is under this principle that Maimonides sets out the four areas mentioned above of doctrines, acts, ethics, and speech. If two or more injunctions or prohibitions lay down one doctrine, or enjoin or prohibit one kind of act, and so on, then those injunctions or prohibitions should be considered as a single commandment, positive or negative as the case may be, unless the Talmud indicates otherwise. We should not literal-mindedly count imperatives. To take one of Maimonides' own examples: the Torah commands us not to retrieve a sheaf left behind in the grain harvest but to leave it for the poor, and also not to retrieve olives left behind in the olive harvest but to leave those for the poor as well. Since there is no contrary indication, these prohibitions should be counted as one commandment not to retrieve forgotten produce.[46] Enumeration of the commandments entails their conceptualization—not at a very advanced level in this case, but nevertheless, the trend is there.

A related principle (and Maimonides explicitly links it to principle 9), is principle 11: 'It is not permissible to include in this Classification as distinct

---

[45] *Book of the Commandments*, 4.

[46] As indeed they are in the *Book of the Commandments*, negative commandment 214, where not retrieving a sheaf is stated to imply a rule that applies to all kinds of harvesting.

commandments the separate parts which in their aggregate constitute but one commandment.'[47]

Under this heading Maimonides deals with an interesting difficulty. In some commandments made up of several elements, each of the elements is a *sine qua non*, so together they clearly form a single commandment, since none can stand by itself. In other cases, however, each element is valid independently, so that it is possible to consider each as a separate commandment. In such cases, Maimonides states, it is necessary to decide whether the different elements constitute one matter or several. He cites the example of the fringes worn on the corners of four-cornered garments. Each fringe comprises several white threads and one blue thread.[48] The white threads, however, are valid without the blue thread, and vice versa.[49] Do white and blue, then, constitute separate commandments? Maimonides cites a ruling in *Mekhilta derabi yishma'el* that they do not, but he adds a reason, which is that the different elements of white and blue thread concern a single matter, or a single aim, namely, to remind the wearer of his obligation to perform all of the commandments, which is the general objective of the commandment to wear fringes. Although principle 5 of the fourteen disqualifies reasons for commandments from being commandments in themselves, it turns out that the reason can nevertheless play a role in defining the commandment. The separate parts of the commandment of fringes are considered one commandment and not two because they relate to one concept. Again, enumeration entails conceptualization. This may seem obvious, but Maimonides writes with some asperity about predecessors who attempted to list the commandments without having grasped it.[50]

In the medieval philosophical language with which we are dealing, 'conceptualization' can be translated as 'form'. Through his fourteen principles, Maimonides begins to impose form on the commandments, or to reveal

[47] *Book of the Commandments*, 5.

[48] The Torah does not specify a number for the white threads, but the sages fixed it at seven. See 'Laws of Fringes', 1: 1 and 6.   [49] See ibid. 1: 4.

[50] See under principle 7. Note that, even though, applying principle 11, Maimonides determines that the phylacteries worn on the head and on the arm constitute two separate commandments, because the Talmud indicates as much (see *The Book of the Commandments*, positive commandment 13). He nevertheless rules, contrary to Ashkenazi custom, that when both are put on at the same time a single blessing should be recited ('Laws of Phylacteries, Mezuzah, and Torah Scroll', 4: 5), on the grounds, stated in a responsum, that both concern the same matter, namely, remembrance (*Mose Ben Maimon Responsa* (Heb.), ed. Freimann, 6). Interestingly enough, this is the same concept as unites the different threads of *tsitsit*. The ruling is in line with those of several previous authorities (see *Rambam la'am* note ad loc.), but it does also evince the drive to unite parts under single, conceptual wholes.

their form—for immediate purposes, the difference is not material. Twersky describes the *Book of the Commandments* as 'intended merely as an exact and exhaustive checklist' in preparation for devising the topical-conceptual arrangement of the commandments in *Mishneh torah*.[51] That the *Book of the Commandments* is the groundwork for *Mishneh torah* is undoubtedly true— Maimonides says as much. Our discussion indicates, however, that Twersky's judgement needs to be modified in its implication that conceptualization enters in only with classification, that is, only with *Mishneh torah*. It actually enters in at an earlier stage: it is part of the definition of what a commandment is. A commandment is a conceptual field, or, as Moshe Halbertal puts it, an 'organizing principle',[52] around which cluster detailed laws that may themselves also be in the Torah, or that may be extensions of the commandment or fences around it of rabbinic origin. A commandment is a form, while the details subsumed under it are matter.

In the introduction to the *Book of the Commandments*, Maimonides states that, in order to facilitate study and committal to memory, he decided that he would arrange the commandments in *Mishneh torah* not according to the tractates of the Mishnah, but by commandment. Each commandment, such as that of the *lulav*, is to have its own section in which all the relevant laws are gathered, divided into chapters as appropriate. Sometimes, however, several commandments will be dealt with in one section because they come under one general topic; Maimonides cites the laws about idolatry as an example of this. The structure of *Mishneh torah* thus builds up from the nature of a commandment as defined by Maimonides' fourteen principles in the *Book of the Commandments*. When, on the festival of Sukkot, someone holds the *lulav*, that act involving a physical object constitutes the commandment. But if someone hurls a stone at a shrine to Mercury (which is apparently how Mercury was venerated), he has performed an act that is a part of a general prohibition against worship of an idol according to the customary mode,[53] which in turn is subsumed under the yet more general concept of not enter-

---

[51] Twersky, *Introduction to the Code*, 253.

[52] Halbertal, 'Maimonides' Book of the Commandments' (Heb.). Twersky constantly draws attention to Maimonides' conceptual arrangement of the halakhah in *Mishneh torah*, stating, for example: 'The classification of the law in the *Mishneh Torah*, with its great self-consciousness concerning every formulation and every grouping, is a prime example of Maimonides' genius for generalization mounted on steady "reflection and deliberation." Its inner structure, particularly the premeditated splitting of laws in deference to a conceptual rather than functional or formal categorization, and the elaborate network of cross references attest to this' (*Introduction to the Code*, 277). On the method and purpose of *The Book of the Commandments* and the concept of a Torah commandment, see now Friedberg, *Crafting the 613 Commandments*.   [53] 'Laws of Idolatry', 3: 5.

taining false notions in religion.[54] What looks like a transgression in the area of acts is really, for the purposes of understanding *Mishneh torah*'s form, a transgression in the area of doctrines. The specific question about the *Book of Knowledge* is thus answered, as is the question of how to characterize the books and sections of *Mishneh torah* in general. We go according to the top-level commandment or idea, and not the details it subsumes. We look upstream, not downstream. To stray for a moment into the Neoplatonic field, Maimonides himself perhaps put this most succinctly in relation to the parallel, cosmic structure: higher-level entities in the cosmos confer benefits on lower-level entities, but this does not mean that the higher serves the lower, for 'the end is nobler than the things that subsist for the sake of the end'.[55] Similarly, concepts confer meaning on commandments, but commandments serve concepts, not the other way round.

If we twist this around just slightly, we also have an answer to the question about the composition of the building blocks of *Mishneh torah*. It turns out to be similar to the composition of the entities that make up the universe. Some consist of form only; some of form and matter. Those that consist of form only are in the *Book of Knowledge*. To take 'Laws of Idolatry' again: if there were no Mercury and no stones, the commandments in it would still remain, and even if the commandment to burn an idolatrous city is just possibly classifiable as a commandment concerning a physical object, in that it is positive while all the other specific commandments are negative, certainly the governing idea of 'Laws of Idolatry' is not. On the other hand, the commandment of *lulav* is not performable without the four kinds: it consists of form and matter.

Remembering that matter and form are mobile categories, there is another level above the commandment, namely, the idea or form in relation to which the commandment is matter. In *Guide* iii. 43, Maimonides explains as follows: 'What seems to me regarding the *four species that constitute a lulab* is that they are indicative of the joy and gladness [felt by the Children of Israel] when they left the *desert*.' This fits the general explanation for the festivals of Passover and Tabernacles, that they 'inculcate both an opinion and a moral quality',[56] the opinion being inculcated by commemorating the events of the Exodus from Egypt, thereby confirming belief in the authenticity of the Bible and in divine providence, while the moral quality is gratitude for prosperity. This could be said to be the idea or form of the commandment as far as the *Guide* is concerned. But in *Mishneh torah*, Maimonides does something else.

---

[54] Ibid. 2: 1–3.   [55] *Guide* ii. 11 (p. 275).   [56] *Guide* iii. 43 (p. 572).

The last four *halakhot* of 'Laws of Ram's Horn, Booth, and Palm Branch' are about the joyous celebrations that took place in the Temple on the festival of Tabernacles.[57] The very last *halakhah* generalizes from that to the spirit in which all the commandments are to be observed: a spirit of joy combined with humility. This constitutes the service of God out of love, as advocated in the *Book of Knowledge*. In this way, the rituals in this section become a tributary of the main stream of *Mishneh torah*, which conducts the person who observes the commandments to the love and knowledge of God.[58] The form and matter of the commandment are subsumed by the higher form of the idea, leading ultimately to the form of forms.

If the commandments—individually, or collectively in a section or book of *Mishneh torah*—correspond to stars and spheres, then ideas of commandments correspond to angels. The idea of the commandment is, then, higher than the commandment as angels are higher than stars and spheres: it represents a greater degree of knowledge. It is the same in science: the status of a theory depends on the number of phenomena it encompasses. Higher-level theories cover more phenomena than lower-level theories.

The idea is to the commandment is to the object, as the intelligence is to the sphere is to the stars and planets. As a sphere is moved by its soul's desire for the intelligence, which itself has at least one thought fixed on the first cause, so performance of the commandment is motivated (or should be) by desire for the idea, which ultimately means love of the source of the commandment.[59]

---

[57] 'Laws of Ram's Horn, Booth, and Palm Branch', 8: 12–15.

[58] Note that 'Laws of Ram's Horn, Booth, and Palm Branch', 8: 14, stresses that the active participants in the Temple celebrations on Sukkot were the scholars and men of virtue. The rest of the people were spectators. This provides another link back to the *Book of Knowledge*: the exemplary scholar discussed in the previous chapter.

[59] From a philosophical rather than a literary direction, Amos Funkenstein arrives at a similar view. Funkenstein's interpretation of Maimonides' theory of the commandments is that, while the generality of a commandment expresses God's wisdom, its particulars are a product of his will, and therefore cannot be rationalized. This is parallel to the operation of God's wisdom and will in nature: 'Maimonides imagines the relationship between commandments and their material manifestation as being like the relationship in nature between form and matter' (*Maimonides: Nature, History*, 27).

Similarly, Josef Stern comments on the problem of the focus on the body in certain commandments, such as circumcision, which would seem to lead away from the apprehension of God: 'With each of these commandments, Maimonides therefore attempts to show that within its bodily subject matter there exists a more abstract form (or forms), an object of the intellect, expressing the practical and theoretical perfections of humanity. The aim of the philosophical interpretation of Scripture, and the explanation of its commandments, is to strip off its outermost matter to reveal this inner form' (*Problems and Parables*, 107). Stern differs from Funkenstein, however, on the question of the intelligibility of the details of the commandments—see below, Ch. 4, n. 74.

So the unifying concept of a book or section is its form; the form of a thing is its essential characteristic, that which makes it what it is, or its highest-level unifying feature. Hence we look to the highest-level idea or commandment in characterizing a book or section. This serves to cement the arguments made earlier about the conceptual justification for the inclusion of such anomalous-looking areas of law as marriage and divorce in the man–God division of *Mishneh torah*. The notion of marriage as holiness with which the *Book of Women* opens sets the book's character, notwithstanding the fact that it contains such mundane matters as laws governing the financial relationship between spouses. Similarly, 'Laws of Oaths' is in book 6, the *Book of Assevera-tions*, partly because, as with 'Laws of Vows' in the same book, its provisions may have to do with self-imposed restrictions, and may therefore be in the 'welfare of the soul' area, but also, mainly, because the swearing of oaths comes under the commandments to swear by God's name and not to take God's name in vain, so that even though some oaths have to do with the kind of commercial transactions treated in books 12 and 13, and obviously come within the scope of court procedure treated in book 14, their man–God aspect prevails;[60] hence they do not alter the man–God character of book 7. The problem of the splitting in the *Guide* of the commandments in 'Laws of Ethical Qualities' between the man–God and man–man categories can also now be resolved more satisfactorily. Many commandments have more than one aspect. To the prosaic viewpoint of the *Guide*, the commandments in 'Laws of Ethical Qualities' chapters 6 and 7 present their man–man aspect, but looking at that section in *Mishneh torah*'s own terms, we see that these commandments are downstream from the commandment of *imitatio Dei*, which forms the governing concept of 'Laws of Ethical Qualities'. The social commandments in 'Laws of Ethical Qualities' chapters 6 and 7 are thus not just statistically overwhelmed by the man–God theme; they are also conceptually subsumed by it.

The understanding of a commandment as form and matter makes possible a more precise definition of the correspondences between God–man commandments and the heavens, and between man–man commandments and sublunary nature. The relationship between form and matter is different on Earth and above the Earth. Above the Earth 'the bodies of the spheres . . . are substrata to permanent forms'.[61] Similarly, although the objects specified by the man–God commandments must necessarily be composed of the four elements, they play the role of heavenly bodies, serving as substrata for the

---

[60] See particularly 'Laws of Oaths', 11: 1.   [61] *Guide* ii. 11 (p. 275).

commandments and the permanent ideas they represent, be it a doctrine or a moral quality (although, as in the example of portions of the harvest given to the poor, the object of a man–God commandment may at the same time also fulfil an earthly function).

On Earth it is different. Forms are temporary, ceasing when the matter changes and decays. Similarly, man–man commandments apply to changing human transactions; there is no role play, and the objects concerned are not substrata and do not move from their earthbound economic or social significance. The man–man commandments relate to a permanent idea, the formation of an ideal society, only in the aggregate. In nature 'every being from among the bodies of the spheres has an existence that is proper to it and that it does not have in common with anything other than itself'.[62] Each is a distinct consciousness with its own level of comprehension of the divine. By contrast, the four elements and everything composed of them are merely changing forms of the same underlying, unconscious matter. Correspondingly, we shall find when we come to examine the dynamics of *Mishneh torah*'s structure in the next two chapters that, whereas the first ten books, although undoubtedly forming a system, can be related individually, or at least in sub-groups, to specific concepts, and each represents a distinct level of intellectual attainment, the last four books must be considered collectively as embodying a single process—they really belong under one title.

I remarked above that, in Maimonides, the distinction between man–God and man–man commandments ultimately falls away. This too can be expressed in terms of form and matter, for the ultimate aim is the realization of the uniquely human capacity to convert a temporary form, the hylic intellect that perishes with the body, into a permanent form, the acquired intellect that is immortal, and this requires the conversion of all human concerns, social, material, appetitive, and emotional, into the substrate of a developing intellect.

Maimonides' practice of rounding off books and sections of *Mishneh torah* with a homiletic or spiritual flourish promotes this view of the commandments as form. To the reader who has come through an entire book filled with myriad particulars of a division of the law, the final paragraph can make that book seem like a black and white picture suffused at a touch with colour. But the force of the impression derives from a rigorous method that shapes the book and *Mishneh torah* as a whole, from the sense that the discussion of the particulars of the body of the law is motivated by desire for the idea.

[62] *Guide* ii. 22 (p. 319).

The classification of the law in *Mishneh torah* is not a filing system that serves the commandments, but a system of ideas that the commandments serve.

The idea–commandment–object hierarchy is the tool with which Maimonides analyses the commandments and carves them into shape. This is what is meant by calling *Mishneh torah*'s form organic. It grows out of the nature of its elemental components. *Mishneh torah* is, then, not just clothed in cosmic form. The inner workings of the book correspond to the workings of the cosmos; the inner principle matches the outer form of expression.[63]

From 'Knowledge That' to 'Knowledge Of'

Table 4 above can be read in two directions. In the vertical plane, it gives a hierarchy stretching from intellect down to matter, represented in the composition of *Mishneh torah* by the idea–commandment–object hierarchy,

---

[63] The idea–object–commandment hierarchy might possibly provide a way of resolving a difficulty in Maimonides' explanation for the order of the twice-daily Shema recital. Explanation is called for because the three passages in the recital are not in the order in which they appear in the Torah: the passage recited third is earlier than the first two. 'Laws of Recitation of the Shema', 1: 2, states:

The paragraph *Hear* is recited first because it contains commandments concerning God's unity, the love of God, and the study of God, which is the basic principle on which all depends. After it, *If, then, you obey* is recited since the passage commands obedience to all the other commandments. After that, the paragraph concerning the fringes is recited, since it contains a command to recall all the commandments.

Leḥem mishneh (Abraham ben Moses de Bouton, sixteenth century) points out that a perfectly good explanation is to be found in the Talmud (BT *Ber.* 13*b*):

R. Yehoshua ben Korha said: Why does the passage of *shema* [*Hear*] precede that of *vehayah im shamo'a* [*If, then, you obey*]? So that one will first accept upon oneself the yoke of heaven, and after that the yoke of the commandments; and *vehayah im shamo'a* precedes *vayomer* [the paragraph concerning the fringes] because *vehayah im shamo'a* applies both by day and by night, while *vayomer* only applies during the day [there being no obligation to wear a fringed garment at night].

Surely, *Leḥem mishneh* comments, Maimonides should have furnished this explanation, and not one of his own invention.

Leḥem mishneh gives an answer (which seems partly based on a variant reading criticized by *Kesef mishneh* ad loc., in a note that itself reconciles Maimonides' and the Talmud's explanations of the Shema order) but his question draws attention to Maimonides' reformulation of the Talmud. 'The yoke of heaven' becomes 'the unity of the name and the love and study of him', precisely as set out in the *Book of Knowledge*; that is, Maimonides turns submission to divine authority into something intellectually tractable. Thereby, with the merest touch, and without straying very far at all from it, he transforms his source in line with his framework of the commandments. *Shema* becomes the idea, *vehayah im shamo'a* represents the commandments themselves, and *vayomer* is about the object (fringed garment), which, as in many of Maimonides' explanations of the man–God commandments, is presented as a reminder. On the phrase 'the study of him' as meaning the study of metaphysics, see Kellner, 'Philosophical Themes', 18 ff. See also Kellner's translation of the *Book of Love*, 184 n. 15.

where the object is the material substratum of the commandment. But read horizontally, from left to right, it is a diagram of the way the cosmos shapes human beings via the law. The cosmos is the form of the commandments, and the commandments are the form of man and of human society. In other words, for idea–commandment–object, substitute idea–commandment–reader. This makes the relationship of the author to his material the same as the relationship of the author to the reader, for the form he gives his material is a pattern of the idea he wishes to generate in the reader. We have reached the idea of an objective correlative broached in the Introduction. The form represents the web of thought and feeling behind *Mishneh torah* that is waiting to be reconstituted in the reader's mind.

An objection might be raised as follows: the evidence adduced so far proves nothing of the sort, because to justify the invocation of a term like objective correlative, and to make *Mishneh torah* qualify as a work of art in the sense that we normally attribute to that term, it has to be shown that it engages the reader. Form is not enough. It is fine and admirable that Maimonides symbolically represents the idea that the commandments are supposed to align a human being with the cosmos, but how does he make that correlate with anything in the reader's experience? Is this not precisely where his whole approach falls down? That he should begin his code with God as the non-contingent existence on which everything depends, and with an account of the heavens and the earth, is magnificent, and even more magnificent when that account is seen to underlie the form of the entire work; that his theory of the commandments mirrors his cosmology is wonderful; but all this is liable to leave the reader cold. If Maimonides intended not only to codify the law, but also to induce acceptance and observance of the law, this can't work. How much more effective is Judah Halevi who, in the *Kuzari*, bases Jewish truth claims on the direct, concrete manifestation of the divine in human affairs, and thereby begins to apply balm to the Khazar king's distress, sceptical though the king is at first, and via him to the distress of the Jewish reader.

Fairly obviously, the characterization of *Mishneh torah* that this implies is unfair. Maimonides constantly shows awareness of the reader, guiding and coaxing, anticipating and smoothing out perplexities, and, through his homiletic and philosophical interjections, making the legal details understandable and relevant.[64] Altogether, the persona of the narrator in *Mishneh*

---

[64] Twersky sums up his discussion of Maimonides' use of direct address to the reader in *Mishneh torah* thus: 'Direct address seems to be not mere literary convention but an educational device which both flatters and fascinates the reader, who is now and then encouraged to see himself as a one-man

torah is that of a stern but compassionate teacher. Nevertheless, I will try to meet the objection head on, for it presents an opportunity to examine the projected stance of the reader in relation to *Mishneh torah*.

A glance at the *Guide* will help to clarify what is meant. Maimonides addressed the *Guide* to his favourite pupil, Joseph ben Judah. This arose out of their situation: after Joseph left Fostat, where he studied with the master, he continued his education by correspondence. The *Guide* was indeed sent to Joseph in parts.[65] The epistolary or monologue form, though, is also a literary conceit. It has the entertainment value of making us eavesdroppers, and it also buys our confidence and makes us feel privileged. Joseph ben Judah is a proxy with whom the reader can identify, and thus feel as though the *Guide* cares particularly about him or her. At the same time, the form establishes a certain distance, as from a theatrical performance that we observe but in which we do not physically participate, allowing the imagination to be liberated. Maimonides gauged his relationship to the reader of the *Guide* carefully, adopting a form that renders us more amenable to persuasion than if we were lectured at directly, and that wins imaginative participation.

The question is whether he did anything similar in *Mishneh torah*. If it is accepted that the use of Hebrew indicates a poetic genre, which precise genre does *Mishneh torah* exemplify, and what relationship with the reader does that genre determine?

The answer is in fact a continuation of the observation above about Maimonides' interjections in *Mishneh torah*. *Mishneh torah* has characteristics of epic, a form midway between lyric and dramatic, retaining the personal urgency of lyric poetry, and combining it with controlled drama.[66] Its theme is a quest (a usual feature of epic) for the knowledge of God.[67] That it deftly combines the individual, national, and universal dimensions of this quest is further confirmation of epic status. *Mishneh torah*'s narrative kinship with the

---

audience receiving exclusive attention' (*Introduction to the Code*, 137). The reader is supposed to take *Mishneh torah* personally. In the last four books there is a feeling that Maimonides does not see himself as just recording the civil law, but as sitting at the judge's elbow—this sometimes surfaces quite clearly, for example, at the end of 'Laws of Agents and Partners', 10: 5. At the very least we can say that Maimonides the pedagogue is never far beneath the surface of Maimonides the legislator.

[65] On the way the *Guide* was actually composed, see Langermann, 'Fusul Musa'; Kasher, 'Early Stratum'.

[66] The definition is adapted from *A Portrait of the Artist as a Young Man*, chapter 5, in which James Joyce has his hero Stephen Dedalus say of epic: 'The personality of the artist passes into the narration itself, flowing round and round the persons and the action like a vital sea.'

[67] The quest is, of course, the underlying theme of Hartman, *Maimonides: Torah and Philosophic Quest*.

Torah was discussed in the Introduction, and the Torah itself is an epic of the establishment of God's kingdom on earth. The initial attempt, with all of humanity (represented by Adam and Eve), fails, and humanity is expelled from the Garden of Eden. The attempt then shifts to an individual, a family, and ultimately a nation, and the Torah ends with the nation about to re-enter the Garden of Eden, represented by the Land of Israel—from which it will eventually be expelled. The Torah contains much drama, but all is under divine control, and the reader's response to events is continually guided.

Mishneh torah has a similar theme, but going beyond the Torah to the prophets, it ends with a restoration that is both national and universal. All the time, its dramatic tension, between monotheism and idolatry, between intellect and matter, between love and awe, is under firm authorial control.

But how does the author win the reader's imaginative participation in this epic? To revert to the comparison with the *Kuzari*, the contrast between Maimonides' reference point in philosophy and Halevi's in history is a standard way of distinguishing the two most reverberative Jewish thinkers of medieval times, and of accounting for the former's alleged remoteness and the latter's immediacy. In the case of *Mishneh torah*, however, Maimonides does begin with history: the reader's history.

Mishneh torah could have opened thus: 'The foundation of foundations and the pillar of the sciences is that there is a First Being who brought every existing thing into being.' That is essentially how Alfarabi opens his *Al-madinah al-fadilah*: 'The First Existent is the First Cause of the existence of all the other existents.'[68] Ibn Pakuda, using imagery similar to that of Maimonides, begins chapter 1 of the *Book of Direction to the Duties of the Heart* with a more personal touch: 'When I searched for the most important pillar of our religion and the main root, I found this basic principle in the pure assertion of the unity of our Creator.'[69]

Ibn Pakuda here opens with his own history ('When I searched'), and thus invites the reader to join his quest. Maimonides, by contrast, with a single word, makes the quest the reader's own, for, in fact, *Mishneh torah* begins thus: 'The foundation of foundations and the pillar of the sciences is *to know* that there is a First Being who brought every existing thing into being.'[70]

This *halakhah* is not so much about God's existence as about consciousness of God's existence. The addition of the verb 'to know' transforms a statement of dogma about a remote 'First Being' (compare Ibn Pakuda's 'our

---

[68] Alfarabi, *Perfect State*, 57.   [69] Ibn Pakuda, *Duties of the Heart*, 109.

[70] In Hebrew 'to know' is a single word, *leida*.

Creator') into something requiring the reader's participation. At this stage, that participation could be seen as restricted to assent to the dogma, with its implication that God as the origin of all existing things has the authority to impose the commandments. Such is the basic meaning of the Hebrew *leida she*. The static image of 'foundation of foundations and the pillar of the sciences' reinforces the impression of something fixed and established.

On the other hand, Bernard Septimus argues that Maimonides' use of the word *mada*, as in *Sefer hamada* (*The Book of Knowledge*), refers to 'a property of mind' rather than to a body of learning, and comments, 'In *Mishneh Torah*, *yada* means both "to know" and "to come to know".'[71] In the particular case of the opening *halakhah*, Septimus seems to regard *leida* (the infinitive from the root *yada*) as meaning simply 'to know', but there is perhaps room for taking it in both senses, as referring both to recognition of God's existence as an objective fact, and to the start of a process of coming to know God.

Certainly, for Maimonides, to know something is not simply to be informed of it or to assent to its truth, but to internalize it. In the *Guide*, he maps the route from belief to knowledge:

> belief is the affirmation that what has been represented is outside the mind just as it has been represented in the mind. If, together with this belief, one realizes that a belief different from it is in no way possible and that no starting point can be found in the mind for a rejection of this belief or for the supposition that a different belief is possible, there is certainty. When you shall have cast off desires and habits, shall have been endowed with understanding, and shall reflect on what I shall say in the following chapters, which shall treat of the negation of positive attributes, you shall necessarily achieve certain knowledge of it.[72]

Achieving knowledge is a process that is moral as well as intellectual ('When you shall have cast off desires and habits'). *Mishneh torah* says, and its form shows, that all the commandments, in fact, all actions whatsoever, come under the rubric of knowing God.[73] It can be regarded as a transformation of 'knowledge that' into 'knowledge of'. Its opening can be read both as a demand to become convinced beyond doubt of God's existence, which is certainly required, and also as an open invitation to join an intellectual and moral process of developing the knowledge of God, a process that *Mishneh torah* instructs in, and embodies. This is not just a matter of objective, deductive proof; it reaches into every aspect of ritual, moral, and social experience.

---

[71] Septimus, 'What Did Maimonides Mean by *Madda*?', 86.

[72] *Guide* i. 50 (p. 111). On the stages of cognition, see Nuriel, 'Maimonides' Epistemology'.

[73] 'Laws of Ethical Qualities', 3: 3.

Mishneh torah is entirely true to its doctrine that there is no direct knowledge of God to be had; we can know God only through the things he has made, and we can do that only by becoming like the things he has made. *Mishneh torah* is a long process of 'becoming like', an epic of evolving human consciousness.

Nor does it lack *dramatis personae*. The first of them is unnamed:

And what is the way that will lead to the love of Him and the fear of Him? When a person contemplates His great and wondrous works and creatures and from them obtains a glimpse of His wisdom which is incomparable and infinite, he will straightway love Him, praise Him, glorify Him, and long with an exceeding longing to know His great Name, even as David said 'My soul thirsteth for God, for the living God' (Ps. 42: 3). And when he ponders these matters, he will recoil affrighted, and realize that he is a small creature, lowly and obscure, endowed with slight and slender intelligence, standing in the presence of Him who is perfect in knowledge. And so David said 'When I consider thy heavens, the work of Thy fingers—what is man that Thou art mindful of Him?' (Ps. 8: 4–5).[74]

This passage precedes the account of physics and metaphysics in 'Laws of the Foundations of the Torah'. It could be seen simply as a prelude to a fairly standard account of the universe, or it could be seen as an invitation, such as great art offers, to forget, at least for an instant, our accustomed concepts and categories, to experience afresh. If this seems too paradoxical to bear for a code of law, for law is all about imposing rules and conventions, it should be remembered what Torah is for Maimonides: not a conventional *nomos* designed to regulate the affairs of the state, but a divine law that brings about intellectual perfection in the knowledge of God. And if, as suggested in the Introduction, the first four chapters of that section are equivalent to the first chapters of Genesis, then the unnamed protagonist here is Adam as Everyman, looking at the universe as though for the first time.

As with the *halakhah* on the ascent of the prophet discussed in the Introduction, Maimonides uses language poetically in order to dramatize this moment, imbuing it with psychological truth and emotional force. In the Hebrew, in the phase of love, the sounds and cadences are firm, expansive, and resonant, with the words dividing into phrases that give a satisfyingly resolved, quasi-verse pattern of two metrical feet with two stresses followed by two with three stresses: *miyád hu ohév / umeshabé'aḥ umefa'ér / umitavéh ta'aváh gedoláh / leidá et hashém hagadól* ('he will straightway love Him / praise Him, glorify Him / and long with an exceeding longing / to know His great

---

[74] 'Laws of the Foundations of the Torah', 2: 2.

Name'). This gives way to an altogether different cadence in the phase of awe: *miyád hu nirtá la'ahoráv / veyirá veyifhád / veyedá shehu beri'áh ketanáh shefeláh afeláh / omédet bedá'at kaláh me'utáh / lifnei temím de'ót* ('he will recoil / affrighted / and realize that he is a small creature, lowly and obscure / endowed with slight and slender intelligence, standing / in the presence of Him who is perfect in knowledge'). Here we have timorous, open sounds, an uncertain rhythm, a deflated, even mournful tone.

In the previous chapter, the transition from love to awe was shown to be reflected in the transition from 'Laws of the Foundations of the Torah' to 'Laws of Ethical Qualities', but in fact this moment energizes all of *Mishneh torah*: the oscillation between love and awe is a pulse that beats right through it.[75] The twin emotions of desire to come close to God and abashed retreat find expression in several ways in the work, but what runs through its entire length and sustains this initial energy is a dramatic tension between the cosmic form, perpetuating the instant of wonder and signifying intellect unbound, and the halakhic content, embodying awe, and representing the need to conduct our material existence in the constant awareness of God's admonishing presence. This casting of the cosmic form as love and the halakhic content as fear is justified by the roles that Maimonides assigns to 'opinions' (i.e. physics and metaphysics) and to the commandments in the *Guide*: 'For these two ends, namely, love and fear, are achieved through two things: love through the opinions taught by the Law, which include the apprehension of His being as He, may He be exalted, is in truth; while fear is achieved by means of all actions prescribed by the Law.'[76]

Note that what overwhelms the Adamic protagonist is not the vastness of the universe, a created thing like him- or herself, but the thought of God's knowledge of the universe, which bears no comparison with human knowledge.[77] (Being awed by the universe itself turns out to be the beginning of idolatry.[78]) The person who gazes at the universe and is seized by the desire to know the Creator is thrown back by meeting the Creator's knowledge coming the other way, as it were.

[75] Compare Halbertal's remark on this passage: 'Cognition is not a neutral activity, devoid of desire and emotion, because enfolded within it is the kernel of the religious experience, which is built upon the pairing of attraction and recoil' (*Maimonides* (Heb.), 175); my translation.

[76] *Guide* iii. 52 (p. 630).   [77] See 'Laws of the Foundations of the Torah', 2: 10.

[78] See 'Laws of Idolatry', 1: 1. It must be acknowledged that 'Laws of the Foundations of the Torah', 4: 12, in which awe is associated with awareness of the superiority of the spheres and separate intellects, blurs the distinction. The point is perhaps that once the essential meaning of awe is understood, then knowledge of the universe feeds both love and awe of God. In *Guide* iii. 14 (pp. 456–9) Maimonides does use cosmic magnitudes as a stepping stone to the understanding of God's qualitative

The reader who appreciates the intensity of the Adamic moment, its evocation of the dawn of consciousness, begins to become involved in the process of transformation of 'knowledge that' into 'knowledge of', and thereby also capable of appreciating the artistic crystallization in *Mishneh torah*'s form of the drives set going. The depiction of the cosmos is a necessary stock of ideas, but also a template, a way of knowing.

In depicting wonder at the universe as the beginning of the desire for knowledge ('His great and wondrous works') our *halakhah* has an Aristotelian flavour, for Aristotle states in the *Metaphysics* that 'it is owing to their wonder that men both now begin and at first began to philosophize',[79] and in the same passage mentions the wonder of myth. Whereas, for Aristotle, wonder was the starting point of an intellectual journey to cognitive knowledge, Avicenna granted wonder, particularly wonder at poetry and myth, a validity in its own right: poetry affects us with a sense of pleasurable awe.[80] In this light, the idea of the form of *Mishneh torah* as an objective correlative of the feelings of love and awe looks less unlikely.[81]

The Adamic figure in 'Laws of the Foundations of the Torah', 2:2, is joined by other actors. We saw in the last chapter that Maimonides embodies the religious experience in role models, the nearer one of the scholar, and the more remote one of Abraham. If we are talking about the literary qualities of *Mishneh torah*, this is a further example of the way Maimonides creates depth of perspective, and involves the reader imaginatively as well as cognitively. The evidence of the existence of the First Being, or God, is the motion of the sphere: 'For the Sphere is always revolving; and it is impossible for it to revolve without someone making it revolve. God, blessed be He, it is, who, without hand or body, causes it to revolve.'[82] This is precisely how Abraham arrived at the knowledge of God:

By day and by night he was thinking and wondering: How is it possible that this (celestial) sphere should continuously be guiding the world and have no one to guide

difference from the world. 'Laws of the Foundations of the Torah', 4:12, and love and fear in *Mishneh torah* generally, are revisited in Ch. 6 below.

[79] Aristotle, *Metaphysics*, 982*b*.

[80] See Kemal, *Poetics of Alfarabi and Avicenna*, 157–69. Just as love and awe give rise here to the desire for knowledge, and at the end of the *Book of Knowledge*, knowledge leads to love, so *Mishneh torah* itself can be said to lead from wonder to educated wonder—cf. Black's remarks on Avicenna in *Logic and Aristotle's* Rhetoric *and* Poetics, 256–8.

[81] Contrasting the approach to rationalization of the commandments in the *Guide* with that in *Mishneh torah*, R. Joseph B. Soloveitchik writes, 'The *Code* does not pursue the objective causation of the commandment, but attempts to reconstruct its subjective correlative' (*The Halakhic Mind*, 94). Further on this, see pp. 307–9 below.   [82] 'Laws of the Foundations of the Torah', 1:5.

it and cause it to turn round; for it cannot be that it turns round of itself. He was submerged, in Ur of the Chaldees, among silly idolaters. His father and mother and the entire population worshipped idols, and he worshipped with them. But his mind was busily working and reflecting till he had attained the way of truth, apprehended the correct line of thought and knew that there is One God, that He guides the celestial Sphere and created everything, and that among all that exists, there is no god beside Him.[83]

Abraham recapitulates the opening of *Mishneh torah*, but in a specific historical time and place. *Mishneh torah*'s opening is even linked to him by an image: recognizing that there is a God is 'the pillar of the sciences';[84] Abraham is 'the pillar of the world'.[85]

The effect of this is twofold: it integrates the individual intellectual quest with the history and the mission of the Jewish people; and, conversely, it intellectualizes that history and that mission. The reader is in history, and history is in the reader. Being related in the same terms as the current command to know God, the story of Abraham's overthrow of idolatry becomes contemporary.[86] To adapt Aristotle, we are encouraged to philosophize in the same way as Abraham at first began to philosophize. There is here a kind of staging or activation of history that draws the reader in, as there is in the likenesses to Abraham in the portrait of the ideal scholar. Through narrative depth as well as structure, *Mishneh torah*'s form can be transformative.

Admittedly this lands Maimonides in a certain difficulty. The Jews in Maimonides' time and place were pressed by the claim of Islam to be the true heir to Abraham's legacy, and Islam is not idolatrous. If it adhered to the ideological tenets of monotheism, what was the point of paying the high price of maintaining the detailed observances of the law and the peculiar identity of the Jewish people?[87] By intellectualizing Jewish history, and making Abraham a self-selecting missionary, of independent mind and high courage but not distinguished by lineage—his parents were idolaters—or by a call from God, Maimonides apparently leaves Judaism all the more vulnerable to this pressure. Somehow he will have to show that his philosophical premises

---

[83] 'Laws of Idolatry', 1: 3.   [84] 'Laws of the Foundations of the Torah', 1: 1.

[85] 'Laws of Idolatry', 1: 2. The epithet is repeated at *Guide* iii. 29 (p. 516).

[86] Compare Josef Stern's comment on Maimonides' explanations in the *Guide* of the commandments as designed to counter Sabian cult practices: 'By uncovering the ancient Sabian myths that explain the Mosaic legislation of the *huqqim*, Maimonides believes that he is thereby exposing a major myth of his own day—astrology and the culture surrounding it—and thus a primary form of idolatry that the Law is still engaged in battling' (*Problems and Parables*, 111).

[87] See the analysis of *The Epistle to Yemen* in Halbertal, *Maimonides* (Heb.), 48–54.

entail continued adherence to the Mosaic legislation, the next event in his account in 'Laws of Idolatry' of the repeated lapses and recoveries of monotheism. We shall see the solution to this difficulty shortly.

Origin of the Commandments

There is also a more direct connection between the structure of the cosmos and the structure of the commandments. If, as Alfarabi held, 'everything which the state and the nation contains has its counterpart in what the entire universe contains', it follows that understanding of what the universe contains confers understanding of what the state contains. The person with the greatest understanding of what the universe contains is the prophet, who is also the highest type of legislator.[88] Once he has attained moral and intellectual perfection and understood all that he is capable of understanding of God's governance of the world, the prophet applies that understanding in governing the state. Moses, the greatest of the prophets, obtained complete knowledge of 'all existing things . . . their nature and the way they are mutually connected so that he will know how He governs them in general and in detail'.[89] When Moses made his request of God 'Show me thy ways',[90] what he was asking, according to Maimonides, was to be granted understanding of God's governance of the world in order to be able to govern the people, 'a people for the government of which I need to perform actions that I must seek to make similar to thy actions in governing them'.[91]

This, Howard Kreisel argues, 'alludes to the view that the legislation of the law is the product of Moses' translation of the theoretical knowledge of all of existence into a system of ideal rule in the human context'.[92] *Mishneh torah*'s microcosmic form supports his interpretation. The form reflects 'all of existence'; the content is 'a system of ideal rule'. The implication is that the law has microcosmic form because the cosmos is the law's origin. 'The great thing' begat 'the small thing', and eternally begets in the artistic suspension in time that is *Mishneh torah*.

Consistent with this is Maimonides' stress, in the first two of his fourteen principles in the *Book of the Commandments*, on the Torah commandments as comprising only the Mosaic legislation. This excludes from Torah status all rabbinical ordinances, and even laws derived from the Torah using the tradi-

---

[88] See *Guide* ii. 40 (p. 382).   [89] *Guide* i. 54 (p. 124).
[90] Exod. 33: 13.   [91] *Guide* i. 54 (p. 125).
[92] Kreisel, *Maimonides' Political Thought*, 15. See also id., '*Imitatio Dei* in "Guide"', 177 n. 23, and 'The Voice of God' (Heb.); Ivry, 'The Image of Moses in Maimonides'.

tional thirteen methods of exegesis. This approach is distinctively Maimonidean, representing a break with earlier thinkers, and it was destined to puzzle
Nahmanides.[93]

The uniqueness of the Mosaic legislation is paralleled by the uniqueness
of Moses' understanding of the cosmos. For in asserting that Maimonides
sees the cosmos as a model of the perfect human personality and the perfect
state, I have so far overlooked a fundamental difficulty: divine though the
source of intellect may be, in practice intelligibility is limited, and Maimonides did not believe that human beings were likely to be able to understand
the cosmos without the aid of prophetic insight. The difficulty lay in the gap
between theory and observation. Aristotelian physics, which posited a universe consisting of concentric spheres each in uniform motion, could not
account for the actual movements of the stars and planets. Ptolemy's astronomy, with its eccentrics and epicycles, did take care of the particular movements, and could be used to make very accurate predictions of the positions
of stars and planets, but it could not be reduced to general laws, certainly not
anything compatible with Aristotle. This is Maimonides' famous 'true perplexity'. How then, if we want to move beyond generalities, is a person supposed to find in the macrocosm a pattern of behaviour capable of imitation?

As far as *Mishneh torah*'s content is concerned, the answer is that he is not.
Imitatio Dei in 'Laws of Ethical Qualities', 1: 5–6, refers to God's governance
of the sublunary world,[94] and there Maimonides was sure that Aristotle had
got it right.[95] Besides, the commandment to be like God is presented as a matter of imitating the qualities attributed to God, rather than deriving understanding of God's ways from nature: 'Even as God is called gracious, so be
thou gracious.' Acquiring intellectual virtue might mean getting out the tele-
scope, but for moral virtue one need only read the Bible.

Mishneh torah's form, as we have seen, tells a different story. The model is
the cosmos as a whole, not just the part beneath the Moon. In that case, won't
'the true perplexity' stymie the quest for virtue?

The solution lies in the commandments of the Torah. They represent
Moses' unsurpassed, and unsurpassable, prophetic understanding of the cosmos translated into norms of behaviour. In *Guide* ii. 24, where 'the true perplexity' is presented, Maimonides recommends abandoning the futile effort
of trying to overcome it. Not for nothing does he make his recommendation

---

[93] See Halbertal, 'Maimonides' Book of the Commandments' (Heb.).
[94] With the possible exception of the injunction to be holy, on which see the next chapter.
[95] See *Guide* ii. 24 (p. 326).

in the following terms: 'Let us then stop at a point that is within our capacity, and let us give over the things that cannot be grasped by reasoning to him who was reached by the mighty divine overflow so that it could fittingly be said of him: *With him do I speak mouth to mouth*.'[96]

The one with whom God spoke mouth to mouth was, of course, Moses.[97] The mention of Moses here is not just pious acknowledgement of his superiority. It is crucial to the status of the law that Moses was uniquely capable of exceeding the reach of normal human understanding in penetrating, or receiving, the secrets of the cosmos.[98] That makes the commandments precious indeed. On this basis, the meaning of *Mishneh torah's* form is not just that observance of the commandments is a way of aligning the individual and the state with the cosmos: except for people of extraordinary talent—an Aristotle perhaps—it could be the only way.[99]

Performance of the Commandments and Immortality

Just as microcosm–macrocosm theory can help in understanding the origin of the commandments, their formal cause, it can perhaps also help in understanding how the commandments attain the purpose, or final cause, of winning immortality, and in resolving some apparent inconsistencies in Maimonides' statements on this matter.

As far as Maimonides is concerned, what survives death, if anything, is the acquired intellect, which becomes permanent through its apprehension of, and hence identity with, an incorporeal, imperishable form.[100] Performance of the commandments assists by laying the moral and political foundations for intellectual pursuits, but good deeds as such will not get a person into heaven.

Yet there are places where Maimonides seems to say that they will, or at least that they have a more direct part to play. Take, for example, the following from 'Laws of Repentance': 'The Holy One Blessed be He gave us this

---

[96] See *Guide* ii. 24 (p. 327).   [97] See Num. 12: 8.

[98] This, of course, is the reverse of the idea of the Torah as the blueprint for creation. See Kellner, 'Did the Torah Precede the Cosmos?' (Heb.).

[99] Note, however, that, according to Strauss, this was only a public teaching, and Maimonides in fact allowed for later prophecy to exceed that of Moses in 'the science of the Law'—see Strauss, 'How to Begin to Study *The Guide*', pp. xxxii–xliii. Levinger understands Maimonides as having an evolutionary view of the law itself—see his *Maimonides as Philosopher and Codifier* (Heb.), 56–66.

[100] See 'Introduction to *Perek ḥelek*' (*Commentary on the Mishnah*, Order *Nezikin*, 138)—for the translation, see Twersky, *Maimonides Reader*, 412; 'Laws of Repentance', 8: 2; Kellner, *Maimonides' Confrontation with Mysticism*, 220–9; Davidson, *Moses Maimonides*, 164.

Torah, "a tree of life", and anyone who does all that is written in it, and knows it completely and accurately, merits the life of the world to come, and his merit is in accordance with the extent of his deeds and the extent of his wisdom.'[101]

This puts knowledge and deeds on an equal footing as far as qualification for immortality is concerned, and moreover, the knowledge mentioned is of the Torah, not of incorporeal forms. It could be argued that what Maimonides really means here is deeds as preparatory to the acquisition of knowledge, but in the same *halakhah* he goes on to explain that the earthly rewards promised for fulfilling the commandments are in order that we 'will have leisure to become wise in the Torah and engage in it, and thus attain life in the World to Come', and concludes 'for when one is troubled here on earth with diseases, war or famine, he does not occupy himself with wisdom or the commandments, by which life hereafter is gained'. If life hereafter is actually only gained by apprehending a non-corporeal form, the insistence in this *halakhah* on fulfilment of the commandments seems overdone, even if we assume a need to accommodate conventional religious notions.

The idea that the commandments realize a human being's microcosmic form possibly provides a way out of the difficulty. It means that fulfilment of the commandments has intrinsic value as a means of attaining the kind of knowledge through the self discussed above in Chapter 1. The commandments also achieve that displacement of the ego from the centre of human concern described in *Guide* iii. 12 as the beginning of knowledge.[102] Knowledge objectifies nature and the commandments, making them avenues of love rather than means of gratification. Hence the greater the knowledge, the greater the love. When we identify with creation as a whole, we can perceive it as good, unperturbed by nature's indifference to human wishes. This would explain the mention of the commandments in that context:

On the other hand, men of excellence and knowledge have grasped and understood the wisdom manifested in that which exists, as *David* has set forth, saying: *All the paths of the Lord are mercy and truth unto such as keep His covenant and His testimonies.*[103] By this he says that those who keep to the nature of that which exists, keep the commandments of the Law, and know the ends of both, apprehend clearly the excellency and the true reality of the whole. For this reason they take as their end that for which they were intended as men, namely, apprehension.[104]

---

[101] 'Laws of Repentance', 9: 1.   [102] See Halbertal, *Maimonides* (Heb.), 177.
[103] Ps. 25: 10.   [104] *Guide* iii. 12 (p. 446).

In the microcosmic form of *Mishneh torah*, 'that which exists' and 'the commandments of the Law' come together, symbolizing the role envisaged in this passage for the commandments in bringing about 'apprehension'. Of course, mere performance of the commandments could never be enough. In 'Laws of Repentance', the world to come is not promised to someone who only 'does all that is written'; one must also know the Torah 'completely and accurately'. Similarly, in *Guide* iii. 12, we must 'know the ends of both'. But the implication is that someone who performs the commandments out of understanding of their form and purpose is aligned with a permanent form and on the way to securing some kind of immortality.[105] *Mishneh torah* promotes both performance and understanding. If we understand its form, we can see how it is designed to escort human beings to the world to come.[106]

Fourteen

The question arises whether any general significance can be found for the recurrence of the number fourteen in Maimonides' works. It could be co-incidence that, in the *Book of the Commandments*, the number of criteria for deciding what constitutes a commandment is the same as the number of books in *Mishneh torah*.[107] That his early work *The Treatise on Logic* discusses terms of logic under fourteen headings could also be coincidence, as could the later classification of the commandments in the *Guide*, where, although they are reshuffled to give an arrangement different from that of *Mishneh torah*, they again fall into fourteen classes.

We are not compelled to find a single explanation for all this, but an attempt can be made as follows.

A modern-day physicist may perhaps construct a mathematical model that predicts the existence of a hitherto unknown sub-atomic particle. When the particle is duly detected, the physicist may sense a certain mystery, there being no a priori reason that the structures of nature should correspond to the constructs of the human mind. As one prominent scientist has put it, 'Why the world should conform to mathematical descriptions is a deep question. Whatever the answer, it is amazing.'[108]

[105] Avicenna both describes grades of immortality and assigns morality a role in achieving them. See Davidson, *Alfarabi, Avicenna and Averroes on Intellect*.

[106] Further on the cognitive aspect of the commandments, see pp. 317–19 below.

[107] Fourteen may also be significant in the groupings of the commandments in *The Book of the Commandments*—see above, Introduction, n. 267.

[108] Wolpert, *The Unnatural Nature of Science*, 7. Compare Einstein's remark, 'One may say "the eternal mystery of the world is its comprehensibility"' (*Later Years*, 61). As a non-scientist, I accept

For Maimonides, things work the other way round. Knowledge is not produced by the human mind projecting its constructs onto the universe, but by the universe projecting forms onto the mind, via the agent intellect.[109] There is no mystery of intelligibility, for the universe *is* intelligibility. It is the complete manifestation of God's wisdom, and it actively communicates that wisdom, each mind comprehending it according to its capacity.

That is what Maimonides' signature number fourteen represents. It is the number of the cosmos, the sum total of its components (the ten angels with their spheres and the four elements), and so stands for completeness and rationality as the cosmos is complete and rational. In order to receive the emanation from the agent intellect, a human being must be brought to correspond to the structure of nature, in particular to the relationship between the superlunary world and the world of matter. In symbolic terms, a human being must be brought into line with the number fourteen. Furthermore, because knowledge is radiated from the universe, cosmology becomes epistemology; knowledge is organized according to the same form–matter hierarchy that prevails in the cosmos, a principle that Maimonides applies consistently in the way that he defines and explains the commandments.

The terms of logic are the manifestation of human intellect, and the means by which a human being strives for receptivity to God's wisdom in the cosmos. *The Treatise on Logic* purports to give a complete account of them. In it the number fourteen symbolizes this match between reason, or the tools of reason considered as a complete system, and the universe.

Through the fourteen principles set out in the *Book of the Commandments*, Maimonides defines the commandments as organizing principles, or forms. Here too, he aims at completeness, for the principles enable him to list the entire set of 613 commandments, and at rationality, for those same principles are in themselves wonderfully coherent and rational, and their product is an enumeration of the commandments that is the basis for their classification, that is, the discernment of their form. In other words, as the terms of logic are to nature, the principles of enumeration are to the commandments. The basis

Wolpert's testimony, and make no pretence at being able to judge the merits of attempts to dispel the mystery using the anthropic principle. The point here is only to clarify Maimonides' world-view.

[109] See *Guide* ii. 4 (p. 257); ii. 12 (p. 280); ii. 37 (pp. 373–5); Davidson, *Alfarabi, Avicenna and Averroes on Intellect*; Ivry, 'Arabic and Islamic Psychology'. Kraemer sums this up as follows: 'We humans think by means of the same (Agent) Intellect, as though our minds were our personal computers tapping into a main-frame computer, the cosmic mind, or Agent Intellect . . . The universe has a mind and we think with it. The universe is rational and knowable because the same cosmic mind that determines its order (the laws of nature) illuminates human intelligence' ('Islamic Context', 55).

for the assumption of intelligibility in the commandments is the same as its basis in nature: God is the source of the commandments and the source of reason. Completeness and rationality apply to the commandments not just in the principles of their enumeration, but because they are themselves onto-logically complete and rational, the entire manifestation of God's wisdom as a code of law, to which nothing can be added and from which nothing can be taken away.

I have already described *Mishneh torah* as the complete account of a com-plete and perfect law that originates in supreme insight into the cosmos and is designed to align human beings with the cosmos. Within *Mishneh torah*, as explained above, the rationale of the idea–commandment–object formation according to which the commandments are organized and are to be under-stood reflects the intellect–sphere–star formation, underlying which is the universal form–matter hierarchy.

Similarly, the *Guide*, although its method of rationalization of the com-mandments is different from that of *Mishneh torah*, presents the law as rational and complete, and organizes it according to general concepts, under which are listed particular commandments and their physical details.

To sum up, *The Book of the Commandments*, *Mishneh torah*, and the *Guide* are exercises in bringing reason, or form, to bear on the commandments, while *The Treatise on Logic* is an exercise in organizing the principles of reason itself. All four works aim at completeness. It is apt that all four should bear the stamp of the number fourteen, representing the ideal of rationality and com-pleteness which is the cosmos itself.[110]

[110] Strauss makes a similar connection between reason and law in Maimonides via the number fourteen as the number of chapters in the *Treatise on Logic* and the number of books in *Mishneh torah*, but without the cosmic dimension:

Should there be a connection between the number 14 on the one hand, and logic and law on the other? In the 14th chapter of the *Guide*, he explains the meaning of 'man'. We suggest this expla-nation: Man, being the animal which possesses speech, is at the same time the rational animal which is perfected by the art of reasoning, and the political animal which is perfected by law. ('Maimonides' Statement', 126)

It is possible, though, that at least one earlier writer did perceive more penetratingly the significance of the number fourteen in Maimonides' works. R. Nissim b. Moses of Marseilles wrote a commentary entitled *Ma'aseh nisim*, in which he set out to demonstrate that the miracles in the Torah could be explained by natural causation. Kreisel finds that the chief influence behind R. Nissim's rationalist approach was Maimonides (*Ma'aseh nisim*, 1). The first part of R. Nissim's commentary is a philosophi-cal introduction, in the course of which he associates the verse 'Let us make man in our image, after our likeness' (Gen. 1: 26) with the idea of man as microcosm (*Ma'aseh nisim*, 245), an association we found in the previous chapter in 'Laws of the Foundations of the Torah' and 'Laws of Ethical Quali-ties'. That first part has fourteen chapters. Kreisel remarks, 'It is no coincidence that the first part numbers fourteen chapters, a prominent number in the writings of Maimonides' ('Philosophical-

Some Contrasts

In order to bring the meaning of *Mishneh torah*'s structure into sharper relief, it will be useful to contrast Maimonides' use of the concepts of form and matter and the macrocosm–microcosm theory with the use made of them by other Jewish thinkers writing against the same philosophical background.

Judah Halevi and the Commandments as Matter

If Maimonides identified the law with reason, Judah Halevi had a quite different approach. Of Halevi's *Kuzari* (*The Book of Argument and Proof in Defence of the Despised Faith*) Guttmann writes, 'Halevi's apology, unlike that of his rationalist predecessors, does not attempt to identify Judaism with rational truth, but, elevating it above the rational sphere, claims for it exclusive possession of the full truth.'[111] Whereas for Maimonides knowledge of physics and metaphysics leads to the love of God, for Halevi the two things are discontinuous. 'The pious man is driven to God not by desire for knowledge, but by his yearning for communion with him . . . The yearning heart seeks the God of Abraham; the labor of the intellect is directed toward the God of Aristotle.'[112] The final aim of religion is not intellectual virtue, but rather cultivation of a 'supraintellectual religious faculty',[113] and it is towards this faculty that the commandments are directed; communion with the supernatural, rather than alignment with the natural. Although he is not unappreciative of nature, Halevi ultimately finds God in the miraculous, in the exceptions to the rules,[114] whereas Maimonides finds God in the rules; he does allow for miracles, but as far as he is concerned, nature is really miracle enough.[115]

In essence, for Halevi, there is no relationship between the law and nature. He sometimes uses nature for the purposes of analogy, but the commandments and nature remain on different planes. He insists that the only route to the divine and immortality lies through the commandments, so that, for example, when the Khazar king remarks that the Karaites, against whom

---

Allegorical Interpretation of the Torah' (Heb.), 301 n. 19). It could be that R. Nissim did not just mimic Maimonides' prominent number, but understood very well what it meant and intended to import its cosmic and rationalist significance. Following Colette Sirat, Kreisel puts the date of the commentary at 1315–25 ('Philosophical-Allegorical Interpretation of the Torah' (Heb.), 299 n. 12).

[111] Guttmann, *Philosophies of Judaism*, 121. Maimonides was, of course, a successor, not a predecessor.   [112] Ibid. 125.   [113] Ibid. 126.   [114] e.g. in *Kuzari* 5: 22.

[115] His impatience with those who prefer the miraculous to seeing the divine in nature is expressed in *Guide* i. 6 (pp. 263–4).

the rabbi has been inveighing, appear more devout than do adherents of rabbinic Judaism, the response is that the Karaites simply do not have the right formula, so that their piety, however sincere, is in vain.[116] The right formula can only be known through revelation. Halevi compares this to form and matter in nature. Just as it is impossible for man to replicate the precise proportions of the elements required to receive any particular form, such as that of a lion or that of a horse, so it is impossible for him to work out the precise rituals that will invoke the divine.

This comparison involves no real connection between the commandments and nature; Halevi only uses the one to illustrate a point about the other. But the point of comparison on which his illustration turns is a very telling one. Whereas Maimonides sees the commandments as form, Halevi sees them as comparable to matter. This makes the commandments unintelligible, for intellection is the perception of form: the commandments become intelligible only in the mind of God, as it were, and only if they are performed correctly. Maimonides makes the commandments and nature equally knowable, while Halevi makes them equally mysterious, and whereas for Maimonides the details of the commandments are arbitrary, for Halevi they are all-important. In Maimonides' system, the commandments operate through the human mind, and are a way of enabling the mind to impose the idea of the unity of God on a disintegrative material reality, but Halevi sees them as a separate reality, and a direct line to God. In his casting of *Mishneh torah* in cosmic form, Maimonides took a definite position on an issue over which the Jewish tradition is divided.

Sa'adyah and the Microcosmic Temple

Maimonides was not the first to see a microcosm–macrocosm dimension to the commandments. One set of commandments attracted cosmic musings from quite ancient times, namely, those about the Tabernacle and the Temple. Certain expressions in the account of the construction of the Tabernacle in Exodus that echo the account of creation in Genesis stimulate *midrashim* that elaborate on correspondences between the two events, taking in hints from all over Scripture, in the usual way of Midrash. Cosmic parallels for Temple furnishings are also to be found in Josephus, and in Philo, who attributed cosmic significance to both the Temple and the High Priest's garments.[117] Maimonides would not have known about Josephus or Philo, but he would

---

[116] *Kuzari* iii. 23.

[117] See above, Introduction, n. 185. For a full account and references see Klawans, *Purity, Sacrifice, and the Temple*, 111–44.

certainly have been aware of the *midrashim*, and almost certainly of the later development of the midrashic ideas by Sa'adyah Gaon. Of Sa'adyah's approach, Henry Malter states:

The 'Commentary on the Book of Creation' is, so far as I know, the only extant work of Saadia in which he touches also upon the ancient idea of the parallelism existing between the universe as a macrocosm and man as a microcosm . . . Following a Midrash, Saadia interposes between these two worlds an intermediary world, which is represented by the Holy Tabernacle. He refers the reader to his 'Commentary on the Construction of the Temple'.[118]

We do not have the *Commentary on the Construction of the Temple*, but R. Abraham Ibn Ezra cites it in his *Long Commentary* on Exodus 25: 40, where he states: 'For one who knows the secret of his soul and the formation of his body can know the things of the upper world. For man is the figure of a small world . . . The Gaon mentioned that there are eighteen things in the Tabernacle, which is the middle world, and their likenesses are in the upper world, and similarly in the small world.'[119] Ibn Ezra himself, in the same place, compares the Temple to the small world, that is, man, in order to argue that just as in a human body certain parts, such as the heart, are more important than others, so in the world, although God is everywhere, certain locations are more imbued than others with his presence.

Maimonides' view of the Temple's status differs from the essentialist view of Ibn Ezra; he does not consider the Temple to be inherently holy,[120] and would presumably have regarded Ibn Ezra's comparison with the human body as specious. In fact, we saw in the previous chapter exactly how Maimonides retreated from just such a comparison. Having suggested that God is to the world as the heart is to the body, he points out that the analogy is invalid because the heart is in the body but God is not in the world. Ibn Ezra's attempted analogy would fail the Maimonidean test because it violates the doctrine of God's absolute non-physicality, his separateness from the world, and from all human concepts, which cannot escape the physical human condition.[121] Maimonides' version of the microcosm–macrocosm theory supports argument by analogy from God to man, but not the other way round.

---

[118] Malter, *Saadia Gaon*, 186.

[119] See also the *Short Commentary* on Exod. 25: 7.

[120] 'Laws of the Temple', 6: 16 could be viewed as saying the opposite, but see Kellner, *Maimonides' Confrontation with Mysticism*, 107–15.

[121] On Maimonides and Ibn Ezra, see Twersky, 'Did Ibn Ezra Influence Maimonides?' (Heb.). On Maimonides' use of analogy in the *Guide*, see Schwartz, 'Maimonides' Philosophical Methodology' (Heb.).

More interesting for present purposes is the kind of parallelism suggested by Sa'adyah, because it is so close to, yet so different from, that suggested by Maimonides. For the middle panel in Sa'adyah's triptych of man, Tabernacle, and cosmos, Maimonides substitutes the commandments. Whether or not he was responding specifically to Sa'adyah in this matter, the Temple-as-microcosm idea had currency, and so it is legitimate to present it in Sa'adyah's version as a foil to Maimonides' approach to microcosm–macrocosm theory.

Maimonides does not ascribe cosmic significance to the Temple.[122] In the *Guide*, he classes the Temple ritual as part of the second intention of the law, the accommodation of human nature and the gradual weaning of it from paganism.[123] As such, the Temple has no absolute value. It is designed to instil awe only; the cosmos instils both awe and love. The Temple ritual cannot, then, of itself lead to the knowledge and love of God, and so there are no grounds for comparison with the absolute and perfect system of the cosmos. Any such comparison would have been quite incongruous in the *Guide*.

In *Mishneh torah*, matters are more complicated. There, as will be shown in the forthcoming chapters, Maimonides evinces a dual attitude to the Temple. The form of *Mishneh torah* can be interpreted both as exalting the Temple's importance and also as deprecating it in line with the attitude of the *Guide*: exalting in the law's public aspect; deprecating in its private aspect. How the duality arises will be explained later; the point here is that even on the exalted interpretation, there is no cosmic parallelism. No doubt with the exercise of a little ingenuity a cosmic correspondence *could* be read into the *Book of Temple Service*, but, unlike 'Laws of the Foundations of the Torah' and 'Laws of Ethical Qualities', and *Mishneh torah* taken as a whole, that book provides no surface hint that I can detect inviting such a reading. Assuming that none exists, the contrast between Maimonides and Sa'adyah can, then, be expressed both in the negative and in the positive: Sa'adyah sees the Tabernacle/Temple as a microcosm; Maimonides does not, but rather presents the law as a whole as a microcosm.

To make parts of the Tabernacle/Temple correspond to parts of the heavens is to start to make the elementary mistake made by the generation of Enosh, who considered the heavenly bodies intrinsically worthy of respect as God's ministers, setting off a process of degeneration that ended with temples being built to the stars.[124] At the most basic level, the error was one of logic,

---

[122] But see Hadad, 'Nature and Torah in Maimonides' (Heb.), 132–47. Hadad interprets Maimonides' account of the Temple as a parable designed to replace a pagan understanding of cosmic processes with a true one.　　　[123] See *Guide* iii. 32.　　　[124] See 'Laws of Idolatry', i: 2.

consisting of the kind of illegitimate (from a Maimonidean standpoint) application of analogy as we saw being made by Ibn Ezra. Maimonides would not
countenance anything that might accidentally send us down that slippery
slope.

We have already noted that for Maimonides, sin or error consists in taking
means for ends or the part for the whole, and unfortunately that is exactly
what Sa'adyah does with the Temple. He makes a part of the system of commandments—the Tabernacle/Temple—transcendent by linking it to the cosmos, thereby granting it the status of an end, the place where human beings
meet the universal. Since, for Maimonides, the Tabernacle/Temple belongs
to the second intention of the commandments, it is no more than a means; it
is just a part of the commandments and does not stand for the whole. The
parts attain their full significance only in relation to the whole, and only the
whole can be transcendent, never the parts. So Maimonides shifts the cosmic
parallel from the part to the whole.

Another approach to the same idea is via the concept of *imitatio Dei*.
According to Jonathan Klawans, *imitatio Dei* underlies the Temple-as-
microcosm idea. As he puts it in relation to Josephus's version of that idea,
'Just as God creates the world, so too people create the earthly symbol of that
world, the temple.'[125] Maimonides, as we have seen, works with a very different notion of *imitatio Dei*, one located not in the Temple but in the intellect.
The intellect, not the Temple, is the centre from which enlightenment and
morality spread abroad, and *imitatio Dei* is a matter of bringing oneself under
the rule of intellect as the universe is under the rule of God.

This is the end which the commandments serve, but again, they do so as
a complete system, and no one commandment or set of commandments
makes man God-like. If the commandments derive in their entirety from
the cosmos through the intellect of the prophet, they cannot lead back to the
cosmos, that is, back to conjunction with the agent intellect, except through
the intellect of the person who observes and comprehends them in their
entirety: there are no short cuts via the Temple. Hence the commandments as
a whole, rather than the Temple, occupy the middle panel as the medium
for the apprehension of God, or of God's works, which are all that can be
apprehended of him.

But wait: did we not spend the previous chapter demonstrating that a
microcosm–macrocosm relationship exists between 'Laws of Ethical Qualities' and 'Laws of the Foundations of the Torah'? Does this not mean that

[125] Klawans, *Purity, Sacrifice, and the Temple*, 115.

one set of commandments does make man God-like, and that one set of commandments can be a microcosm? In that case, the difference between Sa'adyah and Maimonides is not between a partial and a holistic approach to applying microcosm–macrocosm theory to the commandments; it is rather a matter of the selection of two different sets of commandments for the purpose—still an interesting difference, but not as dramatic or fundamental as made out above.

Such an objection is based on an incomplete picture of how the microcosm–macrocosm theory operates in *Mishneh torah*. The next chapter will seek to supply the missing element, namely, emanation. For now, it will simply be asserted that 'Laws of Ethical Qualities' and 'Laws of the Foundations of the Torah' are not to be regarded as separate sets of commandments. Within the system that is *Mishneh torah*, they, along with the rest of the *Book of Knowledge*, form a pattern that is projected onto *Mishneh torah* as a whole, and all flows, logically and formally, from the basic principle enunciated at the beginning, that everything is contingent upon God. The parallelism between *Mishneh torah* and the cosmos is an amplification of the parallelism between 'Laws of Ethical Qualities' and 'Laws of the Foundations of the Torah', not a separate instance.

This awaits elucidation. The point here is that Maimonides re-engineered Sa'adyan microcosm theory as applied to the commandments, transferring the interface between man and God from the Temple to the mind.

Proto-Kabbalah and the Mystical Microcosm

The fact that there were previous applications of microcosm theory of which he could not approve, as well as his apparent downgrading of the Temple, which might be unacceptable to some, are possible reasons that Maimonides preferred to signal his parallelism between the commandments and the cosmos covertly rather than overtly. He was probably wary of the risk of confusion with astrological and theurgic notions on the part of people without a proper grounding in science.[126] At the covert level, the polemic is not only aimed at Sa'adyah. Moshe Idel has portrayed Maimonides as standing in opposition to antique mystical trends that, in reaction to him, regrouped as kabbalah.[127] In that case, the cosmic symbolism of *Mishneh torah* can be

---

[126] See also Gersonides, *Commentary on Song of Songs*, trans. Kellner, Translator's Introduction, pp. xxix–xxxi.

[127] See Idel, *Kabbalah: New Perspectives*, 253. Idel writes from the point of view of kabbalah. For a treatment of the subject from the point of view of Maimonides, see Kellner, *Maimonides' Confrontation with Mysticism*.

seen as a silent argument against what Kellner, following Idel, calls 'proto-kabbalah'.[128] For the motif of man as microcosm and the attribution of cosmic significance to the number ten are found in mystical writings too, but in very different form and with very different implications.

Three features of Maimonides' thought differentiate his application of microcosm–macrocosm theory from that of the mystics. The first is that the relationship that the cosmic form of *Mishneh torah* implies between the law and nature is within a single, post-Creation reality. As Stern puts it, 'the parallel Maimonides constantly emphasizes between the Law and divine, i.e. natural, acts is not a parallel between two *different* domains but *within* one domain'.[129]

Secondly, no direct connection is implied between particular commandments and particular constituents of the cosmos. The correspondences work through analogous structures and functions. The likenesses between the parts of the two systems are conceptual, not real. Thus the *Book of Knowledge* is like the diurnal sphere in that it moves the rest of the commandments; or the *Book of Love* is comparable to the second sphere, that of the fixed stars, in that the defining characteristic of the commandments it contains is that they are constant. What that means is that, just as the fixed stars move in constant motion relative to the diurnal sphere, and thus make the motion of the latter visible, so the commandments in the *Book of Love*, such as the Shema recital, act as constant reminders of the doctrines in the *Book of Knowledge*, making them too, as it were, visible. What it does not mean is that reciting the Shema somehow puts the reciter in touch with the *ofanim*, the second order of angels that governs the sphere of the fixed stars. The fact that Maimonides gives a different classification of the commandments in the *Guide* yet within the same cosmic scheme denoted by the number fourteen, though it requires further explanation, is at least evidence that there is no real connection between commandments or groups of commandments and the heavens.

Thirdly, traffic between the heavens and the earth is strictly one-way. Performance of the commandments has a reflexive effect on the performer, and also affects his or her social surroundings, but has no effect whatsoever on any higher realm. Similarly, saying that the commandments derive from Moses' perfect understanding of the cosmos does not mean that Moses was a super-astrologer who saw the commandments written in the stars. It means that he understood the governance of the cosmos as a whole system, and could extract its forms, and translate them into legislation. Maimonides'

---

[128] Ibid. 5–31.   [129] Stern, 'Idea of a Hoq', 97.

motive in denouncing astrology is to maintain the doctrine of free will, and to preserve monotheism, but the ground of his objection is that astrology is unscientific.[130] In Maimonides' system, the superlunary world certainly influences the sublunary world, but he insists that such influence must be described by a general theory that traces cause and effect. The commandments are therefore not a means of drawing down heavenly forces in a supernatural way, and certainly not a means of manipulating such forces. Lower entities can have absolutely no effect on higher ones.

In all these respects, Maimonides differs from mystical conceptions whereby Torah and the form of man precede creation, so that the commandments and the idea of man as microcosm are ways of connecting with, and even influencing, a higher, supernatural reality.

Maimonides' opposition to views arising from certain *midrashim* that depict God as consulting the Torah in creating the world, or which claim that the patriarchs observed the commandments and that the commandments represent a fixed secret pattern of creation and therefore a key to theurgic manipulation of supernatural influences, has been documented by Kellner.[131]

As for the form of man, this too, as the *adam elyon*, the supernal man, functions in mystical thought as a pattern for creation, and it is linked to the number ten. The native Jewish tradition of cosmic significance for the number ten is quite different from the Aristotelian philosophical tradition on which the cosmology underlying *Mishneh torah*'s form is based. Idel writes, 'the motif of a divine anthropomorphical decad, instrumental in the creational process, was part of ancient Jewish thought. This decad was presumably the source of the ten *sefirot* of *Sefer yetsirah*.'[132]

In the mystical version of macrocosm–microcosm theory, there is an actual one-to-one relationship between parts of the microcosm and parts of the macrocosm, with the commandments mediating between the two. As Idel puts it:

there was more than a pure structural correspondence between the Supernal *Merkavah*, alias the *Adam Elyon* or Sefirotic Realm, and the 613 commandments; the

---

[130] Here I follow Tzvi Langermann's line on Maimonides' critique of astrology. Gad Freudenthal considers that Maimonides failed to muster a coherent case. See Langermann, 'Maimonides' Repudiation of Astrology'; Freudenthal, 'Maimonides' Philosophy of Science'.

[131] Kellner, 'Did the Torah Precede the Cosmos?' (Heb.). Kellner opines that the *midrashim* themselves are simply intended to express the notion that the existence of the universe is not value-free, and that it took over-literal interpretation to make them support the kind of ideas that Maimonides confronted.

[132] Idel, *Kabbalah: New Perspectives*, 112. Judah Halevi rejected the theory of emanation in favour of the *sefirot*—see *Kuzari*, iv. 25, v. 22.

latter were conceived as instrumental for the Kabbalists' power to influence Divinity as theurgical practices which constituted the very core of the mainstream of Kabbalah.[133]

The direct link between the commandments and *ma'aseh merkavah*, contrasting with the analogical relationship posited by Maimonides, is made very clearly in a statement by Rabbi Menahem Recanati (*c.*1250–*c.*1310): 'The commandments depend on the Supernal Merkavah . . . and each and every commandment depends upon one part of the Merkavah.'[134] The source is of course anachronistic, but the idea is an outcome of the mystical trends traced by Idel that pre-date Maimonides.

To sum up, the application of microcosm–macrocosm theory in the mystical stream of Judaism stands opposed to the application embodied in *Mishneh torah*'s form on all three counts enumerated above: Torah and the form of man exist in a separate domain from nature; the connection between halakhah and *ma'aseh merkavah* is direct and real; and the commandments have theurgic power.

That said, it must be acknowledged that not all strands of Jewish mysticism are antithetical to Maimonides in the same degree. Gershom Scholem described kabbalah as 'the product of the interpenetration of Jewish Gnosticism and Neoplatonism'.[135] Idel disputes this formulation, on the grounds that it makes kabbalah too thoroughly non-native to Judaism, but acknowledges that kabbalah owes a debt to Neoplatonism.[136] Although Maimonides took a different fork in the Neoplatonic road from the one that would be taken by the kabbalists, it is open to question just how different the ultimate destinations are. Prophecy in Maimonides has a well-defined theoretical framework and its content is transmittable, useful knowledge, but all the same, the prophet's near-disembodiment as described in 'Laws of the Foundations of the Torah', 7:2, bears comparison with the ecstasy of the mystic.[137] Moreover, it will be argued in Chapter 4 that the Neoplatonic aspect of *Mishneh torah*'s form includes what is generally regarded as a motif of mystical thought, namely, the ladder of ascension.

---

[133] Idel, 'Maimonides and Kabbalah', 44.

[134] *Commentary on* Ta'ame ha-Mitzvot, ed. H. Lieberman (London, 1963), fo. 3*a*, cited in Idel, 'Maimonides and Kabbalah', 44.

[135] Scholem, *Kabbalah*, 45.   [136] See Idel, 'Maimonides and Kabbalah'.

[137] See Blumenthal, 'Maimonides' Intellectuallist Mysticism'. According to Idel, Maimonides did find greater favour among some of the ecstatic kabbalists than among the theurgical kabbalists—see 'Maimonides and Kabbalah', 70.

In the end, though, the very status of *Mishneh torah* as a work of art, its transformation of the commandments from *kinesis* to *stasis*, is counter-mystical. Idel describes the limits of kabbalistic symbolism thus:

The Kabbalist is, however, far more than one who has succeeded in understanding a given event in the divine world. As Ricoeur aptly puts it, symbols 'invite thought'. But interesting as this diagnosis of symbolism may be for Christian thought, in mystical Judaism it is still only a preliminary step. Understanding the higher structures and dynamics, the Kabbalist is invited, even compelled, to participate in the divine mystery, not by understanding, faith, and enlightenment, but primarily by an *imitatio* of the dynamics. The transparency of the divine world through symbols is secondary to the pedagogic role of bringing someone to action. The comprehension of the 'mystery' is meaningless if not enacted in every commandment, even in every movement one performs. In other words, the main role of Kabbalistic symbolism is the presentation of a reflection of the theosophical structure. This dynamic structure functions as a powerful instrument of ensuring the dynamism of human activity and endowing it with a sublime significance, which is why the 'pure contemplation' of Kabbalistic symbolism falls short of penetrating its ultimate nature . . . The Kabbalistic symbols strove to induce an active mood or approach to reality rather than to invite contemplation.[138]

By contrast, the symbolism of *Mishneh torah* is not a set of levers, as it were, but a set of interrelated signs, the function of which is precisely to invite contemplation. The commandments prescribe acts, but, again, these acts are reflexive. They shape the human actor into an analogy of cosmic form, making him or her capable and worthy of perceiving form, and ultimately of knowing God, the form of forms. The kabbalist rebounds from symbolism to action. *Mishneh torah* takes us through symbol and action to knowledge.

The aesthetic difference begins with differing attitudes to nature. By positing a dual reality, mysticism turns nature into a veil between man and God, hiding the divine as a garment hides its wearer, but giving clues about the wearer to those who can decode it. Maimonides too speaks of a veil, but in a very different sense. Matter, he says, is 'a strong veil preventing the apprehension of that which is separate from matter as it truly is' so that 'we are separated by a veil from God'.[139] The veil here is not the world hiding God like a garment; it is not a fact about the world at all, but a fact of the human condition: as physical creatures, human beings have a limited ability to perceive forms, separate or immanent in matter, and are absolutely unable to perceive God as he is.

---

[138] Idel, *Kabbalah: New Perspectives*, 252–3.   [139] *Guide* iii. 9 (pp. 436–7).

Alongside this limitation lies an inestimable gain. Since God produces nature yet is utterly separate from it, nature is not a garment, but simply itself, complete and perfect, and bare to reason's gaze. It is through reasoning about nature, stimulated by the love of God arising from wonder at creation, that a human being activates what in him or her is potentially God-like. In short, whereas, for the mystic, nature conceals God, for Maimonides nature reveals God, or all of God that will ever be revealed.

It follows that, while room can be found in Maimonides' system for valuing art as the imitation of nature, in the eyes of a kabbalist, as in the eyes of Plato, it is liable to be worse than valueless, a distraction from reality.[140] As was stressed in the Introduction, the imitation of nature does not, fundamentally, mean the representation of natural objects, but the reproduction of a natural state or process. Nature is prior to the commandments and to art, but each, in parallel, is, or strives to bring into being, that to which nothing can be added and from which nothing can be taken away. It is in this that beauty consists, and it is for this reason that Maimonides can approve of art in the right circumstances.

It is for this reason too that the commandments are susceptible of artistic treatment; their ethical values are translatable into aesthetic values. But this does not endow the commandments with any inherent symbolism. Whatever symbolic significance is attributed to them, whether individually or as a whole, is a construct. In its poetic aspect, *Mishneh torah* gives a possible, but not necessarily definitively true, symbolic representation of the meaning of the commandments. In the phrase Maimonides consistently uses to qualify intellectual attainment, it is *kefi koho*, in accordance with his capacity and understanding.

In the kabbalistic conception, by contrast, the commandments are imbued with symbolism.[141] They relate to the supernal structure in a direct, fixed, objective way. Kabbalistic aesthetic values too are vertically orientated, towards the absolute. As Kalman Bland writes, the kabbalists 'renounced the strictly psychological, relativistic, and anti-metaphysical foundations of Maimonidean aesthetics' in favour of a notion that 'cosmic beauty originates within the mysterious depths of God's being'.[142]

---

[140] 'According to Maimonides himself, nature was an important avenue, and according to S. Pines' view, the single way open to the apprehension of the reality of the divine. Therefore, actual interest in natural phenomena was a religious requirement, almost an obligation . . . The Kabbalists, on the other hand were not interested in nature as an actual domain of contemplation' (Idel, *'Deus Sive Natura'*, 100).   [141] See Idel, *Kabbalah: New Perspectives*, 227–8.

[142] Bland, 'Beauty, Maimonides, and Cultural Relativism', 103. See also above, Introduction, n. 71.

Maimonides allows no ontological, ideal status to beauty, divine or otherwise, but locates it in the mind. Just as, in his view, the commandments are self-reflexive, his artistic meditation on them is self-reflective, and stimulates self-reflection in the reader—and therein lies its ultimate beauty.[143] It discloses the commandments' immanent form, or rather its author's perception of that form, to the reader *kefi koḥo*, to the extent of his or her own individual, developing apprehension. Rather than evoking the splendour of a divine realm, a frequent subject of mystical poetry, it suggests epiphanies reachable within natural boundaries. Altogether, *Mishneh torah* presents a poetic alternative to mysticism as much as a philosophical one.

Since the visions of the prophets embody their understanding of nature, they, like nature, are bare before reason, so that, for example, the first chapter of Ezekiel can be interpreted according to scientific cosmology, without the aid of tradition.[144] Maimonides' identification of the esoteric lore of *ma'aseh bereshit* and *ma'aseh merkavah* with the natural philosopher's physics and metaphysics was one of the main elements of his thought to provoke criticism by the kabbalists.[145] But, cast in symbolic form, what they saw as profanation is what conveys Maimonides' motivation of love and lends *Mishneh torah* the repose of art.

Summary

Mishneh torah's microcosmic form reflects the various parallels that Maimonides draws more or less explicitly in the *Guide* between the laws of nature and the law of the Torah: both are perfect; both are permanent; both are accessible to reason. It implies the Torah's derivation from nature via the uniquely comprehensive prophecy of Moses, who understood God's gover-

---

[143] Compare Kemal on the poetics of Alfarabi:

By explaining that poetic discourse is imaginative, al-Farabi implies that poetry either lacks concern with truth or is false. Poetic discourse consists in statements which are meaningful and which, while neither true nor false, at best *show* the connections it seeks to make . . . That is, poetry is self-reflective in spite of its basis in imaginative representations. The simple and essentially correct reason for this is that poetic discourse, being constituted of imaginative representations, cannot be true of the world for reasons given above, but does reveal something of the minds that construct those representations. (*Poetics of Alfarabi and Avicenna*, 123)

Similarly, the point of *Mishneh torah*'s form, according to my interpretation, is to show certain connections, and reveal the mind that constructed it. The question how far Maimonides considered his representations to be true of the world and how far they are an imaginative construct is taken up again in Ch. 6.

[144] See *Guide* iii, Introduction (p. 416). 'Received tradition' is the basic meaning of 'kabbalah'.

[145] See Idel, 'Maimonides and Kabbalah'.

nance of the world more perfectly than anyone before or since, and translated this understanding into a system of laws.

The literary form of *Mishneh torah* leads to an understanding of the commandments as form. The 'great thing', the order of nature, is the form of the commandments, and the commandments form human individuals and society as microcosms. The inner principle that gives life to these structures is *imitatio Dei*, the ideal of the commandments, and the mover of the universe itself. As transmitters of form, the commandments are also conduits of knowledge, the knowledge of God constituted by the realized microcosmic form of man as discussed in the previous chapter. Spanning the entire gamut of human existence, from its most physical to its most intellectual aspects, the commandments dissolve the Aristotelian partition between moral and intellectual virtue, directing, even converting, experience to knowledge.

Mishneh torah does not just convey this through objective form, but engages the reader in a process of developing the knowledge of God through imaginative participation in its narrative.

Despite Maimonides' programmatic remarks about ease of reference and so forth, the classification of the commandments in *Mishneh torah* is above all a rationalization of the commandments. Through its form, *Mishneh torah* presents them *sub specie aeternitatis*: they condense the rationality of the cosmos. Its treatment is to be distinguished from mystical interpretations that link the commandments to a supernal domain rather than to nature.

CHAPTER THREE

EMANATION

IN THE PREVIOUS CHAPTER the cosmic system of spheres and elements was presented as the model for the superstructure of *Mishneh torah*. In this chapter and the next we shall look at the Neoplatonic infrastructure, adding movement to the model, and exploring ways in which *Mishneh torah*'s inner dynamics correspond to cosmic processes. The Aristotelian model explains why *Mishneh torah* has fourteen books, but it does not wholly explain the sequence of those books. That sequence can be accounted for by the idea of emanation. As a reminder, this applies only to the sequence of the first ten books, on the man–God commandments. The last four, on the man–man commandments, will be considered in the next chapter.

Emanation, the idea that existence flows from higher hypostases to lower ones, was invoked in Chapter 1 in discussing the relationship between 'Laws of the Foundations of the Torah' and 'Laws of Ethical Qualities'. Although it is one concept, it will be convenient to split it into two components: hierarchy itself, and the flow from higher entities in the hierarchy to lower ones. This will be applied to the first ten books of *Mishneh torah* by arguing two propositions:

1. The first ten books of *Mishneh torah* are arranged according to a hierarchy from higher to lower.

2. A formal pattern originating in 'Laws of the Foundations of the Torah' is repeated first in the *Book of Knowledge* as a whole, and then over the first ten books. This pattern carries the basic concepts set out in 'Laws of the Foundations of the Torah' and the *Book of Knowledge* into the rest of *Mishneh torah*. The flow of both content and form from the *Book of Knowledge* corresponds to the Neoplatonic idea of the Forms emanating from the One.

Plotinus posited a twofold process of emanation, from the One to Intellect, and from Intellect to Soul. Alfarabi subsequently applied emanation to the

Aristotelian system of the spheres, to give ten levels, each produced from the one above it, from the first cause down to the agent intellect.[1] The descent from one level to the next is also a decline in reality and value, until the process peters out, to leave matter, which has no reality, and no value. Reality, contrary to our usual notion of it as the sensible and concrete, means having independent, permanent existence, which ultimately is true only of the One, whereas matter is considered an absence, rather as darkness is an absence of light. Value is almost synonymous with unity: the higher up the scale we go, the greater the degree of unity we find, until we reach the transcendent, incomprehensible unity of the One.

This is why it is assumed that the flow from higher to lower in *Mishneh torah* is manifested only in the first ten books, which are about the man–God commandments. They will be shown to be in descending order of reality and value. The last four books, which deal with the man–man commandments and the world of sublunary matter, are assumed to exhibit no such hierarchy, since the notions of reality and value do not apply beyond the ten levels of emanation; the sequence of those books will therefore need to be explained differently.

I shall look first at Maimonides' own version of the concept of emanation, and then apply it to *Mishneh torah* to observe the hierarchy of its first ten books. After that, the pattern of those first ten books will be traced to 'Laws of the Foundations of the Torah' via the *Book of Knowledge*. As a demonstration of its usefulness, this microcosmic model will be brought to bear on the well-known problem of Maimonides' attitude to animal sacrifices, which are deprecated in the *Guide*, yet treated as eternally relevant, with their laws fully expounded, in *Mishneh torah*. Lastly, I shall look at how the metaphor of water, which Maimonides uses as an image of emanation in the *Guide*, is also deployed to similar effect in *Mishneh torah*.

A note of caution must be sounded. Whereas, in the previous chapter, it was possible to establish a one-to-one correspondence between *Mishneh torah*'s superstructure and the components of Maimonides' cosmology, when it comes to its inward workings, matters are less straightforward. Patterns are not necessarily rigidly symmetrical, themes cut across one another, structures are looser, and altogether the model is less mechanical. We are dealing with an original, artistic rendition of the Neoplatonic model, not a slavish copy, and the model itself is not fixed—it developed over centuries. It becomes pointless to strain to find precise and consistent equivalences; sometimes one

---

[1] See Davidson, *Alfarabi, Avicenna and Averroes on Intellect*, and Appendix II.2.

can only point to tendencies and trends. Nevertheless, I believe that a plausible case emerges that the form of *Mishneh torah* embodies a Jewishly modified Neoplatonic world picture.

Maimonides on Emanation

As just noted, the change in viewpoint from that of superstructure has produced a switch of metaphor. Whereas up to now the basic image has been architectural, taking a cue from 'the foundation of foundations and the pillar of the sciences', the universe and *Mishneh torah* being seen as great edifices, now, to convey the idea of a flow from higher to lower, we have introduced the image of water. This is the main metaphor Maimonides uses in the *Guide* to describe the relationship between God and creation, and between the different levels of creation, in his version of the concept of emanation:[2]

It [our purpose] is further to show that governance overflows from the deity, may He be exalted, to the intellects according to their rank; that from the benefits received by the intellects, good things and lights overflow to the bodies of the spheres; and that from the spheres—because of the greatness of the benefits they have received from their principles—forces and good things overflow to this body subject to generation and corruption.[3]

The attempt to describe the indescribable gives rise to some mixing of metaphors ('lights overflow'), but the underlying image is of a cascade of water.

Maimonides is careful to state that the image of an overflow from the higher to the lower does not imply the absurdity that the higher exists for the purpose of benefiting the lower. That would make the lower being the end, and the end is always nobler than the means to the end. No, the higher being is perfect, but it has 'a residue of perfection . . . left over from it for something else'.[4]

In the following chapter Maimonides refines the overflow metaphor. There, he explains that the action of the separate intellects in giving form to matter is not describable in the same way as the actions of physical entities on one another, which take place because of proximity, or at a distance through intermediary agencies. This is because the separate intellects, as non-physical beings, do not possess the physical property of location. The effects of actions of the separate intellects are therefore not a function of proximity or connection to the cause, but rather, the action of the separate intellect is constant and

---

[2] For the idea of emanation in Islamic philosophy and in Arabic sources, see Fakhry, *A History of Islamic Philosophy*, 22–33.   [3] *Guide* ii. 11 (p. 275).   [4] Ibid.

indiscriminate; how it manifests itself depends on the preparedness of matter to receive it. Hence, says Maimonides,

the action of the separate intellect is always designated as an overflow, being likened to a source of water that overflows in all directions and does not have one particular direction from which it draws while giving its bounty to others. For it springs forth from all directions and constantly irrigates all the directions nearby and afar . . . Similarly with regard to the Creator, may his name be sublime . . . it has been said that the world derives from the overflow of God and that He has caused to overflow to it everything in it that is produced in time. In the same way it is said that He caused His knowledge to overflow to the prophets. The meaning of all this is that these actions are the action of one who is not a body. And it is His action that is called overflow.[5]

Here, the water metaphor becomes explicit, and Maimonides is at pains to make the reader aware that it is a metaphor, and only a metaphor, for he continues:

This term, I mean 'overflow', is sometimes also applied in Hebrew to God, may He be exalted, with a view to likening Him to an overflowing spring of water, as we have mentioned. For nothing is more fitting as a simile to the action of one that is separate from matter than this expression, I mean 'overflow'. For we are not capable of finding the true reality of a term that would correspond to the true reality of the notion. For the mental representation of the action of one who is separate from matter is very difficult, in a way similar to the difficulty of the mental representation of the existence of one who is separate from matter.

The twin effects of overflow mentioned here, which are creation ('the world derives from the overflow of God'), and prophecy ('In the same way it is said that He caused His knowledge to overflow to the prophets'), are the two main subjects of 'Laws of the Foundations of the Torah', the initial receptacle, as it were, of the overflow in *Mishneh torah*.

We can thus begin to see how what Maimonides tells us about emanation in the *Guide* is reflected in the form of *Mishneh torah*. It will be more satisfying, though, more in accord with notions of artistic self-containment, if *Mishneh torah* tells us about its Neoplatonic principle of organization itself. Let us, therefore, see what is intimated there about cosmic hierarchy and flow.

'According to Greatness and Degree'

To sum up what we saw in the *Guide*, the intellects, or angels, receive goodness from God 'according to their rank'. Goodness flows from each intellect

---

[5] *Guide* ii. 12 (p. 279).

to its corresponding sphere, so that the spheres are also ranked accordingly, and via the spheres to the sublunary world. Similarly, in 'Laws of the Foundations of the Torah' we read:

Every star and sphere has a soul and is endowed with knowledge and intelligence. They are living beings who apprehend 'Him who spake and the world was'. They praise and glorify their Creator, just as the angels do, each according to its greatness and degree. And as they apprehend God, so are they conscious of themselves and of the angels above them. The knowledge possessed by the stars and spheres, is less than that of angels, more than that of human beings.[6]

We have looked at this passage twice before: in Chapter 1 for the sphere's awareness of itself, and in Chapter 2 for the hierarchy of angel and sphere. Let us now move on to consider the hierarchies within categories. Here we find that the spheres and angels 'praise and glorify their Creator . . . each according to its greatness and degree'.

Angels know more than spheres, but also between angels, and by implication between spheres, 'greatness and degree' depends on knowledge: 'All these forms live, realize the Creator, and possess a knowledge of Him that is exceedingly great—a knowledge corresponding with the rank of each . . . the highest angelic form apprehends and knows more than the one below it; and so on, through all the degrees down to the tenth.'[7]

So we have angels ranked from one to ten, and spheres ranked from one to nine, on the basis of their knowledge of God.

I have said that in Maimonides' concept of a commandment there is an idea–commandment–object hierarchy, so that, for each of the first ten books of *Mishneh torah*, the content of the book corresponds to the sphere, while the idea of the book, the motivating concept that unifies the commandments it contains, corresponds to the intellect of the sphere, desire for which induces the sphere's motion. This corresponds to the first hierarchy, in which angels are superior to spheres. If our system holds, then we should also be looking for a hierarchy between the books, and one somehow based upon knowledge. And just as the cosmic hierarchy is primarily a hierarchy of angels, and only secondarily a hierarchy of spheres, what we should primarily be ranking is the unifying concept of each book, and not the detailed commandments that the book contains.

The case of the first book, the *Book of Knowledge*, is very easy. Its unifying concept is knowledge itself, which clearly places it highest in a knowledge-

---

[6] 'Laws of the Foundations of the Torah', 3: 9.   [7] Ibid. 2: 8.

based ranking, and the sphere to which it corresponds is clearly top-ranked, not just because it is physically highest, but also because it imparts motion to the rest of the system.[8] For the rest, it may be less obvious why, say, the *Book of Seasons* should be at number three while the *Book of Women* is number four. A conceptual reason is that the commandments in the *Book of Seasons* are partly explained in the *Guide* as serving to remind us of basic doctrines—the sabbath, for example, being a reminder of the doctrine of creation—so that they have to do with knowledge, whereas the *Book of Women* has no such knowledge component. I shall come to the conceptual side shortly, but the first task is to establish the hierarchy of books in a formal way on the Neoplatonic model.

Here we need to invoke the principle that intellect and matter are opposites, and that matter is the inhibitor of knowledge.[9] Accordingly the rank of any book in the hierarchy depends on the degree to which it has a material substrate. The more it is involved in matter, the lower a book comes, because the admixture of matter drags it down the scale of reality and value, that is, of knowledge. This is the basic scheme, to which further layers will be added later as we delve more deeply into the application to *Mishneh torah* of the doctrine of emanation.

It emerges that over the first ten books Maimonides plays a brilliant counterpoint. If we consider those books as proceeding from first to last, they begin from basic principles in the *Book of Knowledge*, and apply those principles in an ever widening social sphere, climaxing with the Temple, the central institution of the Jewish nation, the focus of its messianic hope, and the place where it meets God. This foreshadows the climax to the work as whole: in 'Laws of Kings and Their Wars', the restoration of the Temple is one of the key achievements of the messiah. But if we bring into play the cosmic structure behind those first ten books, we find a counter-movement from higher to lower, from the *Book of Knowledge* corresponding to the highest sphere, to the *Book of Sacrifices*, which corresponds to the ninth sphere, followed by the *Book of Purity*, which corresponds to no sphere at all but to the feeblest of the Alfarabian intellects, the agent intellect. It is pointless to ask which element of this double movement represents Maimonides' true position; the truth can be taken to lie in the combination, for they represent the ontological and teleological axes of *Mishneh torah*.

Before we consider in detail how the books of *Mishneh torah* conform to the ontological hierarchy, it will be as well to make clear certain guidelines,

---

[8] Ibid. 3: 1.   [9] See above, Ch. 2, n. 40.

mainly deriving from the analysis of the structure of the commandments in the previous chapter:

1. The hierarchy is one of concepts. As already mentioned, this reflects the idea–commandment–object hierarchy. The ranking of books is according to the top-level idea or commandment in each, not the particulars it contains. It depends upon the degree to which the idea of the book is an idea about matter, or how closely the commandments in the book, taken as a whole, are bound to their material substrates, if any. The book as a whole is coloured by its general concept.

2. The hierarchy is one of rationality. A sign of rank is the degree to which the details of the commandments in a book can be rationalized, on a scale from completely logical (to know there is a God) down to completely arbitrary (to sacrifice a lamb rather than a ram).[10] This is supplementary to the first point: the hierarchy is one of concepts, and of the depth to which the details of a book can be conceptualized.

3. The hierarchy is analogical. As we go through the ten books, we will find some direct points of comparison between them and their corresponding spheres in the heavenly hierarchy, but the chief point is the analogy between the organizing principles of each system.

4. Consideration will be given to commandments in their Torah rather than their rabbinic guise. Sufficient justification for this is the first of the fourteen criteria for determining the 613 commandments set out in the *Book of the Commandments*, which excludes rabbinic commandments. The implication is that the Torah remains the determinant of a commandment's nature.

5. The internal organization of a book is not to be taken into account. Some books do reflect the general hierarchy in their internal organization, proceeding from the non-physical to the semi-physical to the physical, and such cases will be pointed out, but this is not a rigid pattern, because other considerations may apply. Torah commandments tend to have priority over rabbinic commandments, and sometimes the sequence of commandments within a book is determined by practical and associative connections. In what is meant as a brief survey to establish the general principle of a hierarchy between the books, it is not possible to give a thorough account of the internal organization of each one. The point to

[10] See *Guide* iii. 26 (p. 509).

stress is that, whatever the sequence of the subsequent commandments, it is the lead commandment that determines a book's ranking.

The pinnacle of the hierarchy has already been effectively dealt with in Chapter 2. The *Book of Knowledge* and the diurnal sphere are both 'uninformed': the diurnal sphere contains no stars; the *Book of Knowledge* contains no practical commandments. The diurnal sphere moves the lower spheres; the *Book of Knowledge* provides the concepts that motivate performance of the commandments in the subsequent books. The commandments in the *Book of Knowledge* have no material substrate.

With *Mishneh torah*'s second book, the *Book of Love*, we move slightly down the scale. To love God is the fourth commandment in the *Book of Knowledge*. The first three, concerning God's existence, uniqueness, and unity, are in the realm of pure logic. The love of God is the first commandment to introduce an element of emotion, of material things the least material, while of emotions, love is the highest. It also orientates us in the direction of the material universe, for it is by contemplation of the universe that the love of God is aroused, that is to say, it does not involve divine science, about God in himself, but natural science. In short, for all Maimonides' intellectualist understanding of love, the idea of the *Book of Love* begins to tilt towards matter. To anticipate somewhat, the book's form emanates from the second level down in the internal hierarchy of 'Laws of the Foundations of the Torah'.

As already mentioned briefly in Chapter 2, it is also possible to see a correspondence between the *Book of Love* and the sphere next to the diurnal sphere, that of the fixed stars. In the *Guide*, Maimonides states the reason for the commandments in that book as 'the constant commemoration of God, the love of Him and the fear of Him, the obligatory observance of the commandments in general, and the bringing-about of such belief concerning Him, may He be exalted, as is necessary for everyone professing the law'.[11] Two characteristics emerge from this statement. One is constancy: the commandments in the *Book of Love* are designed to be permanent or at least frequently recurring reminders of God. This matches the fixed stars, which move with the revolution of the diurnal sphere but whose position is otherwise constant. The other characteristic is generality: the commandments in question do not motivate the rest of the commandments, but they are meant to bring to mind 'the obligatory observance of the commandments in general', that is, they serve as expressions of the concepts found in the *Book of Knowledge*, in the

---

[11] *Guide* iii. 44 (p. 574).

same way as the fixed stars do not drive the motions of the rest of the universe, but do make visible the motion of the diurnal sphere.[12] As Maimonides puts it in the *Guide*: 'The utility of this class is manifest, for it is wholly composed of works that fortify opinions concerning the love of the deity and what ought to be believed about Him and ascribed to Him.'[13]

The *Book of Love* thus has general application, although not in as fundamental a way as the *Book of Knowledge*, and so is appropriately placed after it. All this is in contrast with the commandments in Books 3 to 10 of *Mishneh torah*, which are less constant and have more specific functions.

The *Book of Love* opens with the commandment to recite the Shema. In both content and form this is the most intellectual of the active commandments. The form is speech, the least physical of human acts. The content is the proclamation of God's existence and unity, and of the duty to love God and teach the Torah, to shun idolatry, and to perform the commandments—almost a recapitulation of *Book of Knowledge*.

After the Shema, the *Book of Love* deals with prayer, again a commandment that is almost non-physical. In fact, in its original Torah format, prayer was a daily extempore utterance of praise, supplication, and thanks, as Maimonides takes care to point out.[14] Fixed times, and forms, came later. Applying guideline 4 above, prayer therefore counts as a commandment not bound to any property of matter.

We then encounter in the *Book of Love* several commandments that do have material substrates. It discusses blessings, the most common of which are those recited over food. It contains the laws about phylacteries, *mezuzah*, Torah scrolls, and fringed garments, all of them physical objects. Finally, it presents what is perhaps the most physical commandment of all, namely, circumcision.

The grouping of commandments in the *Book of Love* is largely practical and associative. The lead commandment in the book is the Shema recital. In practice, this is part of the daily prayers, while phylacteries, fringed garments, and Torah scrolls serve, among other things, as accoutrements of prayer. Along with *mezuzah*, they are specifically mentioned in the Shema recital. *Mezuzot* and the parchments in phylacteries contain the first two paragraphs of the Shema. As for blessings, they are very close to prayer, and, like prayer and the Shema, are treated in tractate *Berakhot* of the Mishnah. In short, the Shema brings in train all these other topics. To some extent, Mishnah

---

[12] See 'Laws of the Foundations of the Torah', 3: 7.
[13] *Guide* iii. 35 (p. 537).   [14] 'Laws of Prayer', 1: 2.

Berakhot also explains the arrangement of the *Book of Love*, in that the Shema, prayer and blessings appear in that order in both, though interspersed with additional matters, from other sources, in the latter.

However, the main organizing principle is the top-level idea of love. This is proven by the commandment of circumcision, which is not directly connected with the preceding topics, and is of course the test of the whole approach that has been developed here about the basis of the hierarchy of the books of *Mishneh torah*. For the commandment of circumcision most certainly has a material substrate, so what is it doing so high up the hierarchy, in the *Book of Love*? In the *Guide*, it appears in class number 14.

The *Guide* ascribes two purposes to circumcision.[15] One is that it diminishes sexual desire; the other is that it is a sign of belief in God's unity. The classification of circumcision is determined in the *Guide* by the first reason and in *Mishneh torah* by the second. Circumcision has no fixed character; it changes colour according to its context. As a damper on desire, its purpose and physical performance are one. As a sign of belief in God's unity, the act requires conceptual, indeed cultural, support in order to be understood aright. In *Mishneh torah*, therefore, circumcision takes its meaning from being in the *Book of Love*. Its purpose is understood from the unifying general concept under which all the commandments in the *Book of Love* are gathered, the form they have in common, to 'fortify opinions concerning the love of the deity and what ought to be believed about Him and ascribed to Him'.[16] All of the commandments in the *Book of Love* play a part in inculcating and reinforcing the principles set out in the *Book of Knowledge*. They represent the first step towards translating those principles into everyday behaviour. That, and their constant nature, gives them primacy among the practical commandments.[17] Maimonides' treatment of circumcision thus validates the proposition that the hierarchy of *Mishneh torah* is a hierarchy of ideas. As the angel, or intelligence, begets the sphere that contains the stars, so the idea, as it were, begets the book that contains the commandments. The study and performance of the commandments reverse the process and lead back to the idea.

Within the *Book of Love*, however, the hierarchy is commandment-based. Whereas in considering the hierarchy of books the commandments were matter to the book's form, within the book they are form and their objects or substrates are matter. Hence, as the above summary of its content shows, the

---

[15] *Guide* iii. 49 (pp. 609–10).
[16] See also Twersky, *Introduction to the Code*, 283.   [17] See ibid. 261.

Book of Love moves down the scale of materiality from the Shema to circumcision. It is probably no coincidence that such close co-ordination of
the internal organization of a book with the general structure occurs in the
second-highest book in the list.

The next book, the *Book of Seasons*, introduces the concept of time.
According to Maimonides, time is something created, a property of the physical universe,[18] and the book's title indicates that time is of its essence.[19] In
Plotinus, the transition from Intellect to Soul is a transition from simultaneity to succession in time.[20] We are thus another step down the scale towards
materiality. The commandments in the book are in line with this. In moving
from the *Book of Love* to the *Book of Seasons*, we move from doctrines about
God as first existence and commandments that are mostly meditative, to God
as Creator and commandments that have other purposes besides indoctrina-
tion. The sabbath, as already noted, is a reminder that the world was produced in time, while the festivals commemorate historical events and remind
us of God's providence, so that these events are not only 'appointed times' but
are about time itself. But in addition to this, the sabbath provides a day of
rest;[21] and the festivals have the social purpose of providing an opportunity
for family and communal rejoicing.[22] All in all, then, the *Book of Seasons* represents a step towards physicality and a step away from pure contemplation.

To a degree, the internal organization of the *Book of Seasons* exhibits the
non-physical to physical gradient. It starts with the 'Laws of the Sabbath', the
sabbath being the most metaphysical, as it were, of the seasons in question,
since it is a reminder of creation,[23] and with an exposition of the abstract principles that determine what constitutes forbidden labour on the sabbath,
which apply to festivals as well.[24] The book moves on to the laws of rest on
festivals, which are chiefly occasions for rejoicing, while the fact that they also
commemorate miracles for the children of Israel in their wanderings in the

---

[18] See *Guide* ii. 30 (pp. 349–50).

[19] The name of the order of the Mishnah that deals with these topics, *Mo'ed*, usually translated as
'appointed time' or 'festive season', also clearly incorporates the idea of time (see Jastrow, *Dictionary*).
Mo'ed is used in the Torah of the sabbath and festivals, but Maimonides' title, *The Book of Seasons* (*Sefer
zemanim*), which uses a term found in the liturgy of the festivals, places more emphasis on periodicity;
zeman can refer to time as a concept; *mo'ed* never does.

[20] 'The lower principle fragments the life of its prior and the result in this case is the generation of
time' (Wallis, *Neoplatonism*, 53).

[21] See *Guide* iii. 43 (p. 570).   [22] See ibid. (pp. 571–2).   [23] See ibid. (p. 570).

[24] In a detailed example of the relationship between nature and the law, Hadad draws a comparison
between the kind of acts forbidden on the sabbath and the characteristics of God's actions as described
in the *Guide* (Hadad, 'Nature and Torah in Maimonides' (Heb.), 82–6).

desert ranks below the sabbath in Maimonides' scheme of things, since he rates the natural order as celebrated by the sabbath above miraculous disruptions to that order. Then come 'Laws of Leavened and Unleavened Bread', taking us closer to the physical, and only after that do we find, grouped together, commandments that require specific physical objects, in 'Laws of Ram's Horn, Booth, and Palm Branch'. However, other principles clearly do operate in the organization of the *Book of Seasons*. The sabbath in any case has primacy in the Torah and Mishnah, while the placement of 'Laws of Megilah and Hanukah' at the end of the book is due to their being rabbinical rather than Torah institutions.[25]

From the physical but still fairly abstract property of time in *Book of Seasons* we switch in the *Book of Women* to human beings with their physically prompted desires and emotions. In the *Book of Women* the stress is on the social aspect of relations between man and wife. The book opens with the sanctification of those relations and their conversion to the regulated social institution of marriage.

The first part of the *Book of Holiness*, which deals with forbidden sexual relations, is in a sense a continuation of *Book of Women*, but the stress now is on the carnal aspect of relations between the sexes. The second part of the book is about forbidden foods, an even more thoroughly physical aspect of human existence.

The *Book of Asseverations* continues the theme of curtailing the appetites, but now the restrictions are self-imposed, assumed in addition to those laid down in the *Book of Holiness*. It represents an intensification of the human being's struggle to impose mind on material existence.

With the *Book of Agriculture* we reach the earth itself, inanimate matter, for the commandments in this book, as its name indicates, primarily concern agriculture. Again it should be stressed that Maimonides uses a double scheme. Undoubtedly the laws in the *Book of Agriculture*, which include care for the poor, and for the priest and Levite (who have no land of their own and therefore, in an economy based on subsistence agriculture, no independent means of support), represent a widening of the social context, so that we feel we have moved on from the personal and private concerns of the previous three books. Because it deals with the tithes and gifts due to the priest and Levite, the *Book of Agriculture* also clearly provides a lead-in to the *Book of Temple Service*. There is, then, a sense of progress. At the same time, from the cosmic point of view that the symbolic structure of *Mishneh torah* gives us,

---

[25] But see below, Ch. 4, n. 156.

there is decline. The commandments broaden in scope, but their substrata become ever more material.[26]

After the *Book of Agriculture* come the *Book of Temple Service* and the *Book of Offerings*. The first deals with the Temple structure and administration and with public sacrifices; the second with private sacrifices. The Temple and its ritual are the most tangible possible representations of the Divine. In these books, the commandments and their material substrata practically fuse. We have reached the apogee of national and religious aspiration, but, Neoplatonically speaking, we are at a low.

Finally in the series of man–God books comes the *Book of Purity*, which deals with the laws of ritual impurity. It completes the laws relating to the Temple, for, as Maimonides stresses, 'this matter of uncleanness and cleanness concerns only the Holy Place and holy things, nothing else'.[27] As we get closer to matter, intelligibility also diminishes. In the *Guide*, it is chiefly commandments that are part of Temple and purification procedures that Maimonides finds difficult to understand in detail, or concerning which he simply denies that there is any point in looking for explanation of the details: 'The offering of sacrifices has in itself a great and manifest utility, as I shall make clear. But no cause will ever be found for the fact that one particular sacrifice consists in a *lamb* and another in a *ram* and that the number of the victims should be one particular number.'[28]

Three other scales of value, closely related to it, can be overlaid upon this hierarchy. The first is to do with Maimonides' view of the intention of the law; the second with love versus awe; and the third with the elusive, but perhaps in the end most fundamental, value of holiness.

First and Second Intention

I have divided the law into man–God commandments and man–man commandments, and found that the first ten books of *Mishneh torah* deal with the

[26] As noted in the Introduction, Maimonides split up the topics of Order *Zera'im* of the Mishnah, placing the less materially connected topic of blessings high up his order in the *Book of Love*, while agricultural laws proper are lower down in the *Book of Agriculture*.   [27] *Guide* iii. 47 (p. 594).

[28] Maimonides gives up trying to explain the show bread (*Guide* iii. 45 (p. 578)), the offering of wine (*Guide* iii. 46 (p. 591)), and the items used in purification rites (*Guide* iii. 47 (p. 597)). Of course his difficulties in these three cases may be seen as stemming from lack of historical information rather than as examples of unintelligibility in principle, although it could also be argued that the very dependence on such information for understanding the commandments, as well as its irretrievability, are themselves limitations imposed by matter, and are in any case symptomatic of commandments belonging to the second intention rather than the first and therefore of lower account—see Stern, 'Idea of a Hoq'.

first division and the last four books deal with the second, and this is indeed the fundamental division of *Mishneh torah*'s fourteen books. But Maimonides has another division of the commandments, between what he calls the first intention and the second intention of the law. The first intention is 'to put an end to idolatry, to wipe out its traces and all that is bound up with it',[29] and 'the abolition of mutual wrongdoing' among people.[30] The second intention is to use idolatry against itself by adapting accustomed modes of worship to the service of God.[31] Since the man–man commandments are all about abolishing wrongdoing, and so belong entirely to the first intention, the division between first and second intentions is really a subdivision of the man–God commandments, which means that, in *Mishneh torah*, it applies only within the first ten books.

The laws in the *Book of Knowledge* are pure first intention, establishing basic doctrines about God and commanding the avoidance of idolatry. The laws in the *Book of Love* are close to the first intention, and are supportive of it. As Maimonides states: '*sacrifices* pertain to a second intention, whereas invocation, prayer, and similar practices and modes of worship come closer to the first intention and are necessary for its achievement'.[32] He also explicitly puts 'the *fringes*, the *doorposts*, and the *phylacteries*', all matters dealt with in the *Book of Love* in addition to prayer, on the same level.[33]

The language here ('come closer to the first intention') indicates that Maimonides did not think of the first intention and the second intention as a dichotomy; rather, he allows for a gradual transition from the one to the other, which is in line with the similes with which he opens the discussion of the subject, of the gradations of the nervous system, and of the gradual weaning of an infant and its introduction to solid food.[34] The *Book of Love* belongs, on the whole, to the first intention, but, by comparison with the *Book of Knowledge*, it has something of the second intention about it, for prayer and its rituals, as we have them, are, like sacrifices in their day, concessions to convention. Maimonides is quite explicit about this. To make understandable the impossibility of an immediate, outright ban on sacrifice as a form of worship when the children of Israel left Egypt, he writes:

At that time this would have been similar to the appearance of a prophet in these times who, calling upon the people to worship God, would say: 'God has given you a Law forbidding you to pray to Him, to fast, to call upon Him for help in misfortune. Your worship should consist solely in meditation without any works at all.'[35]

---

[29] *Guide* iii. 29 (p. 517).   [30] *Guide* iii. 32 (p. 531).   [31] See ibid. (pp. 525–31).
[32] Ibid. (p. 529).   [33] Ibid. (p. 530).   [34] See ibid. (p. 525).   [35] Ibid. (p. 526).

The sabbath also belongs to the first intention: it is a reminder of the doctrine of creation, and it was part of the initial Mosaic legislation, before Sinai, at Marah, which was all of the first intention type.[36] Nevertheless, the sabbath, and certainly the festivals, exhibit more than a touch of second intention, for religions generally have their festivals, and they also satisfy the need for rest and for leisure to socialize.[37] The *Book of Seasons* thus uses social instinct and social convention to bring about an opportunity for recognition of the truth of certain doctrines. It also veers away from the purely philosophical notion of God to the more popular notion of a God who intervenes in history and institutes festivals commemorating those events. That book therefore finds its place after the *Book of Love*.

And so on. Linking this scale of value to the intelligibility/materiality scale, we can see, without at this stage going into too much detail, that the first ten books of *Mishneh torah* progressively accommodate, even exploit, the human need for concrete acts and representations to prompt towards appreciation of the Divine, until we arrive at the Temple ritual, which is at the other end of the scale from the *Book of Knowledge*, pure second intention. In fact, the analogy of the nervous system at the beginning of *Guide* iii. 32 fits the first ten books of *Mishneh torah* rather well, with the *Book of Knowledge* as the brain, and the following books corresponding to the nerves and sinews, becoming ever tougher and more solid as they ramify.

The Love–Awe Polarity

The next additional scale of value derives from the pendulum that swings between love and awe. We have seen that man's first response on contemplating the universe is a rush of delighted wonder and an access of love of the creator and desire to know him, but, in the same moment, he recoils in awe, suddenly aware of his insignificance and low, material condition.[38] In that moment, love and awe are the upbeat and the downbeat of an intense awareness of God, but as that primary experience recedes and the commandments start to run into the channels of everyday life, love and awe separate out into different planes. The service of God out of sheer love is on the highest plane, worth more even than service out of the expectation of the world to come, while service out of awe, when awe means the fear of punishment, is the least worthy form.[39]

---

[36] See *Guide* iii. 32 (p. 531).

[37] See *Guide* iii. 43 (p. 570).

[38] See 'Laws of the Foundations of the Torah', 2: 2.

[39] See 'Laws of Repentance', ch. 10.

Love depends upon knowledge, and inspires desire for knowledge, hence the *Book of Knowledge* is book 1. The *Book of Love* as book 2 scarcely requires explanation, while the high position of the *Book of Seasons* on this scale is also understandable, since the commandments it contains have to do with awareness of God as creator. The *Book of Women* concerns love on the human plane, while the historical preamble at the beginning of it converts what was originally a purely consensual arrangement between a man and a woman into an arrangement governed by the commandments, directing this love to a higher end. With the *Book of Holiness*, we begin to tip in the direction of awe. The book deals with commandments that restrain the appetites, meaning that we are now at the level of the self-consciousness as material creatures that triggered the sense of awe in 'Laws of the Foundations of the Torah', 2: 2. Knowledge is no longer a factor.

By the time we reach the books on the Temple and associated matters, we are completely in the realm of awe. The commandment to be in awe of the Temple is the only commandment associated with it that is addressed to the emotions, and one to which Maimonides devotes an entire chapter.[40] Moreover, he stresses at the beginning of that chapter that 'you are not in awe of the Temple, but of the one who commanded the awe of it'.[41] The Temple stands for the awe of God, pure and simple. In the *Guide*, too, Maimonides is emphatic that the function of the Temple is to inspire awe:

You know to what extent the Law fortifies the belief in the greatness of the Sanctuary and the awe felt for it, so that on seeing it, man should be affected by a sentiment of submission and servitude. It says: And ye shall fear My Sanctuary, an injunction that He has coupled with the precept to keep the Sabbath in order to strengthen fear of the Sanctuary.[42]

Maimonides further explains that the purpose of the laws of purity is to prevent people from visiting the Temple often, so that their awe of the place will not be diminished by familiarity.[43] By contrast, the love of God is a constant desire for closeness. This is also consonant with what Maimonides says in *Guide* iii. 52 about actions teaching fear while opinions teach love.[44] The *Book of Knowledge* is the book with the greatest concentration of opinion, while the books on the Temple and its rites are the most action-intensive. So the love–awe polarity is not just a matter of a single moment; it plays out over

---

[40] 'Laws of the Temple', ch. 7. However, love is not entirely absent from Maimonides' treatment of the Temple in *Mishneh torah*, for the motto of the *Book of Temple Service* is 'Pray for the peace of Jerusalem: they shall prosper that love thee' (Ps. 122: 6).   [41] 'Laws of the Temple', 7: 1.
[42] *Guide* iii. 45 (p. 577).   [43] See *Guide* iii. 47 (p. 593).   [44] p. 630.

the first ten books of *Mishneh torah*, love gradually giving way to awe, until awe takes over completely.

The Hierarchy of Holiness

There is a narrow approach and a broad approach to the concept of holiness in Maimonides. Kellner, for example, tends to seek to cut it down to size. He sees holiness of person in Maimonides as a matter of obeying those commandments designed to restrain physical appetites, preparatory to the pursuit of intellectual virtue, and stresses Maimonides' denial to holiness of ontological status.[45] Twersky is more expansive: from Maimonides' negation of being holy as a commandment in itself, he derives the positive implication that holiness is the goal of the entire law.[46] The position that will be presented here is that holiness is a fundamental scale of value that underlies the others already mentioned, spanning all of the first ten books of *Mishneh torah* and running through every moral and intellectual endeavour in Maimonides. To arrive at that position will require close analysis of the way he adapts his rabbinic sources to forge a comprehensive, malleable idea of holiness, religious in appearance but with a philosophical sinew running through it, revealing something of the synthetic power that is no small part of his literary art.

The place where holiness is ruled out as a commandment is in the introduction to *The Book of the Commandments*, where, under principle number 4, the various injunctions to be holy in the Torah are cited as examples par excellence of general exhortations that must not be taken as commandments in themselves. Holiness, says Maimonides, is an aspect of every commandment, and therefore the imperative 'be holy' amounts to no more than saying 'perform my commandments'.[47]

If that is so, why is a book of *Mishneh torah* named the *Book of Holiness*, as though holiness were a discrete concept around which cluster certain commandments but not others? It could also be seen as surprising that 'be holy' turns up as an independent imperative in 'Laws of Ethical Qualities':

And we are commanded to walk in these middle ways, and they are the good and straight ways, as it says: And you shall walk in his ways. Thus they taught this com-

[45] Kellner, 'Spiritual Life'; id., *Maimonides' Confrontation with Mysticism*, 85–126.

[46] This idea is stated briefly in Twersky, *Introduction to the Code*, 442 n. 209, and amplified in id., 'Martyrdom and the Sanctity of Life' (Heb.).

[47] See also *Guide* iii. 47 (pp. 595–6), where Maimonides states that uncleanness has three meanings, one of them being disobeying the commandments, and that holiness is the opposite of uncleanness in all its three meanings; hence we understand that holiness means obeying the commandments.

mandment explicitly: Just as he is called gracious, so should you be gracious; just as he is called merciful, so should you be merciful; just as he is called holy, so should you be holy.[48]

If holiness is such a general concept, why does it appear here not even as a commandment, but as a detail of a commandment, one more item in a list of virtues?

These questions may seem artificial, deliberately deaf to the tone of 'Laws of Ethical Qualities'. It may also seem disingenuous to represent principle 4 of the *Book of the Commandments* as meaning that 'be holy' is exactly equivalent to other general exhortations cited there, such as 'keep my covenant' (Exod. 19: 5). In contrast to the summary treatment of the other statements, 'be holy' is discussed at some length, and emerges as a subtle notion that is not simply reducible to a meta-commandment. It may be too general in scope to qualify as a commandment, but as an aspect of the commandments it does apparently have specific content. The point of the questions raised is to probe the meaning of holiness, and, what is most relevant to this study, to bring out the ways in which *Mishneh torah*'s form expresses it, mediating between the narrow and the broad interpretations of the term.

A tour of the probable sources of 'Laws of Ethical Qualities', 1: 6, will help to give a more precise understanding of what Maimonides intends by this *halakhah*, and, as mentioned, will have the side benefit of providing an example of the way in which he adapts Midrash.

First, let us analyse the *halakhah* itself a little more closely. It is really *derash*, a piece of homiletic exegesis, working according to the associative method of Midrash, whereby a verse that requires explanation (which will be called the 'explicandum verse') is linked to another verse (which will be called the 'explicans verse'), which is used to gloss or explain it, giving rise to a moral conclusion. In our *halakhah* the verse that requires explanation is 'And you shall walk in his ways'. What can this mean? The explicans verse appears to be Exodus 34: 6, part of the narrative of Moses' audience with God in which he pleads for forgiveness for the Children of Israel following the worshipping of the golden calf. The verse reads: 'The Lord, the Lord, mighty, merciful, and gracious, long-suffering, and abundant in goodness and in truth.' Our *halakhah* does not directly cite this verse, but it is distinctly echoed in the conclusion: 'Just as he is called gracious, so should you be gracious; just as he is called merciful, so should you be merciful' and so on. The association between the two verses is actually made somewhat earlier in Moses' audience,

---

[48] 'Laws of Ethical Qualities', 1: 5–6.

when he requests of God, 'show me now thy way, that I may know thee'.[49] The verse 'The Lord, the Lord, mighty, merciful' is taken to be the response to this request;[50] this, then, is 'thy way', and so 'And you shall walk in his ways' means imitating the characteristics mentioned in that verse. The structure of our *halakhah* is thus rather like a syllogism from which the middle term has been omitted:

'And you shall walk in his ways' (Deut. 28: 9, explicandum verse)

God's ways are: 'The Lord, the Lord, mighty, merciful, and gracious' (Exod. 34: 6, explicans verse—omitted)

Therefore 'Just as he is called gracious, so should you be gracious; just as he is called merciful, so should you be merciful; just as he is called holy, so should you be holy' (conclusion)

This is where the problems begin. Exodus 34: 6, the explicans verse, does not list holiness as one of God's characteristics, and so the question arises, where does 'just as he is called holy, so should you be holy' spring from? There certainly are other biblical verses that do call for imitation of God in respect of holiness, as we shall very shortly see, but, by the sentence 'Thus they taught this commandment explicitly', our *halakhah* seems to intend the rabbinic *midrashim* that refer to Exodus 34: 6, and those fail to mention holiness in their elaboration of the commandment. This sharpens the question raised above: if to be holy is too general a concept to qualify as a specific commandment, why does Maimonides insert it here when nothing in his sources compels him to do so? Moreover, against the background of the relevant *midrashim*, the explicandum verse is also problematic: the *midrashim* in question do not set out to explain this particular verse, but, at best, other verses that sound similar.

In Deuteronomy 28: 9, from which Maimonides quotes it, the plain meaning of 'and you shall walk in his ways' is 'do as God says'; it is part of an exhortation to keep the commandments.[51] In the derivation of the idea of *imitatio Dei* (which for the moment we shall take to mean imitating God in the sense of doing as God *does*) from this phrase, Maimonides seems in fact to combine and adapt three pieces of rabbinic *derash*. One, in BT *Shabat* 133*b*, links Exodus 15: 2, 'The Lord is my strength and song, and he is become my salvation; he is my God, and I will prepare him an habitation', to Exodus 34: 6–7 (referred to above): 'The Lord, the Lord, mighty, merciful, and gracious'.

---

[49] Exod. 33: 13.   [50] See also *Guide* i. 54 (p. 124).
[51] One of many in the book of Deuteronomy, and compare 1 Kgs. 2: 3.

The passage in BT *Shabat* reads: 'Abba Shaul says: "And I will prepare him an habitation",[52] [which means] be like him: as he is gracious, so you be gracious, as he is merciful, so you be merciful.' There is no sign of holiness here, and Abba Shaul does not base his homily on the verse in our *halakhah*, 'And you shall walk in his ways'.

The other *derash* is found in BT *Sotah* 14*a*, this time based on Deuteronomy 13: 5: 'Ye shall walk after the Lord your God, and fear him, and keep his commandments'. As in Deuteronomy 28: 9, the plain meaning is clear: to walk after the Lord means to do what the Lord says, but in *Sotah*, R. Hama in the name of R. Hanina interprets it as meaning to do what the Lord does,[53] and cites instances of God's compassion in the Bible as examples that human beings should emulate.[54] Again, holiness does not come into it, while the verse commented upon, though it sounds closer to the verse in our *halakhah*, is still not the same one.

The third source is *Sifrei* on Deuteronomy 11: 22. That verse reads: 'For if ye shall diligently keep all these commandments which I command you to do

---

[52] The verse is taken from the 'Song of the Sea'. 'I will prepare him an habitation' is the way the King James Bible renders the Hebrew word *ve'anvehu*, a translation that follows Onkelos, who gives *ve'evnei lei makdash*, 'and I will build him a temple'. Onkelos was perhaps swayed by the use of the word *neveh* later in the 'Song of the Sea', in Exod. 15: 13, where it clearly does mean 'habitation', and so took *nvh* to be the root of *ve'anvehu*, and also by Exod. 15: 17, towards the end of the Song, which reads, 'Thou shalt bring them in, and plant them in the mountain of thine inheritance, in the place, O Lord, which thou hast made for thee to dwell in, in the sanctuary, O Lord, which thy hands have established'. *Ve'anvehu* can also be interpreted as meaning 'And I will beautify him'. The latter is the interpretation given to the word in the talmudic passage from which the statement of Abba Shaul is taken, although Rashi ad loc. explains Abba Shaul's statement itself as a play on the words *ani* (I) and *vehu* (and him), that is, I should strive to be like him (like God). It is also possible that Abba Shaul has in mind the interpretation 'I will prepare him an habitation', and that he makes the verse mean that by becoming like God I make him dwell in me. Rashi's commentary on the Torah mentions both interpretations of *ve'anvehu*, 'habitation' and 'beautify', but not the play on words. Among the other medieval commentators, Rashbam denies that the interpretation 'I will prepare him an habitation' makes sense in context, while Ibn Ezra goes with Onkelos.

[53] Perhaps seeing redundancy in the verse rather than rhetorical expansiveness—if it mentions 'and keep his commandments' specifically, then 'ye shall walk' must refer to something else.

[54] 'R. Hama son of R. Hanina said: What means the text: Ye shall walk after the Lord your God? Is it possible for a human being to walk after the Shekhinah; for has it not been said: For the Lord thy God is a devouring fire? [Deut. 4: 24] But [the meaning is] to walk after the attributes of the Holy One, blessed be He. As He clothes the naked, for it is written: And the Lord God made for Adam and his wife coats of skin, and clothed them [Gen. 3: 21], so do thou also clothe the naked. The Holy One, blessed be He, visited the sick, for it is written: And the Lord appeared unto him by the oaks of Mamre [Gen. 18: 1], so do thou also visit the sick. The Holy One, blessed be He, comforted mourners, for it is written: And it came to pass after the death of Abraham, that God blessed Isaac his son [Gen. 25: 11], so do thou also comfort mourners. The Holy One, blessed be He, buried the dead, for it is written: And He buried him in the valley [Deut. 34: 6], so do thou also bury the dead.'

them, to love the Lord your God, to walk in all his ways, and to cleave unto him'.[55] Like the *midrash* in *Sotah*, the *midrash* in *Sifrei* (which has overlaps with both *Sotah* and *Shabat*) also reads 'do as God does', or even 'be as God is', into a verse the plain meaning of which is 'do as God says'. *Sifrei*'s comment on the verse, citing Deuteronomy 34: 6 ('The Lord, the Lord, mighty etc.'), is:

> *To walk in all His ways*: These are the ways of God, *The Lord, God, merciful, and gracious* (Exod. 34: 6). Scripture says, And it shall come to pass, that whosoever shall call by the name of the Lord shall be delivered (Joel 3: 5)—how is it possible for man to be called by the name of the Lord? Rather, as God is called merciful, so should you be merciful; as the Holy One, blessed be He, is called gracious, so too should you be gracious, as it is said, *The Lord is gracious and full of compassion* (Ps. 145: 8), and grants free gifts. As God is called righteous, *For the Lord is righteous, He loveth righteousness* (Ps. 11: 7), so you too should be righteous. As God is called merciful, as it is said *For I am merciful* [*ḥasid*], *saith the Lord* (Jer. 3: 12), so too should you be merciful.[56]

Sifrei, in the freewheeling way of Midrash, explains the verse 'To walk in his ways' through characteristics of God mentioned in other verses; holiness is not among these characteristics, and once again, the explicandum verse does not match the one in our *halakhah*.

So, in order to provide biblical warrant for the idea of *imitatio Dei*, Maimonides uses an explicandum verse different from the ones quoted in *Sotah* and *Sifrei*, though similar to those verses in its language, and uses the explicans verse from BT *Shabat*, which is also one of the explicans verses in *Sifrei*, tacking onto it the concept of holiness.

When it comes to *imitatio Dei* in respect of holiness, there is hardly any need for *derash*, for the Torah enjoins it almost explicitly, for example, in Leviticus 11: 44–5: 'For I am the Lord your God: ye shall therefore sanctify yourselves, and ye shall be holy; for I am holy: neither shall ye defile yourselves with any manner of creeping thing that creepeth on the earth. For I am the Lord that bringeth you up out of the land of Egypt, to be your God: ye shall therefore be holy, for I am holy'; Leviticus 19: 2: 'Speak unto all the congregation of the children of Israel, and say unto them, Ye shall be holy: for I the Lord your God am holy,' and Leviticus 21: 8, on the subject of whom a priest may marry: 'Thou shalt sanctify him therefore; for he offereth the

---

[55] Rashi seems to have had this verse, somewhat conflated, at the back of his mind in making his comment on the statement of Abba Shaul in BT *Shab.* 133*b*, for in full his comment reads, 'The expression *ve'anvehu* [means] *ani* (I) *vehu* (and him), I will make myself like him to cleave to his ways.'

[56] *Sifre*, trans. Hammer, 105–6.

bread of thy God: he shall be holy unto thee: for I the Lord, which sanctify you, am holy.'

The sense of these verses is really 'be holy *because* I am holy', but it is a very short, though still significant, step from that to 'be holy *as* I am holy'. This step is taken by, for example, *Sifra* on Leviticus 11: 44: 'ye shall therefore sanctify yourselves, and ye shall be holy; for I am holy: just as I am holy, so should you be holy; just as I am separate, so should you be separate.'[57]

Maimonides could therefore have based the idea of *imitatio Dei* on these verses, and in fact, in *Guide* i. 54, he did: 'For the utmost virtue of man is to become like unto Him, may He be exalted, as far as he is able; which means that we should make our actions like unto His, as the sages made clear when interpreting the verse, *Ye shall be holy*. They said: *He is gracious, so be you also gracious; He is merciful, so be you also merciful*.'[58]

As we have seen, and as far as I have been able to ascertain, the sages never did interpret 'Ye shall be holy' to mean 'He is gracious, so be you gracious', and so forth. *Sifra* points in that general direction, but this precise interpretation is the one placed by Abba Shaul on the verse 'he is my God, and I will prepare him an habitation'.

But are we not being pedantic? After all, the rabbis did make the statement 'just as I am holy, so should you be holy', only not in relation to the verse Maimonides happens to hang it on in 'Laws of Ethical Qualities'—not something to become exercised about. Marc Shapiro warns against over-intense efforts to account for apparent lapses by Maimonides in citation of sources, arguing that such efforts smack more of hagiography than of scholarship, and cites our passage from *Guide* i. 54 as an example of probable inadvertence.[59] We do not even have to accuse Maimonides of a lapse; perhaps he simply took a short cut.

On the basis of what we have seen so far, there is room to argue that actually Maimonides was aware of what he was doing in *Guide* i. 54, but at any rate, our main concern is with 'Laws of Ethical Qualities', 1: 6, and there, I believe, it can be shown that he manipulated his sources with intent.

Unlike in the *Guide*, in *Mishneh torah* Maimonides could not base *imitatio Dei* on 'Ye shall be holy', because *Mishneh torah* is a work of halakhah; its currency, as we must again remind ourselves, is the commandments, and

---

[57] *Leviticus Rabbah* on Lev. 24: 4 is in a similar vein, and in fact *Yad peshutah* suggests that in 'Laws of Ethical Qualities', 1: 6 Maimonides conflated this *midrash* and *Sifrei* on Deut. 9: 22 (ad loc.).
[58] See also *Guide* iii. 33 (p. 533).   [59] M. B. Shapiro, *Studies in Maimonides*, 47.

'Ye shall be holy' is excluded from the list of 613 commandments by principle 4 of the *Book of the Commandments*. What did he do instead?

It has already been noted that the explicandum verse in 'Laws of Ethical Qualities', 1: 6, is not identical with the verses in the sources.[60] For that matter, were it not for the background *midrashim*, the verse Maimonides uses, 'And you shall walk in his ways', would be no better than 'Ye shall be holy' from the point of view of the fourth principle in the *Book of the Commandments*, since, as we have seen, its meaning in context is simply 'keep the commandments'.[61] He invokes those *midrashim*, but casts them on a verse that is apparently of his own choosing.

It could be that Maimonides was looking at a different text, but we do have evidence that suggests that his substitution of the explicandum verse found in the Talmud and Midrash was deliberate. In the *Book of the Commandments*, positive commandment 8, as sources for *imitatio Dei*, he first cites Deuteronomy 28: 9 ('and walk in his ways'), the same verse as he cites in 'Laws of Ethical Qualities', 1: 6, but in addition he cites Deuteronomy 11: 22 ('to walk in all his ways'), the verse on which *Sifrei* comments, and he goes on to quote from *Sifrei* extensively, citing his source.[62] This makes it rather likely that *Sifrei* is the source in 'Laws of Ethical Qualities', 1: 6, as well, and indicates that Maimonides was aware that 'to walk in all his ways', rather than 'and walk in his ways', was *Sifrei*'s point of departure. That being the case, we can be reasonably sure that, when he came to write 'Laws of Ethical Qualities', 1: 6, there was no confusion: in expounding the idea of *imitatio Dei*, Maimonides consciously took a statement by *Sifrei* and attached it to a verse different from

[60] Shapiro remarks, 'Use of this verse seems to be original to Maimonides, as nowhere in earlier rabbinic literature is the teaching מה הוא נקרא חנון אף אתה היה חנון וכו (or variations) connected to this verse' (*Studies in Maimonides*, 47). See, however, *Eliyahu Rabbah* (Ish Shalom), 24.

[61] The question why 'And you shall walk in his ways' is considered a separate commandment when it appears to be just the kind of general exhortation excluded from canonical status by principle 4 of the *Book of the Commandments* was addressed to Maimonides' son Abraham. See *Responsa of R. Abraham Maimonides* (Heb.), ed. Freimann, 65–8 (no. 63). Freimann surveys the various possible sources of 'Laws of Ethical Qualities', 1: 6, and also mentions a post-Maimonidean work that uses his explicandum verse (*Responsa of R. Abraham Maimonides* (Heb.), 67 no. 13). The responsum is discussed by Twersky in 'Law and Ethics'.

[62] There is no explicit mention of holiness in this commandment, but it is adjacent to the commandment of *kidush hashem*, sanctification of God's name, at number 9. This juxtaposition perhaps implies that *kidush hashem* flows from *imitatio Dei*. In the *Book of the Commandments*, the treatment of *kidush hashem* is restricted to martyrdom and is not broadened, as it is in 'Laws of the Foundations of the Torah', to include everyday behaviour, but this can be explained by the earlier work's brevity—it is unlikely that Maimonides only thought of *kidush hashem* in everyday terms when he came to write 'Laws of the Foundations of the Torah'. On holiness as sanctification of the name, see Twersky, 'Martyrdom and the Sanctity of Life' (Heb.).

the one on which the statement originally comments, an explicandum verse peculiar to himself.

Altogether, there is a choice of seven verses in the Torah that contain the expression 'walk in his ways' or some near variant of it, and that could therefore be considered candidates to be the basis for the commandment to become like God.[63] Having discarded the ones used by his talmudic and midrashic sources, why did Maimonides pick Deuteronomy 28: 9 in particular?

What this verse has, and the others do not, is holiness. In full, the verse reads: 'The Lord shall establish thee an holy people unto himself, as he hath sworn unto thee, if thou shalt keep the commandments of the Lord thy God, and walk in his ways.' So in 'Laws of Ethical Qualities', 1: 6, not only did Maimonides tack holiness onto the explicans verse; he also introduced it via his choice of explicandum verse, making it frame the commandment: 'as it says: And you shall walk in his ways [verse referring to holiness and the commandments]. Thus they taught this commandment explicitly: Just as he is called gracious, so should you be gracious; just as he is called merciful, so should you be merciful; just as he is called holy, so should you be holy.'

Whatever the truth about sources, this is an arresting coincidence. Maimonides wove together the *midrashim* found in BT *Shabat*, BT *Sotah*, *Sifrei*, *Sifra*, and elsewhere to give a compact, synthesized derivation of *imitatio Dei* as a commandment, and to make it begin and end with holiness.[64] The implication is that holiness is both the way, or perhaps one should say the ways, and the goal. Interpretation risks tearing Maimonides' delicate web, but, in conjunction with the ideas developed in Chapter 2, I take him to mean that, while holiness is the element of *imitatio Dei* in every commandment, it is ultimately an inward condition, the condition that the commandments are meant to bring about by aligning a person with the cosmos. To imitate the attributes of God's actions by being gracious and merciful is not an end in itself. It has aspects of holiness, but it is a process the end of which is to be holy as God is called holy.

If to be holy is a process, then there is holy, holier, and holiest. Some commandments may be holier, that is, have more of *imitatio Dei* about them, than others. Holiness covers all the commandments, but the term also has a core

[63] Deut. 8: 6; 10: 12; 11: 22; 19: 9; 26: 17; 28: 9; and 30: 16, per Even-Shoshan, *New Concordance* (Heb.).

[64] For discussion of the connection between holiness and *imitatio Dei*, see W. Z. Harvey, 'Holiness'; Seeskin, 'Holiness as an Ethical Ideal'; Kreisel, *Maimonides' Political Thought*, 151–6. The point here is the way the connection is expressed through *Mishneh torah*'s form.

meaning of separateness.[65] This is already clear from the discussion under principle 4 in the *Book of the Commandments*, which cites the comment of *Sifra* quoted above, interpreting 'be holy' as 'be separate'.

Separateness as the core meaning, or starting point, for holiness also emerges from another place where *imitatio Dei* and holiness come together, in 'Laws of Impurity of Foodstuffs', 16: 12:

> It is the way of piety that a man keep himself separate and go apart from the rest of the people and neither touch them nor eat and drink with them. For separation leads to the cleansing of the body from evil deeds, and the cleansing of the body leads to the hallowing of the soul from evil traits, and the hallowing of the soul leads to striving for likeness with the *Shekhinah*; for it is said, 'Sanctify yourselves therefore and be holy',[66] 'for I the Lord who sanctify you am holy'.[67]

Here too, Maimonides manipulates his sources. The origin of this ladder of virtues is a statement of R. Pinhas ben Ya'ir that appears in several places in the Talmud and Midrash in different versions, none of which corresponds precisely to this *halakhah*, and none of which mentions 'likeness with the *Shekhinah*'.[68] Once more, therefore, we see Maimonides' determination to bring holiness and *imitatio Dei* together.

It is not just the talmudic sources that are manipulated. The verses cited here are marked separately in order to give their references, but in the original they are run together as though they formed one verse, even though they are actually spaced fairly widely apart. Maimonides moulds the verses to the concept of self-sanctification leading to sanctification by God. The process of self-sanctification becomes ever more inward, beginning with isolating oneself from the profane crowd, leading on to sanctification of the body, then of the character, and finally of the intellect, which is what 'likeness with the *Shekhinah*' seems to mean here: in philosophical terms, receptiveness to the flow of knowledge from God via the agent intellect. Sanctification by God is also the beginning of the process, since God gave the tools of self-

---

[65] Twersky takes a similar line in 'Martyrdom and the Sanctity of Life' (Heb.).

[66] Lev. 11: 44.   [67] Lev. 21: 8.

[68] The version in Mishnah *Sot.* 19: 15 may be taken as representative:

R. Pinhas ben Ya'ir says zeal leads to cleanliness and cleanliness leads to purity and purity leads to separation and separation leads to holiness and holiness leads to humility and humility leads to fear of sin and fear of sin leads to piety and piety leads to the holy spirit and the holy spirit leads to the resurrection of the dead and the resurrection of the dead comes through Elijah of good memory amen.

Other versions are to be found in BT *AZ* 20b; JT *Shab.* 1: 3; JT *Shek.* 2: 12; S. *of S. Rabbah* 1: 5; Midrash Prov. 5: 15.

sanctification in the form of the commandments: 'I the Lord who sanctify you' suits both senses. Looked at this way, the movement in this passage is not dissimilar to that in 'Laws of Ethical Qualities', 1: 6.

It is also worth noting that, in this passage, 'holiness' extends over moral virtue in general ('hallowing of the soul from evil traits') rather than being an element of it. This is in line with *Guide* i. 54, and with the construction placed above on the allusions in 'Laws of Ethical Qualities', 1: 6, that holiness is both the starting point and the end point of *imitatio Dei*.

The ultimate example of the reciprocal process of sanctification is the prophet. Here again is the passage that was quoted in the Introduction to illustrate Maimonides' dramatic ability. Note the resemblance to the ascent to likeness to the Shekhinah in 'Laws of Impurity of Foodstuffs', 16: 12.

When one, abundantly endowed with these qualities and physically sound, enters *pardes* and continuously dwells upon those great and abstruse themes, having the right mind capable of comprehending and grasping them; sanctifying himself, withdrawing from the ways of the ordinary run of men who walk in the obscurities of the times, zealously training himself not to have a single thought of the vanities of the age and its intrigues, but keeping his mind directed upwards as though bound beneath the Celestial Throne, so as to comprehend the pure and holy forms and contemplating the wisdom of God as displayed in His creatures, from the first form to the very centre of the earth, learning thence to realize His greatness—on such a man the Holy Spirit will promptly descend.[69]

Holiness is mentioned three times in this passage: the would-be prophet sanctifies himself by detaching himself from the masses and from physical desire; he comprehends holy, pure forms; and the holy spirit rests on him. Having become morally and intellectually holy, the prophet is sanctified by God who *is* holy, that is, he or she attains prophecy.[70]

All this has to do with holiness of person. Holiness also has other applications: there is holiness of times and places, holiness of relationships, as in the sanctification of marriage, and holiness of objects, such as a Torah scroll. The underlying meaning is always something set aside, but it takes on many guises.

To sum up, and without pretending to have arrived at an exhaustive definition, holiness is a goal, and the way to that goal. God is absolutely holy, that is, an absolute unity utterly separate from matter. The goal is to be as like

---

[69] 'Laws of the Foundations of the Torah', 7: 1.

[70] This is not meant to imply that holiness has ontological status. Calling God holy in Maimonides' terms means that God is totally separate from anything material—it is, in the end, a negative attribute.

God as possible in that respect. The way is via detachment from the crowd, detachment from desire, and intellectual development.

It is now possible to present a view of *Mishneh torah* as a hierarchy of holiness, its books ranked according to distance from the goal.

The highest form of holiness is not to imitate God in his relation to the world, but God as he is, intellect intellecting itself. This is the contemplative mode of the *Book of Knowledge*. The following two books, the *Book of Love* and the *Book of Seasons*, contain commandments designed to inculcate and reinforce concepts found in the *Book of Knowledge*. They do so by sanctifying certain acts, as in blessings over food in 'Laws of Blessings', and certain times, the sabbath and festivals. The *Book of Women* sanctifies sexual intercourse through the institution of certain formalities to bring awareness of God into a natural act.[71] Whereas before the Torah, marriage with its contractual obligations stemmed from sexual intercourse, after it, the act of marriage is separate from, and must precede, intercourse.[72] That is holiness.

There is also a subplot in these opening four books, about social utility. We have already seen this in the case of circumcision, a dual-purpose commandment having both intellectual/theological and moral/social aspects. The sabbath and festivals promote social cohesion by allowing rest days and opportunities for social gatherings,[73] while the institution of marriage and the abolition of prostitution prevent sexual jealousy and disputes over inheritances from destroying the social fabric.[74] The social aspect of the commandments seems to become stronger as we go along, but nevertheless, in *Mishneh torah*, it is the intellectual/theological aspect that dominates, whereas in the *Guide*, the subplot of moral and social utility becomes the main plot. The key

[71] The formalities concerned are known as *kidushin* (or *erusin*, betrothal), and a woman who has undergone *kidushin* is *mekudeshet*, meaning essentially 'set apart' or 'dedicated', from the root *kdsh*, which is also translated as 'sanctified'. Once the formalities have taken place, and even if the marriage has not been consummated, all other men besides the husband are forbidden to have sexual intercourse with this woman. The other change with the giving of the Torah is that prostitution, previously condoned, is banned: a man who has intercourse with a woman without *kidushin* is liable to be flogged. Ironically perhaps, the Hebrew for prostitute in this context is *kedeshah*, associated with the same root as the words for holiness and sanctification. The origin is in prostitution as a part of pagan rites. See under *kadesh* in Even-Shoshan, *New Dictionary* (Heb.).

[72] This is so notwithstanding that, even under the new dispensation, intercourse itself is one of the ways in which a woman may become married (the others are by a bill of marriage, and by accepting something of value), because in order to be valid it requires a declaration on the part of the man, and witnesses to the fact that the couple were alone together (see 'Laws of Marriage', 3: 5), and is therefore on a different, more formal plane to pre-Torah marriage through intercourse. In any case the practice died out under rabbinical disapproval because of people's inability to make that distinction (see 'Laws of Marriage', 3: 21).   [73] See *Guide* iii. 43 (p. 570).   [74] See *Guide* iii. 49 (pp. 601–2).

idea behind these commandments in *Mishneh torah* is sanctification, in its purest form as the acquisition of knowledge, and as reinforcement of that knowledge through physical acts. On the whole, then, the first four books can be said to concern sanctification in the sense of consciousness of God and of God in nature.

Next come two books on the core idea of holiness. The *Book of Holiness* and the *Book of Asseverations* are concerned with restraint of the appetites for food and sex. There is of course continuity between the *Book of Women* and the *Book of Holiness*, the first section of which is 'Laws of Forbidden Intercourse', but there is also a fundamental switch between the two books, from the idea of holiness as sanctification of the material and temporal, to holiness as detachment from the material and temporal

In the introduction to *Mishneh torah*, Maimonides states of the *Book of Holiness*, 'I will include in it commandments concerning forbidden sexual unions and commandments concerning forbidden foods, because in these two respects God sanctified us and separated us from the nations.' *Guide* iii. 33 explains that the restraint of physical appetites is one of the basic purposes of the law, and the way to purity and sanctification, mentioning as examples the ban of sexual intercourse in the period leading up to the revelation at Sinai, and the nazirite's abstention from wine,[75] and again citing *Sifra*. This gives holiness in the sense of separation two aspects: separation from the nations, but also separation from desire. As God is separate from the world, Israel should be separate from the nations, and individuals should separate themselves from their physical appetites. The *Book of Asseverations* concerns renunciations that are self-imposed rather than imposed universally by the Torah, but once they are undertaken, the Torah regulates them. Books 5 and 6 of the first ten books of *Mishneh torah* thus form a central, pivotal unit, dealing explicitly with the subject of holiness.[76]

[75] 'Laws of Nazirites' is the third section of the *Book of Asseverations*.

[76] The following passages epitomize the concept of holiness in these two books: 'Therefore a man should subjugate his desire in this matter and habituate himself to extra holiness' ('Laws of Forbidden Intercourse', 22: 20, on the temptation to incest and adultery); 'And anyone who is careful about these things brings holiness and extra purity to his soul, and cleanses his soul for the sake of the Holy One Blessed be He, as it says, "ye shall therefore sanctify yourselves, and ye shall be holy; for I am holy" (Lev. 12: 44)' ('Laws of Forbidden Foods', 17: 32, on bodily cleanliness and avoidance of disgusting food); 'Anyone who undertakes a vow in order to reform his character and mend his deeds . . . these are all a way of serving the Name, and of these and suchlike vows the sages said: vows are a fence for separation' ('Laws of Vows', 13: 23, on people who ban themselves from things otherwise permitted, separation being a proximate virtue to holiness); 'But if someone makes a vow to God by way of holiness, this is something fine and praiseworthy' ('Laws of Nazirites', 10: 14, on the *nazir*, who circumscribes himself, for a period or for life, with the extra restrictions set out in Num. 6).

The *Book of Agriculture* leads away from this core concept of holiness towards holiness as a social institution, the province of a certain social stratum, the priests and Levites, and a certain place, the Temple. What is more, the Temple does not represent the separation of Israel from the nations; on the contrary, it is a concession to Israel's need to be like the nations. By implication, the Temple and its ritual have little of *imitatio Dei* about them (in contrast to their role for those who would see the Temple as a microcosm).[77] These commandments still reflect the actions of God in nature, which operate through gradual stages to bring about the ultimate divine purpose,[78] and so imitate God in that respect, but they do not to any great extent induce God-like qualities in those who perform them, at least, they are not explained that way in the *Guide*. This is the double scheme mentioned at the start of this chapter. In a way, in respect of holiness, the first ten books of *Mishneh torah* build to a climax in the shape of the Temple, for what could be holier than the Holy of Holies? But looked at another way, holiness is in decline. It began in the mind, as the contemplation of pure form in the *Book of Knowledge*, and evolved into rituals designed to remind one of that ideal, thence into holiness as bodily separation, and is finally centred outside the individual altogether. This is reminiscent of the discussion of perfection at the end of the *Guide*, where the four perfections of wealth, body, morals, and intellect are graded according to their degree of self-sufficiency. Intellectual virtue is the highest perfection because it is completely self-sufficient—as God is self-sufficient.

If a decline in holiness is the trend, we should expect the final book in the sequence of ten, the *Book of Purity*, to be scarcely touched by holiness at all. This is precisely what is said in the *Guide* of the commandments about purity: 'As for His dictum, may He be exalted, *Sanctify yourselves therefore, and be ye holy, for I am holy*, it does not apply at all to uncleanness and cleanness.'[79]

Anyone who undergoes a purification rite emerges qualified to do certain things, such as enter the Temple or partake of tithes, but no holier than before.[80]

Two More *Midrashim*

At the start of this exploration of the subject of holiness in *Mishneh torah*, it was stated that an incidental point would be to show that remoulding Midrash is part of Maimonides' craft. It is by now clear that Maimonides feels at liberty to mix and match *midrashim*. He does not see the sages as telling us

---

[77] See previous chapter.   [78] See *Guide* iii. 32 (p. 525).
[79] *Guide* iii. 47 (p. 595).   [80] See also Kellner, 'Maimonides on Ritual Purity'.

the hidden, or even received, meaning of certain words.[81] Rather, he understands their interpretations as expressing a tendency that can be crystallized into a concept.

Although he does not cite them explicitly, at least two more *midrashim* seem to lie behind his treatment of holiness and *imitatio Dei*. The first is from *Midrash tanḥuma*:

> What does the verse mean 'and God that is holy shall be sanctified in righteousness' (Isa. 5: 16)? That he is sanctified in his world through the righteousness that he pleads for Israel, as it says, 'I that speak in righteousness' (Isa. 63: 1). The Holy One Blessed be He said to Israel, I am sanctified in you, as it says, 'But when he seeth his children, the work of mine hands, in the midst of him, they shall sanctify my name, and sanctify the Holy One of Jacob, etc.' (Isa. 29: 23), and he also says 'Israel in whom I will be glorified' (Isa. 49: 3), and you are sanctified in me, and I am sanctified in you, as it says, 'Ye shall therefore sanctify yourselves, and ye shall be holy; for I am holy' (Lev. 11: 44).[82]

We see here the verse 'Israel in whom I will be glorified' placed in a context of holiness, both the holiness with which Israel endows God, that is, sanctification of the name (*kidush hashem*), and the holiness with which God endows Israel, that is, according to the *Sifra* cited by Maimonides, the commandments. Now that we have seen how closely *imitatio Dei* and holiness are bound up with each other, it is possible to speculate that this *midrash* may partly be what lies behind the duplication discussed in Chapter 1 of the verse 'Israel in whom I will be glorified' at the end of 'Laws of the Foundations of the Torah', 5, and of 'Laws of Ethical Qualities', 5, representing, respectively, sanctification of the name and *imitatio Dei*. It may also be this *midrash* that justified the second appearance of the verse despite the fact that, as noted in Chapter 1, it is strictly speaking out of context at the end of 'Laws of Ethical Qualities', 5. If so, this would be a further example of the general point that Maimonides treats his aggadic sources as pliable.

The second probable source is *Sifra* on Leviticus 19: 1:

> 'And the Lord said to Moses, Speak to all the congregation of the children of Israel, and say to them, You shall be holy'. This teaches us that this chapter was stated in the assembly of all Israel. And why was it stated in the assembly of all Israel? It is because most of the principles of the Torah depend on its contents. 'You shall be holy': 'You shall be separate'. 'You shall be holy for I the Lord your God am holy.' That is to say,

---

[81] See the remarks on Midrash in *Guide* iii. 43 (p. 573).

[82] *Midrash tanḥuma* (Buber), 'Kedoshim', 1 (*Midrash Tanhuma: Leviticus*, trans. Townsend, 300).

'if you sanctify yourselves, I shall credit it to you as though you had sanctified me, and if you do not sanctify yourselves, I shall hold that it is as if you have not sanctified me.' Or perhaps the sense is this: 'If you sanctify me, then lo, I shall be sanctified, and if not, I shall not be sanctified'? Scripture says, 'For I am holy', meaning, I remain in my state of holiness, whether or not you sanctify me. Abba Saul says, 'The king has a retinue, and what is the task thereof? It is to imitate the king.'[83]

Two features of this passage are noteworthy in the light of the present discussion. One is that it recognizes God's objective holiness, yet allows that, by sanctifying themselves, human beings somehow sanctify God, the same complementarity as exists between 'Laws of the Foundations of the Torah', 5, where the name of God is sanctified publicly through martyrdom and exemplary behaviour, and 'Laws of Ethical Qualities', 5, where the scholar sanctifies himself. The other is that here we find Abba Shaul, who provides, as it were, the foundation statement on *imitatio Dei* in BT *Sotah*, but without mentioning holiness, again talking about *imitatio Dei*, 'to imitate the king', this time in a context of holiness. The addition by Maimonides of 'just as he is called holy, so should you be holy' to the first statement of Abba Shaul may have been a shorthand way of invoking the second as well.[84]

Holiness and the Commandments

Just to clear up the difficulties with which this discussion started, it can now be seen that the *Book of Holiness* and 'Laws of Ethical Qualities', 1: 6, do not stand in contradiction to the principle that holiness is an aspect of all the commandments and not a commandment in itself. *Mishneh torah* is indeed all about holiness, but the *Book of Holiness* is the nub, the point at which intellect confronts physical desire, and therefore the point at which holiness is most sharply at stake. It is also a point of transition in the gradual externalization of holiness, from holiness as an inward quality induced by commandments designed to reinforce opinions, through holiness as resistance to the material world, to holiness as an attribute of the material world in the Temple.

For its part, 'Laws of Ethical Qualities', 1: 6, does not really present 'be holy' as an isolated commandment. It rather explains how holiness extends

---

[83]   *Sifra*, 87.

[84]   A further tightening of the connection between *imitatio Dei* and holiness is that in another comment in *Midrash tanḥuma*, 'Kedoshim', 3, on Lev 19: 1 ff., comparing that passage with the Ten Commandments, 'Do not commit adultery' is associated with 'You shall be holy' (*Midrash Tanhuma: Leviticus*, trans. Townsend, 302). *Midrash tanḥuma*, 'Kedoshim', 2 also associates sanctification of God's name with the same verse, and provides midrashic background to the halakhic decision (BT *San.* 74*b*) that this commandment applies only to the Jewish people.

over all the commandments. 'And walk in his ways' is the root commandment of moral virtue. The social commandments have the double purpose of 'the abolition of their wrongdoing each other' and 'the acquisition by every human individual of moral qualities that are useful for life in society'.[85] Throughout, Maimonides tends to explain these commandments as having both direct social utility and a reflexive effect on the doer. Through the donations to the priests and the Temple, for example, 'the moral quality of generosity is acquired', while the 'Laws of Creditor and Debtor' 'are imbued with benevolence, pity, and kindness for the weak'.[86] In other words, the point of these commandments is not just to act with mercy and grace, but to become merciful and gracious, as God is merciful and gracious, and ultimately holy as God is holy.[87]

The Flow of Form from the *Book of Knowledge*

The first ten books of *Mishneh torah* are thus arranged according to a hierarchy. The higher up the hierarchy we go, the closer we become to immateriality, knowledge, the first intention, and love. Conversely, as we descend, we become closer to matter, unintelligibility, the second intention, and awe. Spanning all these oppositions is the idea of holiness, allied to *imitatio Dei*. Emanation, however, is more than a matter of hierarchy. Each level in the hierarchy is produced by the one above it, everything ultimately deriving from the One. To reflect a Neoplatonic model, each book of *Mishneh torah* ought, then, to evolve from the one that precedes it, and also be traceable to an ultimate source.

One device that it has been suggested concatenates the books of *Mishneh torah* is the different biblical verse each bears as a motto.[88] But there is, on the whole, a fairly obvious thematic flow from one book to another in the first ten books, a flow that is not inhibited by the boundaries of the division into three types of holiness just made. As we have just seen, the *Book of Love* emerges clearly from the *Book of Knowledge*, while the *Book of Seasons* continues the theme of commandments that act as reminders of important doctrines. The *Book of Women*, the *Book of Holiness*, and the *Book of Asseverations* also form a coherent series, linked by the theme of restraint on appetite, whether im-

[85] *Guide* iii. 27 (p. 510).   [86] *Guide* iii. 39 (p. 553).

[87] Seeskin comments: 'While some commandments promote the welfare of the body, others promote the welfare of the soul. In either case, the performance of commandments must not only make us better people but bring us closer to God and thus allow us to become God-like in some way' ('Holiness as an Ethical Ideal', 192–3).   [88] Shaviv, 'Motto Verses' (Heb.).

posed by the law or self-imposed. The *Book of Asseverations* concludes with 'Laws of Valuation and Consecration', essentially about donations to the Temple, leading in to the *Book of Agriculture*, which begins with 'Laws of Diverse Kinds', laws that regulate the growth of food just as eating is regulated, but that originate, according to Maimonides, in a drive to stamp out pagan agricultural rites, setting us on the track towards the laws of the Temple, many of which are similarly explained as designed to counter pagan practice.[89] The *Book of Agriculture* moves on to laws about donations to the poor and to the priest and Levite, leading directly into the last three books, which are about the Temple.[90]

There is one juncture where the thematic link is not obvious, between the *Book of Seasons* and the *Book of Women*. A link can be found, however, between the endings of the two books. At the end of 'Laws of Megilah and Hanukah', the final section of the *Book of Seasons*, the discussion is about the priority to be given to commandments in a situation where several need to be performed but there is only money enough for the requirements of one.

If such a poor man needs oil for both a Sabbath lamp[91] and a Hanukkah lamp, or oil for a Sabbath lamp and wine for the Sanctification benediction,[92] the Sabbath lamp should have priority, for the sake of peace in the household,[93] seeing that even a Divine Name might be erased to make peace between husband and wife.[94] Great indeed is peace, forasmuch as the purpose for which the whole of the Law was given is to bring peace upon the world, as it is said, *Her ways are ways of pleasantness, and all her paths are peace* (Prov. 3: 17).[95]

Much could be made of this passage and its placement. For present purposes, the point to note is that by introducing the theme of peace between man and wife, it provides continuity where continuity is not obvious. For its part, the *Book of Women* ends with 'Laws of the Wayward Woman', about the woman

---

[89] *Book of the Commandments*, negative commandment 42; *Guide* iii. 37 (pp. 544 and 548–9).

[90] One reason given for donations to the priest, and this presumably applies also to donations to the Levite and the poor, is 'so that the moral quality of generosity be strengthened and the appetite for eating and for acquisition be weakened' (*Guide* iii. 39 (p. 551)), which again provides continuity from the *Book of Holiness* through the *Book of Asseverations* to the *Book of Agriculture*.

[91] The light lit on Fridays just before the commencement of the sabbath.

[92] i.e. Kiddush—the benediction declaring the holiness of the sabbath or festival, made over a cup of wine, which may be costly.

[93] The home should be cheerful and well lit on the sabbath to help avoid strife.

[94] The procedure followed when a man suspected his wife of infidelity involved a Torah passage written on parchment and containing the name of God being erased in water. Erasing the name of God is a grave matter—see 'Laws of the Foundations of the Torah', 6.

[95] 'Laws of Megilah and Hanukah', 4: 14.

suspected of adultery. This is something Maimonides contrived, for it differs from the arrangement of Order *Nashim* of the Mishnah. 'Laws of the
Wayward Woman' also closes on a note of peace:

It is not fitting for a man to be quick to declare jealousy before witnesses at the beginning, but he should rather do so in private with her, gently, in a pure manner and by
way of warning, to lead her in the right way and remove a stumbling block. And anyone who is not strict with his wife and children and members of his household, and
does not caution them and oversee their conduct constantly until he knows that they
are free of all sin and wrongdoing—he is a sinner, as it says, 'And thou shalt know that
thy tabernacle shall be in peace; and thou shalt visit thy habitation and shalt not sin'
(Job 5: 24).[96]

The *Book of Seasons* thus runs into the *Book of Women*, and the two books have,
as it were, rhyming endings.[97]

So the first ten books of *Mishneh torah* can be read as a serial, each taking
up some theme or motif from the one that precedes it. This does not, however, justify bringing to bear the full philosophical weight of the Neoplatonic
model of emanation. In order to take the argument to the next stage, it will be
as well to remind ourselves of some features of that model, particularly as
presented in the *Book of Knowledge*.

We have seen that the angels exist in a hierarchy determined by degree of
knowledge. In a description that reflects the emanation of the Neoplatonic
hypostases, and the corresponding concatenation of the books of *Mishneh
torah*, Maimonides states that 'Each of them is below another and exists by
the other's power.'[98] But angels, and for that matter everything else in the

---

[96] 'Laws of the Wayward Woman', 4: 19. There is something of a play on words here, as the
Hebrew for peace, *shalom*, is related to the word for perfect or whole, *shalem*, plural *shelemim*. The
original behind 'free of all sin' is *shelemim mikol ḥet*, literally 'whole from all sin'. 'And thou shalt know
that thy tabernacle shall be in peace' carries the overtone 'thou shalt know that thy wife is whole', i.e.
faithful. Similarly, the Hebrew verb behind 'thou shalt visit' is *pakod*, which can also mean to oversee
(reflected in the now almost obsolete use in English of the word 'visitor' to mean auditor ('hearer') or
inspector, cf. the modern Hebrew *mevaker*). Heard in this way, the verse therefore backs Maimonides'
strictures on the master of the house to correct the morals of his wife and family. The idea of domestic
peace nevertheless remains—it will be the result of the balance in this *halakhah* between gentleness
and vigilance. For talmudic expositions of the verse from Job, see BT *Shab.* 34*a*; BT *Yev.* 62*b*; BT *San.*
76*b*. Maimonides' deployment of the verse does not quite correspond to any of the talmudic or
midrashic treatments I have seen.
[97] It may perhaps be stretching a point to read significance into it, but the book after the *Book of
Women*, the *Book of Holiness*, ends on the motif of light, and this is the halfway mark in the ten man–
God books. The repeated motif is perhaps meant to bind the *Book of Holiness* to the preceding books
and distinguish it from the following ones.   [98] 'Laws of the Foundations of the Torah', 2: 5.

cosmos, also derive their existence directly from God. The passage just quoted continues, 'And all exist by the power and goodness of the Holy God, blessed be He'. A little later on, the same idea is repeated: 'All beings, except the Creator, from the highest angelic form to the tiniest insect that is in the interior of the earth, exist by the power of God's essential existence. And as He has self-knowledge, and realizes His greatness, glory and truth, He knows all, and naught is hidden from Him.'[99] In fact, this is stated at the very opening of *Mishneh torah*: 'All existing things . . . exist only through His true Existence.'

These passages could be interpreted as meaning merely that God sets the emanation ball rolling, so that everything ultimately derives its existence from him, though he acts through intermediaries. In that case, their sense is adequately represented in the structure of *Mishneh torah* by the serial model of the books developed above. Neoplatonic cosmology is, however, more complicated than that. Each level of existence derives both from the previous level and from God directly. In the Alfarabian model, it is from each Intelligence's thought of the First Cause, diminishing in power at each successive level, that the next Intelligence emanates. Furthermore, in contrast to the Platonic Demiurge, which creates through contemplation of Forms outside itself, the Neoplatonic Intellect holds the forms within itself. 'Intelligence is unable to receive the vision of the One in its full perfection; it therefore "fragments" it, and the result is the unity-in-plurality of the World of Forms.'[100] Below Intelligence, Soul's role is as an intermediary between the intelligible and sensible worlds, 'conveying into Matter images of the Forms she receives from Intelligence'.[101]

The flow of existence happens because it is in the nature of perfection to give of itself. The One does not give rise to Intelligence because of any lack; on the contrary, the One is absolutely perfect, and it is the overflow of this very perfection that causes Intelligence to exist, and so on down the hierarchy: 'Entities that have achieved perfection of their own being do not keep that perfection to themselves, but spread it abroad by generating an external "image" of their internal activity.'[102]

In *Mishneh torah*, the *Book of Knowledge* corresponds to Intellect or Intelligence, while the following nine books represent gradations of Soul. Intellect

---

[99] 'Laws of the Foundations of the Torah', 2: 9.   [100] Wallis, *Neoplatonism*, 66.   [101] Ibid. 69.

[102] Ibid. 61. Maimonides himself countenances two kinds of perfection: one only sufficient unto itself, and another that flows onward. See *Guide* ii. 11 (p. 275). This is reflected in his doctrine of prophecy, as will be seen later on.

is the highest order of angels, the *ḥayot*, which has the greatest knowledge of God, but is still unable to perceive God in his full perfection.[103] Its vision of God is therefore fragmented into Forms, the immaterial commandments of the *Book of Knowledge*. The following nine 'Soul' books convey those Forms into Matter, into the man–God commandments with their material substrates, and eventually into the the man–man commandments with their essentially material concerns. As we descend, matter becomes more and more predominant: as the perception of God diminishes with each rank of angel, each is apparently able to convey Form more weakly, or perhaps convey a weaker Form.

If this Neoplatonic model of *Mishneh torah*'s form is really justified, then we should expect that, as well as books 2 to 9 emerging one from another, there will be some imprint on all of them of the *Book of Knowledge*; that that book will be perfect in itself, yet project onto the rest an external image of its internal activity.

I shall now look to see whether that expectation is fulfilled, by examining the following propositions:

1. The *Book of Knowledge* is a self-contained unit describing the entire relationship between God and man. The first section, 'Laws of the Foundations of the Torah', represents the divine, and the other sections mankind, in a relationship of reciprocity.

2. The *Book of Knowledge* contains within it the Forms of the rest of *Mishneh torah*, in that the ten chapters of 'Laws of the Foundations of the Torah' are a blueprint for the first ten books.

3. The form of 'Laws of the Foundations of the Torah' flows into books 2 to 10 via the form of the *Book of Knowledge*, imaging the internal activity of that book as described in 1.

The Self-Containment of the *Book of Knowledge*

The *Book of Knowledge* can be divided into two: 'Laws of the Foundations of the Torah', and the rest. 'Laws of the Foundations of the Torah' represents the divine state and divine actions; the remaining sections represent corresponding human states and actions. In this way, 'Laws of the Foundations of the Torah' and the other sections are like two halves of a sphere that, put together, form a perfect whole. This idea was introduced in Chapter 1, with

---

[103] See 'Laws of the Foundations of the Torah', 2: 8.

the discussion of parallel structures in 'Laws of the Foundations of the Torah' and 'Laws of Ethical Qualities' representing man as microcosm, and being versus becoming. What follows continues that discussion.

What is the subject matter of 'Laws of the Foundations of the Torah'? Why are the commandments it discusses to be regarded as the foundations of the law? With some, the answer is straightforward. Since we are dealing with a divine law, 'I am the Lord thy God' clearly forms its basis. Since the law is transmitted by a prophet, obedience to the prophet is fundamental. But what is fundamental about the obligation to sanctify the divine name, through martyrdom if necessary, or the prohibition against erasing it? 'Laws of the Foundations of the Torah' discusses ten commandments. A twenty-first-century observant Jew, asked to compile a list of ten fundamental commandments of the Torah, would be highly unlikely to come up with a list corresponding to Maimonides' ten. For instance, observance of the sabbath, the traditional touchstone for inclusion among the faithful, would almost certainly appear on his or her list, but it finds no place in 'Laws of the Foundations of the Torah'.[104]

Clearly this is a distraction from what Maimonides is about in 'Laws of the Foundations of the Torah': he seeks to set out the conceptual basis of the Torah, not necessarily the most important social or ceremonial commandments. One of the main thrusts of his whole enterprise, and one of the things that made him controversial, was the effort to establish doctrines rather than works as the fundamentals of Judaism and as criteria for inclusion in the community.[105] But the point is worth pressing to bring out his method. For what the commandments in 'Laws of the Foundations of the Torah' appear to have in common is that they concern the ways in which God is revealed in the world, namely, through nature (chapters 1 to 4/commandments 1 to 5), exemplary behaviour (chapter 5/commandment 6), Scripture and the law

[104] In 'Laws of the Sabbath', 30: 15 Maimonides himself pronounces anyone who transgresses the sabbath laws in public a heathen. Incidentally, an English-speaking reader might think that if ten commandments are required, *the* Ten Commandments (which include the sabbath) should serve, but the biblical term for these is *aseret hadevarim*, 'the ten words' or 'things' (Exod. 34: 28; Deut. 4: 13, 10: 4), really the ten clauses of the covenant, generally referred to as *aseret hadibrot*, the ten utterances. The number of commandments they contain is actually more than ten, certainly according to Maimonides' reckoning, in which fourteen commandments arise from the verses in question (Exod. 20: 1–17)—see the key in the *Book of the Commandments*, 334.

[105] See Halbertal, *Maimonides* (Heb.), 119–22; Kellner, *Must a Jew Believe Anything?*, 52–65. One explanation for the commandments included in 'Laws of the Foundations of the Torah' is that they reflect the Thirteen Principles of Faith set out in the *Commentary on the Mishnah*, Introduction to *Perek ḥelek*, Order *Nezikin*, 141–4; see Rabinovitch, *Yad peshutah*, 3–4.

(chapters 6 and 9/commandments 7, 8, and 9), and prophecy (chapters 7 to 10/commandments 9 and 10). These are not unarguable descriptions or categorizations (the law could be grouped with prophecy, for example), but they convey what unites the various topics discussed in 'Laws of the Foundations of the Torah', what makes them foundational.[106]

If 'Laws of the Foundations of the Torah' is about God being revealed in the world, the rest of the *Book of Knowledge* is about the world's answering echo. As far as 'Laws of Ethical Qualities' is concerned, this has already been treated in some detail in Chapter 1: in 'Laws of the Foundations of the Torah' God creates nature, and creates man 'in the image of God' in respect of the intellect; in 'Laws of Ethical Qualities' man creates himself, modelling himself on the attributes of God's actions in nature, and brings his personality under the command of his intellect. As I argued in that chapter, in 'Laws of the Foundations of the Torah' man *is* in the image of God, while in chapter 5 of 'Laws of Ethical Qualities' he *becomes* in the image of God. By so doing, he turns himself, as we have seen, into the exemplar of faith who sanctifies God's name, as he is required to be by 'Laws of the Foundations of the Torah', 5. Furthermore, the requirement of the scholar to be an exemplar can be paired with the corresponding duty to pay respect to the scholar found in 'Laws of Torah Study', again, notably, in chapter 5 (and chapter 6).

Similarly, in 'Laws of the Foundations of the Torah', the Torah is treated in its God-given aspects: unchanging, eternal, inviolable. In 'Laws of Torah Study', on the other hand, the Torah is treated not as something given by God but as something acquired by people, through study.

'Laws of the Foundations of the Torah', 6, deals with damage to the objective representations of God in the world—his written name, the Temple, and books of Scripture. 'Laws of Idolatry' deals with deterioration in human beings' subjective, intellectual representation of God to themselves.

The final pairing is of prophecy, treated in the last four chapters of 'Laws of the Foundations of the Torah', and repentance, the subject of 'Laws of Repentance', the last section of the *Book of Knowledge*.[107]

---

[106] Two things jar here. One is that chapter 6, which is taken as representing Scripture, is negative. It concerns the prohibition against erasing the name of God, under which are subsumed laws against damaging the fabric of the Temple or holy texts. The other is that glaringly absent from the list is the revelation of God through history and miracles. This point is treated in the next chapter, where I show that the solution to the first difficulty is also the solution to the second.

[107] Maimonides' treatment of repentance as a basic conceptual category was unprecedented in a work on Jewish law (as opposed to a work of Jewish thought)—see Kadari, 'Thought and Halakhah in Maimonides' Laws of Repentance' (Heb.), 5–9. This makes the positioning of 'Laws of Repentance',

The correspondence between prophecy and 'Laws of Repentance' works on at least two levels. In chapter 9 of 'Laws of the Foundations of the Torah', Maimonides stresses that, after Moses, the prophet does not come with any new religious dispensation, but only to urge the people to observe the commandments of the Torah.[108] In 'Laws of Repentance' itself we learn that repentance is one of the two main burdens of the message of the prophets,[109] the other being the messiah.[110] The two subjects are of course linked by the fact that repentance on a national scale is a precondition for messianic redemption.[111]

There is also a correspondence on the personal level. Both the prophet and the penitent need to turn away from 'the vanities of the time',[112] and both undergo transformation. Of the prophet it is said,

And when the spirit rests on him, his soul will mingle with the rank of angels called 'Ishim', and he will become a different person, and will understand in his mind that he is not as he was, but that he has become elevated above the level of the rest of the wise, as was said of Saul 'and thou shalt prophesy with them, and shalt be turned into a different man' (1 Sam. 10: 6)[113]

while as for the penitent,

Among the ways of penitence is for the penitent to be constantly crying before God with weeping and supplication, and performing charity as far as he is able, and distancing himself greatly from the thing in which he sinned. And he changes his name, as though to say, 'I am someone else, and not that person who did those deeds'.[114]

The arduous path of the penitent finds at its end a reward similar to the one bestowed on the prophet when his long and difficult self-training is complete. Penitence brings a person close to the divine presence,[115] while the holy spirit rests on the prophet.[116] This is not the place to enquire into the precise

and its structural links to other parts of *Mishneh torah*, as discussed in this chapter and the next, all the more significant.

[108] See 'Laws of the Foundations of the Torah', 9: 2.
[109] See 'Laws of Repentance', 7: 5.   [110] See ibid. 8: 7.
[111] See ibid. 7: 5. See also Blidstein, *Political Concepts* (Heb.), 272–4. Maimonides' position on this was controversial—see Kadari, 'Thought and Halakhah in Maimonides' Laws of Repentance' (Heb.), 236–43.   [112] 'Laws of the Foundations of the Torah', 7: 1; 'Laws of Repentance', 3: 4.
[113] 'Laws of the Foundations of the Torah', 7: 1.
[114] 'Laws of Repentance', 2: 4.   [115] See ibid. 7: 6–7.
[116] 'Laws of the Foundations of the Torah', 7: 1. Technically, what is called here the holy spirit is broadcast unceasingly and indiscriminately by the agent intellect, and the prophet tunes into it, but this description is according to the language of the opening of 'Laws of the Foundations of the Torah', 7: 1: 'God inspires men with the prophetic gift'.

meaning for Maimonides of the term Shekhinah (divine presence or in-dwelling) as opposed to descent of *ruaḥ hakodesh* (holy spirit);[117] what matters for present purposes is that prophecy and repentance have much in common. On the general level the connection lies in the role of the prophet as reprover of the nation,[118] urging it to repent; on the individual level, the prophet is transformed by the holy spirit descending upon him, while the penitent transforms himself in order to remove the barrier between him and God and come close to the divine presence, a further example of the top-down orientation of 'Laws of the Foundations of the Torah' versus the bottom-up orientation of the other sections of the *Book of Knowledge*.

It might be objected that both the prophet and the penitent achieve their transformation through their own exertions, and that the prophet therefore belongs with the penitent on the human side of the divine/human divide, with the consequence that the formal opposition suggested between 'Laws of the Foundations of the Torah' and the other sections of the *Book of Knowledge* fails to hold up.

It is true that the prophet, like everyone and everything in the material world, receives the form that he is prepared to receive. This, however, is not the perspective from which Maimonides presents prophecy in 'Laws of the Foundations of the Torah', for chapter 7 of that section, the first of the chapters on prophecy, opens with the statement, 'It is among the foundations of religion to know that God makes human beings prophesy.' The headline, then, is the top-down process of God bestowing prophecy on people. Maimonides immediately goes on to describe how a person becomes worthy of that bestowal, but the framework has been established. Prophecy can be discussed under the headline of the perfection of man, as it is towards the end of the *Guide*. But that is not where Maimonides puts it in *Mishneh torah*. 'Laws of Repentance', by contrast, does not begin by telling us that God forgives sinners who repent, but rather with the first step in the process of repentance,

---

[117] But see the discussion above on 'Laws of Impurity of Foodstuffs', 16: 12. See also 'Laws of Temple Utensils and Servers', 10: 10 (where the two terms seem almost synonymous); *Guide* i. 10, i. 25, i. 27; Kellner, *Maimonides' Confrontation with Mysticism*, 85–126 and 179–215; Diamond, *Converts, Heretics, and Lepers*, 159–89.

[118] Or as leader of the nation, sometimes effecting immediate penitence, as, for example, in the cases of Samuel and King Saul (1 Sam. 15), Nathan and King David (2 Sam. 12), Elijah and King Ahab (1 Kgs. 21), or Isaiah and King Hezekiah (2 Kgs. 20). Jonah's mission to Nineveh is a further instance of a prophet actually causing people to repent. In fact, a further, if negative, connection between prophecy and repentance is that God may withhold the capacity for both. See *Guide* ii. 32 (p. 361) on God's refusal of prophecy to otherwise qualified individuals, and 'Eight Chapters', 8 on his denying Pharaoh the possibility of repentance.

which is confession. Later on in that section we do find much material on the theological aspects of repentance,[119] but that is not the point of entry. The principle that the top-level or lead idea counts still holds. By mapping *Mishneh torah* in this way we can appreciate the subtle links that connect disparate subjects.

Moreover, we should again recall that *Mishneh torah* deals in commandments. There is no commandment to become a prophet. The commandments relating to prophecy are to obey a genuine prophet and not to put him or her to the test. The emphasis in *Mishneh torah*, then, is not on the subjective experience of becoming a prophet, although that is included, but rather on the prophet's authority, which of course derives from the fact that prophecy comes from God. There definitely is, however, a commandment to confess sins, on which Maimonides builds his laws of repentance.

Of course, the description of the prophet's striving should not be underestimated. Really, there is a double movement here. Within the structure of 'Laws of the Foundations of the Torah', which will be examined shortly, the last four chapters on prophecy represent the human attempt to comprehend the content of the first four chapters, *ma'aseh bereshit* and *ma'aseh merkavah*, and, in that respect, 'Laws of the Foundations of the Torah' turns back on itself. Relative to the rest of the *Book of Knowledge*, however, the chapters on prophecy are a continuation of the divine emanation, which engulfs the prophet, while the counter-movement is the striving of the penitent to mend the rupture with that spirit, even if not on a prophetic level.

Similar considerations apply to all the sections of the *Book of Knowledge* that follow 'Laws of the Foundations of the Torah'. It has already been noted that the opening of 'Laws of Ethical Qualities', with its survey of the variety of human nature, provides an abrupt contrast with the theology and dogma of 'Laws of the Foundations of the Torah'.[120] 'Laws of Torah Study' begins with who is and who is not obliged to study and teach Torah. 'Laws of Idolatry' opens not with the prohibition against idolatry, but with a historical account of how the error of idolatry arose. Maimonides is very consistent in maintaining the human perspective in these sections.

There is also a numerical aspect to the integration of the *Book of Knowledge*. The book has five sections. It is framed by two sections that contain ten chapters each: 'Laws of the Foundations of the Torah' and 'Laws of Repentance'. In between are two sections each of seven chapters, namely, 'Laws of

---

[119] Mainly in chapters 5 and 6, which concern free will.   [120] See p. 90 above.

Ethical Qualities' and 'Laws of Torah Study', and a third, 'Laws of Idolatry', of twelve chapters, which disrupts the symmetry.

Two principles need to be borne in mind in analysing these numbers. The first is the point made in the Introduction, that form and matter are relative terms, so that what is form to the entity below it in the cosmic hierarchy is matter to the entity above it, until we eventually reach the form of forms, which is God. To put it another way, each level of emanation is a manifestation of what is above it, only more involved in matter. The second is that, for Maimonides, it would appear, half of a number may be a proxy for the whole.

Thus the five of the *Book of Knowledge* is equivalent to the ten of 'Laws of the Foundations of the Torah' (although, as we have seen, both numbers can independently represent the superlunary world), meaning that the *Book of Knowledge* is to the first ten books of *Mishneh torah* as 'Laws of the Foundations of the Torah' is to the *Book of Knowledge*.

The framing of the *Book of Knowledge* by two sections containing ten chapters gives an idea of self-containment by its sheer symmetry, and also reflects the content of the sections concerned, for it is appropriate that a section about repentance should restore the perfection of the angelic number ten.

The seven of 'Laws of Ethical Qualities' and of 'Laws of Torah Study' should each be taken as representing fourteen, the number of the heavenly and sublunary worlds together. Ethics and Torah both conduct theory into practice, bringing intellectual awareness to bear on material existence. Again, the signification is not just numerical, but is reflected in the content. The first five chapters of 'Laws of Ethical Qualities' concern moral perfection within the individual, and, as shown in Chapter 1, represent the human being as a microcosm, symbolizing the vertical orientation of a person towards God. The last two chapters are about social ethics, a person's horizontal orientation towards fellow human beings in the world of the four elements, two being half of four. Similarly, the first five chapters of 'Laws of Torah Study' are about study and the relationship of master and pupil, while the last two chapters are about the social standing of the scholar. Even closer parallels can be found between these two sections: both, for example, end on the topic of vengefulness and resentment. The point here, however, is the trend from inner to outer, characteristic of *Mishneh torah* in general, and the proportion governing the man–God relationship versus the man–man relationship, which can appear as 10 : 4 or as 5 : 2, and which reflects the cosmic proportion of angels to elements.

This leaves 'Laws of Idolatry' isolated: no other section matches it numerically, and it does not fit in with the cosmic proportion. This of course is entirely appropriate, since 'Laws of Idolatry' is precisely about what does not fit, about the error that excludes a person from participation in the cosmic order and the flow of emanation. It is very likely, then, that the number twelve as the number of chapters in 'Laws of Idolatry' is meant to represent the signs of the zodiac, and to refer to astrology, which Maimonides regarded as base superstition, the kind of attribution of independent power to heavenly bodies that lay at the root of idolatry, as opposed to the idea of universal forces emanating from God that he advocated.[121]

In sum, the *Book of Knowledge* is unified by more than the fact that it deals with basic principles. The book is a world unto itself, a self-contained unit that, as was claimed above, encapsulates the whole God–man relationship. This quality of the *Book of Knowledge* was illustrated by comparison to a sphere. In fact, circularity is a characteristic of its content as well. 'Laws of Repentance' seeks to put the sinner back into touch with the God from whom he or she has become alienated,[122] the God introduced in 'Laws of the Foundations of the Torah'. At the end of 'Laws of Repentance', we find an explicit *da capo*:

A person ought therefore to devote himself to the understanding and comprehension of those sciences and studies which will inform him concerning his Master, as far as it lies in human faculties to understand and comprehend—as indeed we have explained in 'Laws of the Foundations of the Torah'.[123]

So the *Book of Knowledge* turns back upon itself, one might say contemplates itself, as a self-contained, detached, perfect whole. Its tight integration sets it apart; it embodies the Neoplatonic value of unity to the highest degree. Yet at the same time its perfection overflows, first into the next book, the *Book of Love*, and then down the whole scale of books 3 to 10.

Foundations

That, then, is the perfection of the *Book of Knowledge* and its internal activity: it mirrors itself internally, in that sections 2 to 5 give the human reflection of the divine in section 1. It is as though 'Laws of the Foundations of the Torah' is what Intelligence manages to apprehend of the One, from which it generates within itself the Forms that are the other four sections and that pass

[121] Kraemer makes the same suggestion: see 'How (Not) to Read the *Guide*', 381 n. 107. On pp. 381–3 of that article he mounts a defence of the use of numerology in the study of Maimonides, particularly Strauss's numerology.   [122] See 'Laws of Repentance', 7: 7.   [123] Ibid. 10: 6.

onward onto the gradations of Soul. I shall now examine this process in more detail, by analysing further the divine core of the *Book of Knowledge*, 'Laws of the Foundations of the Torah'.

'Laws of the Foundations of the Torah' contains ten chapters that deal with ten commandments.[124] Ten, as has been pointed out time and again, is the number of books on the man–God commandments, corresponding to the orders of angels. In its subject matter, 'Laws of the Foundations of the Torah' itself encompasses the Alfarabian cosmos, ranging as it does in scope from the First Cause to prophecy (prophecy representing man in closest contact with the agent intellect), even if there is no one-to-one equivalence between its ten chapters and the ten intelligences and spheres.[125] It is a microcosm within a microcosm.

It has already been stated that 'Laws of the Foundations of the Torah' represents the conceptual underpinnings of the law. The point of most of the man–God commandments, as Maimonides explains them in the *Guide*, is to inculcate or preserve the principles that 'Laws of the Foundations of the Torah' expounds. Moreover, those commandments derive their authority from that of the prophet Moses, which 'Laws of the Foundations of the Torah' establishes. So 'Laws of the Foundations of the Torah' is the core of *Mishneh torah*. If so, it is tempting to conjecture that the correspondence between the number of its chapters and the number of man–God books is no coincidence, that it serves as a structural as well as a conceptual foundation.

'Laws of the Foundations of the Torah' as Blueprint

The ten chapters of 'Laws of the Foundations of the Torah' can be divided into three groups. The first, comprising the first four chapters, is about basic concepts in physics and metaphysics. The second group, comprising the middle two chapters, is about holiness: the sanctification of God's name, and the prohibition on damaging the name and sacred objects. The third group,

[124] But not at the rate of one commandment per chapter. When it comes to proofs for the existence of God, Maimonides inverts the argument from design, and asserts that irregularity, or particularization, rather than regularity is the sign of the exercise of will on the part of a sovereign creator (see *Guide* ii. 19 (pp. 304–12), and Davidson, *Maimonides' Secret Position*). It could be that Maimonides applied the example of the heavens to his own work, in this case believing that the number ten would emerge as all the more interesting, more revealing of his intention, for not being deployed with complete regularity. In general, there is a need to guard against looking for absolute system in discussing patterns in the *Mishneh torah*, and in any case, as we have already seen, there can be more than one system in operation at a time. A chapter for every commandment would be the symmetry of a bureaucrat; 'Laws of the Foundations of the Torah' displays the cunning of an artist.

[125] For an examination of the basis in Alfarabi's writings of the content of 'Laws of the Foundations of the Torah', see J. L. Kraemer, 'Alfarabi's *Opinions of the Virtuous City*'.

comprising the last four chapters, is about prophecy. The first four chapters and the last four chapters are balanced against each other, with the two middle chapters about holiness as the pivot.

This is reflected in the similar language with which chapter 1 and chapter 7 open. As a reminder, chapter 1 begins: 'The foundation of foundations and the pillar of the sciences is to know that there is a First Being', while chapter 7 begins: 'It is among the foundations of religion to know that God makes human beings prophesy.'

Chapter 7 starts over again at the foundations. This time, however, it is not the foundation of foundations, but the foundation of religion. The structural symmetry and the verbal echo suggest a parallel between the First Being and the prophet, and indeed there is: the one founds the natural order, while the other founds the social order, which is subordinate to, and imitative of, the natural order.

The parallel does not end there. Just as the natural order is fixed and permanent, yet God can occasionally suspend it to bring about a miracle, so the prophet can occasionally suspend the fixed and permanent provisions of the law.[126] Just as the relationship of God to the world is an overflow of perfection, so prophecy is an overflow of the prophet's perfection to his or her fellow human beings.[127] Perfection does not always overflow, however. In general, Maimonides countenances a perfection that perfects only the thing itself without passing over to anything else,[128] and in the particular case of the prophet he countenances a state of prophecy that only perfects the prophet, without any message being transmitted to society.[129] In all these respects, prophecy and creation correspond. This is a special case of man as microcosm. It might be called superman as super-microcosm. The prophet fulfils *imitatio Dei* to the greatest possible extent, and stands in relation to society as God does to the world, not just in respect of God's actions in nature, which is the status of the ordinarily virtuous person as depicted in 'Laws of Ethical Qualities', but in respect of God as origin of nature.

At any rate, we have a pattern in 'Laws of the Foundations of the Torah' of four chapters on God and nature, two on holiness, and four on society. It is reasonably easy to see a match to the pattern of the first ten books of *Mishneh torah* and the gradations of holiness as presented above. The first four books were characterized as concerning the consciousness of God and of God in

---

[126] See 'Laws of the Foundations of the Torah', 9: 3.   [127] See *Guide* ii. 29 (p. 347).
[128] See *Guide* ii. 11 (p. 275).   [129] See 'Laws of the Foundations of the Torah', 7: 7.

nature. The next two are specifically about holiness.[130] The last four are about the Temple, society's monument to holiness.[131]

At least for the first four books, the pattern applies down to a fine resolution. The first chapter of 'Laws of the Foundations of the Torah' is about God's existence and unity. In laying down fundamental principles, it bears the same relation to the other nine chapters as the *Book of Knowledge*—which, as we have just seen, is itself a unity—bears to the following nine books of *Mishneh torah*. Chapter 2 of 'Laws of the Foundations of the Torah' is about the love of God, giving a clear connection to book 2, the *Book of Love*. Chapter 3 is about the spheres, which generate time, corresponding to book 3, the *Book of Seasons*.[132] Chapter 4 is about the *arba'ah gufim*, the 'four bodies', that is, the four elements of matter, while book 4, the *Book of Women*, brings us to the human body.

The pattern is fairly clear, but perhaps the correspondence between the four chapters of 'Laws of the Foundations of the Torah' on prophecy and the four books on the Temple needs amplification. What substantial connection is there between these two subjects?

What needs to be stressed, as I noted before in comparing prophecy and repentance, is the fact that the commandments that form the basis of the discussion of prophecy in chapters 7–10 of 'Laws of the Foundations of the Torah' are about prophecy in its objective manifestation, and not about being a prophet. They concern the prophet's authority, especially the

---

[130] There may also be Midrash behind this structural parallel—see n. 84 above.

[131] The *Book of Agriculture* is counted as belonging with the Temple group in Berman's account of *Mishneh torah*'s structure, on the grounds that it is a book 'primarily relating to the temple and the priesthood'; see Berman, 'Structure of the Commandments', 55. He too sees the man–God books of *Mishneh torah* as keyed to sections of the *Book of Knowledge*, though he does not extrapolate from 'Laws of the Foundations of the Torah'.

[132] The presence of the sabbath as the very first subject in the *Book of Seasons* might seem to refute this idea, since the periodicity of the sabbath is artificial and not dependent on the spheres. In some respects the sabbath, as a regular though not constant reminder of creation, more properly belongs in the *Book of Love*. The obvious reason for it being in the *Book of Seasons* is that that arrangement corresponds to that of the Mishnah, and in any case, as far as desisting from work is concerned, the laws of the sabbath and of festivals are so closely related that it would make no sense to separate them in different books, so the cosmic parallel has its limits. We should, however, note the juxtaposition that Maimonides creates between circumcision as the closing topic of the *Book of Love* and the sabbath as the opening topic of the *Book of Seasons*. Both these commandments are termed *ot*, 'a sign'. This is mentioned in the final *halakhah* of 'Laws of Circumcision' (3: 9) and of 'Laws of the Sabbath' (30: 15), and, in the case of circumcision, stressed in the description of book 2 in the outline of the fourteen books given in the introduction to *Mishneh torah*. As we saw above in respect of the transition from the *Book of Seasons* to the *Book of Women*, the division into books, each with its own conceptual field, is accompanied by continuity, an aspect of the literary representation of emanation.

supreme authority of Moses as lawgiver. The authority of prophets subsequent to Moses derives from and is defined by the law of Moses. In the love–awe polarity, the four chapters of 'Laws of the Foundations of the Torah' on prophecy are in the same relative position as the four books of *Mishneh torah* about the Temple, on the side of awe, meaning authority, the law, and limit. Or if we want to look at it in terms of the gradations of holiness, the holiness of the prophet is external to the people, as the holiness of the Temple is external. This is as opposed to the commandments to know and love God in the first four chapters of 'Laws of the Foundations of the Torah', which confer inward holiness.

Symptomatic of this opposition is the fact that, whereas the commandment to love God is fulfilled by following the spirit of enquiry in the study of nature, and the further the better, enquiry about the prophet is restricted, for as long as a person fulfils the criteria laid down by the Torah, he or she must be accepted as a prophet and obeyed, without further probing.

All this is relative, of course: on the whole, 'Laws of the Foundations of the Torah' remains in the realm of love, but as with the movement from the non-physical to the physical within the essentially non-physical *Book of Love*, within 'Laws of the Foundations of the Torah' there is a movement from love to awe. This is the awe that is in love, while the Temple is awe distilled.[133]

I have noted above that the language of the beginning of the section on prophecy in 'Laws of the Foundations of the Torah', 7: 1, echoing the language of 'Laws of the Foundations of the Torah', 1: 1, indicates that prophecy is a kind of restart on the social and religious plane of the metaphysical and physical order. A similar restart can be detected at the beginning of the *Book of Agriculture*, which introduces the group of books on the Temple that we have said correspond to prophecy. The first two sections of the *Book of Agriculture* are 'Laws of Diverse Kinds' and 'Laws of Gifts to the Poor'. The ostensible rationale of this sequence is that the first section concerns sowing and the second harvesting. However, as Twersky points out, the commandments grouped in 'Laws of Diverse Kinds' are themselves rather diverse, and include such non-agricultural matters as the prohibition against wearing a blend of wool and linen, while 'Laws of Gifts to the Poor' also branches out: besides the entitlements of the poor at harvest time, it also contains laws about charity in general (an innovative grouping by Maimonides).[134]

What the ban on wool and linen and the laws about sowing diverse seeds have in common is that they are all explained in the *Guide* as countering idol-

---

[133] But see n. 40 above.   [134] See Twersky, *Introduction to the Code*, 291.

atrous practices.[135] The sequence of 'Laws of Diverse Kinds' and 'Laws of Gifts to the Poor' can therefore possibly be read as a reprise on the social plane of the pattern of 'Laws of the Foundations of the Torah' and 'Laws of Ethical Qualities', and the flow of moral virtue from intellectual virtue, the message being: sow truth, and you will reap justice.[136]

The message of the prophet is the emanation of God's goodness objectified into law. At the same time, prophecy itself is an intense, inward experience: 'when they have the prophetic experience, their limbs tremble, their physical strength fails them, their thoughts become confused; and thus the mind is left free to comprehend the vision it sees.'[137]

At the end of the *Book of Agriculture*, in a counter-move to the localization of holiness in the Levites and the Temple that is perhaps his most eloquent expression of universalism, Maimonides reasserts holiness as an attitude of mind:

Why did the tribe of Levi not acquire a share in the Land of Israel and in its spoils together with their brothers? Because this tribe was set apart to serve God and to minister to Him . . .

Not only the tribe of Levi but every individual from among the world's inhabitants whose spirit moved him and whose intelligence gave him the understanding to withdraw from the world in order to stand before God to serve and minister to Him, to know God, and he walked upright in the manner in which God made him, shaking off from his neck the yoke of the manifold contrivances which men seek—behold this person has been totally consecrated and God will be his portion and inheritance for ever and ever.[138]

We have here the same idea of self-sanctification rewarded with consecration by God as we find with the prophet 'when the spirit rests upon him'.[139] In neither case, however, is the individual, subjective quest the main theme of Maimonides' presentation; at any rate, not overtly. What is mainly at stake is the prophet's authority (and hence the authority of the Torah as the product of the prophecy of Moses), and the Levites and Temple as an institution.

---

[135] *Guide* iii. 37 (pp. 544–9). The other laws in 'Laws of Diverse Kinds' are prohibitions against interbreeding of animals and working with two species of animal together, explained in *Guide* iii. 49 (pp. 608–9) as intended to avoid arousing sexual excitement in people engaged in animal husbandry. Maimonides does tend to associate fornication and sexual deviancy with idolatry, *Guide* iii. 37 being a case in point, but the general association with mixing of kinds is probably the stronger motivation here.

[136] See 'Laws of Gifts to the Poor', 10: 3, where denial of charity is compared to idolatry. See the discussion on p. 160 above.   [137] 'Laws of the Foundations of the Torah', 7: 2.

[138] 'Laws of Sabbatical and Jubilee Years', 13: 12–13.

[139] 'Laws of the Foundations of the Torah', 7: 1, cited above, p. 246.

Such passages as these provide an opportunity to stress the point that the correspondences and patterns explored by this study are not something fixed and mechanical. This is not an exercise in decoding the Code, as it were. A text containing a coded message can be discarded once the message is understood. In *Mishneh torah*, by contrast, content and form interact in ways that make it live. These passages, for example, enliven their otherwise technical surroundings. In the chapters about prophecy there is a constructive tension between the inward, self-validating, transcendent experience of the prophet, and the objective rules for certifying a prophet. Similarly in 'Laws of Sabbatical and Jubilee Years', the passage about the person moved by the spirit irrigates with spirituality the dry discussion of the entitlements of the tribe of Levi, the light of the inward quality of holiness shining through even as holiness shifts to become an outward property of physical objects. Such creative tension lends *Mishneh torah* the quality of seeming inexhaustibility found in great art.

The Temple, then, stands as the equivalent of the prophet in the public arena.[140] The prophet trains himself in order to touch the status of the *ishim*, the lowest order of angels, that is, the agent intellect. The nation expends effort and resources to build a place where the divine is made almost concrete. Along with the prophet and the divine law he brings, the Temple is one of the foundations of the social order, the place where the people finds its focus and from where instruction and justice proceed.

This parallelism finds some support in Nachum Rabinovitch's argument that the *Book of Temple Service* marks the switch in *Mishneh torah* from commandments concerning the individual to commandments concerning society.[141] The social order that the prophet founds begins to find concrete expression in the Temple. Although I disagree with Rabbi Rabinovitch's view that the mid-point of *Mishneh torah* represents its main division,[142] there can certainly be sub-patterns in the work, and there is no need to deny all significance to the fact that the books on the laws of the Temple and the ancillary laws of purity precede the books on civil law; they are part of the constitution of the state.[143] I would, however, introduce a modification, and start the sub-

---

[140] José Faur finds a very direct link between prophecy and the Temple. He translates *ruaḥ hakodesh* as 'the spirit of the sanctuary' (*Homo Mysticus*, 74, 82). It is certainly true that prophecy died out with the loss of the Temple and is expected to be restored with the rebuilding of the Temple by the messiah, who will himself be a great prophet.

[141] Rabinovitch, 'Sanctuary, Society, and History' (Heb.).   [142] See pp. 161–2 above.

[143] This would lead to a modification of the view put forward in Chapter 2 that the Temple has no cosmic significance for Maimonides. Insofar as the constitution of the ideal state is a microcosm, as

pattern with the *Book of Agriculture*, in line with the notion discussed above that the extirpation of idolatry in the public sphere starts in that book's first section, 'Laws of Diverse Kinds', and that, structurally, that section marks a new beginning.

The Transfer of Form via the *Book of Knowledge*

We can now consider further the intermediate role of the *Book of Knowledge* in this transfer of form from the ten chapters of 'Laws of the Foundations of the Torah' to the first ten books of *Mishneh torah* as a whole. The first two sections, 'Laws of the Foundations of the Torah' itself and 'Laws of Ethical Qualities', form a pair, in that the one represents the cosmos and the other the microcosm. They chiefly concern individual intellectual and moral virtue. They flow from the first four chapters of 'Laws of the Foundations of the Torah', and flow into the first four books of *Mishneh torah*, adding depth to the idea that the Shema, the sabbath and festivals, and perhaps marriage, originating as it does in Adam and Eve and the commandment to them to 'be fruitful and multiply',[144] are reminders of God's unity and of creation. Remembering these things is not just a matter of holding to correct doctrine: the unity of God and the natural order are things that human beings, each within his or her capacity, have to reproduce in themselves. The holiness of ritual acts, of seasons, and of marriage should infuse the person who performs these commandments with holiness. 'Laws of the Foundations of the Torah' more closely matches the *Book of Knowledge* and the *Book of Love*, in that those books are more theologically orientated, while 'Laws of Ethical Qualities', as it were, funnels theological truths into social relations, matching the structures of the commandments in the *Book of Seasons*—the festivals being designed to promote social solidarity as well as reinforce correct doctrine—and in the *Book of Women*, which clearly is about a social relationship as well as about holiness.

The middle section, 'Laws of Torah Study', concerns holiness in a narrower sense. The Torah is holy because it is God-given, because it contains the commandments that sanctify,[145] and because it is the Torah (and, as far as

---

also discussed in Chapter 2, then the institution of the Temple, in its uniqueness, centrality, and primacy, bears a relationship to the state analogous to that of God to the universe. This is to be distinguished from the view of Ibn Ezra cited in Chapter 2 in that for Maimonides the relationship is purely analogous and works through the consciousness of the citizens, whereas for Ibn Ezra the Temple has this status inherently and the relationship is direct.

[144] Gen. 9: 7. This is the fourth commandment listed in the *Book of Women*.
[145] See *Guide* iii. 47 (p. 595). Holiness is 'sanctification by the commandments'.

Maimonides is concerned, only the Torah) that separates the Jewish people from other peoples. In that way it connects with the middle two chapters of 'Laws of the Foundations of the Torah', which are explicitly about holiness. Chapter 5 of 'Laws of the Foundations of the Torah', as it happens, also introduces the first commandment that distinguishes the Jewish people, the commandment to sanctify God's name, an obligation that falls only on Jews.[146] The theme of holiness in the sense of separation also connects these chapters with the middle two of the first ten books of *Mishneh torah*, which, as we have seen, are about separation from the nations and from the physical.

The final two sections of the *Book of Knowledge*, 'Laws of Idolatry' and 'Laws of Repentance', correspond to the last four chapters of 'Laws of the Foundations of the Torah', on prophecy. We have already seen the connection between prophecy and repentance. As for idolatry, it stems from inaccurate perception of the natural order, while prophecy stems from perfect perception of the natural order. The prophet rescues from idolatry, Abraham and Moses being cases in point in *Mishneh torah*.[147] On the side of the last four man–God books, about the Temple, the Temple belongs to the second intention of the commandments, whereby idolatry is used against itself, directing rituals of pagan origin, or variations on them, to the worship of God. Hence the alignment with 'Laws of Idolatry'. Moreover, one of the main purposes of the Temple is atonement, for an individual bringing a sin offering to atone for an unintentional transgression, and, in its ultimate expression, on the Day of Atonement, when the High Priest performs a rite of atonement for himself, for his family, and for the entire community. As part of this rite, the High Priest enters the Holy of Holies, he being the only person ever allowed to do so, and then only on this one day of the year, so that atonement is the only function that utilizes the whole Temple building, providing that institution's main *raison d'être*.

To recapitulate, the *Book of Knowledge* contains the Form of *Mishneh torah*, in the shape of 'Laws of the Foundations of the Torah', the structural pattern of which is replicated in the first ten books. This emanation of form, a sanctification, in all the range of meanings of that term, of human life, is powered by the inner activity of the *Book of Knowledge*, whereby the four sections that follow 'Laws of the Foundations of the Torah' represent the human striving towards its manifestations of the divine.

All this can be summarized in a table (see Table 5) with the proviso that it should not be applied rigidly; not all the correspondences are absolute.

---

[146] See 'Laws of the Foundations of the Torah', 5: 1.   [147] See 'Laws of Idolatry', 1: 3.

Table 5 The flow of form via the *Book of Knowledge*

'Foundations of the Torah'		*Book of Knowledge*	*Mishneh torah,* books 1–10
1	Knowledge of God	'Foundations'	Knowledge
2	Love/fear of God		Love
3	Spheres and stars	'Ethical Qualities'	Times
4	Matter		Women
5	Sanctification	'Torah Study'	Holiness
6	Desecration		Asseverations
7	Prophecy	'Idolatry'	Agriculture
8	"		Temple
9	"	'Repentance'	Sacrifices
10	"		Purity

It might be felt at this stage that the argument has been stretched too far; that, even if these correspondences exist, there is no need to fetch ideas from Plotinus in order to explain them. Perhaps Maimonides simply liked consistent patterns. We need to engage, however, with an unfamiliar cast of mind that sees the world working by structural correspondences that run through all things, and that endow it with a unity that reflects the unity of God. Besides, the Neoplatonic explanation is not far-fetched, but close to home: its basis lies in the cosmology expounded in 'Laws of the Foundations of the Torah'. Nor have we finished surveying the structural features of *Mishneh torah*. When the survey is complete, we shall find that, taken together, these features fit a higher-level explanation that *Mishneh torah* is a Neoplatonic document. As a single theory covering many structural phenomena, this explanation can claim the virtue of maximum simplicity, even though it contains much complexity.

The final phase of the Neoplatonic patterns in *Mishneh torah*, that of return, remains to be described, and will be the subject of the next chapter. Nevertheless, as far as a table grid can capture them, we see reflected here the Neoplatonic tendencies in *Mishneh torah*'s form, with the hierarchy from the non-physical, the intelligible, love, and holiness as an intellectual quality, down to the physical, the unintelligible, awe, and holiness as an external fact. In addition, the procession from 'Laws of the Foundations of the Torah' to the *Book of Knowledge* to the man–God books gives the sense of an ever-widening circle, reminiscent of Maimonides' metaphor for creation as an infinite overflow from a spring. Just as the universe emanates from God, so *Mishneh torah* emanates from its opening assertion of God's existence, which is like a stone thrown into a pond, the ripples expanding to cover all of reality.

The Sacrifice Paradox

Maimonides' attitude to sacrifices is a well-known puzzle. In the *Guide* he describes them as a concession to people's inability to abandon the tangible and familiar all at once. In the era of the exodus from Egypt, he says, animal sacrifice was the conventional form of worship, and it would have been as disconcerting for the Israelites to be told to forgo it as it would for us to be told to replace prayer with silent meditation.[148] Sacrifices, in that case, were a temporary shift, and are at the bottom of the scale, with prayer being better and meditation best. Yet in *Mishneh torah* Maimonides devotes three out of fourteen books to the Temple ritual, states explicitly that sacrifices will be restored in the days of the messiah,[149] and is emphatic that they belong in the category of *ḥukim* (statutes) that must be obeyed without question even if their rationale is not understood.[150] As David Henshke reminds us in his article on the subject,[151] it was this contradiction that made R. Jacob Emden decide that the *Guide* could not be the work of Maimonides.[152]

In brief, Henshke's solution to the puzzle is that a careful reading of *Mishneh torah* reveals that, in Maimonides' view, sacrifices have no intrinsic value. Their ultimate point, like that of all the commandments (including those that are clearly rational), is obedience to God's will and coming nearer to God. In that respect, the commandments have enduring validity even if the historical explanations for some of them no longer apply. Hence there is no contradiction between *Mishneh torah*'s anticipation of the restoration of sacrifices when historical circumstances permit and the *Guide*'s account of their origin, and so the unity of Maimonides' thought can be preserved.

The problem is that this argument can be regarded as adequate for just about all the apparently non-rational laws, except sacrifices. Maimonides' usual approach to *ḥukim* is to say that they were designed to distance us from

---

[148] See *Guide* iii. 32 (p. 526).   [149] See 'Laws of Kings and Their Wars', 11: 1.

[150] See 'Laws of Trespass', 8: 8. Note also the very positive attitude towards sacrifices, and the regret at the general neglect of the study of this area of the law, expressed at the beginning of Maimonides' introduction to his commentary on tractate *Zevaḥim*.

[151] Henshke, 'Unity in Maimonides' Thought' (Heb.).   [152] See p. 53 above.

some pagan practice.[153] This also applies to the details of worship in the Temple.[154] But his general account of sacrifices is different from his rationalizations of particular laws. Rather than negating a pagan practice, animal sacrifices are an imitation of pagan practice, allowed as a concession because God takes human nature into consideration. Maimonides introduces his account with a comparison to, among other things, the feeding of infants with breast milk until they can digest solid food.[155] This means that, in the case of sacrifices, it is not a question of the historical reason for a law evaporating to leave us with God's bare, enduring command. The restoration of animal sacrifice would actually clash with the historical explanation—it would put history into reverse. Why should we wish to regress to a less worthy, immature form of worship, after we have been weaned off it? Henshke's argument accommodates the non-rational, but this would seem positively irrational. The inconsistency between *Mishneh torah* and the *Guide* remains as glaring as ever.

What is needed to supplement Henshke's argument and to harmonize *Mishneh torah* and the *Guide* is some reflection in *Mishneh torah* of the *Guide*'s scale of value, some indication that prayer is superior to sacrifice and that meditation is superior to prayer. If the theory that the first ten books of *Mishneh torah* are ranked according to a Neoplatonic scale is accepted, this supplies the missing indication. The books dealing with Temple ritual (the *Book of Temple Service*, the *Book of Offerings*, and the *Book of Purity*) are at the bottom of the Neoplatonic hierarchy of reality and value, and at the bottom of the scale from love to awe, while the book dealing with prayer (the *Book of Love*) is next to the top, with meditation, that is, the contemplation of God, at the pinnacle (the *Book of Knowledge*).

Thus *Mishneh torah* presents synchronically and symbolically the same scale of value that the *Guide* presents diachronically and discursively.[156] The message appears to be that human nature will not change in the days of the messiah. People will still need concrete forms of worship, some more than others, and antidotes to idolatry.[157] Even those capable of it will take time to mature into a more intellectual relationship with God, and will never entirely

---

[153] He summarizes his approach this way at the end of *Guide* iii. 49 (p. 612).

[154] For example, the Holy of Holies is placed in the west in contradistinction to pagan worship of the rising sun, while oxen, sheep, and goats are sacrificed in demonstrative rejection of the belief among some sects that they are sacred—*Guide* iii. 45–6. [155] *Guide* iii. 32 (p. 525).

[156] In fact, the other simile Maimonides employs in *Guide* iii. 32 (besides that of the weaning of a child), namely, the nervous system, does suggest a synchronic model.

[157] On this see Seeskin, *No Other Gods*.

leave their material natures behind. *Olam keminhago holekh* (the world continues in its normal course),[158] the great principle underlying the messianic idea as far as Maimonides is concerned, applies to the Temple and its ritual too. Their restoration will of course symbolize restored national unity and independence, but they will remain low on the scale of enlightenment.

Mikveh as Metaphor

The end of the *Book of Purity* marks a break, for this is emanation's furthest edge. Borders are usually interesting places, and we should expect some sign that we have reached the crucial point where emanation ends, and matter begins. We are not disappointed. The last section of the *Book of Purity* is 'Laws of Immersion Pools', about ritual immersion in a *mikveh*, a pool of undrawn water, in order to be cleansed after contact with something impure and to be allowed access to the Temple once more. This is how it closes:

It is plain and manifest that the laws about uncleanness and cleanness are decrees laid down by Scripture and not matters about which human understanding is capable of forming a judgment; for behold they are included among the divine statutes. So, too, immersion as a means of freeing oneself from uncleanness is included among the divine statutes. Now 'uncleanness' is not mud or filth which water can remove, but is a matter of Scriptural decree and dependent on intention of the heart. Therefore the sages have said, if a man immerses himself, but without special intention, it is as though he has not immersed himself at all.

Nevertheless we may find some indication (for the moral basis) of this: just as one who sets his heart on becoming clean becomes clean as soon as he has immersed himself, although nothing new has befallen his body, so, too, one who sets his heart on cleansing himself from the uncleanness that besets men's souls—namely wrongful thoughts and bad character traits—becomes clean as soon as he consents in his heart to shun those counsels and brings his soul into the waters of pure reason. Behold, Scripture says, 'And I will sprinkle clean water on you and you shall be clean; from all your uncleanness and from all your idols will I cleanse you' (Ezek. 36: 25).

May God, in His great mercy, cleanse us from every sin, iniquity, and guilt.[159]

We saw this passage earlier in discussing the idea of knowledge of God through self-knowledge. It is extraordinary. It is the only place that I am aware of in *Mishneh torah*, or in any of his writings, where Maimonides interprets a commandment metaphorically: not as a sign or symbol or reminder of something, but as a true, full-blown metaphor, which arises when two dis-

---

[158] 'Laws of Repentance', 9: 2.   [159] 'Laws of Immersion Pools', 11: 12.

parate things have a quality in common such that the tension between similarity and difference enables the one to stand vividly for the other.[160] Immersion in a *mikveh* is a divine decree, but it becomes accessible to human understanding through water being made a metaphor for the intellect. The effect is more than local, for the metaphor makes meaningful the position of this *halakhah* in the structure of *Mishneh torah* as a whole. The comparison of God's relationship to the world to an overflow of water is the metaphor with which we began. The flow that cascades down the ten first books gathers in the *mikveh*, which stands for the mind receiving the flow of intellect from the agent intellect (the level of the Alfarabian model for which the *Book of Purity* stands), a flow that originates in God.[161]

According to the Neoplatonic model, *mikveh* is a marvellously fitting subject on which to end the man–God books of *Mishneh torah*. Nor was it

[160] In 'Laws of Repentance', 3: 4 we find, concerning the significance of the blowing of the *shofar* on Rosh Hashanah, similar language to that of 'Laws of Immersion Pools', 11: 12: 'Although the blowing of the ram's horn on New Year is a divine decree there is an indication in it, as though to say: Awaken, sleepers from your sleep! And slumberers, rouse yourselves from your slumbers! And examine your deeds and repent and remember your creator, etc.' This supplies a moral function for what would otherwise seem an arbitrary commandment, but it stops short of turning the action commanded into a metaphor. In at least one place in the *Guide*, Maimonides explicitly refers to a commandment as a parable, where he discusses the scapegoat sent to its death in the wilderness as part of the annual Temple ritual of the Day of Atonement: 'No one has any doubt that sins are not bodies that may be transported from the back of one individual to that of another. But all these actions are parables serving to bring forth a form in the soul so that a passion toward repentance should result: We have freed ourselves from all our previous actions, cast them behind our backs, and removed them to an extreme distance' (*Guide* iii. 46 (p. 591)). This does not go all the way to transforming the commandment into a metaphor, as happens in the case of *mikveh*; metonymy is a more appropriate label. Noteworthy, however, is the fact that the *shofar*, the scapegoat, and, as will emerge, the *mikveh* all have to do with repentance. James Diamond construes 'Laws of Impurity of Leprosy', 16: 10 as converting the figure of the leper into 'a metaphor for a far more serious contemplative malady' (*Converts, Heretics, and Lepers*, 36), but the demonstration of this requires some sophisticated analysis, and it is therefore not to be compared with the explicit, dramatic metaphor that *mikveh* becomes in Maimonides' hands. Note too that 'Laws of Impurity of Leprosy', 16: 10 presents a downward moral and intellectual spiral that contrasts with the ladder of virtue at the end of 'Laws of Impurity of Foodstuffs' in the same book. Josef Stern remarks apropos circumcision, 'But the plain fact is that Maimonides makes no attempt to read any symbolism into this ritual—or indeed any other commandment or sacred object or act. On the contrary, the reader senses genuine antipathy on his part to all such hermeneutics' (*Problems and Parables*, 100). This may be true of the prosaic, discursive *Guide*, but it is less true of the poetic, symbolic *Mishneh torah*. Bearing in mind the discussion of symbolism in the Introduction, I think that the reason that Maimonides permits himself to lend symbolic significance to the *mikveh* rite is that he makes it into a summation that stands for all of the commandments. Furthermore, he can, as it were, fill the *mikveh* with metaphorical meaning because he entirely empties it of all inherent meaning.

[161] Mordechai Z. Cohen ('Imagination, Logic, Truth, and Falsehood' (Heb.)) argues that, in the *Guide*, Maimonides abandoned the approach of 'the Torah speaks in the language of human beings' to

obvious that 'Laws of Immersion Pools' should be the closing section. Maimonides had to manoeuvre to set this subject at the end of the *Book of Purity*, for it is some way from that position in Order *Tohorot* of the Mishnah.[162] What is more, although the position of the *Book of Purity* at the end of the man–God division complies with the mishnaic structure, for *Tohorot* is the last order of the Mishnah, on Maimonides' own logic it would have been appropriate to place this book before the *Book of Temple Service*, or even before the *Book of Agriculture*, since he stresses that purification is a precondition for entering the Temple, and is only required for that purpose and for eating tithes.[163] If putting the *Book of Purity* last was a matter of following the Mishnah, then Maimonides could have used the Mishnah's own ending, since Order *Tohorot* ends resoundingly on the subject of peace,[164] for which, as we have seen, he had a penchant when he sought to bring a book to an edifying close. The placement of 'Laws of Immersion Pools' is therefore highly deliberate, and enables Maimonides to close his man–God section with a passage that is resonant and affecting in itself, and also provides an image that perfectly rounds off the theme that, according to the thesis developed here, informs his general structure.

The water metaphor at the end of the *Book of Purity* is also powerfully prospective. At the very end of *Mishneh torah* we find it again, in the quotation from Isaiah describing the days of the messiah that forms the final chord of the whole work:

deal with biblical anthropomorphic descriptions of God (as in 'Laws of the Foundations of the Torah', 1: 12). Instead of this approach, which accommodates the imagination's need for concrete images, he sought in the *Guide* to neutralize anthropomorphisms altogether by treating them as dead metaphors, near-homonyms, that no longer recall their figurative origins. Here, if the analysis is correct, Maimonides invents a metaphor of his own that, if followed through, allows an image to form of God as an overflowing spring, without any of the caveats introduced in *Guide* ii. 12 to the effect that this is only a concession to the difficulty of representing the action of a non-physical entity. This metaphor is very much alive. It could be that the metaphorical treatment of *mikveh* is just the kind of thing Maimonides turned his back on in the *Guide*, but it could equally be that, once again, we are dealing with a difference between genres (noting that Cohen distinguishes between metaphors and parables; Maimonides invents the latter ad lib. in the *Guide*). Apropos the castigation of the imagination cited by Cohen as 'in true reality the *evil impulse*' (*Guide* ii. 12 (p. 280)), it may be worth mentioning that Maimonides also makes allusion to the statement in Mishnah *Berakhot* 9: 5 that the verse 'And thou shalt love the Lord thy God with all thine heart' means with both the good and the evil impulse (*Guide* iii. 22 (p. 489)).

[162] Notice, incidentally, how by changing the name from *Tohorot* ('purifications') to *Tohorah* ('purity'), Maimonides converts a series of rituals into a concept.

[163] See 'Laws of Impurity of Foodstuffs', 16: 8. The specific ritual of *mikveh* is also required for other purposes, chief among them for a woman to become permitted to her husband after menstruation. [164] Mishnah *Uktsin* 3: 12.

In that era there shall be neither famine nor war, neither jealousy nor strife. Blessings will be abundant, comforts within the reach of all. The one preoccupation of the whole world will be to know the Lord. Hence they will be very wise, they will know the things that are now concealed and will attain an understanding of their Creator to the utmost capacity of the human mind, as it is written: 'For the earth shall be full of the knowledge of God as the waters cover the sea' (Isa. 9: 9).[165]

Once more, intellect is likened to water, but the difference between this simile and the previous one reflects the distance travelled between 'Laws of Immersion Pools' and 'Laws of Kings and Their Wars' at the end of *Mishneh torah*. The man–God commandments are meant to inculcate correct opinions, which are a matter of the individual's relationship with God. The aim of the man–man commandments on the other hand is 'the abolishing of their wronging each other', and 'the acquisition by every human individual of moral qualities that are useful for life in society so that the affairs of the city may be ordered'.[166] Immersion in the *mikveh* is an image of the individual perfecting him- or herself; the broad sea is an image of knowledge of God become widespread, permeating social life after society and the state have become perfected, which they do after the four books on the man–man commandments. On the other hand, it should not be forgotten that the sea itself is a valid *mikveh*. Between 'Laws of Immersion Pools' and 'Laws of Kings and Their Wars' we move from individual immersion in the waters of pure reason to collective, universal immersion, from a personal ideal to a political one.

Can we be certain that this double deployment of the metaphor of water is deliberate? We cannot, but its appearance at two critical points, together with the manipulation of the mishnaic material required to put it at those points, its aptly different orientations at each, and the use made of it in the *Guide*, not to mention the sheer originality of the treatment of *mikveh* as metaphor, make it hard to believe in coincidence here. There seems to be a deliberate intent on Maimonides' part to build a pre-climax and a climax for his work using variations on the same image. But consciously or not, he produces a resonance between the endings of the main divisions of *Mishneh torah* that proceeds from a deep level of his conception of God's relationship to the world.

---

[165] 'Laws of Kings and Their Wars', 12: 5. Most editions read 'Hence Israel will be very wise', but the Or Vishua edition notes that some manuscripts omit 'Israel', and this seems a more logical reading.   [166] *Guide* iii. 27 (p. 510).

Intention

The water metaphor at the end of the *Book of Purity* thus looks forward to the end of *Mishneh torah*. Its immediate power, though, is retrospective. It turns the unintelligible commandment of *mikveh* into an image of intelligibility itself, and at the same time reverses the entire trend of the first ten books of *Mishneh torah*, the movement from higher to lower, from intelligible to unintelligible, from non-physical to physical, from love to awe, and, above all, from inward holiness to external holiness. This physical act, which, in Maimonides' view, has no holiness about it at all,[167] symbolizes that which is holiest, the divine in man, reaching back to the source in 'Laws of the Foundations of the Torah' and the idea of man in the image of God.

At the beginning of the *halakhah*, 'human understanding', or the human intellect (*da'ato shel adam*), is prostrate before the divine commandment, powerless to comprehend it. At the end, the waters of intellect (*mei hada'at*) wash away the impediments to human relationship with the divine. The lever that Maimonides uses to make this shift is the notion of intention; it is intention that forms the point of comparison between *mikveh* and intellect. From the laws of cleanness and uncleanness themselves, which deny intellect any role, arises the notion that enthrones intellect as supreme, for it is precisely because immersion in a *mikveh* makes no visible, physical difference[168] that its performance must be accompanied by an intention to fulfil the commandment, otherwise nothing has been done.[169] The mind does not comprehend purification, but only the mind makes it happen. Similarly, the cleansing of the soul from bad traits begins with an intention, and reaches via the consent of the heart to *mei hada'at*.

The central notion of intention in this *halakhah* is expressed in the original by the phrases *kavanat libo* (translated as 'intention of the heart') and *hamekhaven libo* (translated as 'sets his heart'). In 'Laws of Ethical Qualities' the root *kaven*, in the form of the verb *lekhaven*, which has a range of meanings that includes to set, direct, adjust, aim, or tune, is an important one. It occurs when the idea of the middle way is introduced: 'Hence, our ancient

---

[167] And thereby stands for all the commandments, which, as mere acts, do not confer holiness.

[168] One might add—and this must be true for Maimonides' point to work—no magical or mystical difference either.

[169] Maimonides is generalizing in this *halakhah*. What he says applies to purification for the sake of eating tithes and sacrifices and entering the Temple, but in the cases of a married woman after menstruation and purification for the sake of eating profane food, immersion in a *mikveh* without intention is effective—see 'Laws of Immersion Pools', 1: 8.

sages exhorted us that a person should always evaluate his dispositions and so adjust [*umekhaven*] them that they shall be at the mean between extremes',[170] and again when the discussion of the middle way is concluded: 'To sum up, a person should follow the mean in every disposition, until all his dispositions are set [*mekhuvanot*] in the middle.'[171] The word recurs in a key statement in 'Laws of Ethical Qualities': 'A person must direct [*sheyekhaven*] all actions only towards knowledge of God.'[172]

Apparent contradictions in the first two chapters of 'Laws of Ethical Qualities' have provoked debate about what constitutes Maimonides' ideal: the Aristotelian middle way, or the way of the pious, who lean towards more self-denying extremes. Important though that debate is, perhaps the precise way in which one's dispositions are tuned matters less than the very idea of bringing them under the mind's control. On the microcosmic model, this in itself brings one closer to God,[173] and it also enables one to direct all actions towards knowledge of God, as stipulated in the third statement above. All this can be summed up as the conversion of *de'ot* (emotions and appetites) into *da'at* (mind/knowledge) through *kavanah* (intention). This, at any rate, is the summing up of 'Laws of Ethical Qualities' that appears to be presented in 'Laws of Immersion Pools', 11: 12, without prejudice to other allusions in that *halakhah*.

So the end of the *Book of Purity* takes us back to where we began. Then comes a reprise of the idea of reciprocity that has been a main strand of our discussion. The quotation from Ezekiel on which 'Laws of Immersion Pools' ends ('And I will sprinkle clean water on you and you shall be clean; from all your uncleanness and from all your idols will I cleanse you') may possibly be partly intended as reassurance, a scramble back to safe scriptural ground after lurching over the chasm of philosophy, but it also expresses continuity between moral virtue and intellectual virtue, the idea that once we immerse ourselves in intellect, we become receptive to the constant flow emanating from God.[174]

---

[170] 'Laws of Ethical Qualities', 1: 4.   [171] Ibid. 2: 7.   [172] Ibid. 3: 2.   [173] See pp. 110–24 above.
[174] The verse is cited in the last *mishnah* of tractate *Yoma*, which concludes:
R. Akiba said: Blessed are ye, O Israel. Before whom are ye made clean and who makes you clean? Your Father in heaven; as it is written. And I will sprinkle clean water upon you and ye shall be clean [Ezek. 36: 25]. And again it says, O Lord the hope [*mikveh*] of Israel [Jer. 17: 13]— as the *Mikveh* cleanses the unclean so does the Holy One, blessed be he, cleanse Israel. (trans. Danby)
Maimonides may well intend his citation of the verse to invoke this *mishnah*, in which case the final *halakhah* of his *Book of Purity*, seen in relation to the general structure of *Mishneh torah*, may be read as

At this most critical juncture of *Mishneh torah* there is a switch that, in its immediate context, is the conversion of an incomprehensible ritual into a symbol of regeneration, but it can also be seen as a reversal of the whole tendency of the first ten books, once their formal patterns are understood. This is by no means the only example of such reversal in *Mishneh torah*, and, continuing the theme of Neoplatonic ideas shaping that work's form, the idea of reversal or return will be the burden of the next chapter.

Summary

The main theme of this chapter has been the application of the Neoplatonic idea of emanation, as expounded by Maimonides himself in the *Guide*, to the understanding of the structure of *Mishneh torah*. The first ten books are arranged according to a hierarchy of value, corresponding to the hierarchy of the successive levels of hypostases in the Plotinian system, as adapted by Alfarabi, but with the ultimate criterion of rank being the religious value of holiness. Furthermore, those first ten books form a pattern that is a projection of 'Laws of the Foundations of the Torah', expressing the idea that books 2 to 10 emanate from book 1, the *Book of Knowledge*.

The Neoplatonic hierarchy in *Mishneh torah* suggested a way of reconciling the treatment of sacrifices in that work with their treatment in the *Guide*, evaluating them synchronically rather than diachronically.

The underlying model or metaphor for emanation is a flow of water: water flowing downhill, and water flowing outwards from a source. This metaphor surfaces explicitly in 'Laws of Immersion Pools' at the end of the *Book of Purity*, and again at the end of *Mishneh torah* as a whole, pointing up the work's cosmic architecture and adding to it a dynamic element that brings a new level of significance. At the end of the *Book of Purity*, the metaphor serves to direct us back to the beginning of *Mishneh torah* and the ideals of moral and intellectual virtue, leading on to the Neoplatonic idea of return.

a gloss on R. Akiva's statement (which plays on the double meaning of the word *mikveh* as 'hope' and 'immersion pool'), and as an explanation of how the Holy One comes to be like a cleansing *mikveh*. In the *Commentary on the Mishnah*, this *mishnah* goes unremarked.

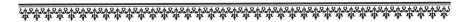

CHAPTER FOUR

RETURN

Neoplatonic cosmogony has two phases: emanation is accompanied by return, as the lower hypostasis turns back yearningly towards the higher one in which it originates. In a Jewish context, 'return' evokes the idea of repentance, the root of the Hebrew word for repentance, *teshuvah*, being *shuv*, meaning to return. It also evokes the political idea of the coming of the messiah, redemption from exile, and return to Zion, which, as far as Maimonides is concerned, depends on repentance.[1] The implication is that Maimonides' concept of repentance is linked to the concept of return in Neoplatonic thought.[2]

The turning back of the lower hypostasis is not a vague longing. It is a dual moment of introspection and retrospection, in which the hypostasis forms a thought of itself and a thought of the First Cause. Through this process, which is a constant of its being, it acquires identity. It is in these two interdependent thoughts that it truly consists. In 'Laws of Repentance', repentance has the same two components of introspection and retrospection. It is a dual process of self-examination and of reconciliation with God.

In Chapter 1 we saw how the structure of human consciousness presented in 'Laws of the Foundations of the Torah' reflects that of the angels, spheres, and stars. The thought of the One or First Cause and the thought of itself in each of the higher entities correspond to the love for God and desire for knowledge of him and the almost simultaneous recoil in self-conscious fear experienced by human beings. In 'Laws of Repentance' the movement is reversed: from consciousness of self in the commandment to confess sins with which that section begins, a human being proceeds towards the love of God via knowledge, the theme on which it ends. Looked at this way,

---

[1] See above, Ch. 3, n. 111.

[2] Ivry, who in general depicts Maimonides' use of Neoplatonic ideas as important but guarded, remarks, 'it is in the Neoplatonic classics that Maimonides would have found the ideal of man's striving for psychic redemption, for returning to his ideal and eternal origins' ('Islamic and Greek Influences on Maimonides', 150). See also Appendix II.1.

repentance can be considered to be the completion of the formation of human consciousness, in the same way as return completes the formation of the Neoplatonic hypostases. This is really a development of the idea put forward in the previous chapter of the self-contained circularity of the *Book of Knowledge*. And just as the structure of that first book was found to be projected onto *Mishneh torah* as a whole, I shall argue that, in a similar fashion, the movement of return represented by 'Laws of Repentance' is a constant in *Mishneh torah*, recurring throughout.

There is, then, a pervasive duality in all created beings possessed of intellect. Aviezer Ravitzky finds a similar duality in Maimonides' model of messianic redemption: redemption is the regeneration of the Jewish nation and the restoration of its political independence, and also the restoration of man's pristine intellectual clarity, of universal recognition of God.[3] We can abstract from this an element of introspection, as the nation rehabilitates itself (this by way of analogy only, since nations do not have intellects), and an element of retrospection, in the reversion to a primordial state of unclouded knowledge. Ravitzky notes the opposite tendencies in these two aspects of redemption: the establishment of a peaceful and stable society creates conditions conducive to intellectual attainment, while, conversely, from the universal recognition of God social harmony and universal peace flow as consequences. It will be immediately obvious that there is a correspondence between this and the two concepts of moral virtue, as preparation for intellectual virtue and as a consequence of intellectual virtue, which, it was argued in Chapter 1, coexist through the form of the *Book of Knowledge*. The content of 'Laws of Ethical Qualities' presents moral virtue as preparation for intellectual virtue, and, at the same time, the derivation of its form from that of 'Laws of the Foundations of the Torah' conveys the idea that intellectual virtue is prior to moral virtue. Just so, the coming of the messiah is described in 'Laws of Kings and Their Wars' as a linear, historical process of social and political renewal leading to enlightenment; at the same time, the overarching cosmic form of *Mishneh torah* can be taken as indicating that enlightenment (which consists of knowledge of the physics and metaphysics that *Mishneh torah*'s form embodies) is prior to that process. That being the case, as Ravitzky points out, individual redemption need not wait for the messiah:

Indeed, an individual may and ought to strive to attain his own spiritual perfection, even in his present, concrete existence, even within the Exile of Israel and in a human

---

[3] Ravitzky, 'Maimonides on the Days of the Messiah'.

society from which war, jealousy, and strife have not been removed. In fact, there is no difference between this world and the times of the messiah in terms of a transformation of the nature of the individual, his destiny, or the content of his intellectual grasp.[4]

The form of *Mishneh torah* conveys the same idea: perfection, in the sense of realization of the human microcosmic form, is always available, as constantly as the movements of the spheres, so that it need not wait for social rehabilitation and the restoration of the political microcosm. Moreover, and apropos the discussion in Chapter 2 of Maimonides' natural microcosm–macrocosm theory versus the mystical variety, Ravitzky contrasts Maimonides' historical messianism, a redemption from human evil in which nothing in the natural order changes, with apocalyptic messianism, which expects a cosmic redemption from ontological evil.[5] This feature, too, is symbolized by the cosmic form of *Mishneh torah*, emblematic of the natural order embracing both the redeemed and the unredeemed states of human affairs. Thus form in *Mishneh torah* effects an artistic reconciliation of the timeless with time, of constancy with process.

The intellectual rehabilitation of humankind in the days of the messiah, Ravitzky argues, is a restoration of the state of consciousness of Adam before his fall, in which he perceived the absolute values of true and false, rather than the conventional values of right and wrong. It is a characteristic of a divine law that it seeks to educate towards the truth, as opposed to a *nomos*, a conventional law that merely regulates society, determining right and wrong.[6] With the completion of the cosmic model of *Mishneh torah*, it will be appropriate to consider it as a means of cognizing the truth in the here and now. At the same time, I shall expand on the theme of repentance in *Mishneh torah*, its role as the agent of redemption, and its relationship to Neoplatonic thought. This will bring into consideration the work's last four books, which have yet to be integrated fully into the microcosmic scheme.

If, in the previous chapter, the idea of emanation was seen converted to Jewish terms as a diminishing flow of holiness, here the idea of return emerges in Jewish guise as repentance. The subtle artistry with which Maimonides produces these transformations reinforces the view endorsed in the Introduction that his declared programme should be taken at face value: he is not temporizing with philosophy but demonstrating how Judaism gives

---

[4] Ibid. 232.   [5] Ibid. 250–6. Further on this distinction, see Kellner, 'Messianic Postures'.
[6] See *Guide* ii. 40 (pp. 381–5).

tangible expression and moral effect to a universally accessible truth that it anciently possessed.

The Ladder of the Commandments and the Ladder of Prophecy

One way of unifying Maimonides' dual model of redemption, if that is required, is to observe that political redemption does not happen by itself: it depends upon the perfection and commitment of an individual. The key figure in the process of return, whereby a lapsed social order is restored to microcosmic perfection, is the prophet, as legislator, as preacher of repentance, as seer of the messiah.[7] It is to this figure, and to the expression of his restorative mission in *Mishneh torah*'s form, that I now turn.

In Chapter 2 the man–God commandments were described as being like the hierarchy of the spheres in that they form a kind of ladder up to God. In the *Guide* Maimonides uses exactly this image, not for the commandments, but for the cosmos and for prophecy. Following and adapting Midrash, he interprets Jacob's dream of angels ascending and descending a ladder as referring to both these subjects.[8]

Jacob's dream is discussed in the *Guide* in three places. In the introduction to Part I it serves as an example of the kind of parable in which every detail and every word carries significance, as opposed to parables like that of the temptress in Proverbs, which are significant only in outline. This point is not germane to the present discussion, but it will be taken up in the next chapter.

In *Guide* i. 15 Maimonides turns to the content of the parable. In this lexicographic chapter he explains that 'to stand erect', when predicated of God, does not refer to a physical posture, but means to be stable and permanent. He goes on to discuss the use of the term in Jacob's dream, in which God is described as standing erect on the ladder.

And, behold, the Lord stood erect upon it, that is, was stably and constantly upon it— I mean upon the ladder, one end of which is in heaven, while the other end is upon the earth. Everyone who ascends does so climbing up this ladder, so that he necessarily apprehends Him who is upon it, as He is stably and permanently on top of the ladder. It is clear that what I say here of Him conforms to the parable propounded. For the *angels of God* are the prophets with reference to whom it is clearly said: *And he sent an angel; And an angel of the Lord came up from Gilgal to Bochim*. How well put is the phrase

---

[7] 'All the prophets enjoined repentance' ('Laws of Repentance', 7: 5); 'The sages said: All the prophets only prophesied about the days of the messiah' (ibid. 8: 7).   [8] Gen. 28.

ascending and descending, in which *ascent* comes before *descent*. For after the *ascent* and the attaining of certain rungs of the ladder that may be known comes the descent with whatever decree the prophet has been informed of—with a view to governing and teaching the people of the earth.

Sarah Klein-Braslavy distinguishes two elements in this passage: a static element and a dynamic element.[9] In the static element the ladder represents all that lies between the earth on which it stands and the heavens that it reaches, that is, the spheres with the stars and planets. The heavens are the outer sphere that moves all the rest. God standing on the ladder refers to God as the permanent, inexhaustible force that moves the outer sphere. The ladder, in other words, is a model of the cosmos. In the dynamic element the prophets, represented as angels, ascend the ladder in the sense that they progress in their knowledge of physics and metaphysics and of God's governance of the world. They then descend, meaning that they apply the knowledge thus gained to the guidance of human society.

Jacob's ladder makes its third appearance in the *Guide* in Part II, chapter 10. Here the parable's cosmic significance is made more explicit, for the chapter explains the relationship between the heavens and the sublunary world. It all hangs on the number four, taking a cue from the *midrash* that the ladder had four rungs. Four spheres (those of the fixed stars, the planets, the Sun, and the Moon), moved by four causes, affect the four sublunary elements (earth, air, fire, and water), by means of four forces. In this interpretation the four angels on the four rungs of the ladder represent the four elements, which move up and down in the vertical plane in response to the circular motion of the spheres.[10] 'This number four is wondrous and should be an object of reflection', Maimonides declares.

All these significances are derivable from the form of *Mishneh torah*. The first ten books represent the spheres, expanded from the four levels in Jacob's dream to nine plus the agent intellect.[11] At the same time, as we saw in the previous chapter, these books also represent a scale of holiness, or, in Neoplatonic terms, gradations of Soul; the process of becoming a prophet is an ascent up this scale, following the way described in the previous chapter:

---

[9] Klein-Braslavy, 'Maimonides' Commentary on Jacob's Dream' (Heb.).

[10] As Sara Klein-Braslavy shows, these interpretations of Jacob's dream make very subtle use of Midrash, and also require the reader to bring together scattered statements in the *Guide*. Further on this see Diamond, *Maimonides and the Hermeneutics of Concealment*.

[11] See pp. 162–5 above for discussion of the different ways in which Maimonides counted the spheres.

detachment from the crowd, detachment from desire, and intellectual development. There is no precise match, but broadly speaking, the stages in a prophet's self-training described in 'Laws of the Foundations of the Torah', 7: 1, correspond to the main groupings of the first ten books of *Mishneh torah*, starting from the *Book of Purity*. The would-be prophet is already a person of high moral and intellectual stature, 'distinguished by great wisdom and strong moral character'—otherwise he would not aspire to prophecy at all. He is, as it were, immersed in the waters of intellect. The prophet 'sanctifies himself and becomes more and more detached from the ways of the people'. At least one aim of the laws of purity is detachment from the masses, as stated in 'Laws of Impurity of Foodstuffs', 16: 12: 'It is the way of piety that a man keep himself separate and go apart from the rest of the people and neither touch them nor eat and drink with them.' The *Book of Purity* therefore represents a first step towards the special holiness of prophecy. Sanctifying oneself in the sense of detachment from physical appetites is the subject of the *Book of Holiness* and the *Book of Asseverations*. Having become as separate from the physical as is humanly possible, the apprentice prophet can begin to comprehend the separate intellects, his mind 'concentrated on higher things as though bound beneath the Celestial Throne, so as to comprehend the pure and holy forms'. This is reflected in the progression from the *Book of Women* to the *Book of Knowledge*, with commandments that bring us ever closer to the essential truths. Eventually, the prophet gains a conspectus of the entire universe, 'contemplating the wisdom of God as displayed in his creatures, from the first form to the very centre of the Earth', as found in 'Laws of the Foundations of the Torah'. At this point the prophet makes contact with the holy spirit and identifies with the emanation of goodness and existence from God, flowing back down to the *Book of Purity*.

The linking of the ascent of the prophet with the Neoplatonic infrastructure of *Mishneh torah* has parallels in allegorical form in medieval philosophy, as described by Eileen Sweeney:

Though Islamic philosophies had an independent tradition of allegorical literature from which they could draw, the allegories from Medieval Islamic thinkers tend to concern the same Neoplatonic themes of the ascent of the soul and the Neoplatonic structure of the cosmos, allegorizing the stages of emanation from and return to the One. The most common form of Islamic philosophical allegory is on the theme of the heavenly ascent or journey, a philosophical rather than prophetic rewriting of the spiritual journey of the prophet Mohammed.[12]

[12] Sweeney, 'Literary Forms'. My reading of Maimonides' interpretations of the ladder in Jacob's

The man–God books of *Mishneh torah*, read in reverse order, are a ten-runged ladder, an allegory of the ascent to prophecy described in 'Laws of the Foundations of the Torah', 7: 1, or the ladder of ascension in 'Laws of Impurity of Foodstuffs', 16: 12, writ large.[13]

It is worth citing that *halakhah* more fully once again, and reminding ourselves that it is Maimonides' own original distillation and adaptation of the midrashic sources:[14]

It is the way of piety that a man keep himself separate and go apart from the rest of the people and neither touch them nor eat and drink with them. For separation leads to the cleansing of the body from evil deeds, and the cleansing of the body leads to the

dream differs in several respects from that of Altmann in 'Ladder of Ascension'. Commenting on *Guide* i. 15, Altmann writes, 'Maimonides' view of the ladder departs from the neo-Platonic pattern' and 'reflects the notion of *sullam ha-hokhmot* rather than that of *sullam ha-aliya*', i.e. progression through the prescribed curriculum of the sciences rather than a spiritual or mystical ascent, although he winds up saying, 'One can only conclude that the Maimonides passage under review represents a curious conflation of two divergent traditions, that is of the one expressed in the term *sullam ha-hokhmot* and of the one denoted by the phrase *sullam ha-aliya*.' Altmann sees the different interpretation of the ladder in *Guide* ii. 10 as betraying uncertainty. He also contrasts Maimonides' interpretation of the dream as 'an ascent to metaphysical truths' with *midrashim* that 'relate Jacob's prophecy to the historical plane' and with the interpretations of later commentators who 'added Jacob's dream to the list of Biblical accounts of the Merkaba'. Altmann seems to have overlooked, or perhaps he did not consider philosophically serious, the interpretation of Jacob's dream in 'Laws of the Foundations of the Torah', 7: 2 as referring to 'the Monarchies and their oppression of Israel', an interpretation based on Midrash (*Gen. Rabbah* 68), and clearly relating the prophecy to the historical plane. In the next chapter a reading of all three of Maimonides' interpretations of Jacob's ladder will be offered that takes in both history and the *merkavah*, and that sees them as different facets of the same prophecy. Steven Harvey also takes issue with Altmann on this point—see his 'Maimonides in the Sultan's Palace', 61 n. 58.

[13] Menahem Mansoor sees Ibn Pakuda's *The Book of Direction to the Duties of the Heart (Al-Hidaya ila Fara'id al-Qulub)* as reversible in a very similar way:

The plan of the book, in keeping with its rational outlook, is deductive. The duties of the heart are deduced from the basic premise, the belief in the unity of God. The deduction goes from the 'root of roots' to the last chapter, or gate, which is 'Love of God.' This is a logico-philosophical procedure. But then it is important to realize that in the *al-Hidaya* Bahya is addressing not the philosopher, but the common believer. For him, the way to the root of roots goes in the opposite direction. Starting with 'Love of God' he will arrive at the 'root of roots', the highest state of belief.

Thus, the hierarchical order of the duties of the heart ascends from 'Love of God', considered at the end of the book, to a religious state in which the soul 'clings' to God, and apprehends Him as One. The believer now apprehends the unity of God, the theme of the opening chapter. (Ibn Pakuda, *Duties of the Heart*, 6—Translator's Introduction)

Perhaps also of significance is that Ibn Pakuda mentions the idea of man as microcosm (*Duties of the Heart*, 158), and that his work is divided into ten chapters.

[14] See the discussion in the previous chapter (p. 232).

hallowing of the soul from evil traits, and the hallowing of the soul leads to striving for likeness with the *Shekhinah*; for it is said, 'Sanctify yourselves therefore and be holy, for I am holy'.[15]

In *Guide* i. 10, which discusses the terms 'ascent' and 'descent' as used in Scripture, descent is said to refer to 'the alighting of the prophetic inspiration upon the prophet or the coming down of the Indwelling to a certain place'.[16] Pines notes that he uses 'Indwelling' to translate '*sakina*, an Arabic word that is the equivalent of the Hebrew *shekhinah*'.[17] A *midrash* associating the descent of 'the Indwelling' with prophecy is also cited in *Guide* ii. 42.[18] For the Shekhinah to descend onto the prophet, the prophet must strive to ascend to the Shekhinah—in fact, strictly speaking, the Shekhinah descends constantly and indiscriminately, and it is only by inward spiritual ascent that the prophet becomes attuned to it. Thus, if it is permissible to use the *Guide* as a gloss here, our *halakhah* is a version of the ascent of the prophet in *Guide* i. 15,[19] as are the first ten books of *Mishneh torah* read from last to first.

Nor is the number four of *Guide* ii. 10 absent; it should be an object of reflection in *Mishneh torah* too. The main groupings in the latter come in fours. Four chapters of 'Laws of the Foundations of the Torah' deal with physics and metaphysics, and four with prophecy. In the previous chapter the first ten books of *Mishneh torah* were grouped into the first four, dealing with sanctification in the sense of enlightenment and rituals as reminders of correct doctrine; the middle two, dealing with sanctification in the sense of restraint of physical appetite, and the last four, on the Temple and attendant laws, or sanctification in the sense of things and places set aside. The books on the man–man commandments are also four. Moreover, if half of a number can stand for the whole,[20] the two central chapters of 'Laws of the Foundations of the Torah', 5 and 6, as well as books 5 and 6, also fit into the pattern.

Ascent is followed by descent, and in this respect something like the dynamic of *Guide* ii. 10 comes into play in *Mishneh torah* too. The four sections on physics and metaphysics ('Laws of the Foundations of the Torah', 1–4) influence the four books on the state (books 11–14 on the man–man commandments) via the four sections on the prophet ('Laws of the Founda-

---

[15] Lev. 11: 44. [16] *Guide* i. 10 (p. 36).

[17] Ibid. (p. 36 n. 8). See also Kellner, *Maimonides' Confrontation with Mysticism*, 198–200.

[18] *Guide* ii. 42 (p. 390), as pointed out by Kellner in *Maimonides' Confrontation with Mysticism*, 199 n. 54.

[19] It may be coincidence, but this *halakhah* does happen to have four 'rungs': separation; cleansing of the body; hallowing of the soul; likeness with the Shekhinah. [20] See above, pp. 248–9.

tions of the Torah', 7–10). The usual caution against over-systematization applies here, but there is enough evidence to suggest that the wondrousness of the number four did not occur to Maimonides for the first time only when he came to write *Guide* ii. 10, and that it is part of *Mishneh torah* as well, along with the association with Jacob's ladder.[21] Maimonides interprets the word 'angel' as referring both to prophets and to natural forces,[22] which confirms the correspondence between the generation of the natural order by God and the generation of the social order by the prophet, seen in the previous chapter as symbolized by the balancing of the first four sections of 'Laws of the Foundations of the Torah' against the last four. In short, the first ten books of *Mishneh torah* symbolize the ladder of holiness that the prophet ascends, and his subsequent descent, which has parallels with the natural hierarchy of emanation and the transmission of natural forces down through the spheres.

On the way down, once we reach the *Book of Purity*, representing the agent intellect in the cosmic scheme, emanation is exhausted. The agent intellect is incapable of emanating another sphere, and can only produce an analogy of a sphere, the sublunary world. Similarly, emanation no longer applies as an organizing principle in *Mishneh torah*, and we enter upon the material world and the man–man laws that govern sublunary affairs. The prophet, having ascended the ladder and attained enlightenment, then descends to inject metaphysical knowledge into the running of the material world; or, to evoke a Platonic rather than a Neoplatonic image, he re-enters the cave.[23]

---

[21] The number four also held a special place in the composition of the universe in the thought of the Brethren of Purity, and, as in Maimonides' account, there too it was a matter of natural entities reflecting supernatural entities. See Fakhry, *A History of Islamic Philosophy*, 173.   [22] See *Guide* ii. 6.

[23] Ravitzky ('Philosophy and Leadership in Maimonides') finds it paradoxical that *Mishneh torah*, a practical work of halakhah, ends on the idea of personal perfection (that is, the knowledge of God), while the *Guide*, a philosophical treatise, ends on the idea of the social responsibility of the enlightened individual, even though the attainment of enlightenment requires isolation from society to the greatest degree possible. In my reading of its form, *Mishneh torah* embodies the idea of the social responsibility of the prophet. Of the reader of the *Guide* Ravitzky says, 'He does not merely follow in the path required of the Mishneh Torah's *reader*; he follows as well in the path of the Mishneh Torah's *author*, the path of leadership' ('Philosophy and Leadership in Maimonides', 263). As is stressed throughout this study, part of the point of discussing *Mishneh torah* as a work of art is to show how, through formal qualities that act on the sensibility and the imagination, Maimonides persuades the reader to follow in his path. On this view, the distance found by Ravitzky between *Mishneh torah* and the *Guide* is much diminished.

Further on reflections in Maimonides' writings of the parable of the cave in Plato's *Republic*, and on the tension between the desire for solitude and political obligation, see S. Harvey, 'Maimonides in the Sultan's Palace'; Lerner, 'Maimonides' Governance of the Solitary'; Melamed, 'Maimonides on the Political Nature of Man' (Heb.), 302–33; and id., *The Philosopher-King*, 26–60.

From Dystopia to Utopia

What he finds on re-entering is human society in disarray. The *Book of Torts*, the eleventh book of *Mishneh torah*, deals with disregard for others and even active wrongdoing: injuries, robbery, and ultimately murder. Characteristically, though, Maimonides gives the *Book of Torts* an uplifting ending, for the final commandment discussed is the obligation to assist an enemy whom one meets on the highway and whose beast is struggling under its load. The ostensible justification for including this commandment in 'Laws of the Murderer and the Preservation of Life', where it does not obviously belong, is that a person who delays on the road is exposed to danger.[24] It is possible, however, to read more into it. This commandment, in this place, can be seen as the beginnings of a process of repair. Hostility is overcome, and wrong-doing is replaced by co-operation. The placement of this commandment also forms an example of the technique of concatenation frequently found in *Mishneh torah*, whereby the ending of one part (book, section, or chapter) alludes to the beginning of the next. Here, the linkage is very general—the next book, the *Book of Acquisition*, does not begin with aid to someone in distress but with the laws of acquisition. Nevertheless, by ending the *Book of Torts* on the subject of constructive relations between people, Maimonides starts to envisage the conditions of solidarity and trust that allow normal commercial transactions and peaceful enjoyment of property. By beginning with disorder and gradually leading towards order, he embodies in his arrangement the first intention of the law: not just the outlawing and punishment of crime, but the more elevated aim of 'the abolition of mutual wrong-doing among men'.[25]

Maimonides' treatment of the commandment in question is yet more subtle and far-reaching. To understand this, we have to understand the circumstances. Two Jews meet on the road. A is driving a donkey that is buckling under its load. B should help, but he hates A. Why? Not out of personal animosity, for such a thing is inconceivable; Jews are forbidden to nurture hatred for one another. No, the reason B considers A his enemy is that he has been a sole witness to A committing some transgression. He is precluded from airing the matter in court, where two witnesses are required, but he is obliged to hate A until the latter repents. However, God cares even for the lives of sinners, for he prefers them to live and repent rather than die. B must therefore

---

[24] 'Laws of the Murderer and the Preservation of Life', 13: 14. See Twersky, *Introduction to the Code*, 289.   [25] *Guide* iii. 32 (p. 531).

assist A. There is an implication that A has found himself in this dangerous position because of the very transgression to which B was witness, yet B is obliged to rescue him because, in God's eyes, A is a potential penitent.

Two things require definition in this scenario: Jew, and sin. 'Laws of the Murderer and the Preservation of Life', 13: 14 states:

and the Torah is very solicitous for the lives of Israelites, whether of the wicked or of the righteous, since all Israelites acknowledge God and believe in the essentials of our religion. For it is said, 'Say unto them; As I live, saith the Lord God, I have no pleasure in the death of the wicked but that the wicked turn from his way and live' (Ezek. 33: 11).

According to this, a Jew is commanded to save a fellow Jew from danger not because of shared ethnicity, but because of shared belief. A Jew may transgress in some practical sense—he may be in breach of the sabbath laws, for example—and deserve to be hated for it, but as long as he subscribes to correct doctrine, 'the essentials of our religion', then his life must be preserved in the expectation of repentance.[26] The wicked person here is, then, presumably someone who commits any sin short of denial of Maimonides' Thirteen Principles of Faith, for Maimonides makes acceptance of those principles the criterion of inclusion in the community of Israel.[27] 'Laws of the Murderer and the Preservation of Life', 13: 14, is thus a direct application of his summing up of the function of his Thirteen Principles:

When a man believes in all these fundamental principles, and his faith is thus clarified, he is then part of that 'Israel' whom we are to love, pity, and treat, as God commanded, with love and fellowship. Even if a Jew should commit every possible sin, out of lust or mastery by his lower nature, he will be punished for his sins but will still have a share in the world to come. He is one of the 'sinners in Israel'. But if a man gives up any one of these fundamental principles, he has removed himself from the Jewish community.[28]

It follows that if A were to declare that he did not believe in, say, the unity of God, he would be left to fend for himself.[29]

---

[26] This is notwithstanding the fact that if there are two witnesses to a deliberate breach of the sabbath laws instead of only one as here, the person in breach may incur the death penalty.

[27] As enunciated in the introduction to *Perek ḥelek* (*Commentary on the Mishnah*, Order *Nezikin*, *San.* 10: 1, pp. 141–4). I take 'the main principle of religion' in 'Laws of the Murderer and the Preservation of Life', 13: 14 to refer to those principles. See Kellner, *Maimonides on Judaism*, 60–2. *Guide* iii. 18 indicates that the unenlightened would not be worthy of concern about their lives in this situation. Kellner finds that 'Maimonides' definition of a Jew by virtue of his beliefs is an absolute innovation in Judaism' (*Dogma in Medieval Jewish Thought*, 19).   [28] Twersky, *Maimonides Reader*, 22.

[29] Actually, A will still be afforded aid in unloading the donkey, though not in reloading it, not out of concern for him, but out of compassion for the suffering animal, which, according to Maimonides,

Thus far we are in well-mapped territory.[30] What is notable for our purposes is that this turning towards rehabilitation of the relations between people depends on an infusion from the *Book of Knowledge*. God commands assistance to the Jew in distress because he cares for believers, which means that, in caring for believers, we are imitating God's providence.[31] The above scenario is thus a vignette of *imitatio Dei*. The beginning of the redemption of society lies in hearing the distant music of 'Laws of Ethical Qualities', of which *imitatio Dei* is the keynote. Individual morality as the basis for a functioning society, specifically the trait of being forgiving of those who wrong us, is the idea on which 'Laws of Ethical Qualities' ends: 'It alone makes civilized life and social intercourse possible.'[32] In the *Book of Torts*, this is the lever for putting society onto a constructive track. What is more, to qualify for aid in his distress, A requires at least a rudimentary grasp of 'Laws of the Foundations of the Torah'. In this divine law, divinity is at work in the regeneration of the state.

The most important echo of the *Book of Knowledge* is of 'Laws of Repentance'. In helping A, B has to overcome hatred (however caused), and does so with the idea of repentance in mind. Repentance is the engine of rehabilitation; it is the activation of the self-reflective capacity that is the form of a human being bestowed by the agent intellect, and the active ingredient in the good that the prophet carries down the ladder, into the cave. Through it, the prophet's descent promotes social ascent, for it gives human affairs direction, in contrast to all other sublunary processes of generation and decay, which are a constant product of the motions of the unreflective elements under the laws of their own natures and the movements of the spheres, and have no *telos*. It seems unlikely that it is coincidence that the *Book of Torts* ends on the idea of

is a Torah commandment. The same applies to the animal of a non-Jew. See *Rambam la'am*, n. 82 to 'Laws of the Murderer and the Preservation of Life', 13: 14. In 'Laws of Mourning', 1: 9–10, where it is ruled that anyone who has excluded him- or herself from the community is not to be mourned, self-exclusion is by deed as well as doctrine. One way of reconciling that with 'Laws of the Murderer and the Preservation of Life', 13: 14 is to observe that the latter *halakhah* is based on the possibility of repentance, which does not exist for the dead.

[30] See Kellner, *Maimonides on Judaism*, 101.
[31] How God's providence works is explained in *Guide* iii. 17–19 (pp. 464–80). Essentially, providence is withdrawn from those who subscribe to incorrect beliefs, not as a punishment meted out to the individual, but because receptivity to the divine overflow, which is what providence consists of, depends on actualization of the intellect, which means, as a minimum, holding correct doctrines. Something of this can be read into the quotation from Ezekiel that closes 'Laws of the Murderer and the Preservation of Life': 'as I live . . . he should live', that is to say, the preservation of life, not to mention life in the world to come, depends on a human being making his or her life as much like God's 'life' as possible, and that means cultivation of the intellect.   [32] 'Laws of Ethical Qualities', 7: 8.

God's desire for the evildoer's repentance rather than his or her punishment. As I have said, for Maimonides, repentance is a precondition for redemption, and the message surely is that redemption starts here.[33]

Following the *Book of Torts*, the *Book of Acquisition*, which, broadly speaking, deals with contract and property, moves away from wrongdoing to find human beings entering into consensual, mutually beneficial commercial relationships. The *Book of Civil Laws*, which comes next, continues in the same vein, covering such topics as hire, loans, and inheritances. The final book, the *Book of Judges*, covers the court system and the constitution of the state, the guarantors of order. This book culminates in the advent of the king messiah, who will establish universal peace and enable humanity to engage fully in the getting of wisdom, which is the purpose of social order. We go from dystopia to utopia in four books.

It will be observed that, as far as hierarchy is concerned, these last four books reverse the trend of the first ten. The *Book of Knowledge* begins with knowledge of the sovereign of the universe, and, as shown in Chapter 3, it represents the highest of the spheres or of the ten orders of angels. From there onwards, also as described in Chapter 3, the ten man–God books work downwards through the levels of the spheres or angels. By contrast, the four man–man books work their way upwards, both in degree of social order and and in rank, concluding with the section 'Laws of Kings and Their Wars', which concerns the earthly sovereign.[34] This arrangement presumably reflects the hierarchy of the four elements described in 'Laws of the Foundations of the Torah', 3: 10, fire being the highest, followed by air, water, and

[33] Hadad sees a structural parallel between 'Laws of Repentance', as the last section of the *Book of Knowledge*, and the last four books of *Mishneh torah*. There is no reason that 'Laws of Repentance' cannot do double duty as patron of both the books on sacrifices and purity and the books on the man–man commandments. Insofar as 'Laws of Repentance' is the conduit of the message of prophecy, it brings to bear the last four chapters of 'Laws of the Foundations of the Torah', which are about prophecy, on the last four books of *Mishneh torah*, on the rehabilitation of society, which I have argued is through repentance, beamed via the Temple, as it were. On this basis we can discern the positive value of the Temple in a redeemed world, as opposed to the negative idea of accommodation. Hadad detects hints at repentance throughout the final four books, and indeed, the idea seems to be mentioned wherever possible—apart from the *halakhah* under discussion: see 'Laws of Damage by Chattels', 5: 10; 'Laws of Robbery and Lost Property', 1: 13; 'Laws of Sales', 14: 13, 20: 3; 'Laws of Creditor and Debtor', 4: 4–5; 'Laws of Pleading', 2: 10–11; 'Laws of Evidence', 6: 7, 12: 3–4, 12: 10; 'Laws of Rebels', 3: 3, 5: 12–13, 6: 11; 'Laws of Mourning', 13: 12. Hadad also notes that, like the *Book of Knowledge*, each of the last four books has five sections—see 'Nature and Torah in Maimonides' (Heb.), 292–5.

[34] Twersky notes that, while in *Mishneh torah* substantive law precedes procedural law, in *Shulḥan arukh* procedural law is placed first (*Introduction to the Code*, 270). There is no inevitability about *Mishneh torah*'s order.

earth (although, as usual, the rider must be added that we are dealing with analogous processes, not one-to-one correspondences, and there is nothing to associate any book with any particular element). At the end, the metaphor of water (not to be confused with the element of water) reappears, consolidating the integration of the last four books into the general structure, and signifying that, although it is a privation, matter is still part of the created universe, not wholly alienated from God.[35]

The switch from a downward-tending hierarchy in the first ten books of *Mishneh torah* to an upward tendency in the last four, with a rise in order and unity until the world is completely united in the knowledge of God, conforms to the Alfarabian cosmological model. It reflects the reversal made by Alfarabi between the decline in degree of perfection in the successively emanated spheres and intellects, and a process of increasing perfection beneath the Moon. As Majid Fakhry states in describing Alfarabi's system, 'Beneath the heavenly region lies the terrestrial, in which the process of development is reversed, so that from the imperfect the more perfect arises.'[36]

The two divisions of *Mishneh torah* comprising its first ten and last four books are thus part of a characteristic descent and ascent pattern. They reflect the relationship between 'Laws of the Foundations of the Torah' and 'Laws of Ethical Qualities', respectively the bases of intellectual virtue and of moral and political virtue; being in the image of God—a descent; and becoming in the image of God—an ascent. Like everything in the material world, and like an individual human being, society needs to achieve maximum order and unity in order to receive the highest form appropriate to it. In the case of society, this form is the reign of the king messiah. The meeting point between the flow downwards from God and the upward striving of human society is the Temple, which is the subject of the last and lowest of the man–God books, and which the messiah is supposed to restore. In the messianic age, knowledge of God becomes as widespread as possible, making mankind as receptive as possible to the downward flow, represented, as suggested in the previous chapter, by the image of water covering the sea on which *Mishneh torah* ends.

There is, then, a teleology in the last four books of *Mishneh torah*. It is the advancement of human society towards perfection, under the guidance of the law provided by the prophet who has ascended the ladder of the first ten

[35] 'For if it so happens that the matter of a man is excellent and suitable, neither dominating him nor corrupting his constitution, that matter is a divine gift' (*Guide* iii. 8 (p. 433)).

[36] Fakhry, *A History of Islamic Philosophy*, 123.

books. Even negative phenomena can ultimately contribute to this advancement. Christians are pronounced idolaters in 'Laws of Idolatry', 9: 5, but in 'Laws of Kings and Their Wars', 11: 4, Christianity and Islam are given credit for having spread the ideas of the commandments and the messiah, albeit in a distorted way.

In general, the distinction that Twersky draws between the topical-conceptual classification of the law in *Mishneh torah* and the philosophical-teleological classification in the *Guide* underestimates the teleological strand of *Mishneh torah*. The law about assisting the traveller with the struggling animal is a case in point. Noting that it seems out of place in 'Laws of the Murderer and the Preservation of Life', Twersky comments:

> We may assume that the apparent incongruity of these laws (*teinah u-perikah*) in this context—other codes have these laws in widely disparate contexts—is clearly on Maimonides' mind when he adds that 'one is obligated to help him load or unload, and not leave him possibly to die . . .' . . . Maimonides' new and highly sensitized interpretation of the law in this case also validates his classification. This two tiered achievement suffices to show that the classification is not inadvertent or idiosyncratic; it may be seen as a thoughtful conclusion, a necessary stratagem, or an unavoidable compromise, but however it is appraised, there is no room for doubt that it was carefully planned.[37]

Maimonides' plans are laid even deeper than this. The classification of the law about helping someone to load and reload an animal is an example of design that presents the law as a philosophically coherent whole and a redemptive force.

Yet, in its sensitivity, Twersky's approach to the classification of *Mishneh torah* contains hints at this extra dimension. Commenting on the wisdom Maimonides displayed in ordering and structuring halakhah, Twersky writes, 'Diderot's evaluation of Leibniz is applicable; "He combined two great qualities which are almost incompatible with one another—the spirit of discovery and that of method."'[38] The method of the last four books of *Mishneh torah* is astounding, and it is Maimonides' own. To cite Twersky once again, and as already noted in the Introduction, he comments on the *Book of Torts*, the *Book of Acquisition*, and the *Book of Civil Laws*, 'None of these three books has even an approximate parallel in any single order of the Mishnah.'[39] The way that the talmudic and other material is reorganized so that later material builds on

---

[37] Twersky, *Introduction to the Code*, 289. Twersky cites 'Laws of the Murderer and the Preservation of Life', 13: 14 in full.   [38] Twersky, *Introduction to the Code*, 274.   [39] Ibid. 271.

earlier enables even a novice to grasp the principles of Jewish civil law. At the same time, the spirit of discovery is ever present, manifested not just in the way an ethical ideal can tie together seemingly disparate laws, but in the drive towards the ideal state.

Of course the *Book of Torts*, the *Book of Acquisition*, and the *Book of Civil Laws*, and for that matter the last book, the *Book of Judges*, are not entirely divorced from the mishnaic arrangement. If despite everything one had to point to a single order of the Mishnah from which they derive, it would be Order *Nezikin*, which covers much of the civil and criminal, as opposed to ritual, law.[40] A clue to the relationship between books 11 to 13 of *Mishneh torah* and the Mishnah may be found in the explanation of the arrangement of *Nezikin* provided in Maimonides' introduction to his *Commentary on the Mishnah*. One thread in that explanation is the role of the judge. The first tractate of *Nezikin* is *Bava kama*, which deals with torts, because 'the judge's duty is to give first priority to removing causes of injury'.[41] This corresponds to the first aspect of the welfare of the body described in the *Guide*: 'the aboli-tion of their wronging each other'.[42] For the ensuing tractates, *Bava metsia* and *Bava batra*, other sorts of explanations are proffered, but when it comes to *Sanhedrin* and the tractates that follow, Maimonides reverts to the judge, now in his role as enforcer. With tractate *Avot*, the second aspect of the welfare of the body is introduced, namely, 'the acquisition by every human individual of moral qualities that are useful for life in society so that the affairs of the city may be ordered'. *Avot*, according to Maimonides, has two aims. One is to assert the authenticity of the tradition, but the other is to perfect the character of the judge, for unethical behaviour by an individual is bad, but in a judge, to whom the masses look for an example, it is catastrophic, liable to undermine all order. The judge is compared to a physician, in his role as

[40] As noted in the Introduction, Joseph Tabory sees the structure of *Mishneh torah* as based on the Mishnah. Specifically, he asserts that the order of the last four books of *Mishneh torah* does reflect the sequence of Order *Nezikin* ('The Structure of the Mishnah versus *Mishneh Torah*' (Heb.)). This is very broadly true as far as it goes, but once those books are examined in any detail, it becomes obvious that the mishnaic material has undergone a thorough reshuffle. For example, while the *Book of Acquisition* largely derives from tractate *Bava batra*, 'Laws of Hiring', which is the first section of the following book, the *Book of Civil Laws*, switches us back to tractate *Bava metsia*—a switch that is readily under-standable, since it makes sense to set out the laws of permanent acquisition and transfer of property before discussing their derivatives, custodianship and hire, which Maimonides defines as a form of temporary sale ('Laws of Hiring', 7: 1). Maimonides' conceptualization of the commandments thus breaks up the mishnaic arrangement, and Twersky's assessment of the lack of a parallel with the Mishnah therefore stands.

[41] Maimonides, *Commentary on the Mishnah*, Order *Zera'im*, 15.   [42] *Guide* iii. 27 (p. 510).

healer of society's ills.[43] He is thus little lower than the prophet in guiding and rehabilitating society.

Having assigned this purposive significance to the sequence of Order *Nezikin*, when it comes to the books of *Mishneh torah* dealing with the same content, Maimonides moulds the material so as to accentuate the pattern he has identified, in similar fashion to what we have seen elsewhere of his treatment of his sources. So, for example, he shifts the laws of murder from their position in tractate *Sanhedrin*, broadly equivalent to his *Book of Judges*, to his *Book of Torts*, making that book a comprehensive account of crimes committed by people against one another, from the lightest to the severest. As for the acquisition of moral qualities and the judge as exemplar, these matters are dealt with in 'Laws of the Foundations of the Torah' and 'Laws of Ethical Qualities', which, as we have seen, inform the books on the man–man commandments. The teleology of the Mishnah, as Maimonides reads it, emerges even more clearly and powerfully in *Mishneh torah*.

The building of an ordered, functional, harmonious society can be summed up in the rabbinic phrase *tikun olam*, the repair or right fashioning of the world. Menachem Lorberbaum has shown how this concept, which in the Mishnah is given as the grounds for certain isolated rulings and institutions (equivalent perhaps to grounds of public policy in modern legal parlance), was adapted by Maimonides to embrace the governance of the state and as the teleology of halakhah in general.[44] That is to say, every commandment builds the world. On this basis, the pattern of social regeneration in the last four books of *Mishneh torah* is not something imposed on the commandments discussed in them, but, like the cosmic pattern of the first ten books, it rather embodies the commandments' inner essence.

Loss and Restoration

The reversal in the last four books of *Mishneh torah* of the trend of emanation in the first ten, whereby a broken society mends itself, sets a pattern repeated at other junctures. It was suggested in the previous chapter that *Mishneh torah* expands outwards from its opening statement of God's existence. The first circle is 'Laws of the Foundations of the Torah', the second is the *Book of Knowledge*, the third is the first ten books up to the *Book of Purity*, and the outermost circle is reached at the end of the *Book of Judges*, the final book. If we

---

[43] This is reminiscent of 'Laws of Ethical Qualities', 2: 1.
[44] M. Lorberbaum, 'Maimonides' Conception of *Tikun olam*' (Heb.).

look at the endpoints of each of these sections or books, a certain pattern emerges which can be described as one of loss and restoration. What is more, at each of these endpoints there is a reference of some kind to knowledge or intellect. This gives rise to a general sense that there is a flux in *Mishneh torah* consisting of loss followed by restoration through the assertion, or reassertion, of intellect, which is a movement of repentance. Let us see how this is borne out in detail.

The last four chapters of 'Laws of the Foundations of the Torah' are devoted to prophecy. The main point of these chapters, as mentioned above in Chapter 3, is to establish the authority of the prophet, particularly of Moses, on which depends the authority of the law. In fact, Moses is unique in combining the roles of prophet and legislator. After him, the prophet's public role is to preach repentance and the hope of the messiah.[45]

Now chapter 6 of 'Laws of the Foundations of the Torah', immediately preceding the chapters on prophecy, is about destruction. It concerns the prohibitions against damaging the fabric of the Temple and erasing the name of God. This is partly a continuation of the previous chapter, which is about the sanctification of God's name and its obverse, desecration of the name, but chapter 6 is unique in 'Laws of the Foundations of the Torah' in that it concerns only a negative commandment. It appears to be entirely technical, but, symbolically, the act of erasing God's name entails the negation of all that has gone before about acknowledgement of God, the love of God, and, at the end of the previous chapter, the duty to enhance respect for God and religion. 'The great name', as we have already observed, is what the person who is inspired by looking at the cosmos in 'Laws of the Foundations of the Torah', 2: 2, desires to know. If up to this point in 'Laws of the Foundations of the Torah' we have been concerned with deepening and spreading the awareness of God in the world, the erasure of his name implies diminution of that awareness, which amounts to betrayal of a human being's primary purpose. What is more, the commandment not to damage the Temple building, though covered in just one short *halakhah*,[46] cannot but remind us that the Temple actually was destroyed, entirely. In short, 'Laws of the Foundations of the Torah' 6 is about loss.

Against this background the chapters on prophecy can be seen as being about restoration. Again, the material is technical, concerning the qualifications for becoming a prophet, the scope of the prophet's authority, and the way his or her authenticity may be tested. The poetry and message of the

---

[45] See n. 7 above.   [46] 'Laws of the Foundations of the Torah', 6: 7.

great prophets of Israel are hardly hinted at. But although the idea of prophecy cannot but be associated with their promise of future national redemption, the restoration here lies in the regaining of the peak of intellectual perfection from which we fell in 'Laws of the Foundations of the Torah', 6.

The theme of the final chapter of 'Laws of the Foundations of the Torah' is knowledge, for it deals with the difficult question of how it is possible to know that a prophet is genuine. Although Maimonides describes the experience of becoming a prophet,[47] only the claimant to prophetic status knows whether he or she has really undergone this experience. From the outside, we have only the signs prescribed by the Torah for identifying a prophet. These signs are certainly valid because, on the basis of the self-validating experience of the revelation at Sinai, undergone by the entire people and passed on as tradition, there is certainty about the authenticity of the prophecy of Moses, and hence of the Torah. If the signs are present, the person who claims to be a prophet must be obeyed, even though there is always room for doubt, just as a court is obliged by the Torah to rule according to the evidence of two witnesses, despite the risk, even after due inquiry, that they may be lying.[48] What constitutes knowledge is thus an underlying theme of the chapters on prophecy. In this context, it turns about to be the application of reason to the evidence of the senses, according to rules and limits prescribed by authentic tradition.[49] The final *halakhah* of 'Laws of the Foundations of the Torah' even connects acknowledgement of the prophet with acknowledgement of God:

We must not be continually investigating his claims, as it is said 'Ye shall not tempt the Lord, your God, as you tempted Him at Massah' (Deut. 6: 16), where the people asked, 'Is the Lord among us or not?' (Exod. 17: 7). Once it is known that a particular individual is a prophet, they must believe and know that God is in their midst and not harbour doubt or suspicion concerning him; as it is said, 'And they shall know that there hath been a prophet among them' (Ezek. 2: 5).

This stress on knowledge takes us back to the very beginning and the commandment to know that there is a first existent. Through prophecy, the knowledge of God is restored.

When we move on to consider the *Book of Knowledge* as a whole, the pattern of loss and restoration becomes obvious in the juxtaposition of 'Laws of

---

[47] Ibid. 7: 1.   [48] Ibid. 7: 7.

[49] Where tradition breaks down and reason fails, as it did in the generation of Enosh, it takes a person of exceptional intellect and integrity, such as Abraham was, to regain truth.

Idolatry' and 'Laws of Repentance', the penultimate and last sections of the book.

'Laws of Idolatry' actually contains within it two narratives about the loss of tradition and the failure of reason, followed by restoration of the truth by a person of supreme integrity and intellect. In what might be called the second fall,[50] the generation of Enosh fell into error, because of which the name of God was eventually erased not from books, but from the minds of men. This intellectual eclipse continued until Abraham rediscovered God and began to spread the knowledge of him. Later the Jewish people were corrupted in Egypt and the knowledge of God was again darkened, until they were rescued physically and intellectually by Moses. But 'Laws of Idolatry' as a whole is a nadir like 'Laws of the Foundations of the Torah' chapter 6, while 'Laws of Repentance' is a restorative not just in the narrow sense that it is about repenting of sins. 'Laws of Idolatry' shows the depravity that results from error: a priest-ridden society oppressed through meaningless rituals, in which people are scarcely capable of correct thought.[51] The intellectual rigour and the courage of Abraham[52] find expression in the spreading of a faith that, initially, entails no rituals at all.[53] 'Laws of Repentance', ending as it does on the service of God out of love and the nurturing of love through the acquisition of knowledge, can be read as an essay in the restoration of that pristine faith, with ritual, and for that matter morality, once more understood rightly as means to an end.[54] Idolatry begins in an erroneous notion of the relationship of God to the world. 'Laws of Repentance' concludes with a reference back to 'Laws of the Foundations of the Torah', setting us once more on the path to correct understanding. In 'Laws of Idolatry' and 'Laws of Repentance' we have not just sin and repentance, but the light of intellect darkened and relit.

Widening the circle yet further, the next boundary is at the *Book of Purity*, which is about the loss of pure status, the chief consequence of which is loss of

---

[50] The representation of the first is discussed in Chapter 6.

[51] For a close reading of this narrative, see J. Cohen, 'Maimonides as Literary Artist'. The stress on continuity between Abraham and Moses may also be intended to counter Islamic claims.

[52] 'Laws of Idolatry', 1: 3.

[53] See Kellner, 'Did the Torah Precede the Cosmos?' (Heb.); Blidstein, 'Maimonides and Me'iri on Non-Judaic Religion'. Blidstein comments, 'we recall that monotheistic man *knew* God, but that *worship* (i.e. sacrifices and prayer) was first introduced along with idolatry—and that Abraham redirected this worship to the true God. Intrinsically, then, ritual worship may always be a bit of a concession to something idolatrous in humanity' (italics original). But note, as Blidstein does, 'Laws of the Temple', 2: 2, where the sanctity of the Temple and sacrifice on its site are traced back beyond Abraham to Noah and ultimately to Adam.   [54] See pp. 32–4 above.

access to the Temple, and the rituals that restore that status, permitting access to the Temple once more. The final section is 'Laws of Immersion Pools', about *mikveh*, the main ritual. As noted in the previous chapter, Maimonides had to rearrange the mishnaic sequence of topics in order to position this section at the end of the book. Among other things, this indicates his intent to close this main division of *Mishneh torah*, the ten books on the man–God commandments, on the motif of restoration.[55]

The remarkable metaphorical interpretation of the commandment of *mikveh* in the final *halakhah* of 'Laws of Immersion Pools' as standing for the immersion of the soul in the waters of intellect was discussed at length in Chapter 3. The Neoplatonic connotations have also been noted. It remains only to stress that there could hardly be a more forceful way of linking repentance, which is the essence of Maimonides' metaphorical meaning, with Neoplatonic return.[56] The idea of repentance emerges as the inner drive of the restoration pattern.

In the light of the discussion above of the last four books of *Mishneh torah* moving from societal breakdown to ideal order, we can also now fit the *Book of Purity* more securely into the cosmic pattern. As the tenth book, the *Book of Purity* corresponds to the tenth separate intellect, the agent intellect, which, it will be recalled, is unable to produce a sphere but instead endows matter with form. Matter has no permanent form, for things on earth are subject to generation and decay, but only permanent processes, influenced by the movements of the stars and spheres, that produce arrangements of matter capable of receiving different forms from the agent intellect.[57] These processes have no teleology, and matter has no consciousness. Human beings, by contrast, are composed of matter and intellect, and in respect of the intellect they do have a *telos*, which is to realize their potential microcosmic form. In fact, a human being has a dual *telos*: to acquire knowledge of God, and to engage in self-reflection, or repentance, from which there evolves moral virtue and a perfect society. This corresponds to the dual consciousness of the separate intellects in Alfarabi's Neoplatonic system: the thought of the First Cause, and the thought of itself, from which evolves a sphere. The *Book of*

---

[55] It must be acknowledged, however, that another purification ritual, sprinkling with the ashes of the red heifer, is treated in the second of the eight sections of the book—this of course looks forward to the restoration of the Temple.

[56] A comparison between repentance and *mikveh* in fact occurs much earlier on in *Mishneh torah*, in 'Laws of Repentance', 2: 3, where confession of a sin without the intention of abandoning it is likened to immersion in a *mikveh* while holding on to something that makes one impure.

[57] See 'Laws of the Foundations of the Torah', 4: 6.

Purity, via the metaphorical treatment of *mikveh* with which it closes, symbolizes the transmission of form to human beings and to human society
through the process of repentance.

Finally we come to the messiah. The messiah is linked to prophecy in two
ways. Anyone who does not believe in the messiah also denies prophecy and
the truth of the Torah, for the Torah and the prophets predict that the messiah will come.[58] Secondly, the age of the messiah will see the restoration of
prophecy, the messiah himself being a great prophet (though not as great as
Moses)[59] who will enforce repentance.[60] The description of the messiah and
his times at the end of *Mishneh torah* thus brings together the themes that
have emerged at each of the junctures we have examined. The recurrence of
those themes at those junctures links them in the unfolding of an original
prophetic vision, the messianic age being a culmination of history, not a break
with history, with nature, or with the commandments.[61] *Olam keminhago
holekh*, the world continues as usual, is Maimonides' watchword in both
'Laws of Repentance' in the first book of *Mishneh torah*,[62] and in 'Laws of
Kings and Their Wars' in the last.[63]

The knowledge of God will become widespread at that time not as
the product of a new revelation, but as the natural result of people having the
leisure and composure to devote themselves to the pursuit of such knowledge.[64] The naturalness of this outcome is not just stated, but felt. The final
triumph of intellect in the closing quotation of *Mishneh torah*, 'for the earth
shall be full of the knowledge of the Lord as the waters cover the sea',[65] is
anticipated discursively, and also symbolically at the junctures just mentioned. Even the use of the verse from Isaiah in this context is anticipated in
the earlier discussion of the messiah in 'Laws of Repentance', where a shorter
excerpt from it appears.[66] Maimonides employs the narrative technique of
foreshadowing to give a sense of development, culmination, and inevitability.

Through the Neoplatonic association, repentance can be understood as
more than an ad hoc correction of vice or even a reconnection to God. Just as
the emanant is self-constituting through its thought of the First Cause and its
thought of itself, it is by virtue of repentance, conceived of as Soul's continual
striving to objectify material existence rather than be submerged by it, and to
reflect the Intellect whence it came, that human beings have meaningful exis-

---

[58] 'Laws of Kings and Their Wars', 11: 1–2.   [59] 'Laws of Repentance', 9: 2.
[60] 'Laws of Kings and Their Wars', 11: 4.   [61] Ibid. 11: 3; 12: 1.
[62] 'Laws of Repentance', 9: 2.   [63] 'Laws of Kings and Their Wars', 12: 1.
[64] Ibid. 12: 5.   [65] Isa. 11: 9.   [66] 'Laws of Repentance', 9: 2.

tence at all. After forgetting itself in 'Laws of Idolatry' by subordinating itself to nature, thereby forgetting God as well, Soul recollects itself in 'Laws of Repentance', and thereby comes into full being in awareness of God. By this means political redemption is portrayed not as something only for the end of days, but as the product of a constant relationship between individual self-elevation and social order, an idea that acquires force, depth, and complexity in *Mishneh torah*'s treatment. This also enables us to understand a little more deeply the notion of the artistic self-containment of the *Book of Knowledge* discussed in Chapter 3. The turning back towards the beginning and the First Cause formally, substantially, and, in its final *halakhah*, literally ('A person ought therefore to devote himself to the understanding and comprehension of those sciences and studies which will inform him concerning his Master . . . as indeed we have explained in "Laws of the Foundations of the Torah"'), lends the book an aesthetically satisfying shape, rhythm, and unity that, transcending consecutive exposition, bring it into artistic being. The recurrence of this motion of return at each significant juncture of the work as a whole pulls it together thematically and artistically.

Rationalizing the Commandments: *Mishneh Torah* versus the *Guide*

It was stated at the outset of this study that the microcosmic form of *Mishneh torah* was a way of rationalizing the commandments. Now that the account of that form is complete, at least for the present, we can take stock of the ways in which the formal patterns in *Mishneh torah* render the commandments intelligible, and compare this with the rationalization of the commandments in the *Guide*.

Intelligibility

That the commandments ought to be intelligible is something Maimonides took to be practically self-evident. To believe otherwise, he thought, would be to disparage the God who commanded them. Against those 'who consider it a grievous thing that causes should be given for any law'[67] he deploys a *reductio ad absurdum*, arguing that, since an intelligent human being does not act without some end in view, if the commandments were purposeless, human beings would appear superior to God. The purpose should be some benefit to human life, in the light of the verse: '[And the Lord commanded us

---

[67] *Guide* iii. 31 (p. 523).

to do all these statutes, to fear the Lord our God,] for our good always, that He might preserve us alive, as it is this day',[68] and the benefit should be discernible by any reasonable person, for we are told that the non-Jews, though not committed to the commandments, will perceive their wisdom: 'Which shall hear all these statutes and say: Surely this great community is a wise and understanding people.'[69] Every commandment must therefore promote some recognizable good in the intellectual, moral, or political sphere.

In this respect, God's act in giving the commandments is similar to his actions in nature, which are not useless or frivolous, but conform to his wisdom,[70] although we must remember that, whereas the commandments are designed for human benefit, nature does not exist for the sake of mankind, and indeed the fallacy that it does is precisely what leads to the failure to understand natural phenomena, and to the conclusion that some of God's actions are pointless. Creation is 'the bringing into being of everything whose existence is possible, existence being indubitably a good',[71] that is to say, good in itself, without reference to human benefit.

We do not always manage to penetrate to the end of God's wisdom in respect of either the law or nature. Although all God's acts proceed from his wisdom, 'we, however, are ignorant of many of the ways in which wisdom is found in His works'.[72] Similarly, 'all the Laws have a cause, though we ignore the causes for some of them and we do not know the manner in which they conform to wisdom . . . either because of the incapacity of our intellects or the deficiency of our knowledge',[73] but not because no cause is discoverable in principle. Still, even if we do know the cause, that does not give us absolute understanding of the commandment, because the cause does not determine all the commandment's details, which remain dependent on God's will.[74]

---

[68] Deut. 6: 24. Maimonides does not cite the part in square brackets.

[69] Deut. 4: 6. The word for statutes is *ḥukim*, conventionally taken to refer to commandments that have no apparent cause or utility, such as the prohibition on wearing a garment woven from wool and linen, as opposed to *mishpatim*, usually translated as 'laws', and taken to refer to commandments for which the rationale is clear, such as 'Thou shalt not steal'.

[70] See Hadad, 'Nature and Torah in Maimonides' (Heb.). [71] *Guide* iii. 25 (p. 506).

[72] Ibid. [73] *Guide* iii. 26 (p. 507).

[74] This follows Funkenstein, *Maimonides: Nature, History*. Funkenstein takes at face value the statement in *Guide* iii. 26 (p. 508) that 'The generalities of the commandments necessarily have a cause and have been given because of a certain utility; their details are that in regard to which it was said of the commandments that they were given merely for the sake of commanding something' (the details of sacrificial rituals being given as examples), and sees Maimonides' view as being that an element of arbitrariness must be present in both the commandments and in nature, in order to leave room for divine providence and divine compulsion, for if the laws of nature were completely deterministic, God would have no continuing role in the world after Creation, and if the commandments were com-

In this way Maimonides avoids two equally repugnant extremes: the Aristotelian idea that everything in nature flows from necessity, leaving no room for God's will, and the opposing occasionalism of the Mutakallimun school of Islamic theology, the doctrine that there is no regularity in nature at all, that perceptions of cause and effect are illusory, and that everything that happens at every instant is a matter of God's will alone. Similarly, with regard to the law, Maimonides steers a course between the position of those who would dismiss any law not immediately accessible to reason, and the opposing position that the law is entirely a matter of divine decree in which reason plays no part.

This middle course is set clearly in *Mishneh torah*, but, appropriately for that work, framed as a duty rather than as a philosophical deduction. At the end of the *Book of Temple Service* we find the following general statement: 'It is fitting for a person to examine the laws of the holy Torah and know their ends according to his capacity, but something for which he finds no reason and knows no cause for it, let it not seem light to him . . . our sages said: I have instituted statutes and you have no permission to criticize them.'[75] Here, Maimonides encourages enquiry into the reason for the laws, but warns that such enquiry must not undermine obedience. At the end of the next book, the *Book of Offerings*, the same tension between enquiry and obedience is dealt with, but matters are put the other way around, giving the opposite emphasis: 'Even though all the statutes of the Torah are decrees, as we explained at the end of "Laws of Trespass", it is fitting to examine them, and for anything that you can give a reason, give it a reason.'[76] We should attend to the language: to give a commandment a reason is not necessarily to claim to have discovered *the* reason for it. The authority for the commandment remains divine decree.

pletely rationalized, they would be obeyed solely on that basis and not at all out of obedience to the divine will. Just as in nature a form cannot determine every detail of its manifestation in matter, or, as we might say, the genotype does not determine every feature of the phenotype, so the idea or purpose of the commandment cannot determine the commandment's every physical detail.

Stern dismisses this statement of Maimonides as 'nothing more than a smokescreen' ('Idea of a Hoq', 102), and takes his real view to be that unknowns in the reasons for commandments are always only epistemic. Nevertheless, Stern and Funkenstein are in agreement about the importance to Maimonides of the comparison between the commandments and nature—see above, Ch. 2, n. 59.

[75] 'Laws of Trespass', 8: 8.

[76] 'Laws of Substituted Offerings', 4: 13. The reason that Maimonides splits the discussion in this way is possibly that the *Book of Temple Service* is about the Temple as an institution and public sacrifices, to which a stress on the ultimate inscrutability of the commandments is appropriate, while the *Book of Offerings* is about private sacrifices, to which a stress on individual enquiry into the meaning of the commandments is appropriate. The texts are discussed in Nehorai, 'The Mitzvot' (Heb.). See also Twersky, *Introduction to the Code*, 407–18.

At any rate, we see that, within the limits of the mind's capacity and of obedience, Maimonides encourages the application of reason to the commandments.

The corresponding limit on enquiry into physics and metaphysics is stated at the end of the *Book of Knowledge*:[77] 'A person ought therefore to devote himself to the understanding and comprehension of those sciences and studies which will inform him concerning his Master, as far as it lies in human faculties to understand and comprehend.'[78]

The symbolic structure of *Mishneh torah*, in which nature encompasses the commandments, thus serves to amplify the explicit message of the text. Nature and the commandments have similar structures that can be probed by the human intellect in similarly limited ways.

So *Mishneh torah* and the *Guide* are in agreement on the ideological basis for rationalization of the commandments, and on the parameters for such rationalization. On the face of it, however, the application of these principles is much more the province of the *Guide* than of *Mishneh torah*. The latter indicates that performance of the commandments is beneficial and wins life in the world to come,[79] and even suggests reasons for some particular commandments, but still, its emphasis appears to be on the 'what' of the commandments rather than the 'why'. It contains nothing to match the systematic analysis of reasons for the commandments that we find in Part III of the *Guide*.

As we have seen, what is lacking in the content is supplied by the form. The cosmic structure of *Mishneh torah*, we have said, implies that the commandments are rationally caused and rationalizing in their effect. In other words, *Mishneh torah* is just as much concerned with justifying the commandments as the *Guide*, but goes about it in a different way. That, however, is a rather unsatisfactorily general observation. The *Guide* signals strongly that it is worth attempting a closer definition of the contrast, for it provides a constant against which the contrast stands out sharply: the number fourteen. I have noted before now that, as the basis for its treatment of their reasons, the *Guide* divides the commandments into fourteen classes that yet do not correspond to the fourteen books of *Mishneh torah*.[80]

Fourteen, we saw in Chapter 2, symbolizes rationality. The constancy of this number should therefore mean that *Mishneh torah* and the *Guide* share

[77] For a controversy on where the limit lies, see Davidson, 'Maimonides on Metaphysical Knowledge', a response to Pines, 'Limitations of Human Knowledge'.   [78] 'Laws of Repentance', 10: 6.

[79] See 'Laws of the Foundations of the Torah', 4: 13; 'Laws of Repentance', 10: 1.

[80] *Guide* iii. 35 (pp. 535–8).

the essential idea that the commandments are rational, while the different classifications of the commandments that are devised on the basis of it would appear to indicate that the same facts can be rationalized in more than one way. That, at least, will be our working assumption: that the changed classification of the commandments in the *Guide* arises from a different approach to the subject of reasons for the commandments from that of *Mishneh torah*. It is this difference that I shall now explore.

This means leaving behind the view of the relationship between Maimonides' two major works that has been maintained so far, which is largely that the form of *Mishneh torah* shows what the *Guide* says. We now encounter sharper divergence. At the same time, the divide between the two works remains, as it has been all along, a matter of genre. The divergence is essentially a literary one. The point is that the poetry of *Mishneh torah* and the prose of the *Guide* are not always two ways of communicating the same thing. A distinct logical method is part and parcel of the literary form of each work.

Axiom and Summa

In her enumeration of the various medieval literary forms of philosophical argument, two of the forms that Eileen Sweeney identifies are 'axiom' and 'summa'.[81] Axiom form emphasizes the internal coherence of an argument. The validity of a series of propositions is guaranteed if, starting from necessary or universally acknowledged first principles, each proposition in the series can be shown to derive by logical steps from the one before it, as with a proof in Euclidian geometry. The summa form, by contrast, provides an external frame of reference. In this form propositions are evaluated according to criteria outside the propositions themselves.

The suggestion is that *Mishneh torah* exhibits axiomatic form, while the *Guide* has the form of a summa, particularly in the way it sets about justifying the commandments.[82] Furthermore, this contrast is a function of the genre distinction we have already drawn between the two works, so that we should speak of Hebrew/poetic/axiomatic form in *Mishneh torah* versus Arabic/prose/summa form in the *Guide*.

This assertion has to be demonstrated in detail, but it is lent initial plausibility by some characteristics of axiom and summa form outlined by Sweeney. The model for axiom form that she finds in Proclus is the cosmos itself: 'the

---

[81] Sweeney, 'Literary Forms'.

[82] This is *contra* Rynhold, who assumes an axiomatic model for the *Guide*'s exposition of the reasons for the commandments—see *Two Models of Jewish Philosophy*, 6–32. Rynhold's approach is discussed more fully below.

axiomatic form mirrors the metaphysical structure of emanation. As all being emanates from the One, all propositions are derived from axioms.' In that case, its microcosmic form, embodying as it does the idea of emanation, would appear to build into *Mishneh torah* an axiomatic structure of argument. This is a more technical way of expressing the idea, mentioned in the previous chapter, that the Neoplatonic hierarchy of its first ten books gives the impression of the commandments emanating from God, whose existence is the undisputable first principle.

As for summa form, one of its chief characteristics is that it aims 'to completely emancipate the subject matter . . . from the structure dictated either by scripture or authoritative sources'.[83] The *Guide* emancipates the commandments from their scriptural and authoritative sources by matching them to general notions of the purposes of a divine law—any divine law—namely, the welfare of the soul and the welfare of the body. These philosophically warranted purposes constitute the *Guide*'s external frame of reference in evaluating the commandments, and they, rather than scripture or authoritative sources such as the Mishnah, dictate the structure or classification of the commandments found in that work.

It will have been noticed that the contrast between the two forms is asymmetrical: in describing axiom form I spoke of 'derivation', while for summa form the key word was 'evaluation'. Axiom form is deterministic: as long as there is no flaw in our logic, then proposition *b* must follow from proposition *a*, and proposition *c* from *b*, and so on, so that the first principle from which we start is the determining cause of the entire series. Summa form, by contrast, is not deterministic: the criteria by which we evaluate something do not cause it to exist, and this applies to propositions just as much as to anything else. The *Guide* does not attempt to demonstrate that the commandments derive from the purposes set out for them, the welfare of the soul and welfare of the body. Such an attempt would be largely futile: no logical procedure can by itself take us from the welfare of the soul to, say, waving a palm branch once a year. To fill the gap between the general purposes of the commandments and the particulars of each one, the *Guide* resorts to historical and cultural factors, especially the practices of the Sabian pagan cult, or rather the need to counter such practices. What the *Guide* does seek to demonstrate is that, once factors of that kind are taken into account, the commandments can be seen to fulfil rational purposes, and can therefore be thought of as the creation of a rational and purposive legislator.

[83] Sweeney, 'Literary Forms'.

In this respect *Mishneh torah* is perpendicular to the *Guide*. It presents the vertical flow of the commandments and their effects from the highest source through to the final product, namely, the perfect society. The *Guide* moves horizontally, proving the worth of Jewish truth-claims, texts, and practices through dialectical engagement with contrary opinion, a procedure that is a further characteristic of the summa form.[84] So while the axiomatic form of *Mishneh torah* is, at least in principle, a matter of logic pure and simple, the summa form of the *Guide* has, even in principle, a large component of rhetoric; in the arena of competing philosophies, poetry is not enough.

Contrary opinion can arise from within the Jewish camp as well as from outside it. As we saw above, on the way to setting out the reasons for the commandments, Maimonides seeks to undermine the arguments of those who prefer to see the commandments as purely a product of God's will, insisting that they are supposed to be intelligible to the nations of the world. This delineates the approach to reasons for the commandments in the *Guide*: the reference point is not the cosmic order, but the reasonable human being.

But how does *Mishneh torah* explain the particulars of the commandments? The answer will be that it does not, because it does not need to. In that work, it will be argued, the question disappears.

That will be for a little later on. The main point for the time being is that *Mishneh torah* and the *Guide* deal in two different, though definitely complementary, kinds of rationalization.

We have seen this relationship before, in the discussion of the treatment of sacrifices. *Mishneh torah*'s vertical, ontological, synchronic evaluation, in

---

[84] Note that this does not turn the *Guide* into a polemic. *Mutatis mutandis*, approximately the same could be said of it as Sweeney says of Aquinas's *Summa Contra Gentiles*:

> It has been argued that the *Contra Gentiles* is not a polemical but a protreptic work, addressed to Christians, calling on them to deepen their understanding of the faith, specifically about how to persuade others to Christian belief (Jordan, 1986, 190, 194). The gentiles in the title are not Muslims and Jews but 'pre- or extra-Christian man, and metaphorically, the human mind under the tutelage of nature' (Jordan, 1986, 184).

Sweeney bases her discussion here on R. Jordan, 'The Protreptic Structure of the *Summa Contra Gentiles*', *The Thomist*, 50/2 (1986), 173–209. A third characteristic of the summa listed by Sweeney, that it aims 'to cover completely an entire discipline', is one that the *Guide* and *Mishneh torah* actually share.

For that matter, *Mishneh torah* is not devoid of dialectic. For example, as noted in the Introduction (p. 5), Maimonides himself points out that in it he adopted the same tactic as in the *Guide* of proving God's existence on the basis of the eternity of the world, even though the Jewish tradition calls for belief in creation—see *Guide* i. 71 (p. 182). In 'Laws of the Foundations of the Torah', chapter 8, the insistence on halakhah as the framework of a prophet's authority and the negation of miracles as a basis for belief are surely aimed at undermining what Maimonides saw as the assumptions behind the supersessionary claims of Islam and Christianity.

which sacrifices are near the bottom of a Neoplatonic hierarchy, was contrasted with the horizontal, chronological evaluation of the *Guide*, in which sacrifices are justified by the conventions of worship prevailing when they were instituted, and become obsolete with the disappearance of the conventions.

The example of sacrifices illustrates a further point, which is that whereas in the *Guide* evaluation and derivation are separate, in *Mishneh torah* they are coeval, for under the Neoplatonic concept of emanation, each entity is inferior in value to the predecessor from which it derives. Here is another example of poetic form conveying simultaneously what discursive prose conveys successively.

The Whole and the Parts

There is another contrast to be drawn between the axiom and summa forms that will be important to our discussion. If, in axiom form, all subsequent propositions derive from the first principle, it means that they are contained by that principle, which is pregnant with them, as it were. The first principle can therefore be thought of as a whole of which the propositions deriving from it are parts. So axiom form is an argument from the whole to the parts. In summa form, on the other hand, the propositions do not derive from first principles, but rather each is tested to determine whether it meets one or more criteria, and then assembled with the others into something that, it is to be hoped, will meet all the criteria adequately. So summa form is an argument from the parts to the whole.

This coincides with the relationship between form and matter. From one point of view, matter is general, and is particularized by form. But when we consider specific material objects, form is general; it is instantiated by the object. Moreover, as we saw in earlier chapters, in the Neoplatonic hierarchy of emanation each level is as matter to the level above it and as form to the level below it. Axiomatic argument, therefore, as an analogy of emanation, is an argument from form to matter, from the general to the particular. Conversely, summa form argues from material instances to form, from the particular to the general.

The whole need not be a single axiom; it can be a set that is perceived as a whole. This can be illustrated by a short anecdote. In a Tel Aviv park, some friends and I came upon a square, stepped pool with nine boulders arranged in and around it. When the question arose what this installation might signify, one of the party joked that the boulders symbolized nine of the twelve tribes of Israel. The absurdity of this mildly cynical remark lies of course in the fact that one would never imagine a boulder to stand for a tribe of Israel unless there were a whole, a 'twelvesome'. The whole would then project its significance onto the parts, and from there we might proceed to ascribe significance to other characteristics of these stones, such as their sizes, shapes, and arrangement. If, on the other hand, twelve boulders were labelled Reuben, Simeon, and so on, we should get the point by proceeding from the parts to the whole.

Similarly, the understanding of the microcosmic significance of *Mishneh torah*'s structure begins with perception of a whole, a form, a 'fourteensome'. From there, we can start to analyse the ways in which the structure and dynamics of *Mishneh torah* are comparable to those of the universe. By contrast, the chapters on reasons of the commandments in the *Guide* are a labelling exercise, matching particular laws to previously enunciated general principles.

In this respect, art is axiomatic, for the appreciation of art begins with perception of a whole, from which the parts derive their significance. The underlying process is emergence. Propositions emerge from axioms; the meaning of a work of art is released, or emerges from it, in the mind contemplating it, so that it is prior to its rationale or meaning. In summa form, by contrast, the rationale is prior to the propositions: in our case, the aims of the welfare of the soul and the welfare of the body exist prior to particular commandments. For the removal of doubt, this does not contradict what was said earlier about propositions in summa form not deriving from first principles. Laws may be formulated, or examined, in the light of certain aims, but the aims do not directly produce the laws, certainly not in all their details. This does not apply only to religious ritual. For example, collisions on the road are clearly an evil, injurious to the welfare of the body. It therefore makes sense to legislate that vehicles should keep to one side. But which side, right or left, is in many cases a matter of the cultural and historical background in the country concerned, and is not derivable from any philosophical principle or consensual *telos*.[85]

---

[85] In England, for example, ancient custom, apparently going back to Roman law, decreed that horse-riders should keep to the left, in order to present their right hand to oncoming riders, for greeting or self-defence. This eventually translated into legislation requiring traffic to keep left, which in turn became the norm in countries of the British empire, and so it has remained in several of them since their independence. So the reasons that they drive on the left in Australia are: (1) philosophical/teleological—to prevent death and injury; (2) historical/cultural—Australia is a former British colony.

Axiom form has the tautness of art. Using the Aristotelian criterion of artistic perfection discussed earlier, nothing can be added to an axiomatic argument (assuming the potential of the first principle has been exhausted) and nothing can be taken away, for if any proposition is missing, the sequence breaks down. With summa form, on the other hand, propositions can be added *ad infinitum*, and subtracted as well. This is reflected in the different bases suggested in *Mishneh torah* and the *Guide* for the prohibitions against adding to or subtracting from the commandments. In the Introduction we saw how these prohibitions are used in *Mishneh torah* descriptively, defining the perfection of the Torah in terms similar to Aristotle's definition of the perfection of art. In *Guide* iii. 41, on the other hand, their suggested basis is political: 'For this might have led to corruption of the rules of the Law and to the belief that the latter did not come from God.' In other words, in *Mishneh torah*, adding to or subtracting from the commandments is unthinkable, whereas in the *Guide* it is inadvisable.

Moreover, in summa form, once they are labelled as satisfying criterion x or y, propositions are meaningful by themselves; they are emancipated not just from traditional structures, but really from all structure. The sabbath, for example, is labelled in *Guide* iii. 43 as procuring rest from labour, thus promoting the welfare of the body, and as perpetuating the doctrine of creation, thus promoting the welfare of the soul. As such, it could survive by itself as a worthwhile and reasonable commandment even if there were no others (apart from knowledge of God's existence)—in fact, according to Maimonides, the sabbath was the only man–God commandment prescribed to the Children of Israel in the immediate aftermath of the Exodus.[86] In axiom form, on the other hand, propositions, and commandments, can only live within the structure, just as Hamlet only lives within the play. Again we find that our two methods are not just directionally opposed but also asymmetrical: in summa form, the whole is the sum of the parts; in axiom form, the whole is greater than the sum of the parts.

Parallel Methods

Since these two modes of thinking are aspects of literary form, defined as a Hebrew/poetic/axiom genre versus an Arabic/prose/summa genre, it follows that, while the classification in *Mishneh torah* may be *sui generis* in Maimonides' oeuvre (*Mishneh torah* being his only major Hebrew work), the classification in the *Guide* is not necessarily unique to that book but may

---

[86] This follows the Talmud: see *Guide* iii. 32 (p. 531) and references there.

share characteristics with discussions of the commandments elsewhere in his Arabic writings. This indeed turns out to be the case: part of the argument will be that the *Guide*'s classification in some ways reverts to the method of *The Book of the Commandments*, which of course pre-dates *Mishneh torah*. In other words, while we must allow for development and for the particular needs of particular works, fundamentally, the approaches of *Mishneh torah* and the *Guide* to rationalization of the commandments represent two logical methods, one associated with Hebrew and the other with Arabic, that accompanied Maimonides in parallel throughout his career.

As discussed in the Introduction, this way of looking at the matter implies disagreement with earlier explanations of the variations between *Mishneh torah* and the *Guide* in their classifications of the commandments. Unlike Hadad, who sees the two classifications as only superficially different, I see them as genuinely distinct, and for profound reasons; while Berman's suggestion of a process of evolution between *Mishneh torah* and the *Guide* is negated by the idea of parallel modes of thinking present in Maimonides' mind all along.

In the case of Twersky, there is both disagreement and agreement. It will be recalled that he sums up the differences between the classifications of the commandments in *Mishneh torah* and the *Guide* as a reflection of the different orientations of the two works, terming the classification in the former topical/conceptual, and that of the latter philosophical/teleological, meaning, roughly, that in *Mishneh torah* commandments are classified according to their legal characteristics, while in the *Guide* they are classified according to their purposes.[87] It has been the burden of this study to show that, once form is taken into account, *Mishneh torah* is no less philosophical/teleological than the *Guide*, and that philosophy shapes its form. To that extent, the approach adopted here to the two classifications, which is essentially that they are philosophical in different ways but in equal measure, is at odds with Twersky.

On the other hand, the way that Twersky, and also Joseph B. Soloveitchik, differentiate the approaches of *Mishneh torah* and the *Guide* at the micro level, in discussing the reasons Maimonides offers for certain specific commandments, will turn out to correspond to the distinction proposed here between the general philosophical methods of the two works.

With that as an outline of the argument, I shall now look in greater detail

---

[87] Twersky, *Introduction to the Code*, 300–8. Such a distinction between conceptual field and practical purpose is normal. For example, a textbook on insurance law will include vehicle insurance, but I find it convenient to file my car insurance certificate under 'Car' rather than under 'Insurance'.

at how the axiom and summa modes apply to our subject, the reasons for the commandments in Maimonides.

The *Guide*: Chronological and Practical

The *Guide* is the more straightforward case. As already indicated, its classification can be accounted for by the general discussion of the purposes of the commandments that leads up to it, which I now need to cite once more. 'The Law aims at two things', Maimonides states at the beginning of *Guide* iii. 27, 'the welfare of the soul and the welfare of the body. As for the welfare of the soul, it consists in the multitude's acquiring correct opinions corresponding to their respective capacity . . . As for the welfare of the body, it comes about by the improvement of their ways of living one with another.' For men to live together in harmony, he goes on to explain, they need laws to prevent wrongdoing but also 'the acquisition by every human individual of moral qualities'. And although the welfare of the soul is 'indubitably greater in nobility', the welfare of the body is 'prior in nature and time'. That is to say, until we have built a society governed by the rule of law, we shall not enjoy the stability and leisure required for study.

Maimonides goes on, in chapters 28 to 32, to describe the kind of idolatrous beliefs that many of the laws are intended to uproot, the role of sacrifices as a concession to conventional forms of worship, and the sabbath and the civil laws as the most basic commandments.

Chapter 33 opens with the statement, 'To the totality of purposes of the perfect law there belong the abandonment, depreciation, and restraint of desires in so far as possible.' We thus have three main external objects for the commandments (although *Guide* iii. 33 does go on to mention additional objects): welfare of the soul; welfare of the body; and restraint of desire.

With this background we can understand the classification Maimonides gives in chapter 35. He starts with fundamental opinions and the prohibition of idolatry, establishing the most important principles. Then, from the third to the seventh class, he sets out the laws that are 'prior in nature and time', that inculcate moral qualities and bring about social harmony. The eighth class comprises the laws of the sabbath and festivals. This is a transitional category, since, as we saw above, these laws have to do both with the welfare of the body, in that they prescribe rest, and with the welfare of the soul, in that they reinforce the belief in Creation and other important doctrines. From the ninth to the twelfth class, Maimonides deals with the rituals that further the welfare of the soul. Finally, in the thirteenth and fourteenth classes, we come to the last of the ideas he discusses in his introductory chapters, the 'restraint of desires', with the laws of forbidden foods and forbidden sexual unions.

Because these general purposes according to which Maimonides classifies the commandments in the *Guide* do not explain the commandments' particulars, especially not of the *ḥukim*, he resorts to historical and cultural explanations to supply the lack. These explanations are based on his knowledge of the Sabian cult, which, according to him, many of the commandments were designed to counter.

So the method of justifying the commandments in the *Guide* fits the summa method as defined above. The object of the law is threefold—welfare of the soul, welfare of the body, and restraint of desire. These objects are external to the law and antecedent to it. Each commandment is inspected and shown to promote one or more of the objects, but the objects may need to be supplemented by historical research in order to explain the commandment's particulars. For convenience, the commandments are assembled into classes, but the sequence of classes does not grow out of a value system inherent in the commandments. Rather, the opposite is the case: those considered nobler are placed later out of the practical consideration that the less noble come first in nature and time. The *Guide* stresses practicality and chronology, not ontology.

Mishneh Torah: Ontological and Theoretical

The way that *Mishneh torah* manifests axiom form is more complicated. It may be most conveniently discussed under two headings with which we are already familiar: the Aristotelian superstructure, and the Neoplatonic infrastructure.

In discussing Maimonides' reasons for the commandments, Daniel Rynhold describes two Aristotelian criteria of scientific explanation. The first is indeed axiomatic derivation: 'a system of scientific knowledge for Aristotle is a stack of demonstrative syllogisms that can be traced back in the first instance to true and non-demonstrable first principles'.[88]

The second criterion is that scientific knowledge 'can only be of necessary rather than contingent truths'. In other words, science tells us about the essence of something, its essential characteristic, or, in philosophical language, its form. This can be explained, according to Rynhold,

by appeal to his [Aristotle's] contention that our scientific deductions must begin from definitions that state the forms of natural kinds. For Aristotle's four 'causes' are

---

[88] Rynhold, *Two Models of Jewish Philosophy*, 16.

not four different ontological causes, but are rather four different ways of referring to the two ontological factors that are fundamental to explanation for Aristotle: form and matter. The material cause refers to the matter and the other three causes refer to the notion of form in differing ways. This latter concept of form is the fundamental explanatory concept in Aristotelian science and is the essential nature of a substance that accounts for its being what it is. Indeed, according to Aristotle the fundamental explanatory premises of science are simply definitions that state what the forms of the various substances are. That Maimonides shares the same fundamental position is clear from the very first chapter of the *Guide* where he writes in his explanation of the term 'image' as predicated of God: 'The term image . . . is applied to the natural form, I mean the notion *in virtue of which a thing is constituted as a substance and becomes what it is*' [*Guide* i. 22].[89]

Rynhold discusses Maimonides' reasons for the commandments in terms of their final cause, which he takes to be the perfection of man, or, since the causes are ways of referring to form, the form of man, that which makes human beings human.

To sum up, the two criteria for explanatory knowledge of the commandments such as would reveal them as necessary are that they should derive axiomatically from first principles, and that they should embody the form of man, or, conflating these two criteria, the commandments should derive from the form of man.

Rynhold seeks to apply these criteria to the exposition of the reasons for the commandments in the *Guide*, positing that the general aims of the commandments cited there, namely, perfection of the soul, perfection of the body, and restraint of desire, outline the form of man. In the end, however, he candidly concedes that the criteria remain unfulfilled, and for the reason I have discussed, namely, that the particulars of the commandments are not in fact derivable from the general principles in the *Guide*, but are instead explained by historical contingencies, so that

it seems fair to say that the form of man does not uniquely determine a specific law or set of laws. The Torah is underdetermined by the form of man in a way that would not allow us to deduce the Torah in all its specificity from the mere positing of that form as its *telos*. But this means that we cannot construct an Aristotelian scientific demonstration of the Torah: there is no necessary deductive chain that leads us from the purpose of man to the commandments.[90]

Rynhold does suggest some ways around this, but it seems simpler to allow that the *Guide*, as a summa, is not aiming at this kind of axiomatic demonstra-

---

[89] Rynhold, *Two Models of Jewish Philosophy*. 16; the emphasis is Rynhold's.   [90] Ibid. 29.

tion at all. *Mishneh torah*, on the other hand, fits Rynhold's model perfectly. There, the form of man is the form of the cosmos, and the form of the cosmos is the form of the commandments. The purpose of the commandments is to translate God's governance of the world into God-like self-governance on the part of those who observe them. There is no gap between rules and their purposes that needs to be filled by resort to historical contingencies. Hence *Mishneh torah* makes the problem of the particulars of the commandments disappear. Making a problem disappear is not the same as solving it; if we really insist on knowing the origin of, for example, the prohibition on wearing a wool and linen blend, we have to refer to the *Guide*. The point, though, is that under *Mishneh torah*'s axiom method, this question is not of very much interest, is in fact intrusive, because our attention is absorbed by the relationship between the commandment and the formal pattern, just as, for example, someone playing chess is absorbed by the relationships between the way a piece moves, the state of the game, and the ultimate object of capturing the opponent's king, and is not interested in how the move may have originated in games played in Persia and India centuries ago, fascinating as he or she might find that information when in another frame of mind. Considered this way, as a relational system, *Mishneh torah* satisfies the criterion of Aristotelian explanation: the commandments are fully determined by the microcosmic form of man. The form finds material causes that make it manifest, but the origins of these are not on our horizon.

Of course something is missing. Where is the stack of syllogisms leading from the structure of the cosmos (which is the form of man) to the commandments? We have no access to it. It belongs to the unique prophecy of Moses and his supreme insight into God's governance of the world. What *Mishneh torah* presents instead is a symbolic representation, substituting poetic syllogism for demonstrative syllogism, using a schematic model of the universe to refer to Moses' perfect, explanatory knowledge, and the way the commandments issue from it.

Similar considerations apply when we look at the dynamic, Neoplatonic aspect of *Mishneh torah*'s form. The first principle, stated in the very first *halakhah*, is the knowledge of God's existence. This is another version of the form of man, since it is through 'true opinions concerning the divine things' that 'man is man'.[91] There follows a series of quasi-Euclidian propositions

---

[91] *Guide* iii. 54 (p. 635). On the basis of the thesis proposed in Chapter 1, that the realization of man's microcosmic form actually constitutes knowledge of God, the two versions are really two ways of expressing the same thing.

demonstrating God's incorporeality, unity, and unique knowledge. This style seems confined to *Mishneh torah*'s opening, fading away within a chapter or two, but in fact the axiomatic opening announces the form of argument of the work as a whole, and the series continues, not through demonstrative logic but through poetic logic (reinforced by the thematic links between books noted in the previous chapter), the structure acting as a model of emanation and thus as a metaphor for axiomatic derivation. The mimesis of emanation is assurance that the commandments follow from the knowledge of God's existence with a deductive inevitability that matches the emanation of the spheres from the first existence,[92] even though, again, the process of deduction may be beyond everyone bar Moses.

Here, too, there is no causal explanation accessible to us of the particulars of the commandments, and here too, the problem disappears. The poetic logic of *Mishneh torah* gives us no objective, communicable knowledge of how the action of waving a palm branch once a year derives from the knowledge of God's existence. It does give a sense of the way in which, as the basis of the commandments and their ultimate object, the knowledge of God charges all of them with significance. The knowledge of God's existence is the whole of which the commandments emanating from it are parts: in this sense, the commandments *are* knowledge of God's existence, fractured into temporal manifestations by the encounter with matter, and leading back, in the human mind, to the original unity. The endowment of the commandments with significance through their unification under a single object absorbs our interest, to the exclusion of the question of the origins of their particulars. We can test this by seeing what happens if the object is changed—in fact we have already seen it, in the *Shulḥan arukh*, which, by adopting the service of God rather than the knowledge of God as the object of the commandments,[93] alters the significance of each of them, although all their particulars remain the same. Again, the relation of the details to the object is the focus; their origins are beside the point.

To sum up, the form of *Mishneh torah* looks back to the derivation of the commandments in the prophecy of Moses, which, as far as Maimonides is

---

[92] Not with complete inevitability, since both nature and the commandments are products of God's will as well as his wisdom—see n. 74 above. In fact, prophecy transcends even demonstrative syllogistic reasoning: see pp. 347–9 below.

[93] Taking its cue from Jacob ben Asher's *Arba'ah turim*, which opens with a discussion of the character traits required of those who would serve God. Compare 'Laws of Ethical Qualities', which is about the character traits required of those who would know God. This is not to deny that the idea of service has its importance in Maimonides too—see e.g. ch. 10 of 'Laws of Repentance'.

concerned, is an objective fact, and also forward to the realization of the form of man in those who study and observe them, which is experienced subjectively. Neither of these things is a subject for normal discourse: the first because of its inaccessibility; the second because of its very subjectivity. Both can only be expressed poetically.

Twersky and Soloveitchik: Subjective Rationalization

The idea of subjectivity brings us to the views of Twersky and Soloveitchik on Maimonides' treatment of the rationalization of the commandments.

Subjectivity is the distinguishing feature that Twersky sees in the rationalizations of specific commandments found in *Mishneh torah*. Throughout his writings on that work, he encourages sensitivity to the ethical and philosophical promptings that transform it from a manual of law into an education in a way of living and being.[94] He focuses on individual commandments in respect of which Maimonides, subtly or forthrightly, urges some ethical point or provides some insight. Since these reflections are intermittent, Twersky determines that jurisprudence still has priority over philosophy in *Mishneh torah*. All the same, the relationship between a commandment and its reason that he describes in specific cases is the same as the general relationship between commandments and their rationalization elucidated here. The meaning of the law emerges from the law as the fragrance from the flower. He is clear that, in *Mishneh torah* and the *Guide*, we are dealing with two different sorts of reasoning, discerning 'two kinds of rationality and intelligibility, with their different levels of meaningfulness and impact, historical and abstract or experiential and immediate'.[95] The experiential kind of meaningfulness that Twersky finds in *Mishneh torah* shares characteristics with poetic/axiomatic form as defined above. As mentioned, it is subjective: 'Halakah, of course, is uniform in its objective determinacy, but the experience accompanying its implementation is quite variable in its subjective understanding.'[96] It also emerges from the commandment rather than preceding it—as Twersky remarks of Maimonides' strictures on the duty to involve the poor and unfortunate in one's rejoicing on festivals:[97] 'This is a particularly clear illustration of how moral insights and imperatives may be *elicited* from formal law.'[98]

---

[94] 'The primary concern of the *Mishneh Torah* with explanations that revolve around ethical-intellectual motifs—law as an educating-edifying force—as distinct from the *Moreh*'s concern with all kinds of intelligibility and rationality, is the crux of the issue' (Twersky, *Introduction to the Code*, 432).

[95] Ibid. 437.   [96] Ibid.

[97] See 'Laws of Resting on Festivals', 6: 18; 'Laws of the Festal Offering', 2: 14.

[98] Twersky, *Introduction to the Code*, 423 (italics original).

Soloveitchik contrasts the *Guide* and *Mishneh torah* in a very similar way, and aligns the difference between them with what he sees as two different approaches to explanations in science: a summative approach, going from the parts to the whole, and a structural approach, going from the whole to the parts, which of course matches our definitions of the summa and axiom modes of argument.[99]

Soloveitchik's definition of the summative method and its application to the *Guide* conforms closely to the description given above; there is nothing important to add. It is worth dwelling, however, on his comments on the method of *Mishneh torah*, where, like Twersky, he resorts to individual examples. The main example he selects is the reason Maimonides gives for the blowing of the *shofar* (ram's horn) on Rosh Hashanah, which is that it is a hint, a wake-up call to repentance.[100] Soloveitchik distinguishes the idea of a 'hint' from the kind of reason found in the *Guide* thus:

The distinction between them is the same as that between the methods of objectification and reconstruction. By establishing the cause, one objectifies the datum and subordinates it to a superior order. However, by exploring the norm retrospectively through vectorial hints which point toward subjectivity, the religious act with its unique structure retains its full autonomy ... The call to repent could have been realized in many ways and there is no necessary reason why the Torah selected the means of the sounding of the shofar. Hence the message of repentance, which for Maimonides is implied in the sounding of the shofar, cannot serve as the cause of the commandment that would assure it a status of necessity, but it must be apprehended rather as an allusion to a correlated subjective aspect.[101]

As with Twersky, the key feature of *Mishneh torah*'s approach to the reason for this commandment in Soloveitchik's view, in contradistinction to the *Guide*'s causal approach, is emergence: the rule precedes its reason, which emanates from it, and is appreciated subjectively.

The outcome, at least in the cases cited by these two thinkers, is that *Mishneh torah*'s method of rationalizing the commandments individually reproduces its method of rationalizing them collectively, a further aspect of its organic nature. The collective rationalization of the commandments in *Mishneh torah* is, like the response to the sound of the ram's horn, a correlated subjective aspect of its form. The perceived rationality of the commandments will depend on how well the form's 'vectorial hints' are absorbed. But the

[99] See J. B. Soloveitchik, *The Halakhic Mind*, 55–61.
[100] 'Laws of Repentance', 3: 4. See above, Ch. 3, n. 160.
[101] J. B. Soloveitchik, *The Halakhic Mind*, 95–6.

form does more than this. By chaining the commandments to the object of knowledge of God, it confers 'a status of necessity' that the emergent reason for an individual commandment, considered by itself, fails to confer. The status is not of absolute necessity. As we are told in the very first *halakhah* of *Mishneh torah*, that status belongs to God alone, and besides, Abraham managed without most of the commandments, and so did the Children of Israel in the wilderness at first, as we saw above. It is a status of formal necessity, in the way that a detail of a work of art is formally necessary.

Mishneh Torah on Its Own Method

This dual reference of the microcosmic form, to the objective but unreachable cause of the commandments and to their palpable but subjective effects, is reflected in the discussion of the idea of reasons of the commandments in *Mishneh torah* itself:

> Although the statutes of the Torah are decrees, as we explained at the end of "Laws of Trespass", it is fitting to contemplate them, and whatever you can give a reason for, give it a reason . . . And most of the laws of the Torah are nothing but counsels from afar from the one who is great in counsel, to right our character traits and to straighten our deeds.[102]

The commandments remain decrees and counsels from afar in the sense that we cannot repeat the Mosaic experience. They reach us from afar to right our character and our deeds in that they realize the microcosmic form of man. As for the reasons that Maimonides envisages that we might give the commandments, these are not, I would suggest, the objective, antiquarian ones of the *Guide*, but rather Soloveitchik's subjective correlatives, to which Maimonides often shows the way, as in the case of the ram's horn, but which are left to each individual to reach in accordance with his or her capacity. In other words, this *halakhah* is the *Mishneh torah*'s methodology in a nutshell.

Echoes of the *Book of the Commandments*

It was suggested above that, in the way it organizes the commandments, the *Guide* exhibits similarities to the *Book of the Commandments*, and that this indicates a consistent literary divide, involving a difference of logical method, between an Arabic mode and a Hebrew mode in Maimonides' writings. Let us now fill out that suggestion by listing some features that the *Book of the Commandments* and the *Guide* share, in contradistinction to *Mishneh torah*.

Like the *Guide*, the *Book of the Commandments* examines and marshals the

---

[102] 'Laws of Substituted Offerings', 4: 13.

facts in the light of pre-announced principles; in its case, the fourteen criteria set out in its introduction. In accordance with those criteria, it labels statements of the Torah as commandment or not commandment, although it only records the former category, those imperative statements that make the grade. To that extent, the *Book of the Commandments* exhibits a characteristic of the summa method.

Next, the way in which the *Book of the Commandments* groups commandments bears comparison with the classification in the *Guide*, as though *Mishneh torah* has been leapfrogged. For example, the commandment 'to swear in his name'[103] is mentioned very early in both the *Book of the Commandments* and the *Guide*. It is positive commandment number 7 in the *Book of the Commandments*, while in the *Guide* it is placed in the first class, and is the second specific commandment mentioned in that class, after a general reference to 'the opinions that we have enumerated in 'Laws of the Foundations of the Torah', and the commandment to honour the bearers of the law.[104] In *Mishneh torah* this commandment comes in 'Laws of Oaths',[105] which is in the *Book of Asseverations*, book 6, a long way from the foundational commandment to know God's existence with which *Mishneh torah*, like the *Book of the Commandments* and the *Guide* (through the reference to 'Laws of the Foundations of the Torah'), begins.

Now in all three of its appearances, in *The Book of the Commandments*, in the *Guide*, and in 'Laws of Oaths' as well, this commandment is given the same reason, namely, that it glorifies God. In the *Guide* the classification is determined by the reason (not surprisingly, since 'reasons for the commandments' is the overt subject there), and the same appears to hold true for the *Book of the Commandments*. There is a general storyline that is consistent between those two works, even though one or two components differ, but it is just that, a story, not an axiomatic series: God exists, so we should love and fear him, pray to him and cleave to his adherents (in the *Book of the Commandments*), honour the bearers of his law (in the *Guide*),[106] glorify him by swearing in his name, cry to him in distress (in the *Guide*),[107] and so on. *Mishneh torah* too begins with God's existence and the commandments to love and fear him, but discusses the subsequent commandments in the above list in separate places, thereby giving them somewhat different orientations. The classifica-

---

[103] Based upon Deut. 10: 20.   [104] *Guide* iii. 36 (p. 539).   [105] 11: 1.

[106] In *The Book of the Commandments* this is positive commandment 209, but clearly cleaving to God's adherents and honouring the bearers of God's law are very similar notions.

[107] Again, crying to God in distress and praying to him have much in common.

tion of the commandment to swear in God's name is determined not by its reason but by its legal character, so that we find it in 'Laws of Oaths'.[108]

Two further examples of commandments in respect of which *The Book of the Commandments* and the *Guide* are arrayed in opposition to *Mishneh torah* are the prohibition on wearing mixed stuff (a blend of wool and linen), and circumcision. In both the *Book of the Commandments*[109] and the *Guide*,[110] the prohibition on wearing mixed stuff is found among laws to do with avoiding idolatrous practices, the reason given for it in both places being that pagan priests wore such garments, whereas in *Mishneh torah* it is to be found in 'Laws of Diverse Kinds', in the *Book of Agriculture*, with no reason given for it. As for circumcision, it is a very good tracer of literary form, because two reasons are suggested for it in the *Guide*: that it damps sexual desire, and that it is a sign of God's unity.[111] The classification in the *Guide* is in accordance with the first, prosaic, functional, reason, as it is in the *Book of the Commandments*, where circumcision is found among commandments to do with sexual relations.[112] In *Mishneh torah* it is placed at the end of the *Book of Love*, which is all about commandments that are constant reminders of correct doctrine, that is, in accordance with the second, symbolic reason.

This is not haphazard. At the jurisprudential level, *Mishneh torah* adopts the method of the Mishnah, which is a 'hub and spoke' method whereby commandments cluster about a halakhic concept that they have in common, or from which they ramify (hence the prohibition on wearing mixed stuff is attached to the concept of diversity), as opposed to a linear sequence determined by narrative or associative connections, which is what we find in the *Book of the Commandments* and, I think, also in the *Guide*.[113]

Another feature that the *Book of the Commandments* and the *Guide* share is that in each of them the material causes of the commandments are prominent. It is true that in Chapter 2 I said that the *Book of the Commandments* treats the commandments as form, conceptualizing them in order to decide when similar imperatives in the Torah express the same idea and should therefore be counted as a single commandment. To that extent, the *Book of the Commandments* indeed points towards the organizational method of *Mishneh torah*. In its groupings of commandments, however, the *Book of the Commandments* looks more at their matter than their form. For example, as noted in the Introduction, it brings together negative commandments concerning food,

---

[108] On this, see also Twersky, *Introduction to the Code*, 304.
[109] Negative commandment 42.   [110] iii. 37 (p. 544).   [111] iii. 49 (p. 609).
[112] Positive commandment 215.   [113] See above, Introduction, n. 4.

regardless of the different ideas behind them. Among these are the commandments forbidding the *nazir* to consume wine or grapes in any form.[114] In the *Guide*, too, these commandments are grouped with laws about food, in the thirteenth class of commandments.[115] Now the discussion of this class, as is made clear in the preamble to it, follows the order of the *Book of Holiness* and the *Book of Asseverations* in *Mishneh torah*: laws about food, followed by vows, that is, extra, self-imposed prohibitions, followed by the nazirite. The subtle difference is that *Mishneh torah* lists the laws of the nazirite under the rubric of the formal category of vows, whereas the particular chapter of the *Guide* in question discusses vows and the nazirite under the rubric of the material category of food, and omits 'Laws of Oaths', with which the *Book of Asseverations* opens, and which is to do with uttering binding statements, but not with food.[116] Circumcision marks this distinction too, being classed according to its material aspect in the *Book of the Commandments* and the *Guide*, and according to its formal aspect in *Mishneh torah*; and clearly, in the discussion of the laws of the Temple and sacrifices in the *Guide*, it is their material manifestations that are the points of departure. Moreover, in discussing dual-purpose commandments such as circumcision and the sabbath and festivals, the *Guide* tends to put the moral, social, or political reason first and the spiritual/intellectual reason second, even when, in the case of circumcision, it actually states that the commandment's second, spiritual purpose, to be a reminder of God's unity, is 'perhaps . . . even stronger than the first', the diminution of sexual desire. In general, then, if a commandment comprises form and matter, *Mishneh torah*, on the whole, proceeds from form to matter, and thus tends to group commandments according to their formal causes, whereas the *Book of the Commandments* and the *Guide*, on the whole, proceed from matter to form, and thus tend to group commandments according to their material causes.

The examples, and the theorizing, could be pursued almost endlessly, but we have seen enough to justify the contention that, in certain respects, the *Book of the Commandments* and the *Guide* have more in common with each other than either has with *Mishneh torah*, that the features they share belong to summa form, and that it is therefore legitimate to speak of a divide between

---

[114] Negative commandments 202–6.   [115] *Guide* iii. 48 (pp. 598–601).

[116] Interestingly in this context, *The Book of the Commandments* places the particular undertakings of the nazirite to grow his hair during his period of naziritehood and to shave his head at the end of it (positive commandments 92 and 93) *before* the general commandment to observe one's vows (positive commandment 94), which is quite the opposite of the treatment in *Mishneh torah*—see 'Laws of Vows', 1: 4.

an Arabic/discursive/summative mode and a Hebrew/poetic/axiomatic mode
that runs throughout Maimonides' great enterprise of identifying, codifying,
and justifying the commandments.

Artificial versus Natural

In the Introduction it was suggested that a work of art can be considered to be
an artificial object that aspires to the condition of a natural object. As a work
of art, *Mishneh torah* treats the commandments as natural objects, whereas
the *Guide* treats them more as artificial objects. The *Guide* tries to put us into
the mind of God the artificer, purposefully designing commandments to
meet certain ends that he has in view, using the materials to hand.[117] The reasons for the commandments can then be analysed as causes. In *Mishneh torah*
the mind extracts reasons from the commandments, individually and collectively, as it extracts forms from nature. *Mishneh torah*'s artistic form is therefore not a matter of presentation only, of a picture being worth a thousand of
the *Guide*'s words, but is integral to a specific mode of comprehension.

Limitations

We must straightaway hedge this in some important ways. First of all, the distinction between the *Guide* and *Mishneh torah* is not absolute. For example,
when the *Guide* comes to consider the reason for the blowing of the ram's
horn, the very example that Soloveitchik uses to distinguish the two works, it
simply provides a reference to *Mishneh torah*.[118] The reason given in the *Guide*
for the ritual of the scapegoat on the Day of Atonement is that 'these actions
are parables serving to bring forth a form in the soul so that a passion toward
repentance should result'.[119] One could not wish for a more succinct description of the method of *Mishneh torah* than 'to bring forth a form in the soul'.
The explanation in *Mishneh torah* of the prohibition on shaving 'the corners
of the beard', that it arises from the practice of pagan priests,[120] is of the *Guide*
type,[121] and we have seen that the explanation of the commandment 'to swear
in his name' is uniform in the *Book of the Commandments*, *Mishneh torah*, and
the *Guide*.

---

[117] As Rynhold notes—see *Two Models of Jewish Philosophy*, 36.   [118] See *Guide* iii. 43 (p. 571).
[119] *Guide* iii. 46 (p. 591).   [120] See 'Laws of Idolatry', 12: 1 and 7.
[121] It has a cross-reference in *Guide* iii. 37 (p. 544). Actually, the rule probably passes the test of this
exception, because the reason that the origin of the commandment not to shave the corners of the
head is mentioned in 'Laws of Idolatry' is not to justify the commandment itself so much as to justify
its inclusion in that section, so that the orientation is still towards the commandment's formal affilia-
tion rather than towards its material cause.

In Chapter 3 I pointed out that 'Laws of Diverse Kinds' is essentially about countering idolatry, and that it bears a similar relationship to the subsequent section, 'Laws of Gifts to the Poor', as 'Laws of the Foundations of the Torah' bears to 'Laws of Ethical Qualities', so that the reason for the prohibition on wearing mixed stuff implied by its placement in 'Laws of Diverse Kinds' is the same as the reason given explicitly in the *Guide*. But this is the point: a reason that emerges poetically, or, in our newly adopted terminology, axiomatically, from structure, versus a reason explained discursively. The reason for swearing in God's name given in 'Laws of Oaths' was seen in Chapter 2 as having a converse role, in that it bestows spiritual significance on the commandments collected under it in that section, enabling their connections to the theme of the knowledge of God to emerge. All in all, as far as reasons for the commandments are concerned, there is no rigorous segregation between *Mishneh torah* and the *Guide* at the level of detail; it is the structure of explanation that is distinct in each case. The difference is not so much a matter of reasons as of reasoning.

Secondly, and more importantly, the foregoing analysis puts a temporary frame around the treatment of the reasons of the commandments in chapters 35 to 49 of Part III of the *Guide*, which is valid and fair for the purposes of comparing the classification of the commandments in that book with the classification in *Mishneh torah*, but clearly does not do justice to the *Guide* as a whole. The symbolism of *Mishneh torah*'s structure integrates *ma'aseh merkavah* and *ma'aseh bereshit* with the commandments through the number fourteen. This entire discussion of the differences between *Mishneh torah*'s and the *Guide*'s classifications was sparked by noticing that they had the number fourteen in common. It could be that in the *Guide* this number only signifies *ratio* in the abstract, and is there simply to certify the rationality of the commandments. Certainly, in the immediate context, it does not appear to have the same reverberations as in *Mishneh torah*. Since, however, the *Guide* is largely about *ma'aseh merkavah* and *ma'aseh bereshit*, and particularly since its third part, where the reasons of the commandments are found, opens with the *merkavah* vision, we ought to consider whether the presence of the number fourteen does not indicate that we should examine how the whole of the *Guide* bears on the reasons for the commandments, and especially what the sequence of topics leading from the explication of Ezekiel's vision of the *merkavah* up to the 'reasons' section, via the discussions of providence, God's knowledge versus human knowledge, and the trials of Job and Abraham, might signify.

Moreover, the *Guide*'s treatment of the reasons for the commandments does not end with the fourteen classes and the political approach of which they form the basis. For on the large scale, too, the *Guide* goes from matter to form, from a largely moral and social justification of the commandments to something that is almost the opposite. Chapters 50 to 53 of Part III go on to mention the mysteries of the Torah, and then, via the parable of the palace and the various grades of proximity to the ruler, to recommend the commandments as spiritual exercises, and as a means of coming nearer to the ruler's presence. In short, the *Guide*'s rationalization of the commandments should be read completely and in context.

Our temporary manoeuvre has, however, achieved its main objects, which were to distinguish two meanings of rationalization, and to highlight an additional aspect of *Mishneh torah*'s artistic integration. In the axiomatic method of *Mishneh torah*, rationalization means a demonstration of formal necessity, while in the summa method of the *Guide*, rationalization means a demonstration of reasonableness. And as in the classification of the commandments, so too in the rationalization of the commandments, the structure of the whole reflects the structure of the parts. *Mishneh torah*'s general structure reflects the same priority of form over matter as exists in the structure of the individual commandment. Similarly, the kind of rationalization of the commandments as a whole implicit in that general structure reflects the method applied to individual commandments. We have two organic systems, one of classification and the other of rationalization, and the latter is born out of the former. *Mishneh torah*'s form is truly a matrix.

On the question of integration, we have also seen that *Mishneh torah*'s form incorporates the mysteries of the Torah and the idea of the commandments as a spiritual ladder that the prophet ascends, topics that, as we saw just now, are discussed successively in the *Guide*. It turns out, then, that *Mishneh torah* displays two of the literary forms of medieval philosophy at once: axiom and allegory. The man–God books represent a ladder that is a metaphor for axiomatic derivation on the way down, that is, when they are read from first to last, and an allegory of the prophet's progress on the way up when they are read from last to first.

From here we can proceed directly to two further questions about the commandments: their authority, and their intelligibility, not in the sense of a commandment having its particular utility explained, but in the more technical, philosophical sense of the body of the commandments being an object of knowledge.

The Problem of Authority

Josef Stern has pointed out that the explanations that Maimonides proffers for the commandments in the *Guide* answer 'the commandment question', 'explaining or demonstrating the rationality of God's legislation', but do not necessarily answer 'the performance question', 'furnishing reasons that a human agent can use to justify his own performance of the commandments'.[122] In cases where the commandment question is answered, as in the *Guide* it often is, by the need to counter an ancient pagan practice, the reason for continued performance remains unclear, to say the least. There is little trace in Maimonides of the covenantal theme of the Bible, and Stern remarks that, altogether, 'we are told disappointingly little about positive grounds of obligation'. He does, however, make a suggestion:

Or perhaps Maimonides' idea is that individual practices should not, and (in some cases) cannot, be justified or be shown to be obligatory each in isolation, taken one by one, but only derivatively as part of the Torah or Prophetic Tradition as a whole, which itself, to borrow a phrase of Quine, faces the tribunal of justification as a single corporate body. Thus the grounds for one's obligation to obey the Torah are not the sum total of the isolable obligations of its component commandments, but the other way around: individual commandments are obligatory only insofar as they belong to the Law as a whole which 'distributes' its 'holistic' justification among its parts.[123]

In *Mishneh torah* this is precisely Maimonides' idea. A fundamental feature of our axiom model of its form is that the parts derive their significance and force from the whole. The cosmic form presents the law of the Torah as a relational system. Even laws, such as the prohibition against murder, that are accepted in any civilized society, are to be obeyed not because of their utility, which would give them independent validity, but because they are part of the law of Moses. No halakhah escapes the boundary of the system, just as no entity in the universe has independent motion.[124] The concept of the law as microcosm justifies the application of Quine's phrase rather literally, since the microcosm idea is introduced in the *Guide* by a comparison of the unity of the cosmos to the unity of the human body,[125] so that it is very apt to think of the law as 'a single corporate body'.

---

[122] Stern, 'The Idea of a Hoq', 93.   [123] Ibid. 121.

[124] 'Such is the belief of the multitude of the men of knowledge in our Law, and this was explicitly stated by our prophets: namely, that the particulars of natural acts are all well arranged and ordered and bound up with one another, all of them being causes and effects; and that none of them is futile or frivolous or vain, being acts of perfect wisdom' (*Guide* iii. 25, 505). For a detailed application of this to Maimonides' exposition of halakhah, see Hadad, 'The Relationship between Nature and Torah'.

[125] See *Guide* i. 72 (p. 184–94).

Moreover, the Aristotelian superstructure and Neoplatonic infrastructure of *Mishneh torah* answer Stern's requirements very well. The first assembles its parts into a whole; the second distributes the justification of the whole, the imperative to know God, among the parts. In Neoplatonic terms, the One is in the All, and the All is in the One.

Ultimately, the law compels because the law is rational, not just in the sense of being internally coherent (legal systems mostly are), or of containing provisions to which most reasonable human beings would consent, but because, taken as a whole, it represents rationality as such, the rationality of the cosmos, which is what a rational person seeks to reproduce in him- or herself.

The Practical Commandments and Cognition

The question whether Maimonides considered the practical realm to be cognitive has already been answered, in the affirmative, in Chapter 1, where it was suggested that moral virtue could constitute knowledge of God. The present discussion presents an opportunity to tackle the same question from a different angle. We shall begin here with a strong hint from 'Laws of the Foundations of the Torah', 2: 2. In proposing the study of physics and metaphysics as a means of cultivating the love and fear of God, Maimonides signs off with a quotation from Midrash: 'For through that, you recognize the one who spoke and the world was.' In fact, this saying of the sages does not refer to the study of the universe, but to meditation on the commandments.[126] It exists in various versions, but the version of *Sifrei* is as follows:

And these words, which I command thee this day, shall be upon thine heart (Deut. 6: 6). Rabbi (Judah the Prince) says: Why did Moses say this? Because Scripture says, *And thou shalt love the Lord, thy God, with all thy heart* (Deut. 6: 5). I do not know how one is to love God. Hence Scripture goes on to say, *And these words, which I command thee this day, shall be in thine heart*, meaning, take these words to heart, for thus will you recognize Him who spoke, and the world came into being, and you will cling to his ways.[127]

In the *Book of the Commandments*, positive commandment 3—which instructs us to love God—Maimonides cites this very passage from *Sifrei*. There, he adheres more closely to the original sense, for he is talking about contemplating God's commandments, but he adds contemplation of God's works, creating equivalence between the two. By the time we reach 'Laws of the Foundations of the Torah', the *midrash* has been fully converted to being

---

[126] This is a noted discrepancy: see Kreisel, *Maimonides' Political Thought*, 227–8.

[127] *Sifrei* on Deut. 6: 6 (*Sifre*, trans. Hammer, 62).

about the contemplation of nature, but the intention is surely not to deny that the commandments are an object of contemplation; rather, it is to leave that as a suggestion for those who recognize the source, and to express it more fully in *Mishneh torah*'s form. The *midrash* itself is certainly open to interpretation as indicating equivalence between the form of the commandments and the form of nature, since it refers to the God who will be recognized through study of the commandments as 'Him who spoke, and the world came into being', and moreover it points to phase two of the relationship between intellectual virtue and moral virtue (as discussed in Chapter 1), in which ethical behaviour flows from theoretical knowledge, since the result of the recognition of 'Him who spoke, and the world came into being' is that 'you will cling to his ways'. There is much Maimonidean potential in this *midrash*.[128]

In the light of the discussion in Chapter 1 on man as microcosm, there is the possibility that performance of the commandments has intrinsic value in that it aligns the mind with a permanent form, and thus secures immortality, at least at some level. As for knowing the Torah, that earns the world to come because, by Maimonides' definition, it includes physics and metaphysics.[129] Could it also count as an intelligible form?

This question is closely related to the rationality and necessity of the commandments, and, in an article on the matter, Daniel Rynhold applies to it the same Aristotelian model of form and matter that we saw him applying to the reasons for the commandments. To meet Aristotelian standards of intelligibility, a phenomenon must be traceable to non-demonstrable first principles. 'What though is the nature of the first principles of such an Aristotelian science? The concept that does the necessary work here for Aristotle is that of form, the fundamental concept in Aristotelian science.'[130] He repeats the idea that, in the *Guide*, by relating the commandments to the welfare of the body and the welfare of the soul that constitute human perfection, Maimonides provides a connection between them and the form of man, thus rendering them intelligible.

An important plank in the argument for the cognitive status of the practical commandments in Maimonides is his distinction between a *nomos*, which has regard only for the welfare of the body, and a divine law, which has

---

[128] Maimonides cuts short the citation of the *midrash* in 'Laws of the Foundations of the Torah', 2: 2, omitting 'and cling to his ways', presumably because it does not serve his purpose in this *halakhah*, since the concept of God's ways, which in the context of the *midrash* fairly clearly means God's commandments, is to be interpreted in 'Laws of Ethical Qualities' as God's actions in nature.

[129] 'Laws of Torah Study', 1: 12. See Kasher, 'The Study of Torah' (Heb.); id., 'Torah as a Means of Achieving the World to Come' (Heb.).   [130] Rynhold, 'Good and Evil', 171.

regard for ultimate truths. In a divine law the end transforms the means, so that the moral injunctions of the divine law are different in kind from those of a *nomos*. Rynhold draws the following conclusion:

What this means is that we can acknowledge that the intellect proper is the theoretical intellect that deals with truth and falsehood and maybe indeed only directly cognises the forms that are its object. However, we can raise the status of our cognition in the practical sphere to that of knowledge by drawing out the relationship of these practical matters to the form of man that serves as their end.[131]

Again, although Rynhold's argument relates to the *Guide*, the standard of intelligibility he cites is actually better met in *Mishneh torah*, which is more thoroughly imbued with the form of man. Insofar as man is, or is capable of becoming, a microcosm, the form of *Mishneh torah* relates the practical commandments to the form of man, which serves as their end.

So rather than to a mystical, quasi-Platonic, pre-Creation *adam elyon*, Maimonides relates the commandments to a form of man that is Aristotelian, immanent, and natural. At the same time as *Mishneh torah* models the way in which the commandments bestow knowledge by realizing the form of human beings, its artistry bestows knowledge of the commandments themselves, by disclosing their form. Since, for Maimonides, knowledge arouses love, *Mishneh torah*, considered as a work of art, can be seen as being meant to induce the performance of the commandments out of love, entirely in keeping with *Sifrei*.

Why Is 'Laws of Mourning' Where It Is?

I return now to the historical dimension and to the loss-and-restoration pattern, in an attempt to solve a well-known puzzle in *Mishneh torah*'s structure: the position of 'Laws of Mourning' as the penultimate section before 'Laws of Kings and Their Wars'. The section appears so strangely out of place, interposed between laws about courts of justice and about kings, that it has been suggested that it is futile to look for an explanation and that its position came about by default.[132]

Actually, Maimonides took care to attach 'Laws of Mourning' to the preceding and following sections. In the preamble listing the commandments

---

[131] Ibid. 177. On the distinction between divine law and *nomos*, Rynhold cites Kreisel, *Maimonides' Political Thought*.

[132] See H. Soloveitchik, 'Thoughts on Maimonides' Categorization'. Moshe Halbertal nevertheless proposes a solution, based on the perception that mourning, in Maimonides' view, is not so much to salve the grief of the bereaved as to honour the dead—see *Maimonides* (Heb.), 204–9. I do not believe that this is incompatible with the solution that is proposed here.

covered in the section, he states: 'To mourn for relatives, and even a priest defiles himself and mourns for relatives. And a person does not mourn for those executed by the court. And because of this I included these laws in this book, for they concern burial on the day of death, which is a positive commandment.'[133]

Execution of offenders by the court is an important subject generally in the *Book of Judges*. 'Laws of Rebels', the section that immediately precedes 'Laws of Mourning', concerns two such offenders: the rebellious elder and the rebellious son. We should note, if we are looking for continuity, that with the rebellious son the view switches from the wide angle of the state to zoom in on the family, which is the basis of 'Laws of Mourning'.

At the other end of 'Laws of Mourning' the lens angle widens again, for we find a description of the burial rites for kings,[134] a clear lead into 'Laws of Kings and Their Wars'.

Twersky sees Maimonides' explanation for the inclusion of mourning laws in the *Book of Judges* quoted above as 'enigmatic and forced',[135] and perhaps it is. There are two ways of looking at this. We could take the hooks that Maimonides contrives at each end of 'Laws of Mourning' as improvisations making up for the lack of any real logical connection, and as amounting to an admission that the section does not really belong where it is, or we could take them as indicating that, despite the apparent incongruity, the juxtaposition of 'Laws of Mourning' with 'Laws of Rebels' and 'Laws of Kings and Their Wars' is deliberate, and that we should try to discover deeper reasons for it.

'Laws of Mourning' can be seen as a *memento mori*. That would make it suitable for last position, but since it would be uncharacteristic of Maimonides to end on such a note, and since 'Laws of Kings and Their Wars' in any

---

[133] Note that all four of the commandments listed, of which this is the first, refer to mourning priests and the circumstances in which they may and may not become defiled by contact with the dead. The laws of mourning hinge upon the laws of cleanness and uncleanness. This will be of importance later in the discussion. Cf. *The Book of the Commandments*, positive commandment 37, where the general obligation to mourn for deceased relatives is derived through an *a fortiori* argument from the particular obligation of the priest to defile himself in order to bury and mourn for the relatives specified in the Torah. In *Mishneh torah* the biblical origin of the commandment of mourning is given as Aaron's refusal to partake of sacrifices after the death of his two eldest sons ('Laws of Mourning', 1: 1), again linking mourning to the priesthood. See Kaplan, 'Unity of Maimonides' Religious Thought'. Kaplan uses the derivation of mourning from the laws about priests and defilement to find the apparently missing reference to mourning in the *Guide* among the laws about the priesthood (*Guide* iii. 47 (p. 596)). His thesis tends to reinforce the argument that the positioning of 'Laws of Mourning' is deliberate, for it shows that this subject could easily have been incorporated into the *Book of Temple Service* or the *Book of Purity*. Halbertal too draws attention to this feature.

[134] 'Laws of Mourning', 14: 25–6.   [135] Twersky, *Introduction to the Code*, 286.

case has other claims to come last, with its ending on the fulfilment of the longing for the age of the king messiah, next to last is appropriate.[136] As I noted previously, in 'Laws of Kings and Their Wars' it is stressed that nature will undergo no change with the advent of the messiah: *olam keminhago holekh*,[137] the world runs its normal course. In 'Laws of Mourning' Maimonides hints at what that implies, for, inveighing against excessive mourning, he uses similar language: death is *minhago shel olam*,[138] the way of the world. So 'Laws of Mourning' serves to damp any exaggerated expectation of the days of the messiah. People will still die. The messianic age is longed for because it will provide ideal conditions for attaining the world to come;[139] that is the only sense in which the messiah defeats death.

Death is also associated with repentance. In fact, the main effect the death of someone close is supposed to have on the bereaved is to spur them to examine their deeds and repent.[140] Moreover, while a corpse is a prime source of impurity, and the laws about such defilement are an important subject in 'Laws of Mourning', death itself is purifying. For the sin of profanation of the name of God, death is the only absolution,[141] and since profanation of God's name is an aspect of just about any wrongdoing,[142] few will reach their end without some taint of it. For the meritorious, death is purification in the highest sense of unification with the agent intellect, and the moment of greatest enlightenment:

Yet in the measure in which the faculties of the body are weakened and the fire of the desires is quenched, the intellect is strengthened, its lights achieve a wider extension, its apprehension is purified, and it rejoices in what it apprehends. The result is that when a perfect man is stricken with years and approaches death, this apprehension increases very powerfully, joy over this apprehension and a great love for the object of

---

[136] It is possible that a similar consideration applies in the placing of 'Laws of Inheritance' as the last section of the *Book of Civil Laws*. Since it concerns legal procedure, the previous section, 'Laws of Pleading', would have made a neat lead-in to the next book, the *Book of Judges*, which opens with the court system. That 'Laws of Inheritance' interrupts is perhaps a reminder of the transience of life and property.

[137] 'Laws of Kings and Their Wars', 12: 1. The principle is established earlier, in 'Laws of Repentance', 9: 2.

[138] 'Laws of Mourning', 13: 11. 'Laws of Mourning' itself refers to mourning after the advent of the messiah. For example, it includes the rules of mourning for the High Priest ('Laws of Mourning', 3: 6; 7: 6), and there will be no High Priest again until the messiah has rebuilt the Temple.

[139] See 'Laws of Repentance', 9: 2; 'Laws of Kings and Their Wars', 12: 4.

[140] See 'Laws of Mourning', 13: 12.   [141] See 'Laws of Repentance', 1: 4.

[142] See 'Laws of the Foundations of the Torah', 5: 10–11.

apprehension become stronger, until the soul is separated from the body at that moment in this state of pleasure.[143]

Is it possible that, by placing it in this strange position before 'Laws of Kings and Their Wars', Maimonides means to hint at the redemptive power of death, at death as a kind of immersion in the waters of intellect, putting it in line with the other endings in *Mishneh torah* that we have examined? If so, it would be another example of form completing meaning: 'Laws of Mourning' is about the formal aspects of death, but its form takes us beyond formality.

If the last four books represent the repair of society and progress towards the ideal state, in a reverse of the movement of the first ten books from the ideal of the pursuit of knowledge down to the most concrete of rituals, then the coupling of 'Laws of Mourning' and 'Laws of Kings and Their Wars' encapsulates that reversal. The first two sections of *Mishneh torah*, 'Laws of the Foundations of the Torah' and 'Laws of Ethical Qualities', move from intellectual virtue to moral virtue, from knowledge to ethics, in the individual. Like 'Laws of Ethical Qualities', 'Laws of Mourning' is a coming to terms with our material, perishable condition, while in the transition from 'Laws of Mourning' to 'Laws of Kings and Their Wars' we move from the ethical society to the knowledgeable society, culminating in the earth being full of the knowledge of God.

'Laws of Mourning' teaches the highest form of moral goodness, namely, kindness (*ḥesed*). To mourn is presented as a Torah commandment. Mourning for close relatives is mandatory, its rituals are prescribed, and even grief is regulated—not too little, and not too much.[144] To comfort mourners, on the other hand, is a rabbinic ordinance. As an act of kindness, it has no limit. Apropos that act of kindness, Maimonides also discusses other, similar ones: visiting the sick, gladdening a bride and bridegroom, and escorting guests homewards, all of which are theoretically unlimited (although, in fact, the ways of performing them are defined fairly closely).[145] They are all rabbinic ordinances, but Maimonides links them to the Torah commandment 'Thou shalt love thy neighbour as thyself',[146] described by R. Akiva as the 'great principle of the Torah'.[147]

That commandment *per se* is discussed in 'Laws of Ethical Qualities', 6: 3. It is part of the progression in the last two chapters of that section from ethical qualities as a way of being, the state of likeness to God, towards prac-

---

[143] *Guide* iii. 51 (p. 627).   [144] See 'Laws of Mourning', 13: 10–12.   [145] See ibid. 14: 1.
[146] Lev. 19: 18.   [147] *Sifra*, ad loc.

tical ethics in the social sphere. This mimics the overflow of God's perfection towards the world, and is the same movement as described at the end of the *Guide* of individual perfection overflowing in kindness.[148] The discussion of social commandments motivated by love also echoes the ending of 'Laws of Repentance', with its call for the service of God out of love.

It is important to distinguish between acts of kindness and charity. Acts of kindness are superior to charity because they are performed in person, rather than with money, and towards all people, not just the poor, and even, in the case of burial, towards the dead.[149] They are portrayed in the Talmud as *imitatio Dei*,[150] the basis of 'Laws of Ethical Qualities'. In other words, 'Laws of Mourning' is about the highest kind of practical ethics.

This lends symmetry to the beginning and end of *Mishneh torah*. In the opening two sections of the first book, the *Book of Knowledge*, knowledge of God precedes *imitatio Dei*; in the closing two sections of the final book, the *Book of Judges*, *imitatio Dei*, as embodied in the acts of kindness prescribed by 'Laws of Mourning', precedes the universal knowledge of God with which the work concludes. This symmetry is expressive of our theme of restoration,[151] especially as it reflects a similar symmetry within the *Book of Knowledge* itself, where we saw love as a stimulus to knowledge in 'Laws of the Foundations of the Torah' matched by knowledge as a ladder back to love in 'Laws of Repentance'.

Altogether, no clearer example could be wished for of the influence of the *Book of Knowledge* percolating through to the last four books of *Mishneh torah*, or, for that matter, of the organic unity of Maimonides' thought.

In a talmudic passage a form of which is part of the daily liturgy, performing deeds of kindness in general, and 'accompanying the dead' in particular, are among those things of which a person enjoys the fruits in this world and the capital in the world to come.[152] The world to come is thus at stake for the mourners as well as the mourned, and it is just possible that Maimonides intends a hint at this greater reward before dealing with the supreme earthly good, the days of the messiah.[153]

Above all, the juxtaposition of 'Laws of Mourning' with 'Laws of Kings and Their Wars' can be seen as a message of hope. In the traditional Jewish

---

[148] *Guide* iii. 54 (p. 638).

[149] See BT *Suk.* 49*b*. In *Guide* iii. 53 (pp. 630–2), charity, or righteousness, is defined as giving someone their due, and kindness as giving them more than their due; both are seen as attributes of God's actions.   [150] See BT *Sot.* 14*a* and above, Ch. 3, n. 54.

[151] For the idea of the end of *Mishneh torah* as a return to the beginning, see Blidstein, *Political Concepts* (Heb.), 249.   [152] BT *Shab.* 127*a*.   [153] See 'Laws of Repentance', 9: 2.

attitude to bereavement, all mourning is related to the national sense of mourning over the destruction of the Temple and the loss of Jerusalem. It is not clear how far that was the case in Maimonides' time and place,[154] but we do find a comparison of national to personal mourning in the chapter of *Mishneh torah* dealing with the customs of the fast of the Ninth of Av, on which date the destruction of both Temples is commemorated,[155] and which, like the other fast days commemorating the destruction and exile, will turn into a day of rejoicing in messianic times.[156] Read in that light, the sequence of 'Laws of Mourning' followed by 'Laws of Kings and Their Wars' carries just such a sense of conversion of woe to weal, the more powerful for being obliquely conveyed. Mourning is followed by national resurrection and salvation, representing the final instance of loss and restoration.

All in all, the position of 'Laws of Mourning' can be seen as an inexplicable anomaly, or as a stroke of artistic genius, a completely fitting prelude to the climactic 'Laws of Kings and Their Wars' and the messianic era.

---

[154] In both the Ashkenazi and Sephardi traditions, the words of condolence to mourners ('May God comfort you among the mourners of Zion and Jerusalem', 'May you be comforted in Jerusalem') link personal mourning to mourning over the destruction of Jerusalem and the Temple. However, the message of condolence recommended in 'Laws of Mourning', 13: 2 is simply 'be comforted from Heaven', which is based on BT *San.* 19a. Then again, Maimonides wrote 'Laws of Mourning' for use even in messianic times, when there will still be death, but no mourning over Jerusalem. In relation to *Mishneh torah*'s messianic ending, Maimonides' more open, though still not completely explicit, message is about death as a constant in all times; his covert message, conveyed solely through structure, is about redemption.

[155] See 'Laws of Fast Days', 5: 11. In fact, a more explicit connection is made at BT *Ta'an.* 30a.

[156] See 'Laws of Fast Days', 5: 19. Note that 'Laws of Fast Days' is the penultimate section of the *Book of Seasons* and is followed by a final section, 'Laws of Megilah [Purim] and Hanukah', which deals with two festivals commemorating redemption, in what appears to be a further instance of the pattern of loss and restoration, with the optimistic ending of 'Laws of Fast Days' priming the reader for what is to come. It could be, of course, that here Maimonides is simply following the sequence in Order *Mo'ed* (which he justifies in the introduction to his *Commentary on the Mishnah* by saying that the fasts were instituted by earlier prophets and Purim and Hanukah by later ones), but a couple of things indicate otherwise. The first is that *Megilah*, which follows *Ta'anit* in Order *Mo'ed*, does treat of Purim, but barely mentions Hanukah, except to stipulate the Torah reading for that festival (Mishnah *Megilah* 3: 6). The second is that *Megilah* is followed in Order *Mo'ed* by *Mo'ed katan* and *Ḥagigah*, whereas Maimonides subsumes the subject matter of *Mo'ed katan* under the rubric of 'Laws of Resting on Festivals', within the *Book of Seasons*, and removes the subject matter of *Ḥagigah* altogether, to the *Book of Offerings*, leaving 'Laws of Megilah and Hanukah' exposed, I would argue significantly so, at the end of the *Book of Seasons*. The resounding ending of 'Laws of Megilah and Hanukah' would seem to confirm this reading: 'Great is peace, for the whole Torah was given to make peace in the world, as it says, "Her ways are ways of pleasantness, and all her paths are peace" (Prov. 3: 17)' ('Laws of Megilah and Hanukah', 4: 14).

Summary

Through the structure of *Mishneh torah* Maimonides imports into it the interpretations of Jacob's dream as representing the workings of the cosmos and the progress of the prophet that he later set forth in the *Guide*. The first ten books are an ascending ladder of perfection and knowledge. Descending again, the prophet applies the knowledge gained to the rehabilitation of human society, seen in the rising degree of harmony and order in the last four books, to the point that the state is capable of receiving the form of the messianic age.

This redemption is further represented as a natural process through an expanding pattern of loss and restoration built into the structure of *Mishneh torah*'s main divisions: 'Laws of the Foundations of the Torah'; the *Book of Knowledge*; the first ten books; and the work as a whole. This pattern links the Jewish ideas of repentance and redemption to the Neoplatonic idea of return.

With the inclusion of this second phase of Neoplatonic emanation, the form of *Mishneh torah* rationalizes the commandments as flowing from a first cause, God's existence (the form of forms), and towards a final cause, the realized microcosmic form of man and of the state. This structural rationalization stands in contrast to the summative explanation of the commandments in the *Guide*. It also provides a solution to the problem of the authority of the commandments, and a positive answer to the question whether the commandments can be cognitive.

The positioning of 'Laws of Mourning' as the work's penultimate section is both a tempering of messianic hopes, signalling that the reality of death will remain after the redemption, and an encouragement to hope, signalling, in alliance with the pattern of loss and restoration, that national mourning will be lifted.

CHAPTER FIVE

FROM THEORY TO HISTORY, VIA MIDRASH

A Commentary on 'Laws of the Foundations of the Torah', 6: 9 and 7: 3

T HE WAY in which Maimonides invokes and subtly adapts aggadah in *Mishneh torah* has been a subsidiary theme throughout this study, but here it will come to the fore. The burden of this chapter will be the analysis of two *halakhot*, each of which contains a series of biblical quotations, with special attention paid to the way Maimonides plays with the midrashic harmonics, as it were, of the biblical verses in question. The aim will be to show how, out of these aggadot, he creates an aggadah of his own, in which the ontological and teleological bearings of *Mishneh torah* are united. For, picking up the thread of the dual model of messianic redemption from the previous chapter, one might ask: how exactly does a book that begins with a timeless account of physics and metaphysics find its way to an ending about the age of the messiah, that is, about history?

The key, once more, is the figure of the prophet, for the answer to this question will be seen to lie in Maimonides' theory of prophecy. As the highest level of intellectual awareness, prophecy is an apex at which ontology and teleology meet. This leads on to a discussion of how far, if at all, *Mishneh torah* itself can be considered prophetic.

Let us begin by observing a distinction between aggadah and halakhah. Once the decisors converge upon a ruling on a point of halakhah, then, for practical purposes, the talmudic to and fro on that point is otiose. By contrast, aggadah is divergent. The point of it is to involve the reader imaginatively and intellectually. Maimonides' use of it is suggestive rather than apodictic.

It will be found that, even where he does seem to approve a single midrashic interpretation of a verse, this is not necessarily the case, and that the deeper intention may be for the reader to play off the suggested interpretation against other possible interpretations. At the same time, the process is not uncontrolled: Maimonides may not exactly rule on Midrash, but he certainly orchestrates it in his own way.

Twersky's stress on the importance of Midrash in *Mishneh torah* was mentioned in the Introduction. What follows could be said to conform with his stricture that 'The student of Maimonidean thought, following an integrative-holistic approach to the development of Maimonides' ideas, will be especially attentive to this material'.[1] Not everyone agrees with Twersky's integrative approach to Maimonides,[2] but, having seen it borne out through an examination of *Mishneh torah*'s form on the macro-scale, I now turn to the micro-scale of individual *halakhot*.

The Problem of 'Laws of the Foundations of the Torah', 6: 9

Chapter 6 of 'Laws of the Foundations of the Torah' deals with one commandment: the prohibition against destroying anything 'called by God's name'. One may not erase any divine name, destroy sacred books, or damage the fabric of the Temple. This chapter is the obverse of the previous one, which is about the positive sanctification of God's name.[3]

The prohibition against erasing God's name can give rise to difficulty, because God has many names, and some of them are words that have other meanings too. For example, the word *adonai* can be simply the plural of *adoni* and mean 'my masters', used as a polite form of address, but it more commonly refers to God (in which case it is generally translated as 'Lord'). Even if a word plainly refers to a deity, it may not always be clear from the context whether the deity meant is the one God of Israel, or a pagan god. Sometimes the meaning does seem clear, but a midrashic interpretation supervenes to change it. Then there is the question of the status of epithets such as 'the merciful'—when they refer to God, do they count as names? In such cases, it may be hard to know for certain whether erasing a particular word is prohibited or not. This is not a light matter; transgression is punishable by flogging.[4]

---

[1] Twersky, *Introduction to the Code*, 153.   [2] See R. L. Weiss, 'Some Notes'.

[3] These two chapters perhaps exemplify, in turn, the love of God and the fear of God, as described in 'Laws of the Foundations of the Torah', 2.   [4] Ibid. 6: 1.

In 'Laws of the Foundations of the Torah', 6: 9, the final *halakhah* of the chapter, Maimonides rules on seven such unclear terms in the Bible. For words that he decides do refer to God and may not be erased, he uses the term *kodesh* (translated as 'sacred'); for words that do not, and therefore may be erased, he uses the term *ḥol* ('non-sacred'). The *halakhah* reads:

All the names (of God) occurring in the account of the Life of Abraham are sacred, including that in the text, 'O Lord, if I have found favour in thy sight' (Gen. 18: 3). All the Names (Adonai) in the Story of Lot are non-sacred, except the one in the text, 'Oh, not so, O Lord; behold now Thy servant hath found favour in Thy sight', (Gen. 19: 18–19). All the names (of God) occurring in the story of Gibeah of Benjamin (Judg. 20) are sacred. Names in the story of Mikhah (Judg. 17–18) are non-sacred. Those in the story of Naboth (1 Kgs. 21) are sacred.

The name Solomon, wherever it occurs in the Song of Songs, is sacred and is like the other divine epithets. The one exception is that of the text 'Thou, O Solomon, shalt have the thousand' (S. of S. 8: 12). Wherever the word King is found in the book of Daniel, it is a non-sacred term except in the text, 'Thou art King, King of Kings' (Dan. 2: 37), where it is like the other divine epithets.

On the face of it, this *halakhah* is straightforward enough. It represents a distillation of the discussion in a *baraita* cited in BT *Shevuot* 35*b*, where most of these *loci* are the subject of controversy. As usual, Maimonides leaves the disputes behind to give a clear decision in each case.

Closer examination reveals some curious features. In the first place, the *halakhah* seems anti-climactic. Maimonides likes to end chapters and sections by pointing a moral, especially in the *Book of Knowledge*, but this chapter fades out on a few minor points of detail, even if, as mentioned, they are details with serious consequences.[5] A comparison with the ending of the previous chapter, where we are given a vivid portrait of the virtuous scholar who leads by example to the general sanctification of God's name, makes the anti-climax seem particularly marked.[6]

It might be countered that not every chapter, even in the *Book of Knowledge*, has a resounding conclusion, and that here, Maimonides simply came to a natural end, and stopped. That argument might be persuasive, but for the fact that our *halakhah* is actually not in its natural place. We said that the chapter in which it occurs deals with three aspects of destroying things called by God's name: erasing the divine name; destroying sacred books; and dam-

---

[5] Rawidowicz also found this worth remarking on. See 'Opening Book of Mishneh Torah' (Heb.), 418.   [6] See pp. 150–4 above.

aging the Temple. The first aspect is dealt with in *halakhot* 1 to 6 of the chapter. *Halakhah* 7 deals with causing damage to the Temple fabric, and *halakhah* 8 with causing damage to holy books. *Halakhah* 9 then takes us back to erasing the name, the subject of *halakhot* 1 to 6. A more logical arrangement would be (using the existing numeration):

halakhot 1–6	erasing the name
halakhah 9	status of ambiguous names
halakhah 8	destroying holy books
halakhah 7	damaging the Temple

That would end the chapter on the Temple, a grander topic than books or erasing words. Moreover, *halakhah* 7 closes by citing the verse: 'And you shall burn their groves in fire . . . you shall not do so to the Lord your God' (Deut. 12: 3–4), a verse that sums up the theme of the chapter, and would have rounded it off well.[7]

The suggested arrangement would also be more in line with the order of the discussion in BT *Shevuot* 35*b*, on which not only the final *halakhah* but also much else in the chapter is based. In that discussion, the subject matter of *halakhah* 9 comes straight after the subject matter of *halakhah* 5, which is about *kinuyim*, that is, references to God through various epithets. In short, Maimonides placed *halakhah* 9 at the end of its chapter deliberately; he had to wrench logic and disrupt the continuity of the Talmud in order to put it there.

The *halakhah* is by no means exhaustive. Chapter 4 of the minor tractate *Soferim* lists dozens of instances of this kind of ambiguity in the Bible.[8] Why then does Maimonides restrict himself to the seven mentioned in BT *Shevuot*? When he wants to, he certainly can give exhaustive treatment to this kind of matter. 'Laws of Phylacteries, Mezuzah, and Torah Scroll', 8: 4 lists every open and closed paragraph ending in the entire Torah, for the guidance of scribes. For that matter, would not that section be an altogether more appropriate place for laws about erasing the name of God? After all, it is the

---

[7] *Yad peshutah*, in an introduction to 'Laws of the Foundations of the Torah', 6, comments at length on the order of the chapter, but not on what appears to me the anomalous position of the final *halakhah*.

[8] *Masekhet soferim*, 140–51. Higger finds that Maimonides refers to *Soferim* in 'Laws of the Foundations of the Torah', 6: 2–4 (*Masekhet soferim*, 59), in which case it is unlikely that he did not have the additional list of ambiguities, for they are the continuation of the same chapter that contains the source material for those *halakhot* at its start (*Masekhet soferim*, 137–40, *Soferim* 4: 1–4). JT *Meg.* 1: 9 also gives additional cases of the same kind of ambiguous terms.

Table 6 The order of 'Laws of the Foundations of the Torah', 6:9, versus its sources

Bible		BT *Shevuot* 35*b*		'Foundations' 6:9	
1	Abraham	1	Abraham	1	Abraham
2	Lot	2	Lot	2	Lot
3	Mikhah	5	Navot	4	Givat Binyamin
4	Givat Binyamin	3	Mikhah	3	Mikhah
5	Navot	4	Givat Binyamin	5	Navot
6	Solomon	6	Solomon	6	Solomon
7	Daniel	7	Daniel	7	Daniel

scribe who will most commonly need to consult those laws, for whenever he makes an error, he needs to know what he can do to correct it. So what are they doing in 'Laws of the Foundations of the Torah'? What is fundamental about them? 'Laws of Phylacteries, Mezuzah and Torah Scroll' would also be an appropriate niche for the prohibition against damaging sacred books in general, while the prohibition against damaging the fabric of the Temple could have been included in 'Laws of the Temple', which is about the Temple building.[9] The *raison d'être* of this chapter starts to look weak.[10]

Within the *halakhah* itself, the arrangement needs to be accounted for. As may be seen from Table 6, the *baraita* cited in the Talmud keeps to the sequence in which the various verses occur in the Bible, with the exception of Navot (Naboth), which comes third instead of fifth. Maimonides restores Navot to its rightful place, but reverses the order of the episodes of Mikhah and Givat Binyamin; that is to say, he maintains neither the biblical nor the talmudic order.[11]

[9] In fact, there is a reference back to this prohibition in 'Laws of the Temple', 1:17. See *Kesef mishneh*, ad loc.

[10] That is, as far as its content in concerned. Its formal function as part of a general structure in 'Laws of the Foundations of the Torah' that is reflected in the *Book of Knowledge* and in *Mishneh torah* as a whole was discussed in Chapter 4. That discussion only took account of the general idea of the chapter: that of the holiness of the name. Part of the point of the analysis here is to reconcile the formal function with the detail of the content.

[11] I have found no variant reading of the passage in the Talmud that might explain Maimonides' order here, and in fact the passage is prefaced with a mnemonic that lists the cases in the order given, although the mnemonic leaves out Mikhah. Nor does the phrasing of the talmudic passage give the impression that it could have been edited differently. As for the *Mishneh torah* text, the authorized Huntington 80 manuscript gives 'Laws of the Foundations of the Torah', 6:9, as cited here, and shows minor corrections to that *halakhah*, indicating that close attention was paid to it (see *Authorized*

The solution to this last puzzle will set us on the road to possible solutions to the others. A case can be made that our *halakhah* represents a worthy conclusion to 'Laws of the Foundations of the Torah', chapter 6, and that that chapter earns its place among the foundations of the Torah. First, though, it is necessary to fill out the contexts of the expressions about which the *halakhah* rules, and to explain why each expression is problematic.

The Scriptural Contexts

The first four instances all revolve around the word *adonai*, which, as already mentioned, is sometimes ambiguous, because it can refer to 'the Lord' or to men. The first example of such ambiguity occurs in the story in Genesis of the visit paid by three angels to Abraham. They stop to announce to him the birth of Isaac, on their way to destroy the Cities of the Plain. Abraham takes them for wayfarers, and, anxious that they should accept his hospitality, accosts them with the words: *adonai im na matsati ḥen*—'*Adonai*, please, if I have found favour'.[12]

The word *adonai* here is apparently spoken to the disguised angels, and in fact the first opinion cited in the Talmud conforms to the plain reading. However, some sages in the Talmud put a different gloss on it. We should recall that the appearance of the angels comes immediately after God himself appears to Abraham.[13] The passage in the Talmud reads:

All the Names mentioned in Scripture in connection with Abraham are sacred, except this which is secular: it is said: And he said, 'My Lord, if now I have found favour in thy sight'. Hanina the son of R. Joshua's brother, and R. Eleazar b. Azariah in the name of R. Eliezer of Modin, said, this is also sacred. With whom will [the following] agree? R. Judah said that Rab said: Greater is hospitality to wayfarers than receiving the Divine Presence. With whom [will this agree]? With this pair.[14]

The first opinion is that the word *adonai* refers to the wayfarers (in which case it ought to be translated 'my lords') and is therefore non-sacred, but according to R. Hanina and R. Eleazar, with the expression *adonai*, Abraham is speaking to God, disengaging from him in order to perform the more impor-

---

Version of the Code). The texts therefore seem to be reliable. Parallel talmudic passages that I have examined that deal with at least some of the same problem episodes differ in their ordering from BT *Shevu.* 35*b*, but none corresponds exactly to 'Laws of the Foundations of the Torah', 6: 9. The passages in question are at JT *Meg.* 1: 9 (Abraham, Mikhah, Navot); JT *Sefer torah* 4: 4 (Abraham, Lot, Mikhah, Navot); *Masekhet soferim* 4: 10 (Abraham, Lot, Mikhah, Navot, Givat Binyamin).

[12] Gen. 18: 3.   [13] Gen. 18: 1.

[14] 'i.e. R. Hanina and R. Eleazar, who say that Abraham addressed the Lord, asking him not to withdraw His Presence while he entertained the angels' (Soncino translator's note).

tant duty of welcoming guests. The word is therefore sacred and may not be erased. Maimonides rules in favour of this perhaps surprising homiletic reading, so that, where Abraham is concerned, *adonai* always refers to God, even in this instance.

The second case concerns Abraham's nephew Lot. The same angels who visited Abraham have as their next mission the rescue of Lot from Sodom, as they destroy the city for its crimes. They tell him to run for his life, but Lot pleads to be allowed to escape to a neighbouring city, which should be spared for his sake, rather than flee to the hills. Lot's plea includes the phrase *al na adonai* ('oh not so my lord'). While this is apparently addressed to Lot's escorting angel, the phrase has been interpreted as being part of an appeal to God, once more giving rise to a halakhic question. In the case of Lot, Maimonides rules that all possibly ambiguous references are to be taken as non-sacred, except for this one. Anyone who erases the *adonai* in this particular verse will therefore have transgressed.

There is already some indication that there may be more to this *halakhah* than meets the eye. Besides ruling on the technical question of whether erasing a certain word is a culpable act, it invites comparison of the characters of Abraham and his nephew. In Abraham's case, holiness is the rule; in Lot's it is the exception. Lot was brought up in Abraham's household and absorbed his uncle's values, but his own leanings result in those values becoming confused. When he has to choose, Abraham places hospitality above speaking to God. Lot too espouses hospitality; in its name he is prepared to perform the ungodly act of sacrificing his own daughters to pacify a mob out to rape his guests.[15] Something has become distorted in his outlook; Abraham, we may be sure, would not have done the same, but then Lot's choice is the product of an earlier choice, namely, to live in a place like Sodom at all.

In other words, in Lot's character worldliness prevails, but in his moment of distress he turns to God, and the (in his case) normally profane *adonai* becomes sacred. Even this moment of transcendence arises from Lot's own need rather than from the kind of awareness of the needs of others displayed by Abraham. This idea could be expounded on at length, and of course the character of Abraham is more complicated than emerges from this particular episode. The point here is to indicate that there may be some homiletic intent behind the halakhic ruling. The implied question is, whom should one emulate, Abraham or Lot?

[15] Gen. 19: 8.

For the next two cases of ambiguity on which Maimonides rules, we jump from Genesis to Judges. Givat Binyamin was a city in the territory of the tribe of Benjamin that was besieged by the rest of the tribes of Israel on account of an outrage that was perpetrated there. The tribes are twice repulsed with heavy losses. Before each assault, the besieging army consults *adonai* to ask whether its campaign is approved, and each time, the answer is positive, but it is only on the third attempt, through improved tactics, that the tribes gain victory.

Now the book of Judges chronicles a period of frequent anarchy in which idolatry is rife, so that it is sometimes unclear, when the word *adonai* is used, whether it means the God of Israel or a pagan deity. In this case, Maimonides decides according to the opinion in the Talmud that, notwithstanding the initial setbacks, the *adonai* whom the besieging army petitioned was God, and the 'names' are sacred.

In the next case Mikhah, an apparently well-to-do 'man of mount Ephraim' set up a pagan shrine and employed a Levite as its priest. Both idol and priest were kidnapped by troops from the tribe of Gad, on an expedition to carve out an inheritance for themselves by capturing the city of Layish. Maimonides rules that the frequent mentions of *adonai* in this story are all non-sacred.

The next episode cited is the story in Kings about the vineyard of Navot. The king, Ahab, coveted it, and in the end acquired it through the murderous intervention of his queen, Jezebel. All 'names' here are ruled sacred.[16]

The verse cited next, 'Thou, o Solomon, have the thousand', comes from the close of Song of Songs. In Hebrew, Solomon is *shelomoh*. Besides meaning King Solomon, the word *shelomoh* has, throughout Song of Songs, the status of a *kinui*, a substitute or oblique expression for God, because it is interpreted as referring to *hamelekh shehashalom shelo*, 'the King who bestows peace'. In the verse in question, however, the word *shelomoh* is ruled to be non-sacred, meaning that it only refers to King Solomon himself.[17]

Finally, we come to the book of Daniel. Maimonides tells us that, in that book, the Aramaic word *malkhaya*, 'king', is non-sacred, because it refers to

---

[16] The 'names' to which the Talmud refers are in 1 Kgs. 21: 10 and 13. See Rashi and Maharsha ad loc.

[17] The medieval authorities are divided as to whether the intention of the Talmud here is that the word *shelomoh* in Song of Songs may not be erased, or that it may be erased, but anyone who swears an oath in the name of 'the *shelomoh* in Song of Songs' has sworn a fully valid oath incorporating a reference to God, with all the very severe consequences of such an act. (The opinions are summarized in

the king of Babylon only, apart from one instance of the use of the expression 'king of kings'. Though apparently addressed to Daniel's earthly sovereign, Nebuchadnezzar, in that one case *malkhaya* is to be taken as meaning God.

We can now turn to the questions raised at the outset. To explain the anomalous order of 'Laws of the Foundations of the Torah', 6: 9, it is necessary to widen the view and see what preceded the siege of Givat Binyamin. The concubine of a certain Levite has run home to her father. The husband goes to seek her return. This is arranged amicably, and on the journey home the couple decide to spend the night at Givah. No one will give them hospitality, until an old man, not a native of the town, takes them in. The rest of the townspeople surround his house, demanding: 'Bring out the man that came into thy house, that we may have our desire of him.'[18] They are offered the concubine instead. She is raped all night, and in the morning she is found dead on the threshold.

It is impossible to miss the parallels with the story of the visit of the angels to Lot in Sodom: the hospitality offered by a non-citizen, the mob's demand that the stranger be brought out, and the counter-offer of the females in the house. In the text, the very language is similar. The author of Judges ironically echoes the earlier story, perhaps to make a bitter comment on his times. When angels walked the earth, there was salvation for the innocent, and fire and brimstone from heaven to punish the guilty. Not now. By rearranging the order of his quotations, Maimonides brings the reference to Givat Binyamin next to the reference to Lot in his list, drawing attention to the similarities and differences between the two stories. It would seem difficult to argue that this juxtaposition is not deliberate, or not meant to be significant.

the note ad loc. in the Steinsaltz edition of BT *Shevu.*) Maimonides rules that in this and the next case the status of the expression in question is *kishe'ar hakinuyin*, 'like other indirect expressions', which *Kesef mishneh* at least takes as indicating that he is of the latter opinion. *Halakhah* 4 of this chapter states explicitly that *she'ar kinuyin* may be erased. (The Or Vishua edition, which follows the Vilna edition's numbering of the *halakhot* but shows paragraph divisions within *halakhot* where these are indicated in the manuscripts, places the last two cases in *halakhah* 9 in a separate paragraph, indicating that they should be distinguished in some respect from the first five.) This presumably means that if someone were to swear in the name of the *shelomoh* in the verse *ha'elef lekha shelomoh*, there would be no liability, since Maimonides rules according to the opinion that this verse is an exception, and therefore there has been no oath incorporating a reference to God. All this serves as a reminder that Maimonides has taken these rulings out of context, or, more precisely, has split a talmudic discussion that combines laws to do with oaths and laws to do with sacrilege into its component parts. The aspect of oaths is dealt with in 'Laws of Oaths', 2: 2–7. This is further evidence of the care taken in composing 'Laws of the Foundations of the Torah', 6. The chapter should be seen as an example of Maimonides' creativity in halakhah as well as in aggadah.

[18] Judg. 19: 22.

Rather than through direct divine intervention, justice is done at Givah by human agency; the rest of the tribes fight against the Benjamites and eventually conquer their city. But can such a campaign, attended initially by such lack of success, really be seen as the operation of divine justice? That seems to be the point of comparison between the case of Givat Binyamin and the next example on the list, the story of Mikhah. When the men of Gad ask *adonai*, through the Levite whom Mikhah has hired as a priest for his shrine, whether their mission will be successful, they are told, 'Go in peace: before the Lord [*adonai*] is your way wherein ye go.'[19] Indeed, the tribe of Gad encounters no difficulty at all in conquering the peaceful city of Layish and putting its inhabitants to the sword, whereas the tribes besieging Givah at first keep failing despite receiving similar encouragement from *adonai*, although they do prevail in the end. So where is God in this tale of two besieged cities? Is the holiness of an enterprise measured by its outcome, or by its inherent rightness?[20] The answer suggested by the halakhic ruling is that the siege of Layish, despite being crowned with immediate success, is not blessed by divine favour, while the siege of Givah, though fraught with setbacks, is. The moral scarcely needs to be laboured.

The next two quotations, 'Navot' and 'Solomon', also offer an interesting point of comparison. The full verse in Song of Songs from which Maimonides quotes is: *karmi sheli lefanai ha'elef lekha shelomoh umatayim lanotrim et piryo*, and, in translation (including the previous verse): 'Solomon had a vineyard at Ba'al Hamon; he let out the vineyard to keepers: everyone for its fruit was to bring a thousand pieces of silver. My vineyard, which is mine, is before me: you, o Solomon, may have the thousand and those that keep its fruit two hundred.'

It will be recalled that Maimonides rules that Solomon (*shelomoh*), while it can refer to God, here only means King Solomon. What is intriguing is that, both here and in the story of Navot, we have the same elements, namely: a king and a vineyard. The difference is that the vineyard in Navot's case is a real one, whereas the vineyard in the quotation from Song of Songs is

---

[19] Judg. 18: 6.

[20] The debate in the Talmud on the status of the word *adonai* in these episodes perhaps centres on this question: 'All the Names mentioned in connection with Gibe'ah of Benjamin, R. Eliezer said, are secular; R. Joshua said, are sacred. R. Eliezer said to him: Does He then promise, and not fulfil? R. Joshua replied to him: What He promised, He fulfilled; but they did not enquire whether [the result would be] victory or defeat; later, when they did enquire [of the Urim and Tummim], they approved their action.' See Rashi ad loc.

presumably metaphorical; the speaker is talking about her beloved, more precious than King Solomon's wealth.[21]

In the final case in the *halakhah* we stay with kings. Maimonides tells us that, in the book of Daniel, the word *malkhaya*, 'king', is non-sacred, except in one instance. Full explication of this case will be deferred a little. For the time being, it will suffice to observe that the connection between it and the previous one is perhaps similar to that between Abraham and Lot, with the comparison this time being made between territories rather than personalities. In Song of Songs, set in the Land of Israel, references to God are the rule; in Daniel, set in exile, they are the exception.[22]

We have seen enough to realize that there is more going on in this *halakhah* than rulings on ambiguous expressions. The cases are linked to one another in different ways, forming a kind of Bible commentary. In his approach to the underlying talmudic passage, Maimonides simultaneously codifies it as halakhah and interprets it as aggadah. He does here what we have seen him doing before, emphasizing through slight modification a tendency that he has identified in his source. The switch in the order of 'Givat Binyamin' and 'Navot', bringing similar yet subtly different stories into juxtaposition, should leave us in no doubt that Maimonides found in that source some extra-halakhic significance.

How to Read

How does the aggadic aspect of this *halakhah*, with its series of pointed juxtapositions, help to explain its position at the conclusion of the chapter?

In the *Guide* one of Maimonides' central concerns is how to read Scripture and Midrash. The chief problem is that so much of them seems incompatible with science and experience, not to mention correct doctrine, as, for example, anthropomorphic descriptions of God. A literal reading of this material leads either to foolish and even heretical beliefs, or to dismissive contempt.

One solution is to read it as parable. Once that solution is broached, however, the challenge arises of deciding where and how to apply it.[23] Does every-

---

[21] Since the *shelomoh* of the first verse is the same as the *shelomoh* of the second, it follows that it too ought to be non-sacred, but no specific ruling is given on this point.

[22] *Guide* ii. 36 (p. 373) makes it clear that the problem of exile is not the place itself, but the depressing condition of being subordinate to people of low spiritual worth.

[23] Warren Zev Harvey notes that it was the seeming arbitrariness of the procedure that led Spinoza to reject allegorical interpretation as a way of redeeming Scripture from primitiveness. See 'Maimonides' Allegorical Readings'. See also Twersky, *Introduction to the Code*, 366.

thing have another level of meaning? Maimonides' answer to this question is no. Allegory is not to be wielded as a blunt instrument. The first safeguard against its abuse is a general conservatism. Where the literal meaning of a passage does not conflict with demonstrable truth, it should be left alone. Hence the theory of the creation of the world, as presented in Genesis, should be allowed to stand, because 'the eternity of the world has not been demonstrated'.[24]

The next safeguard is sensitivity to the surface quality of the text. Scripture and Midrash are not made out of one cloth. The first question that needs to be answered about any portion of them is, what sort of writing is it? Is it to be taken literally or metaphorically? If metaphorically, what line of interpretation is appropriate, and how far should interpretation go? Maimonides addresses this in the introduction to the *Guide*, where he interprets the verse 'A word fitly spoken is like apples of gold in settings of silver'[25] as meaning that, for any obscure saying, 'Its external meaning also ought to contain in it something that indicates to someone considering it what is to be found in its internal meaning.'[26] As we have already seen, he goes on to class parables as being of two kinds. In the one, exemplified by Jacob's dream of a ladder with angels ascending and descending on it, every detail of the narrative is significant. In the other, exemplified by the blandishments of the temptress in Proverbs, the narrative is allegorical in outline, referring in the example to matter as a trap for intellect, but no particular significance is to be attached to its details. It is vital to be able to characterize texts in this kind of way.[27]

It is extending Maimonides' discussion just a little to say that such characterization also depends on context. The context may be immediately adjacent material, or something elsewhere linked to the text in question through similarity of narrative structure or of imagery, or some other device. Here again, it is necessary to exercise judgement, to contrast as well as to compare.

Can these things be taught? In very general terms, yes, as Maimonides does in the introduction to the *Guide*. Even there, it is with the aid of parables about parables. But at bottom what he is really trying to convey is not readings of Scripture (though he offers plenty) but a way of reading Scripture. Since each text is unique, it is hard to provide anything more than very broad

---

[24] *Guide* ii. 25 (p. 328).   [25] Prov. 25: 11.   [26] *Guide* i, Introduction (p. 12).
[27] On the contrast between this approach to the Bible and the midrashic method, see M. Z. Cohen, *Three Approaches to Biblical Metaphor*, 184 n. 20 and references cited there. If, in our *halakhah*, Maimonides means to criticize the midrashic method, or perhaps rather the literal approach to Midrash, that would be a further reason for him to make his point obliquely, whereas in the *Guide* he allows himself to be more explicit.

guidance, such as the analysis of parables into two types. All Maimonides can do is to multiply examples, in the hope that understanding will dawn by itself.

That, at any rate, seems to be the point of 'Laws of the Foundations of the Torah', 6: 9. It presents us with seven texts that, as we have seen, have links between them. But each text is of a different kind, and the links are just as varied. Perception of the particular qualities of each is vital in making sense of them and of the relationships between them. At this level, we have here a continuation of the discussion about the workings of language from 'Laws of the Foundations of the Torah', chapter 1: from a theological point of view, one must accept that, in descriptions of God, a leg is not a leg, an eye is not an eye, a finger is not a finger; from a literary point of view, one must be alert to the possibility that, for example, a vineyard may not be a vineyard,[28] but equally capable, where appropriate, of letting it be just a vineyard. There is a middle path to be trodden between literal-mindedness, whether of the slavish or contemptuous kind, and an uncontrolled urge to allegorize. In aesthetics as in ethics, finding the middle way is a matter of bringing the intellect to bear to train oneself to find the appropriate response in the circumstances of the case.

With this in mind, it is possible to make a suggestion as to the message Maimonides seeks to convey by ending 'Laws of the Foundations of the Torah', chapter 6, in the way he does. Just as, at the end of chapter 5, he broadens the concept of *kidush hashem*, the sanctification of God's name, to include not just the extreme case of martyrdom, but also the everyday behaviour of the scholar, so in the closing *halakhah* of chapter 6 one senses a broadening of the topic. That *halakhah* can be interpreted as implying that there is more than one way of desecrating a text. A text can be damaged physically, but it can also be spoilt by being insensitively read. Clumsy interpretation is a far more common form of textual vandalism than deliberate physical damage.[29] There is a body of traditional commentary to guide the reader, and to

[28] The interpretation of biblical terms is, of course, a central theme throughout the *Guide*, but see esp. ii. 47 (pp. 407–9).

[29] If Maimonides does intend *halakhah* 9 as a coda that broadens the theme of chapter 6 in this way, there is a midrashic comment that may have a bearing here. The prohibition against defacing or damaging sacred texts and objects derives from Deut. 12: 3–4: 'and you shall wipe out their name from that place. You shall not do likewise to the Lord your God.' *Sifrei* on these verses states: 'Raban Gamliel says: And is it conceivable that Israel will demolish the altars? Rather what it means is that you should not behave like them (the pagans) or your evil deeds will cause the Temple of your fathers to be destroyed' (*Sifrei* Deut., ed. Finkelstein).

If Raban Gamliel could treat this commandment non-literally, the way was certainly open for Maimonides to do so. (Rashi, ad loc., cites this *midrash*, but in all the editions I have seen he attributes it to R. Ishmael, who in *Sifrei* is cited as the author of the statement immediately before this one.)

bring out hidden possibilities, as with the readings on which Maimonides adjudicates here. There are also the nuances of tone, style, and character, verbal and thematic echoes, and so forth. Appreciation of these qualities is hard to teach by precept; it must be done by example, just as the scholar of 'Laws of the Foundations of the Torah', 5: 11, must lead by example in order to inculcate certain attitudes and moral qualities. In both cases, we are *lifnim mishurat hadin*. So Maimonides concludes his discussion of sacrilege with a *halakhah* that, if one pays close attention, compels one to compare and contrast different characters, different narratives, and different kinds of writing, providing an object lesson in hermeneutics.[30]

Where Holiness Lies

Ultimately, by concluding 'Laws of the Foundations of the Torah', chapter 6, in the way he does, Maimonides makes a value judgement. It is not just that misinterpretation of texts is more common than physical vandalizing of them; it is also more heinous. With due respect to the status of the written name of God, scriptural texts, and the Temple, real sacrilege is committed in the mind, in the maintenance of faulty concepts and through the propagation of misguided readings. Holiness lies in the richness of Scripture's content more than in the physical container.[31]

Similarly, the ending of 'Laws of the Foundations of the Torah', 5, on the theme of the exemplary scholar is not just a matter of bringing sanctification of the name down to an everyday level. The everyday is actually preferable. Accepting martyrdom rather than transgressing the law is mandated in

---

[30] In *Guide* ii. 42 (p. 389) Maimonides gives an interpretation of the visit of the angels to Abraham that is in line with the opinion in the Talmud that the *adonai* in Gen. 18: 3 is non-sacred, contradicting the ruling in 'Laws of the Foundations of the Torah', 6: 9. In the *Guide* the entire episode is stated to have been part of a vision, thus avoiding the notion of angels taking physical form, while the opinion of R. Hiya that *adonai* was addressed to the greatest of the angels (*Gen. Rabbah* 48) is cited approvingly, thus avoiding the notion of a man talking to God. The commitment to philosophical truth here overrides both *derash* and what Maimonides decided was halakhah. It is debatable how strenuously one should try to reconcile or distinguish Maimonides' two readings. In any case, what is interesting in 'Laws of the Foundations of the Torah', 6: 9 is the interplay of the *midrashim* about Abraham and Lot. In pt. 1, ch. 8 of *Maimonides as Philosopher and Codifier* (Heb.), Jacob Levinger considers the question whether Maimonides allowed philosophical considerations to affect his halakhic rulings, and on the whole exonerates him from this charge. Here we have an example of Maimonides actually ruling against his philosophical position (thereby yielding aggadic interest), although 'Laws of the Foundations of the Torah', 6: 9, too, could be explained as referring to a prophetic vision, rendering the representation of Abraham talking to God harmless. I have found no commentator who disputes the ruling itself.

[31] On Maimonides' attitude to the sanctity of Torah scrolls, see Kellner, *Maimonides' Confrontation with Mysticism*, 116–23.

certain circumstances, and Jewish history holds very many examples of people who sacrifice their lives rather than betray their faith. At the same time, we cannot help but observe that people are prepared to die for all kinds of causes. It would be presumptuous, perhaps even nonsense, to say that to live nobly is harder than to die nobly, but it certainly appears that Maimonides regards a righteous life as a more effective example to others than a brave death. He lays down as the basic rule that one should submit to the oppressor and transgress rather than defy him and die.[32] The circumstances in which martyrdom is demanded are the exception. The hero of the chapter on sanctification of the name is therefore the person every day of whose life inspires true belief, not only the last.

This is of a piece with Maimonides' general preference for the usual over the unusual. He regards miracles as an ineffectual means of instilling faith. They may be necessary in some circumstances, but the people of Israel acquired true and lasting belief from the revelation at Sinai,[33] a unique event, but, for Maimonides, a continuation of nature rather than a disruption of it like the miraculous events of the Exodus. In this case, the preference for intellectual revelation over miracle is explicit, but in our analysis of 'Laws of the Foundations of the Torah', chapters 5 and 6, it is a pleasing paradox that the content concerns the form of the law, while it is the work's form that conveys the law's inner content. The obliqueness allows a message that might otherwise be found trite by some, or disturbing by others, to emerge subtly, evenly, and persuasively, in simple outline yet with its complexity intact. The method, then, embodies the message. Without disruption to its flow, *Mishneh torah* draws the reader into its intricacies, aligning him or her with its steady focus on the purified knowledge of God, even in its most technical or quotidian concerns. This is not the art of persuasion, but the persuasiveness of art.

The Four Kingdoms

Let us now take a closer look at the last case that Maimonides deals with in 'Laws of the Foundations of the Torah', 6: 9, from the book of Daniel.

Chapter 2 of Daniel, from which the phrase at issue is taken, is about Nebuchadnezzar's dream of a figure with a head of gold, breast and arms of silver, belly and thigh of brass, legs of iron, and feet part iron and part clay. Daniel interprets this dream as symbolizing four successive kingdoms, with a fifth kingdom, the kingdom of God, to come after. The rabbis associated the four kingdoms with four empires: Babylon, Medes and Persians, Greece, and

---

[32] 'Laws of the Foundations of the Torah', 5: 1.   [33] Ibid. 8: 1.

Rome.[34] Our *halakhah* is thus capped by a reference to a vision of human history and the advent of the age of the messiah.

This ending sets off several further associations via a cluster of *midrashim*. *Song of Songs Rabbah* associates the verse 'My vineyard that is mine is before me' with the Babylonian exile and Nebuchadnezzar:

R. Hiyya taught on Tannaic authority, 'The matter may be compared to the case of a king who was angry with his son and handed him over to his servant. What did he do? He began to beat him with a club. He said to him, "Don't obey your father."

'The son said to the servant, "You big fool! The very reason that father handed me over to you was only because I was not listening to him, and you say, "Don't listen to father!"

'So too, when sin had brought it about that the house of the sanctuary should be destroyed and Israel was sent into exile to Babylonia, Nebuchadnezzar said to them: "Do not listen to the Torah of your father in heaven, but rather, 'fall down and worship the image I have made' (Dan. 3: 15)."

'The Israelites said to him, "You big fool! The very reason that the Holy One, blessed be He, has handed us over to you is because we were bowing down to an idol: 'She saw . . . the images of the Chaldeans portrayed in vermillion' (Ezek. 23: 14), and yet you say to us, 'fall down and worship the image I have made'. Woe to you!"

'It is at that moment that the Holy One, blessed be He, said, "My vineyard, my very own, is for myself."

'Said before him that wicked man, "There were a thousand [righteous] and they are now cut down in numbers here and are only two hundred."

'Said to him the Holy One, blessed be He, "Woe to that wicked man, rotten spit! There were a thousand and their numbers have increased here and they are now two hundred thousand."'[35]

This *midrash* connects the final ruling of the *halakhah* with the penultimate one, on Song of Songs. For a reader who has the *midrash* in mind, this final pair of references conveys the message that Israel remains loyal to God in exile and God does not abandon his people. The intimacy and faithfulness between God and the Jewish people portrayed by Song of Songs will survive, even through the tribulations portrayed in Daniel.[36]

---

[34] See Raviv, 'Talmudic Formulation of the Prophecies' (Heb.). For Maimonides' own interpretation of the four kingdoms or empires, see *Epistles*, ed. Halkin and Hartman, 135 n. 55.

[35] *S. of S. Rabbah*, trans. Neusner, ii. 240 (I have emended Neusner's 'two thousand' in the last sentence to 'two hundred thousand').

[36] In the *Guide* Maimonides treats Song of Songs as an allegory of the relationship between the individual and God. See particularly *Guide* iii. 54 (p. 636), where an earlier appearance of the motif of the vineyard in S. of S. 1: 6 is interpreted as referring to cultivation of the rational faculty. In the *Epistle*

The reference to the prophecy of the four kingdoms also brings the *halakhah* full circle, via *Mekhilta derabi yishma'el*, which interprets a verse in the episode of the 'covenant between the pieces' made by God with Abraham[37] as referring to that prophecy.[38] This creates a loop back to Abraham, who was the subject of the first reference in the *halakhah*. It creates a forward link as well: *halakhah* 2 of the next chapter of 'Laws of the Foundations of the Torah', 7, describes the terror that overcomes the prophet as he receives the prophetic vision. As examples, Maimonides mentions none other than Abraham and Daniel:[39]

And all of them, when they prophesy, their limbs shudder, their bodily strength fails, and they lose their senses, and the mind remains free to understand what it sees, as it says of Abraham, 'and lo, an horror of great darkness fell upon him' (Gen. 15: 12); and as it says of Daniel, 'for my comeliness was turned in me into corruption, and I retained no strength' (Dan. 10: 8).[40]

The verse from Genesis is precisely the one interpreted in *Mekhilta derabi yishma'el* as referring to the four empires, while the verse from Daniel is a prelude to Daniel's vision of the end of days. The allusions are tightly packed.

---

to *Yemen*, however, Song of Songs is treated as an allegory of the relationship between God and the Jewish people. See *Epistles*, ed. Halkin and Hartman, 104. It would be in keeping with the distinction drawn between *Mishneh torah* and the *Guide* in the Introduction that the latter, nationalist interpretation should be invoked by our *halakhah*.

[37] Gen. 15: 9–21.

[38] 'R. Nathan says: Whence can you prove that God showed to our father Abraham Gehenna, the giving of the Law, and the division of the Red Sea? . . . He also showed him the four kingdoms that would in the future oppress his children. For it is said: "And it came to pass that, when the sun was going down, a deep sleep fell upon Abram, and, lo, a dread, even a great darkness, was falling upon him" (Gen. 15: 12). "A dread," refers to the Babylonian Empire. "Darkness," refers to the empire of Media. "Great," refers to the Greek Empire. "Was falling," refers to the fourth empire, wicked Rome. There are some who reverse the order by saying: "Was falling," refers to the Babylonian Empire, as it is said: "Fallen, fallen is Babylon" (Isa. 21: 9). "Great," refers to the empire of Media, as it is said: "King Ahasuerus made great" (Esther 3: 1). "Darkness," refers to the Greek Empire which caused the eyes of Israel to become dark from fasting. "A dread," refers to the fourth kingdom, as it is said: "Dreadful and terrible and strong exceedingly" (Dan. 7: 7)' (*Mekhilta*, trans. Lauterbach, 268–9).

[39] As he also does in *Guide* ii. 41 (p. 385), although in *Guide* ii. 45 (pp. 398–400) Daniel is ranked below the fully fledged prophets.

[40] Incidentally, note that the beginning of this *halakhah* refers to degrees (*ma'alot*) of prophets, the same term as applied to angels in 'Laws of the Foundations of the Torah', 2: 6–7. We saw in the previous chapter that, in one of Maimonides' interpretations of Jacob's dream (*Guide* i. 15), the angels on the ladder are prophets. *Guide* ii. 45 lists eleven degrees of prophecy, although the first two are really only 'stepping stones toward prophecy'. This could possibly be reconciled with the ten degrees of angels.

The Problem of 'Laws of the Foundations of the Torah', 7: 3

The association with the four empires is cemented in the very next *halakhah*, which reads as follows:

The things made known to the prophet in the prophetic vision are made known to him through a parable, and the meaning of the parable is instantly engraved on his heart in the prophetic vision, and he will know what it is: like the ladder that Jacob our father saw, and angels were ascending and descending on it (Gen. 28: 12), which was a parable of the kingdoms and subjugation to them; and like the living creatures that Ezekiel saw (Ezek. 1), and the seething pot and the rod of an almond tree that Jeremiah saw (Jer. 1), and the scroll that Ezekiel saw (Ezek. 2: 9–3: 3), and the basket that Zekhariah saw (Zech. 5).[41]

Since the figures of Abraham and Daniel and the prophecy of the four kingdoms bridge the end of chapter 6 and the beginning of chapter 7 of 'Laws of the Foundations of the Torah', the statement in this *halakhah* that Jacob's dream symbolizes the kingdoms or empires can hardly be coincidental. Again, Midrash is the source. Several *midrashim* suggest that the angels in Jacob's dream stand for the four empires.[42] All of them assume that the angels were four in number, and offer proofs of different kinds for that assumption. *Genesis Rabbah* 68: 13 makes explicit reference to Daniel and Nebuchadnezzar, so that a reader with that *midrash* in mind gains a strong impression of continuity from 'Laws of the Foundations of the Torah', 6: 9 through 'Laws of the Foundations of the Torah', 7: 2 to this *halakhah*.[43] The *midrashim* do, however, offer several other possibilities for the meaning of Jacob's dream, some of which are made use of in the *Guide*, as we saw in the previous chapter. That Maimonides chose this particular interpretation at this point confirms a concern on his part to form a connection between chapters 6 and 7 of 'Laws of the Foundations of the Torah' based on a vision of the unfolding of history. I shall return to this theme presently, but, in order to appreciate fully the invocation

[41] 'Laws of the Foundations of the Torah', 7: 3.

[42] *Pesikta derav kahana* (ed. Mandelbaum), 23: 2; *Gen. Rabbah* 68: 13; *Lev. Rabbah* 69: 12; *Midrash tanḥuma* (Vilna), 'Vayetse', 2.

[43] The *midrash* actually makes a series of associations of elements in Jacob's dream with Daniel and Nebuchadnezzar, culminating in a direct allegorization of the angels as the four kingdoms. Sara Klein-Braslavy prefers to see *Pesikta derav kahana* as Maimonides' primary source here (she cites the Mandelbaum edn., 334–5) because of similarities of language. She also mentions *Midrash tanḥuma*. See Klein-Braslavy, 'Maimonides' Commentary on Jacob's Dream' (Heb.).

of history at this juncture, it is necessary first to explore some other curious features of 'Laws of the Foundations of the Torah', 7: 3.

The order of the biblical references with which the *halakhah* continues is at least as strange as the order of the references in 'Laws of the Foundations of the Torah', 6: 9. From Ezekiel, it jumps backwards to Jeremiah, then forwards to Ezekiel again. What is more, the examples from Jeremiah are themselves reversed: in Jeremiah 1, the vision of the rod of an almond tree precedes the vision of the seething pot. It is as though Maimonides has laid speed bumps in the text to make us slow down and consider more closely. The indications are that what we have here is probably not a random sample of prophetic parables.

Of all the examples, Jacob's vision stands out the most. It is the only one from the Torah rather than from the Prophets; it is the only one for which an interpretation is given; and in order to give that interpretation, instead of referring to Jacob's ladder in a shorthand way as he does to all the other parables, Maimonides has to lengthen the description to include an extra detail, 'and angels were ascending and descending on it', because, in the *midrash*, the kingdoms are symbolized by the angels, not the ladder.

Jacob's vision also stands out because of the classification of prophetic parables in the second part of the *halakhah*. There are three types:

And likewise the other prophets—there are those of them that state the parable and its interpretation, like these, and there are those of them that state the interpretation only. And sometimes they state the parable alone, without an interpretation, as in some of the sayings of Ezekiel and Zechariah—and all of them prophesy through parable and riddle.

Jacob's ladder is a parable of the third type, in which the parable alone is stated, without an interpretation—Maimonides has to supply one from Midrash. Therefore, from an organizational point of view, this parable belongs with the final list, which ought to read: 'And sometimes they state the parable alone, without an interpretation, as in the ladder that Jacob our father saw, and as in some of the sayings of Ezekiel and Zechariah'. Why then does it appear by itself at the beginning?

Admittedly, the episode of Jacob's ladder is third-person rather than first-person narrative (another exceptional feature) but that hardly seems an insuperable difficulty.

It might be objected that these questions see complications where none exists. Jacob's ladder may be exceptional for being from the Torah, but it is placed first precisely for that reason. The extra detail and the interpretation are supplied for that parable because, as the first in the list, it is meant as a paradigm: the rest should be interpreted in similar ways. The interpretation of the empires and their domination is given because it is the simplest and most concise that the Midrash offers, and so suits the style of *Mishneh torah*, enabling a point to be made without causing distraction.

If we want complication, we can find it in the *Guide*, where the interpretations of Jacob's ladder are seemingly much more sophisticated, making very subtle use of Midrash, as Klein-Braslavy shows, and moreover requiring the reader to gather together scattered statements in order to appreciate those interpretations fully.[44] *Mishneh torah*, as mentioned, simply lifts a straightforward interpretation from the Midrash as is. That would appear to fit the usual view of the different orientations of the two books. Klein-Braslavy characterizes the interpretation in 'Laws of the Foundations of the Torah', 7: 3, as concerned with revelation of the future, and the interpretations in the *Guide* as concerned with 'secrets of the Torah'.

One could even surmise that, because the prophecy of the four empires is associated with Daniel and, through Midrash, with Abraham, and because these figures are mentioned in 'Laws of the Foundations of the Torah', 6: 9 and 'Laws of the Foundations of the Torah', 7: 2, Maimonides picked Jacob's dream and the *midrash* about the four empires to begin illustrating the use of parables in prophecy in 'Laws of the Foundations of the Torah', 7: 3, simply because, consciously or unconsciously, his mind was running on that theme.

Such speculation-damping readings are plausible enough, but they stumble on the peculiarity of the sequence of the parables in 'Laws of the Foundations of the Torah', 7: 3. The two possible organizing principles considered so far, namely, the biblical order and classification by type of parable, both fail to account for the sequence satisfactorily, so that the opening with Jacob's dream of the ladder followed by Ezekiel's vision of the creatures remains anomalous. Once one feature of the *halakhah* indicates something contrived, everything needs to be probed. All the questions are therefore thrown open again.

To sum up, we are left needing to explain why Maimonides was so determined (*a*) to mention 'the ladder that Jacob our father saw' prominently; (*b*) to interpret that parable as symbolic of the four empires; and (*c*) to juxtapose it with 'the living creatures that Ezekiel saw'. In the course of answering these questions, we shall find that the treatment of Jacob's vision of the ladder

---

[44] See also Diamond, *Maimonides and the Hermeneutics of Concealment*.

is actually no less sophisticated in *Mishneh torah* than in the *Guide*, and that this is another example of compressed, poetic presentation in the one versus discursive presentation in the other.

Theory and History in the Prophet's Epiphany

The categorical statement that the angels on Jacob's ladder symbolize the empires and their domination, perhaps meant as a palliative for the ordinary reader, is a provocation to the expert reader aware of the many possibilities Midrash offers. For such a reader, the juxtaposition of that vision with 'the living creatures that Ezekiel saw' might arouse curiosity not just because of the contortion required to bring it about, but also because of the following *midrash*: 'Said R. Shimon b. Lakish. "The patriarchs are themselves the chariot [of God]: 'God went up from Abraham' (Gen. 17: 22). 'And God went up from upon him [Jacob]' (Gen. 35: 13), 'And behold the Lord stood upon him' (Gen. 28: 13)."'[45]

The chariot (*merkavah*) is, of course, the vision of 'the living creatures' in Ezekiel chapters 1 and 10, the primary texts of Jewish mysticism, while what 'the Lord stood upon' was the ladder in Jacob's dream.[46] That is to say, R. Shimon ben Lakish (Resh Lakish) preceded Maimonides in bringing 'the ladder that Jacob our father saw' and 'the living creatures that Ezekiel saw' together. Whatever this *midrash* means, the hint to it in our *halakhah*, if we are right to see one,[47] should put the expert reader on the alert. But on the alert to what? It still remains to be shown just how 'the ladder that Jacob our father saw' and 'the living creatures that Ezekiel saw' are connected.

For this we need finally to turn to the *Guide*. Just before we do so, however, let us note a couple of points. One is that, through the reference to the succession of dominant empires, Maimonides has introduced a historical dimension into a theoretical discussion of prophecy. The other is that *malkhuyot*

---

[45] *Gen. Rabbah* 47: 8 (trans. Neusner, iii. 19). Note that the last quotation is from Jacob's dream, and can also read 'stood upon it' (i.e. upon the ladder)—see following note. Steven Harvey comments, 'That Maimonides considered the parable of Jacob's ladder to be a description of the Chariot is clear to me, and I believe quite important', and notes the juxtaposition of the two in our *halakhah* ('Maimonides in the Sultan's Palace', 61 n. 58).

[46] The verse can also be interpreted as meaning 'the Lord stood above him', or even 'beside him', so that it is not absolutely clear whether, in his dream, Jacob saw God on top of the ladder or was simply aware of God's presence. The alternative interpretation is perhaps more consistent with the other verses in the *midrash* (see previous note), but 'stood above it' rather than 'stood above him' is given here because Maimonides clearly favours that interpretation in the *Guide*, as will be seen below.

[47] Maimonides cites this *midrash* in the *Epistle to Yemen*, where he says, 'The meaning is that they [the patriarchs] have attained a true conception of the deity' (*Epistles*, ed. Halkin and Hartman, 118).

veshi'abudan ('empires and their oppression') is a highly charged phrase, for Maimonides adopts the view of the *amora* Samuel[48] that the end of imperial oppression represents the only difference between the pre- and post-messianic eras.[49] That is to say, he has invoked history in its most momentous aspect.

The three discussions of Jacob's dream in the *Guide* were set out in the previous chapter. The first of them, in the introduction, already presents an interesting parallel with *Mishneh torah*. In both 'Laws of the Foundations of the Torah' and in the introduction to the *Guide*, this dream serves as the chief paradigm of a parable. It is the first in the list of examples in 'Laws of the Foundations of the Torah', 7: 3, while in the introduction to the *Guide* it is the example of a parable in which every detail is significant. In both places, I believe, notice is being served that this parable will be highly important. Moreover, insofar as the *Guide* can be used retrospectively,[50] the discussion there assures us that, in Maimonides' eyes, minute examination of Jacob's dream and a high degree of sensitivity to any reference to it are fully justified.

The remaining discussions in the *Guide* give us two additional allegorical referents for Jacob's dream of the ladder to put alongside the four empires in *Mishneh torah*, namely, the double referent of the cosmos and the prophet ascending and descending in *Guide* Part I, and the four elements of matter in *Guide* Part II. This multiplication of interpretations itself gives rise to a question: if Maimonides believes in authorial intention, and we have seen that he does, how can he put forward three different interpretations of the same parable? Do we have to resort to multiple intention, or are they three interpretations that are really one? I suggest that the answer is the latter, and that the link between the different interpretations is to be found in Maimonides' theory of prophecy.

Someone who aspires to prophecy must perfect both their rational and their imaginative faculties. In *Guide* ii. 36,[51] prophecy itself is defined as 'an overflow overflowing from God, may He be cherished and honored, through the intermediation of the Active Intellect, toward the rational faculty in the first place and thereafter toward the imaginative faculty'. Kraemer paraphrases this as follows:

The prophet receives theoretical truths from the emanation of the Agent Intellect upon his rational faculty. This emanation actuates his faculty of imagination, thus giving rise to symbolic representations of the truth on a level the common folk can

---

[48] BT *Shab.* 63*a*.   [49] 'Laws of Repentance', 9: 2.
[50] It can, for reasons discussed below.   [51] p. 369.

understand. The prophet communicates these symbols to the public by way of myth and ritual.[52]

Two chapters later, this definition is expanded in order to account for the prophet as both communicator of theoretical knowledge and foreteller of future events. First we are told that, just as everybody possesses reason, so everybody possesses imagination, and is therefore to some extent capable of foretelling the future. What marks out the prophet is that he has developed his rational faculty to the utmost degree of which he is capable, making him receptive to the flow from the agent intellect that confers intuitive, perfect knowledge instead of painstaking deduction of one proposition from another through reason. This translates into clear and accurate knowledge of future events perceived in the imagination, instead of the fitful and unreliable intimations of the future which ordinary people with strong imaginations may receive. The difference in degree precipitates a difference in kind. It must be, argues Maimonides, that the difference is felt in both faculties:

Know that the true prophets indubitably grasp speculative matters; by means of his speculation alone, man is unable to grasp the causes from which what a prophet has come to know necessarily follows. This has a counterpart in their giving information regarding matters with respect to which man, using only common conjecture and divination, is unable to give information.[53]

In other words, ordinary people cannot through reasoning reach the knowledge of physics and metaphysics conferred upon the prophet by the agent intellect, because they lack the premises from which this knowledge follows. The prophet attains knowledge of good government and of the future that the ordinary, unaided imagination cannot grasp. The passage continues:

For the very overflow that affects the imaginative faculty—with a result of rendering it perfect so that its act brings about its giving information about what will happen and its apprehending those future events as if they were things that had been perceived by the senses and had reached the imaginative faculty from the senses—is also the overflow that renders perfect the act of the rational faculty, so that its act brings about its knowing things that are real in their existence, and it achieves this apprehension as if it had apprehended it by starting from speculative premises ... This should be even more fitting for the rational faculty. For the overflow of the Active Intellect goes in its true reality only to it [that is, to the rational faculty], causing it to pass from potentiality to actuality. It is from the rational faculty that that overflow comes to the imaginative faculty. How then can the imaginative faculty be perfected in so great

---

[52] J. L. Kraemer, *Maimonides*, 388.   [53] *Guide* ii. 38 (p. 377).

a measure as to apprehend what does not come to it from the senses, without the rational faculty being affected in a similar way so as to apprehend without having apprehended by way of premises, inference, and reflection?

The senses are to the imaginative faculty what logic is to the rational faculty. If the flow from the rational faculty to the imaginative faculty makes the imaginative faculty capable of perceiving in concrete form things that were never present to the senses, particularly future things, it must be that the rational faculty is vouchsafed scientific knowledge without having to go through the steps of logical deduction.

In short, in the true prophet, theoretical knowledge of physics and metaphysics and practical knowledge of the future are really two sides of the same coin, a result of the same communion with the agent intellect affecting the rational faculty. If we want to understand how it is that the same inspiration conveys both kinds of knowledge, we can refer to the discussion of the influence of the movements of the heavenly bodies on earthly events in the interpretation of Jacob's dream in *Guide* ii. 10. The implication is that anyone who has perfect knowledge of those movements and their effects will be able to predict such events. In the most finely attuned mind, knowledge of future history flows from knowledge of physics.[54] Discussing *Guide* ii. 38, Kreisel writes: 'In knowing all the universal laws of nature, the prophets divine about individual matters based on their all-encompassing theoretical knowledge of nature . . . Maimonides intimates that it is the overflow from the theoretical faculty that forms the basis for prophetic prediction.'[55]

We can now suggest a reason for the juxtaposition in 'Laws of the Foundations of the Torah', 7: 3, of 'the ladder that Jacob our father saw' and 'the living creatures that Ezekiel saw'. A Jewish thinker's approach to Ezekiel's vision of the living creatures, *ma'aseh merkavah*, is the touchstone of their position on the scale that runs from unadorned naturalism to other-worldly mysticism. The exposition of the vision of Ezekiel in *Guide* iii. 1–7 is meant to be obscure,[56] but in fact it is reasonably clear that it treats the vision as a

---

[54] This naturalistic approach is broadly in line with Avicenna's theory of divination. See Fakhry, *A History of Islamic Philosophy*, 146–7. In *Mishneh torah* Maimonides states that, while a true prophet's prognostications of good will always come about down to the last detail, evil ones can be confounded through repentance, so that the prophet's knowledge of the future is to some extent conditional—see 'Laws of the Foundations of the Torah', 10: 4. If we regard repentance as a change in the disposition of matter resulting in receptivity to a higher form, it is possible to understand how prophecy is at once conditional and scientific.

[55] Kreisel, *Maimonides' Political Thought*, 87. See also id., *Prophecy*, 254–5.

[56] *Guide* iii, Introduction (pp. 415–16).

representation of the motions of the spheres and the elements. The great secret of the *merkavah* is, then, no more than the philosopher's system. Maimonides was certainly understood this way in the fourteenth century by Moses of Narbonne (Narboni), who approved,[57] and in the fifteenth by Isaac Abravanel, who was dismayed.[58]

By placing Jacob's ladder and Ezekiel's living creatures together in 'Laws of the Foundations of the Torah', 7: 3, Maimonides conveys some of the profounder implications of the statement that 'The things made known to the prophet in the prophetic vision are made known to him through a parable'. The parable will reflect both the theoretical and the divinatory aspects of the insight gained through the prophet's conjunction with the agent intellect. As received in the rational faculty, the content of prophecy must presumably always be the same, although one prophet may receive more of it than another, just as, while one person may know more mathematical formulae than another, what they both know is part of the same whole. When it comes to the imaginative, symbolic representation of that content, however, there is room for variation. No two people will paint the same landscape the same way, and no two people are likely to produce identical symbolic expressions of an abstract concept. In the *Guide*, the very different parables of Jacob's ladder and Ezekiel's creatures both reflect the workings of nature. In the interpretation set out in *Guide* i. 15, Jacob's ladder also conveys truths about prophecy itself, especially that the prophet's knowledge of particulars and his ability to divine the future in the sublunary region of generation and corruption derive from his knowledge of the constant motions of the everlasting spheres. His 'descent' comes after his 'ascent'.

So the juxtaposition of Jacob's ladder and Ezekiel's creatures tells us about prophecy. The prediction of the rise and fall of the empires derives from the kind of theoretical knowledge that the creatures represent. Events on Earth are influenced by the movements of the spheres and stars, and so knowledge of those events derives from knowledge of those movements and their effects.[59]

What Maimonides omits from his *halakhah* is any mention of the number

---

[57] In commenting on *Guide* iii. 1, Narboni mentions the significance of the number four in *Guide* ii. 10.   [58] See Lawee, '"The Good We Accept"', 149–53.

[59] The multiplicity of interpretations of Jacob's ladder is permissible within Neoplatonic canons of exegesis, according to which 'the same thing by virtue of different aspects of itself can show an *analogia* to different elements of reality' (Dillon, 'Image, Symbol and Analogy', 256).

four, which clearly links Jacob's four-rung ladder and the four angels on it, as expounded by the Midrash,[60] with Ezekiel's four living creatures. If he leaves that connection, obvious to anyone who knows Bible and Midrash, for the reader to make, this is, in the first place, a further signal inviting a closer look at our *halakhah*, and, secondly, a possible indication that the connection should be made at a profounder level than mere numerical coincidence. It seems not unlikely that Maimonides saw the succession of four empires as linked to the number of the spheres, with the fifth age, that of the messiah, associated with the diurnal sphere, which, with its constant motion, most directly evidences God's existence and non-physicality,[61] or perhaps the correspondence is with the four elements and the fifth body.

Another question that arises is what Maimonides can possibly mean by including 'the living creatures that Ezekiel saw' among prophecies 'that state the parable and its interpretation'. He spends the first seven chapters of the third part of the *Guide*, plus the introduction to that part, elucidating this vision, and even then only in 'chapter headings'. This is supposed to be the mystery of mysteries; how can Maimonides say that it was stated with its interpretation, as though the interpretation were straightforward?

Two possible answers suggest themselves. One is that 'the living creatures that Ezekiel saw' is indeed a deep and difficult vision, but it does not come without an aid to understanding, for in *Guide* iii. 3, Maimonides treats the second version of the vision of the creatures, in Ezekiel 10, as a gloss on the first, in Ezekiel 1. This would be the accompanying interpretation referred to in our *halakhah*. A second possibility is that the *Guide* treats Ezekiel's vision on the esoteric level, as a parable about physics and metaphysics, but that the vision also has a plainer meaning, in the admonitions and predictions that follow each of the visions of the creatures and that are perhaps to be understood as having been apprehended through them, so that when Ezekiel says, 'And the word of the Lord came unto me', he refers to a transcript 'in clear' of something encrypted in a vision. This is not an answer that sits very comfortably with the text, which is full of further visions and symbols along the way, such as the scroll that Ezekiel sees and ingests in chapters 2 and 3. It would mean, though, that the juxtaposition with Jacob's ladder points to a parallel duality: each vision has a political/historical interpretation in our *halakhah* and a scientific/metaphysical interpretation in the *Guide*.

It might be objected that, when he wrote 'Laws of the Foundations of the

---

[60] With the exception of *Pesikta derav kahana*, where the angels are four but the ladder has many rungs.   [61] 'Laws of the Foundations of the Torah', 1: 7.

Torah', Maimonides did not know what he was going to write in the *Guide*. The *Guide* therefore cannot be used as an aid to the interpretation of 'Laws of the Foundations of the Torah', 7: 3. It is one thing to suggest that matters discussed at length in the *Guide* are hinted at in *Mishneh torah*, and quite another to suggest that *Mishneh torah* is written as though the *Guide* will complement it. In fact, the temporal relationship between the two is complicated. In part, the *Guide* is a revised attempt at conveying the meanings of prophetic parables and rabbinic Midrash after Maimonides abandoned earlier works meant to explicate these matters,[62] works that are already projected in the *Commentary on the Mishnah*.[63] It seems most likely, then, that Maimonides had worked out his various interpretations of Jacob's dream and Ezekiel's vision before he wrote 'Laws of the Foundations of the Torah', 7: 3, in which case it is legitimate to see the *Guide* as reflecting ideas that would have already been in his mind at that earlier time.[64]

If the derivation of knowledge of the future from knowledge of physics is part of the meaning of 'Laws of the Foundations of the Torah', 7: 3, we can also see why such a message should be given in coded fashion in *Mishneh torah*. Anyone not properly trained in logic and science might confuse it with the position of the astrologers that Maimonides condemns, namely, that the future is in the stars. He certainly saw a link between the heavens and life on Earth, but he believed in, and contributed to, a systematic science asserting a chain of cause and effect that explained general processes, rather than the reading of the fates of individuals or groups in the positions of the heavenly bodies.[65] Usually, this science is acquired through long mental toil, but rare individuals, who have already toiled all they can, may receive a sudden inundation of knowledge from the agent intellect.

At any rate, what Maimonides has done in our *halakhah* is to play one biblical reference against another, and both against their midrashic resonances, to combine revelation of the future with the secrets of the Torah.

We now move to the last pair of parables cited in 'Laws of the Foundations of the Torah', 7: 3, Ezekiel's scroll and Zechariah's basket. We have seen

---

[62] See *Guide* i, Introduction (pp. 9–10).

[63] See 'Introduction to *Perek ḥelek*' (*Commentary on the Mishnah*, Order *Nezikin*, 140). The work on prophecy is stated to have been commenced.

[64] See Langermann, 'Fusul Musa'. Langermann suggests that the *Guide* brings together short memoranda that Maimonides composed over a long period, which supports the idea that *Mishneh torah* and the *Guide* can to some extent be viewed in parallel. See, however, Kasher, 'Early Stratum'.

[65] See Langermann, 'Maimonides' Repudiation of Astrology' and 'Astronomical Problems in Maimonides' (Heb.).

at least a possible reason that Maimonides juxtaposes Jacob's dream and the four creatures seen by Ezekiel. The reason that he then interrupts with two references to Jeremiah before returning to Ezekiel seems to be that he also wanted to create the juxtaposition of Ezekiel and Zechariah, for this juxtaposition is also significant. Ezekiel was not the only prophet who saw a scroll in one of his visions: Zechariah did too, as is related just before the vision of the basket that Maimonides cites.[66] Ezekiel's scroll is an indictment of Israel. The meaning of Zechariah's scroll is obscure, but it appears to be an indictment of the non-Jews who impeded the rebuilding of the Temple after the Babylonian exile.[67] Zechariah's vision of the basket seems to have similar significance, namely, that the opponents of the work of rebuilding the Temple will be removed. So between Ezekiel and Zechariah we move from rebuke and punishment to redemption.

If it has been hinted that we should look at what precedes the vision of the basket in Zechariah, perhaps we should also be prepared to look at what follows it.

And I turned, and lifted up mine eyes, and looked, and behold, there came four chariots out from between two mountains; and the mountains were mountains of brass. In the first chariot were red horses; and in the second chariot black horses. And in the third chariot white horses; and in the fourth chariot grisled and bay horses. Then I answered and said unto the angel that talked with me, What are these, my lord? And the angel answered and said unto me, These are the four winds of the heavens, which go forth from standing before the Lord of all the earth.[68]

Maimonides cites this passage in *Guide* ii. 10, where he expounds on the number four, continuing from his 'physical' interpretation of Jacob's dream:

In his parables, *Zekhariah*—when describing that *there came out four chariots from between the two mountains, and the mountains were mountains of brass*—says in interpretation of this: *these are the four airs of the heavens which go forth after presenting themselves before the Lord of all the earth.* They are accordingly the cause of everything that comes to pass in time.[69]

Is this, too, meant to be one of the overtones of 'Laws of the Foundations of the Torah', 7: 3? It may be stretching a point to see the *Guide* as supplementing *Mishneh torah* to such an extent, but it should come as no surprise that there are those who interpret the four chariots/winds as referring to the four kingdoms.[70] We have here another instance of a parable like Jacob's ladder,

---

[66] Zech. 5: 1–4.   [67] See *Tanakh da'at mikra, zekharyah*, 18–19.
[68] Zech. 6: 1–5.   [69] *Guide* ii. 10 (pp. 272–3).
[70] See *Tanakh da'at mikra, zekharyah*, Introduction, 11–12.

one that has a theoretical interpretation in the *Guide*, and besides that also a historical interpretation, one that may possibly be alluded to in *Mishneh torah*, bearing in mind that the four chariots are 'the cause of everything that comes to pass in time'.

It remains to try to understand the references to Jeremiah and their inverted order. It could be that this requires leaving exegesis and returning to basics. The main point of 'Laws of the Foundations of the Torah', 7: 3, is to inform us that the prophets speak in parables. In that respect, the *halakhah* can be regarded as a condensed version of *Guide* ii. 43, which explicitly refers back to it. In that chapter of the *Guide*, Maimonides discusses different kinds of parables (using some of the same examples as in the *halakhah*), and the different ways in which their meanings are made known to the prophets who receive them. The rod of an almond tree is there contrasted with the seething pot (and other parables) in that while the latter conveys its meaning through visual symbolism, the former does so through a play on words. It could therefore be that the parables Maimonides cites in our *halakhah* have a similar function, namely, to illustrate different parabolic styles, as well as to serve as examples of the point that parables are sometimes accompanied by explanations and sometimes not. In that respect, as a visual symbol, the seething pot that Jeremiah saw has more in common with the living creatures that Ezekiel saw than does the rod of an almond tree, hence the order of creatures–pot–almond rod in the *halakhah*. As it happens, the two visions of Jeremiah are discussed in reverse order in *Guide* ii. 43 as well, and the chapter in general jumbles the examples it cites as far as their biblical order is concerned, without that seeming particularly significant. It is the more taut style of *Mishneh torah* that makes one sensitive to such anomalies.

There is, however, an intriguing point of connection, in content rather than in style, between Ezekiel's living creatures and Jeremiah's seething pot: the creatures come from the north, and the pot points north, indicating that evil will come from that direction.

And I looked, and behold, a whirlwind came out of the north, a great cloud, and a fire infolding itself, and a brightness was about it, and out of the midst thereof as the colour of amber, out of the midst of the fire. Also out of the midst thereof came the likeness of four living creatures.[71]

Then the Lord came unto me the second time, saying, What seest thou? And I said, I see a seething pot; and the face thereof is toward the north. Then the Lord said unto me, Out of the north an evil shall break forth upon all the inhabitants of the land.[72]

[71] Ezek. 1: 4–5.   [72] Jer. 1: 13–14.

It is hard to know what, if anything, to make of this. The connection, if it is intentional, may possibly only be meant to indicate that the references to the prophets in 'Laws of the Foundations of the Torah', 7: 2–3 are concatenated, representing, perhaps, the idea of Abraham's vision being transmitted to his grandson and to the prophets, as related in 'Laws of Idolatry', 1: 3.

Alternatively, Maimonides could be indicating that, although he eschews the midrashic method, which flattens the Bible and treats it as a homogenous text, and instead respects the contours and climate of each book and each kind of writing—this is the lesson of the previous *halakhah* we looked at—nevertheless, since all prophecy is of common origin in the agent intellect, there is room for prophecies to comment on one another and for treating them as a single system of symbols, somewhat midrashically, despite the individuality of imagination. If that is so, then our two neighbouring *halakhot* represent two halves of a balanced and nuanced essay on Bible interpretation.

Perhaps it is time to take up again the thread that was left hanging in the discussion above of the transition from chapter 6 to chapter 7 of 'Laws of the Foundations of the Torah', and the unfolding of history.

'Laws of the Foundations of the Torah', 6: 9, left us in exile with Daniel and Nebuchadnezzar's dream about the four empires. This historical nadir coincides with the spiritual and intellectual nadir that 'Laws of the Foundations of the Torah', chapter 6, represents: the erasure of God's name. In Chapter 4 above, a pattern was noted in *Mishneh torah* of loss followed by restoration, and the transition in 'Laws of the Foundations of the Torah' from chapter 6 to chapter 7 was mentioned as the first example, the theme of erasure of God's name and destruction giving way to the theme of prophecy, with its promise of redemption and ultimate universal knowledge of God at the end of the period of domination of the fourth and last empire. That is the transition described in general terms. It is now possible to see it in finer detail, in the particular prophecies and *midrashim* that Maimonides cites and evokes.

Looked at as aggadah, 'Laws of the Foundations of the Torah', 7: 2, with its pairing of Abraham and Daniel, is a kind of recapitulation of 'Laws of the Foundations of the Torah', 6: 9. This time, however, via the *midrash* in *Mekhilta derabi yishma'el*, the four empires are associated with Abraham. In part, this *midrash* is consolatory. The thought behind it appears to be that if, in the episode of 'the covenant between the pieces', Abraham was vouchsafed a prophecy of his descendants' enslavement in Egypt and their eventual deliverance, then he surely must also have had some intimation of their later exile, and of their eventual redemption. By reading such an intimation into Genesis 15: 12, *Mekhilta derabi yishma'el* gives comfort to a dispossessed and vulnerable people: their plight was foreknown to their progenitor, is part of a plan, and, most importantly, has a destined end. Association of the four empires with the more ancient and revered figure of Abraham, rather than just with Daniel, makes that plight easier to come to terms with: it is built into the original programme.

The figure of Jacob also provides comfort. Midrash *Genesis Rabbah* sees his departure from Beersheba for Haran, on which journey he has the dream of the ladder, as foreshadowing the exile of his descendants.[73] But Jacob eventually returned home. Similarly, Jeremiah's prophecy is one of destruction, and Ezekiel's scroll contains rebuke, but the *halakhah* closes with Zechariah and his vision of restoration.

This reading may seem more like *derash* than *peshat*, but our two problematic *halakhot* do seem to call for some kind of constructive explanation. If the one offered here is considered fanciful, then some other must be sought, for while the overtones created by the arrangements of biblical references may be subtle, they cannot be ignored.

Maimonides' own historical situation should also be borne in mind. One only has to read the *Epistle on Martyrdom* and the *Epistle to Yemen* to understand how keenly aware he was of the precarious state of the Jewish people in his time, and how anxious he was to comfort them and instil confidence in the prophecies of redemption, while at the same time disabusing them of false and dangerous hopes. So, in the *Epistle to Yemen*, he invokes the prophecy of Daniel about the four empires in order to assure the Jews of Yemen that the tyrannous Islamic empire will come to an end,[74] but inveighs against the notion that eras in history have anything to do with astrological periods, dismissing as fraud astrological calculations of the date of the advent of the messiah.[75] In his youth, Maimonides himself, along with his family, was buffeted by Islamic persecution, and his messianic ideal envisaged an age in which truth could be pursued without disturbance.

For Maimonides then, prophecy was not just a theoretical subject, a matter of defining the intellectual perfection of the individual. As well as the truth of the prophecy of Moses as the basis of the authority of the law, which is discussed at length in 'Laws of the Foundations of the Torah', the historical

---

[73] *Gen. Rabbah* 68: 13. It may be noteworthy that Jacob is referred to as 'Jacob our father', perhaps indicating that he is to be thought of typologically, whereas in the previous *halakhah* Abraham is plain Abraham.   [74] *Epistles*, ed. Halkin and Hartman, 100–1.   [75] Ibid. 114–18.

truth of the prophecies of the patriarchs, of Daniel, and of Isaiah, Jeremiah, and the other prophets of Israel was of real, practical and emotional, concern to him. This concern would have been a good reason for Maimonides to have inserted into his discussion of the theory and legal framework of prophecy hints at the content of the messages of the prophets, and at the scientific basis for believing in them. By being oblique he could link theory and history without nourishing the kind of superstition and febrile speculation that elsewhere in his writings he forcefully combated.[76]

Maimonides and Historical Process

Does the link between theory and history give us a theory of history? The effect of the motions of the spheres on the elements has no particular *telos*. In the previous chapter we saw that lack being supplied by repentance, but repentance does not account for the rise and fall of empires. Is it, then, possible to fill the gap between the four empires and the four spheres? Does the way Maimonides conveys a sense of destiny imply anything about how that destiny will come to pass?

Opinion is divided on these questions, and it is not possible to deal with them here other than in very general terms, to see whether our textual analysis comes down on one side or other of the argument. Salo Baron saw Maimonides as without any systematic theory of history. 'Whatever the reasons, Maimonides undoubtedly was consciously "unhistorical"', he wrote, although he added, 'Unconsciously, however, he could not help referring to the history of his people when he wished to explain certain contemporary phenomena.'[77] Baron sees this unhistorical attitude partly as a reaction against the approach of such as Abraham bar Hiyya, who, following Arabian historians, combined astrology and history and tried to explain historical developments through the influence of the stars.[78] 'Among the other methodical problems his rejection of the astrological method stands out', he writes.[79]

Baron refers to Maimonides' interpretation of Daniel: 'The four beasts as well as the four words "return" are allusions to the four empires of Greece, Rome, Persia and Islam which were to exercise domination over the Jews before the advent of the messiah',[80] but cautions, 'This optimistic view of the ultimate future should not be mistaken for a belief in the idea of progress.'[81]

By contrast, Amos Funkenstein describes Maimonides as seeing the same

---

[76] On prophecy in its political context see Ravitzky, 'Maimonides on the Days of the Messiah', and Blidstein, *Political Concepts* (Heb.), 269–82.   [77] Baron, 'Historical Outlook', 113–14.
[78] Ibid. 112.   [79] Ibid. 161.   [80] Ibid. 157.   [81] Ibid. 158.

dialectical principle of divine accommodation at work in nature, the commandments, and history. On Maimonides' explanation of sacrifices as a way
of directing pagan means to monotheistic ends, Funkenstein writes, 'Just as
Hegel's *objektiver Geist* uses the subjective, egotistic freedom of man to further the objective goals of history . . . so also Maimonides' God fights poly-
theism with its own weapons and uses elements of its worship as a fruitful
deceit.'[82]

The idea of progress is, in Funkenstein's view, very much present in
Maimonides: 'The messianic age crowns a didactic and dialectical process
which began with the modest establishment of a monotheistic community by
Abraham, continued with the fortification through laws of this community
after its relapse, advanced with the growing hold of the monotheistic imagery
in Israel, and made a decisive progress even in the time of the Diaspora.'[83]

Again, after surveying Maimonides' comments on the function of Christianity and Islam in spreading knowledge of the commandments, he writes,
'These and other scattered passages add up to a distinct view of the course
and phases of human history seen as a history of monotheisation.'[84]

Funkenstein notes that, in *The Epistle to Yemen*, the four empires are
loosely associated with the sects described as using different stratagems for
undermining Judaism,[85] stratagems that ultimately work in Judaism's favour,
another manifestation of a divine ruse. The four empires are not just successive world powers: they have ideological significance, and the eras that pass
before the messiah are therefore not just periods of time to be waited
through, but processes to be undergone, bringing the messiah in train.

Baron's remarks about Maimonides' aversion to contemporary astrological approaches to history provide yet clearer motivation for the oblique way
in which the relationship between theory in history is expressed in *Mishneh
torah*. The idea that knowledge of the movements of heavenly bodies is connected to knowledge of the future might have been thought to coincide with
the claims of astrology. The idea could therefore not be discussed explicitly,
but, at the same time, a discussion of prophecy would not be complete without it.

In the main, though, the analysis suggested above coincides more with
Funkenstein's view. Maimonides does seem to have thought that there was

[82] Funkenstein, *Perceptions of Jewish History*, 143.   [83] Ibid. 148.   [84] Ibid. 149.
[85] Ibid. 151. Interestingly, in commenting that 'Maimonides, unlike some Jewish and most
Christian philosophers of history, did not pay specific attention to detailed periodizations. Nor was he
interested in history as such', Funkenstein cites Baron, yet it seems to me that their views do diverge.
(Funkenstein, *Perceptions of Jewish History*, 151 n. 66).

progress in history. He was not especially interested in particular historical events, which tend to excite astrologers, but he was very interested in historical processes, and he believed that they were connected to the motions of the spheres. So history exhibits a pattern of generation, decay, and regeneration symbolized by the pattern of loss and restoration in *Mishneh torah* as described above in Chapter 4, a pattern that can be seen as parallel to the natural processes engendered in sublunary nature through the circular motions of the spheres inducing vertical movement in the elements.

Above all, the different symbolic significances of Jacob's dream, stated separately in the *Guide*, but suggested simultaneously in 'Laws of the Foundations of the Torah', 7: 3, bring together natural and historical processes, in what looks like support for Funkenstein's way of linking the two.

That said, it must be borne in mind that, for Maimonides, progress in history is always restorative, and not towards any unfolding, yet to be understood ideal. As Kenneth Seeskin puts it, modifying Baron's verdict, 'it would be better to say that what Maimonides lacked is not a sense of history but the sense of history that measures change in terms of conceptual revolution'.[86] The ideal remains the state of Adam before the Fall, possessed of the knowledge of true and false rather than good and evil, and history cannot improve on it.

Mishneh Torah as Prophecy

It was argued in the previous chapter that *Mishneh torah* meets the criteria for intelligibility. Can it go one step further and qualify as prophecy? If its structure is a representation of the ascent and descent of the prophet, and if it contains such subtle references to the theory of prophecy and the message of the prophets, is it telling us something about itself? If its content fulfils the purposes of teaching correct opinions, inculcating sound morals, and abolishing wrongdoing, while its form reflects God's governance of the universe, does it not embody the mentality of the prophet-king, ordering human affairs while fixed on God?

R. Hayim Joseph David Azulai, also known by the acronym Hida (1724–1807), believed that the holy spirit (*ruaḥ hakodesh*), which is at least a state of readiness for prophecy, rested on Maimonides, and he is not alone.[87] In the

---

[86] Seeskin, 'Maimonides' Sense of History', 137. See also Spero, 'Maimonides and the Sense of History'.

[87] See M. B. Shapiro, *Studies in Maimonides*, 88. Shapiro cites a passage in which, referring to Maimonides, Hida echoes precisely the language of 'Laws of the Foundations of the Torah', 7: 1 about the holy spirit resting on the prophet.

world of the yeshiva it is a commonplace that *Mishneh torah* is imbued with *ruaḥ hakodesh*. The late Lubavitcher Rebbe, Menachem Mendel Schneerson, would even apply to it methods of biblical exegesis, finding parables in seemingly mundane *halakhot*.[88] Such things attest to the aura that *Mishneh torah* possesses. In his essay 'Did Maimonides Believe that He Had Attained the Rank of Prophet?', Heschel wrote:

> From hints in Maimonides' writings one suspects that this master rationalist and the teacher of all future generations, concerning whom modern scholars would claim that his soul recoiled from all taint of mystery-mongering obscurantism and would have totally rejected anything which lay beyond the bounds of the human intellect, was himself a seeker after prophecy,[89]

and went on to list the hints he had found.[90] Heschel's notion that Maimonides had prophetic longings has not gained widespread acceptance, but in the light of what has been asserted here about *Mishneh torah*'s form, it is worth revisiting.

  A cardinal feature of Maimonides' doctrine of prophecy is that all prophets after Moses derive their legitimacy from the law of Moses, and their prophecies have force only within the scope permitted by the law. A prophet may not introduce any permanent change in the law,[91] and may not invoke prophetic insight—from a heavenly voice, for example—to settle a dispute about the law in a particular case.[92] This is Maimonides' view of the tradition, one well grounded in the Talmud,[93] and also clearly intended to counter Christian and Islamic claims of a new divine dispensation. These limitations, however, only apply to the prophet *qua* prophet. They do not mean that the same person cannot be both prophet and sage, and in the latter capacity engage in legal disputation on the same terms as other sages, using the same tools of logic and interpretation. The biblical prophets were, after all, part of the chain of trans-

---

[88] See Gotlieb, *Habad's approach to Maimonides* (Heb.).   [89] Heschel, *Prophetic Inspiration*, 70.

[90] Heschel also cites a very early association of the holy spirit with Maimonides, in Samuel ibn Tibbon's *Ma'amar yikavu hamayim*. On the *Guide*'s allusions to secrets of creation, Ibn Tibbon wrote, 'it is as if they came to me via the Holy Spirit' (Heschel, *Prophetic Inspiration*, 124). The original is: *ukhe'ilu ba li beruaḥ hakodesh* (Ibn Tibbon, *Ma'amar yikavu hamayim*, 9). Incidentally, in his preface to Heschel's book, Moshe Idel points out an ambiguity in the expression *ruaḥ hakodesh*: it is not always clear whether it is being used metaphorically, 'to enhance the authority of a certain type of teaching', or whether the intended meaning is 'a feeling of revelation from above in the proper sense of the word' (*Prophetic Inspiration*, p. ix).

[91] 'Laws of the Foundations of the Torah', 9: 1.   [92] Ibid. 9: 4.

[93] See e.g. BT *BM* 59b, alluded to in 'Laws of the Foundations of the Torah', 9: 4 through the biblical phrase 'it is not in heaven' (Num. 30: 12).

mission of the law.[94] Moreover, Maimonides observes that a prophet does not necessarily have a public mission; prophecy may be a matter of personal enlightenment only.[95] The possibility therefore remains open of a sage possessed of prophetic qualities. That is how Kreisel interprets Maimonides' portrait of R. Judah the Prince in the introduction to the *Commentary on the Mishnah*:

Significantly, Maimonides in the introduction to his *Commentary on the Mishnah* treats R. Judah the Prince, the compiler of the Mishnah, as a person whose intellectual and moral perfection was exceeded only by that of Moses. In ascribing to him all the qualifications for prophecy, Maimonides essentially indicates that while there were no postbiblical *public* prophets, those possessing prophetic perfection continued to arise on the stage of history. They functioned as great sages. R. Judah the Prince is the model of such a sage. The product of his activity had a singular impact both in preserving and adapting the Law to his period. More than any other postbiblical figure, he served as the model for Maimonides' own activity.[96]

In the introduction to *Mishneh torah*, by way of justifying his audacity in compiling the work, Maimonides describes the circumstances of the Jewish people and their deleterious effect on Jewish learning in his time in terms very similar to those in which he describes the historical circumstances that prompted R. Judah the Prince to compile the Mishnah.[97] Without making a direct comparison, Maimonides clearly implies that the Mishnah is a precedent and that R. Judah the Prince is indeed a role model. The conclusion that begs to be drawn is that Maimonides attributed to himself qualities similar to those attributed to R. Judah the Prince in the introduction to the *Commentary on the Mishnah*.

---

[94] Mishnah *Avot* 1: 1, and see Maimonides' introductions both to his *Commentary on the Mishnah* and to *Mishneh torah*.

[95] 'Laws of the Foundations of the Torah', 7: 7; *Guide* ii. 37 (p. 375): 'Sometimes the prophetic revelation that comes to a prophet only renders him perfect and has no other effect. And sometimes the prophetic revelation that comes to him compels him to address a call to the people, teach them, and let his own perfection overflow toward them.'

[96] Kreisel, *Maimonides' Political Thought*, 27. A speculation: Maimonides describes himself in his rhyming prose Hebrew prologue to the *Epistle to Yemen* as *katan mikotnei ḥakhmei sefarad*, 'the least of the least of the sages of Spain' (*Letters*, ed. Shailat (Heb.), 82). In BT *Suk.* 28a, R. Yohanan ben Zakai is described as *katan shebekulan* 'the least [youngest?] of them all', i.e. of the eighty pupils of Hillel; but of course it fell to him to rescue Jewish learning from the catastrophe of the destruction of the Second Temple. Did Maimonides identify with this earlier saviour of the Jewish people in time of crisis as well as with R. Judah the Prince, and hint as much in his letter, in an expression that is self-deprecating but at the same time, possibly, self-mythologizing?   [97] See above, Introduction, n. 238.

So much for circumstantial evidence. Is there internal evidence in the body of *Mishneh torah* of prophetic intent?

Prophecy, we have seen, derives from 'all-encompassing theoretical knowledge of nature', as Kreisel put it. This finds expression in *Mishneh torah* in the final stage of the prophet's progress as described in 'Laws of the Foundations of the Torah', 7: 1, when he 'gazes at the wisdom of the Holy One Blessed be He in its entirety, from the first form to the earthly globe, and recognizes His greatness from them—immediately, the holy spirit (*ruaḥ hakodesh*) rests upon him'.

The key phrase for our purposes is 'in its entirety' (*kulah* in the Hebrew). Taking our cue from this phrase, and bearing in mind what we have learned about prophecy from the *Guide*, we might interpret the thought behind this passage in the following way. The universe is greater than the sum of its parts. As the product of God's creative act, it is a complete manifestation of his wisdom. The point of creation, Maimonides says in the *Guide*, is 'the bringing into being of everything whose existence is possible, existence being indubitably a good'.[98] God does not stint. When we look at the universe, we see not what happens to exist, but everything that could possibly exist, all that God's wisdom can contrive.[99] We are, as it were, looking at God's reflection, all of the divine that a human being is capable of apprehending. If we understand a part of the universe, we see God's wisdom at work, and our knowledge thereby increases; but if we understand it all, we see God's wisdom itself, and this pitches us into an altogether different order of knowledge, or at least into a state in which we are capable of a different order of knowledge.[100] This order of knowledge is called *ruaḥ hakodesh*, the transformed state in which the

---

[98] *Guide* iii. 25 (p. 506).

[99] On Maimonides and the 'principle of plenitude' see Leaman, *Moses Maimonides*, 178; Manekin, 'Problems of Plenitude'. On the principle in Neoplatonic thought generally, see Wallis, *Neoplatonism*, 69.

[100] Knowledge can never, however, really be complete; the would-be prophet is restricted to knowledge gained from observation of the artifice, and can never penetrate to the mind of the artificer—see *Guide* iii. 21 (pp. 484–5). See also *Guide* iii. 8 (p. 432) on the highest rank of human beings, who 'only reflect on the mental representation of an intelligible, on the grasp of a true opinion regarding everything, and on union with the divine intellect, which lets overflow towards them that through which form exists', and Kreisel's comment, '"Union" or "conjunction" in this passage does not refer to the point at which one attains a "mental representation of an intelligible." It refers to the end result of the process of attaining *all* the intelligibles, or "true opinion regarding everything"' (*Maimonides' Political Thought*, 145). Note that this leaving behind of the material claims of one's body to identify with the universe as a whole is the fulfilment of a Neoplatonic ideal. See Wallis, *Neoplatonism*, 77.

would-be prophet communes with the lower angels, the *ishim* (also known as the agent intellect), and is ready to receive the prophetic gift.

Comprehensive knowledge, then, gives rise to *ruaḥ hakodesh*. Now comprehensiveness is a noted feature of *Mishneh torah*'s content. In his introduction to the work, Maimonides himself draws attention to its comprehensive treatment of halakhah:

On these grounds, I, Moses the son of Maimon the Sephardi, bestirred myself, and relying on the help of God, blessed be He, intently studied all these works, with the view of putting together the results obtained from them in regard to what is forbidden or permitted, clean or unclean, and the other rules of the Torah—all in plain language and terse style, so that thus the entire Oral Law might become systematically known to all, without citing difficulties and solutions or differences of view, one person saying so, and another something else—but consisting of statements, clear and convincing, and in accordance with the conclusions drawn from all these compilations and commentaries that have appeared from the time of Moses to the present, so that all the rules shall be accessible to young and old . . . so that no other work should be needed for ascertaining any of the laws of Israel, but that this work might serve as a compendium of the entire Oral Law . . . Hence, I have entitled this work *Mishneh torah* (Repetition of the Law), for the reason that a person who first reads the Written Law and then this compilation, will know from it the whole of the Oral Law, without having occasion to consult any other book between them.

This passage is quoted at length in order to bring out three ways in which Maimonides claims that *Mishneh torah* is comprehensive: he says that it draws upon all sources of the law; that it includes all the laws; and that it is accessible to all—which is perhaps not comprehensiveness, but is, at any rate, universal comprehensibility.[101] For present purposes, the most important of these

---

[101] How far Maimonides actually fulfilled this programme is another matter. In fact, *Mishneh torah* does not entirely consist of lapidary statements of the law. It sometimes mentions divergent opinions, most commonly when Maimonides is concerned to overturn a ruling of the *ge'onim*, and once famously when he overturns a ruling of his father ('Laws of Slaughter', 11: 10). Now and again, the reasoning behind a *halakhah* is given (e.g. in 'Laws of Entrance into the Sanctuary', 2: 7). As far as comprehensibility goes, there are parts of *Mishneh torah* in which Maimonides imports swathes of Mishnah almost unedited (in 'Laws of the Sabbath', for example), with all the original's disadvantages of extreme terseness and obscure vocabulary, and without necessarily pausing to distil general principles from lists of cases (although such lists are organized with characteristic logic and method). It is hard to understand such passages without the aid of a commentator learned in the Talmud, which means that *Mishneh torah* does not render the Talmud altogether dispensable. The focus on particular cases rather than on legal principles was one of the grounds on which Crescas challenged its pretension to being a final repository of the law—see W. Z. Harvey, *Rabbi Hisdai Crescas*, 42; Ackerman, 'Hasdai Crescas on the Philosophic Foundation of Codification'. Ackerman demonstrates how

claims is the second. On the face of it, all three claims relate to the work's practical reliability and usefulness, but, as Twersky notes, we have already a hint of something beyond that is to be found in the sheer number of times that Maimonides uses the word 'all': 'The word "all" and variations of it occur with the rhythmic regularity of a lyrical refrain; comprehensiveness is the hallmark of these programmatic pronouncements and all-inclusiveness is their goal. Holism is another aspect of making the "Torah great and glorious," commodious and comprehensive—it helps transcend functionality.'[102]

Holism is indeed transcendent, as the passage about the prophet tells us. Since the law, like nature, is a product of God's wisdom,[103] the same kind of argument applies to it as was outlined above in relation to science. The *Sifrei* on Deuteronomy 6: 6, 'take these words to heart, for thus will you recognize Him who spoke, and the world came into being', and the interchangeability that Maimonides sees between the commandments and the cosmos as paths to recognition, are again relevant. Someone who knows a commandment understands a small part of God's wisdom, and of course knows what to do in particular circumstances. Someone who knows all of the commandments is beyond doing; he has absorbed God's wisdom into his very being, and his mind is transformed.

Treatment of the whole of the law is in fact *Mishneh torah*'s motto: 'Then shall I not be ashamed, when I have respect unto all thy commandments.'[104] In full, the passage from which the motto is taken reads:

1. Blessed are the undefiled in the way, who walk in the law of the Lord.
2. Blessed are they that keep his testimonies, and that seek him with the whole heart.
3. They also do no iniquity: they walk in his ways.
4. Thou hast commanded us to keep thy precepts diligently.
5. O that my ways were directed to keep thy statutes!

Crescas' own programme (never fulfilled) for a Jewish legal code was of a piece with his general philosophy, a conclusion similar to the argument here about Maimonides' plan in *Mishneh torah*.

[102] Twersky, *Introduction to the Code*, 189 (this passage was cited in the Introduction). A caveat should be added that the word *kol* in Maimonides does not always necessarily mean 'all'; sometimes it means 'most' or 'many'. For example, in 'Laws of Kings and Their Wars', 11: 3 he asserts that 'R. Akiva and all [*kol*] the sages of his generation' saw Kozba (Bar Kokhva) as the messiah, when in fact there were dissenters—see Ravitzky, 'Maimonides on the Days of the Messiah', 244. An even clearer example is 'Laws of Joining Domains', 3: 1. Nevertheless, in our passage the sense does seem to be the usual one.   [103] See *Guide* iii. 26 (pp. 506–10).

[104] Ps. 119: 6. That this motto serves to stress the comprehensiveness of *Mishneh torah* is noted by Twersky—*Introduction to the Code*, 190. All of ch. 3 (pp. 188–237, entitled 'Scope') of Twersky's *Introduction* is especially pertinent to this discussion.

6. *Then shall I not be ashamed, when I have respect unto all thy commandments.*

7. I will praise thee with uprightness of heart, when I shall have learned thy righteous judgments.

8. I will keep thy statutes: O forsake me not utterly.[105]

In its context, the verse probably means 'I shall not be ashamed when I look at all your commandments if I have directed myself towards keeping them all.' Quoted out of context, it could mean that looking at the commandments in their entirety itself removes shame—the shame of ignorance, or the shame of separation from the agent intellect and being locked in one's material existence.[106] In other words, the motto could be taken as a reference to the transforming effect of knowing the law in its entirety.[107]

Mishneh torah's microcosmic structure can be taken as implying that comprehensive knowledge of nature and comprehensive knowledge of the law are equivalent. By placing its exposition of the law in a cosmic setting, *Mishneh torah* fulfils its own precept that all actions should be directed towards the knowledge of God. It also holds out a kind of promise that whoever reads and comprehends it acquires not just information but knowledge. It is a kind of lens through which God may, within the limits of human capacity, be perceived. For Maimonides, such perception is the ultimate goal of the commandments, and the communication of it may be supposed to be the motive and ultimate goal of *Mishneh torah*. The prophet's ascent and descent are therefore also the ascent and descent of the reader of *Mishneh torah*. The dynamic of that work transforms the commandments from a series of practices to a scale of values, by ascending which we can transcend right and wrong to reach a restored consciousness of true and false. This is the recovery of the Adamic state of consciousness that Ravitzky describes as the universalist aspect of Maimonides' dual model of the messianic era, as mentioned above, at the beginning of Chapter 4. *Mishneh torah* thus appears to offer the possibility of redemption in the here and now, or, at least, an analogy of the redemption to come.[108]

---

[105] Ps. 119: 1–8 (italics added).

[106] The comma in the *Authorized Version* after 'Then shall I not be ashamed' tends to indicate that the original sense is close to this interpretation, and that the verse means, 'Looking at your commandments will remove my sense of shame.' This reading takes 'then' as looking forward, rather than back to the preceding verse. Radak, ad loc., favours the latter reading, Ibn Ezra the former.

[107] Perhaps even in the psalm itself there is a hint that performance of the commandments after learning them all (verses 6 and 7) is different from performance of them before they are learnt.

[108] See also Blidstein, *Political Concepts* (Heb.), 269.

Mishneh torah is also historically comprehensive. Its coverage of all of human intellectual history and destiny, from the first disturbance in intellectual balance 'in the days of Enosh' (before which human beings were presumably serenely certain in their knowledge of God and therefore nothing of consequence happened) to Abraham's mission, the Exodus and the giving of the Torah, to final restoration of universal knowledge of God in the age of the messiah, and its mobility on the level of halakhah between the unredeemed present and the redeemed future, was noted in the Introduction. The effect is to make all time seem eternally present—another transcendent effect of holism, and, possibly, a reflection of the dual insight of the prophet, whose intuitive knowledge of cosmic processes makes the future present to his mind. The pattern of loss and restoration that was found in the previous chapter to link individual and national destiny, and to be powered by repentance, might be regarded as prophetic, a distillation of the message of the biblical prophets built into *Mishneh torah*.

All in all, *Mishneh torah* performs the function of the prophet, converting intellectually cognized truths into symbolic figures proceeding from and acting upon the imagination. It can therefore be considered, in Maimonides' own terms, if not a work of prophecy, then at least an analogy of prophecy.

The answer to the question whether *Mishneh torah* should be regarded as prophecy perhaps depends on the answer to another question, raised by Moshe Halbertal, which is whether *Mishneh torah* is halakhah, in the same way that the Mishnah is halakhah, or only a textbook about halakhah.[109] If it is halakhah, then Maimonides can indeed be thought of as having taken on a prophetic mantle that passed from Moses to R. Judah the Prince, and features of *Mishneh torah* such as its comprehensiveness and its cosmic symbolism can be seen as of a piece with that. If it is only about halakhah, then its prophetic features are only analogies. Halbertal's answer is that Maimonides himself was ambivalent, leaving the halakhic status of his work to be determined by its reception among the Jewish people. He must have known whether he had experienced anything like a prophetic vision, but the question of the objective status of *Mishneh torah* as prophecy is similarly left open.

Summary

Maimonides deploys aggadah to add extra layers of meaning in *Mishneh torah*. Where he makes intense use of biblical reference, close reading and attention

---

[109] Halbertal, 'What Is *Mishneh Torah*?'

to midrashic resonances can be rewarding. Two examples of this were analysed. 'Laws of the Foundations of the Torah', 6:9, was interpreted as broadening the chapter's theme of avoiding desecration of sacred objects and texts to include the need for sensitive reading of texts. In 'Laws of the Foundations of the Torah', 7:3, the juxtaposition of Jacob's dream of the ladder with Ezekiel's vision of the chariot was found to refer to the combination of theoretical knowledge and insight into historical process in the vision of the prophet. This is reflected in the ontological and teleological dimensions of *Mishneh torah*'s form. That in turn suggests that there may be grounds for renewing speculation that Maimonides aspired to prophetic status.

CHAPTER SIX

CONCLUSION: *MISHNEH TORAH* AS PARABLE

ONE OF THE PURPOSES of the *Guide of the Perplexed*, as stated in its introduction, is 'the explanation of very obscure parables occurring in the books of the prophets, but not explicitly identified there as such'.[1] A discussion on the interpretation of parables follows. It will be an appropriate way of pulling together the ideas on the interpretation of *Mishneh torah* put forward in this study to review them in the light of that discussion, on the suspicion that Maimonides' remarks on reading Bible and Midrash may well tell us as much about his own methods of composition as they do about those texts. In other words, I shall treat *Mishneh torah* as a great parable that is not explicitly identified as such.[2]

The Lost Language of the Commandments

A sub-theme of this study has been Maimonides' manipulation of rabbinic sources. As it happens, his account of the function of parables is itself an example of such manipulation. *Song of Songs Rabbah* says of that biblical book: 'This matter may be compared to the case of a king who lost gold in his house or pearls. Is it not through a wick that is worth a penny that he finds it again? So let a parable not be despised in your view, for it is through the parable that a person can master the words of the Torah.'[3] The message is that scholars should not regard studying the works of Solomon as beneath their dignity. Even a king uses a cheap taper to find something precious. Similarly, although Proverbs, Ecclesiastes, and Song of Songs have little value for halakhah, they should not be dismissed, because they serve as parables that cast light on the Torah.

---

[1] *Guide* i, Introduction (p. 6).

[2] As Stern points out, in Maimonidean parlance, a parable is not just a story with a moral, but 'any text, narrative or not, with multiple levels of external and internal meaning' (*Problems and Parables*, 10). [3] *S. of S. Rabbah* 1: 8 (*S. of S. Rabbah*, trans. Neusner, i. 47).

Maimonides first paraphrases and then explains this parable about parables, one of a series on which he bases his discussion:

About this it has been said: *Our Rabbis say: A man who loses a sela or a pearl in his house can find the pearl by lighting a taper worth an issar. In the same way this parable in itself is worth nothing, but by means of it you can understand the words of the Torah.* This too is literally what they say. Now consider the explicit affirmation of [the sages], *may their memory be blessed*, that the internal meaning of the *words of the Torah* is a *pearl* whereas the external meaning of all the parables *is worth nothing*, and their comparison of the concealment of a subject by its parable's external meaning to a man who let drop a pearl in his house, which was dark and full of furniture. Now the pearl is there, but he does not see it and does not know where it is. It is as though it were no longer in his possession, as it is impossible for him to derive any benefit from it at all until, as has been mentioned, he lights a lamp—an act to which an understanding of the meaning of the parable corresponds.[4]

A subtle shift has taken place. Maimonides wants the message of the *midrash*, that parables are not to be despised, for that is also part of his argument, but his analysis carries us elsewhere. If the *midrash* was concerned with prestige, Maimonides' reworking of it concerns hermeneutics.

Let us note the differences. In the original the person who has lost something precious is a king, as of course was Solomon, who wrote the parables in question. In Maimonides' paraphrase the person in the parable is demoted. The *midrash* treats the parable as something easy that clarifies something difficult: the taper appears lit, ready to illuminate 'the words of the Torah'. In Maimonides' version, the taper still needs to be lit before the pearl can be found, corresponding to the intellectual effort required to illuminate the parable's obscure meaning. The house is now 'full of furniture',[5] a detail that was not in the *midrash*; nor is there any reference there to 'concealment'. By furniture Maimonides appears to mean the furnishings of the parable itself, its 'external meaning', the story or the images over which a person will stumble while trying to discern the inner meaning. Instead of being an aid to understanding, the parable is now presented as an impediment to understanding, for rather than revealing words of Torah, it disguises them. In general, Maimonides' explication stresses loss and the difficulty of finding the precious object, rather than the status and attitude of the person who lost it.

Clearly, the *midrash*, too, is saying that Song of Songs should not be taken at face value. Maimonides' changes of emphasis are small, but still significant. His rebalancing seems designed to make this *midrash* lead up to his idea of

[4] *Guide* i, Introduction (p. 11).   [5] Schwarz gives *gruta'ot.*

layers of meaning in parables, which will be considered shortly.[6] Taking a wider view, it is possible that it also reflects the decline of Jewish learning Maimonides saw between the time of the Talmud and Midrash and his own time. He takes 'the words of Torah' on which the *midrash* says parables shed light as referring to 'obscure matters',[7] that is, *ma'aseh bereshit* and *ma'aseh merkavah*, which, as we have seen, he identifies with physics and metaphysics. As we have seen, in making that identification, Maimonides regarded himself as restoring to the Jewish tradition knowledge that the sages of the Talmud and Midrash possessed but that had been lost, and that could be reconstructed only from the works of the philosophers and through speculation. But what was lost, it seems, was not just the knowledge, but also the language in which it was expressed, that is, the parables of the prophets (with Solomon counting among the prophets for this purpose) and the Midrash. For example, of the *midrashim* on the story of Adam and Eve in the Garden of Eden, Maimonides states: 'Know that those things that I shall mention to you from the dicta of the *sages* are sayings that are of utmost perfection; their allegorical interpretation was clear to those to whom they were addressed, and they are unambiguous.'[8]

The position of the enlightened Jew of Maimonides' day is therefore comparable to that of communities of our own day that still maintain the ancient practice of having an Aramaic rendition declaimed alongside the public reading of the Torah in its original Hebrew. Whereas at one time this was a matter of translating the Torah from a language the hearers did not understand into a language that they did, now the translation is from a language that (in Israel at least) they do understand into one that they mostly don't. Similarly, while the prophetic parables were always meant to conceal matters from the multitude,[9] to the talmudic sages they shed light on 'the words of the Torah', but now they are dark, while, thanks to Aristotle and his Arab followers, *ma'aseh bereshit* and *ma'aseh merkavah* are at least approximately known. Much of the *Guide* is devoted to recovering this lost parabolic language. Maimonides might well acknowledge that he has adapted our *midrash*, and argue that times have changed.

In Maimonides' treatment of them, the commandments too can be compared to a lost language. In their original cultural context many of the ritual

---

[6] Mordechai Cohen sees the discussion of the parable of the taper as being about the rabbinic method of interpreting parables, in contrast to Maimonides' own. According to my analysis, Maimonides subtly alters the rabbinic parable, and thereby co-opts it. See M. Z. Cohen, *Three Approaches to Biblical Metaphor*, 122–4.

[7] *Guide*, Introduction (p. 11).   [8] *Guide* ii. 30 (p. 355).   [9] See *Guide*, Introduction (p. 9).

commandments were understood to refer to pagan practices. By banning, countering, or adapting such practices, they shed light on the truth. When knowledge of those practices died out, it became necessary to clarify the commandments themselves. Thanks to his knowledge of the Sabian cult, Maimonides is able to do so. He works out the commandments' etymologies, as it were, and reconstructs their meaning as an anti-pagan vocabulary (in keeping with the *Guide*'s lexicographical approach to the meaning of parables). The whole enterprise of the reasons for the commandments in the *Guide* and their classification in that book is in relation to certain external, pre-announced, philosophically determined goods: the welfare of the soul; the welfare of the body; and the restraint of desire. The concern is with how the commandments refer to the world.

To continue with the language simile, *Mishneh torah* is not so much about the semantic references of the commandments as about their grammar and syntax, or, more generically, their form. The cosmic model, together with the direct insights into their moral and philosophical import, teaches us to parse the commandments. It enables us to understand how the significance of each commandment depends on its relationship to the others, and how it can be analysed into form and matter. The frame of reference is not an external, substantial one of defined goods, but an internal, formal one—or axiomatic, as it was defined in Chapter 4.

Mishneh torah's structure is based upon the description of the cosmos contained within it, in 'Laws of the Foundations of the Torah'. This is emblematic of the organic nature of *Mishneh torah*'s literary form, arising out of the priority of form over matter that is also the basic structure of the commandments. Just as the existence of the cosmos flows continually from the first existent, the form of forms, the impression is created of the commandments as a continual flow from the same source, and thereby of *Mishneh torah* as a continually self-replenishing work of art.

Understanding the structure of the commandments means that, instead of stumbling in the dark over their material manifestations, their 'furniture', we can extract from them 'a form in the soul'. That form is a microcosm, the inward reproduction of *ma'aseh merkavah* and *ma'aseh bereshit*. The form of *Mishneh torah* in the literary sense is a parabolic representation of the form of the commandments in the technical, philosophical sense.

A Jacob's Ladder

In the introduction to the *Guide* Maimonides chooses Jacob's dream of the ladder with the angels ascending and descending to illustrate the complex type of parable that is significant in all its details, as opposed to parables that are significant only in outline. He thus announces the centrality of this parable to his vision. In its later appearances in the *Guide*, it serves to concentrate that book's ideas in the realms of physics, metaphysics, and prophecy.

Mishneh torah embodies all that Jacob's dream stands for in the *Guide*. The first ten books represent everything that lies between the Earth and the outermost sphere, reflecting the static aspect of the interpretation of the ladder in *Guide* i. 15.[10] The hierarchical arrangement of those books, informed by the Neoplatonic concepts of emanation and return, reflects the dynamic aspect of Maimonides' interpretation, the ascent and descent of the prophet. The overall form of the work's fourteen books suggests the effect of the circular movements of the spheres on the linear movements of the elements of matter, which the ladder is taken to represent in *Guide* ii. 10. To this, as discussed in Chapter 5, *Mishneh torah* adds the dimension of time, signalled in 'Laws of the Foundations of the Torah', 7: 3, where the angels on Jacob's ladder are the four empires, an interpretation that combines with the cosmological and psychological significances of the dream to give a vision of the gradual perfection of society until it reaches a condition in which it is capable of receiving the messianic form.

This would appear to make *Mishneh torah* a parable of the complex type, organic and compact.[11] On the other hand, not every word in it, and not every detail of every commandment, is of transcendental significance, so that it also appears to have characteristics of a parable of the simpler type, in which the details contribute to the general effect but are not separately meaningful.

It is possible to seek aid here in Mordechai Z. Cohen's criticism of Sara

---

[10] As discussed in Chapter 2, the way the spheres are counted is flexible, and so the four spheres (corresponding to the four rungs of Jacob's ladder) of the *Guide* can be the nine spheres plus agent intellect of *Mishneh torah*.

[11] The term 'organic' is used in awareness of the metaphysical freight it bears as a critical term. See Benziger, 'Organic Unity'. Benziger stresses the dependence of the idea of organic unity in art on the idea of artistic creation 'in the image of the Divine work of art' ('Organic Unity', 37). This resembles, and partly derives from, the idea of art as *imitatio Dei* in the Neoplatonic critical tradition, in which I have suggested that Maimonides worked, and which is traceable back to Plato and Aristotle. It is probably no coincidence, then, that it is Jacob's dream, the example of the type of parable possessed of organic unity, that later in the *Guide* turns out to represent the workings of the cosmos.

Klein-Braslavy's methodology for its ascription of significance to individual words in Jacob's dream on the basis of Maimonides' lexicography, rather than to the components of the dream. Cohen writes:

Instead of a lexical division, he [Maimonides] divides the vision itself into distinct scenes, each of which represents another element in the *batin* [the hidden meaning]. This does not imply semantic reconstrual; the language retains its normal literal sense and conveys what Jacob actually saw in his dream, which Maimonides neither negates nor erases. We can thus conclude that in the first type of *mashal* [parable] every detail of the *zahir* [the external meaning]—not every word—has a deeper meaning.[12]

Similarly, and further to the idea of the commandments as a language, Maimonides in *Mishneh torah* leaves them in what could be termed their literal sense, in that he does not invest them individually with transcendental or mystical significance, but he does arrange them into 'scenes', it being a question of judgement what level of detail constitutes a scene. On the basis of Cohen's approach, a temptress-type parable could be called mono-scenic, while a Jacob's ladder-type is multi-scenic. *Mishneh torah* qualifies as a parable of the Jacob's dream kind in that all its components co-ordinate with the idea of the knowledge of God, but we need to be as sensitive to the various kinds of writing it contains as to different kinds of writing in the Bible. Some parts are more intensely written than others, and some are more directly related to the cosmic model than others. So, while *Mishneh torah* is multi-scenic, on the whole, as we descend from the *Book of Knowledge*, the scenes expand, and the details become less significant. We found that the *Book of Knowledge* itself could be seen as corresponding to the uninformed, diurnal sphere, and that the *Book of Love* could be compared to the sphere of the fixed stars, but that thereafter there was no isomorphic correspondence between books and particular spheres. By the time we arrive at the Temple ritual, we are presented with something rather like the temptress type of parable; meaningful as a whole, but not necessarily so in all its component parts.

Literary Devices

This study has surveyed some of the formal devices that shape the law into a coherent parable. In Chapter 1 we saw repeated patterns and biblical allusion

---

[12] M. Z. Cohen, *Three Approaches to Biblical Metaphor*, 133. Apropos the treatment of *Mishneh torah* as a parable, Cohen does consider parallels between Maimonides' approaches to parables and to *ta'amei hamitsvot*—see ibid. 184–6. See also Twersky, *Introduction to the Code*, 397–400.

deployed to introduce the idea of man as microcosm, and a motif of descent and ascent, or, more abstractly, the absolute projected onto the contingent and the contingent striving for the absolute, in this case man created in the image of God in respect of his intellect striving to become like God in his whole moral being. In Chapter 2 the general structure of *Mishneh torah* was shown to be a microcosm, a device that symbolizes the relationship between Torah and nature. Combined with the idea of man as microcosm, it also symbolizes the role of the commandments as mediators between the absolute and the contingent, offering human beings the possibility of inwardly replicating the permanent, love-induced motions of the heavens and their influence on the permanent processes beneath the Moon.

Sequence and metaphor were other elements of literary form that Maimonides had at his disposal. Chapter 3 showed them operating in tandem, the sequence of the first ten books of *Mishneh torah* embodying the idea of emanation, underlain by the metaphor of a flow of water, implying a hierarchy of the ritual commandments from the most purely intellectual, nearest the source, down to the most materially bound. After that descent Chapter 4 completed the Neoplatonic picture with the idea of return. The endpoint of the metaphorical flow of water, the *mikveh*, becomes the starting point of the spiritual ascent of the prophet, who then descends to reform human society.

This brought in the last four books of *Mishneh torah*, on the man–man commandments, corresponding to the elements of matter in the microcosmic structure, and forming an ascent from chaos to order. A pattern of loss and restoration, a variation on the descent–ascent theme, was discerned running right through *Mishneh torah*, beginning in the *Book of Knowledge*, and culminating in the ultimate restoration, the advent of the messiah.

In Chapter 5 the device of biblical and midrashic reference again came to the fore, and the historical/teleological axis of *Mishneh torah* was found to meet the ontological axis in Maimonides' theory of prophecy.

A specific application of this device worth highlighting is the use of the figures of Abraham and Moses. Time and again they appear as a pair. As noted in Chapter 1, Abraham is portrayed as the progenitor not only of a people, but also of moral and divine science, derived from observation of nature. Moses the legislator later embodied these sciences in the commandments. This historical process reflects, and helps to justify, the idea of religion devolving from philosophy within Moses' prophecy, as presented on the ontological axis by the relationship between *Mishneh torah*'s microcosmic form and its religious content.

Unifying all these devices and patterns is an organic or crystalline form, in which the parts, down to individual commandments or groups of commandments, and the whole, the microcosm, share the same basic principles: the hierarchy of form and matter, and structure endowing meaning. This form translates the Neoplatonic idea that the One is in the All and the All is in the One into an aesthetic ideal of the whole distributed among the parts and the parts reflecting the whole.[13]

Thus, beyond even the stupendous achievement of codifying halakhah, in *Mishneh torah* Maimonides meshes halakhah with physics and metaphysics, and with his concept of history and his messianic teleology. In addition, conceptual differences between *Mishneh torah* and the *Guide* have turned out to be explicable by their different literary forms: the latter discursive/prosaic, the former symbolic/poetic; a philosophical and theological discourse versus what is at one and the same time an individual spiritual quest and a national epic. The *Guide* tells us about the ladder; *Mishneh torah* invites us to imagine the ladder and the prophet ascending and descending it, or even our own ascent and descent. In short, if the *Guide* is *about* Jacob's ladder, *Mishneh torah* *is* Jacob's ladder.

The Problem of Obsolescence

Here it is appropriate to raise a difficulty that has been suppressed all along: the ladder has been taken away. The spheres and the four elements have gone, and along with them the underlying idea of a cosmic hierarchy. We live in what Nigel Calder has termed 'Einstein's democratic universe':[14] the laws of nature are held to be the same everywhere, with no point in our inanimate universe privileged over any other. Psychology and cosmology have gone their separate ways, and few believe in microcosms any more.[15]

---

[13] Compare Schelling's formulation: 'The relationship between the individual parts in the closed and organic world of philosophy resembles that between the various figures in a perfectly constructed poetic work, where every figure, by being part of the whole, as a perfect reflex of that whole is actually absolute and independent in its own turn' (*Philosophy of Art*, 282).   [14] Calder, *Einstein's Universe*, 11.

[15] The loss is expressed by Kreisel thus:

By rooting his approach to *imitatio Dei* in his metaphysical views, specifically the view of emanation, Maimonides not only is able to reconcile the practical and theoretical aspects of human perfection, but also to develop a highly integrated philosophical conception of the world. Ethics and human perfection are inseparably bound to the activity of God and the structure of the world. Yet this interpretation raises the question of the philosophical relevance of Maimonides' approach to *imitatio Dei* for the modern reader. It would appear that Maimonides' approach can serve as a viable model only for those who accept his metaphysical views. The fundamental

If the account of physics and metaphysics in 'Laws of the Foundations of the Torah', chapters 2–4, is there because, following his assertion that the way to the love and fear of God lies through the study of creation, Maimonides sees fit to provide a potted version of the science of his day, this need not be fatal. Those chapters can then be regarded as a separate module that, arguably at least, could be replaced by the science of our own day, with little incidental damage.

If, however, Maimonides' physics and metaphysics are not confined to 'Laws of the Foundations of the Torah', chapters 2–4, but, as foundations, underpin the whole of *Mishneh torah*, we have a disaster, for the foundations have crumbled, and the cracked edifice must collapse. If halakhah was supposed to have been made meaningful by being erected as a rational system parallel to a cosmic hierarchy, to which the virtuous personality also corresponds, it now looks meaningless, as obsolete as the science with which it was associated. Its harmonization of subjective self and objective law is destroyed. It is one thing to propound naturalistic explanations of parables and prophecy, and even of the commandments, in a speculative work like the *Guide*. It is quite another to make that approach the pillar of a book with pretensions to defining halakhah. The risk of marrying the commandments to a concept of the natural order is one Maimonides should never have taken.

Silver and Gold

It looks as though, rather as Haym Soloveitchik has argued, *Mishneh torah*'s very sophistication could be its downfall. Yet it does not feel outmoded; it still seems to speak to us on the narrative level, and it is necessary to try to analyse how that is accomplished on the formal level as well.

> changes in the conception of the world since Maimonides' time thus undermine the model of human perfection developed by him. ('*Imitatio Dei* in "Guide"', 213)

Kreisel goes on to state:

> Maimonides' implicit claim, reflecting the classical Greek and Islamic philosophic traditions, is that the philosophic enterprise must be 'holistic.' 'Practical' philosophy (i.e., ethics and politics) is inseparable from theoretical philosophy (i.e., physics and metaphysics) . . . Maimonides' approach to *imitatio Dei* and human perfection, for all the problems it raises, is profound for the manner in which it integrates these topics. It forces us to rethink the question, recently raised in the philosophic literature, whether we can develop viable approaches to ethics and human perfection which are not part of a holistic world view . . . The hold Maimonides' philosophy continues to exert on modern students of philosophy stems in no small part from the longing shared by many for such a holistic approach to philosophy. ('*Imitatio Dei* in "Guide"', 214)

The argument developed here is that the artistic form makes the holism transmittable across different conceptions of the world.

Lenn Goodman has tackled the question of the enduring value of the Maimonidean world picture to philosophy.[16] The discussion here will be from a literary point of view; the question is whether *Mishneh torah* survives as a work of art 'not of an age, but for all time',[17] or whether the obsolescence of its science renders its design an antique curiosity.

First of all, we should be precise about what in Maimonides' cosmology is strange to us. The medieval picture of Earth at the centre of a system of spheres is sometimes misunderstood, as though human beings claimed pride of place in a universe that existed for their sakes, until they were disabused and humbled by Copernicus. If anything, the opposite is true. To the medieval mind it was not the centre but the circumference of the universe, and even more so what lay beyond the circumference, that was most glorious. As C. S. Lewis puts it, 'The Medieval Model is, if we may use the word, anthropoperipheral. We are creatures of the Margin.'[18] People thought the spheres and stars far above them not just physically, but also in happiness and intelligence. It was absurd to imagine that such majesty could exist for the sake of lowly human beings, as Maimonides himself states.[19] With the new science, we eventually shed our sense of inferiority towards the heavens. In this respect 'the Copernican Revolution', once it had run its course, indeed wrought a fundamental change in the self-image of that part of humanity that had subscribed to the Ptolemaic system; the very idea of above and below no longer holds. At the same time, this feature makes 'the Model' at least superficially similar to a modern non-teleological view of the physical world. Maimonides is very clear on this: 'It should not be believed that all the beings exist for the sake of the existence of man. On the contrary, all the other beings too have been intended for their own sakes and not for the sake of something else.'[20]

Maimonides himself did not regard his science as necessarily all factually true. It approaches a Platonic 'likely tale'.[21] He was committed to the

---

[16] See Goodman, 'Maimonidean Naturalism'.

[17] 'He was not of an age, but for all time' (Ben Jonson, *To the Memory of My Beloved Master William Shakespeare and What He Hath Left Us*). [18] Lewis, *The Discarded Image*, 58. [19] See p. 210 above.

[20] *Guide* iii. 13 (p. 452). In the introduction to the *Commentary on the Mishnah*, Maimonides states that things beneath the Moon (though not those above it) exist for man's sake, but he appears to have moved from that view, for in *Guide* iii. 13 the most he will allow is that plants may have been created in order to feed animals. In this respect there is tension between the Aristotelian/Neoplatonic model and a religious viewpoint. For Christians, Lewis writes, 'I think that there remained throughout the Middle Ages an unresolved discord between those elements in their religion which tended to an anthropocentric view and those in the Model which made man a marginal—almost, as we shall see, a suburban creature' (*The Discarded Image*, 51). In *Guide* iii. 13 Maimonides offers explanations for those biblical verses that seem to contradict his position.

[21] Goodman also makes the comparison with Plato ('Maimonidean Naturalism', 182).

Aristotelian account of the sublunary world, but as far as things above the Moon were concerned, he was well aware of the discrepancy between theory and observation.[22] It was argued in Chapter 2 that the system of spheres outlined in 'Laws of the Foundations of the Torah', 3: 1, on which *Mishneh torah's* structure is based, is schematic, and not meant as a picture of reality.[23] Nor, on the other side of the equation, was Maimonides wedded to a fixed structure of the commandments; as we have seen, the form in which he cast them depended on the genre in which he was writing. To reject his concept of the commandments, as reflected in the form of *Mishneh torah*, because his science is outdated betrays something of the literal-mindedness that he spent his career combating.[24] The status of his cosmology as presented in *Mishneh torah* lies somewhere between reality and metaphor. Even if that work's microcosmic form cannot be as immediately compelling as it would have been to someone whose imagination was dominated by 'the Model', and the likely tale now seems much less likely, it is possible to suspend disbelief. We come back to the notion of a parable.

But what sort of a parable? After we emerge from an imaginative engagement with *Mishneh torah*, and disbelief reasserts itself, what do we have in hand, if the matter may be put so crudely? What is at stake, after all, is not poetic faith, but faith.

It is not possible to be categorical about this, but some suggestions can be put forward with the aid of Maimonides' discussion of layers of meaning in parables:

The Sage has said: *A word fitly spoken is like apples of gold in settings (maskiyyoth) of silver.*[25] Hear now an elucidation of the thought that he has set forth. The term *maskiyyoth* denotes filigree traceries; I mean to say traceries in which there are apertures with very small eyelets, like the handiwork of silversmiths. They are so called because a glance penetrates through them ... The Sage accordingly said that a thing uttered with a view to two meanings is like an apple of gold overlaid with silver filigree-work having very small holes. Now see how marvellously this dictum describes a well-constructed parable. For he says that in a saying that has two meanings—he means an external and an internal one—the external meaning ought to be as beautiful as silver, while its internal meaning ought to be more beautiful than the external one,

---

[22] As already noted, *Guide* ii. 24 (pp. 322–7), with its 'true perplexity', is the main expression of this.

[23] This was not just Maimonides' attitude: 'On the highest level, then, the Model was recognized as provisional' (Lewis, *The Discarded Image*, 16).

[24] This is to be contrasted with the more rigidly welded correspondence between Torah and medieval science in Gersonides, which really did render his system obsolete as science progressed. See Kellner, *Torah in the Observatory*, 17.   [25] Prov. 25: 11.

the former being in comparison to the latter as gold is to silver. Its external meaning also ought to contain in it something that indicates to someone considering it what is to be found in its internal meaning, as happens in the case of an apple of gold overlaid with silver filigree-work having very small holes. When looked at from a distance or with imperfect attention, it is deemed to be an apple of silver; but when a keen-sighted observer looks at it with full attention, its interior becomes clear to him and he knows that it is of gold. The parables of the prophets, peace be on them, are similar. Their external meaning contains wisdom that is useful in many respects, among which is the welfare of human societies, as is shown by the external meaning of Proverbs and of similar sayings. Their internal meaning, on the other hand, contains wisdom that is useful for beliefs concerned with the truth as it is.[26]

Josef Stern sees a parallel between this approach to interpreting parables and the way that the commandments are explained in the *Guide*. He notes the *Guide*'s two sets of reasons for the commandments: one in *Guide* iii. 26–49, based upon the aims of inculcating correct doctrine, abolishing wrongdoing, and restraining desire, and the other in *Guide* iii. 51–2 that presents the commandments as aids to meditation on God. Stern argues that the relationship between these two kinds of reasons for the commandments is the same as the structure of Maimonides' interpretation of parables in that, like a parable, a commandment has an external and an internal significance. The former consists in its usefulness for the welfare of society; the latter consists in its usefulness for 'beliefs concerned with the truth as it is'. He concludes the argument thus:

In sum, the general structure under which we might subsume Maimonides' two different explanations of the commandments, in III:26–49 and in III:51–52, seems to fit exactly the two-leveled structure of his idea of parabolic interpretation . . . At the external level, their reasons are oriented toward anthropomorphic communal well-being; at the internal level, toward the theocentric (intellectual) perfection of individuals who are capable of such perfection.[27]

Applying this to the form of *Mishneh torah*, the two-levelled structure could be seen as represented by the form's static and dynamic aspects. The static aspect is the well-ordered personality and society, conceived as microcosms. The dynamic aspect is the intellectual perfection of the individual climbing the ladder of ascension. This also epitomizes the contrast between *Mishneh torah* as poetry and the *Guide* as prose, the way in which a complex of ideas will receive successive, discursive treatment in the latter, but simultaneous, sym-

---

[26] *Guide* i, Introduction (pp. 11–12).   [27] Stern, *Problems and Parables*, 75–6.

bolic expression in the former. In the *Guide* the chapters on the internal level of meaning of the commandments follow consecutively those on the external level; in *Mishneh torah*, resembling more closely the image of the golden apple overlaid with silver in Maimonides' parable about parables, the internal, golden level emerges from within the external level.

This is to see *Mishneh torah* in two dimensions. There is, however, a third dimension: that of the reader's experience. From this perspective the silver and gold layers can be seen as corresponding to the two levels of response to *Mishneh torah*'s form put forward at the outset: the level of ideas and the level of inspiration. In Neoplatonic terminology these are the eiconic and entheastic levels, and in that of Aquinas, *consonantia* and *claritas*. Maimonides' use of the image from Proverbs of a filigree of silver surrounding an apple of gold to illustrate the point that the external meaning indicates what is to be found in the internal meaning is, then, very apt. The way in which *Mishneh torah*'s form networks the commandments into a system, so that the interconnections of the parts convey what Twersky terms 'supra-halakhic' meanings, indeed forms a kind of ideational filigree-work. But the more one becomes involved in tracing it, the more one senses something underlying it that is not reducible to ideas.

In Chapter 5 it was proposed that *Mishneh torah* is at least a quasi-prophetic book. Maimonides himself looked at prophecy as concerned both with the welfare of society and with the truth as it is, and sometimes only the latter: 'The prophet's message may be for himself alone: to expand his heart and enlarge his mind until he knows what he did not know about those great matters.'[28]

Awareness of *Mishneh torah*'s artistic form gives access to its inner workings, to a mind bent on knowledge of 'those great matters', through communion with which the reader too may 'expand his heart and enlarge his mind'.[29] Alongside the objective fixing of halakhah, the experience of *Mishneh torah* is the kind of guided subjectivity that is the experience of art. In this way, the book is reborn in every reader.

Goodman paraphrases Maimonides' assertion that natural objects are 'intended for their own sakes and not for the sake of something else' thus: 'Maimonides holds that God made all things in the first instance for their own sakes. Things glorify God in pursuing their own perfection.'[30] Nature is

---

[28] 'Laws of the Foundations of the Torah', 7: 7.
[29] For the idea in medieval theory of poetic discourse as reflecting the mind of the author rather than objective truth, see Ch. 2, n. 143 above.   [30] Goodman, 'Maimonidean Naturalism', 182.

ineluctably separate from God. Things in nature are not allegories of, or even dissolvable barriers to, the divine, for they have nothing whatsoever in common with it and share no boundary with it. Hence things glorify God most when they are most themselves, following their own laws, and hence, too, God is understood to the greatest extent possible through understanding those laws. Human beings are part of nature. Accordingly, as we saw in Chapter 1, it is through pursuing his own perfection that the scholar of 'Laws of the Foundations of the Torah', 5: 11 and 'Laws of Ethical Qualities', 5: 13 becomes 'my servant Israel, in whom I will be glorified'.

As a work of art, *Mishneh torah*, too, needs to be understood in the first instance on its own terms. If it is an imitation of nature and an aesthetic equivalent of the ethical ideal, as this study argues, then its most profound, golden level is its pursuit of its own perfection, a perfection that lies in unity. The filigree of ideas integrates *Mishneh torah* in the image of the cosmic unity that is all that can be comprehended of divine unity. The contemplation of that emergent aesthetic unity quickens a sympathetic movement in the reader's own mind, generating 'a form in the soul'—a subjective, integrative process that goes beyond ideas, resembling more and more, though never reaching, the ineffable unity of God.

The autonomy of created things is reproduced in the relationship between *Mishneh torah*'s form and its content. The intricacy of Maimonides' art is such that, although it presents philosophy as the inspiration of the commandments, philosophy does not swamp halakhah, which retains its rabbinic consistency, its own perfection.

Yet though separate from nature, God works through nature. The process of enlightenment, of knowing God, is gradual, proceeding within the constraints that the material condition of human beings imposes. The possibility is offered, within natural bounds, of ascending levels of integrity, understanding, and worship. The rationalization of the commandments as embodied in *Mishneh torah*'s form is that they are a way of attuning human beings to the idea that all things flow from intellect and to intellect return. It is a rationalization that presents the commandments as designed to realize nature, to make human nature know what it truly is.

The form of *Mishneh torah* contributes to the sensitizing quality that Twersky so much stresses. If, in Chapter 2, the cosmic structure was seen as part of making the commandments 'great and glorious', by the same token it infuses the performance of them with grace, for it connects the smallest acts to the source of being, and makes God, though unfathomable, not remote, but present, via the stages of emanation, in those acts. As we saw in Chapter 4, the occasional moralizing and philosophical interpolations in *Mishneh torah*, Rabbi J. B. Soloveitchik's 'subjective correlatives', intended to make perform-ance of the commandments more thoughtful and humane, co-ordinate with the grand design. The sense of grandeur combined with fineness of sensibil-ity survives the vicissitudes of science.

Of course, it is only 'in the first instance' that things exist for their own sakes. *Mishneh torah* is a code of law; it exists for the sake of moral and social order. Its identity as a code of law, however, is not separate from its identity as a work of art: the two originate in a single point.

The portal through which we enter *Mishneh torah* is the consciousness of God's existence. This entails the primacy of form over matter that prevails throughout creation and is also the fundamental structure of the command-ments. In human beings, whose form is an intellectual capacity like that of the angels and spheres but who, unlike them, consist of degenerative matter, establishing the proper order is a conscious task. *Mishneh torah* derives its dramatic energy and tension from the moment where this contest begins, in 'Laws of the Foundations of the Torah', 2: 2, to which I have referred so many times, and in which the archetypal, Adamic human being, seeing the cosmos as though for the first time, is seized by wonder and love, and then by fear. From love springs the desire for knowledge of God, the actualization of the human form, while fear is the awareness of the material impediment to knowledge. In the *Guide*, fear is associated with the commandments; love with philosophy.[31] But whereas the *Guide* treats philosophy and command-ments as different departments of Torah, *Mishneh torah* combines them. From the point of origin, love precipitates as *Mishneh torah*'s form, while fear precipitates as its content, and in those guises they continue to interact, animating each other throughout.

Fear has several connotations in Maimonides. As a concomitant of love, a self-conscious reaction upon recognition of the infinite gap between divine and human knowledge, it is necessary and healthy; detached from love, it becomes pathological.[32] In the narrative in chapter 1 of 'Laws of Idolatry', the avenue of love and knowledge becomes blocked, and error and ignorance give rise to an exploitative regime based upon fear: the false prophets would

---

[31] See *Guide* iii. 52 (p. 630).

[32] This also goes for love detached from fear, as seen in the confusion and corruption that result from the pursuit of knowledge without the discipline of moral training and an orderly course of studies. See above, p. 100 n. 67.

'tell all the people that this particular figure conferred benefits and inflicted injuries and that it was proper to worship and fear it'.[33] It was Abraham 'my lover' who broke the hold of this fear.[34]

Just such self-interested fear of punishment and hope of reward, though directed towards God, are castigated in 'Laws of Repentance', 10:1, as unworthy motives for keeping the commandments. Even less edifying is the 'confusion and terror' that in 'Laws of Repentance', 9:1, overtakes those given over to the pursuit of physical satisfactions and bereft of knowledge, so abject that they are rendered incapable of observing the commandments. In Neoplatonic terms this is the consequence of Soul becoming too much involved with matter and forgetting its origin in Intellect. By contrast, the fear spoken of in connection with the commandments in the *Guide* is of an elevated kind, the laudable *outcome* of observing the commandments conscientiously, which induces constant awareness of being in God's presence, via the intellect, by means of which 'He, may He be exalted, is constantly with us, examining from on high'.[35]

The Adamic moment of 'Laws of the Foundations of the Torah', 2:2, prefaces the description of a sentient, hierarchical cosmos, but its poetic impact does not depend on that description being true. This can be appreciated by contrasting it with the *halakhah* that concludes the summary of natural science, in which the same moment is recapitulated in slightly different terms:

When a man reflects on these things, studies all these created beings, from the angels and spheres down to human beings and so on, and realizes the Divine Wisdom manifested in them all, his love for God will increase, his soul will thirst, his very flesh will yearn to love God. He will be filled with fear and trembling, as he becomes conscious of his own lowly condition, poverty and insignificance, and compares himself with any of the great and holy bodies; still more when he compares himself with any one of the pure forms that are incorporeal and have never had association with corporeal substance. He will then realize that he is a vessel full of shame, dishonour, and reproach, empty and deficient.[36]

The repetition here of the idea that contemplating creation induces love and the desire for knowledge and also fear is a measure of the distance covered since the idea was first introduced in 'Laws of the Foundations of the Torah', 2:2. The initial wonder is now an educated wonder, through understanding

---

[33] 'Laws of Idolatry', 1:2.

[34] See also *Guide* iii. 24 (pp. 500–1), where Abraham personifies the ideal combination of love and fear in the trial of the binding of Isaac.

[35] *Guide* iii. 52 (p. 629).   [36] 'Laws of the Foundations of the Torah', 4:12.

of the system of spheres and stars. Moreover, this passage emphasizing man's lowly, marginal place in the universe is almost immediately followed, in 'Laws of the Foundations of the Torah', chapter 5, by the commandment to sanctify the name of God; a dramatic turn, since one would not have thought so squalid a creature capable of sanctifying anything. Through the leverage of a heteronomous commandment to sanctify God's name, a human being is set upon the path from 'shame, dishonour and reproach' towards the status of the scholar at the end of the chapter, who glorifies God in pursuing his own perfection.

All the same, the feeling behind this *halakhah* cannot really be recaptured in any authentic way. Since we do not now see our physicality as different from that of anything else in the universe, comparison with the stars cannot put us to shame for our bodily existence. In 'Laws of the Foundations of the Torah', 2: 2, on the other hand, fear (at this point the Hebrew *yirah* should more properly be rendered 'awe') arises out of comparison with God himself, or rather out of the realization that there is no comparison. There, the yearning and recoil are more like the *mysterium tremendum et fascinans* of which theologians, including Jewish theologians, speak in our time.[37] This is a depiction of the human condition with which it is possible to identify. It may now be challenged, but it is also challenging, even though our universe is not the one in which Maimonides thought he lived. In the axiomatic form that is *Mishneh torah*, it is a proposition one down from the existence and unity of God, a whole that gives life to the parts even when they are no longer viable by themselves, so that the structure leading off from this source, though outmoded as cosmology, can still serve to irrigate and vitalize halakhah, and orientate it towards a vision of human perfection.

From this point onwards the story of *Mishneh torah* is an epic of love lost and regained. A sane balance of love and fear is necessary, but self-conscious fear also casts Adamic man down from a state of pure knowledge, of outwardly directed contemplation of God and of true and false, to a state of perception of good and bad, sequestered in his materiality, with which he is in constant struggle.[38] The commandments order material existence, but because they are part of a divine law, and everything in a divine law is

---

[37] Examples of the invocation of Rudolf Otto's phrase by Jewish writers are J. B. Soloveitchik, 'The Lonely Man of Faith', 17; Berkovits, *God, Man and History*, 52. Apropos Soloveitchik, it is not claimed that the analysis of Adamic man's dual response to nature offered here necessarily coincides with his interpretation of the two versions of the creation of Adam in Genesis.

[38] On the fall of Adam and form succumbing to matter in human beings, see *Guide* i. 2 (pp. 23–6); ii. 30 (pp. 355–8); and iii. 8 (pp. 430–5).

directed towards knowledge, they also have the function of educating the self-reflective phase of consciousness, of converting action into contemplation.

The commandments instil fear, in the sense of the constant awareness of being in God's presence, but at the same time purge the lower kind of fear, reclaiming material existence for the intellect and transmuting fear into self-knowledge. They lead back from matter to form, to the knowledge of how 'all existing things' flow from God, the form of forms, and to a perspective of educated wonder from which all that exists, for its own sake and regardless of human concerns, is 'indubitably a good'.[39] *Mishneh torah* conveys the idea that goodness means alignment through knowledge with the permanent whole, the divine reflection, of which we are part. What more can we ask of it as a work of art than that it should thus teach us to value existence?

Love and fear finally assume, or reassume, their proper roles in the closing vision of the days of the messiah. *Mishneh torah* wins through to restored intellectual clarity in relations between man and God, and to a humane material, social order that serves enlightenment rather than power. Through the embodiment of this process in the interplay of form and content, *Mishneh torah* enacts its ideal of repentance, thereby earning the hope of redemption on which it ends. As much as anything it is this artistic coherence and vitality that make Maimonides' natural messianic model a match for the apocalyptic kind and a still relevant point of view from which to judge contemporary reality.[40] Meanwhile, until the model is realized, an individual human being may at any time dare climb the ladder from fear back to love.

These aspects of *Mishneh torah* should not be thought of as a current running only beneath the surface. The intricacies of its form affect even the reader who is not directly aware of them. The lucidity and felt purpose of each *halakhah* is due not only to the weight of scholarship and the incisive mind behind it, but also to the fact that it is like a wave upon a mighty tide driving towards the work's conclusion; its beauty derives not only from elegant expression, but from its being a detail of a grand architecture.

But love, Maimonides tells us, is commensurate with knowledge. The greater our consciousness of *Mishneh torah*'s art, the more we shall be moved by the love of God of which it is the sublime expression.

---

[39] *Guide* iii. 25 (p. 506).

[40] For this characterization of Maimonides' idea of the messiah, see Ravitzky, 'Maimonides on the Days of the Messiah' (discussed on pp. 270–1 above) and Hartman, 'Maimonides' Approach to Messianism'.

APPENDIX I

THE BOOKS AND SECTIONS OF *MISHNEH TORAH*

ENGLISH TITLE	HEBREW TITLE	NO. OF CHAPTERS
1. *Knowledge*	***Mada***	**46**
Foundations of the Torah	*Yesodei hatorah*	10
Ethical Qualities	*De'ot*	7
Torah Study	*Talmud torah*	7
Idolatry	*Avodah zarah vehukot hagoyim*	12
Repentance	*Teshuvah*	10
2. *Love*	***Ahavah***	**46**
Recitation of the Shema	*Keriyat shema*	4
Prayer and the Priestly Blessing	*Tefilah uvirkat kohanim*	15
Phylacteries, Mezuzah, and Torah Scroll	*Tefilin, mezuzah, vesefer torah*	10
Fringes	*Tsitsit*	3
Blessings	*Berakhot*	11
Circumcision	*Milah*	3
3. *Seasons*	***Zemanim***	**97**
Sabbath	*Shabat*	30
Joining Domains	*Eruvin*	8
Resting on Tenth of Tishrei (Day of Atonement)	*Shevitat asor*	3
Resting on Festivals	*Shevitat yom tov*	8
Leavened and Unleavened Bread	*Hamets umatsah*	8
Ram's Horn, Booth, and Palm Branch	*Shofar vesukah velulav*	8
Shekel Dues for Temple	*Shekalim*	4

ENGLISH TITLE	HEBREW TITLE	NO. OF CHAPTERS
Sanctification of the New Moon	*Kidush haḥodesh*	19
Fast Days	*Ta'aniyot*	5
Megilah (Purim) and Hanukah	*Megilah veḥanukah*	4
4. *Women*	***Nashim***	**53**
Marriage	*Ishut*	25
Divorce	*Gerushin*	13
Levirate Marriage	*Yibum veḥalitsah*	8
Virgin Maiden	*Na'arah betulah*	3
Wayward Woman	*Sotah*	4
5. *Holiness*	***Kedushah***	**53**
Forbidden Intercourse	*Isurei bi'ah*	22
Forbidden Foods	*Ma'akhalot asurot*	17
Slaughter	*Sheḥitah*	14
6. *Asseverations*	***Hafla'ah***	**43**
Oaths	*Shevuot*	12
Vows	*Nedarim*	13
Nazirites	*Nezirut*	10
Valuation and Consecrations	*Arakhim veḥaramim*	8
7. *Agriculture*	***Zerai'm***	**85**
Diverse Kinds	*Kilayim*	10
Gifts to the Poor	*Matnot aniyim*	10
Heave Offerings	*Terumot*	15
Tithe	*Ma'aser*	14
Second Tithe and Fourth Year's Fruit	*Ma'aser sheni veneta reva'i*	11
First Fruits and Other Priestly Offerings	*Bikurim ushe'ar matnot kehunah*	12
Sabbatical and Jubilee Years	*Shemitah veyovel*	13
8. *Temple Service*	***Avodah***	**95**
Temple	*Beit habeḥirah*	8
Temple Utensils and Servers	*Kelei hamikdash veha'ovdim bo*	10
Entrance into the Sanctuary	*Bi'at mikdash*	9

ENGLISH TITLE	HEBREW TITLE	NO. OF CHAPTERS
12. *Acquisition*	***Kinyan***	**75**
Sales	*Mekhirah*	30
Acquisition and Gifts	*Zekhiyah umatanah*	12
Neighbours	*Shekhenim*	14
Agents and Partners	*Sheluḥin veshutafin*	10
Slaves	*Avadim*	9
13. *Civil Laws*	***Mishpatim***	**75**
Hiring	*Sekhirut*	13
Borrowing and Depositing	*She'elah ufikadon*	8
Creditor and Debtor	*Malveh veloveh*	27
Pleading	*To'en venitan*	16
Inheritance	*Naḥalot*	11
14. *Judges*	***Shofetim***	**81**
Sanhedrin	*Sanhedrin*	26
Evidence	*Edut*	22
Rebels	*Mamrim*	7
Mourning	*Evel*	14
Kings and Their Wars	*Melakhim umilḥamotehem*	12
Total number of chapters		1,000

THE PHILOSOPHICAL BACKGROUND

1. Outline of Neoplatonism

The school of thought known as Neoplatonism arose in Rome in the third century CE.[1] It is so called because it represents a return, with modifications, to the doctrines of Plato after his pupil Aristotle's rejection of them. Plotinus, who studied philosophy in Alexandria and arrived in Rome in about 244, is generally considered to be the first and foremost figure of the school. His pupil Porphyry collected and edited his writings, and between 300 and 305 published them as the *Enneads*. Aristotle, it is worth recalling, died in 322 BCE, so that the interval between him and Plotinus is five and a half centuries.

In the Islamic world Plotinus was hardly known by name.[2] Parts of the *Enneads* circulated in Arabic paraphrases, such as *The Theology of Aristotle*. The medieval Islamic philosophers attributed this and other versions of Plotinus' works to Aristotle,[3] and tend to amalgamate the thought of both of them in their metaphysics. Whether or not Maimonides read *The Theology of Aristotle* or any similar work is not known for sure. Herbert Davidson detects no reference or allusion to such works in the *Guide*.[4] Alfred Ivry, on the other hand, states forthrightly, on the basis of a comparison of some of the teachings of the *Guide* with those of the *Enneads*, that 'The striking parallels that emerge offer persuasive evidence that this text, originally in Greek, had considerable

[1] The summary is chiefly based on Wallis, *Neoplatonism*; Dominic J. O'Meara, *Plotinus*; *The Oxford Classical Dictionary*, 2nd edn. (Oxford, 1970), s.v. 'Plotinus'.

[2] Fakhry, *A History of Islamic Philosophy*, 22.

[3] The misattribution may or may not have been deliberate. See Adamson, 'The Theology of Aristotle'.

[4] See Davidson, *Moses Maimonides*, 111. Reviewing the authors mentioned in Maimonides' letter to Samuel ibn Tibbon, Steven Harvey comments, 'With regard to the inquiry into Maimonides' Neoplatonism, it seems to me that one must confront the simple fact that in the letter he eschews the many Neoplatonic texts translated into Arabic' ('Maimonides' Letter to Samuel ibn Tibbon', 70). See also Galston, 'A Re-examination of Al-Farabi's Neoplatonism' (cited by Harvey).

influence in its Arabic versions upon Maimonides' thinking, directly as well as indirectly, and that it is a major source of Maimonides' philosophy.'[5] At any rate, familiarity with Neoplatonic ideas was guaranteed by Maimonides' reading of Alfarabi and Avicenna, whose writings contain a noted Neoplatonic strain,[6] and also through his knowledge of Ismaili writings.

Aristotle differed from Plato on the status of universals, that is, properties such as 'chair-ness', 'humanity', 'right-angled triangle'. Plato was a realist, holding that universals really exist as ideal Forms, and that the chairs, human beings, and right-angled triangles we see are but imperfect copies of the Forms. Aristotle held form to be immanent in matter, inseparable from it but distinguishable in the mind.[7] Both these philosophers considered knowledge to be the perception of form, but whereas for Plato this ultimately meant seeing beyond material existence to the realm of the Forms, for Aristotle it meant extracting form from matter; the universal property 'humanity', for example, from encounters with many human beings.

Plotinus resuscitated the Forms but placed them in a universal mind, and provided a mechanism whereby they reach matter, namely, emanation.

In Plotinus' system, existence is hierarchical. Movement up the hierarchy is towards unity, simplicity, consciousness, and reality; movement downwards is towards multiplicity, complexity, lack of consciousness, and unreality. 'Real' here means permanent, unchanging, and intelligible, that is, perceptible by the intellect without the mediation of the senses—like Plato's Forms. Perishable, sensible matter is thus the least real thing in existence. Although the system is derived from the bottom upwards, using the argument that a composite being must be preceded by a simpler one, it is easier to describe it from the top downwards.

Above matter the hierarchy has three levels, occupied by three entities, or hypostases. The supreme hypostasis is the One or the Good, a being of absolute unity and perfection, the only absolute reality,[8] of which, beyond that, nothing can be said. Although it might be thought that nothing could derive from absolute perfection that would not impair it, Plotinus asserts that the very perfection of the Good entails that it should not keep goodness within itself but that goodness should flow from it. An analogy he uses is that of heat

---

[5] Ivry, 'Neoplatonic Currents in Maimonides' Thought', 117. Pines gives no entry for Plotinus in his 'Philosophic Sources'. He does mention the fifth-century Neoplatonist Proclus ('Philosophic Sources', p. lxxviii.).

[6] See Davidson, *Alfarabi, Avicenna and Averroes on Intellect*; Netton, *Al-Farabi and his School*, 43.

[7] Compare 'Laws of the Foundations of the Torah', 4: 7.   [8] Compare ibid. 1: 1–4.

radiating from fire. In Neoplatonic metaphysics everything seeks to return to its cause, and in doing so becomes self-aware and shapes itself.[9] The flow, or emanation, from the One is an infinite, formless stream, but as it turns back towards the One, it acquires definition, becoming Intellect, the next hypostasis. This turning back is actually a double movement: the hypostasis turns back to contemplate its source, and also turns back in contemplation on itself. In contemplating the One, Intellect is unable to comprehend it in its entirety and truth, and fragments it into the Forms.

An overflow from Intellect in turn produces the third hypostasis, which is Soul. As it turns back to Intellect, Soul carries the process of fragmentation further, so that Intellect's timeless, whole vision of the Forms becomes successive, bringing time and space into existence. Nature, which is sometimes described as a lower level of Soul and sometimes as a separate entity, imposes shadows of the Forms onto matter, resulting in the multiplicity of the physical world, while the higher level of Soul remains in contemplation of Intellect. With Soul the process of emanation is exhausted, and we reach matter, 'the point at which the outflow of reality from the One fades away into utter darkness'.[10] This also marks the end of the chain of value. Matter is evil, not as a malevolence, but as a deprivation, an utter lack of determination. It emerges that the highest entity, the One, is, as an indescribable unity, formless, yet the source of form, while the lowest, matter, is formless, indeed hardly even an entity, but apt to receive form.

Emanation is a one-way process. It involves no change in the higher entity, which has no knowledge of the entity below it. The lower entity, on the other hand, only possesses form through its contemplation of the higher one, in its desire to return to it. Nevertheless, the One cannot be described as detached from existence: through the process of emanation the One is in All and All is in the One.[11] An analogy that has been suggested for this is Euclid's theorems, each of which implies the whole of his geometry, yet has independent value.

The link between this ontology and psychology/morality is the idea of microcosm. Human beings have the three levels of existence within themselves. Human consciousness usually operates at the level of Soul, the level of successive, logical, discursive reasoning, but it can reach the intuitive, holistic thought identified with Intellect, and can even aspire to transcendent unity

[9] Wallis, *Neoplatonism*, 65–6. [10] Ibid. 50.
[11] Maimonides acknowledges the tension between this idea and the doctrine of God's separation from the world in *Guide* i. 72 (p. 193).

with the One. Soul, however, tends to be distracted by matter and to operate on the lower level of Nature rather than at its higher level. It needs to become purified and to calm the passions so that at its higher level it can contemplate, and become a reflection of, the timeless order of Intellect.

The attitude of the Neoplatonists towards the body was not entirely negative: 'the body is not seen as an enemy, the keynote remains Hellenic moderation and self-discipline rarely turns into self-torture',[12] but taking the path to enlightenment means turning away from the sensible world towards the One in love, for which moral virtue is a prerequisite.

2. The World According to Alfarabi and Avicenna

The opposing ideas of Aristotle and Plotinus were synthesized by later thinkers, so that the picture of the world that Maimonides received from the Islamic philosophers Alfarabi (d. 950) and Avicenna (980–1037) can roughly be described as a combination of Aristotelian cosmology and Neoplatonic cosmogony.[13] From Aristotle derives the model of transparent, revolving spheres containing the stars and planets. This model is meant to account for the apparent motions of the heavenly bodies for an observer on earth. From this point of view the motions of the stars and planets are very complicated. The number of spheres required to account for them is quite large, in fact indeterminate, and the system includes some spheres that are not Earth-centric, to accommodate planets whose motions do not conform to a smooth, regular orbit around the Earth.[14] However, the basic model assumed by Alfarabi is of nine nested spheres with the Earth at their centre.

The outer or diurnal sphere revolves once every twenty-four hours. It contains no stars or planets; its function is to impart motion to the other spheres. Within the diurnal sphere is the sphere of the fixed stars, that is to say, stars that are fixed in relation to the diurnal sphere, so that they appear to revolve around the Earth once every twenty-four hours. Within that are five spheres containing the known planets;[15] within them is the sphere of the

[12] Wallis, *Neoplatonism*, 9.

[13] As Davidson puts it, 'The universe envisioned by Alfarabi is fashioned of Aristotelian bricks and of mortar borrowed from Neoplatonic philosophy' (*Alfarabi, Avicenna and Averroes on Intellect*, 44). The account here is largely based on Davidson's book, but is greatly simplified, ignoring important differences between Alfarabi and Avicenna, and between Maimonides and both of them, that Davidson describes. See also Netton, *Al-Farabi and his School*.

[14] This is mentioned in 'Laws of the Sanctification of the New Moon', 11: 13–14.

[15] Jupiter, Saturn, Mars, Venus, and Mercury.

Sun; and lowest of all, immediately surrounding the Earth, is the sphere of the Moon.

In Aristotle's system there is no causal connection between one sphere and the next, and although the motion of each sphere is controlled by an Intelligence, the Intelligence is not the cause of the sphere's existence.

Alfarabi supplies these connections by invoking, and expanding, the Neoplatonic concept of emanation. To combine the Neoplatonic system with the Aristotelian model of the universe, he divides the phase of Intellect into ten intellects. From the First Cause (which corresponds to the Neoplatonists' One or Good) proceeds a first intellect. This intellect has two thoughts: a thought of its own essence, from which proceed the soul and the body of the first sphere; and a thought of the First Cause, from which emanates a second intellect. This second intellect in turn produces the body and soul of the second sphere from its thought of itself and emanates a third intellect from its thought of the First Cause. The process continues until there are nine intellects and nine corresponding spheres with their souls.

The tenth phase is a little different. Here Alfarabi brings into play the Aristotelian concept of the agent intellect (also known as the active intelligence, or active intellect), the status and function of which in Aristotle's system is not entirely clear but which Alfarabi and Avicenna interpret as an entity that emanates forms that are projected onto sublunar matter. What has happened is that the decline in value represented by the phases of emanation is also a decline in power. By the time the tenth phase is reached, there is not enough power to emanate another sphere or a subsequent intellect. All the agent intellect can accomplish is something analogous to the activity of the higher intellects: instead of emanating another intellect, it gives human intellects a thought of itself (what we call simply thoughts), and instead of emanating a sphere, it gives form to matter. In Alfarabi's system prime matter (that is, matter before it receives the basic forms of fire, air, water, and earth) is produced by the revolutions of the spheres, while according to Avicenna it is emanated by the agent intellect itself. Either way, the agent intellect stands in relation to the sublunar world as the higher intellects do to their corresponding spheres.[16]

[16] This, according to Davidson, is an innovation by Alfarabi. See his *Alfarabi, Avicenna and Averroes on Intellect*, 18. In Maimonides' angelology the agent intellect corresponds to the lowest order of angels, the *ishim*—see 'Laws of the Foundations of the Torah', 4: 6. From the point of view of the human microcosm I have treated this hierarchy as a gradation of Soul rather than Intellect; the point is that the purer a human being's soul becomes, the greater becomes their capacity for intellectual perception.

THE ALFARABIAN/MAIMONIDEAN COSMOS

The diagram shows the emanation of the ten separate intellects, or angels (named as in 'Laws of the Foundations of the Torah', 2:7), and the spheres. The separate intellects do not actually have physical locations.

Emanation is unidirectional from the First Cause down to the *ishim*, or agent intellect. Lower entities have thoughts of higher ones, but do not affect them in any way.

As shown in the enlarged diagram of the activity of the separate intellect, each angel/separate intellect has two thoughts: a thought of the First Existence, or God, and a thought of itself. From its thought of God, it emanates the next angel/separate intellect, while from its thought of itself, it emanates the intellect, soul, and body of a sphere. It is also aware of the separate intellect above it (not drawn).

The sphere's intellect represents to its soul the separate intellect that emanated it. This makes the soul of the sphere love the separate intellect and desire to unite with it. Since the sphere cannot move from its position, this desire causes it to rotate.

The power of emanation diminishes as we descend the hierarchy, so that the agent intellect is too weak to emanate another separate intellect. Instead, by analogy with emanation, it projects forms onto the various combinations of the elements, and assists human beings in attaining knowledge.

The number and order of the spheres shown here accords with 'Laws of the Foundations of the Torah', 3:1. *Guide* ii. 9 (pp. 268-9) puts Venus and Mercury above the Sun.

The four elements are arranged in spherical layers, but, having no souls, they do not rotate. Under the influence of the rotating spheres, small amounts of them move up and down and mingle to form different combinations, though each element tends to return to its original, natural place—see 'Laws of the Foundations of the Torah', 3:10–4:6.

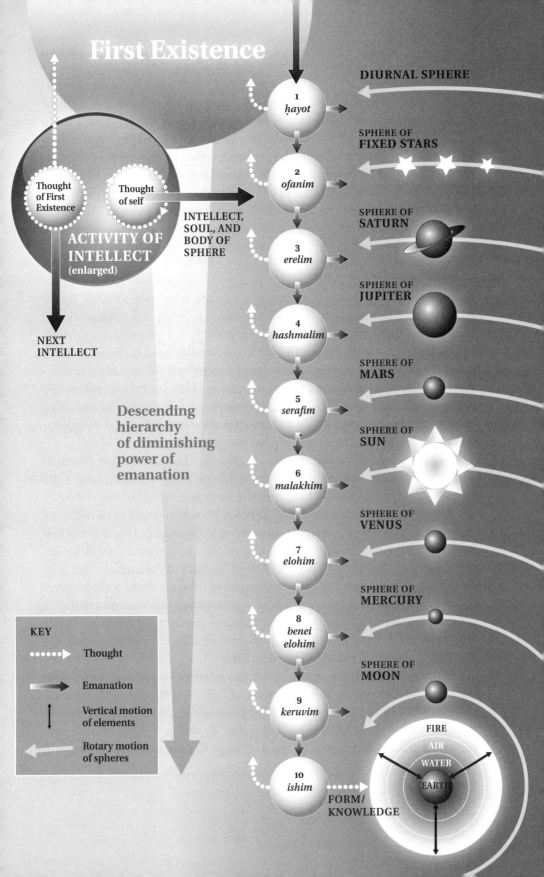

First Existence

DIURNAL SPHERE

1 ḥayot

SPHERE OF **FIXED STARS**

2 ofanim

SPHERE OF **SATURN**

3 erelim

SPHERE OF **JUPITER**

4 hashmalim

SPHERE OF **MARS**

5 serafim

SPHERE OF **SUN**

6 malakhim

SPHERE OF **VENUS**

7 elohim

SPHERE OF **MERCURY**

8 benei elohim

SPHERE OF **MOON**

9 keruvim

10 ishim

FORM/ KNOWLEDGE

FIRE
AIR
WATER
EARTH

Thought of First Existence

Thought of self

ACTIVITY OF INTELLECT
(enlarged)

INTELLECT, SOUL, AND BODY OF SPHERE

NEXT INTELLECT

Descending hierarchy of diminishing power of emanation

KEY

••••••▶ Thought

▬▬▶ Emanation

↕ Vertical motion of elements

◀▬▬ Rotary motion of spheres

The idea underlying the role of the agent intellect in giving form to matter is that a potential cannot become actual unless the actuality already exists.[17] A piece of wood, for example, may be potentially a table, but it cannot become one unless the idea of a table already exists in the carpenter's mind. Similarly, natural forms pre-exist in the agent intellect. Any blend of the elements of matter receives the form appropriate to it, to become a palm tree, say, or a human being. The agent intellect, as it were, broadcasts simultaneously and constantly on all frequencies, and any particular blend of matter is tuned to receive a particular frequency which gives it its form.

Intellect and Immortality

The acquisition of knowledge too is a passage from potential to actual, requiring an external agent in which the knowledge pre-exists. (Knowledge here means theoretical knowledge, pure science, not practical knowledge, which derives from experience.) To say that forms pre-exist in the agent intellect is the same as saying that knowledge pre-exists in it—knowledge, as mentioned, being the perception of form. So, just as a blend of matter will receive the broadcast form appropriate to it, a human mind will receive the broadcast knowledge that, through moral and intellectual effort, it is tuned to receive, and is thereby assisted in actualizing its intellectual potential.

The actualization of the intellect is gradual. The intellectual potential with which human beings are born is a hylic (material) intellect, one of the faculties of the human soul along with the nutritive, reproductive, and other faculties that perish with the body. When a person engages in thought, he or she begins to receive concepts from the agent intellect. This is the actual intellect, or intellect *in actu*. We do not, of course, constantly think in any conscious way about everything we know. This state of the intellect that possesses thoughts but is not at present engaged in thinking them is the intellect *in habitu*. Once the intellect reaches the highest state of knowledge of which it is capable, it achieves the status of an acquired intellect, which exists separately from the body. The acquired intellect is capable of comprehending the source of knowledge, the agent intellect itself.

Alfarabi compares the operation of the intellect to physical sight, with the agent intellect as the Sun, the source of light, and the forms that are the objects of knowledge as the colours of physical objects. At first, light activates the eye, making potential sight actual. Then, by means of light, the eye perceives the colours of objects. In the next stage the eye perceives light itself,

---

[17] For Maimonides' explanation of this principle, see *Guide* ii. 4 (pp. 257–8).

until finally it perceives the Sun, corresponding to the human intellect's perception of the agent intellect.

The acquired intellect is immortal like the agent intellect, because we are what we know. To understand this, we must begin with Aristotle's theory of perception, according to which a perceiving mind grasps the object perceived by becoming like it.

'Perception comes about with <an organ's> being changed and affected . . . for it seems to be a kind of alteration' (*De Anima* ii 5, 416b 33–34) . . . Aristotle is happy to speak of an affected thing as receiving the form of the agent which affects it and of the change consisting in the affected thing's 'becoming like' the agent (*De Anima* ii 5, 418a 3–6; ii 12, 424a 17–21) . . . Just as perception involves the reception of a sensible form by a suitably qualified sensory faculty, so thinking involves the reception of an intelligible form by a suitably qualified intellectual faculty (*De Anima* iii 4, 429a 13–18). According to this model, thinking consists in a mind's becoming enformed by some object of thought, so that actual thinking occurs whenever some suitably prepared mind is 'made like' its object by being affected by it.[18]

The perception of objects is the function of the senses, and the storage of such sense impressions is a function of the imagination. These impressions are separate from the object perceived, and in some way separate from the perceiving subject. But when the intellect, aided by the agent intellect, strips an object's form, or essential characteristic, from the sense impression of it, then, in that act, form, intellect, and perceiving subject are one. Hence what the intellect is depends on what it is thinking about.

Herbert Davidson explains the application of this to the idea of immortality as follows (apropos Maimonides' statement in his commentary on Mishnah *Sanhedrin* 10: 1 that ultimate human felicity consists in the 'permanence of the soul through the permanence of its object of knowledge and through its becoming identical therewith'):

In every act of thinking, the human intellect becomes identical with its thought: When the intellect has something belonging to the physical world as the object of its thought, it becomes identical with the form abstracted from the thing in question; during the time that it thinks a thought of a tree or a cat, the intellect is identical with the form abstracted from the tree or cat. It is possible, however, for the human intellect to have as the object of its thought not only beings within the physical world, but beings belonging to the incorporeal, imperishable realm as well. Since incorporeal beings possess no material side, their forms do not have to be abstracted

---

[18] Shields, 'Aristotle's Psychology', 10–12.

from a material substratum. Consequently, when a human intellect succeeds in having a being of that sort as the object of its thought, what it takes hold of is the incorporeal being in its entirety.[19]

The fully actualized human intellect, having the agent intellect as the object
of its thought, becomes immortal like it.

God's knowledge is different. The above process involves change, caused
by an external stimulus, from not knowing to knowing, and also multiplicity,
since we speak of the person, or the intellecting subject, the intellect itself,
and the intellected object, three components that conjoin in the act of perception. Since God is an unchanging, absolute unity, unaffected by anything
outside himself, we must say that he is constantly, simultaneously, and inseparably subject, intellect, and object.

Prophecy

Prophecy is the highest level that a human intellect can reach. It is not a
supernatural communication bypassing the natural channels of emanation,
but the natural outcome of the would-be prophet's moral and intellectual
striving, making him or her supremely receptive to the knowledge constantly
transmitted via those channels. In other words, prophets are self-selecting.
With differing nuances, Alfarabi and Avicenna see prophecy as a direct emanation from the agent intellect passing through the rational faculty of the
prophet to his or her imaginative faculty. The human imagination is in any
case capable of fitful knowledge of the future. In the prophet's more highly
developed imagination, the abstract knowledge received in the emanation
from the agent intellect can become applied knowledge that is reliable, and
communicable to the masses. This may be in the form of accurate predictions
about the real world, or parables, or a system of law. Joel Kraemer describes
Alfarabi's position on the prophetic origin of the law thus: 'Alfarabi had
asserted that humans are united by love (*mahabba* = *philia*) as the various parts
of the universe are united by justice and concord. Social order is natural and
reflects the cosmic hierarchy. The true prophet, who is also a philosopher,
translates this cosmic hierarchy into a social order.'[20]

In general, the world-view described here assumes structural, functional,
and psychic correspondence between different parts of existence, correspondence that embraces the human mind as well. For medieval thinkers this is
what makes the world understandable.[21] This seems strange and fanciful to a

---

[19] Davidson, *Moses Maimonides*, 164.   [20] Kraemer, 'Naturalism and Universalism', 54.
[21] 'Essences, or forms, exist as paradigms in the Agent Intellect, abstractly in the human mind

modern sensibility, a projection of the self onto reality of the kind that we outgrew long ago. Nevertheless, for all the strangeness, the thinkers surveyed here constructed their models of existence in large part in order to deal with such perennial concerns of philosophy as perception, knowledge, mind and body, and universals. In the case of Maimonides, it may be added that he strove precisely to emancipate people from the bonds of a self-centred world-view, and that his major works serve as guides to moral, intellectual, and spiritual maturity.

and concretely in objects. The truth is therefore defined by a correspondence theory, the intelligible forms in the mind conforming to forms in sensible objects. The correspondence between mind and the world order is then both noetic and ontological. The universe is rational and can be understood by the human mind. There is a commensurability and reciprocal linkage between human beings and the universe' (Kraemer, 'Islamic Context', 54).

Glossary

꿇

aggadah (Heb.) Lore and legend in the form of elaborations on the biblical narrative collected in compilations of Midrash, and these together with stories about the sages incorporated in the Talmud

amora (pl. **amora'im**) (Aram.) Sage of the Talmud

batin (Arab.) The hidden meaning of a text

da'at (Heb.) Intellect, mind

de'ah (pl. **de'ot**) (Heb.) 1. Intellect; 2. character trait; 3. separate (i.e. incorporeal) intellect, angel

fasl (pl. **fusul**) (Arab.) A short paragraph, an aphorism

gaon (pl. **geonim**) (Heb.) Title given to the heads of the Babylonian yeshivas, in Sura and Pumbedita, in the period 589–1040 CE. Subsequently, heads of the Baghdad yeshiva also assumed the title.

gematria (Heb.) System of numerical values of Hebrew letters, often employed to lend symbolic significance to words and phrases in Scripture and generally

Genesis Rabbah (Heb.) Legendary midrashic commentary

halakhah (pl. **halakhot**) (Heb.) 1. Practical Jewish law in general; 2. a specific provision of the law; 3. *halakhah* (italicized): a paragraph of *Mishneh torah*, its smallest unit

Hanukah Eight-day festival of lights commemorating the second-century BCE Jewish victory over the Seleucids and restoration of the Jerusalem Temple

hok (pl. **hukim**) (Heb.) Statute; in rabbinic usage, a Torah law the purpose of which is not readily apparent

lulav (Heb.) Date palm shoot, used together with citron, myrtle, and willow in the Sukkot festival rite—see Lev. 23:40; *lulav* is often used synecdochically to refer to all four kinds

ma'aseh bereshit (Heb.) 'Account of the beginning'—the exposition of the story of Creation in Genesis, held by Maimonides to refer to physics

ma'aseh merkavah (Heb.) 'Account of the chariot'—the exposition of the vision of Ezekiel in Ezek. 1, held by Maimonides to refer to metaphysics

mashal (Heb.) A parable

Mekhilta derabi yishma'el (Heb.) A midrashic legal and legendary commentary on Exodus

Midrash Legal (*midrash halakhah*) and legendary (*midrash aggadah*) exegesis of and elaboration upon the verses of the Bible, in various compilations redacted between the fifth and the sixteenth centuries CE

midrash (pl. *midrashim*) (Heb.) A particular instance of Midrash

Midrash tanḥuma (Heb.) A legendary midrashic commentary on the Torah

mikveh (Heb.) Immersion pool of natural ('undrawn') water used in purification and conversion rites

Mishnah Redaction of the halakhah under R. Judah the Prince in the third century CE

mishnah (pl. *mishnayot*) (Heb.) An individual paragraph of the Mishnah

nazirite A person who adopts more stringent practices than are required in normative Jewish law (not to cut their hair, not to consume wine or any product of grapes, and not to become impure through contact with a dead body), either for a specified period or for life

pardes (Heb.; lit. 'orchard') 1. The term used to refer collectively to *ma'aseh bereshit* and *ma'aseh merkavah*; 2. used as an acronym to refer to four levels of biblical exegesis: *peshat*—the plain meaning of a verse or passage; *remez*—'hint' or symbolic meaning; *derash*—an implied meaning, often derived through echoes in passages elsewhere in Scripture, the method of Midrash; *sod*—the esoteric or mystical meaning

paytan (Heb.) A composer of liturgical poetry

Pesikta derav kahana (Heb.) Legendary midrashic commentary on selected portions of the Torah and prophets

piyut (pl. *piyutim*) (Heb.) 1. Liturgical poetry as a genre; 2. an individual liturgical poem

Purim (Heb.) Festival commemorating the salvation of the Jews of the Persian empire from a decree of extermination, as recounted in the book of Esther

Rambam (Heb.) The acronym of Maimonides' name by which he is generally known in Hebrew (*rabi mosheh ben maimon*)

sefirah (pl. *sefirot*) (Heb.) The emanations or attributes, ten in number, through which, in kabbalah, the Ein Sof (Infinite) creates and is manifest in the physical and metaphysical realms

Shema (Heb.) Twice-daily mandatory recital of Torah verses, incorporated into the morning and evening prayers, and comprising three sections: Deut. 6: 4–9 (which begins *Shema yisra'el*—'Hear, O Israel'); Deut. 11: 13–21; Num. 15: 37–41

shofar (Heb.) Horn of an animal, usually a ram, blown as part of the Rosh Hashanah (New Year) rite

Sifra (Heb.) A midrashic legal commentary on Leviticus

Sifrei (Heb.) A midrashic legal commentary on Numbers and Deuteronomy

Song of Songs Rabbah (Heb.) Legendary midrashic commentary *sukab* (Heb.) Structure with roof of unprocessed vegetation (in Israel, often palm branches) inhabited during the seven days of the Sukkot festival

talit (Heb.) Fringed prayer shawl

Talmud (Heb.) 1. Discussions of the rabbis largely elucidating the Mishnah, and the second most important source for the Oral Law. The Jerusalem Talmud records discussions of rabbis in the Land of Israel and was redacted in the fourth century CE. The Babylonian Talmud, recording discussions of the rabbis of the academies in Iraq, was redacted later—according to tradition, in the fifth century CE. In this sense, Talmud is also known as Gemara; 2. Mishnah and Gemara collectively; 3. in Maimonides' definition (see 'Laws of Torah Study', 1: 11–12), *talmud* is the derivational study of the Oral Law, and also includes *pardes*

taryag (Heb.) Acronym formed of the Hebrew letters *tet*, *resh*, *yod*, *gimel*, the numerical equivalents of which total 613, by tradition the number of commandments in the Torah

Torah (Heb.) 1. The Five Books of Moses; 2. Jewish law and doctrine in general

yeshiva (Heb.) Institute of Jewish religious study

zahir (Arab.) The plain meaning of a text

Bibliography

Works by Maimonides

Mishneh Torah

The Authorized Version of the Code of Maimonides: Sefer Hamada, Sefer Ahavah. Facsimile Edition of Oxford Manuscript Huntington 80, ed. Shlomo Zalman Havlin (Jerusalem and Cleveland, 1997).

The Code of Maimonides, 13 vols. (New Haven, 1949–2004): *The Book of Agriculture*, trans. Isaac Klein (1979); *The Book of Cleanness*, trans. Herbert Danby (1954); *The Book of Judges*, trans. A. M. Hershman (1949); *The Book of Love*, trans. Menachem Kellner (2004); The Book of Offerings, trans. Herbert Danby (1950); *The Book of Seasons*, trans. Solomon Gandz and Hyman Klein (1961); *The Book of Temple Service*, trans. Mendel Lewittes (1957); *The Book of Torts*, trans. Hyman Klein (1954); *The Book of Women*, trans. Isaac Klein (1972).

Introduction and *Book of Knowledge*, trans. Moses Hyamson (Jerusalem, 1965).

Mishneh torah, ed. Shabse Frankel, 15 vols. (Benei Berak, 1985–2006).

Mishneh torah, Vilna edn. with commentaries (repr. Jerusalem, 1975).

Mishneh torah, ed. Yohai Makbili (Haifa, 2006).

Rambam la'am, 15 vols. (12th imprint, Jerusalem, 1993).

Sefer hamada im perush yad peshutah, ed. Nachum L. Rabinovitch, 2 vols. (Jerusalem, 1990).

Other Works by Maimonides

Book of the Commandments [Sefer hamitsvot], trans. Charles B. Chavel, 2 vols. (London, 1940); Heb. trans. Joseph Kafih (Jerusalem, 1989/90).

Commentary on the Mishnah [Mishnah im perush rabenu moshe ben maimon], ed. and trans. from Arab. Joseph Kafih, 6 vols. (Jerusalem, 1963–7).

'Eight Chapters' [Shemonah perakim] (introd. to commentary on Mishnah *Avot*), trans. in Raymond L. Weiss and Charles E. Butterworth (eds.), *Ethical Writings of Maimonides* (New York, 1975).

'Epistle to Yemen', trans. in Abraham Halkin and David Hartman, *Epistles of Maimonides: Crisis and Leadership* (Philadelphia, 1985), 91–131.

'Essay on Resurrection', trans. in Abraham Halkin and David Hartman, *Epistles of Maimonides: Crisis and Leadership* (Philadelphia, 1985), 209–33.

Guide of the Perplexed [Arab.: Dalalat al-ḥa'irin; Heb.: Moreh nevukhim], Eng. trans. from Arab. Shlomo Pines, 2 vols. (Chicago, 1963); Heb. trans. Michael Schwarz, 2 vols. (Tel Aviv, 2002); Heb. trans. Samuel ibn Tibbon, with commentaries by Shem Tov, Efodi, Crescas, Abravanel (Lvov, 1866; repr. Jerusalem, 1960).

Letters and Essays of Moses Maimonides [Igerot harambam], Heb. trans. Itzhak Shailat, 2 vols. (3rd imprint, Ma'aleh Adumim, 1995).

Mose Ben Maimon Responsa [Teshuvot harambam], ed. Alfred Freimann (Jerusalem, 1934).

Treatise on Logic, trans. Israel Efros (New York, 1938).

Other Works

ABRAMS, M. H., *The Mirror and the Lamp: Romantic Theory and the Critical Tradition* (Oxford, 1953).

ACKERMAN, ARI, 'Ḥasdai Crescas on the Philosophic Foundation of Codification', *AJS Review*, 37/2 (2013), 315–31.

ADAJIAN, THOMAS, 'The Definition of Art', in Edward N. Zalta (ed.), *The Stanford Encyclopedia of Philosophy*, Fall 2008 edn. (21 Sept. 2008), <http://plato.stanford.edu/archives/fall2008/entries/art-definition/>.

ADAMSON, PETER, 'The Theology of Aristotle', in Edward N. Zalta (ed.), *The Stanford Encyclopedia of Philosophy*, Fall 2008 edn. (21 Sept. 2008), <http://plato.stanford.edu/archives/ fall2008/entries/theology-aristotle/>.

ALFARABI, ABU NASR, *On the Perfect State* [Al-madina al-fadila], trans. Richard Walzer (Oxford, 1985).

ALLEN, GRAHAM, *Intertextuality* (London, 2000).

ALLONY, NEHEMYA, *The Jewish Library in the Middle Ages: Book Lists from the Cairo Genizah*, ed. Miriam Frenkel and Haggai Ben-Shammai with the participation of Moshe Sokolow (Jerusalem, 2006).

ALTMANN, ALEXANDER, 'The Delphic Maxim in Medieval Islam and Judaism', in id. (ed.), *Studies in Religious Philosophy and Mysticism* (Ithaca, NY, 1969), 1–40.

—— 'The Ladder of Ascension', in Efraim Elimelech Urbach, Raphael Jehudah Zwi Werblowsky, and Chaim Wirszubski (eds.), *Studies in Mysticism and Religion Presented to G. G. Scholem* (Jerusalem, 1967), 1–32.

—— 'Maimonides' "Four Perfections"', *Israel Oriental Studies*, 2 (1972), 15–24.

ANNAS, JULIA, *Platonic Ethics, Old and New* (Ithaca, NY, 1999).

ARISTOTLE, *Metaphysics*, trans. W. D. Ross, in *The Complete Works of Aristotle*, ii, ed. Jonathan Barnes (Princeton, NJ, 1984), 1552–1728.

—— *Nicomachean Ethics*, trans. W. D. Ross and J. O. Urmson, in *The Complete Works of Aristotle*, ii, ed. Jonathan Barnes (Princeton, NJ, 1984), 1729–1867.

ARMSTRONG, A. HILARY, 'The Apprehension of Divinity in the Self and Cosmos in Plotinus', in R. Baine Harris (ed.), *The Significance of Neoplatonism* (Norfolk, 1976), 187–98.

Babylonian Talmud, trans. various, ed. Isidore Epstein (London, 1935–52).

BANETH, DAVID H., 'On the Philosophic Terminology of Maimonides' (Heb.), *Tarbiz*, 6/*Sefer harambam* (1935), 10–40.

BARON, SALO WITTMAYER, 'The Historical Outlook of Maimonides', in Arthur Hertzberg and Leon A. Feldman (eds.), *History and Jewish Historians: Essays and Addresses* (Philadelphia, 1964), 109–63.

BARTHES, ROLAND GÉRARD, *Image—Music—Text*, trans. Stephen Heath (London, 1977).

BELL, CLIVE, *Art* (London, 1914).

BEN-SASSON, MENAHEM, 'Maimonides' *Mishneh Torah*: Towards Canon Formation in the Life of an Author' (Heb.), in Robert Brody et al. (eds.), *Uncovering the Canon* [Hakanon hasamui min ha'ayin] (Jerusalem, 2010), 133–201.

BENZIGER, JAMES, 'Organic Unity: Leibniz to Coleridge', *PMLA*, 66/2 (1951), 24–48.

BERKOVITS, ELIEZER, *God, Man and History*, 4th edn. (Jerusalem, 2004).

—— 'Torah and Nature in the Philosophy of Maimonides' (Heb.), in Menahem Zohori, Arie Tartakover, and Haim Ormian (eds.), *Studies on Jewish Themes by Contemporary American Scholars* [Hagut ivrit be'amerikah], ii (Tel Aviv, 1973), 9–17.

BERMAN, LAWRENCE V., 'The Ethical Views of Maimonides within the Context of Islamicate Civilization', in Joel L. Kraemer (ed.), *Perspectives on Maimonides* (Oxford, 1991), 13–32.

—— 'Maimonides the Disciple of Alfarabi', *Israel Oriental Studies*, 4 (1974), 154–78.

—— 'The Political Interpretation of the Maxim: The Purpose of Philosophy is the Imitation of God', *Studia Islamica*, 15 (1961), 53–61.

—— 'The Structure of the Commandments of the Torah in the Thought of Maimonides', in S. Stein and R. Loewe (eds.), *Studies in Jewish Religious and Intellectual History in Honor of Alexander Altmann* (Tuscaloosa, Ala., 1979), 51–66.

BIRNBAUM, RUTH, 'Maimonides, Then and Now', *Judaism: A Quarterly Journal of Jewish Life and Thought* (Jan. 2005), 66–78.

BLACK, DEBORAH L., 'Aesthetics in Islamic Philosophy', in Edward Craig (ed.), *The Routledge Encyclopedia of Philosophy Online* (London, 1998).

—— *Logic and Aristotle's* Rhetoric *and* Poetics *in Medieval Arabic Philosophy* (Leiden, 1990).

BLAND, KALMAN P., *The Artless Jew* (Princeton, NJ, 2000).

—— 'Beauty, Maimonides, and Cultural Relativism in Medieval Jewish Thought', *Journal of Medieval and Early Modern Studies*, 26/1 (1996), 85–112.

—— 'Medieval Jewish Aesthetics: Maimonides, Body, and Scripture in Profiat Duran', *Journal of the History of Ideas*, 54/4 (1993), 533–59.

BLIDSTEIN, GERALD J. (YA'ACOV), 'Art and the Jew', *The Torah u-Madda Journal*, 10 (2001), 163–72.

—— 'Maimonides and Me'iri on the Legitimacy of Non-Judaic Religion', in *Scholars and Scholarship: The Interaction Between Judaism and Other Cultures. The Bernard Revel Graduate School Conference Volume* (New York, 1990), 27–35.

—— *Political Concepts in Maimonidean Halakhah* [Ekronot mediniyim bemishnat harambam], 2nd edn. (Ramat Gan, 2001).

—— 'Where Do We Stand in the Study of Maimonidean Halakhah?', in Isadore Twersky (ed.), *Studies in Maimonides* (Cambridge, Mass., 1990), 214.

BLOOM, HAROLD, *Wallace Stevens: The Poems of Our Climate* (Ithaca, NY, 1977).

BLUMENTHAL, DAVID R., 'Maimonides' Intellectualist Mysticism and the Superiority of the Prophecy of Moses', *Studies in Medieval Culture*, 10 (1977), 51–67.

BREUER, EDWARD, 'Maimonides and the Authority of Aggadah', in Jay M. Harris (ed.), *Be'erot Yitzhak: Studies in Memory of Isadore Twersky* (Cambridge, Mass., 2005), 25–45.

BRODY, ROBERT, 'The Influence of Sa'adyah Gaon's Halakhic Monographs on Maimonides' *Mishneh Torah*' (Heb.), in Aviezer Ravitzky (ed.), *Maimonides: Conservatism, Originality, Revolution* [Harambam: shamranut, mekoriyut, mehapkhanut], i (Jerusalem, 2008), 211–22.

BUCHMAN, ASHER BENZION, '*Mishneh Torah*: Science and Art', *Hakirah, The Flatbush Journal of Jewish Law and Thought*, 9 (2010), 199–220.

BUTCHER, SAMUEL HENRY, *Aristotle's Theory of Poetry and the Fine Arts*, 4th edn. (London, 1951).

CALDER, NIGEL, *Einstein's Universe* (London, 1979).

CARONE, GABRIELA ROXANA, *Plato's Cosmology and its Ethical Dimensions* (Cambridge, 2005).

COHEN, BOAZ, 'The Classification of the Law in the *Mishneh Torah*', *Jewish Quarterly Review*, 25 (1935), 519–40.

—— 'The Responsum of Maimonides Concerning Music', in id. (ed.), *Law and Tradition in Judaism* (New York, 1969), 167–81.

COHEN, JONATHAN, 'Maimonides as Literary Artist: The Philosopher Tells a Story', in Felice Ziskin (ed.), *The Pardes Reader* (Jerusalem, 1997), 13–19.

COHEN, MORDECHAI Z., 'Imagination, Logic, Truth and Falsehood: Moses Ibn Ezra and Moses Maimonides on Biblical Metaphor in Light of Arabic Poetics and Philosophy' (Heb.), *Tarbiz*, 73/3 (2005), 417–58.

—— *Three Approaches to Biblical Metaphor: From Abraham Ibn Ezra and Maimonides to David Kimhi* (Leiden, 2003).

COLLINSON, DIANÉ, 'The Aesthetic Theory of Stephen Dedalus', *The British Journal of Aesthetics*, 23/1 (1983), 61–73.

CONGER, GEORGE PERRIGO, *Theories of Macrocosms and Microcosms in the History of Philosophy* (New York, 1922).

CORNFORD, FRANCIS MACDONALD, *Plato's Cosmology: The* Timaeus *of Plato*, translated with a running commentary (London, 1937).

COULTER, JAMES A., *The Literary Microcosm: Theories of Interpretation of the Later Neoplatonists* (Leiden, 1976).

DAHIYAT, ISMAIL M., *Avicenna's Commentary on the* Poetics *of Aristotle* (Leiden, 1974).

D'ANCONA, CRISTINA, 'Greek into Arabic', in Peter Adamson and Richard C. Taylor (eds.), *The Cambridge Companion to Arabic Philosophy* (Cambridge, 2005), 10–31.

DANTO, ARTHUR C., *The Transfiguration of the Commonplace* (Cambridge, Mass., 1981).

DAVIDSON, HERBERT A., *Alfarabi, Avicenna, and Averroes, on Intellect: Their Cosmologies, Theories of the Active Intellect, and Theories of Human Intellect* (Oxford, 1992).

—— 'Maimonides on Metaphysical Knowledge', *Maimonidean Studies*, 3 (1992/3), 49–103.

—— 'Maimonides' Secret Position on Creation', in Isadore Twersky (ed.), *Studies in Medieval Jewish History and Literature* (Cambridge, Mass., 1979), 16–40.

—— 'Maimonides' *Shemonah Peraqim* and Alfarabi's *Fusul al-Madani*', *Proceedings of the American Academy for Jewish Research*, 31 (1963), 33–50.

—— 'The Middle Way in Maimonides' Ethics', *Proceedings of the American Academy for Jewish Research*, 54 (1987), 31–72.

—— *Moses Maimonides: The Man and His Works* (Oxford, 2005).

DAVIES, STEPHEN, *Definitions of Art* (Ithaca, NY, 1991).

DE BRUYN, FRANS, 'Reading Virgil's "Georgics" as a Scientific Text: The Eighteenth-Century Debate between Jethro Tull and Stephen Switzer', *English Literary History*, 71/3 (2004), 661–89.

DIAMOND, JAMES A., *Converts, Heretics, and Lepers: Maimonides and the Outsider* (Notre Dame, Ill., 2007).

—— *Maimonides and the Hermeneutics of Concealment* (Albany, NY, 2002).

DILLON, JOHN, 'Image, Symbol and Analogy: Three Basic Concepts of Neoplatonic Allegorical Exegesis', in R. Baine Harris (ed.), *The Significance of Neoplatonism* (Norfolk, 1976), 247–62.

DODGE, BAYARD, *The Fihrist of al-Nadim: A Tenth Century Survey of Muslim Culture*, ii, trans. Bayard Dodge (New York, 1970).

DRORY, RINA, *Models and Contacts: Arabic Literature and Its Impact on Medieval Jewish Culture* (Leiden, 2000).

ECO, UMBERTO, *Art and Beauty in the Middle Ages*, trans. Hugh Bredin (New Haven, 1986).

EINSTEIN, ALBERT, *Out of My Later Years* (New York, 1950).

EISEN, ROBERT, '*Lifnim Mi-Shurat ha-Din* in Maimonides' *Mishneh Torah*', *Jewish Quarterly Review*, 89/3–4 (1999), 291–317.

ELIOT, T. S., *The Sacred Wood: Essays on Poetry and Criticism*, 7th edn. (London, 1950).

EMDEN, JACOB, *Mitpaḥat sefarim* (Lvov, 1870).

ENDRESS, GERHARD, *Proclus Arabus: Zwanzig Abschnitte aus der Institutio Theologica in arabischer Übersetzung* (Beirut and Wiesbaden, 1973).

EPSTEIN, JACOB N., *Introduction to the Mishnaic Text* [Mavo lenusaḥ hamishnah], ii, 3rd edn. (Jerusalem, 2000).

ERAN, AMIRA, 'Al-Ghazali and Maimonides on the World to Come and Spiritual Pleasures', *Jewish Studies Quarterly*, 8 (2001), 137–66.

EVEN-SHOSHAN, ABRAHAM, *A New Concordance of the Bible* [Konkordantsiyah ḥadashah letorah, nevi'im ukhetuvim] (Jerusalem, 1988).

—— *The New Dictionary* [Hamilon heḥadash], 4 vols. (Jerusalem, 1987).

FAKHRY, MAJID, *A History of Islamic Philosophy* (New York, 1970).

FAUR, JOSÉ, *Homo Mysticus: A Guide to Maimonides's Guide for the Perplexed* (Syracuse, NY, 1998).

—— 'Maimonides on Imagination: Towards a Theory of Jewish Aesthetics', in Mayer I. Gruber (ed.), *The Solomon Goldman Lectures*, vi (Chicago, 1993), 89–104.

FELDMAN, SEYMOUR, 'The End of the Universe in Medieval Jewish Philosophy', *AJS Review*, 11/1 (1986), 53–77.

Fox, Marvin, 'The Doctrine of the Mean in Aristotle and Maimonides: A Comparative Study', in Raphael Loewe and Siegfried Stein (eds.), *Studies in Jewish Religious and Intellectual History in Honor of Alexander Altmann* (Tuscaloosa, Ala., 1980), 114–15.

—— 'Maimonides and Aquinas on Natural Law', *Dine Israel*, 3 (1972), pp. xxii–xxiii.

Frank, Daniel H., 'Anger as a Vice: A Maimonidean Critique of Aristotle's Ethics', *History of Philosophy Quarterly*, 7 (1990), 269–81.

—— '"With All Your Heart and Soul . . .": The Moral Psychology of the *Shemonah Peraqim*', in Robert S. Cohen and Hillel Levine (eds.), *Maimonides and the Sciences* (Dordrecht, 2000), 25–33.

Freudenthal, Gad, 'The Biological Limitations of Man's Intellectual Perfection According to Maimonides', in Georges Tamer (ed.), *The Trias of Maimonides* (Berlin, 2005), 137–49.

—— 'Four Observations on Maimonides' Four Celestial Globes (*Guide* 2:9–10)', in Aviezer Ravitzky (ed.), *Maimonides: Conservatism, Originality, Revolution* [Harambam: shamranut, mekoriyut, mehapkhanut], ii (Jerusalem, 2008), 499–527.

—— 'Maimonides' Philosophy of Science', in *The Cambridge Companion to Maimonides* (Cambridge, 2005), 134–66.

Friedberg, Albert, *Crafting the 613 Commandments: Maimonides on the Enumeration, Classification, and Formulation of the Scriptural Commandments* (Boston, Mass., 2013).

Friedman, Shamma, '*Mishneh Torah*: The Great Composition' (Heb.), in Karmiel Cohen and Zvi Heber (eds.), *From the Blessing of Moses: A Collection of Articles on the Thought of Maimonides in Honour of Rabbi Nachum Rabinovitch* [Mibirkat mosheh— kovets ma'amarim bemishnat harambam likhvodo shel harav nakhum eliezer rabi- novich], i (Jerusalem, 2012), 311–43.

—— 'The Organizational Pattern of the *Mishneh Torah*', *The Jewish Law Annual*, 1 (1978), 37–41.

Funkenstein, Amos, *Maimonides: Nature, History, and Messianic Beliefs* [Teva, histori- yah umeshiḥiyut etsel harambam] (Tel Aviv, 1983).

—— *Perceptions of Jewish History* (Berkeley, Calif., 1993).

Gallagher, Daniel, 'The Platonic-Aristotelian Hybridity of Aquinas's Aesthetic Theory', *Hortulus: The Online Graduate Journal of Medieval Studies*, 2/1 (2006), <http://hortulus.net/journal/20061Gallagher.pdf>.

Galston, Miriam, 'A Re-examination of Al-Farabi's Neoplatonism', *Journal of the History of Philosophy*, 15/1 (1977), 13–32.

Genesis Rabbah: The Judaic Commentary to the Book of Genesis Rabbah: A New American Trans- lation, trans. Jacob Neusner (Atlanta, Ga., 1985).

Gersonides, *Commentary on Song of Songs*, trans. Menachem Kellner (New Haven, 1998).

Goodman, Lenn E., 'God and the Good Life: Maimonides' Virtue Ethics and the Idea of Perfection', in Georges Tamer (ed.), *The Trias of Maimonides* (Berlin, 2005), 123–35.

—— 'Maimonidean Naturalism', in id. (ed.), *Neoplatonism and Jewish Thought* (Albany, NY, 1992), 157–94.

GOTLIEB, JACOB, 'Habad's Harmonistic Approach to Maimonides' [Hatefisah hahar-monistit shel mishnat harambam beḥasidut ḥabad] (Ph.D. diss., Bar Ilan University, 2003).

GRAETZ, HEINRICH, *History of the Jews*, 5 vols., vol. iii (Philadelphia, 1891).

GREENBERG, MOSHE, 'Bible Interpretation as Exhibited in the First Book of Mai-monides' *Code*', in id., *Studies in the Bible and Jewish Thought* (Philadelphia, 1995), 421–45.

GUTTMANN, JULIUS, *Philosophies of Judaism*, trans. David W. Silverman (New York, 1964).

HADAD, ELIEZER, 'The Relationship between Nature and Torah in the Works of Mai-monides' [Hayaḥas bein hateva latorah bekhitvei harambam] (Ph.D. diss., Hebrew University of Jerusalem, 2008). Published as *The Torah and Nature in Maimonides' Writings* [Hatorah vehateva bekhitvei harambam] (Jerusalem, 2011).

HALBERTAL, MOSHE, *Concealment and Revelation: Esotericism in Jewish Thought and its Philosophical Implications*, trans. Jackie Feldman (Princeton, NJ, 2007).

——*Maimonides* [Harambam] (Jerusalem, 2009); English edn.: *Maimonides: Life and Thought*, trans. Joel Linsider (Princeton, NJ, 2013).

——'Maimonides' Book of the Commandments and the Architecture of the Halakhah' (Heb.), *Tarbiz*, 59 (1989–90), 457–80.

——'What Is the *Mishneh Torah*? On Codification and Ambivalence', in Jay Harris (ed.), *Maimonides after 800 Years: Essays on Maimonides and His Influence* (Cambridge, Mass., 2007), 81–111.

HALKIN, ABRAHAM, and DAVID HARTMAN, *Epistles of Maimonides: Crisis and Leader-ship* (Philadelphia, 1985).

HARTMAN, DAVID, 'Maimonides' Approach to Messianism and its Contemporary Implications', *Da'at*, 2–3 (1978-9), 5–33.

——*Maimonides: Torah and Philosophic Quest*, 1st paperback edn. (Philadelphia, 1976).

HARVEY, STEVEN, 'Alghazali and Maimonides and their Books of Knowledge', in Jay M. Harris (ed.), *Be'erot Yitzhak: Studies in Memory of Isadore Twersky* (Cambridge, Mass., 2005), 99–117.

——'Did Maimonides' Letter to Samuel ibn Tibbon Determine which Philosophers Would Be Studied by Later Jewish Thinkers?', *The Jewish Quarterly Review*, 83/1/2 (1992), 51–70.

——'The Greek Library of the Medieval Jewish Philosophers', in Cristina D'Ancona (ed.), *The Libraries of the Neoplatonists* (Leiden, 2007), 493–506.

——'Maimonides in the Sultan's Palace', in Joel L. Kraemer (ed.), *Perspectives on Maimon-ides* (Oxford, 1991), 47–75.

HARVEY, WARREN ZEV, 'Aggadah in Maimonides' *Mishneh Torah*', *Dine Israel*, 24 (2007), 197–207.

HARVEY, WARREN ZEV, 'Ethics and Meta-Ethics, Aesthetics and Meta-Aesthetics in Maimonides', in Shlomo Pines and Yirmiyahu Yovel (eds.), *Maimonides and Philosophy: Papers Presented at the Sixth Jerusalem Philosophical Encounter, May 1985* (Dordrecht, 1986), 131–8.

—— 'Holiness: A Command to Imitatio Dei', *Tradition: A Journal of Orthodox Jewish Thought*, 16/3 (1977), 7–28.

—— 'How to Begin to Study the *Guide of the Perplexed*, i.1' (Heb.), *Da'at*, 21 (1988), 5–23.

—— 'Maimonides' Critical Epistemology and *Guide* 2:24', *Aleph: Historical Studies in Science and Judaism*, 8 (2008), 213–35.

—— 'The *Mishneh Torah* as a Key to the Secrets of the *Guide*', in Ezra Fleischer et al. (eds.), *Me'ah She'arim: Studies in Medieval Jewish Spiritual Life in Memory of Isadore Twersky* [Me'ah she'arim: iyunim be'olamam haruḥani shel yisra'el biyemei habeinayim, lezekher yitsḥak tverski] (Jerusalem, 2001), English section, 11–28.

—— 'On Maimonides' Allegorical Readings of Scripture', in Jon Whitman (ed.), *Interpretation and Allegory: Antiquity to the Modern Period* (Leiden, 2000), 181–8.

—— *Rabbi Hisdai Crescas* (Heb.) (Jerusalem, 2010).

HENSHKE, DAVID, 'On the Question of Unity in Maimonides' Thought' (Heb.), *Da'at*, 37 (1996), 37–52.

HERZOG, ISAAC HALEVI, 'The Order of the Books in Maimonides' *Mishneh Torah*' (Heb.), in J. L. Fishman (ed.), *Rabbi Moses Maimonides* [Rabenu mosheh ben maimon], ii (Jerusalem, 1935), 257–64.

HESCHEL, ABRAHAM JOSHUA, *Prophetic Inspiration After the Prophets: Maimonides and Other Medieval Authorities* (Hoboken, NJ, 1996).

—— *The Sabbath*, introd. Susannah Heschel, paperback edn. (New York, 2005).

HUGHES, AARON, '"The Torah speaks in the language of humans": On Some Uses of Plato's Theory of Myth in Medieval Jewish Philosophy', in Robert M. Berchman and John F. Finamore (eds.), *History of Platonism: Plato Redivivus* (New Orleans, 2005), 237–52.

HYMAN, ARTHUR, 'Divine Law and Human Reason', in Leo Landman (ed.), *Scholars and Scholarship: The Interaction between Judaism and Other Cultures. The Bernard Revel Graduate School Conference Volume* (New York, 1990), 37–52.

IBN PAKUDA, BAHYA BEN JOSEPH, *The Book of Direction to the Duties of the Heart*, trans. Menahem Mansoor (London, 1973).

IBN TIBBON, SAMUEL, *Ma'amar yikavu hamayim* (Pressburg, 1837).

IBN ZADDIK, JOSEPH BEN JACOB, *The Microcosm of Joseph Ibn Saddiq*, trans. Jacob Haberman, ed. Saul Horovitz (Madison, NJ, 2003).

IDEL, MOSHE, '*Deus Sive Natura*: The Metamorphosis of a Dictum from Maimonides to Spinoza', in Robert S. Cohen and Hillel Levine (eds.), *Maimonides and the Sciences* (Dordrecht, 2000), 87–110.

—— *Kabbalah: New Perspectives* (New Haven, 1988).

—— 'Maimonides and Kabbalah', in Isadore Twersky (ed.), *Studies in Maimonides* (Cambridge, Mass., 1990), 31–81.

INBARI, MOTTI, *Jewish Fundamentalism and the Temple Mount: Who Will Build the Third Temple?* (Albany, NY, 2009).

IVRY, ALFRED L., 'Arabic and Islamic Psychology and Philosophy of Mind', in Edward N. Zalta (ed.), *The Stanford Encyclopedia of Philosophy*, Fall 2008 edn. (21 Sept. 2008), <http://plato.stanford.edu/archives/fall2008/entries/arabic-islamic-mind/>.

—— 'The Image of Moses in Maimonides' Thought', in Jay M. Harris (ed.), *Maimonides after 800 Years: Essays on Maimonides and His Influence* (Cambridge, Mass., 2007), 113–34.

—— 'Islamic and Greek Influences on Maimonides' Philosophy', in Shlomo Pines and Yirmiyahu Yovel (eds.), *Maimonides and Philosophy* (Dordrecht, 1986), 139–56.

—— 'Neoplatonic Currents in Maimonides' Thought', in Joel L. Kraemer (ed.), *Perspectives on Maimonides* (Oxford, 1991), 115–40.

JACOB BEN ASHER, *Arba'ah turim*.

JANAWAY, CHRISTOPHER, *Images of Excellence: Plato's Criticism of the Arts* (Oxford, 1995).

JASTROW, MARCUS, *A Dictionary of the Targumim, the Talmud Babli and Yerushalmi, and the Midrashic Literature*, 2 vols. (New York, 1903).

KADARI, ADIEL, 'Thought and Halakhah in Maimonides' "Laws of Repentance"' [Hagut vehalakhah behilkhot teshuvah larambam] (Ph.D. diss., Ben Gurion University of the Negev, 2000). Published as *Studies in Repentance: Law, Philosophy, and Educational Thought in Maimonides' 'Hilkhot Teshuvah'* [Iyunei teshuvah: halakhah, hagut, umaḥshavah ḥinukhit behilkhot teshuvah larambam] (Beersheva, 2010).

KAFIH, JOSEPH, *The Hebrew Bible in Maimonides* [Hamikra barambam] (Jerusalem, 1972).

KAMPINSKY, YEHOSHUA, 'Saint and Sage in Maimonides' Teaching' (Heb.), *Shma'atin*, 35/132 (1998), 87–92.

KAPLAN, LAWRENCE, 'An Introduction to Maimonides' "Eight Chapters"', *Edah Journal*, 2/2 (2002), 2–23.

—— 'The Unity of Maimonides' Religious Thought: The Laws of Mourning as a Case Study', in Jonathan W. Malino (ed.), *Judaism and Modernity: The Religious Philosophy of David Hartman* (Jerusalem, 2001), 411–34.

KARO, JOSEPH, *Shulḥan arukh*.

KASHER, HANNAH, 'Is There an Early Stratum in the *Guide of the Perplexed*?', *Maimonidean Studies*, 3 (1992–93), 105–29.

—— 'Maimonides' Philosophical Division of the Law' (Heb.), *HUCA*, 56 (1985), 1–7.

—— 'On the Form of the "Images" (Further Clarifications of *Guide of the Perplexed* i.1)' (Heb.), *Da'at*, 53 (2004), 31–42.

—— 'Self-Cognizing Intellect and Negative Attributes in Maimonides' Theology', *The Harvard Theological Review*, 87/4 (1994), 461–72.

—— 'The Study of Torah as a Means of Apprehending God in Maimonides' Thought' (Heb.), *Jerusalem Studies in Jewish Thought*, 5 (1986), 71–81.

—— 'The Torah as a Means of Achieving the World to Come' (Heb.), *Tarbiz*, 64 (1995), 301–6.

Kellner, Menachem, 'Did the Torah Precede the Cosmos? A Maimonidean Study' (Heb.), *Da'at*, 61 (2007), 83–96.

—— *Dogma in Medieval Jewish Thought from Maimonides to Abravanel* (Oxford, 1986).

—— 'The Literary Character of the *Mishneh Torah*', in Ezra Fleischer et al. (eds.), *Me'ah She'arim: Studies in Medieval Jewish Spiritual Life in Memory of Isadore Twersky* [Me'ah she'arim: iyunim be'olamam haruḥani shel yisra'el biyemei habeinayim, lezekher yitsḥak tverski] (Jerusalem, 2001), English section, 29–45.

—— *Maimonides' Confrontation with Mysticism* (Oxford, 2006).

—— *Maimonides on Human Perfection* (Atlanta, Ga., 1989).

—— *Maimonides on Judaism and the Jewish People* (Albany, NY, 1991).

—— 'Maimonides on the Nature of Ritual Purity and Impurity', *Da'at*, 50 (2003), pp. i–xxx.

—— 'Messianic Postures in Israel Today', *Modern Judaism*, 6/2 (1986), 197–209.

—— *Must a Jew Believe Anything?* (London, 1999).

—— 'On the Status of the Astronomy and Physics in Maimonides' *Mishneh Torah* and *Guide of the Perplexed*', *British Journal for the History of Science*, 24 (1991), 453–63.

—— 'Philosophical Themes in Maimonides' *Sefer Ahavah*', in Idit Dobbs-Weinstein, Lenn E. Goodman, and James Allen Grady (eds.), *Maimonides and His Heritage* (Albany, NY, 2009), 13–35.

—— 'Spiritual Life', in Kenneth Seeskin (ed.), *The Cambridge Companion to Maimonides* (Cambridge, 2005), 273–99.

—— *Torah in the Observatory* (Boston, Mass., 2010).

—— 'The Virtue of Faith', in Lenn E. Goodman (ed.), *Neoplatonism and Jewish Thought* (Albany, NY, 1992), 195–205.

Kemal, Salim, 'Aesthetics', in Oliver Leaman and Seyyed Hossein Nasr (eds.), *History of Islamic Philosophy*, ii (London, 1996), 969–78.

—— *The Poetics of Alfarabi and Avicenna* (Leiden, 1991).

Kirschenbaum, Aaron, '*Middat Hasidut* and Supererogation', *Da'at*, 44 (2000), 5–58.

Klawans, Jonathan, *Purity, Sacrifice, and the Temple: Symbolism and Supersessionism in the Study of Ancient Judaism* (New York, 2006).

Klein-Braslavy, Sara, 'The Creation of the World and Maimonides' Interpretation of Gen. I–V', in *Maimonides and Philosophy: Papers Presented at the Sixth Jerusalem Philosophical Encounter, May 1985* (Dordrecht, 1986), 65–78.

—— 'Maimonides' Commentary on Jacob's Dream of the Ladder' (Heb.), *Bar-Ilan*, 22–3 (1987), 329–49.

Kraemer, Joel L., 'Alfarabi's *Opinions of the Virtuous City* and Maimonides' *Foundations of the Law*', in Joshua Blau et al. (eds.), *Studia Orientalia Memoriae D. H. Baneth Dedicata* (Jerusalem, 1979), 125–53.

—— 'How (Not) to Read the *Guide of the Perplexed*', *Jerusalem Studies in Arabic and Islam*, 32 (2006), 350–409.

—— 'The Islamic Context of Medieval Jewish Philosophy', in Daniel H. Frank and Oliver

Leaman (eds.), *The Cambridge Companion to Medieval Jewish Philosophy* (Cambridge, 2003), 38–68.

—— *Maimonides: The Life and World of One of Civilization's Greatest Minds* (New York, 2008).

—— 'Maimonides and the Spanish Aristotelian School', in Mark D. Meyerson and Edward D. English (eds.), *Christians, Muslims, and Jews in Medieval and Early Modern Spain: Interaction and Cultural Change* (Notre Dame, Ill., 1999), 40–68.

—— 'Naturalism and Universalism in Maimonides' Political and Religious Thought', in Ezra Fleischer et al. (eds.), *Me'ah She'arim: Studies in Medieval Jewish Spiritual Life in Memory of Isadore Twersky* [Me'ah she'arim: iyunim be'olamam haruḥani shel yisra'el biyemei habeinayim, lezekher yitsḥak tverski] (Jerusalem, 2001), English section, 47–81.

KREISEL, HAIM (HOWARD), 'Asceticism in the Thought of R. Bahya Ibn Paquda and Maimonides', *Da'at*, 21 (1988), pp. v–xxii.

—— '*Imitatio Dei* in Maimonides' "Guide of the Perplexed"', *AJS Review*, 19/2 (1994), 169–211.

—— *Maimonides' Political Thought: Studies in Ethics, Law, and the Human Ideal* (Albany, NY, 1999).

—— 'Philosophical-Allegorical Interpretation of the Torah in the Middle Ages: *Ma'aseh Nisim* by R. Nissim of Marseilles' (Heb.), in Ezra Fleischer et al. (eds.), *Me'ah She'arim: Studies in Medieval Jewish Spiritual Life in Memory of Isadore Twersky* [Me'ah she'arim: iyunim be'olamam haruḥani shel yisra'el biyemei habeinayim, lezekher yitsḥak tverski] (Jerusalem, 2001), Hebrew section, 297–316.

—— *Prophecy: The History of an Idea in Medieval Jewish Philosophy* (Dordrecht, 2001).

—— 'The Voice of God in Medieval Jewish Philosophic Exegesis' (Heb.), *Da'at*, 16 (1986), 29–38.

LAHEY, STEPHEN E., 'Maimonides and Analogy', *American Catholic Philosophical Quarterly*, 67/2 (1993), 219–32.

LANGERMANN, Y. TZVI, 'Astronomical Problems in Maimonides' Thought' (Heb.), *Da'at*, 37 (1996), 107–18.

—— 'Fusul Musa; or, On Maimonides' Method of Composition', *Maimonidean Studies*, 5 (2008), 325–44.

—— 'Maimonides' Repudiation of Astrology', in Robert S. Cohen and Hillel Levine (eds.), *Maimonides and the Sciences* (Dordrecht, 2000), 131–57.

—— 'The True Perplexity: The *Guide of the Perplexed* Part II, Chapter 24', in Joel L. Kraemer (ed.), *Perspectives on Maimonides* (Oxford, 1991), 159–74.

LAWEE, ERIC, '"The good we accept and the bad we do not": Aspects of Isaac Abarbanel's Stance Towards Maimonides', in Jay Harris (ed.), *Be'erot Yitzhak: Studies in Memory of Isadore Twersky* (Cambridge, Mass., 2005), 119–60.

LEAMAN, OLIVER, 'Maimonides and the Development of Jewish Thought in an Islamic Structure', in Georges Tamer (ed.), *The Trias of Maimonides* (Berlin, 2005), 187–97.

—— *Moses Maimonides*, 2nd edn. (London, 1997).

LEAMAN, OLIVER, 'Poetry and the Emotions in Islamic Philosophy', in Anna-Teresa Tymieniecka and Nazif Muhtaroglu (eds.), *Classic Issues in Islamic Philosophy Today* (Dordrecht, 2010), 139–50.

LERNER, RALPH, 'Maimonides' Governance of the Solitary', in Joel L. Kraemer (ed.), *Perspectives on Maimonides* (Oxford, 1991), 33–46.

LEVINGER, JACOB S., *Maimonides as Philosopher and Codifier* [Harambam kefilosof ukhefosek] (Jerusalem, 1989).

LEWIS, C. S., *The Discarded Image* (Cambridge, 1964).

LOBEL, DIANA, 'Being and the Good: Maimonides on Ontological Beauty', *The Journal of Jewish Thought and Philosophy*, 19/1 (2011), 1–45.

LORBERBAUM, MENACHEM, 'Maimonides' Conception of *Tikun olam* and the Teleology of Halakhah' (Heb.), *Tarbiz*, 64/1 (1994–5), 65–82.

LORBERBAUM, YAIR, '"The men of knowledge and the sages are drawn, as it were, toward this purpose by the Divine Will" (*The Guide of the Perplexed*, Introduction): On Maimonides' Conception of Parables' (Heb.), *Tarbiz*, 71 (2002), 87–132.

McKEON, RICHARD, 'The Philosophic Bases of Art and Criticism', *Modern Philology*, 41/2 (1943), 65–87.

MALTER, HENRY, *Saadia Gaon: His Life and Works* (Hildesheim, 1978).

MANEKIN, CHARLES H., 'The Limitations of Human Knowledge According to Maimonides: Earlier vs. Later Writings' (Heb.), in Aviezer Ravitzky (ed.), *Maimonides: Conservatism, Originality, Revolution* [Harambam: shamranut, mekoriyut, mehapkhanut], ii (Jerusalem, 2008), 297–316.

—— 'Problems of "Plenitude" in Maimonides and Gersonides', in Ruth Link-Salinger (ed.), *A Straight Path: Studies in Medieval Philosophy and Culture: Essays in Honor of Arthur Hyman* (Washington, DC, 1988), 183–94.

MASCALL, ERIC L., 'The Doctrine of Analogy', in Robert E. Santoni (ed.), *Religious Language and the Problem of Religious Knowledge* (Bloomington, 1968), 156–81.

Masekhet soferim [Tractate Scribes], ed. Michael Higger (New York, 1937).

MATHIS, C. K. II, 'Parallel Structures in the Metaphysics of Iamblichus and Ibn Gabirol', in Lenn E. Goodman (ed.), *Neoplatonism and Jewish Thought* (Albany, NY, 1992), 61–76.

MELAMED, ABRAHAM, 'Maimonides on the Political Nature of Man: Needs and Obligations' (Heb.), in Moshe Idel, Devora Dimant, and Shalom Rosenberg (eds.), *Tribute to Sara: Studies in Jewish Philosophy and Kabbala Presented to Professor Sara O. Heller Wilensky* [Minḥah lesarah: meḥkarim befilosofyah yehudit vekabalah mugashim liprofesor sarah orah heler vilenski] (Jerusalem, 1994), 292–333.

—— *The Philosopher-King in Medieval and Renaissance Jewish Political Thought* (Albany, 2003).

Mekilta de-Rabbi Ishmael: A Critical Edition on the Basis of the Manuscripts and Early Editions, trans. and ed. Jacob Z. Lauterbach, 2 vols. (Philadelphia, 1949).

Midrash Tanhuma Translated into English with Introduction and Brief Notes: Exodus and Leviticus: S. Buber Recension, trans. John T. Townsend (Hoboken, NJ, 1989).

Midrash tanḥuma with commentaries *Etz yosef* and *Anaf yosef* (Vilna, 1833, repr. Tel Aviv, n.d.).

MOORE, EDWARD, 'Neoplatonism', *The Internet Encyclopedia of Philosophy* (2005), <http:// www.iep.utm.edu/neoplato>.

MULGAN, R. G., 'Aristotle's Doctrine That Man Is a Political Animal', *Hermes*, 102/3 (1974), 438–45.

MURRAY, PENELOPE ANNE, and T. S. DORSCH, *Classical Literary Criticism* (London, 2000).

NEHORAI, MICHAEL ZVI, 'The Mitzvot: A Decree of God or an Intellectual Challenge?' (Heb.), in Aviezer Ravitzky (ed.), *Maimonides: Conservatism, Originality, Revolution* [Harambam: shamranut, mekoriyut, mehapkhanut], ii (Jerusalem, 2008), 367–74.

NETTON, IAN RICHARD, *Al-Farabi and his School* (London, 1992).

NISSIM B. MOSES OF MARSEILLES, *Ma'aseh nisim* [commentary on the Torah], ed. Haim (Howard) Kreisel (Jerusalem, 2000).

NORRIS, CHRISTOPHER, *Deconstruction: Theory and Practice*, rev. edn. (London, 1991).

NOVAK, DAVID, *Natural Law in Judaism* (Cambridge, 1998).

NURIEL, ABRAHAM, *Concealed and Revealed in Medieval Jewish Philosophy* [Galui vesamui bafilosofyah hayehudit biyemei habeinayim] (Jerusalem, 2000).

—— 'Remarks on Maimonides' Epistemology', in Shlomo Pines and Yirmiyahu Yovel (eds.), *Maimonides and Philosophy: Papers Presented at the Sixth Jerusalem Philosophical Encounter, May 1985* (Dordrecht, 1986), 36–51.

O'MEARA, DOMINIC J., *Plotinus: An Introduction to the Enneads* (Oxford, 1993).

PARRY, RICHARD, 'Empedocles', in Edward N. Zalta (ed.), *The Stanford Encyclopedia of Philosophy*, Fall 2008 edn. (21 Sept. 2008), <http://plato.stanford.edu/archives/fall2008/entries/empedocles>.

Pesikta derav kahana, ed. Bernard Mandelbaum, 2 vols. (New York, 1962).

PESSIN, SARAH, 'The Influence of Islamic Thought on Maimonides', in Edward N. Zalta (ed.), *The Stanford Encyclopedia of Philosophy*, Fall 2005 edn. (21 Sept. 2005), <http://plato.stanford.edu/archives/fall2005/entries/maimonides-islamic/>.

PINES, SHLOMO, 'The Limitations of Human Knowledge According to Al-Farabi, ibn Bajja, and Maimonides', in Isadore Twersky (ed.), *Studies in Medieval Jewish History and Literature* (Cambridge, Mass., 1979), 82–109.

—— 'The Philosophical Purport of Maimonides' Halachic Works and the Purport of *The Guide of the Perplexed*', in Shlomo Pines and Yirmiyahu Yovel (eds.), *Maimonides and Philosophy: Papers Presented at the Sixth Jerusalem Philosophical Encounter, May 1985* (Dordrecht, 1986), 1–14.

—— 'Translator's Introduction: The Philosophic Sources of the *Guide of the Perplexed*', in *The Guide of the Perplexed*, i (Chicago, 1963), pp. lvii–cxxxiv.

—— 'Truth and Falsehood Versus Good and Evil: A Study in Jewish and General Philosophy in Connection with *The Guide of the Perplexed*, I, 2', in Isadore Twersky (ed.), *Studies in Maimonides* (Cambridge, Mass., 1990), 95–157.

PLATO, *Laws*, trans. Trevor J. Saunders, in *Plato: Complete Works*, ed. John M. Cooper (Indianapolis, 1997), 1318–1616.

RABINOVITCH, NACHUM L., 'Sanctuary, Society, and History' (Heb.), in Aviezer Ravitzky (ed.), *Maimonides: Conservatism, Originality, Revolution* [Harambam: shamranut, mekoriyut, mehapkhanut], i (Jerusalem, 2008), 63–77.

RAVITZKY, AVIEZER, 'God and Nature, Religion and Science: Did Maimonides Anticipate Scholastic and Modern Views?' (Heb.), in id., *Maimonidean Essays: Society, Philosophy, and Nature in Maimonides and his Disciples* [Iyunim maimoni'im] (Tel Aviv, 2006), 157–80.

—— '"To the Utmost of Human Capacity": Maimonides on the Days of the Messiah', in Joel L. Kraemer (ed.), *Perspectives on Maimonides: Philososophical and Historical Studies* (Oxford, 1991), 221–56.

—— 'Philosophy and Leadership in Maimonides', in Jay M. Harris (ed.), *Maimonides after 800 Years: Essays on Maimonides and His Influence* (Cambridge, Mass., 2007), 257–90.

RAVIV, RIVKA, 'The Talmudic Formulation of the Prophecies of the Four Kingdoms in the Book of Daniel', *JSIJ: Jewish Studies, an Internet Journal*, 5 (2006), 1–20, <http://www.biu.ac.il/JS/JSIJ/5-2006/Raviv.doc>.

RAWIDOWICZ, SIMON, 'The Opening Book of *Mishneh Torah*' (Heb.), in id., *Studies in Jewish Thought* [Iyunim bemaḥshevet yisra'el], i (Jerusalem, 1970), 381–464.

—— 'The Structure of the *Guide for the Perplexed*' (Heb.), in id., *Studies in Jewish Thought* [Iyunim bemaḥshevet yisra'el], i (Jerusalem, 1969), 237–96.

Responsa of Abraham Maimonides [Teshuvot rabenu avraham], ed. Alfred Freimann (Jerusalem, 1938).

ROBINSON, JAMES T., 'Some Remarks on the Source of Maimonides' Plato in *Guide of the Perplexed* I.17', *Zutot: Perspectives on Jewish Culture*, 3 (2003), 49–57.

ROSNER, FRED, 'Moses Maimonides on Music Therapy and His Responsum on Music', *Journal of Jewish Music and Liturgy*, 16 (1993), 1–16.

RYNHOLD, DANIEL, 'Good and Evil, Truth and Falsity', *Trumah*, 6 (2002), 163–82.

—— *Two Models of Jewish Philosophy: Justifying One's Practices* (Oxford, 2005).

SATTERLEE, THOM, 'Thom Satterlee Delves into Robert Frost's Views on Translation', *Delos: A Journal on and of Translation* (1996), 46–52.

SCHACTER, JACOB J., 'R. Jacob Emden, Philosophy, and the Authority of Maimonides', *Tradition: A Journal of Orthodox Jewish Thought*, 27/4 (1993), 131–9.

SCHELLING, FRIEDRICH WILHELM JOSEPH, *The Philosophy of Art*, trans. Douglas W. Stott (Minneapolis, 1989).

SCHIRMANN, JEFIM HAYYIM, 'Maimonides and Hebrew Poetry' (Heb.), *Moznayim*, 3 (1935), 432–6.

SCHOLEM, GERSHOM, *Kabbalah* (Jerusalem, 1974).

SCHWARTZ, DOV, 'Maimonides' Philosophical Methodology: A Reappraisal' (Heb.), in Aviezer Ravitzky (ed.), *Maimonides: Conservatism, Originality, Revolution* [Harambam: shamranut, mekoriyut, mehapkhanut], ii (Jerusalem, 2008), 413–36.

SCHWARZSCHILD, STEVEN, 'Moral Radicalism and "Middlingness" in the Ethics of Maimonides', in Menachem Kellner (ed.), *The Pursuit of the Ideal* (Albany, NY, 1990), 137–60.

Seeskin, Kenneth, 'Holiness as an Ethical Ideal', *Journal of Jewish Thought and Philosophy*, 5/2 (1996), 191–203.

—— 'Maimonides' Sense of History', *Jewish History*, 18 (2004), 129–45.

—— *No Other Gods: The Modern Struggle Against Idolatry* (New York, 1995).

—— *Searching for a Distant God: The Legacy of Maimonides* (Oxford, 2000).

Septimus, Bernard, 'Literary Structure and Ethical Theory in *Sefer ha-Madda*', in Jay M. Harris (ed.), *Maimonides after 800 Years: Essays on Maimonides and His Influence* (Cambridge, Mass., 2007), 307–25; a longer version is published in Hebrew as 'Mivneh veti'un besefer hamada', in Aviezer Ravitzky (ed.), *Maimonides: Conservatism, Originality, Revolution* [Harambam: shamranut, mekoriyut, mehapkhanut], i (Jerusalem, 2008), 223–46.

—— 'Maimonides on Language', in Aviva Doron (ed.), *The Culture of Spanish Jewry: Proceedings of the First International Congress* (Tel Aviv, 1994).

—— 'What Did Maimonides Mean by *Madda*?', in Ezra Fleischer et al. (eds.), *Me'ah Shearim: Studies in Medieval Spiritual Life in Memory of Isadore Twersky* [Me'ah she'arim: iyunim be'olamam haruḥani shel yisra'el biyemei habeinayim, lezekher yitsḥak tverski] (Jerusalem, 2001), English section, 83–110.

Shapiro, David S., 'The Doctrine of the Image of God and *Imitatio Dei*', *Judaism: A Quarterly Journal of Jewish Life and Thought*, 12 (1963), 57–77.

Shapiro, Marc B., *Studies in Maimonides and His Interpreters* (Scranton, Pa., 2008).

Shatz, David, 'Maimonides' Moral Theory', in *The Cambridge Companion to Maimonides* (Cambridge, 2005), 167–92.

Shaviv, Yehudah, 'The Motto Verses of the Books of *Mishneh Torah*' (Heb.), *Essays on Maimonides* [Kovets harambam] (Jerusalem, 2005), 60–78.

Shields, Christopher, 'Aristotle's Psychology', in Edward N. Zalta (ed.), *The Stanford Encyclopedia of Philosophy*, Spring 2011 edn. (21 March 2011), <http://plato.stanford.edu/archives/spr2011/entries/aristotle-psychology/>.

Shiloah, Amnon, 'Maïmonide et la musique', in Nicole S. Serfaty and Joseph Tedghi (eds.), *Présence juive au Maghreb: Hommage à Haïm Zafrani* (Paris, 2004), 497–506.

Sifra: An Analytical Translation, iii, trans. Jacob Neusner (Atlanta, Ga., 1988).

Sifre: A Tannaitic Commentary on the Book of Deuteronomy, trans. Reuven Hammer (New Haven, 1986).

Sirat, Colette, *A History of Jewish Philosophy in the Middle Ages* (Cambridge, 1985).

Soloveitchik, Haym, '*Mishneh Torah*: Polemic and Art', in Jay Harris (ed.), *Maimonides after 800 Years: Essays on Maimonides and His Influence*, i (Cambridge, Mass., 2007), 327–43.

—— 'Thoughts on Maimonides' Categorization of the Commandments in the *Mishneh Torah*: Real and Imagined Problems', *Maimonidean Studies*, 4 (2000), 107–15.

Soloveitchik, Joseph B., *The Halakhic Mind* (New York, 1986).

—— 'The Lonely Man of Faith', *Tradition: A Journal of Orthodox Jewish Thought*, 7/2 (1965), 5–67.

Song of Songs Rabbah: An Analytical Translation, trans. Jacob Neusner, 2 vols. (Atlanta, Ga., 1989).

SPERO, SHUBERT, 'Maimonides and the Sense of History', *Tradition: A Journal of Ortho-dox Jewish Thought*, 24/2 (1989), 128–38.

STERN, JOSEF, 'The Enigma of *Guide of the Perplexed*, i. 68' (Heb.), in Aviezer Ravitzky (ed.), *Maimonides: Conservatism, Originality, Revolution* [Harambam: shamranut, mekoriyut, mehapkhanut], ii (Jerusalem, 2008), 437–51.

—— 'The Idea of a Hoq in Maimonides' Explanation of the Law', in Shlomo Pines and Yirmiyahu Yovel (eds.), *Maimonides and Philosophy: Papers Presented at the Sixth Jerusalem Philosophical Encounter, May 1985* (Dordrecht, 1986), 92–130.

—— 'The Knot That Never Was', *Aleph: Historical Studies in Science and Judaism*, 8 (2008), 319–39.

—— *Problems and Parables of Law: Maimonides and Nahmanides on Reasons for the Command-ments* (Albany, NY, 1998).

STRAUSS, LEO, 'How to Begin to Study *The Guide of the Perplexed*: Introductory Essay', trans. Shlomo Pines, in *The Guide of the Perplexed*, i (Chicago, 1963), pp. xi–lvi.

—— 'The Literary Character of the *Guide of the Perplexed*', in Salo Wittmayer Baron (ed.), *Essays on Maimonides: An Octocentennial Volume* (New York, 1941), 37–91.

—— 'Maimonides' Statement on Political Science', *Proceedings of the American Academy for Jewish Research*, 22 (1953), 115–30.

—— 'Notes on Maimonides' Book of Knowledge', in *Studies in Mysticism and Religion Presented to Gershom G. Scholem* (Jerusalem, 1967), 269–83.

SWEENEY, EILEEN, 'Literary Forms of Medieval Philosophy', in Edward N. Zalta (ed.), *The Stanford Encyclopedia of Philosophy*, Fall 2008 edn. (21 Sept. 2008), <http://plato.stanford.edu/archives/fall2008/entries/medieval-literary/>.

TABORY, JOSEPH, 'The Structure of the Mishnah versus the Structure of *Mishneh Torah*' (Heb.), in Uri Ehrlich, Howard Kreisel, and Daniel J. Lasker (eds.), *By the Well: Studies in Jewish Philosophy and Halakhic Thought Presented to Gerald J. Blidstein* [Al pi habe'er: meḥkarim behagut yehudit uvemaḥshavat hahalakhah mugashim leya'akov blidshtein] (Beersheva, 2008), 675–90.

TANENBAUM, ADENA, *The Contemplative Soul: Hebrew Poetics and Philosophical Theory in Medieval Spain* (Leiden, 2002).

TA-SHMA, ISRAEL, 'Was Maimonides' Position on Talmud Study Truly Revolutionary?' (Heb.), in Aviezer Ravitzky (ed.), *Maimonides: Conservatism, Originality, Revolution* [Harambam: shamranut, mekoriyut, mehapkhanut], i (Jerusalem, 2008), 111–17.

TOBI, JOSEPH, 'The Hebrew and the Arabic Poetry in Spain: Affinity and Uniqueness' (Heb.), in Aviva Doron (ed.), *The Heritage of the Jews of Spain* [Tarbut yahadut sefarad] (Tel Aviv, 1994), 43–60.

TOLSTOY, LEO NIKOLAYEVICH, *What Is Art? What Is Religion?*, trans. Aylmer Maude (Rockville, Md., 2008).

Torah, Prophets, and Writings with Da'at Mikra Commentary [Torah, nevi'im ukhetuvim im perush da'at mikra], ed. Yehudah Kiel et al. (Jerusalem, 1990).

TWERSKY, ISADORE (YITZHAK), 'A Clarification of Maimonides' Remarks in "Laws of Trespass", 8: 8: Towards Understanding Maimonides' Reasons for the Command-ments' (Heb.), in Emmanuel Etkes and Yosef Salmon (eds.), *Studies in the History of Jewish Society in the Middle Ages and in the Modern Period, Presented to Professor Jacob Katz* [Perakim betoledot haḥevrah hayehudit biyemei habeinayim uva'et heḥadashah: mukdashim leprofesor ya'akov kats] (Jerusalem, 1980), 24–33.

—— 'Did R. Abraham Ibn Ezra Influence Maimonides?' (Heb.), in Isadore Twersky and Jay M. Harris (eds.), *Rabbi Abraham Ibn Ezra: Studies in the Writings of a Twelfth-Century Polymath* (Cambridge, Mass., 1993), 21–48.

—— *Introduction to the Code of Maimonides (Mishneh Torah)* (New Haven, 1980).

—— *A Maimonides Reader* (West Orange, NJ, 1972).

—— 'Martyrdom and the Sanctity of Life: Aspects of Holiness in Maimonides' (Heb.), in Isaiah M. Gafni and Aviezer Ravitzky (eds.), *Sanctity of Life and Martyrdom: Studies in Memory of Amir Yekutiel* (Jerusalem, 1992), 167–90.

—— 'On Law and Ethics in the *Mishneh Torah*: A Case Study of *Hilkhot Megillah* II:17', *Tradition: A Journal of Orthodox Jewish Thought*, 24/2 (1989), 138–49.

—— 'Some Non-Halakic Aspects of the *Mishneh Torah*', in Alexander Altman (ed.), *Jewish Medieval and Renaissance Studies* (Cambridge, Mass., 1967), 95–118.

WALLIS, RICHARD T., *Neoplatonism* (London, 1972).

WEISS, RAYMOND L., *Maimonides' Ethics: The Encounter of Philosophic and Religious Morality* (Chicago, 1991).

—— 'Some Notes on Twersky's "Introduction to the Code of Maimonides"', *The Jewish Quarterly Review*, NS 74/1 (1983), 61–79.

WEISS, ROSLYN, 'Maimonides on the End of the World', *Maimonidean Studies*, 3 (1992–3), 195–219.

WHITMAN, JON, 'Present Perspectives: Antiquity to the Late Middle Ages', in id. (ed.), *Interpretation and Allegory: Antiquity to the Modern Period* (Leiden, 2000), 33–72.

WOLPERT, LEWIS, *The Unnatural Nature of Science* (London, 1992).

YAHALOM, YOSEF, 'Maimonides and Hebrew Poetic Language' (Heb.), *Pe'amim*, 81 (1999), 4–18.

ZIEMLICH, BERNHARD, 'Plan und Anlage des Mischne Thora', in W. Bacher, M. Brann, and D. Simonsen (eds.), *Moses ben Maimon, sein Leben, seine Werke und sein Einfluss*, i (Leipzig, 1908), 248–318.

ZIMMERMANN, FRITZ, 'Proclus Arabus Rides Again', *Arabic Sciences and Philosophy*, 4/1 (1994), 9–51.

Index of Citations

Letters

Index of Subjects